# Prisoners

law and practice

Simon Creighton and Hamish Arnott

LAG Legal Action Group
2009

This edition published in Great Britain 2009
by LAG Education and Service Trust Limited
242 Pentonville Road, London N1 9UN
www.lag.org.uk

British Library Cataloguing in Publication Data
a CIP catalogue record for this book is available from the British Library.

ISBN    978 1 903307 71 7

Typeset by Regent Typesetting, London
Printed in Great Britain by Hobbs the Printer, Totton, Hampshire

# Foreword

Stephen Shaw, Prisons and Probation Ombudsman

Most of those picking up this book will have no doubt of the proposition that prisoners, however grievously they may have offended against the rights of others, retain inalienable human rights. Indeed, few readers would regard the proposition as other than axiomatic and as a simple statement of international and domestic law. Nor would they question the idea that, because of the extent of their dependence upon the state, prisoners are actually owed a special duty of care from those charged with their custody. Yet it is also manifest that this approach to prisoners' rights is not one that is recognised or approved of by many sections of the British media, nor to be frank by many of our fellow citizens.

For that reason, this book is much more than a guide to the present state of prison law – although it serves that purpose splendidly. It is also a polemic, or perhaps more aptly, a work of advocacy. Because beyond the expert analysis, beyond the Prison Service Orders and Instructions, beyond the many citations of domestic and international case law, there is at the heart of the text an intrinsic belief in the right of prisoners to be treated fairly, respectfully, and in a manner that recognises their inherent vulnerability.

That vulnerability is acknowledged in the raft of inspection and oversight mechanisms to which prisons are properly subject. For ten years as Ombudsman I have played my part in those processes, and as Ombudsman it will be no surprise if I say that I do not believe that recourse to the law is always the best way of resolving problems – whether in a custodial environment or in the world at large. Ask any prisoners about their experience and the conversation invariably turns to the quality of relationship they enjoy with prison staff. Jails are what were once known as total institutions (for some reason, the term seems to have lost its currency). They operate on what we would now call 24/7. They encompass every human activity: eating, working, bathing, contact with family, learning, exercising, and sleeping. Each one of these activities is subject to regulation and each one generates hundreds of staff-prisoner interactions (and hundreds of discretionary decisions in the interpretation of the regulations). For this reason, the quality of relationships is not some confection designed to sweeten the necessarily (and legitimately) coercive nature of imprisonment. Relationships – whether good or ill – are the very means by which authority is enforced.

But the law, whether at a United Nations, European or national level, is the bedrock on which those relationships are based. Because without law, the ever-present danger of neglect or abuse may go unchecked – as the woeful examples from Abu Ghraib and Guantanamo Bay and the so-called War against Terror have illustrated. As a consequence, much of what is in this book is of as much value to would-be and current prison staff as it is to would-be and current legal practitioners. The sub-title, Law *and* Practice, is well-judged.

Before the late 1960s, any guide to prison law would have been a thin volume indeed. But from that point on, prison litigation played a leading part in the development of public law as a whole. The landmark cases: *Silver, Golder,* the two *St Germain* cases, *Tarrant, Campbell and Fell,* transformed prisons from a legal no-go area into one of the most interesting and progressive fields of law. It may be that the high weather mark has now been passed, but there remain important topics where the jurisprudence is uncertain. To take an issue close to my own interests and experience, in what circumstances is the ECHR article 2 investigative obligation triggered by a 'near death' in custody or an actual death immediately following release? Surprisingly, the second of these matters is wholly untested in the courts so far as I am aware.

As in any work of advocacy, the reader will find some judgements which they may not wholly agree. Again to give an example, I am more critical than the authors of the absence of a power to quash a finding of guilt at prison adjudications conducted by District Judges acting as Independent Adjudicators. I may add that I also think the authors are not entirely fair in everything they say about the Ombudsman's office! And things are always changing: for example, complainants to my office now have three months (not one) within which to refer matters for investigation.

All that said, I judge these to be small quibbles given a book of this length and depth. This is a magisterial study of the interface between prisons and the law.

Stephen Shaw
Prisons and Probation Ombudsman for England & Wales
July 2009

# Preface

We finished writing this book at the same time as the prison population reached another record high, as the number of prisoners serving indeterminate sentences in England and Wales has outstripped the combined lifer population for the rest of Europe and as the Legal Services Commission announced significant cutbacks to both the scope and payment rates for publicly funded prison law work. Sadly, it appears that the decision to carve out the Ministry of Justice from the Home Office has allowed the Justice Secretary, Jack Straw, to pursue an ever more punitive and reactionary approach to the principles and purposes of imprisonment.

At the same time as the political atmosphere has hardened against prisoners, there has been a growing body of opinion that the risk of committing crimes – and in particular the risk of recidivism – can be predicted through the application of quasi-scientific behavioural assessment and treatment techniques. This neo-Victorian approach to criminal behaviour has contributed to the drive for more and more indeterminate sentences and has created such a risk-averse approach to imprisonment that the release rates on parole have dropped alarmingly over the past four years. Interestingly, this approach appears to be little more than a modern version of phrenology with very little change having been brought about in rates of recidivism or overall crime rates.

One of the effects of prison overcrowding generally is to add to the pressure on family ties, resulting in prisoners being held further away from their homes making visiting difficult. This does little to aid prisoners to remain connected to their families and wider social networks and places additional pressure on prisoners' community ties, even though it is those ties that are generally accepted to be one of the most effective protective factors against further offending. Alongside the general rolling back of attitudes to prisoners, foreign nationals and young people have faced particular demonisation and we have tried to pay particular attention to the issues affecting these two groups in this book.

Tony Blair's promise that the government would be 'tough on the causes of crime' appears to have been abandoned in favour of simply being tough on criminals and it is perhaps unsurprising that for young people in custody, the 'causes of crime' do not appear to have been addressed with any great success. Whilst there has been an increase in the numbers of children under the age of 15 who are imprisoned of over 800 per cent in the 15 years up to 2006,[1] children in custody still have severe literacy problems and the vast majority have been excluded from school or have spent time in care or outside the family home.[2] It is still the case that the prison population contains an unnecessarily large number of remand prisoners and in 2007, figures indicated that 24 per cent of young people remanded into custody were acquitted and 51 per cent received non-custodial sentences.[3] The damage that is done by these unnecessary remands is huge and can be irreparable.

Foreign nationals have faced a particularly virulent campaign in the tabloid press in recent years leading to further marginalisation. There has been an exponential increase in the numbers of foreign nationals sent to prison of 144 per cent between 1997 and 2007, whereas the equivalent increase in British nationals has been just 20 per cent.[4] The particular problems that are faced by those people imprisoned in a foreign country are far more acute and this is graphically and tragically illustrated by the fact that 16 per cent of all self inflicted deaths in prison custody in 2008 were of foreign national prisoners.[5]

One of the themes that commonly arises when trying to addressing the issues around imprisonment is that prisoners are somehow undeserving of sympathy or that a lesser value should be placed upon their rights than for those at liberty. This was a theme that the Justice Secretary recently repeated in his highly misleading assault on the provision of public funding for prisoners in which he has sought to prevent prisoners from having access to publicly funded lawyers before they have raised their complaints within the prison system.[6]

1    Youth Justice Board (2006) Annual Statistics 2005/2006.
2    Prison Reform Trust: Bromley Briefing Factfile, June 2009, p29.
3    Prison Reform Trust: Bromley Briefing Factfile, June 2009, p27.
4    Prison Reform Trust: Bromley Briefing Factfile, June 2009, p 26.
5    HMCIP, Annual Report 2007/8.
6    http://www.justice.gov.uk/consultations/docs/legal-aid-refocusing-on-priority-cases-consultation.pdf

As the criminal justice system has become more focussed on the needs of victims, the current thinking appears to be to try and characterise victims' rights as being in conflict with the rights of those in custody and that respect for victims' rights requires a rolling back of the rights of those who have been imprisoned. This is a false dichotomy and there is no such conflict between the two groups – the issues of openness and accountability being at the heart of the concerns of both victims and prisoners. Attempts to limit the rights of those in the custody of the state are particularly disturbing as this group are dependent upon the state to provide the mechanisms for their protection. As with all attacks on vulnerable members of society, the erosion of the rights of prisoners should stand as a stark forewarning of the general erosion of wider rights in society.

Against this rather depressing political backdrop, we have been able to find some comfort in the cyclical nature of these attacks on prisoners' rights which provides some hope that alternative models may be explored in the future. We are able to remind ourselves of the resourcefulness that prisoners have long demonstrated in challenging abuses of power by the state. As the ability of prisoners to access legal advice and representation is likely to suffer significantly in the coming years, we are very pleased to have had the opportunity to work with Legal Action Group to provide what we hope is a comprehensive guide to the law and practice relating to prisoners and imprisonment which we hope will prove accessible and informative to prisoners and practitioners alike. The structure of the book seeks to follow the path of a prisoner through the custodial process by looking at the prison into which one is first received and following through the issues of categorisation and allocation, the conditions that exist in prisons and the right prisoners have while detained through to the various mechanisms for release. Although the routes for challenging adverse decisions are mentioned in context in which they arise, we have concluded with a chapter seeking to provide a more thorough exploration of the main remedies available to prisoners.

We have received important contributions to this book from a number of people: our colleague Nancy Collins contributed the chapters on healthcare and contact with the outside world; Siobhan Grey who assisted with the writing of the section on criminal offences committed in prison; Naomi Lumsdaine who wrote about discrimination issues and Nicki Rensten who wrote about living conditions in prison. We are generally indebted to Nicki and her colleagues at the Prisoners' Advice Service for their assistance and expertise in all areas of prison law.

As well as receiving formal contributions, we have also been greatly assisted both in our practices and in our writing by a number of colleagues specialising in prison law, particularly Phillippa Kaufmann, Tim Owen QC, John Dickinson, Hugh Southey, Ed Fitzgerald QC and Pete Weatherby. We are also very grateful to all of our colleagues at Bhatt Murphy for their support and tolerance as we have written this book whist simultaneously trying to keep up with our normal caseloads and responsibilities.

As with any piece of writing, in the time between concluding the final draft and receiving the proofs, there have been a number of important developments in this field. During that time the Lifer Manual (PSO 4700) was renamed as the Indeterminate Sentence Manual with the eligibility criteria for town visits being extensively re-written; the system of Prison Service Orders has been rationalised to provide one system covering all of NOMS including the probation service; and, the Legal Services Commission has reported back on its consultation on public funding with the introduction of fixed and standard fees having been approved. We have sought to flag up these changes in the main body of the text where possible. Otherwise the text aims to reflect the law as it was at 30 April 2009.

Simon Creighton
Hamish Arnott
31 July 2009

# Contents

## APPENDICES

# Table of cases

References in the right-hand column are to paragraph numbers.

# Table of statutes

References in the right-hand column are to paragraph numbers.

# Table of statutory instruments

References in the right-hand column are to paragraph numbers.

# Abbreviations

| | |
|---|---|
| ACCT | Assessment Care in Custody Teamwork |
| AG | Advice to Governors |
| AI | Agency Instructions (NOMS) |
| ALO | Adjudication Liaison Officer |
| BCU | Briefing and Casework Unit |
| CALM | Controlling Anger and Learning to Manage it |
| CART | category A review team |
| CCTV | Close Circuit Television |
| CCRC | Criminal Cases Review Commission |
| CDA 1988 | Crime and Disorder Act 1988 |
| CDS | Criminal Defence Service |
| CHR 2001 | Children's Home Regulations 2001 |
| CICA | Criminal Injuries Compensation Authority |
| CJA | Criminal Justice Act |
| CJIA 2008 | Criminal Justice and Immigration Act 2008 |
| CJPOA 1994 | Criminal Justice and Public Order Act 1994 |
| CNA | certified normal accommodation |
| CPR | Civil Procedure Rules |
| CPS | Crown Prosecution Service |
| CPT | Committee for the Prevention of Torture |
| C & R | Control and Restraint |
| CRD | Conditional Release Date |
| C(S)A 1997 | Crime (Sentences) Act 1997 |
| CSBS | Cognitive Skills Booster System |
| CSC | Close Supervision Centres |
| CSCP | Cognitive Self-Change Programme |
| CSRA | Cell sharing risk assessment |
| DCR | Discretionary Conditional Release |
| DDA | Disability Discrimination Act |
| DHSP | Directorate of High Security Prisons |
| DLO | Disability Liaison Officer |
| DOM | Director of Offender Management |
| DSPD | Dangerous and Severe Personality Disorder Unit |
| DTO | Detention and Training Order |
| DVCVA 2004 | Domestic Violence, Crime and Victims Act 2004 |
| ECHR | European Convention on Human Rights |
| ECtHR | European Court of Human Rights |
| ECL | End of Custody Licence |

| | |
|---|---|
| EPR | European Prison Rules |
| ETS | Enhanced Thinking Skills |
| FLO | Family Liaison Officer |
| HDC | Home Detention Curfew |
| HMCIP | Her Majesty's Chief Inspector of Prisons |
| HMP | Her Majesty's Prison |
| HMP detention | Detention at Her Majesty's Pleasure |
| HRA 1998 | Human Rights Act 1998 |
| HSF | Healthy Sexual Functioning |
| HSU | High Secure Unit |
| IA | Independent Adjudicator |
| IA 1971 | Immigration Act 1971 |
| ICCPR | International Covenant on Civil and Political Rights |
| ICM | Intensive Case Management |
| IEPS | Incentives and Earned Privileges System |
| IG | Instructions to Governors |
| IMB | Independent Monitoring Boards |
| IND | Immigration and Nationality Directorate |
| IPP | Indeterminate sentence for public protection |
| IRMTs | Inter-departmental Risk Management Teams |
| LAP | Local Advisory Panel |
| LED | Licence Expiry Date |
| LIDS | Local Inmate Database System |
| LSC | Legal Services Commission |
| MALRAP | Multi-agency lifer risk assessment panel |
| MAPPA | Multi-Agency Public Protection Arrangements |
| MAPPP | Multi-Agency Public Protection Panels |
| MBU | Mother and Baby Unit |
| MDT | Mandatory drug test |
| MHA 1983 | Mental Health Act 1983 |
| MoJ | Ministry of Justice |
| NDPB | Non-Departmental Public Body |
| NIAA 2002 | Nationality, Immigration and Asylum Act 2002 |
| NIS | National Identification Service |
| NOMS | National Offender Management Service Agency |
| NSF | National Security Framework |
| OASys | Offender Assessment System |
| OCA | Observation, Classification and Allocation |
| OM | Offender Manager |
| OMA 2007 | Offender Management Act 2007 |
| OMM | Offender Management model |
| OPCAT | Optional Protocol to the Convention |
| OPV | Official Prison Visitor |
| OS | Offender Supervisor |
| PA 1952 | Prison Act 1952 |
| PBR | Parole Board Rules |
| PCC(S)A 2000 | Powers of the Criminal Courts (Sentencing) Act 2000 |
| PCO | Prison custody officer |
| PCT | Primary Care Trust |

| | |
|---|---|
| PED | Parole Eligibility Date |
| PER | Prisoner Escort Record form |
| PI | Probation Instruction |
| PMU | Prison Service's Population Management Unit |
| POA | Prison Officers' Association |
| PPO | Prisons and Probation Ombudsman |
| PPU | Public Protection Unit |
| PR | Prison Rules |
| PSI | Prison Service Instructions |
| PSO | Prison Service Orders |
| PWU | Protected Witness Unit |
| RA | Responsible authority |
| REO | Race Equality Office |
| ROTL | Release on Temporary Leave |
| RPA | Repatriation of Prisoners Act |
| RRA | Race Relations Act |
| RRLO | Race Relations Liaison Officer |
| SCH | Secure children's home |
| SDS | Standard determinate sentence |
| SED | Sentence Expiry Date |
| SGC | Sentencing Guidelines Council |
| SIR | Security intelligence reports |
| SLA | Service level agreements |
| SMR | Standard Minimum Rules |
| SO | Standing orders |
| SOTP | Sex Offender Treatment Programme |
| SSU | Special Secure Unit |
| STC | Secure training centres |
| STCR | Secure Training Centre Rules |
| TC | Therapeutic Community |
| UAL | Unlawfully at large |
| UKBA | UK Border Agency |
| UNCRC | United Nations Convention on the Rights of the Child |
| ViSOR | Violent and Sexual Offenders Register |
| YJB | Youth Justice Board |
| YOI | Young offender institution |
| YOIR | Young Offender Institution Rules |
| YOT | Youth offending team |

# CHAPTER 1

# Introduction

1.1    Prisoners are in a very vulnerable position, the deprivation of liberty leaving them dependent upon the prison authorities for the provision and protection of their basic needs and rights. The aim of this book is to explore and seek to explain what duties the state has to those in detention and the nature of the rights that survive imprisonment. In the ten years following the enactment of the Human Rights Act (HRA) 1998, cases concerning imprisonment have continued to occupy the courts with diverse matters such as the provision of healthcare for drug users, the use of pain compliance techniques on young offenders and the right to vote or start a family dividing public opinion. The development of a substantial body of domestic jurisprudence on prisons and the treatment of prisoners has undoubtedly been a positive development, but paradoxically it can also serve to dislocate the legal issues from the underlying principles that originally generated the concept of prison law, allowing these principles to be read through the prism of short-term government policies.

1.2    The United Nation's International Covenant on Civil and Political Rights (ICCPR) articulates the fundamental principles upon which the rule of law should be based and in relation to imprisonment, it commences with the principle that, 'all persons deprived of their liberty shall be treated with humanity and with respect for the inherent dignity of the human person'.[1] It goes on to articulate the aim of imprisonment as being rehabilitation and the social reintegration of prisoners into the community.[2] The mechanism that has been identified for achieving these aims is through 'the minimisation of [the] differences between prison life and liberty'.[3] It is

---

1  ICCPR art 10(1).
2  ICCPR art 10(3).
3  UN Standard Minimum Rules on the Treatment of Prisoners, rule 60(1).

possible to identify three categories of rights within the context of imprisonment:

1) Imprisonment automatically involves the forfeiture of liberty and freedom of movement.
2) Certain rights cannot be circumscribed such as the right to life, respect for physical and mental integrity and freedom from torture or other cruel or inhuman treatment or punishment, freedom from slavery and the right of access to the law.
3) Rights that are necessarily interfered with by the fact of imprisonment but which are not extinguished, such as freedom of thought and expression, rights associated with personal expression such as voting and marriage and the right to family contact.

1.3   Prison law essentially looks at these three categories and seeks to define the parameters of the state in relation to these rights. The structure of this book seeks to explain the manner in which deprivation of liberty is authorised, the steps that have to be taken to uphold and protect non-derogable rights and the extent to which the requirements of imprisonment can interfere with those rights that are necessarily circumscribed by the fact of imprisonment.

1.4   The reason why such a large body of prison law has developed to resolve these issues and the reason why the HRA 1998 has been so frequently relied upon is probably attributable to the very sparse statutory framework that governs the prison estate. The Prison Act 1952 and the Prison Rules 1999 primarily contain a framework for the regulation and management of prisons, enabling the executive to formulate the policies that govern the day to day life for prisoners. The policy documents do not provide a set of enforceable minimum standards and prisoners have no more than an expectation that they will be treated in accordance with the policy as it currently stands, thereby leaving no protection when policies are changed as can frequently happen when politicians respond to perceived public concerns about the penal system.

1.5   The suggestion that the administration of prisons would be improved by the introduction of such standards is neither new nor does it appear to be contentious. The Woolf Report into the Prison Disturbances in April 1990 made a number of recommendations to improve prison administration and conditions. These included:

- clearer information being provided to prisoners about expectations through the introduction of compacts;
- a set of required accredited standards and conditions;
- control over prisoner numbers within individual prisons;

- improved sanitation;
- a greater emphasis on community links; and
- a formal grievance procedure with 'prisoners normally being given reasons for decisions'.[4]

1.6 Although twenty years have passed since those recommendations were made and largely endorsed by the subsequent government white paper, *Custody Care and Justice*,[5] the commitment to implement these changes has been extremely patchy. For example, whilst the complaints process in prisons was completely overhauled, the recommendation for a complaints adjudicator that is independent of the Prison Service has only been partially implemented with the Prisons and Probation Ombudsman continuing to bemoan the lack of a statutory basis for his office. The recommendation for enforceable minimum standards has never been mooted as a serious plank of prison policy. The Prison Service Performance Standards are a managerial audit tool, rather than a source of protection for prisoners.

1.7 The decision of the House of Lords in relation to the provision of offending behaviour programmes for prisoners serving indeterminate sentences[6] provides an illustration of the worrying results that can arise in the absence of such standards and also of the importance that international standards should have in shaping prison policy. The European Prison Rules (EPR) and the Standard Minimum Rules (SMR) suggest that prisoners should receive treatment that takes into account their individual needs – referred to as the principle of individualised treatment – and is tailored to their individual sentence and rehabilitation plan.[7] This requirement is in effect a corollary of the rehabilitative aim of imprisonment. This was a requirement that was patently missing in relation to the planning for indeterminate sentences with prisoners reaching their first possible release dates with no sentence planning having been conducted, no treatment having been given and no reports being written. The Lords variously described this situation as 'unacceptable', a 'systemic breach of a public law duty' and Lord Hope went so far as to call it 'deplorable'. However, the application of public law principles, even with the added bolster of the engagement of article 5 rights under

4 *Report of an Inquiry into Prison Disturbances*, April 1990, Cmnd 1456, HMSO, p26.
5 HMSO Cmnd 1647.
6 *James (formerly Walker), Lee and Wells v Secretary of State for Justice* [2009] UKHL 22.
7 EPR 103; SMR 63(1).

the European Convention on Human Rights (ECHR) was unable to provide a resolution to the problem. The resulting judgment arguably emptied parole reviews for this class of prisoner of any meaning, reducing them to a formalistic process. Had the prisoners been able to access enforceable standards in relation to their treatment throughout their sentences, it is arguable that this situation could have been addressed more effectively.

1.8     These tensions and the continuing public debate about the nature and purpose of imprisonment mean that prisoners' cases will almost certainly continue to be a major area of law for many years to come. This book reflects the law as at 30 April 2009 but as prisons standards and practices are so policy driven, it is necessary for practitioners and advisers to be aware of changes in penal policy and practice. *Legal Action*[8] contains regular legal updates and the Prisoners' Advice Service publishes and distributes quarterly bulletins on legal developments and it is strongly recommended that these are utilised by anyone providing advice in this area.

8  *Legal Action* is published by Legal Action Group: see www.lag.org.uk/legalaction

## CHAPTER 2

# Legal framework and supervision

*continued*

# Who makes up the prison population?

2.1    The number of people detained in penal institutions in England and Wales remains of high concern when compared with other Western European countries.[1] The actual figures are regularly published by the Ministry of Justice.[2] The prison population has been inexorably rising over recent years and throughout most of 2008 and 2009 it operated well in excess of the certified normal accommodation (CNA) figure with no obvious end to the problem in sight. This has an inevitable impact on the quality of life in prisons, the possibility of prisoners being located in institutions close to their homes and families, and the ability of the Prison Service to provide access to offending behaviour programmes on a timely basis.

2.2    The prison population at 31 March 2009 provides a useful snapshot. At that date there was a total of 83,346 (in prisons, young offender institutions (YOIs), secure training centres (STCs) and secure children's homes (SCHs)) 4,410 of whom were female. The total was made up of:

- *Remand prisoners* – those who have been refused bail and the courts have ordered to be detained pending trial. There were a total of 12,987 held in prisons or YOIs, 537 of which were under 18.
- *Fine defaulters and non-criminal prisoners* – a total of 1,744. This included those detained under the Immigration Act 1971 after completion of their criminal sentences in either prisons or the Prison Service run immigration detention centres.
- *Sentenced adults* – those 18 or over serving determinate sentences, extended sentences or one of the types of indeterminate sentences. There was a total of 66,688. Of these 12,151 were serving indeterminate sentences.
- *Sentenced children in YOIs* (15- to 17-year-olds) – there was a total of 1,593 including 34 females.
- 255 children in *secure training centres* – including 87 females.
- 198 children in *secure children's homes* – including 35 females.

1   A prison population of 152 per 100,000 of population: 73 per cent more than in 1992, as against 96 in France or 88 in Germany. Of course the other contrast is with the USA which imprisons 760 per 100,000, or Russia where the figure is 626 (figures from the King's College International Centre for Prison Studies: www.kcl.ac.uk/depsta/law/research/icps/worldbrief/wpb_stats.php).

2   www.justice.gov.uk/latest-updates/populationincustody.htm

# The agencies of imprisonment

## The Ministry of Justice

2.3   The Ministry of Justice was created in May 2007 and the new Secretary of State for Justice took over the primary statutory duty to supervise and maintain prisons,[3] and the statutory duty to provide probation services[4] from the Home Secretary. The day to day management and commissioning of prison and probation services is in fact delegated to the National Offender Management Service (NOMS) Agency (see para 2.5 below), which in turn oversees the operations of the Prison Service and the National Probation Service.

2.4   The NOMS framework document issued in July 2008 states that as the responsible minister the Secretary of State for Justice is accountable and responsible to Parliament for the NOMS Agency. The Secretary of State is advised by the Permanent Secretary of the Ministry and may delegate his responsibilities set out below to a junior minister. As at April 2009 there was a minister for the NOMS Agency and youth justice. The Secretary of State's responsibilities under the framework document include:

- setting the strategic direction, objectives, key performance indicators and targets of the NOMS Agency;
- determining the policy and financial framework within which the NOMS Agency operates;
- annually approving the NOMS Agency corporate and business plans;
- holding the NOMS Agency Director General to account for the performance of the Agency and the delivery of its plans, objectives and targets;
- publishing and laying before the House of Commons the NOMS Agency annual report and accounts;
- approving any policy or operational practice, or a revision of the same, determined by the Agency which is likely to arouse parliamentary, media or public interest or concern; and
- approving revisions to the Agency Framework Document, obtaining approval from HM Treasury ministers as appropriate.

The Permanent Secretary also acts as the Ministry of Justice's departmental sponsor. As such he or she is responsible for advising the

---

3   Under Prison Act (PA) 1952 ss1 and 4.
4   Offender Management Act (OMA) 2007 s2 and see also Secretary of State for Justice Order 2007 SI No 2128.

Secretary of State for Justice on how well NOMS and its Director General are performing, and also chairs the Offender Management Supervisory Board which provides 'strategic supervision' of the agency.

## The National Offender Management Service Agency

2.5 NOMS[5] is an executive agency of the Ministry of Justice currently operating under a framework document issue in July 2008.[6] NOMS was first created in 2004 following the recommendations of the report of Lord Carter *Managing Offenders, Reducing Crime.*[7] This report made three broad recommendations – that there should be 'end to end' supervision of offenders from their first contact with the Probation Service to the end of the sentence, that there should be a clear distinction between the commissioning and provision of services, and finally that there should be 'contestability' between providers. The last principle clearly envisaged the possibility of privatisation of probation as well as Prison Services. When NOMS was first created the Prison Service remained a distinct executive agency with its own Director General.

2.6 The current framework document for NOMS was issued following a ministerial statement issued in January 2008 which in turn responded to Lord Carter's more recent review of prisons.[8] These changes effectively amalgamated NOMS and the Prison Service into one headquarters with a single Director General. The framework document states that the responsibility of the NOMS Agency is to deliver the sentences and orders of the courts of England and Wales by:

- commissioning adult offender services in custody and the community from public, private and non-governmental organisations;
- managing the Prison Service; and
- overseeing the Boards and Trusts which provide probation services.

2.7 NOMS is managed by a Director General who in turn manages regional Directors of Offender Management (DOMs) who are responsible for the provision of both prison and probation services in their respective areas. They have since April 2009 replaced the previous

---

5  www.noms.justice.gov.uk
6  www.justice.gov.uk/docs/noms-agency-framework.pdf
7  Which reported in December 2003.
8  *Securing the Future – proposals for the efficient and sustainable use of custody in England and Wales*, Ministry of Justice, December 2007.

system of separate area managers for the Prison Service, and regional offender managers within the Probation Service. There are 11 areas each with their own DOM. The organisational structure for NOMS is available at the Prison Service website.

2.8     In relation to prisons, the framework document states that public sector prisons and YOIs are run by NOMS and managed through service level agreement (SLAs) agreed between DOMs and individual Governors. Private sector prisons operate under contract to NOMS. NOMS is responsible for managing the prison population, including Prisoner Escort and Custody Services, maintaining the existing estate and building prison capacity. In addition, the NOMS Agency is commissioned by other organisations, in particular by the Youth Justice Board to provide secure accommodation places and attendance centres for young people, and by the UK Border Agency to provide places for immigration detainees.

From 1 August 2009 a new system of issuing policy guidance has been introduced to harmonise procedures throughout NOMS. Prison Service Instructions will continue to be issued to prisons. However, Probation Circulars are to be replaced with Probation Instructions (PIs).[9] NOMS Agency Instructions (AIs) will provide guidance to NOMS headquarters, and regional management, staff. Clearly it will be some years before existing guidance is replaced.

## The Prison Service

2.9     As noted above, the Prison Service[10] has now effectively been subsumed into the NOMS Agency and is managed by the NOMS Director General. However it remains a separate agency. Its statement of purpose says 'Her Majesty's Prison Service serves the public by keeping in custody those committed by the courts. Our duty is to look after them with humanity and help them lead law-abiding and useful lives in custody and after release'.

2.10    The Chief Operating Officer, who reports to the NOMS Director General, supervises the Directors of Offender Management, the Office of National Commissioning (which oversees the private prisons), the Public Protection Unit and the Mental Health Unit. There is a separate Director of High Security, who also reports to the Director General, who has responsibility for general security policy, and management of the eight high security prisons. There are also Directors of

---

9   PSI 23/2009, PI 1/2009, AI/2009.
10  www.hmprisonservice.gov.uk

Commissioning and Operational Policy, and of Offender Health. The various policy leads at Prison Service Headquarters are responsible for issuing the guidance contained in PSOs and PSIs (see below).

## The statutory and policy framework of the Prison Service

### The Prison Act 1952

2.11    The Secretary of State for Justice retains responsibility for the management of the prisons[11] although the operational management of prisons is now delegated to the NOMS Agency. The Prison Act 1952 also requires the Secretary of State for Justice to ensure compliance with the Act and the Prison Rules 1999.[12] The Prison Act does not include a comprehensive code for the administration of prisons but sets out the key legal responsibilities and office holders in connection with them.

2.12    As the Prison Act 1952 itself contains relatively few provisions a key section is that which allows the making of Rules for the management of prisons.[13] These are contained in the Prison Rules (PR) 1999 as amended for adult prisons[14] and the Young Offender Institution Rules (YOIR) 2000 as amended for YOIs.[15] These are issued by statutory instrument and therefore have legal force as with other secondary legislation.

### The Prison Rules and Young Offender Institution Rules

2.13    The PR 1999 and YOIR 2000 contain broadly similar provisions (the differences are highlighted where necessary throughout the text of this book). These range from setting out the purpose and aims of imprisonment,[16] to provisions relating to food health and hygiene, to those dealing with discipline and use of force. As delegated legislation provisions of the Rules can be quashed if found to be ultra vires the Prison Act itself.[17]

---

11  PA 1952 ss1 and 4.
12  PA 1952 s4(2). This duty clearly does not prevent prisoners bringing judicial reviews of breaches of the Act – *Leech v Deputy Governor of Parkhurst Prison* [1988] AC 533.
13  PA 1952 s47.
14  SI 1999 No 728.
15  SI 2000 No 3371.
16  PR rule 3, YOIR rule 3.
17  For example *R v Secretary of State for the Home Department ex p Leech (No 2)* [1994] QB 198.

*Centrally issued policies*

2.14    Beyond the Prison Act and the Rules, the Prison Service issues a large
amount of policy guidance. This is now largely issued through Prison Service Orders (PSOs) and Prison Service Instructions (PSIs).[18]
These replaced the previous systems of issuing policy guidance
that were contained in Standing Orders (SOs) and Instructions and
Advice to Governors (IGs and AGs). The new system commenced
in 1997 and although PSIs and PSOs have been issued for several
years there are still some issues covered by earlier guidance. A very
helpful guide is available at the Prison Service which references the
appropriate document by subject matter.[19]

2.15    PSOs tend to be long-term policy documents that cover a whole
area such as segregation[20] or prison discipline.[21] PSIs are usually
shorter term and often will provide updates to PSOs. All PSOs and
PSIs are available on the Prison Service website and should also be
available to prisoners through prison libraries.[22] PSOs and PSIs contain both general guidance and mandatory requirements, the latter
always being italicised in the text. This system was introduced in
order to introduce more clarity and certainty into the issuing of policies following a recommendation of the Woodcock report into the
escapes from Whitemoor, which criticised the then systems of issuing policies.[23] From 1 August 2009 there will be a single system of
issuing policy guidance across NOMS. New Prison Service guidance
will from now on be issued as PSIs only (PSI 23/2009).

2.16    The Prison Service does issue other policy guidance that is not
in the form of PSOs or PSIs. Most notable is the National Security
Framework (NSF) which sets out national policy on important issues
such as categorisation, searching, intelligence and other security
issues. This is only available on the Prison Service intranet. This
book has been written with access to the version from 2004 but the
Prison Service has refused to disclose the most recent and up to date
version. The non-disclosure of the NSF is potentially unlawful. Non-
statutory policies are capable of providing the lawful basis for interference with Convention rights, but where this is the case such policies

18  PSO 0001.
19  www.hmprisonservice.gov.uk/assets/documents/1000462Dsubject_index_
    apr09.pdf
20  PSO 1700.
21  PSO 2000.
22  PSO 0001 section 5.
23  December 1994 Cm 2741.

must be adequately accessible.[24] Other policies not available on the internet include the Special Secure Unit (SSU) operating standards and the guidance on procedures relating to Close Supervision Centres (CSCs).

2.17 The Prison Service also has published a set of Performance Standards.[25] These standards define the baselines against which prisons are audited. Although they are designed to form the basis of such audits, they are sometimes useful to identify policy aims the breach of which may afford prisoners a remedy.

## Local policies

2.18 The centrally issued policies include mandatory requirements, but will also often require local prisons to have their own policies. For example the NSF requires prisons to have local searching and security strategies, and the PSO on incentives and earned privileges sets out a National Framework under which prisons are expected to devise their own schemes in order to meet specific requirements of the institution. Accordingly in order to understand the legal basis of a decision it may be necessary to obtain a copy of the local policy.

## Policies generally

2.19 Although policies do not have the force of law in the same way as primary or secondary legislation it is misleading to suggest that they have no legal effect. The courts have often commented upon the desirability of the adoption of policies to ensure that wide statutory discretions are exercised reasonably and consistently, as long as policies are not so inflexible so as to fetter discretion.[26] Policies may provide the lawful basis for interferences with Convention rights (see above). In such circumstances if they are not followed such rights may be breached.[27] They may also provide prisoners with a legitimate

---

24 In *Silver v UK* (1983) EHRR 347 the European Court of Human Rights accepted that Standing Order 5 could provide the basis by which the UK ensured interferences with prisoner communications were 'in accordance with the law' for the purposes of article 8, but found the UK in breach by not ensuring that Standing Order 5 was available to prisoners.

25 Available at www.hmprisonservice.gov.uk

26 See *R (Pate) v Secretary of State for the Home Department* [2002] EWHC Admin 1018.

27 For example in *Wainwright v UK* (2007) 44 EHRR 40 a failure to follow searching policy gave rise to a breach of article 8.

expectation that they are followed.[28] The courts will quash policies that are unlawful as ultra vires either the Prison Act or the Rules.[29]

## Prison Service personnel

2.20    The Prison Act[30] requires each prison to have a 'governor, a chaplain[31] and such other officers as may be necessary'.[32] Prisoners are deemed to be in the legal custody of the Governor of the prison.[33] Prisons holding women are specifically required to have sufficient numbers of women officers.[34]

2.21    Each publicly run prison and YOI in fact will have a Governor,[35] who has the support of Operational Manager grades who in turn manage the prison officer grades. The Act also confirms that prisons that are large enough may have a deputy governor.[36] Governors are permitted under the Rules, with the leave of the Secretary of State for Justice, to delegate any of their powers and duties to another officer.[37]

### Operational managers

2.22    Each prison will also have a number of operational managers.[38] These will either be senior operational managers (on pay band A to D) or operational managers (pay band E and F). Such managers will be known by their job title (such as Head of Security) and may be

---

28  *R v Secretary of State for the Home Department ex p Hargreaves* [1997] 1 WLR 906 – although in the prison context legitimate expectation has to date been construed as only giving the prisoner the right to benefit from the policy as promulgated from time to time, not a substantive benefit that can survive a change of policy.

29  For example the cell searching policy in *R (Daly) v Secretary of State for the Home Department* [2001] 2 AC 532.

30  PA 1952 s7.

31  This must be a Church of England chaplain (s7(4)) – although where the numbers of prisoner warrant it, visiting Ministers of other faiths can be appointed (s10).

32  PA 1952 s7(1).

33  PA 1952 s13(1).

34  PA 1952 s7(2) – although what is 'sufficient' is not defined.

35  Sometimes also known as the 'number one Governor'.

36  PA 1952 s7(3).

37  PR rule 81, YOIR rule 85 – generally the level of officer permitted to carry out specific tasks will be specified in the relevant PSO.

38  Which used to be known as 'governor grades' – which led to the confusing position that the actual Governor of the prisoner was known as the 'governing governor'.

authorised to carry out functions on behalf of the Governor.[39] They are officers for the purposes of the Prison and YOI Rules.

## Prison officers

2.23 There are three uniformed prison officer grades. Prison officers, senior officers (SOs) who act as first line managers, and principal officers (POs) who manage senior officers and may have responsibility for managing accommodation units or operational tasks such as security under the supervision of an operational manager. Officers are required to conform to the Prison or YOI Rules and are under a duty to report to the Governor any 'abuse or impropriety' which comes to their knowledge.[40] The Rules also include prohibitions on officers accepting any gift in connection with their office, engaging in any business activity with prisoners, bringing any item in or out of a prison for a prisoner, without the Governor's knowledge knowingly communicating with former prisoners or their friends or family, or making unauthorised communications to the press on matters relating to their work.[41] There is also a specific code of discipline to deal with misconduct by prison officer.[42] A prohibition on the right of prison officer's to strike[43] was disapplied due to an agreement with the Prison Officers' Association (POA) to a procedure for resolving disputes, but in May 2008 the POA withdrew from these arrangements. New legislation was then introduced to reinstate the statutory prohibition on prison officers striking.[44]

## Other staff

2.24 Within a prison there will also be many non-uniformed staff such as administrators, catering staff, along with those working in education. These do not have the general powers of prison officers, but may in some circumstances be able to carry out some functions such as searching.

39 For example a 'suitably trained' Operational Manager can act as an adjudicator in prison disciplinary proceedings – see PSO 2000.
40 PR rule 62, YOIR rule 67.
41 PR rules 63, 65–67, YOIR rules 68, 70–72.
42 PR rule 69, YOIR rule 73.
43 Criminal Justice and Public Order Act (CJPOA) 1994 s127.
44 Criminal Justice and Immigration Act (CJIA) 2008 s138.

## Private prisons

2.25    The first statutory authority for the privatisation of prisons was contained in the Criminal Justice Act (CJA) 1991.[45] Although the official Labour Party line in opposition was that private prisons would be returned to public management[46] this policy was reversed within weeks of the 1997 election. Since then all newly built prisons have been contracted out and England and Wales now has a greater percentage of its prison population held in private prisons than the US.[47] There are now 11 private prisons and YOIs which are run under contracts with NOMS in England and Wales. Nine prisons have been financed, designed, built and run by the private sector under PFI contracts – Dovegate, Altcourse, Ashfield, Forest Bank, Lowdham Grange, Parc, Rye Hill, Bronzefield and Peterborough. In addition Wolds and Doncaster were built and financed by the public sector but are run by private companies under management-only contracts.[48]

2.26    Private prisons do not have Governors. They are instead managed by a Director and a Controller.[49] The Director is employed by the private company contracted to run the prison and is the day to day manager. The Controller is a Ministry of Justice employee whose role is to review the running of the prison and to report on this to the Secretary of State, and to investigate and report on allegations made against prison custody officers.[50] The Secretary of State for Justice has the power to take over temporarily the management of a private prison if the Director has lost effective control.[51]

2.27    Private prisons are subject to the legislative framework of the Prison Act and the Prison and YOI Rules which apply with appropriate amendments.[52] PSOs and other centrally issued mandatory policy guidance also applies to private prisons. When the legislation

---

45  CJA 1991 s84.
46  Jack Straw famously stated in March 1995 '[I]t is not appropriate for people to profit out of incarceration' two years before becoming Home Secretary.
47  About 11% as against 7.2% in the US: see the Prison Reform Trust website.
48  Two former privately managed prisons, Blakenhurst and Buckley Hall, are now publicly run.
49  CJA 1991 s85(1): who together have the functions of the governor in publicly run prisons for the purposes of the Prison Act 1952: CJA 1991 s87(2).
50  CJA 1991 s85(4).
51  CJA 1991 s88.
52  CJA 1991 s87, PR 1999 r82 and YOIR 2000 r86 – which provide, for example, that references to an 'officer' in the Rules includes references to a prison custody officer.

enabling the privatisation of prisons was first brought into force the
Director was not permitted to make conduct disciplinary hearings or
make decisions relating to the segregation or use of mechanical restraints. These functions were reserved to the Controller. In a move
that demonstrates how uncontroversial the privatisation of the state's
coercive functions has become, this position was changed in November 2007 when changes to the Prison and YOI Rules facilitated by the
Offender Management Act (OMA) 2007[53] were brought into force.
Accordingly references to the Governor throughout this book should
also be taken, unless stated otherwise, to include Directors.

2.28    The statutory framework permits the contract to provide that
the running of part of a private prison can be sub-contracted.[54] This
permits, for example, the running of health care services to be sub-
contracted to separate private suppliers. The fact that more than one
private company may be involved in the running of a prison can
lead to complexity in attempting to allocate legal responsibility when
something goes wrong (see chapter 12).

2.29    Privately run prisons have prison custody officers (PCOs) who do
not have the general powers of a constable that prison officers in publicly run prisons have.[55] Accordingly the powers of PCOs have to be
more closely prescribed by legislation.[56] PCOs also have to be certified by the Secretary of State for Justice to carry out custodial duties.[57]
Changes were made to the powers of PCOs in November 2007 by
OMA 2007 that increased their powers of search so that they are now
broadly in line with prison officers in public prisons.[58] Private prisons are subject to inspections by the Chief Inspector of Prisons in the
same way as public prisons.

### Escorts and escort contractors

2.30    The Prison Act confirms that prisoners remain in the legal custody
of the Governor if outside the prison in the custody of a prison officer.[59] Accordingly this gives lawful authority for prison officers of

---

53  OMA 2007 s19 removed the bar previously contained in s85(3) on directors
    performing these functions.
54  CJA 1991 s84(1).
55  CJA 1991 s87(3).
56  CJA 1991 s86 as amended.
57  CJA 1991 s89 and Sch 10 – and such certification can be suspended or revoked
    where it appears that to the Secretary of State that the PCO is not a proper or fit
    person to carry out these functions.
58  CJA 1991 s86.
59  PA 1952 s13(2).

public prisons to escort prisoners between institutions, and to and from court.

2.31    However CJA 1991 also includes provisions to allow for the privatisation of prisoner escort functions.[60] The provisions[61] allow for the contracting out of the following functions:

- Escorting prisoners between courts, prisons (including temporary custody at prisons during the journey), police stations and hospitals. This can include travel to or from institutions within the British Isles outside England and Wales, as long as one end of the journey is in England and Wales.
- The custody of prisoners held at court or while they are outside of the prison for other temporary purposes.

2.32    Privatised escort functions must be carried out by PCOs who are subject to the same certification requirements as those employed in private prisons.[62] Such PCOs are also given similar powers of search and use of force as PCOs employed in the private prisons.[63] The statute also requires there to be appointed a prisoner escort monitor who has the duty of keeping privatised escort arrangements under review and to report on them to the Secretary of State for Justice. The escort monitor is also required to investigate allegations made against escorting PCOs and alleged breaches of discipline by prisoners being escorted.[64] A panel of lay observers must also be appointed by the Secretary of State which has a duty to inspect the conditions in which prisoners are transported and to make recommendations.[65]

2.33    The Prison Service has contracted out the national inter-prison escorting arrangements to be run by GSL UK Ltd.[66] Some escorting functions, such as those relating to category A or provisional category A prisoners, are not contracted out. The various NOMS regions have individual contracts to cover escorts from prisons to local courts and police stations. These are covered by a number of different private companies.

---

60  CJA 1991 s80 as amended by the CJPOA 1994.
61  CJA 1991 ss 80(1) and 80(1A).
62  CJA 1991 s80(1) and (2).
63  CJA 1991 s82.
64  CJA 1991 s81.
65  CJA 1991 s81(1)(b).
66  A successor business to Group Four which was first given the national escorting contract in 1999 – see PSI 23/1999, PSO 6200, PSI 8/2006.

### International standards relating to management

2.34   The European Prison Rules (EPR) (see below) record that the observance of prisoners' rights is dependent upon appropriate prison management as well as the way in which prison staff treat prisoners in
their day to day contact.[67] The guidance contained in the EPR and UN
Standard Minimum Rules on the Treatment of Prisoners states that:

- There must be an ethical basis of the prison management that
  recognises the principle of humane treatment and rehabilitation
  as one purpose of the prison system.[68]
- Prison work should be recognised as a valuable public service and
  there should be provision of civil service status to prison staff with
  security of tenure and adequate salary.[69]
- Staff should be properly selected and trained and given regular
  in-service training (including on prisoners' rights).[70]
- There should be a sufficient number of specialists, such as psy-
  chiatrists, psychologists, social workers, teachers and vocational
  and sports instructors, as part of full-time prison staff.[71]

2.35   Along the same lines, the Committee of Ministers of the Council of
Europe adopted a set of European guidelines applicable to prison
staff, which emphasise their responsibility to maintain constructive,
non-discriminatory and respectful relations with prisoners under
their care.[72]

## The Probation Service

2.36   In 1907, probation supervision was given a statutory basis which allowed courts to appoint and employ probation officers. Probation officers were then formally empowered to 'advise, assist and befriend'[73]
those placed under supervision by the courts. The last 15 years have
seen a marked shift away from the original ethos of the Probation
Service accompanied by the move towards the language of 'offender
management'. The Secretary of State for Justice said to the NOMS

---

67   EPR rule 74.
68   EPR rule 72.
69   EPR rules 78 and 79(1); Standard Minimum Rules rule 46(3).
70   EPR rules 76 and 81; Standard Minimum Rules rules 46 and 47(3).
71   EPR rule 89; Standard Minimum Rules rule 49.
72   Council of Europe, Committee of Ministers, recommendation No R(97) 12,
     appendix II, 10 September 1997, at paras 11–19.
73   Probation of Offenders Act 1907 s4: a phrase that re-appeared in the Criminal
     Justice Act 1948.

annual conference in February 2009 '[g]one are the days when the main duty of probation officers was to "advise, assist and befriend" offenders. The new stated aim of the probation service: to "punish, help, change and control" offenders'.

2.37   The Probation Service is in a transition phase at the time of writing. Although the Probation Service is managed under the NOMS Agency, it is a statutory body. The National Probation Service was created by the Criminal Justice and Court Services Act (CJCSA) 2000. This divided the service into local probation boards[74] that cover the same geographical area as the different police areas. The aim of this was to better facilitate multi-agency working such as that under MAPPA (see below). However, in a process that must feel like permanent revolution to those working in probation, the local probation boards are in the process of being replaced with 'probation trusts' under OMA 2007. Under the Act the 'probation purposes' for which the Secretary of State for Justice has ultimate responsibility, include 'the supervision and rehabilitation of persons charged with or convicted of offences',[75] and this in turn includes:[76]

- assisting in the rehabilitation of offenders who are being held in prison;
- supervising persons released from prison on licence;
- providing accommodation in approved premises.[77]

2.38   Probation trusts created by OMA 2007 have statutory power to contract the provision of probation services from the private or voluntary sector.[78] The trusts are therefore being created to faciliate 'contestability' (or as their critics fear privatisation) which has been at the core of the NOMS project since its inception. As at April 2009 only eight probation boards had been transferred into trusts. The aim is to complete the transfer of the remaining 34 into trusts by April 2010. There remains a Director of Probation in NOMS who reports to the Director General. The National Probation Service issues central policy guidance in the form of Probation Circulars which are available at its website.[79] From 1 August 2009 policy guidance will be issued

---

74  CJCSA 2000 s4.
75  OMA 2007 s1(1)(c).
76  OMA 2007 s1(2).
77  This is a target duty and does not amount to a duty to individual prisoners to provide hostel accommodation to individual prisoners – *R (Irving) v London Probation Board* [2005] EWHC 605 (Admin).
78  OMA 2007 s5(3).
79  www.probation.homeoffice.gov.uk/files/pdf/MAPPA%20Guidance%202009%20Version%203.0.pdf

in the form of Probation Instructions (PIs) (PI 1/2009). Probation Officers also act under Offender Management National Standards (last issued in 2007).

2.39 Under the Offender Management Model (see chapter 4) prisoners will have allocated to them an Offender Manager (OM) (this role has replaced that of the 'home probation officer'). The OM will be a probation officer based in the prisoner's local probation area whose function is to manage the sentence from imposition until the sentence expiry date. The OM will therefore be responsible for developing the sentence plan, drafting key reports such as those required in the parole process, and also enforcing the licence (recommending recall where considered necessary). Individual prisons also have probation staff seconded from the Probation Service who also will contribute to sentence planning, the delivery of offending behaviour courses or treatment, and the provision of reports for parole or other processes.

2.40 There is a statutory duty on probation boards and trusts to ascertain whether victims of crimes, where the offender receives a sentence of 12 or more months for a sexual or violent offence, wish to make representations to the courts or the Parole Board as to whether a prisoner should be subject to any particular licence conditions on release, and further whether they want to receive information about licence conditions actually imposed.[80] If the victim does wish to make such representations it is the duty of the probation board or trust to ensure that they are forwarded to the court or the Parole Board.[81] A detailed Code of Practice relating to the treatment of victims in the criminal justice system has been in force since 2006[82] giving guidance on these powers.[83]

2.41 Probation services are subject to inspection by Her Majesty's Chief Inspector of Probation (see further below).

## The Youth Justice Board

2.42 The Youth Justice Board (YJB)[84] is a non-departmental public body that was created by the Crime and Disorder Act (CDA) 1988.[85] CDA

80 Domestic Violence, Crime and Victims Act (DVCVA) 2004 s35.
81 DVCVA 2004 s35(6).
82 Issued under DVCVA s32.
83 www.homeoffice.gov.uk/documents/victims-code-of-practice
84 www.yjb.gov.uk/en-gb/
85 CDA 1988 s41.

1988 sets out as the principal aim of the youth justice system to prevent offending by children and young people aged 10 to 17.[86] It is a body corporate and consists of up to 12 members appointed by the Secretary of State for Justice. The YJB is responsible for the allocation of prisoners under 18 and for the commissioning of secure places for such prisoners.[87] The YJB has also issued detailed policy guidance on how such allocations are made, and on the regimes that should be applicable for children in detention including on segregation and use of force.

## Youth Offending Teams

2.43    CDA 1988 also requires local authorities to put in place an annual youth justice plan, and to establish youth offending teams (YOTs).[88] Each YOT brings together professionals with a range of disciplines. Statutory involvement is required from local authority social services and education departments, the police, probation service and health authorities; other agencies, such as housing and youth and community departments, are also encouraged to contribute resources to YOTs. Each team is led by a YOT manager, who is responsible for coordinating the work of the local youth justice services.

2.44    YOTs are required to provide a supervising officer for those young people who receive custodial sentences. The supervising officer should complete a structured risk assessment known as ASSET (equivalent to the OASys assessment for adults) for each young person who come into the youth justice system. This is designed to identify why the young person has offended, what their family and lifestyle circumstances are, whether they have specific mental health or drug and alcohol-related problems, if they are engaged in learning, their level of educational attainment, and what level of risk they pose to themselves and others. The supervising officer will also work with the secure establishment to draw up a sentence plan. This should seek to address the young person's education, health and accommodation needs and resettlement issues must be addressed from the beginning of the sentence. The YOT worker will also write reports where appropriate for parole applications.

---

86   CDA 1988 s37.
87   Youth Justice Board for England and Wales Order 2000 SI No 1160 art 4.
88   CDA 1988 s39.

# UK Border Agency

2.45    The UK Border Agency (UKBA) is an executive agency of the Home Office, which is responsible for immigration services and policy. Immigration detention is authorised by the provisions of the Immigration Act (IA) 1971 as amended, and section 62 of the Nationality, Immigration and Asylum Act (NIAA) 2002.[89] Those who are both serving a sentence and are liable to be detained under the Immigration Act are held in prisons. Those detained under the Immigration Act may be held in such places as the Home Secretary may direct.[90] Those detained solely under the Immigration Act are usually held in one of the 11 immigration detention centres (two of which are managed by the Prison Service, Haslar in Gosport, and Lindholme in South Yorkshire). The primary statutory provisions concerning the management of detention centres are contained in the Asylum and Immigration Act (AIA)1999 as amended, and more detailed provisions on conditions are contained in the Detention Centre Rules 2001.

## The detention of Immigration Act detainees in prisons

2.46    In some circumstances immigration detainees will be held in prisons even though they are not serving criminal sentences. Immigration detainees should only be held in prisons when they present specific risk factors that indicate they are unsuitable for immigration detention centres, for reasons of security or control. There is a protocol between the NOMS and UKBA which sets out the criteria for allocation which states that in general terms immigration detainees will only normally be held in prison accommodation in the following circumstances:[91]

- *National security* – where there is specific verified information that a person is a member of a terrorist group or has been engaged in terrorist activities.
- *Criminality* – those detainees who have been involved in the importation of Class A drugs, committed serious offences involving

---

89  The UKBA policy on when detention under the IA 1971, including for those who have been reached the end of their criminal sentence, is contained in Enforcement Instructions and Guidance chapter 55 – at www.ukba. homeoffice.gov.uk/sitecontent/documents/policyandlaw/enforcement/detentionandremovals/

90  IA 1971 para 18 Sch 2, and para 2(4) Sch 3 – such directions are contained in the Immigration (Place of Detention) Direction 2009 which includes police cells, the 11 detention centres, prisons or hospitals.

91  PSO 4630 para 5.1.

violence, or committed a serious sexual offence requiring registration on the sex offenders' register.

- *Security* – where the detainee has escaped prison or immigration
custody, or planned or assisted others to do so.
- *Control* – engagement in serious disorder, arson, violence or damage, or planning or assisting others to so engage.

2.47　It follows that transfer to prison accommodation must never be used
as a punishment but only for genuine reasons of security or control.
Accordingly these criteria must be applied flexibly and a detainee who
falls within them may still be suitable for non-prison accommodation depending on behaviour, and for example where a ex-prisoner
has been located in an open prison, it should be accepted that they
will be suitable for an immigration detention centre.[92] In exceptional
circumstances detention in prison may be justified for the detainees
own protection.[93] Where a detainee has been in a detention centre
for some time, failure to properly consider whether their behaviour
genuinely warrants transfer to a prison may render a decision unlawful.[94] Where those detained solely under the Immigration Act are held
in prisons they should be treated as, and given access to the same
privileges as, unconvicted prisoners.[95]

## Multi-Agency Public Protection Arrangements (MAPPA)

2.48　There is a statutory duty for area chief police officers, local probation
boards or trusts and the Prison Service to establish arrangements
to assess the risks posed by serious sexual and violent offenders.[96]
These arrangements are known as Multi-Agency Public Protection
Arrangements or 'MAPPA'. The Secretary of State has, through the
Public Protection Unit at NOMS, issued statutory guidance under
section 325(8) of CJA 2003 on how the various bodies are to exercise
their functions under their MAPPA functions.[97] The Prison Service

---

92　PSO 4630 para 5.1.
93　*R (T) v Secretary of State for the Home Department* [2007] EWHC 3074 (Admin)
　　– where the Home Office claimed that a Jamaican police informer could only
　　be kept safe in prison accommodation because of the risk of reprisals in the
　　immigration detention estate.
94　*R (Ahmed and another) v Home Secretary* [2007] EWHC 1300 (Admin).
95　PSO 4360 para 3.9.
96　CJA 2003 ss325–326.
97　The third version of the MAPPA guidance was issued in 2009: www.probation.
　　homeoffice.gov.uk/files/pdf/MAPPA%20Guidance%202007%20v2.0.pdf

has also issued a Public Protection Manual which also gives guidance on MAPPA.[98]

2.49      The statutory framework of MAPPA places duties on the 'responsible authority' (RA), which collectively consists of the police, prison and probation services.[99] The relevant RA will be determined by the location of the prisoner's offender manager.[100] Other public bodies have a duty to co-operate with the responsible authority[101] including local social services departments, NHS trusts, YOTs, local authority housing and education departments, and social landlords. The MAPPA guidance includes sections on when MAPPA agencies will share and disclose information regarding offenders.[102]

2.50      The purpose of MAPPA is to facilitate multi-agency working in order to devise and implement Risk Management Plans for specific categories of sexual and violent offenders.[103] There is a specific electronic database which holds details of all MAPPA managed offenders, and onto which MAPPA meeting minutes are entered. This is the Violent and Sexual Offenders Register, or ViSOR.[104] The practical workings of the MAPPA scheme are discussed in detail in chapter 10.

## The Parole Board

2.51      Most prisoners are now released automatically on licence. However the release of all indeterminate sentenced prisoners, and the earliest possible release of some determinate sentenced prisoners convicted of violent or sexual offences,[105] and the re-release of recalled prisoners, are dependent upon a decision of the Parole Board. The board is a statutory body[106] that operates as a Non-Departmental Public Body (NDPB) sponsored by the Access to Justice unit of the Ministry of Justice.

---

98   This was last updated in 2009 – it is not available on the Prison Service website, the Manual has replaced PSO 4745.

99   CJA 2003 s325(1).

100   MAPPA guidance, 4.19.

101   CJA 2003 s325(3).

102   Sections 5 and 6.

103   See para 1.2 of the MAPPA guidance.

104   Para 2.5 of the MAPPA guidance – ViSOR is available to all police, probation and Prison Services.

105   For full details of the role and functions of the board see chapters 10 and 11.

106   CJA 2003 s239 and Sch 19.

# The places of imprisonment

## Prison Service institutions

2.52    There are 140 prisons and YOIs in England and Wales.[107] As noted above the prison population currently exceeds the Certified Normal Accommodation (CNA). The government response to the severe problems of overcrowding has been to increase prison capacity, although this continues to lag behind the increased numbers caused by, amongst other things, changes to sentencing regimes including the introduction of IPP sentence in 2005. This has in turn required the introduction of policies to ease overcrowding temporarily by letting prisoners out early (such as the end of custody licence, see chapter 11) and the increase of the maximum period prisoners can spend on an electronic tag. The Secretary of State for Justice has, however, rejected the idea, recommended by Lord Carter, to created 'titan' prisons, holding 2,500 prisoners. Instead the intention is to bring prison capacity up to a total of 96,000 by 2014 primarily by the creation of five smaller prisons holding a total of 1,500 prisoners, each divided into smaller units.[108] The type of institution in which prisoners are held primarily depends upon whether they have been sentenced and their security categorisation. Both prisons and YOIs are inspected by the Chief Inspector of Prisons (see below).

## Adult male prisons

### High security prisons

2.53    There are eight prisons in what is known as the High Security Estate:

- Belmarsh
- Frankland
- Full Sutton
- Long Lartin
- Manchester
- Wakefield
- Whitemoor
- Woodhill

---

107 www.hmprisonservice.gov.uk/prisoninformation/locateaprison/
108 Statement to Parliament by Secretary of State for Justice, 27 April 2009. See www.justice.gov.uk/news/announcement270409a.htm

The high security prisons used to be known as 'dispersal' prisons. This dated from the 1960s when it was decided that prisoners that posed a high degree of security or control problems should be dispersed into establishments throughout the country rather than concentrated into a single maximum security prison.[109] The extra security measures involved in holding prisoners in high security prisons result in a significant cost. In a written answer of 11 March 2008[110] the prisons minister confirmed that the annual cost per place was £47,613 as against £27,713 for a category B prison, £22,707 for category C, and £20,687 for a place in an open prison.

2.54    The high security prisons are managed centrally as a group by the Directorate of High Security within the Prison Service. The high security prisons hold category A and provisional (that is unsentenced) category A prisoners, although they will also hold other types of prisoner depending on their role. Belmarsh and Manchester also act as a local prisons and so will hold a large remand population, prisoners serving short sentences, as well as other category B prisoners. Conversely category A prisoners cannot be held outside the high security estate without the authority of the Director of High Security Prisons.[111]

2.55    The high security prisons are where the specialist units that deal with the prisoners assessed as most dangerous, or that pose the greatest control problems are located. Exceptional escape risk category A prisoners are held in High or Special Secure Units. Close Supervision Centres are located in Wakefield, Whitemoor and Woodhill with an assessment centre at Long Lartin. Dangerous and Severe Personality Disorder (DSPD) units are located in Frankland and Whitemoor.

## Local prisons

2.56    Local prisons are category B prisons, normally located in cities and towns, which serve the local criminal courts. They hold a large number of remand prisoners – who are normally required to be held in category B conditions – although they will also hold sentenced prisoners on short sentences, and other types of prisoner depending on their role. Local prisons have a high turnover and are especially

---

109 This was a recommendation of the 1968 Advisory Council on the Penal System report chaired by Leon Radzinowicz. The 1966 Mountbatten inquiry into Security and Escapes by contrast recommended concentration.
110 *Hansard* 11 March 2008 Col 380W.
111 See written answer of David Hanson 13 October 2008.

susceptible to problems of prison overcrowding as they are the institutions that receive prisoners direct from the courts, and can also face problems moving prisoners onto suitable prisons due to overcrowding in the rest of the system. The introduction to an inspection report from HMCIP of HMP Brixton in 2008 summarises conditions often found in local prisons:

> Brixton prison in many ways exemplifies all the problems of our overcrowded prison system. It has old, cramped and vermin-infested buildings, no workshops to provide skills training, and two prisoners eating and living in a cell with an unscreened toilet no more than an arm's length away. A visit to the top landings of Brixton's old wings would quickly dispel any notion that our prisons are 'cushy'.[112]

2.57   There is greater unpredictability in the local prison population because of uncertainty about how many prisoners will be arriving from the courts, or returning from court if escorted there. When local prisons become too overcrowded to accept further prisoners, 'Operation Safeguard' is utilised which is the protocol for holding prisoners in police cells at times of high overcrowding.[113]

## Category B and C training prisons

2.58   These constitute the majority of male, adult prisons and are where prisoners serving longer sentences are likely to be held whilst they are required to undertake offending behaviour courses designed to address risk factors identified by the sentence planning process. Category B prisons are significantly more secure than category C prisons although the regimes within them may not differ greatly. Category C prisoners may be held in category B prisons, but not vice versa. A limited number of closed prisons include resettlement units.

## Open prisons

2.59   These have a relaxed regime and will take category D prisoners. Accordingly the prisoners will have been sentenced for less serious offences or will have reached the end of a longer sentence and have been assessed as both low risk to the public and of escape. Life-sentenced prisoners can only be allocated to open conditions once a

---

112 *Report on an announced inspection of HMP Brixton* 28 April – 2 May 2008 by HM Chief Inspector for Prisons. Available at http://inspectorates.homeoffice. gov.uk/hmiprisons/inspect_reports/hmp-yoi-inspections.html/547854/ Brixton_2008.pdf?view=Binary

113 PSI 30/2006 – it is lawful for prisoners to be held in police cells by virtue of Imprisonment (Temporary Provisions) Act 1980 s6.

Parole Board recommendation has been accepted on behalf of the Secretary of State for Justice. There is little in the way of perimeter security at open prisons and prisoners are likely to be spending a great deal of time in the community engaged in community or paid work. Prisoners will also be able to spend time at home on resettlement leave in preparation for release.

## Women's prisons

2.60    Women are required to be held separately from men.[114] There are 14 prisons and YOIs for women. Women prisoners are not allocated the same range of security categories as men. There are currently no women's prisons for category A prisoners and women assessed as high risk are instead given 'restricted status' (see chapter 3). Women's prisons are closed (including local), semi-open, or open. Because the female prison population is relatively small (about five per cent of the total) there is a comparative lack of variety of regime and opportunity to engage in activities. The small number of institutions also means that, although women are far more likely to be primary carers, they are also more likely to end up further away from their families. There are seven mother and baby units in women's prisons. Prior to April 2004 the women's prisons were managed centrally as a group. However, they are now managed within the same geographical areas as the male prisons in those areas. However, there remains the Women and Young People's Group at the Prison Service Headquarters, which provides Directors of Offender Management with specialist expertise and support including on issues relating to the operation of mother and baby units. The Head of the Women and Young People's Group reports to the Director of Commissioning and Operational Policy.

2.61    PSO 4800 on Women Prisoners was introduced in April 2008. This gives guidance on the specific issues that arise in the regimes and facilities that arise for this group. The PSO was designed to ensure that the Prison Service complies with the 'gender equality duty'.[115] This duty requires public authorities to promote equality between men and women and eliminate unlawful sex discrimination. Instead of depending on individuals making complaints about sex discrimination, the duty places a positive legal responsibility on public sector bodies such as the Prison Service demonstrate that they

---

114  PR 1999 r12(1).
115  Introduced by the Equality Act 2006, which inserted a new section 76A into the Sex Discrimination Act 1975.

actively promote equality between men and women. Accordingly the PSO gives very detailed guidance on how prisons should ensure that the Prison Service takes into account the particular needs and vulnerability of women.

## Children and young adult prisons

2.62   The terminology now used by the Prison Service is that under 18-year-olds are known as 'young people' (they used to be known as 'juveniles') and the 18- to 21-year-olds as 'young adults'. Those under 21 do not receive sentences of 'imprisonment'[116] but various orders of 'detention'. Under 18-year-olds can receive the following sentences:

- A Detention and Training Order (DTO).[117]
- A determinate sentence where the offence would attract a maximum term of 14 years or more for someone over 18 (or for certain sexual offences or those involving weapons).[118]
- An extended sentence for sexual or violent offences where the court also is satisfied that the offender poses a risk of serious harm (made up of a custodial term and an extension period to be served on licence in the community).[119]
- Detention 'during Her Majesty's Pleasure' – the mandatory life sentence for those who commit murder when under 18.[120]
- Detention for life or indeterminate detention for public protection ('IPP') imposed for other offences where the offender is assessed as posing a risk of serious harm.[121]

2.63   18- to 21-year-olds can receive the following sentences:

- Detention in a YOI – which is equivalent to a normal determinate sentence for someone 21 or over.[122]
- 'Custody for life' – the mandatory life sentence for those convicted of murder when 18-years-old or over but under 21.
- Life detention or indeterminate detention for public protection for other offences where the court assesses the offender as posing a risk of serious harm.[123]

116  Powers of Criminal Courts (Sentencing) Act 2000 s89.
117  Imposed under PCC(S)A 2000 s100.
118  PCC(S)A 2000 s91.
119  CJA 2003 s228.
120  PCC(S)A 2000 s90.
121  CJA 2003 s226.
122  PCC(S)A 2000 s96.
123  CJA 2003 s225.

- An extended sentence for sexual or violent offences which again requires a finding of serious harm by the court.[124]
- 18- to 21-year-olds can also be sentenced for non-payment of fines or contempt in the same way as other adults.[125]

2.64 Those children or young adults serving long sentences (not including DTOs) have their sentences converted into the equivalent sentence of imprisonment to enable the remainder to be served in adult prisons from the age of 21.[126] There is otherwise wide statutory power as to where children and young adults can be held. Those serving DTOs can be held in YOIs, STCs, Secure Children's Homes or 'such other accommodation' as the Secretary of State for Justice may specify.[127] Children serving other determinate sentences, HMP life sentences, or indeterminate or extended sentences under the CJA 2003 can be held in such places and under such conditions as the Secretary of State for Justice may direct or may arrange with any person.[128] In practice, the allocation of under 18-year-olds has been delegated to the YJB which has detailed guidance on where children should be detained (see chapter 3).

2.65 In 2008 the UK removed its long standing reservation in relation to article 37(c) of the United Nations Convention on the Rights of the Child (UNCRC) which states that detained children (those under 18) should be kept separately from adults (see para 2.105). The UK had been unable to comply with this requirement primarily due to the lack of spaces in dedicated units for under 18-year-olds. In a statement on 22 September 2008 the Secretary of State for Justice said:

> We have conducted a review of the arrangements for accommodating young people who are remanded or sentenced to custody. It concluded that all custodial establishments for under-18s in England and Wales are now able to comply with the terms of article 37(c). Scotland and Northern Ireland have confirmed that they too no longer need the reservation.
>
> This is a sign of the change that has occurred in the secure estate for children and young people, following my announcement as Home Secretary in 1999 that we intended to remove all girls under 17 from Prison Service establishments. Since then we have set up a separate

124 CJA 2003 s227.
125 PCC(S)A 2000 s108.
126 PCC(S)A 2000 s99 – this power can be exercised at the age of 18 if the Secretary of State directs where the IMB has reported that the prisoner is a disruptive influence.
127 PCC(S)A 2000 ss102 and 107.
128 PCC(S)A 2000 s92 and CJA 2003 s235.

estate for boys and transformed provision for girls, a process which involved building new units for 17-year-old girls and separate mother and baby facilities for under-18s. It is a major achievement.

2.66    Whilst the creation of dedicated units for children has to be seen as an improvement, the spirit of the UNCRC and notably the requirement in article 37(b) that detention of children should be 'used only as a measure of last resort and for the shortest appropriate period of time' would seem to indicate an emphasis on the reduction in the numbers of children held in prisons, rather than the creation of more places for them.

2.67    18- to 21-year-olds serving either detention in a YOI sentences, custody for life, or terms for default or contempt can serve these sentences in YOIs, or in adult prisons where the Secretary of State for Justice directs.[129]

## Young offender institutions

2.68    YOIs are run either by the Prison Service or by the private sector, and hold 15- to 21-year-olds. The YJB commissions and purchases the places for under 18-year-olds who are held in units that are completely separate from those for 18- to 21-year-olds. The YJB and Prison Service have an SLA which sets out the standards to be delivered in YOIs. YOIs operate under the Young Offender Institution Rules (YOIR).[130] These largely mirror the adult prison rules although include some key differences which are highlighted in the relevant sections of this book. PSOs and PSIs apply to YOIs as they do to adult prisons.

2.69    The vast majority of detained children are held in YOIs, about 78 per cent of the total population as at 31 March 2009. Notwithstanding the creation of discrete units for children who are held in YOIs there remains real concern about the appropriateness of these institutions for children. The prisoner to staff ratio is much higher in YOIs than in STCs or SCHs, and so YOIs are less able to deal with individual needs of vulnerable children. The legal framework of YOIs is also of concern. For example it appears wholly anomalous that the courts have held that it would breach article 3 of the ECHR for children held in STCs to be exposed to the risk of restraint or segregation for general purposes of 'good order or discipline'[131] when children

---

129  PCC(S)A 2000 ss95, 98 and 108(5).
130  Issued by statutory instrument under PA 1952 s47.
131  *R (C) v Secretary of State for Justice* [2008] EWCA Civ 882.

in YOIs can face use of force or segregation on these grounds. The concerns over the holding of children in YOIs was highlighted by the Howard League case that confirmed that local authority social services departments continue to owe duties under the Children Act 1989 to children held in custody.[132] The Prison Service response has been the creation of dedicated units for young people, and also the development of detailed policy guidance on regimes applicable for children held in YOIs. Since the Howard League case, the YJB has also funded social work posts, and advocacy services located within the children's units in YOIs.

2.70    The policy on regimes for children in YOIs is contained in PSO 4950. The Women's and Young Peoples Group at Prison Service Headquarters is responsible for providing support in application of this policy. The policy is also designed to ensure that the Prison Service complies with its statutory duty to make arrangements to safeguard and promote the welfare of children.[133] The policy is expressed to apply mainly to those serving DTOs, but also expressly states that its principles, insofar as they are designed to safeguard the welfare of children, are applicable to all under 18-year-olds. The key feature of the policy is that YOIs holding children must have a Safeguarding Children Policy which is promoted by a dedicated manager and monitored by a Safeguarding Children Committee.[134] It also provides specific guidance on particular aspects of regimes as they apply to children, including complaints procedures, use of force and searching and contact with the outside world.

### Secure Training Centres

2.71    Secure Training Centres (STCs) are purpose-built centres for young people up to the age of 17.[135] They are all run by private operators[136] under Youth Justice Board for England and Wales (YJB) contracts, which set out detailed operational requirements. There are four STCs in England:

- Oakhill in Bedfordshire
- Hassockfield in County Durham

---

132  *R (Howard League) v Secretary of State for the Home Department* [2002] EWHC 2497 (Admin).
133  Children Act 2004 s11.
134  PSO 4950 chapter 2.
135  They were first introduced by the CJPOA 1994, which amended PA 1952 s43 to allow for the provision of STCs.
136  The contracting out of STCs is permitted under CJPOA 1994 s7.

- Rainsbrook in Northamptonshire
- Medway in Kent

The typical staff to young people ratio in an STC is 3:8.[137]

2.72    STCs house vulnerable young people who are sentenced to custody or remanded to secure accommodation. They aim to provide a
secure environment where they can be educated and rehabilitated.
They have a higher staff to young offender ratio and are smaller in
size, which means that individuals' needs can, in principle, be met
more easily. Detainees should be provided with formal education 25
hours a week, 52 weeks of the year.[138]

2.73    STCs are subject to the Secure Training Centre Rules (STCR).[139]
These are similar to the Prison Rules in format although there are
significant differences. Following high profile deaths of detainees in
STCs following use of unauthorised restraint the Court of Appeal
declared unlawful an attempt to amend the Rules to widen the circumstances in which force or segregation could be used. The Rules
require contracted STCs to have a director rather than a governor,[140]
responsible for day to day management, and a 'monitor' appointed
by the Secretary of State who has similar functions as the controller
in private prisons. The monitor accordingly must be informed of key
decisions such as the segregation or use of force on a detainee. There
is also policy guidance issued by the YJB on regimes in STCs.[141] STC
inspections are carried out by Ofsted and the inspection reports are
available at the Ofsted website.[142]

## Secure children's homes

2.74    Secure children's homes (SCHs)[143] are run either by local authority
social services departments or by private companies, overseen by the
Department of Health and the Department for Education and Skills
in England, and Social Services for Wales and Estyn in Wales. Out
of the three types of establishment, secure children's homes have
the highest ratio of staff to young people, and are generally smaller,
ranging in size from six to 40 beds. They are usually used to accom-

---

137  See information at www.yjb.gov.uk/en-gb/yjs/Custody/
      SecureTrainingCentres/
138  STCR rule 28(2).
139  SI 1998 No 472 as amended, issued under CJPOA 1994 s7 and PA 1952 s47.
140  STCR rule 46.
141  www.yjb.gov.uk/en-gb/practitioners/Custody/
142  www.ofsted.gov.uk/
143  See www.yjb.gov.uk/en-gb/yjs/Custody/SecureChildrensHomes/

modate younger children (those aged 12 to 14), young women up to the age of 16, and 15- to 16-year-old boys who are assessed as needing extra care.

2.75 As with STCs they are inspected by Ofsted. Historically the inspection reports for secure children's homes have not been published but following consultation Ofsted decided in December 2008 that the reports would be made available, but with all information that might identify the home removed. SCHs are governed by the Children's Home Regulations (CHR) 2001.[144] Policy guidance on regimes is issued by the Secure Accommodation Network.[145]

# Supervision of imprisonment

## Introduction

2.76 Aside from the courts and formal legal procedures, there are a number of bodies and statutory agencies that have responsibility for monitoring and supervising prisons. By and large, these bodies do not have direct power to interfere in the running of prisons but are restricted to supervisory or administrative roles. One body, the Prisons and Probation Ombudsman provides a direct mechanism for resolving individual complaints while the remainder are more concerned with ensuring compliance with legal requirements and good practice. This means that while they can form an important resource to obtain information in support of prisoners' cases, they are not mechanisms for individual dispute resolution.

## Domestic monitoring bodies

### Independent monitoring boards

2.77 It is a statutory requirement for the Secretary of State to appoint a group of independent monitors for each prison[146] whose task is to 'pay frequent visits to the prison and hear any complaints which may be made by the prisoners and report to the Secretary of State any matter which they consider it expedient to report'.[147] In order to discharge that function, the prison are required to admit members of

144 SI No 3967, issued under the Care Standards Act 2000.
145 www.secureaccommodation.org.uk/practiceguidelines.htm
146 PA 1952 s6(2).
147 PA 1952 s6(3).

the board at any time and the members are to have free access to any part of the prison.[148]

2.78    Independent Monitoring Boards (IMBs) replaced the old boards of visitors in 2003.[149] Historically, the boards of visitors were required to play a role in disciplining prisoners as well as hearing prisoners' complaints. Until the Criminal Justice Act 1991 was enacted in 1992, boards of visitors were required to hear the more serious charges against prison discipline and had virtually unlimited powers to award loss of remission to prisoners (for further discussion of prison discipline, see chapter 9). This disciplinary role was ended on the recommendation of the Woolf Report as it was considered to conflict with the role as a watchdog.

2.79    Although the formal adjudicatory role was ended in 1992, IMBs were still required to authorise segregation for prisoners who were to remain segregated for three days or longer. Presumably, this requirement was considered to be a safeguard against the misuse of informal disciplinary powers by prison staff and so was retained without there being any conflict with their other roles. However, this obligation was ended in 2005[150] leaving IMBs with no formal role to play in any aspect of prison discipline.

2.80    PR rules 74–80 set out the range of specific responsibilities that IMBs now have. Appointment is by the Secretary of State for periods of three years[151] and Boards are required to meet monthly, or at the very least, eight times a year.[152] They are required to satisfy themselves about the physical conditions of the prison and prisoners,[153] to inspect food[154] and to hear prisoners' requests and complaints.[155] Annual reports have to be issued to the Secretary of State.[156] Annual reports, which may provide useful information on individual prisons are available at the IMB website.[157]

2.81    Although the boards are required to take an active role in the day to day running of prisons, there are no corresponding powers of

---

148  PA 1952 s6(3).
149  The formal statutory name change coming with the OMA 2007 s26.
150  SI 2005 No 3437 r2, Sch para 9(a).
151  PR rule 75.
152  PR rule 76.
153  PR rule 77(1).
154  PR rule 78(2).
155  PR rule 78(1).
156  PR rule 80.
157  www.imb.gov.uk/annual-reports/

enforcement. This does mean that their effectiveness in relation to resolving problems and complaints is entirely dependent upon the willingness of individual members to pursue matters for prisoners. There is no requirement to raise matters with Boards before pursuing any other remedy, either internal or external to the prison.

2.82    There is also a National Council for IMBs, a non-statutory body which aims to 'provide strategic leadership, policy development, guidance, and quality control, including identifying good practice, to Boards to help ensure they fulfill their statutory duties efficiently and effectively'.[158]

2.83    Members of the IMB should not be confused with Official Prison Visitors (OPVs). OPVs are independent volunteers appointed by prisons, who visit prisons in order to offer friendship to prisoners. They have no statutory basis or formal monitoring role.[159]

## Prisons and Probation Ombudsman

2.84    The office of the Ombudsman was originally created in 1994 in response to the Woolf Report. The full role and remit of the Prison and Probation Ombudsman (PPO) with particular reference to the complaints system in prisons is discussed in more detail in chapter 12. The background to the post is contained in Lord Woolf's 1991 report on the Strangeways Riot. He envisaged the need for a complaints adjudicator who was entirely separate from the prison system with the power to resolve prisoners' disputes with the prison authorities. The Ombudsman was a partial concession to this proposal. On the one hand the Ombudsman can consider and adjudicate upon complaints made by individual prisoners. However, there is no statutory footing for this position and there are no enforceable powers attached to his decisions.

2.85    The Ombudsman's remit was originally confined to investigating complaints against the Prison Service. In 2004 this role was expanded to include the Probation Service and subsequently, from 1 October 2006, complaints from those within immigration detention. The Ombudsman can currently investigate complaints made by individuals who are, or who have been in prison or an immigration centre, under the supervision of the probation service or have had a

---

158  See first annual report of the National Council produced in 2008: www.imb. gov.uk/docs/IMB_National_Council_AR09_F1.pdf.

159  For guidance see PSO 4410 section 5 – prisons are required to have an Official Prison Visitor Scheme through which prisoners can apply to have visitors unless there are 'demonstrable reasons why this is not appropriate'.

probation report written about them. The internal complaints procedure for the relevant organisation must be used before the Ombudsman will investigate and the matter must be within his remit. This
remit currently excludes ministerial decisions, including advice to
ministers and clinical decisions on healthcare. It is also important
to remember that any organisations or bodies that are independent
of the prison and probation services do not fall within this remit so,
for example, complaints against the Parole Board are excluded. If the
Ombudsman finds in favour of the person making the complaint, a
report will be issued with recommendations for the resolution of the
problem. There are no powers of enforcement if the recommendation is rejected.

2.86    The other major change in 2004 was that the Ombudsman was
also instructed by the Secretary of State to take responsibility for investigating the deaths of:

- prisoners, including young people held in YOIs;
- residents of probation approved premises, including voluntary
  residents; and
- residents of immigration removal centres and those under immigration service managed escort.

The purpose of this expansion in his remit was to enable pre-inquest
investigations into custodial deaths to be carried out by a body with
some measure of independence from the Prison Service.

2.87    This expansion of the Ombudsman's role has also lead to him
being asked to undertake special investigations into matters as diverse
as near-deaths in custody, through to disturbances in Immigration
Detention Centres and allegations made of racism and mistreatment
by immigration detainees.[160]

2.88    The major concern that has been raised about the Ombudsman's
office is the lack of any statutory underpinning and this naturally
causes concern about his independence from the Ministry of Justice.
This independence is important in relation to general complaints investigations, not least because many of the Ombudsman's staff are
seconded from or have worked for the Prison Service at some point.
However, it is arguably even more important for the investigations
into deaths in custody, as these investigations have to comply with the
state's article 2 obligations. The original bill that formed the basis for
CJIA 2008 did envisage reconstituting the Ombudsman as HM Com-

---

160 Copies of these reports can be found on the Ombudsman's website: www.ppo.
    gov.uk/publications/index.html

missioner for Offender Management and Prisons (as had previous draft legislation) and providing a range of powers including the same powers as the High Court to issue witness summons and require the production of documents. When the bill finally reached the Lords, these proposals were dropped and the question of whether a statutory Ombudsman's scheme is necessary has gone back to consultation, leaving the current office of Prisons and Probation Ombudsman as a purely administrative arrangement.

2.89    In 2007/2008 the Ombudsman received 4,750 individual complaints, a figure that remained virtually the same as the preceding year. Of those complaints, only one third were eligible for investigation.[161] The majority of complaints made by prisoners were in relation to 'general conditions' followed by complaints about property and race relations. Interestingly, complaints about prison adjudications have now dropped to just six per cent of the overall total. The vast majority of complaints are made by men and this possibly reflects the longstanding difficulty that the Ombudsman has in providing an effective service to those who are not serving long sentences. The difficulty is that the procedures for investigations are so long that it is of little practical help to those serving shorter sentences. The overall uphold rate for prison complaints was 26 per cent and for probation complaints, 32 per cent.[162]

## Her Majesty's Chief Inspector of Prisons

2.90    There is a statutory duty requiring the Secretary of State to appoint a Chief Inspector of Prisons (HMCIP) to inspect prisons and report upon prison conditions and the treatment of prisoners.[163] This duty also now extends to Immigration Detention Centres.[164] In addition, the Secretary of State can direct the Chief Inspector to investigate and report on specific issues.[165] The mission statement for the Inspectorate is:

> To provide independent scrutiny of the conditions for and treatment of prisoners and other detainees, promoting the concept of 'healthy prisons' in which staff work effectively to support prisoners and detainees to reduce reoffending or achieve other agreed outcomes.

161  See the PPO Annual Report 2007/2008, p 55.
162  The first Ombudsman's Annual Report in 1996/1997 recorded an uphold rate of 44 per cent.
163  PA 1952 s5A.
164  PA 1952 ss5A(5A) and (5B).
165  PA 1952 s5A(4).

2.91   The Inspectorate is not a body that can investigate complaints from in-dividuals, although information from individuals can help inform the Inspectors about which prisons to inspect and current issues of concern amongst prisoners. Instead of processing individual complaints, inspections of all adult prisons will be conducted once every five years and once every three years for establishments holding juveniles. Immigration Detention Centres are also inspected at least once every three years. The establishment being inspected will be notified of the visit in advance and the Inspectorate will physically visit the prison. The normal practice is for inspection reports to be prepared within 16 weeks of the physical visit to the prison. The prison will be expected to produce an action plan addressing any concerns raised within the report.

2.92   Follow up inspections will be arranged on a risk assessed basis depending on the concerns raised at the full inspection. The follow up inspection will either be a 'short inspection' in cases where there are few concerns or a 'full follow-up inspection' where more serious concerns have been uncovered. In both cases, the follow up inspection is unannounced to the establishment.

2.93   HMCIP has produced a set of 'expectations' – essentially the criteria against which conditions and treatment of prisoners are assessed.[166] These are extremely useful reference documents they cross-reference subject areas of inspection against both the requirements of domestic law, and also international instruments such as the UN Standard Minimum Rules for the Treatment of Prisoners, and the European Prison Rules (see para 2.103).

2.94   In addition to the inspections of individual establishments and the preparation of an annual report, the Inspectorate also conducts thematic reviews that are relevant to prison conditions. The thematic reviews have covered a wide range of diverse areas including: older prisoners; juveniles in prison; treatment of IPP prisoners; close supervision centres; recalls to custody. These thematic reviews have proven to be extremely valuable sources of information and evidence in legal challenges about the reality of prison conditions.

## Her Majesty's Inspectorate of Probation

2.95   The Probation Inspectorate was first set up in 1936 as a hybrid body dealing with recruitment, training and standards. Following a review in 1987 where the educational and training role was divested to educational establishments, it was given a statutory footing in CJA 1991.

166  http://inspectorates.homeoffice.gov.uk/hmiprisons/our-work/

The new statutory agency retained the duties of an Inspectorate. Its current statutory authority derives from the Criminal Justice and Court Services Act 2000 s6.

2.96    The statement of purpose for this body explains that its role is to:

- reportto the Secretary of State on the effectiveness of work with individual offenders, children and young people aimed at reducing reoffending and protecting the public, whoever undertakes this work under the auspices of the National Offender Management Service or the Youth Justice Board
- reporton the effectiveness of the arrangements for this work, working with other Inspectorates as necessary
- contributeto improved performance by the organisations whose work we inspect
- contribute to sound policy and effective service delivery, especially in public protection, by providing advice and disseminating good practice, based on inspection findings, to Ministers, officials, managers and practitioners
- promoteactively race equality and wider diversity issues, especially in the organisations whose work we inspect
- contributeto the overall effectiveness of the Criminal Justice System, particularly through joint work with other inspectorates.[167]

2.97   As with the prisons inspectorate, the probation inspections are conducted both of the regional probation services, and on thematic issues. The probation inspectorate will sometimes undertake joint inspections with that of prisons. For example, the review of IPP prisoners was a joint thematic review by both organisations. Joint inspections of criminal justice services also take place with the Inspectorate of Constabulary. The most well publicised reports prepared have related to risk of harm investigations that have been ordered where serious offences have been committed by people under licence in the community. The two most high profile of those investigations in recent times have been the reviews into the further convictions of Damien Hanson and Anthony Rice.[168] Both cases involved released prisoners who went onto commit murders whilst under supervision in the community and the reports have been hugely influential in shaping practice and risk assessment in the parole review process. The Hanson report highlighted the distinction to be drawn between people convicted of crimes involving instrumental violence and those convicted of

---

167 http://inspectorates.homeoffice.gov.uk/hmiprobation/about-us.html/
statement-purpose.html/?version=1

168 These reports can be found on the HMIP website: http://inspectorates.
homeoffice.gov.uk/hmiprobation/

violence following a loss of control. This resulted in much closer scrutiny being given to the selection of prisoners for offending behaviour programmes. The Rice report emphasised the need for more robust risk assessment for lifers before they are moved to open prisons resulting in the Parole Board deciding to conduct oral hearings before recommending that any lifer is moved to open conditions.

2.98    There is a concern that these investigation reports look across too many disciplines to be safely conducted by a body that only specialises in the probation service's models of risk assessment and risk management. For example, in the Rice report it was stated that the move towards a properly judicialised system of release for lifers following a parole hearing had created a situation where it had become:

> a challenging task for people charged with managing offenders effectively to ensure that public protection considerations are not undermined by human rights considerations.[169]

2.99    This is an extraordinary comment to make on a judicial process, particularly one where the rules of evidence and procedure are flexible, where there is no defined burden or standard of proof and where the vast majority of the evidence is prepared by prison and probation staff. It is not clear whether commenting on the Parole Board procedures actually falls within the Inspector's remit but these comments have undoubtedly had a chilling effect on the Parole Board with its release rate plummeting since the report was issued.

## Key international bodies and instruments

### The Council of Europe

#### Committee for the Prevention of Torture

2.100    Article 1 of the European Convention for the Prevention of Torture and Inhuman or Degrading Treatment established a Committee (CPT) whose task is to 'by means of visits, examine the treatment of persons deprived of their liberty with a view to strengthening, if necessary, the protection of such persons from torture and from inhuman or degrading treatment or punishment'. The United Kingdom is a signatory to the Convention and has been the subject of regular visits and inspections for many years.

2.101    The CPT is administered by the Council of Europe and has a role that is akin to a domestic Inspectorate. It comprises lawyers, doctors and experts in the fields of policing imprisonment, these mem-

169  Para 10.12.2.

bers being appointed for terms of four years. Following visits, the CPT will publish reports on the conditions it has found but does not have any directive powers. Its reports can be useful material in cases where prison conditions are under scrutiny. For example, in the report delivered after an inspection of a number of police and prison establishments in 2001 the CPT paid particular attention to the conditions of the Close Supervision Centre at Woodhill (see chapter 8) and expressed concern at the provision of facilities for inmates and the rate of transfers to special hospitals.[170] As might be expected, more recent visits by the CPT have looked at the position of foreign national terrorist suspects detained in custody without charge.[171]

2.102    A set of standards have been published by the CPT[172] that examine issues such as the appropriate use of restraints in custody, juveniles in detention and the appropriate training of law enforcement personnel. These standards stress the need to 'combat impunity' and to create a culture where ill treatment of those in custody is not tolerated. They place particular emphasis on the requirement for effective state investigations of potential abuses backed up by a suitable legal framework. These standards obviously feed into the appropriate method of investigating alleged mistreatment in custody as well as article 2 investigations into deaths and near deaths.

## The European Prison Rules

2.103    The Council of Europe has also issued the European Prison Rules (EPR)[173] which set out minimum standards on the treatment and conditions of prisoners. Whilst the EPR and CPT standards are not binding they can be relevant in deciding whether there have been breaches of the ECHR.[174]

## The United Nations

### Convention Against Torture

2.104    The United Nations Convention Against Torture prohibits torture of or other cruel and inhuman or degrading treatment or punishment.[175]

---

170  CPT/Inf (2002) 6 paras 59–68.

171  CPT/Inf (2006) 28.

172  Available on the Council of Europe website at: http://cpt.coe.int/en/documents/eng-standards.doc

173  https://wcd.coe.int/ViewDoc.jsp?id=955747

174  See *Gülmez v Turkey*, application no 16330/02 and *Mouisel v France* (2004) 38 EHRR 34 respectively where these standards are referred to.

175  Article 1.

The United Kingdom is a signatory and the duties imposed by the Convention include taking effective measures to prevent torture and to make torture a criminal offence.[176] It also requires the creation of universal jurisdiction to enable torturers to be tried wherever the offence was committed.[177] The Convention carries an investigative duty[178] and interestingly in light of the developments in 'war against terror', prohibits the use of evidence gained by torture in domestic courts.[179] The Optional Protocol to the Convention (referred to as OPCAT) of which the United Kingdom is one of 40 signatories, provides for visits and inspections to be made by a Sub-Committee on Prevention of Torture. The implantation of the Convention is overseen by a Committee which receives regular reports from member states. The Committee does have the power to examine individual complaints.

## UN Convention on the Rights of the Child

2.105   This Convention was adopted by the United Nations in 1989 and is the most widely ratified UN Convention.[180] States which are party to the convention, including the UK, have to report to the Committee on the Rights of the Child. This United Nations treaty monitoring body assesses how well states are implementing the Convention, reports on progress and makes recommendations. The Committee comprises 18 independent children's rights experts who are elected in their personal capacity to four-year terms and is responsible for examining the progress made by state parties in fulfilling their obligations under the Convention. The Committee does not have the power to examine individual complaints concerning violations of the rights of a child.

2.106   Article 37(c) provides that:

> Every child deprived of liberty shall be treated with humanity and respect for the inherent dignity of the human person, and in a manner which takes into account the needs of persons of his or her age.

2.107   In *R(C) v The Secretary of State for Justice* [2008] EWCA Civ 882 the Court of Appeal confirmed that article 3 of the ECHR prohibiting torture has to be applied consistently with this article 37(c) of this

---

176  Article 8.
177  Article 5.
178  Articles 12 and 13.
179  Article 15.
180  Having been ratified by all UN member states except Somalia and the United States.

Convention[181] when applied to children and the views of the Committee as the expert monitoring body charged with the implementation of the state's obligations under the Convention must be taken into account. The Court of Appeal in that case were mindful of the Committee's indication that deliberate infliction of pain is not permitted as a form of control of juveniles as helping form their judgment that a policy of using pain compliance techniques on children in custody was unlawful.

### UN Standard Minimum Rules for the Treatment of Prisoners

2.108   These were adopted in 1977[182] and state that

> [t]hey seek only, on the basis of the general consensus of contemporary thought and the essential elements of the most adequate systems of today, to set out what is generally accepted as being good principle and practice.

As with the EPR the UN minimum rules contain largely uncontroversial provisions such as the requirement to keep sentenced and unconvicted prisoners separate, and the need to ensure restraint is not used as punishment.

181   The article prohibits the detention of children with adults and the UK Government removed its reservation in relation to this article in 2008. See para 2.65.
182   www.unhchr.ch/html/menu3/b/h_comp34.htm

## CHAPTER 3

# Starting a prison sentence

*continued*

# Reception

3.1   The primary guidance on the procedure.
      and Young Offender Institutions (YOIs) wh.
      from the courts is contained in PSO 0500. Th

      - to ensure that prisoners are properly identi.
      - to ensure that prisoners are accompanied wı
        tation providing a legal basis for detention;
      - identify those who should be given category A st.
        the escape list; and
      - to ensure that they are properly searched but also
        immediate health needs or other vulnerabilities are i.

      The policy includes guidance on the types of information
      staff should seek to obtain in order to inform these asses
      Specific extra guidance on particular issues that arise for
      prisoners is contained in PSO 4800, and for children held in YC
      PSO 4950.

3.2   There are core activities identified by the policy that must take pla
      before the prisoner leaves the reception process, and some that mus
      take place before the prisoner is locked up for the night. The prison
      must ensure that in reception:[3]

      - *The prisoner's identity is confirmed.* If the prisoner denies they are
        the person named on the warrant they should be given an op-
        portunity to contact family or friends and seek legal advice. The
        prison should record the prisoner's name as that on the warrant
        even if this is different to that used on a previous sentence.[4] Pris-
        ons are required to have local policies on how to deal with prison-
        ers who present themselves claiming to be unlawfully at large.
        Prisons should contact the last holding prison for documentation,
        and place the prisoner on report.

      - *The legal basis for detention is confirmed.* The policy gives detailed
        guidance on the various kinds of document that will provide
        authority to hold the prisoner such as an order for imprisonment
        from the Crown Court.[5] The policy further states that if there is
        no such document but evidence that one exists (for example an

---

1  PSO 0500 para 1.3.
2  PSO 0500 chapter 4.
3  PSO 0500 para 1.10.
4  PSO 0500 paras 2.9–2.10.
5  PSO 0500 Annex A.

on the prisoner escort record) then the prisoner can be held the Governor should obtain a copy of the warrant within six s. This policy of course will not provide any defence to a claim false imprisonment if in fact there is no lawful warrant for tention.[6]

ssential information is checked or recorded. This is recorded on form 2050 and the Local Inmate Database System (LIDS). There is a statutory requirement for prisons to maintain a personal record for all prisoners.[7] This will entail an interview with the prisoner at reception so that information such as religion[8] and next of kin are recorded. Prisoners are fingerprinted and photographed on reception.[9]

- *At risk prisoners are identified and kept safe.* Prisoners may arrive from other prisons whilst on self-harm measures, or from court with a prisoner escort record (PER) that should alert staff. Such prisoners must be kept safe under local policies until referred to the reception healthcare screener.[10]

- *The prisoner is searched.* On reception prisoners should immediately undergo a rub down search, and at a later stage of the process a full strip search.[11] Property should also be searched and recorded and prisoners should only be allowed property in-possession which is listed on the prisons facilities list, which should be displayed in reception. Other property will be recorded, sealed and stored.[12] Specific guidance on the searching of women on reception is contained in PSO 4800, and of under 18-year-old prisoners in PSO 4950.

- *That any immediate potential risks to other prisoners, staff or the public are identified.*

3.3    The following activities must take place before the prisoner is locked up for the first night:[13]

---

6   PSO 0500 para 2.3.
7   PR rule 42, YOIR rule 47.
8   The recording of the prisoner's religion is a statutory requirement – PA 1952 s10(5) and PR rule 13, YOIR rule 30.
9   PA 1952 s16, PR rule 42(2)–(2A), YOIR rule 47(2)–(2A), PSO 0500 chapter 3 and the NSF.
10  PSO 0500 para 4.4.
11  PR rule 41(1), YOIR rule 46(1), PSO 0500 para 5.3, NSF.
12  PR rule 43(5), YOIR rule 48(4), PSO 0500 paras 5.4–5.6, NSF.
13  PSO 0500 para 1.11.

- *A suicide/self-harm screening.* Where prisoners are identified as being at risk of suicide or self-harm the normal procedures should be adopted.[14]

- *A cell sharing risk assessment* (CSRA). Such assessments should take place:
  - where a prisoner is new to custody, or
  - a prisoner transferring from another establishment arrives without an up-to-date CSRA on their records, or
  - a prisoner transfers from another establishment and arrives with an up-to-date CSRA but contra-indications related to the transfer process indicate that their risk assessment should be reviewed.[15]

- *Medical and risk assessments.* There is a distinction in the level or medical assessment to be carried out depending on whether the prisoner is entering custody for the first time, or is transferring from another prison, or is returning from court. Those entering custody for the first time should have an assessment on reception to detect immediate physical and mental health problems, drug and alcohol abuse and risk of suicide or self-harm. A more general health assessment should then take place in the week immediately following reception. In cases where prisoners are transferred or return from court the assessment will generally be limited to a screen for risk of suicide or self-harm.[16] The policy states that prisoners need only see a doctor where there is a reason for this, although it is good practice for a doctor to be available for consultation during the normal reception period.[17] Prisons are required to have local policies on dealing with those who are withdrawing from alcohol and/or drugs, and on which types of medication are allowed in possession.[18]

3.4 The policy confirms that for under 18-year-olds held in Prison Service establishments, and for those serving DTOs over that age, the reception interview must take place within one hour of the prisoner's arrival so that an assessment of needs and vulnerability is carried out.[19] They should also be given an opportunity within two hours of

14  PSO 2700.
15  PSO 2750 and PSI 49/2008.
16  PSO 0500 paras 6.7–6.9.
17  PSO 0500 para 6.11.
18  PSO 0500 paras 6.13–6.14.
19  See also PSO 4950 para 5.6.

their arrival to telephone 'someone who may be concerned about their well-being'.[20]

3.5     At reception prisoners should be provided with food and drink when appropriate.[21] They should also be allowed to make phone calls if they have any urgent needs (for example where they need to make alternative arrangements for the care of children).[22] They should also be told of their entitlement to a reception visit which should be permitted within 72 hours.[23] They should be given clothing and toiletries to meet essential needs for at least 24 hours[24] and provided with information about the reception and first night process. There is a statutory requirement on prisons to provide within 24 hours of reception information about the Prison Rules, the Incentives and Earned Privileges scheme, and on how to make complaints.[25]

## Unconvicted prisoners and civil prisoners

3.6     PR rule 7(2) stipulates that unconvicted prisoners, and this includes those detained solely under the Immigration Act, shall be kept out of contact with convicted prisoners as far as the governor considers it can reasonably be done, and 'shall under no circumstances be required to share a cell with a convicted prisoner'. The Rules refer to unconvicted prisoners and so between conviction and sentence prisoners generally lose the advantages given by the Rules. The definition of 'convicted prisoner' in PR rule 2(1) includes someone who has pleaded guilty and so if there is a long period between such a plea being entered at court and sentence, then the prisoner will not be treated as 'unconvicted'.[26]

3.7     As noted below, remand prisoners are given category U and normally located in category B prisons, most commonly in a 'local' prison to the appropriate court, although in some circumstances they

---

20  PSO 4950 para 5.9.
21  PSO 0500 para 7.3.
22  PSO 4800 suggests women should be allowed at least a five-minute free phone call to sort out child care issues.
23  PSO 0500 para 7.6.
24  PSO 0500 para 7.9.
25  PR rule 10(1), YOIR rule 7(1) – on specific information to be given to under 18-year-olds see PSO 4950 para 5.16.
26  *R (Edwards-Sayer) v Secretary of State for the Home Department* [2008] 1 WLR 2280.

can be allocated to category C prisons. There has long been concern over the fact that those who are yet to be found guilty by the criminal courts are commonly held in the worst conditions in the prison estate, namely the Victorian local prisons such as Wandsworth, Wormwood Scrubs and Chelmsford. Such prisons tend to be the most overcrowded with a transient population and life in such prisons is 'dominated by the need to find space for prisoners, often for very short periods of time, rather than doing anything constructive with, and for, them'.[27]

3.8    Guidance on the treatment of unconvicted prisoners is contained in PSO 4600. This confirms that their unconvicted status means that they should not lose

> their normal rights and freedoms as citizens, except where this is an inevitable consequence of imprisonment, of the court's reason for ordering their detention and to ensure the good order of the prison.
>    Instructions or practices that limit their activities must provide only for the minimum restriction necessary in the interests of security, efficient administration, good order and discipline and for the welfare and safety of all prisoners.[28]

Accordingly they should be allowed all 'reasonable facilities' to:

- seek release on bail;
- preserve their accommodation and employment;
- prepare for trial;
- maintain contact with relatives and friends;
- pursue legitimate business and social interests; and
- obtain help with personal problems.[29]

3.9    A summary of the special entitlements of unconvicted prisoners, and accordingly immigration detainees, in addition to the above is contained in Annex B to PSO 4600, namely that they are entitled to:

- Have supplied at his or her own expense, books, newspapers, writing materials and other means of occupation.[30]
- Have items for cell activities and hobbies handed in by relatives or friends, as well as to purchase them from private cash or pay.
- Carry out business activities.

---

27  Unjust Deserts: a thematic review by HM Chief Inspector of Prisons of the treatment and conditions for unsentenced prisoners in England and Wales, HMCIP, December 2000.

28  PSO 4600 para 1.1.

29  PSO 4600 para 1.2.

30  PR rule 43(1).

- Wear his or her own clothing, unless considered inappropriate or unsuitable (and unconvicted prisoners can be required to wear distinctive clothing if considered an escape risk).[31]
- Take part in the Incentives and Earned Privileges scheme, entering at standard level. Movement to basic level should be based on behaviour only.[32]
- Send and receive as many letters as he or she wishes[33] including two statutory letters at public expense per week.
- Be attended by his or her own registered medical practitioner or dentist, at his or her own expense.[34]
- Have in possession a greater quantity of smoking materials, and bring in tobacco and cigarettes on reception, or have them sent in by friends.
- Receive as many visits as he or she wishes, within reasonable limits.[35]
- Not to work unless he or she chooses to.[36]

3.10   The Rules also contain special provisions about civil prisoners, namely those 'committed or attached for contempt of court, or failing to do or abstain from doing anything required to be done or left undone'.[37] They should be treated as a separate class but permitted to associate with any other class of prisoner if willing to do so. Like unconvicted prisoners, they may access their own medical practitioner, to wear their own clothes, send as many letters and receive as many visits as they wish within limits.[38] However unless their sentences are so short they should be categorised like other convicted prisoners.[39]

## Induction

3.11   The Prison Service has also a detailed policy on induction procedures which should aim to 'inform prisoners about prison life, the regime and their responsibilities and privileges and to begin to prepare them

31  PR rules 23, 40(3).
32  PSO 4000.
33  PR rule 35(1).
34  PR rule 20(5).
35  PR rule 35(1).
36  PR rule 31(5).
37  PR rule 7(3).
38  PR rule 7(3).
39  PSO 4600 para 3.3.

for their return to the community'.[40] An induction process is mandatory for all those who are new to custody, those who have changed
status from remand to convicted and who are new to a particular
prison.[41] Some prisons will have a separate wing which is used for
induction purposes.

3.12      Prisons and YOIs are required by the policy to have local policies
that ensure:[42]

- Prisoners after reception are treated as being on the induction
  process until they are integrated into the prison regime.
- Arrangements are in place for staff to ensure the safety and well-
  being of the prisoner during the first night. In particular the cell-
  sharing risk assessment must be completed before lock up on
  the first night. Guidance in the policy states that prisons should
  ensure that a specific member of staff provides assistance and
  information.
- The induction process is tailored to the specific needs of prisoners. Clearly prisoners who have previously spent time in the prison
  may need less induction than a first-time or vulnerable prisoner.

3.13   The policy specifies the types of information that the prisoner should
be provided with including details of the prison's race relations
policy, suicide prevention procedures, facilities for religious observance, healthcare, expected standards of behaviour and access to the
prison shop.[43] Information must also be given about sources of assistance, such as the CARATs team or disability liaison officer, and on
resettlement opportunities.[44] The focus on resettlement needs at the
induction stage reflects the statutory requirements to help prisoners
prepare for their return to the outside community.[45]

3.14      The induction policy applies to under 18-year-old prisoners with
some modifications, such as the need to provide information about
advocacy services, and carry out a full educational assessment.[46]

40  PSO 0550 para 1.1.
41  PSO 0550 para 1.2.
42  PSO 0550 sections 2–4.
43  PSO 0550 para 6.6.
44  PSO 0550 paras 6.7–6.9.
45  PR rules 3 and 5, YOIR rule 3.
46  PSO 4950 paras 5.19–5.25.

# Sentence calculation

## Introduction

3.15   In a case heard in 1987 involving how remand time should be taken into account when calculating a sentence it was said that:

> [t]he determination of a man's [release date] is something which should be beyond dispute. Parliament must have intended the provision whereby the determination is made to be easy to apply.[47]

It is of obvious importance both for the good administration of justice, and for the rights of prisoners, that there is no doubt as to the term of imprisonment to be served. In fact the courts have regularly had to struggle with an increasingly labyrinthine set of statutory provisions which determine the calculation of sentences. When trying to discern how release dates should be worked out when a prisoner was serving sentences administered both under the 1991 and 2003 Criminal Justice Acts (CJAs) a judge in 2008 commented:

> [i]t is simply unacceptable in a society governed by the rule of law for it to be well nigh impossible to discern from statutory provisions what a sentence means in practice.[48]

The complexity of the legislative framework also frustrates the ability of judges to comply with the duty to explain the effect of sentences in 'ordinary language'.[49]

## An overview of the principles of sentence calculation

3.16   Release mechanisms are more fully discussed in chapters 10 and 11. However in order to understand the principles of sentence calculation it is important to have an overview of the different statutory regimes applicable to early release (the release dates referred to here do not deal with Home Detention Curfew or end of custody licence, but to the statutory entitlement to release):

- Determinate sentences imposed prior to 1 October 1992[50] are governed by CJA 1967 – the prisoner is eligible for release on licence if the Parole Board so recommends at one third of the

---

47  *R v Secretary of State for the Home Department ex p Read* (1987) 9 Cr App R (S) 206.

48  *R (Noone) v Governor of Drake Hall Prison* [2008] EWHC 207 (Admin).

49  CJA 2003 s174(1)(b).

50  The date of the coming into force of the relevant sections of the CJA 1991: SI 1992 No 333.

sentence, and is released unconditionally at two-thirds (CJA 1967 sentences). [51]

- Where the determinate sentence is imposed on or after 1 October 1992 for an offence committed before 4 April 2005 (CJA 1991 sentences) prisoners serving less than four years are known as 'short-term prisoners' and those serving four or more years as 'long-term prisoners':
  - if the sentence is less than 12 months release is automatic with no licence at the halfway point;
  - for sentences of 12 months or more, but less than four years release is automatic at the halfway point on licence;
  - for sentences of four years or more release on licence is automatic on licence at the halfway point except for specified violent or sexual offences[52] when the Parole Board must approve release (and if it does not release is automatic on licence at the two-thirds point);
  - for extended sentences release on licence is at the halfway point of the custodial term, and is automatic if the custodial term is less than four years, but depends on a Parole Board recommendation if the custodial term is four or more years and the sentence is for a specified violent or sexual offence.[53]

- For offences committed on or after 4 April 2005 (CJA 2003 sentences):
  - for sentences of 12 months or more release is on licence at the halfway point of the sentence;
  - sentences of under 12 months are still governed by the CJA 1991 which creates some complexities where multiple sentences are imposed (see below);
  - for extended sentences release on licence is at the halfway point of the custodial term (automatic for sentences imposed on or after 14 July 2008, on a direction by the Parole Board for sentences imposed before that date).

3.17 The determinate sentence of detention in a YOI, and the determinate sentence imposed on under 18-year-olds under the Powers of the Criminal Courts (Sentencing) Act (PCC(S)A) 2000 are calculated in the same way as adult determinate sentences (but DTOs have their own rules, see below).

---

51  CJA 1991 Sch 12 para 8.
52  Contained in CJA 2003 Sch 15.
53  Contained in CJA 2003 Sch 15.

3.18    For indeterminate sentences prisoners are eligible for release on a direction by the Parole Board once they have served their 'minimum term' (see chapter 10 for more detail on life sentences). It is now established that further sentences can be made consecutive to an indeterminate sentence. Accordingly a determinate sentence, or a further indeterminate sentence can be ordered to run from the date of expiry of the minimum term of an existing indeterminate sentence.[54]

3.19    Prisoners' release dates are arrived at by proper consideration of the statutory provisions and no policy issued by the executive can determine them. However the Prison Service has issued very detailed guidance on applying the very complicated statutory framework as interpreted by the courts in PSO 6650.

## Calculating Criminal Justice Act 1967 sentences

3.20    There will be very few prisoners serving sentences that still fall to be administered under the procedures for release first introduced by the 1967 Act. As noted above only sentences imposed prior to 1 October 1992 will be administered in this way. However if such a prisoner has remained in custody since the imposition of the sentence and then receives another sentence imposed for an offence committed prior to 4 April 2005, or a sentence of 12 months the result will be a 'single term' (see below) which preserves the entitlement to consideration for conditional release at the one-third point, and to automatic and unconditional release at the two-thirds point of the entire term.

## Calculating Criminal Justice Act 1991 sentences

### Remand time

3.21    The prison, when calculating sentences imposed under the CJA 1991, deducts the appropriate remand time.[55] The sentence should be reduced by the 'relevant period' which is defined as:

- any period during which the prisoner was in police detention in connection with the offence for which the sentence was passed;
- any period during which he or she was remanded in custody by a court in connection with any proceedings relating to that sentence or the offence for which it was passed (where a charge on an

54   PCC(S)A 2000 s154; *R v Hills and others* [2008] EWCA Crim 1871.
55   CJA 1967 s67.

indictment is reduced, for example, periods of custody in relation
to the first charge are 'relevant' to the sentence for the second);

- any period during which he or she was remanded in custody by
  a court in connection with any proceedings from which the proceedings referred to above arose relating to that sentence (where a
  prisoner is remanded for burglary, for example, and on sentence
  this matter is not proceeded with but he is sentenced for handling
  the same stolen goods on the day in question, the remand time is
  'relevant' to the sentence);

- days in which the prisoner was remanded into the care of a secure
  children's home.[56]

3.22   Any relevant period relating to any offence forming part of a 'single
term' (see below) must all be counted, but only counted once.[57] So all
remand time relevant to any of the sentences forming a single term is
added together and the total deducted from the single term.

3.23   Time spent on remand does not count if the prisoner is at the
same time also serving a sentence of imprisonment (although if the
prisoner is detained under the Immigration Act 1971, concurrently served remand time will count).[58] However the reduction in the
length of a sentence by counting of remand time will not affect the
applicable release regime (so if a sentence of the court is four years
and relates to the kind of offence that requires the Parole Board to
determine release, deduction of remand time will not give the prisoner an entitlement to automatic release[59]).

3.24   Time spent awaiting extradition from abroad will only count if
the sentencing judge so directs.[60] Time spent surrendering to bail at
court, or in the custody of the court during a trial (where the judge for
example directs that the defendant should be held in custody during
recesses) will not count.[61]

---

56  Guidance on CJA 1967 s67 contained at PSO 6650 para 4.1.2 – *R v Secretary of
State for the Home Department ex p A* [2000] 2 AC 276 confirmed that it was only
a remand to a secure children's home that should be deducted from a sentence.

57  *R v Governor of Brockhill Prison ex p Evans* [1997] 2 WLR 236.

58  CJA 1967 s67(1A)(b), PSO 6650 para 4.1.4.

59  *R v Secretary of State for the Home Department ex p Probyn* [1998] 1 WLR 809 and
PSO 6650 para 4.1.5.

60  CJA 1991 s47(2) although courts should normally direct that such time will be
taken into account, time taken up by 'impudent' appeals resisting extradition
may not be – *R v Howard (Curtis)* [1996] 2 Cr App R (S) 419, *R v Scalise* (1985) 7
Cr App R (S) 395.

61  *Burgess v Secretary of State for the Home Department* [2001] 1 WLR 93.

## Multiple sentences

3.25   When a court imposes more than one sentence it can either order that the sentences are served concurrently (overlapping), or consecutively (one after another). Where multiple CJA 1991 sentences are imposed (which, as noted above, include sentences of less than 12 months imposed for offences committed after 4 April 2005) a key concept is that of the 'single term'.[62] Where sentences form a single term, the relevant release mechanism is applied to that single term. In a simple example: if two sentences, one of six months and one of three and a half years, are ordered to be served consecutively this produces a single term of four years. The prisoner would then be eligible for release on licence at the two-year period (and whether Parole Board approval is necessary for release would depend on whether the offences were sexual or violent). If concurrent, a single term of three and a half years results as the shorter sentence is wholly subsumed into the longer. The prisoner would then be automatically released on licence at the halfway point.

3.26   For sentences imposed before 30 September 1998[63] all sentences served were single termed.[64] This was so whether or not the prisoner had been released and recalled in relation to one sentence before having a further sentence imposed. This situation created uncertainty as to release dates, as changes to the length of a single term caused by later sentences being incorporated could alter the applicable release scheme (by turning a short-term prisoner into a long-term one for example). Accordingly, for all CJA 1991 sentences imposed on or after 30 September 1998 a single term will only be created if:

- they were passed on the same occasion; or
- where they were passed on different occasions the prisoner has not been released at any time between the first and last of those occasions (release on ROTL does not count for this purpose, although release on HDC does).

3.27   So if a prisoner is given a sentence of 18 months, and six months later whilst in prison receives a sentence of three years, if the latter sentence is consecutive a single term of four and a half years is created, if it is concurrent a single term of three and a half years results. If however the prisoner is released from the 18-month sentence at nine

---

62   CJA 1991 s51.
63   When amendments to section 51 were made by the CDA 1998.
64   *R v Secretary of State for the Home Department ex p Francois* [1999] 1 AC 43.

months and then recalled and subsequently given a second sentence, no single term can be created.[65] However periods of imprisonment for default of payment of fines and civil sentences do not form part of the single term.[66]

3.28    Where CJA 1991 extended sentences form part of a single term, only the custodial term of the sentence is included in the single term.[67] Accordingly a prisoner who receives a six-year extended sentence with a three-year custodial term, and a consecutive one-year sentence, a single term of four years is created. The prisoner is therefore eligible for release on licence at the two-year point. The extension period is applied to the single termed custodial sentence. The fact that two short term sentences of under four years can be single termed into long term sentence, which makes the prisoner subject to less favourable release arrangements, was upheld by the House of Lords who considered this to be an inevitable consequence of the statutory framework.[68]

### 'At risk' sentences or 'orders to return'

3.29    Under the CJA 1991 whenever a new offence is committed before the final sentence expiry date, when the court imposes a sentence for the new offence, it may also make an order requiring the prisoner to serve an additional period. The maximum such period is that between the date of commission of the new offence and the sentence expiry date of the first sentence.[69] Such periods are to be treated as terms of imprisonment in their own right and so are subject to the relevant release mechanism depending on the length of the term. The new sentence can accordingly be ordered to run consecutively to the order to return, as although the prisoner has been released from the original sentence, the order to return is a fresh sentence in its own right.[70]

---

65  And the in such circumstances the sentencing court cannot impose consecutive sentences PCC(S)A 2000 s84 – and so the multiple sentences run in parallel and the prisoner remains in prison until the latest release date.

66  PSO 6650 para 3.2.6.

67  CJA 1991 s44(2).

68  *R v Secretary of State for the Home Department ex p Francois* [1999] 1 AC 43.

69  PCC(S)A 2000 s116.

70  *R v Lowe, R v Leask* [2000] 1 WLR 153.

## Calculating Criminal Justice Act 2003 sentences

### Remand time

3.30   For CJA 2003 sentences the prison is no longer responsible for crediting remand time. It is now the responsibility of the sentencing court to give a direction which specifies the amount of remand time to be deducted from the sentence.[71] The court can include time spent on bail subject to curfew and electronic tagging conditions from 3 November 2008.[72]

3.31   Although the change to requiring the court to specify remand time to be taken into account, rather than making it an administrative procedure dealt with at the prison, was designed to bring greater clarity to the sentencing process, it can lead to confusion. This can occur when the sentencing court has insufficient information to make an accurate calculation at the time of sentencing. Whilst magistrates' courts can rectify a mistake at any time there is a time limit of 56 days for the Crown Court to do so.[73] If the time limit is missed in the Crown Court the only way to correct any error is by way of appeal to the Court of Appeal which is timely and costly. In light of these problems the Court of Appeal has given guidance that if judges are in any doubt about the correct amount of remand time to be taken into account they should effectively make a provisional order as to the number of days which can be amended administratively if it turns out to be wrong. If the judge fails to make such a direction, the time limit has passed, and the parties agree, then the appeal should be dealt with in a streamlined procedure without attendance.[74]

3.32   Where a prisoner commits a further offence on licence and there is a considered decision not to recall them, it is wrong for the judge sentencing for the new offence to refuse to direct that time spent in custody awaiting trial should not be taken into account. Moreover a judge minded to direct that remand time should not count should raise this issue with the defence before the decision is made so that submissions on that point can be made.[75] Time spent abroad awaiting extradition falls to be considered in the same way as other remand time and so must be dealt with by the sentencing judge.[76]

---

71   CJA 2003 s240.
72   CJA 2003 s240A.
73   Magistrates' Courts Act 1980 s142, PCC(S)A 2000 s155.
74   *R v Nnaji and Johnson (RT)* [2009] EWCA Crim 468.
75   *R v Metcalfe* [2009] EWCA Crim 374.
76   CJA 2003 s243.

## Multiple sentences

3.33　The CJA 2003 does not include provisions for single term sentences. Instead concurrent sentences are served in parallel so that the prisoner is released only at the latest release date, and remains on licence until the latest sentence expiry date.[77] Consecutive sentences[78] are aggregated in order to calculate release dates and sentence expiry.[79] For example a three-year sentence consecutive to a two-year sentence will result in the prisoner being released two and a half years after sentence on licence to five years after sentence.

3.34　As with extended sentences imposed under the CJA 1991, where an extended sentence is imposed under the CJA 2003 consecutively with other sentences, it is only the custodial term of the sentence that is aggregated with the other terms.[80] The Court of Appeal has given guidance that courts should avoid making normal determinate sentences consecutive to extended sentences. This is because if there is no single term and release from the extended sentence depends on a Parole Board decision, then there will be difficulties in deciding the point at which the determinate sentence should be deemed to run from.[81] Accordingly determinate sentences should be ordered to be served first. This problem does not apply for CJA 2003 sentences imposed after 14 July 2008 as release is automatic at the halfway point of the custodial term.

3.35　There are no 'at risk' provisions for CJA 2003 sentences and so sentencing courts cannot impose further terms when new offences are committed during the currency of a sentence.

## Where a prisoner is serving both CJA 1991 and CJA 2003 sentences

3.36　The different sentencing regimes are fixed with reference to the date when offences were committed and so there are commonly situations where prisoners are serving both kinds of sentences. Also, prison sentences of under 12 months remain subject to the CJA 1991 whenever committed and so where a prisoner is serving a mix of sentences of fewer and more than 12 months, both schemes will apply to the respective sentences. This can give rise to complicated issues of sentence calculation.

77　CJA 2003 s263.
78　Which, as with the CJA 1991 regime, cannot be imposed where the prisoner has been released from a sentence: CJA 2003 s265.
79　CJA 2003 s264.
80　CJA 2003 s264(2) and (6)(a)(i).
81　*R v C and others* [2007] EWCA Crim 680.

3.37    All CJA 1991 sentences (including sentences of fewer than 12 months imposed for offences committed after 4 April 2005) imposed on the same occasion, or different occasions as long as the prisoner has not been released, will be single termed. However CJA 2003 sentences cannot be single termed with CJA 1991 sentences but will be given separate release dates. The complexities that this can give rise to were demonstrated by the *Noone* case.[82] In that case the prisoner was given consecutive sentences of 22 months, four months and one month. As the two shorter sentences were under 12 months they fell to be single termed under the CJA 1991 provisions. However the 22-month period could not form part of the single term. Moreover, as this was the sentence first handed down by the court the prison determined that it had to be served first. Accordingly the sentence was calculated so that the prisoner would first serve the CJA 2003 sentence and then the five-month single term of the CJA 1991 sentences. This in turn meant that the prisoner was only eligible for a period on HDC referable to the five-month sentence rather than the total 27-month term, the impact of which was that she was eligible for HDC for a period of 38 days rather than the maximum 135 days.

3.38    If all the sentences had been imposed under either the CJA 1991 or CJA 2003 regimes the prisoner would have been entitled to have her HDC eligibility calculated with reference to the entire sentence length. However, the Court of Appeal held that the Prison Service was bound to calculate the sentences as it had due to the fact that sentences under both regimes could not be aggregated or single-termed with each other. Further it would be improper for prisons to calculate a sentence by changing the order of the sentences as handed down by the court. As a result of the litigation involving this issue guidance has been given to courts as to the potential effect of the order in which sentences are ordered to be served on HDC eligibility.[83]

## Detention and Training Orders (DTOs)

3.39    Where children or young offenders receive determinate sentences other than DTOs,[84] these are largely calculated in the same way as sentences for adults and remand time is taken into account in the same way. However DTOs[85] are served in a different way. They are divided

---

82   [2009] 1 WLR 1321.
83   *R v Isse* [2009] EWCA Crim 1354.
84   Under PCC(S)A 2000 s91 for those under 18 years old, or detention in a YOI under section 96.
85   Imposed under PCC(S)A 2000 s100.

into two parts – the period of detention and training and the period of supervision. The period of detention is usually one-half the whole DTO. Whilst the court can impose consecutive DTOs, it must avoid imposing an order that results in a DTO exceeding 24 months.[86]

## Default terms, civil prisoners and contempt

3.40 Terms of imprisonment imposed for failure to pay financial penalties in criminal proceedings, or for contempt of court[87] are subject to special release provisions. Prisoners are released unconditionally at the halfway point of the sentence if the term is less than 12 months, or unconditionally at two-thirds if the term is 12 months or over.[88] Custodial terms of imprisonment for non-payment are not treated as sentences of imprisonment and will generally be served in full.[89]

## Time spent unlawfully at large (UAL)

3.41 Time spent UAL is not taken into account in calculating sentences unless the Secretary of State for Justice directs otherwise.[90] Time is considered to be spent UAL where the prisoner has escaped from custody, has absconded from custody, has had the licence revoked or has failed to return from a period of temporary release as required. Whether a prisoner is UAL is a matter of fact. There is accordingly no mental element and a prisoner can be UAL if a licence has been revoked and they are not returned to prison, even where they have no knowledge of the revocation,[91] or where they unknowingly become unlawfully at large due to the amendment to a court order.[92] This can clearly result in unfairness which is why the Secretary of State for Justice's power to direct that time spent UAL should count towards sentence is important.

3.42 PSO 6650 contains a detailed policy on the circumstances in which the power to direct that UAL should count towards the sentence will be exercised.[93] This states that each case will be considered on its individual merits, having regard to the following factors:

86  PCC(S)A 2000 s101(4).
87  PCC(S)A 2000 s108.
88  CJA 1991 s45.
89  PSO 6650 Annex I for summary.
90  PA 1952 s49(2).
91  *R (S) v Secretary of State for the Home Department* [2003] EWCA Civ 426.
92  *R (Lunn) v Governor of Moorland Prison* [2006] EWCA Civ 700.
93  PSO 6650 para 7.1. NB the exercise of this power is separate to that relating to special remission.

- The length of time before the prisoner is informed that they are UAL. In cases of mistaken release, if the prisoner is informed that they are UAL relatively quickly, then their case may be less deserving than those who are informed after a lengthy period.
- The extent to which the prisoner has been severely disadvantaged by their return to custody. For example, if the prisoner will lose irreplaceable employment and accommodation links.
- Whether the prisoner has deliberately withheld knowledge of the error. If it can be established that the prisoner was well aware that they were released too soon then this would render the exercise of the Secretary of State's discretion inappropriate.
- Public protection issues. Consideration must be given to the circumstances of a prisoner's release, in particular the security conditions under which they were held immediately prior to release, and any outstanding and existing risk factors.
- Family issues. Where the prisoner is a primary carer, regard must be paid to the care and wellbeing of the child or other person for whom they have been caring.

3.43   A prisoner who is UAL and is recaptured in a foreign country will not normally have time spent awaiting extradition taken into account, although they will be able to apply under the above policy.[94] The Secretary of State may be entitled to refuse to direct that such time should count where he decides that the prisoner is responsible for the time spent UAL awaiting extradition.[95] The policy states that only in very exceptional circumstances will the Secretary of State for Justice consider allowing UAL time amounting to more than 25 per cent of the sentence term to count. Short periods (less than one month) of UAL may be allowed to count at the discretion of the DOM. Longer periods will require ministerial approval on the recommendation of the DOM. When re-calculating the sentence the time spent UAL is added to all release dates, licence expiry dates and the date of sentence expiry.[96]

94  PSO 6650 para 7.2.5.
95  See for example *R (Murphy) v Secretary of State for the Home Department* [2005] EWHC 3116 (Admin) – which also confirmed that as the decision was only concerned with how a sentence was executed it did not raise issues under either article 5 or 6 of the ECHR.
96  PA 1952 s49(2), PSO 6650 para 7.2.1 – all release dates are effectively postponed by the number of days UAL. Accordingly where a prisoner released on HDC is recalled, his release at the halfway point of the sentence will be postponed by the number of days UAL, as will any future release date should he be recalled again – this does not amount to having to serve the UAL days twice but reflects the fact that UAL time puts back all relevant dates – *R (Lindo) v Secretary of State for the Home Department* [2004] EWCA Civ 491.

## Sentence calculation procedure

3.44  Chapter 2 of PSO 6650 contains detailed guidance on how prisons should calculate sentences. Release dates should be calculated by the prison within two working days of reception.[97] The calculation must be made on the basis of the order of the court, even if this does not accurately reflect the judge's intention.[98] The calculation should be checked by a second member of staff.[99] The prison should ensure that the prisoner is notified of the sentence calculation in writing within, at most, two working days after the calculation has been made.[100] Two weeks, and then two days before the anticipated release date the calculation must be checked by different members of staff to ensure that it is correct.[101]

3.45  Where the warrant or sentence appears ambiguous or invalid, the prison should contact the sentencing court so that if necessary an amendment can be made.[102] The magistrates' courts can re-open a case at any time after sentencing to rectify a mistake[103] although Crown Courts can only do so within 56 days of sentencing.[104]

3.46  Any time spent in custody beyond that authorised by the sentence of the court will give rise to a claim for false imprisonment, even if the calculation was made in good faith and on the basis of an accepted interpretation of the law which turns out to be wrong.[105] A mistake in sentence calculation made prior to release which gives a prisoner an expectation that they are to be released earlier may give rise to an entitlement to special remission (see chapter 11). If a prisoner is released early by mistake, they will be classified as UAL but the Secretary of State has the power to direct that the time will be taken into account in calculating the sentence in order to mitigate the unfairness that may result (see above paras 3.42–3.43).

---

97  PSO 6650 2.1.1.
98  *R (Lunn) v Governor of Moorland Prison* [2006] EWCA Civ 700 – the prison was bound to calculate the sentence as contained in the order of the court until it had been corrected in line with the judge's intention.
99  PSO 6650 para 2.5.1.
100 PSO 6650 para 2.1.2.
101 PSO 6650 paras 2.5.2–2.5.3.
102 PSO 6650 para 2.6.
103 Magistrates' Courts Act 1980 s142.
104 PCC(S)A 2000 s155 – for sentences imposed prior to 14 July 2008 the time limit was 28 days.
105 *R v Governor of HM Prison Brockhill ex p Evans (No 2)* [2001] 2 AC 19.

# Categorisation and allocation

## Introduction

3.47    As noted in chapter 2, there is a wide range of institutions in which prisoners can be held. The decision as to where a prisoner is located may have a massive impact both on the conditions of their detention, and on their ability to maintain family and other ties with those outside. There are two distinct processes which will determine where and in which kind of institution a prisoner will be located; these are categorisation and allocation. Categorisation refers to the decision as to the prisoner's appropriate *security category*. This decision-making process will broadly encompass three factors; likelihood of escape, risk to the public and the kinds of control problems that the prisoner may pose (although the relevance of this third factor is variable). It is only when a decision has been made as to which security category is appropriate that the *allocation* decision is made. This is the decision as to which particular institution is appropriate for the prisoner.

## Legal principles

### The distinction between categorisation and allocation

3.48    The Prison Act 1952 s12 states that prisoners may be lawfully confined in any prison and can, on the Secretary of State's direction, be moved to other prisons during the term of imprisonment.[106] The courts have traditionally construed these statutory provisions as giving the Secretary of State a wide degree of discretion especially where the decision to move a prisoner is based on operational or security grounds.[107] However courts have made a distinction between allocation decisions, which due to issues of security may have to be taken urgently and categorisation decisions, which need not be, as a proper review can take place once the prisoner has been transferred.

3.49    Where, for example, the Secretary of State decided to recategorise 22 prisoners who had more than five years of their sentences left to serve from category D (which meant that they were suitable for open conditions) to category C, the categorisation decisions were held to be unlawful as the individual circumstances of each prisoner had

---

106  PA 1952 s12(1) and (2).
107  *R v Secretary of State for the Home Department and another ex p McAvoy* [1984] 1 WLR 1408.

not been properly considered.[108] This can be contrasted with the case where in May 2006 all foreign national prisoners serving life sentences were transferred out of open conditions (but were not recategorised) due to concerns that there was an increased risk of such prisoners absconding. This concern followed an announcement by the Home Secretary that there was a presumption that all prisoners liable to deportation would actually be deported. About 25 such prisoners were removed from open conditions due to the perceived security concerns, without any consideration being given to their individual circumstances. The court that analysed this decision decided that it was lawful as the prisoners had not been formally recategorised. Individual assessments as to suitability for open conditions took place once they were held in the closed prison.[109]

### Principles of decision-making

3.50    The courts have also accepted that the principles of procedural fairness apply to categorisation decisions. There is a requirement to give reasons for such decisions[110] and the Prison Service's policies reflect this (see further below). The extent of the requirements imposed upon the Prison Service will depend on the nature of the decision. For example decisions to recategorise life sentence prisoners, who have served their minimum term, from category C to category B will clearly impact on the prospects of release as lifers are generally required to spend some time in an open prison before being released by the Parole Board and this decision will affect that progress. Accordingly such prisoners are entitled to be informed of any prospective recategorisation, the reasons behind the proposal and given a reasonable opportunity in which to make representations before a decision is taken. This does not prevent the transfer taking place pending such steps, if such a move is justified on operational or security grounds.[111]

---

108  *R (Vary and others) v Secretary of State for the Home Department* [2004] EWHC 2251 (Admin) – the decisions were taken pending a review into categorisation policy following the absconding and death of a prisoner from open conditions who was only six and a half years into a 21-year sentence.

109  See *R (Chindamo) v Secretary of State for the Home Department* [2006] EWHC 3340 (Admin) – however a number of those transferred were in fact British citizens and subsequently successfully sought compensation for the decisions to move them under RRA 1976 and DPA 1998.

110  *R v Secretary of State for the Home Department ex p Peries* [1997] EWHC 712 (Admin).

111  *Hirst v Secretary of State for the Home Department* [2001] EWCA Civ 378.

This principle clearly applies even more forcefully for decisions relating to the transfer of post-minimum term lifers from category D to category C.[112] Similarly, as category A decisions have a serious impact both on prospects of release and the conditions in which prisoners are held, they are entitled to disclosure and an opportunity to make representations prior to such decisions being taken. In some cases fairness will require an oral hearing in the category A context. The full requirements of a category A review are examined in detail below.

3.51    These rigorous standards of procedural fairness have not been extended to other categorisation decisions. Accordingly it has been held that as long as a determinate sentence prisoner is given proper reasons and an opportunity to make representations through the complaints process, then he or she does not need to be given prior disclosure or an opportunity to make representations before a decision is taken to recategorise, even from D to C.[113]

### The ECHR, categorisation and allocation

3.52    In a large number of cases it has been held that article 5 does not apply to decisions relating to the conditions in which a prisoner is held (subject to the need for there to be a proper relationship between the place of detention and its purpose).[114] Accordingly, the procedural safeguards that apply when article 5(4) is engaged do not apply to categorisation or allocation decisions. The justification for this is that article 5(4) is only involved in decisions directly affecting liberty and so it is not engaged by decisions that may impact on the timing of eventual release, but only involve the conditions in which the prisoner is held, such as decisions as to whether a lifer should go to open conditions, or whether a prisoner is held in category A.[115]

3.53    Furthermore article 6 is not engaged in categorisation decisions because the courts have held that an administrative decision to recategorise a prisoner is not a determination of civil rights or a criminal charge.[116] As categorisation decisions are primarily about prison security the prison authorities are not required to take into account

---

112  *R (Blagden) v Secretary of State for the Home Department* [2001] EWHC 393 (Admin).

113  *R (McLeod) v HM Prison Service* [2002] EWHC 390 (Admin), *R (Palmer) v Secretary of State for the Home Department* [2004] EWHC 1817 (Admin).

114  *Aerts v Belgium* (1998) 29 EHRR 50.

115  *R (Burgess) v Secretary of State for the Home Department* [2000] Prison LR 257, *R (Sunder) v Secretary of State for the Home Department* [2001] EWCA Civ 1157.

116  *R (Sunder) v Secretary of State for the Home Department* [2001] EWCA Civ 1157.

the impact of them on family circumstances even where these engage article 8 of the Convention.[117]

3.54　　Individual *allocation* decisions may, however, engage a range of rights under the Convention. The positive duty to protect prisoners that arises under articles 2 and 3 may, for example, require placement in a vulnerable prisoners or protected witness unit (see chapter 4). A transfer of a prisoner pending trial that prejudices the right to a fair trial may breach article 6 of the Convention.[118]

3.55　　A prisoner's rights to family or private life can also be breached by a particular allocation. Although prisoners have been able to argue that article 8 is engaged in such cases, the prison authorities have usually been able to successfully argue that the decision is nonetheless justifiable and proportionate by reference to security issues. In *McCotter v UK*[119] it was stated that only in 'exceptional circumstances' would the detention of a prisoner a long way from home breach article 8. This should be read as meaning that the reality of the application of article 8 to the position of serving prisoners is such that very few allocation decision will be capable of breaching the article.[120]

3.56　　The risk of breaching article 8 will obviously be heightened where a decision to locate a prisoner a long way from family and support involves those who are young or vulnerable. Decisions as to whether babies should be kept with their mothers in detention have provided the clearest analysis as to how article 8 will apply:

> (i) the right to respect for family life is not a right which a prisoner necessarily loses by reason of his/her incarceration; (ii) on the other hand, when a court considers whether the state's reasons for interfering with that right are relevant and sufficient, it is entitled to take into account (a) the reasonable requirements of prison organisation and security and (b) the desirability of maintaining a uniform regime in prison which avoids any appearance of arbitrariness or discrimination; (iii) whatever the justification for a general rule, Convention law requires the court to consider the application of that rule to the particular case, and to determine whether in that case the interference is proportionate to the particular legitimate aim being pursued; (iv) the more serious the intervention in any given case (and interventions

---

117　*R (Bryant) v Secretary of State for the Home Department* [2005] EWHC 1663 (Admin).

118　*R v Secretary of State for the Home Department ex p Quinn* [1999] Prison LR 35.

119　(1993) 15 EHRR CD 98.

120　Not that there is in reality a test of 'exceptionality' that must be met – see the discussions in *Gilbert v Secretary of State for the Home Department* [2002] EWHC 2832 (Admin) and *R (Shaheen) v Secretary of State for Justice* [2008] EWHC 1195 (Admin).

cannot come very much more serious than the act of separating a mother from a very young child), the more compelling must be the justification.[121]

## Statutory and policy framework

### Adults

3.57    For adults, PR rule 7(1) requires prisoners to 'be classified, in accordance with any directions of the Secretary of State, having regard to their age, temperament and record and with a view to maintaining good order and facilitating training and, in the case of convicted prisoners, of furthering the purpose of their training and treatment'. This broad duty to classify is then subject to detailed guidance set out in the NSF and PSO 0900.

### Young offenders

3.58    YOIR rule 4 states that prisoners 'may be classified, in accordance with any directions of the Secretary of State, taking into account their ages, characters and circumstances'. Again this power to classify is subject to the detailed guidance in the NSF and PSO 0900.

### Children

3.59    Although the statutory responsibility for the conditions in which the under-18s are held lies with the Minister of Justice[122] the Youth Justice Board has delegated responsibility for the placement.[123] The YJB policy on where children will be detained is contained in its Secure Facilities Placement Guidance.[124]

## E List prisoners in prisons and YOIs

3.60    This is not a formally a security category, but the NSF contains detailed procedures for identifying those who pose a risk of escape (this is

---

121  *R (P and Q) v Secretary of State for the Home Department* [2001] 1 WLR 2002.
122  For those serving DTOs see PCC(S)A 2000 ss102(1) and 107(1); s92 for those serving a sentence imposed under PCC(S)A 2000 s91, and CJA 2003 s235 for those under 18-years-old sentenced to indeterminate or extended sentences under that Act.
123  This is expressed as a concurrent duty with the Secretary of State for Justice – see article 4. The Youth Justice Board for England and Wales Order 2000 SI No 1160.
124  Available at www.yjb.gov.uk/Publications/Resources/Downloads/ SecFacPlacGuide.pdf

unrelated to any assessment of risk to the public). Prisons and YOIs are required to consider the following when deciding who should be placed on the 'E List':

- whether there is there reliable intelligence that the prisoner is planning to escape;
- whether the prisoner escaped or made a credible attempt to escape;
- whether the prisoner escaped or tried to escape before and the circumstances and whether similar circumstances apply now; and
- whether the prison's physical and procedural security is sufficient to deal with the perceived threat without placing the prisoner on the E List.

3.61 Where a prisoner is placed on the E List the following measures must be applied:

- If the prisoner is in category C, D or open conditions then their security category should be reviewed and the prisoner transferred to more appropriately secure conditions as soon as possible. In the meantime, the Governor should make arrangements to ensure that the prisoner is held in as secure conditions as possible to prevent an escape.
- A standard risk category A prisoner (see below) who presents a high risk of escape must be reported to the Directorate of High Security for consideration for reclassification to high risk category A. The prisoner must be placed on the E List pending the decision from Prison Service Headquarters.
- The decision to place the prisoner on the E List must be reviewed by a manager at least every 28 days. The prisoner must be removed from the list as soon as he or she no longer presents a risk of escape.

3.62 The NSF says nothing about the procedural safeguards of decisions to place prisoners on the E List. However it is certain that prisoners are entitled to reasons for such decisions. That said, the decision making will usually have been made on the basis of sensitive security information, and so the reasons given may not provide the prisoner with much to go on in order to make representations. Decisions can be challenged through the normal complaints procedure. The Prisons and Probation Ombudsman as part of any investigation will be able to examine any non-disclosed material.

3.63 Life for prisoners on the E List is far more restricted. The NSF requires all prisons to have a local security strategy dealing with the movement and supervision of E List prisoners which must include as a minimum:

- A system to record the location of E List prisoners and the member of staff responsible for them at any one time should be in place. Handover arrangements must also be specified.
- Instructions for the Control Room to follow regarding the movement of E List prisoners within the establishment.
- An outline of the work and activity areas that E List prisoners may be allocated to. The use of outside facilities by E List prisoners may only be given approval if appropriate levels of security are in place.
- E List prisoners must wear clothing that distinguishes them from other prisoners. Traditionally E List prisoners wear prison clothing with bright yellow markings (known as 'patches').

## Categorisation and allocation: adult males

*The categories and principles of categorisation*

3.64    There are four security categories for sentenced adult males:[125]

### Category A

Prisoners whose escape would be highly dangerous to the public or the police or the security of the state and for whom the aim must be to make escape impossible.

### Category B

Prisoners for whom the very highest conditions of security are not necessary but for whom escape must be made very difficult.

### Category C

Prisoners who cannot be trusted in open conditions but who do not have the resources and will to make a determined escape attempt.

### Category D

Prisoners who can be reasonably trusted in open conditions.

3.65    PSO 0900 states that 'prisoners must be categorised objectively according to the likelihood that they will seek to escape and the risk that they would pose should they do so'. Although the policy states

---

125  NSF and PSO 0900 para 1.1.1.

that the consideration of these two factors will normally be sufficient to determine a prisoner's category, it also recognises that there may be a small number of prisoners who, despite posing little risk, may because of their behaviour 'require a higher category so that they may be sent to a prison commensurate with the risk they pose to control'. No other considerations aside from risk to the public, of escape and relevant control issues should be taken into account.[126] In particular, control issues not directly relevant to security (such as ability to mix with other prisoners, educational, medical or offending behaviour needs) should not be taken into account as these are issues relating to allocation rather than security.[127]

3.66    Prisoners 'must be placed in the lowest security category consistent with the needs of security and control' and so the correct category must be assigned even if it is clear that it will not be possible to arrange a transfer to a prison of that category. '[O]n no account should a prisoner's security category be adjusted to enable a better match with available spaces throughout the estate'.[128]

3.67    Formal categorisation is a process that takes place after sentencing is complete as sentence length is one of the key considerations in deciding the appropriate security category. Therefore, all prisoners on remand awaiting trial, or convicted and awaiting sentence, other than those provisionally categorised A, are placed in category U (unclassified). Category U prisoners are normally held in local (category B) prisons but where there is 'adequate information' to suggest that category B accommodation is not needed they can be transferred to category C prisons with the approval of the DOM. Each case should be considered on its individual merits.[129]

## Category A status

### Introduction

3.68    Category A prisoners are subject to a detailed set of security procedures commensurate with the aim of making escape impossible for those prisoners identified as posing a very high risk to the public. In November 2008, out of a total population in custody of about 83,000, the Directorate of High Security Prisons stated that there were about

---

126  PSO 0900 1.2.1.
127  PSO 0900 1.2.2.
128  NSF and PSO 0900 para 1.2.3.
129  See NSF and PSO 0900 para 1.4.1.

930 category A prisoners.[130] Unlike the other security categories, category A status is decided centrally, by the Directorate of High Security Prisons at Prison Service headquarters. Those detained under the Immigration Act can be classified as category A and will have annual reviews in the same way as sentenced prisoners.

## The definition of category A status

3.69    Because of the level of risk posed by this class of prisoners, the definition of category A set out above previously stated that the category would apply 'no matter how unlikely that escape may be'. This aspect of the policy was successfully challenged by a prisoner who argued that, although the Prison Service was clearly entitled to have a policy the aim of which was to make escape impossible for highly dangerous prisoners, it would be unlawful to give no consideration in such a policy to the individual's ability to escape. The prisoner in that case was aged and infirm and stated he was incapable of escaping (although it was accepted that he was still dangerous).[131] In such cases the legitimate aim of the policy might be met by confining the prisoner to conditions of lesser security (where for example a dangerous prisoner is so infirm that escape is a practical impossibility).

3.70    As a result of the challenge the definition of category A was amended and the relevant policy guidance to the Prison Service now states that 'consideration may also need to be given to whether the stated aim of making escape impossible can be achieved for a particular prisoner in lower conditions of security, and that the prisoner is categorised accordingly. However this will only arise in exceptional circumstances since escape potential will not normally affect the categorisation as it is rarely possible to foresee all the circumstances in which escape may occur'.[132]

3.71    Although the policy states that it will only be in 'exceptional circumstances' that escape potential will be relevant, such circumstances are not limited to physical infirmity. For example, in one case a prisoner argued that his location in a Protected Witness Unit was relevant to whether he was properly category A on the basis that he had an incentive not to escape. The Court of Appeal agreed that this was a relevant consideration that should have been taken into account

---

130  With a breakdown of 915 adult males, six females and nine male young offenders on 'restricted status' see para 3.150.

131  *R (Pate) v Secretary of State for the Home Department* [2002] EWHC 1018 (Admin).

132  PSO 1010 para 1.3.

(although it would clearly not be determinative).[133] However, despite the need to consider, in exceptional circumstances, whether a highly dangerous prisoner may be held in category B conditions because of limited escape potential, it is unclear whether any prisoner has ever been downgraded from category A on this basis.[134]

## Escape risk classification

3.72 Within category A there are three further subdivisions which relate to the assessed escape risk posed by the prisoner. These are:

**Standard escape risk**
Most category A prisoners are classified as standard escape risk. They are not considered to have the determination and skill to overcome the range of security measures which apply to the custody and movement of category A prisoners. There is no current information to suggest that they have external resources which could be used to assist them to overcome those measures. They have no history of escape or determined escape planning. *Even so, the Prison Service must assume that they would take any opportunity to escape and that, if unlawfully at large, they would pose a very serious threat to the public, the police, or the security of the state.*

**High escape risk**
They have a history and background which suggest that they have the ability and determination to overcome the range of security measures which apply to the custody of standard risk category A prisoners. There may be current information to suggest that they have associates or resources which could be used to plan and carry out an assisted escape attempt. If there is information that the prisoners or associates have access to firearms or explosives, and have been willing to use them in committing crime or in avoiding capture, high risk is the expected category.

**Exceptional escape risk**
A small number of category A prisoners are classified as exceptional escape risk. These are usually cases having the same features which apply to high escape risk, but where the nature and extent of the external resources which could be called upon to mount an escape attempt are such that the level of threat posed requires that the prisoner be held

133 *G v Secretary of State for the Home Department* [2006] EWCA Civ 919 – this case also confirmed generally that where a prisoner's representations raised a relevant issue as to escape potential this should be dealt with in the decision.

134 *R (Pate) v Secretary of State for the Home Department* [2002] EWHC 1018 and *G v Secretary of State for the Home Department* [2006] EWCA Civ 919 were successful procedural challenges, but neither led to the downgrading of the prisoners concerned.

in the most secure accommodation and conditions available to the Prison Service in order to achieve the aim of making escape impossible. Prisoners who have a history and background which suggest that they have the personal resourcefulness to overcome, with or without any external assistance, all but the highest conditions of security available, may also warrant an exceptional escape risk classification.[135]

3.73   The decisions as to whether a prisoner should be given category A status, and to which escape risk classification they should be allocated are distinct although factors might be relevant both to assessing dangerousness and escape risk (such as association with criminal gangs). The escape risk allocation should be kept under constant review so that a prisoner classified as either high or exceptional risk should be downgraded as soon as the grounds for such status are no longer present. In practice the DHSP does not invite representations on the issue of escape risk classification when it is reviewed outside the annual category A process and the courts (perhaps unsurprisingly) have considered that the requirements of fairness do not entitle prisoners to an opportunity to make such representations in advance of the decision.[136] Reasons for such decisions should be sought (which are likely to be limited for security reasons) so that representations can be then be made.

## The development of procedures for determining category A status

3.74   The impact that category A status has both on the day to day living conditions of a prisoner, and on their prospects of release if they are assessed as dangerous (for prisoners whose release is dependent on a positive consideration by the Parole Board) was recognised in the case of *R v Secretary of State for the Home Department ex p Duggan*[137] where the court required enhanced standards of fairness in determining that status by comparison with other categorisation decisions. The court highlighted the more onerous regimes to which such prisoners are subjected:

> It is common ground that a prisoner in category A endures a more restrictive regime and higher conditions of security than those in other categories. Movement within prison and communications with the outside world are closely monitored; strip searches are routine; visit-

---

135  PSO 1010 para 1.4.

136  *R (Allen) v Secretary of State for Justice* [2008] EWHC 3298 (Admin) – this was only an application for permission.

137  [1994] 3 All ER 277.

ing is likely to be more difficult for reasons of geography, in that there are comparatively few high security prisons; educational and employment opportunities are limited. And as, by definition, a category A prisoner is regarded as highly dangerous if at large, he cannot properly be regarded by the Parole Board as suitable for release on licence.

3.75  Until 1993, prisoners were not provided with any disclosure of the material upon which category A decisions were made, and were given no proper reasons for those decisions. The *Duggan* decision established that prisoners were at least entitled to a 'gist' of the material that was to be used in the decision-making process so that meaningful written representations could be submitted. The rationale of the case was that it was unfair for a decision potentially impacting on liberty being taken in secret and with no reasons being given.[138]

3.76  This resulted in prisoners being provided with a summary of the reports compiled by the holding prison and any external police information. The 'gist' would not particularise allegations and would not usually identify the report writers responsible for specific allegations or opinions.

3.77  Although at the time the entitlement to the gist was a significant development for prisoners, over time the category A process became more anomalous. This was because in other areas, such as parole hearings, prisoners were increasingly being given access to the full body of information that decision makers were relying upon. Despite this, prisoners were unsuccessful in arguing that there was no justification for withholding full reports in the category A process (subject to the right to withhold sensitive information) where full disclosure was the norm in parole cases.[139] This limited disclosure of a gist was subject to the proviso that there may be exceptional circumstances where full disclosure of the reports might be required, for example where it was impossible to fairly reconcile the content of the gist with reports put before the Parole Board without such disclosure.[140] There was also a growing concern about the quality of gists being prepared. Prisoners would sometimes be informed by staff of positive

138  As it was put in the parole context '[a] prisoner's right to make representations is largely valueless unless he knows the case against him and secret, unchallengeable reports which may contain damaging inaccuracies and which result in continuing loss of liberty are, or should be, anathema in a civilised, democratic society'. *R v Secretary of State for the Home Department ex p Creamer and Scholey* [1993] COD 162.

139  *R v Secretary of State for the Home Department ex p McAvoy* [1998] 1 WLR 790.

140  As was the case in *R (Williams) v Secretary of State for the Home Department* [2002] 1 WLR 2264.

recommendations in reports that were not then reflected in the gist. There was also a tendency for gists to be standardised in format and formulaic in their phraseology.

3.78    These problems were highlighted in the case of *Lord*, which finally established the right, subject to exceptions, to full disclosure of the category A reports.[141] The judgment quoted from an investigation by the Prisons and Probation Ombudsman that raised similar concerns:

> [i]f a gist renders itself so anodyne that it could equally apply to any number of prisoners then its effectiveness in providing a prisoner with credible material to understand the reasons behind their categorisation is open to question.

The facts of *Lord* itself also demonstrated that gists were in reality being drafted with little care that the reports were accurately reflected. For example the gist under challenge in this case suggested that the reports were unanimously against downgrading, when in fact two out of the total of six were supportive of such a course (and one made no recommendation). The court in *Lord* decided on the facts of the case that the prisoner had not been fairly treated. The judge concluded:

> A gist which, like the gist in the present case, entirely omits – conceals and suppresses – what from the perspective of the prisoner is the vital information that the adverse views on him are *not* unanimous, that some of the views are indeed decidedly favourable to him, in my judgment falls far short of what both the law and elementary principles of fairness require. Worse than that: it goes a long way to depriving him of any meaningful ability to make worthwhile representations.

3.79    The outcome in *Lord*, namely that all prisoners should have disclosure of the full reports relied upon in the category A process subject to limited exceptions, did not, however, rely upon the principles of fairness. The judge instead held that a blanket policy of non disclosure of reports was in breach of the Data Protection Act 1998. This was on the basis that the category A reports were properly to be considered as personal data under the Act, and that the Prison Service failed to establish that, in principle, there were any grounds under the statute for withholding disclosure. Following this case the current category A procedure was amended to that set out below, which include an entitlement to disclosure of the reports.

---

141  *R (Lord) v Secretary of State for the Home Department* [2003] EWHC 2073 (Admin).

## Category A procedures

3.80   In summary category A decisions take place at the following times:

- Local prisons identify potential category A prisoners when remanded and report them into the DHSP which then decides whether the prisoner should be given provisional category A status.
- Once convicted and sentenced the first formal review takes place with disclosure (although this is limited) and an opportunity for the prisoner to make representations.
- If the prisoner remains category A after the first formal review then the next review normally takes place two years later, with annual reviews thereafter.

## Provisional category A status

3.81   As noted above the responsibility for deciding which prisoners should be given category A status lies with the DHSP at Prison Service Headquarters. However the holding prison has responsibility for 'reporting in' potential category A prisoners when received on remand. The DHSP will decide whether they should be placed *provisionally* in category A pending conviction and sentence. Prisoners detained under the Immigration Act who pose a high security risk will also be reported in for provisional category A status.

The prison first identifies prisoners with the following convictions which is the first indication that a prisoner may need to be reported in to the DHSP:

- murder
- attempted murder
- manslaughter
- wounding with intent to do grievous bodily harm
- rape
- buggery
- robbery
- attempted robbery
- conspiracy to rob
- importing, producing or distributing drugs
- arson with intent to endanger life
- offences under the Official Secrets Act 1989
- offences connected with terrorism
- any other offences likely to result in sentences in excess of ten years.[142]

142  See NSF and PSO 1010 para 3.1.

3.82    The guidance states that prison staff should contact the police officer in charge of the case to obtain information about the offence charged, including whether the victim was known to the prisoner; possible motives; the extent of violence and injuries received; whether a weapon was carried or used; and whether drink, drugs or the prisoner's mental state were relevant. The police should also provide an assessment of the prisoner's dangerousness and escape potential.[143]

3.83    More specific guidance is then given as to when those convicted of the above offence should have their cases reported in, namely:

- where the serious offences of violence, including serious sexual offences, were serial in nature or represented an escalating pattern of offending;
- where an offence involving a particularly high level of violence, especially if of a frenzied or sadistic nature, was committed against a victim who was not related to, or closely associated with, the prisoner;
- where a serious sexual offence was randomly committed and involved life-threatening levels of violence and very serious injury additional to the sexual element of the attack;
- where a serious offence, including sexual offences, has been committed against children;
- where an attempted or actual robbery involved acts of life-threatening violence to the public or police;
- where loaded firearms were discharged at people;
- where an offence of armed robbery committed by a professional robber of considerable standing resulted in large amounts of money being stolen;
- where the arresting authorities indicate that an offender charged with serious drug importation or production offences is a senior member of a well researched criminal gang prepared to use firearms in an escape attempt, and who would violently resist any attempt at re-arrest putting the police and public at serious risk;
- where an arsonist with a history of fire raising endangers the lives of strangers;
- terrorist or Official Secrets Act offences;
- prisoners charged with the offences listed above who are subsequently convicted and sentenced to custody for ten years or more should also be reported in.[144]

---

143  See NSF and PSO 1010 para 3.1.
144  NSF and PSO 1010 para 3.2.

3.84 Prisoners not convicted of one of the offences listed above may still be reported in if any special features of their case justify this. Examples include:

- prisoners who, during a sentence, are charged with or convicted of any offence which meets the above criteria;
- where the subject of fresh information about the prisoner or associates suggests that category A should be considered;
- prisoners who behave in prison in a way which suggests that escape would be highly dangerous to the public, the police or the state.[145]

3.85 Additionally prisoners held under the Immigration Act who are believed to have committed serious offences abroad, or those held under anti-terrorism legislation, or detained pending extradition for serious offences abroad should also be reported in.[146]

3.86 The operations unit within DHSP will then decide whether a prisoner should be treated as a provisional category A prisoner pending conviction and sentence. The prison will be informed of the decision and the escape risk classification and if necessary transfer to an appropriate high security prison will be arranged.[147] Exceptional risk category A prisoners will be transferred to a High Security Unit. This first decision by DHSP that prisoners pending conviction should be provisional category A prisoners is not made with any disclosure being made to the prisoner, and the process does not allow for any representations to be made. This is because the decision is made on an assessment of the offence as charged. In the *Duggan* case,[148] although the court held that fairness required disclosure and an opportunity to make representations in the first and subsequent reviews of a category A decision, the judge stated that, 'I see nothing unfair in that initial categorisation being undertaken without the substance of reports being revealed or reasons being given'.

3.87 Although the Prison Service policy does not state that prisoners should even be given reasons for their provisional category A status, there is clearly scope for errors that could be corrected by representations even at this stage. If prisoners or their advisers are concerned about a decision to treat a remand prisoner as provisional category A, it is possible to seek reasons from DHSP and in light of those reasons, to seek a review if there are concerns whether the relevant

145 NSF and PSO 1010 para 3.2.
146 PSO 1010 para 3.4.
147 PSO 1010 para 3.5.
148 [1994] 3 All ER 277.

criteria have been properly applied. Pending the decision from the
DHSP prisoners who have been reported-in should be treated as category A, and where the prison consider the prisoner might warrant
high or exceptional escape risk classification DHSP should be contacted for advice on cell location and security procedures.[149]

### The first formal review

3.88    Following conviction and sentence all provisional category A prisoners must have their security category reviewed by DHSP as soon as
practicable.[150] The purpose of this review by the Director of High
Security Prisons is to decide whether the provisional decision on category A should be confirmed. The prison should fax to the DHSP
within five days after sentence copies of the warrant from the court,
the indictment and the court form 5089.[151] The category A review team
(CART) at the DHSP will then review the case, if necessary seeking
advice from the police advisers section and if the recommendation is
that the prisoner remains category A, written representations will be
sought from the prisoner following disclosure of the material relied
upon, and a gist of any non-disclosable material.[152] The prisoner will
be given one month to make representations on disclosure of the
material, CART will then make a recommendation to the Director of
High Security within a further month and the Director should then
make a decision within two weeks.[153]

### Subsequent reviews

3.89    The first review following the first formal review will take place two
years later unless:

- the Director of High Security decides, at the first formal review,
  that the case should be reviewed within a shorter timescale; or
- the Governor of the holding prison makes a recommendation for
  an earlier review on the basis of evidence of diminished risk.[154]

---

149  PSO 1010 para 3.6 and PSI 38/2005 para 1.1.
150  PSO 1010 para 2.5.
151  PSO 1010 para 2.5.
152  PSO 1010 paras 2.4 and 5.1 – the format of the reports for the first formal
     review is at Annex B.
153  PSO 1010 para 5.1.
154  PSO 1010 para 2.6. Such recommendations require 'cogent evidence of reduced
     risk' evidenced by, for example, offending behaviour programme reports
     and/or psychological assessments which show a 'significant reduction in the
     likelihood of re-offending in a similar way if unlawfully at large', see para 2.7.

3.90    These subsequent reviews must then take place annually on a timescale for the individual prisoner that has to be agreed with the CART.[155] Prisons are able to synchronise reviews with other processes such as sentence planning reviews as long as the requirement for annual reviews is not seriously affected[156] and as long as CART agrees the review process can be delayed for offending behaviour courses to be completed, although this should not then affect the timing of the original cycle of reviews.[157]

3.91    The reviews take place in a two-stage process. After preparation of the reports which will be disclosed to the prisoner, a Local Advisory Panel (LAP) at the prison meets and makes a recommendation. This recommendation is then considered by CART. However only the Director of High Security can actually make the decision to downgrade a prisoner from category A.

### The category A reports

3.92    The format of reports in the annual reviews is set out in Annex C to PSO 1010. The aim is to focus the report-writer's mind on the prisoner's level of dangerousness.[158] However, the policy asks report-writers *not* to make recommendations.[159] Section 1 of the reports gives the basic details of the prisoner, and any previous convictions. There will also be a description of the 'index' offence (that is the offence giving rise to the sentence being served), and details of any breaches of bail, probation supervision or other court orders.

3.93    The description of the index offence can be contentious. The account should as far as possible reflect the findings of the criminal court. Clearly comments of the sentencing judge may be included so long as they reflect the findings of the jury. However no judicial or other comments should be included that suggest that the prisoner should have been convicted of a more serious offence.[160] Category

---

155  PSO 1010 paras 2.9 and 4.1.
156  PSO 1010 para 4.2.
157  PSO 1010 para 4.3.
158  PSO 1010 para 5.3.
159  PSO 1010 para 5.3.
160  *R v Secretary of State for the Home Department ex p Daly* [2000] Prison LR 133
     – the trial judge in tariff setting papers stated that the prisoner, who had been convicted of manslaughter, was 'more deeply involved that the verdicts showed and ... his evidence that he did not know in advance that anybody was going to be killed was frankly incredible'. The court held that it was unlawful to include this suggestion that he should have been convicted of murder, notwithstanding that it came from the trial judge, in the category A papers.

A decisions can lawfully take into account convictions that are spent under the Rehabilitation of Offenders Act 1974 so the reports can properly refer to such convictions.[161]

3.94    Section 2 of the reports cover the prison history. Information should be obtained from the prisoner's core records and sentence planning documents. Report-writers are asked to discuss the prisoner's 'response to authority' (giving examples of 'compliance, co-operation and reasonableness'), their relationship with other prisoners (including any manipulative or bullying behaviour), and whether they have faced any formal disciplinary proceedings over the previous reporting period. Other sections of the reports cover offending behaviour work undertaken by the prisoner, sentence planning information, reports of any substance misuse, healthcare information including reports regarding mental health and security information reports (SIRs). Reports on offending behaviour work completed will be important as these may give evidence of sufficient reduction in risk to warrant downgrading.[162] There will normally be a psychology report and in keeping with the general current reliance upon the psychological assessments as providing the most authoritative assessments of dangerousness, this report will often be critical to the decision.

3.95    The assessment of dangerousness will always proceed on the basis that the prisoner is correctly convicted.[163] Prisoners who maintain their innocence are put into a difficult position in the categorisation process. As with parole, although denial of guilt cannot be determinative of category A status (in that it would be unlawful to refuse to downgrade solely on the basis of such a denial[164]), it will inevitably make it far more difficult for the prisoner to demonstrate that risk to the public has reduced. Prisoners who maintain innocence can of course complete offending behaviour courses that do

---

161  *R v Secretary of State for the Home Department ex p Purcell* [1998] EWHC 236 Admin – convictions become 'spent' under the Act not by reference to the seriousness of the offence, but by the length of the sentence.

162  And a failure to properly take into account offending behaviour work may render a decision unlawful – eg *R (Lynch) v Secretary of State for Justice* [2008] EWHC 2697 (Admin).

163  See *R (Roberts) v Secretary of State for the Home Department* [2004] EWHC 679 (Admin).

164  *R (Roberts) v Secretary of State for the Home Department* [2004] EWHC 679 (Admin): where the analogy with the parole situation was accepted by the Secretary of State – albeit that the assessment of risk in the category A process has to focus on what would happen if the prisoner escapes, rather than if released into the supervision of the Probation Service.

not require admission of guilt, or demonstrate a reduction in the risk they pose through developing maturity or changes in attitude evidenced through contact with staff.[165]

3.96 Section 7 of the reports is where any non-disclosable information is recorded. This is information that is only withheld in line with exemptions under the Data Protection Act 1998 in accordance with the *Lord* decision.[166]

3.97 Once the reports are disclosed to the prisoner, there should be a period of at least one month for representations to be submitted to the prison's LAP. The prisoner can of course seek the advice of a solicitor in preparing and submitting representations. These may seek to correct inaccuracies about the offence, allegations relating to behaviour in prison and details of offending behaviour work undertaken as well as addressing the substantive risk assessment that has been made. The prisoner may also submit expert reports, for example from an independent psychologist, as part of the review. If such reports are to be commissioned it will normally be necessary to seek an extension of time for submitting representations.

3.98 The LAP should be made up of the Governor or Deputy Governor of the prison, and the report writers – for sex offenders this should include staff involved in delivering any offending behaviour work, and for others security staff or the police liaison officer.[167] The LAP will consider the reports and the prisoner's representations. Following the meeting of the LAP the Governor or Deputy Governor completes section 6 of the reports which sets out the prison's recommendation as to whether the prisoner should remain category A or be downgraded. Section 6 directs consideration as to whether the prisoner has 'demonstrated evidence of a significant reduction in his risk of re-offending in a similar way if unlawfully at large' and requires reasons for the recommendation, whether it is for downgrading or not.

165 *R (Roberts) v Secretary of State for the Home Department* [2004] EWHC 679 (Admin): these were examples given in evidence by the Secretary of State in the case of matters that might demonstrate reduced risk.

166 The most common exemptions relied upon by the Prison Service are that the information would prejudice the detection and prosecution of crime (including crime committed in prison), legally privileged material and information relating to third parties (which does not include Prison Service staff) – see PSO 9020 para 10.1.3.

167 PSO 1010 para 5.4.

## Consideration by the DHSP

3.99   Officials in the CART will then consider the local prison's recommendation, the reports and the prisoner's representations. Although PSO 1010 does not specify that the LAP recommendation should be disclosed to the prisoner prior to consideration by the DHSP, it is clearly arguable that fairness requires this (most obviously so that any factual errors made by the local prison can be corrected). When making representations to the LAP prisoners and their advisers should ask that the LAP recommendation be disclosed so to enable a further opportunity to make further representations if necessary. Most prisons do in fact give the LAP recommendations to the prisoner.

3.100   Only the Director of High Security has the authority to downgrade a prisoner from category A[168] but not all final decisions are taken by the Director. The CART in some respects acts as a gate-keeper:

- if the CART supports a prison recommendation that the prisoner remains category A then a decision will be issued by the head of CART;
- if the CART supports a recommendation for downgrading it will draft a decision letter that will then go to the Director for approval (although clearly the Director would be entitled to veto such a recommendation);
- if CART does not support a prison recommendation (either way) then the case is referred to the Director; and
- all cases will be referred to the Director every five years.

3.101   Where cases are referred to the Director he or she makes the final decision and may seek the advice of the headquarters advisory panel. The advisory panel at the DHSP is made up of:

- the Director of High Security;
- the head of Resettlement and Programmes Group;
- the Police Advisers Section Commander;
- the head of DHSP operations unit; and
- the head of the category A review team.[169]

---

168  PSO 1010 para 5.6.
169  PSO 1010 para 5.6 – the policy makes clear that the Director can make decisions alone and does not need to consult the panel. It is unclear how often such consultation is made as the Director's decisions do not clarify whether it has taken place. Before the policy change effected by PSO 1010 the 'Category A Review Panel' (a body with a similar make up as the headquarters advisory panel) met bi-monthly and was responsible for all downgrading decisions.

3.102 Although the category A review process as set out in PSO 1010 is predicated on the right of the prisoners to make only written representations, the courts have recognised that there may be circumstances where fairness requires an oral hearing. This was first recognised in the *Williams* case[170] where the Parole Board conducted an oral hearing and recommended that the prisoner should be downgraded from category A. The DHSP then decided, at a time when there was no full disclosure of reports but only a gist in line with the *Duggan* case, that he should remain category A. The Court of Appeal held that in those circumstances, fairness required an oral hearing to determine category A status so that,

> the reasons for the contradictory views [could] be examined on behalf of the claimant and for the contents of any adverse reports to be directly addressed. In the final analysis the review team would, of course, have reached its own decision, but an oral hearing, and proper disclosure, would have ensured that the decision was the result of a better informed process.[171]

3.103 Oral hearings to determine category A status remain extremely rare.[172] The *Williams* decision predated full disclosure of category A reports and the Parole Board is now specifically asked not to comment on whether a prisoner is correctly categorised (save for the issue of suitability for open conditions for lifers). The combination of a stark disagreement between the Parole Board and the DHSP, together with only the gist of the category A reports being disclosed is now far less likely to happen. However, there have been at least two reported cases since these changes where the court has stated that the failure to convene an oral hearing was unfair.[173]

3.104 The director's decision will provide reasons both for the category A decision and the escape risk classification. Such decisions can be challenged through the Prison Service complaints procedure, and thereafter to the Prisons and Probation Ombudsman, or by applications for judicial review.

---

170 *R (Williams) v Secretary of State for the Home Department* [2002] 1 WLR 2264.

171 *R (Williams) v Secretary of State for the Home Department* [2002] 1 WLR 2264 para 32.

172 Aside from in *Williams* it is unclear whether any other prisoner has actually had the benefit of one.

173 *R (H) v Secretary of State for Justice* [2008] EWHC 2590 Admin – where the prisoner was a tariff expired lifer, in a Protected Witness Unit and so opportunities for offending behaviour work were limited, and the local prison had twice recommended downgrading. In *R (Wilkinson) v Secretary of State for Justice* [2009] EWHC 878 (Admin) the court considered fairness required an oral hearing where the Parole Board had recommended downgrading, as had the LAP, of a post tariff mandatory lifer who had been category A for 20 years.

3.105    It is of note that all the successful challenges to category A status have been on procedural grounds. The courts have shown a great deal of deference to the director's decisions on the merits of individual cases, such as in *R (Mackenzie) v Secretary of State for Justice*[174] where the court refused to interfere with a decision where a 62-year-old sex offender whose testes had been removed as a result of prostate cancer treatment was retained as a category A prisoner.

## Consequences of category A status

3.106    Category A prisoners are subject to a wide range of security measures (detailed in the NSF) that impact both on the conditions in which they are held, and the extent of their contacts with the outside world.

## The Approved Visitors Scheme

3.107    All social visitors to category A prisoners have to be approved. This entails the proposed visitor having to complete an application form together with two photographs which will be security checked by the police. In relation to standard and high risk category A prisoners, the Governor will decide whether the prisoner should be approved in light of the information provided by the police. The NSF notes that it is rare, especially for close relatives, for visitors not to be approved although the Governor may refuse if the police suspect that they would pose a threat to security or control. For exceptional risk and high risk prisoners on terrorist charges the application must be referred to the police advisers section. If the Governor does not accept its recommendation then the matter must be referred to the Director of High Security Prisons. Prisons have discretion to allow visits from close relatives pending the approval of an application under the scheme.

## Monitoring

3.108    The NSF specificies that the prison's Local Security Strategy must set out:

- Procedures for the observation of those in special security categories (eg category A, escape list, and those at risk of self-harm).
- All exceptional and high risk category A prisoners, all potential and provisional category A prisoners held temporarily outside the

---

174  [2008] EWHC 3382 (Admin), although the Court of Appeal allowed an appeal ([2009] EWCA Civ 669) on the basis that the Director had given insufficient weight to the impact of castration on risk of sexual offending.

category A estate, and all E List prisoners must be checked at least hourly while locked up.

- For standard risk category A prisoners held in the category A estate, Governors must agree with the Director of High Security the frequency of overnight checks.[175]

3.109 Local instructions, agreed between the Governor and Director of High Security Prisons, must be in place to cover the use of exercise areas and sportsfields by category A prisoners. Exceptional and high risk category A prisoners must only take their exercise in an enclosed yard, protected by anti-helicopter measures. The NSF also states that the Local Security Strategy should outline the work/activity areas that category A prisoners may be allocated to. The use of outside facilities by category A prisoners may only be given approval if appropriate levels of security are in place.

3.110 Any potential exceptional risk prisoner who is temporarily, due to exceptional or unforeseen circumstances, held on remand, or otherwise held in a non-SSU (Special Secure Unit) location, will be subject to the security measures appropriate to high risk prisoners. The Director of High Security Prisons should be consulted about whether any supplementary measures will be required.

3.111 Where possible, category A prisoners will be housed in cells which comply with the current physical security standard for category A cells. Prisoners held in non-compliant cells outside of the high security estate should have a change of accommodation on a frequent basis, at a level to be agreed between the Governor and DOM. High and exceptional risk category A prisoners must normally be in single cells wherever they are held. But they may exceptionally share a cell in certain circumstances with the agreement of the Director of High Security Prisons. Standard risk category A prisoners held in the high security estate may be accommodated two to a cell provided the cells are of category A standard and that the Director of High Security Prisons is satisfied that the searching strategy is adequate and effective, effective cell inspections (locks, bars and bolts) are carried out daily, local consideration is given to those who are to be doubled up to ensure they are suitable and vulnerable cells are not used (such as those at the end of the landing).

175 Regular checks at night, even where there is evidence that this sometimes wakes the prisoner, have been held to come 'nowhere near' the threshold of severity to engage article 3 of the ECHR and to be justified insofar as they engage article 8: *R (Mackenzie) v Governor of HMP Wakefield* [2006] EWHC 1746 (Admin).

3.112     Standard risk category A prisoners held in prisons outside the high security estate will normally be accommodated in single cells. Such prisoners may share a cell if the medical officer assesses the prisoner as a suicide risk who would benefit from the company of a cell mate, the Governor or head of custody, taking advice from the security department, approves the medical officer's recommendation and the shared cell is constructed to category A standards. All category A prisoners must have a change of accommodation on a regular basis, the frequency of which is to be stated in the local security strategy. An examination of the vacated cell and furniture must be undertaken after each move and a permanent record of cell changes recorded.

3.113     An up-to-date photograph of every category A prisoner should be on display in the residential unit office. The security department should be notified of any change in appearance and a new photograph taken within 24 hours. A category A prisoner should not go on escort (save for an emergency) without an up-to-date photograph. Form F1352 is used to maintain a continuous, auditable record of the supervision, location and movement of category A prisoners, incorporating movements to and from residential units (this is why prisoners call category A status being 'on the book').

3.114     All in-cell possessions must be authorised and in compliance with national and local volumetric control instructions. There must be instructions setting out arrangements for controlling and monitoring high and standard risk category A prisoners' written communications and telephone calls. There must be instructions setting out the extent to which category A prisoners are permitted to assemble together and with other categories of prisoner and to participate in activities/use facilities.

### Special Secure Units

3.115     Special Secure Units (SSUs) are the dedicated, self contained units which hold prisoners who are exceptional risk category A. They are effectively prisons within a prison and are subject to much higher security and searching procedures than the rest of the high security estate. SSUs have their own operating standards although these are not in the public domain.[176]

3.116     Security measures applicable to this class of prisoner were radically tightened following the escape of six exceptional risk category A prisoners from the SSU at HMP Whitemoor in September 1994 following

176   For a history from the 60s to the 90s see Roy Walmsley, *Special Secure Units*, HO Research Study 109.

the recommendations of the report into that escape.[177] Some changes went beyond those recommendations. For example, visits, including legal visits to such prisoners are closed unless an exceptional open visit is authorised by the Director of High Security Prisons, a policy that was upheld as lawful by the Court of Appeal in *R v Secretary of State for the Home Department ex p O'Dhuibir*[178] although the court was applying a reasonableness test, rather than assessing whether the restrictions were proportionate.[179] However even since the coming into force of the Human Rights Act (HRA) 1998 the courts have not been willing to hold that closed legal and family visits for this class of prisoner are necessarily disproportionate so as to breach either articles 3 or 8 of the Convention.[180]

3.117     There are obvious concerns about the impact on the physical and mental health of those held in SSU conditions for long periods. In May 1996 the Director-General of the Prison Service commissioned an inquiry by Sir Donald Acheson, the former Chief Medical Officer, into the effects of the SSUs on prisoners' health. It recommended that prisoners should be held in SSUs for as short a period as possible, that more opportunities for mental stimulation and physical exercise should be provided, including the provision of meaningful activities, and that prisoners should have access to open visits with members of their immediate family. It criticised the cramped conditions and lack of natural daylight at Belmarsh and Full Sutton Prisons in particular and stated that they could lead to mental health problems. The report concluded that:

> the combination of uncertainty concerning the sentence plan and the length of stay on the unit, together with lack of: opportunities for meaningful work, natural visual and auditory stimuli, social contact outside a small group of prisoners, incentives, and physical contact with families and friends, if sustained for several years is likely to lead to significant adverse effects on mental health in a proportion of prisoners.[181]

177 The Woodcock report, December 1994 Cm 2741.

178 [1997] COD 315.

179 Such closed visits were not recommended by the Woodcock report, but were by the Learmont report into the escapes from Parkhurst.

180 See the decision refusing permission to bring judicial review proceedings in *R (Allen) v Secretary of State for Justice* [2008] EWHC 3298 (Admin) – this case involved at that time the only remand prisoner held as an exceptional escape risk in the whole prison system, and so had no association except with prison officers.

181 The report itself has never been made publicly available and this was quoted in *United Kingdom: Special Secure Units Cruel, Inhuman or Degrading Treatment*, Amnesty International, March 1997.

3.118   Although detention in extreme high security conditions may give rise to breaches of article 3 of the ECHR, the courts will of course take into account the particular security risk posed by the individual prisoner in determining whether any given measure is in breach of that article. In *Ramirez Sanchez v France*[182] a period of solitary confinement of a high profile terrorist in high security conditions of over eight years did not breach article 3. The court did comment that such measures as location in a 'prison within a prison' should be resorted to exceptionally, that the prisoner's physical and mental condition should be closely monitored and that solitary confinement cannot be imposed indefinitely. Article 3 can be breached due to the cumulative effect of a number of different measures or conditions in prison.[183]

## Initial categorisation for other categories

3.119   Categorisation for prisoners other than category A or lifers (where suitability for open conditions is under consideration) is administered by the Observation, Classification and Allocation (OCA) unit within the local prison which receives the prisoner from court. OCA staff should be specifically trained for the role.[184] Prison overcrowding has had the greatest impact on closed prisons and historically open prisons have a lower occupancy rate than closed prisons. Accordingly during 2007 and 2008 a number of policy initiatives were introduced to ensure that as many prisoners as possible are considered suitable for category D status.

### Streamlined process for short sentences

3.120   A distinct policy is in place to determine suitability for open conditions for those serving sentences of under 12 months. Such prisoners should be subjected to a streamlined risk assessment subject to a requirement that they must spend a minimum of seven days in closed conditions.[185] They should be placed in category D unless:

- convicted of a sexual offence;
- serving a sentence for an offence of violence;
- serving a sentence for an offence under terrorism legislation;
- undergoing detoxification, otherwise requiring 24-hour medical

---

182  (2007) 45 EHRR 49.
183  *Dougoz v Greece* (2002) 34 EHRR 61.
184  PSO 0900 para 1.3.3.
185  PSI 16/2008 para 10.

cover, or has medical appointments that may be cancelled if transferred;
- identified as medium or high on a cell-sharing risk assessment;
- identified as level 2 or 3 under MAPPA;
- the prison has been notified that further charges are pending; or
- there are other factors indicating that the prisoner is likely to present a high risk of harm to the public if placed in open conditions.[186]

3.121 As the Criminal Casework Directorate of the UKBA has stated that it does not generally have an interest in pursuing for deportation foreign national prisoners serving sentences of less than 12 months, this streamlined assessment applies to this class of prisoner unless:

- they were sentenced to less than 12 months but the current sentence plus one or two previous sentences within the last five years (taking account of the most significant sentences during the period) total 12 months or more; or
- there is a court order recommending deportation at the end of the sentence; or
- the prison has been notified by UKBA of an intention to deport; or
- the prison is in possession of an IS91 form (authority to detain under the Immigration Act) for the prisoner.

## Categorisation for other cases

3.122 For prisoners who do not qualify for category D status under the streamlined assessment, the categorisation process should be completed within two working days of receipt of the essential documents.[187] The documents which as a minimum must be considered are:

- current custodial records and previous records where available;
- schedule of previous convictions;
- details of the offences giving rise to the current sentence;
- the Prisoner Escort Record (PER) form where comments on risks the prisoner poses have been entered;
- any OASys assessment completed prior to conviction; and
- risk assessment form for foreign nationals where appropriate.[188]

3.123 The OCA unit should also consider whether other documents should be obtained or whether reports, for example from the healthcare,

186 PSI 16/2008 Annex A.
187 NSF.
188 NSF and PSO 0900 para 1.5.3.

psychology or probation departments, should be obtained.[189] The form ICA 1 is an open document that should be made available to the prisoner on application. If a categorisation decision is going to take into account security information or other material that is to be withheld from the prisoner, then such a decision must be taken by a governor grade or equivalent and in any event the 'nature and reliability' at least of the information should be disclosed to the prisoner if not its source.[190]

3.124    The OCA unit uses the Form ICA 1 to determine the prisoner's security category. This sets out a two-stage process:

- a provisional assessment is made by application of an algorithm; then
- consideration of any issues that might override the provisional category suggested by the algorithm.[191]

## Category B

3.125    The initial algorithm determines that all prisoners are probably suitable for category B if any of the following applies:

- the current sentence is ten years or more;
- the prisoner has been category A during a previous sentence;
- the current sentence or any previous sentences are for offences of terrorism; or
- the prisoner has been treated as a provisional category A prisoner whilst on remand.

## Category C

3.126    If none of the above apply then the prisoner should be considered as probably suitable for category C unless more than one of the following apply:

- the prisoner has a previous sentence of ten years or more;
- the prisoner has previously escaped from a closed prison, the police or an escort;
- the current sentence or any previous sentence is for a serious offence involving violence, threats to life, firearms, sex, arson, drugs or robbery.

189  PSO 0900 para 1.5.7.
190  PSO 0900 para 1.5.2.
191  PSO 0900 para 1.5.1.

## Category D

3.127    If none or only one of the above apply then the prisoner should be considered as probably suitable for category D unless more than one of the following apply:

- they have a previous sentence of 12 or more months for offences of violence, threats of violence, arson, sex or drug dealing/ importation;
- their current sentence is for 12 or more months for offences of violence, threats of violence, arson, sex or drug dealing/ importation;
- they have within the last three years absconded from prison, failed to surrender to custody, breached bail or failed HDC or ROTL;
- they have an outstanding confiscation order or further charges.[192]

3.128    The criteria outlined above are not to be seen as either exhaustive or inflexible[193] and so it is incumbent upon the prison to consider whether there are exceptional reasons why a prisoner should be placed within a provisional category not suggested by the algorithm.

3.129    Following an incident in 2003 when a prisoner serving a 21-year sentence absconded from an open prison after only having served six and a half years of his sentence and was subsequently found dead, the Prison Service introduced a policy that prisoners should only normally be considered suitable for category D:

- if serving long sentences when they have served a sufficient proportion of their sentence in a category C prison to enable them to settle into their sentence and access appropriate offending behaviour work;
- in the majority of cases if there is less than five years until the automatic release date, or less than two years until the parole eligibility date.[194]

3.130    The policy is not to be applied inflexibly but if, in 'exceptional circumstances' a decision to categorise a prisoner as D outside these time limits is made, the decision must be taken by the Governing Governor in order to 'minimise the risk of damage to public confidence'.

192  See form ICA 1 – the current version of PSO 0900 is now out of date.
193  PSO 0900 para 1.2.6.
194  PSI 45/2004. See also PSI 3/2009 and paras 4.8–4.10.

### Overriding the provisional assessment

3.131    The next stage of the process is the consideration of whether there are any reasons to override the provisional assessment of category. The policy guidance states that such a decision, which must be justified on form ICA 1, could relate either to matters not covered by the algorithm (for example a previous sentence served successfully in an open prison, or in the other direction a known tendency to violence in an apparently minor offender), or to an unusual combination of factors which produces an unreasonable result via the algorithm.[195] The form ICA 1 itself refers to 'security information, significant control problem, circumstances of offence, pattern or offending, or facing further charges of a serious nature' as issues that might warrant overriding the provisional categorisation decision. It is therefore clear from the policy that the provisional categorisation can be overridden either way.

### Allocation

3.132    The policy guidance on allocation, where the prisoner will go once the initial categorisation process has been completed, makes it clear that the process is distinct from categorisation.[196] This decision is also normally carried out by the OCA unit within the prison. The guidance confirms that an interview should be arranged with the prisoner before the final allocation decision to ensure that all relevant issues have been identified, although such an interview may be dispensed with for prisoners sentenced to less than six months.[197] OCA staff are warned not to allow views on appropriate allocation to influence the categorisation decision. Because of the need to start sentence planning promptly allocation must be completed '*as soon after sentence as practical*'.[198]

3.133    There are three priorities that prisons are required to take into account when deciding which prison adult males should be allocated to, namely:

195  PSO 0900 para 1.5.11 – the NSF gives another example of where the algorithm should be overridden – 'an armed robber sentenced to seven years would emerge as a category C prisoner. If there is also information to suggest that that prisoner has contacts on the outside that would be able to help in an escape and if the prisoner has previously indicated an intention to escape then it would be inappropriate to categorise him as C'.

196  PSO 0900, para 1.6.1.

197  Para 1.7.5 PSO 0900 – and the prisoners comments should be recorded on Form ICA 1.

198  Para 1.6.2 PSO 0900.

- the needs of security, including control;
- the need to make maximum use of available spaces in training prisons; and
- the needs of individual prisoners.[199]

3.134  The policy recognises that these priorities are not always compatible. In recent years the ability of the Prison Service to give real effect to these priorities has been seriously compromised by serious over-crowding with the result that prisoners can either end up spending far too long in local prisons following conviction where no meaning-ful sentence planning can take place, or being moved to unsuitable or distant prisons.

3.135  The policy guidance also states that OCA departments must also take account of the following factors:

- suitability for particular types of accommodation (in light of vul-nerability, age etc);
- medical and/or psychiatric needs that may require a particular type or level of care;
- the need for identified offence related behavioural programmes to confront assessed risk;
- the home area, or that of likely visitors;
- educational/training needs or potential; and
- published allocation criteria for individual establishments reset-tlement needs.[200]

3.136  The decision on allocation should be recorded by the OCA depart-ment on the form ICA 1 and must be 'justifiable' in light of the prior-ities and considerations referred to above. Any allocation to a prison of a higher security category that of the prisoner himself must be referred to at least a Senior Officer rank and the reasons for the allo-cation recorded on the form ICA 1.[201] Resettlement needs are only one of the factors to be taken into account and may be outweighed by other considerations, '*to the extent permitted by operational require-ments and a balanced assessment of the prisoner's overall needs, alloca-tion decisions must seek to reinforce the resettlement process*'.[202] So that prisons can properly take the resettlement needs into account, OCA departments are required to have information on educational and training programmes available at relevant prisons, and must ensure

199  Para 1.6.3 PSO 0900.
200  PSO 0900 para 1.6.4.
201  PSO 0900 para 1.6.6.
202  PSO 2300 para 4.6.

that they are aware of any courses the prisoner is currently under-taking, any courses or programmes that are part of the sentence plan and details of the prisoner's family ties.[203] Allocation decisions should be informed by available documentation relating to current and previous offending and custodial behaviour, and OCA staff are required to consider whether specific further reports are required.[204] OCA staff should also obtain advice on the level of healthcare required by the prisoner and this should also be recorded on the form ICA 1.[205]

3.137    There may be circumstances when the OCA unit will be unable to allocate a prisoner to the most appropriate prison, for example, where the prison lacks vacancies or in the case of some open prisons, where the offence or length of sentence is not within the selection criteria. OCA staff are under mandatory instructions not to modify the categorisation process in order to achieve a better match between prisoners and available spaces. In the last resort a prisoner can be allocated to a higher category prison 'solely on the ground that no alternative space is available in prisons of the correct category' and the reasons recorded on the ICA 1 form.[206]

3.138    Allocation to category C prisons does raise some additional issues relating to control which may determine allocation. Following riots at HMP Wymott in 1993 the Prison Service carried out research that identified the characteristics of prisoners more likely to commit disciplinary offences and concluded that a high proportion of such prisoners in any prison will make riots more likely. Therefore, OCA staff are instructed to identify such prisoners to ensure that they are sent to appropriate prisons in appropriate numbers.[207] Form ICA 1 requires OCA staff to identify those prisoners:

- who are under 25;
- who are serving a sentence for robbery or burglary; and
- whose sentence is less than four years.

3.139    These are known as 'score 3' prisoners and should only make up a specified percentage of the category C prison's population depending on its control rating to avoid a concentration of prisoners assessed as liable to cause trouble. Category C prisons are accordingly designated as having a control rating of very good (which can hold 18 per cent

203  PSO 2300 para 4.7.
204  PSO 0900 para 1.7.2.
205  PSO 0900 para 1.7.4.
206  PSO 0900 para 1.6.9.
207  PSO 0900 para 1.7.3.

score 3 prisoners), good (which can hold 14 per cent), medium (which can hold 10 per cent) or poor (which can hold 8 per cent).[208] Once an allocation decision has been made the movement of the prisoner will be arranged centrally by the Prison Service's Population Management Unit (PMU).

## Categorisation and allocation: women prisoners

### Categorisation

3.140 The security categories for women prisoners are slightly different to those for adult males:

**Category A**
The definition is the same as for adult males (but see below).

**Closed conditions**
Prisoners for whom the very highest conditions of security are not necessary but who present too high a risk for semi-open or open conditions or for whom semi-open or open conditions are not appropriate.

**Semi-open conditions**
Prisoners who present a low risk to the public but who require a level of physical perimeter security to deter abscond.

**Open conditions**
Prisoners who present a low risk; can reasonably be trusted in open conditions and for whom open conditions are appropriate.[209]

3.141 Although PSO 0900 and the 2004 version of the NSF refer to category A status for women, the practical reality is now different. In 2005 all category A women prisoners were downgraded to what is known as 're- stricted status' which has a similar definition as applies to male young offenders (see below). This coincided with a decision to remove HMP Durham, which was the only prison to hold category A women prison- ers, from the high security estate. It therefore appears that the decision to introduce restricted status into women prisoners' categorisation was made so that the Prison Service could avoid having to have provision for women in the high security estate. There are therefore currently no category A status women prisoners, and very few 'restricted status' women[210] and reviews of this category are similar to those that apply to category A. There are presently two prisons which hold restricted status women prisoners, HMP Bronzefield and HMP Low Newton.

208 PSO 1701.
209 NSF.
210 Six at the time of writing this book.

3.142    Prison Service policy states that all women prisoners '*must be categorised objectively according to the likelihood that they will abscond and the risk that they would pose should they abscond*'.[211] As with male prisoners, control factors are relevant when considering categorisation but only where the issue is suitability for open or semi-open conditions. The streamlined process for consideration of suitability for open conditions also applies to women prisoners.[212] Similarly factors such as ability to mix, or educational and training needs should not factor into the categorisation decision as they are relevant to allocation.[213]

3.143    If none of the following apply then open conditions should be considered as providing an appropriate level of security on initial categorisation, subject to the suitability assessment (see below):

- the current sentence is three years or more;
- the current offence is a serious offence
  - of actual or threatened violence or harm
  - of a sexual nature
  - of drug dealing or importation;
- the prisoner has previously received a sentence of three years or more within the past five years, or has a previous conviction within the past five years for a serious offence as defined above, or the pattern of previous offending gives cause for concern;
- the offence is against a child and gives cause for concern;
- there are concerns about the prisoner's association with serious criminals;
- the prisoner is diagnosed or is suspected of suffering from any psychiatric or psychological problems;
- there are further charges outstanding or the prisoner is awaiting further sentencing;
- there is concern about any escape or abscond from any form of custody, breach of licence, community service order or community sentence during the past three years;
- the prisoner is subject to enforcement action under the Immigration Act 1971.[214]

3.144    If only either one of the last two bullet points above apply, then semi-open conditions should be considered as providing an appropriate level of security on initial categorisation.[215] Otherwise, on

211  PSO 0900 para 6.2.1.
212  PSI 16/2008 para 15.
213  PSO 0900 para 6.2.2.
214  PSO 0900 para 6.2.3.
215  PSO 0900 para 6.2.5.

initial categorisation women prisoners should be assigned to closed conditions.[216]

3.145    If women prisoners are assigned to closed conditions then there is no need to complete the suitability assessment. This is designed to determine whether those provisionally assessed as needing only open or semi-open conditions to meet the needs of security are in fact suitable. Prisoners should be so considered unless one of the following applies:

- there are issues of control which warrant close levels of supervision;
- there is a genuine need for 24-hour medical oversight;
- the prisoner is considered likely to be unable to cope in semi-open or open conditions;
- the prisoner is on self-harm measures and the case conference has decided that a transfer to semi-open or open conditions would not be in the prisoner's best interest; or
- the prisoner is known or suspected of currently using drugs; is undergoing a detoxification programme or has recently completed a detoxification programme.[217]

## Allocation

3.146    Where it is decided that women prisoners are not suitable for open or semi-open conditions, they will be allocated to a closed prison. A prisoner categorised as open or semi-open but who is 'deemed unsuitable' for open or semi-open conditions must be allocated to a closed establishment.[218]

3.147    The policy states that allocation assessment should recognise that there may be significant factors which influence the prisoner's allocation. These may sometimes override a semi-open or open categorisation and suitability assessment and so result in the prisoner being retained in closed conditions if this is the most appropriate. Care must be taken, however, to ensure that the allocation of such prisoners is kept under regular review and they are not retained in conditions of higher security longer than is necessary or appropriate. Examples of significant allocation issues which may need to be considered include:

- to facilitate visits from children, or other family members;
- to enable child-care arrangements to be sorted out;

216  PSO 0900 para 6.2.6.
217  PSO 0900 para 6.3.2.
218  PSO 0900 para 6.4.1.

- to complete any necessary offending behaviour work; and
- to facilitate any resettlement needs.

3.148   Prisoners categorised and suitable for open or semi-open conditions should be transferred to a suitable prison as soon as possible. As with male prisoners, the OCA department of the prison is responsible for categorisation decisions not involving category A or the allocation of life sentence prisoners to open conditions. Women prisoners should be held as close to their home and family as possible unless they are intending to resettle in a different area.

3.149   Wherever possible, women serving long sentences – which are classified as those over three years in the policy – should be transferred back closer to home (or to a new area if appropriate), before release to take advantage of resettlement opportunities.[219]

## Categorisation and allocation: male young offenders

### Categorisation

3.150   The different security categories for male young offenders as set out in the NSF are:

**Category A**
Prisoners whose escape would be highly dangerous to the public or the police or the security of the state and for whom the aim must be to make escape impossible.

**Restricted status**
Offenders sentenced to detention in a Young Offender Institution (YOI) whose escape would present a serious risk to the public and who are required to be held in designated secure accommodation.

**Closed conditions**
Young offenders for whom the very highest conditions of security are not necessary but who present too high a risk for open conditions or cannot be trusted in open conditions.

**Open conditions**
Young offenders who present a low risk and can reasonably be trusted in open conditions.

The streamlined process for consideration of suitability for open conditions set out above also applies to young offenders.[220]

3.151   As with other prisoners, young offenders must be categorised objectively according to the likelihood that they will abscond and the

219  PSO 4800 Issue E.
220  PSI 16/2008 para 16.

risk that they would pose should they do so. They are categorised according to an algorithm contained in form ICA 2 which takes into account factors relating to the prisoner's current offending, previous history of offending and any history of escape or abscond.[221] Application of the algorithm will determine provisionally whether the young offender should be placed in closed or open conditions of security. The criteria used in the algorithm must not be seen as either exhaustive or inflexible. However, every instance of departure from the prescribed criteria must be justified and documented and countersigned by a Senior Officer rank or above. As with adult prisoners, for those other than category A or restricted status, or lifers being considered for open conditions, the categorisation process is dealt with by the OCA department in the prison. It should in most cases involve an interview with the prisoner.[222]

## Allocation

3.152 Prison Service policy recognises that there are two, often conflicting, priorities governing the allocation of young offenders:

- the needs of security; and
- the needs of the individual.[223]

3.153 It states that while the main factor to be considered in determining a young offender's allocation must always be his security category, account must also be taken of:

- his or her suitability for particular types of accommodation (factors such as vulnerability or immaturity);
- his or her medical and/or psychiatric needs that may require a particular level of care;
- need for identified offence related behavioural programmes to address assessed risk;
- his or her home area, or that of his visitors and the need to maintain family ties;
- his or her educational or training needs; and
- any restrictions on allocation criteria agreed with local authorities, governors, Area Managers or Estate Planning Section in Headquarters.[224]

---

221 PSO 0900 para 3.2.1.
222 PSO 0900 para 3.5.1.
223 PSO 0900 para 3.7.3.
224 PSO 0900 para 3.7.4.

3.154   There may be occasions when the OCA Unit will be unable to allocate a young offender to the establishment for which he or she is
most suited in terms of category and needs. This may arise either
because the YOI concerned lacks vacancies, or because certain ac-
ceptance criteria are imposed. But as with adults, it is not acceptable,
under any circumstances, to modify the process or outcome in order
to achieve a better match between prisoners and available spaces. In
the last resort only, a young offender categorised as suitable for open
conditions may be allocated to a closed YOI solely on the grounds
that no alternative space is available in the open estate. A young offender categorised for closed conditions must not, however, be allocated to an open YOI.[225]

3.155   An initial allocation assessment on paper will normally be followed by an interview.[226] Any personal comments the offender may
wish to make in relation to his or her allocation should be recorded.
Having completed this process, the officer must then decide which
establishment is suitable, giving reasons for the decision.

3.156   Once young offenders reach 21 years old their sentences of detention, except DTOs, can be treated as if they have been sentenced to
an adult sentence of imprisonment of the same length when they are
transferred into the adult prison system. The same statutory provision allows the Secretary of State to direct that the young offender
is serving a adult sentence to allow transfer to an adult prison where
the IMB reports that the prisoner is 'exercising a bad influence on
the other inmates of the institution or as behaving in a disruptive
manner to the detriment of those inmates'.[227]

## Categorisation and allocation: children

### Categorisation

3.157   The responsibility for deciding where children are either remanded or sent to following sentence lies with the Youth Justice Board
(YJB).[228] The YJB allocates children to the various types of custodial
establishment based upon:[229]

---

225  PSO 0900 para 3.7.8.
226  PSO 0900 para 3.8.4.
227  PCC(S)A 2000 s99.
228  See chapter 2.
229  See www.yjb.gov.uk/en-gb/yjs/Custody/PlacingChildrenandYoungPeople
inCustody/

- vulnerability;
- specific needs, such as a disability or need for a specific programme;
- available beds;
- competing demand for beds;
- location; and
- age.

3.158 The vulnerability of a young person is determined by an assessment, completed by the Youth Offending Team (YOT), called Asset, which the YOT then sends to the YJB. The key factors from this assessment that determine the vulnerability of a young person, and therefore influence which institution they are sent to include:

- risk of self-harm;
- having been bullied, abused, neglected or depressed;
- separation, loss or care episodes;
- risk taking;
- substance misuse;
- other health-related needs;
- the ability to cope in a YOI or other custodial establishment.

## Allocation

3.159 The YJB states that it aims to ensure that children will be sent to an institution that is close to their family and home and provides an environment that is suited to their needs, based on the information from their assessment. However as the YJB makes clear when the detained population is high, it is not always possible to place young people in the kind of institution that is most appropriate for their needs. The YJB aims to follow the criteria overleaf as to how children are allocated by reference to their age and vulnerability:

| Gender and vulnerability | Status | Institution |
|---|---|---|
| Male and female (12–14yrs) | secure remand or sentenced | SHC or STC |
| Vulnerable males (15–16 yrs) | secure remand or sentenced | SHC or STC |
| Non-vulnerable males (15–16 yrs) | remanded or sentenced | YOI |
| Females (15–16 yrs) | secure remand or sentenced | SCH or STC |
| Males and females (17 yrs) | remanded | YOI |
| Vulnerable males and females (17 yrs) | sentenced | YOI, SCH or STC |
| Non-vulnerable males and females (17 yrs) | sentenced | YOI |

3.160    The catastrophic effects of getting the allocation of vulnerable children wrong was demonstrated in the case of Joseph Scholes, a 16-year-old sentenced to a two year DTO for robbery in 2002. Despite a history of self-harm and serious concerns about his welfare being expressed by his social worker he was allocated to a YOI. He killed himself only nine days into the sentence. The case raised serious concerns both about the procedures in place to ensure that vulnerable children were not allocated to unsuitable institutions, but also the inability of YOIs to deal with such vulnerability. Crucially it highlighted the problem that vulnerable children might be sentenced on the basis that appropriate secure accommodation is available, when due to resources this might not be the case. The Coroner at the inquest into his death stated:

> It seemed clear to me that the allocation of disturbed and vulnerable young children (typically 15- and 16-year-old boys) should be determined on a needs basis and not a resources basis. This is all the more important if Courts are sentencing such vulnerable and disturbed young offenders in the belief, mistaken or not, that recommendations, such as that contained in the pre-sentence report and endorsed by the Sentencing Judge can be implemented.[230]

230 However the Court of Appeal rejected a claim that following the case there should be a public inquiry to look into the sentencing and allocation to custody of vulnerable children – *Scholes v Secretary of State for the Home Department* [2006] EWCA 1343 Civ.

3.161   Similar concerns about the unsuitability of YOI accommodation for vulnerable children had been raised some years before in the landmark case brought by the Howard League that established that social services departments continued to owe duties to detained children under the Children Act 1989.[231] At that time there were over 3,000 children in YOIs and the judge commented that 'they are, on any view, vulnerable and needy children. Disproportionately they come from chaotic backgrounds. Many have suffered abuse or neglect'.

3.162   The YJB did respond to concerns about the effectiveness of its placement policies, partly in response to the Howard League case and the death of Joseph Scholes. In 2005 it issued a strategy document in which it described how it anticipated the provision of custodial institutions for children should be developed.[232] However, this strategy itself recognises that perhaps the two key factors that determine where children are detained are matters beyond the YJB's powers, namely sentencing trends and the availability of resources: the same matters raised by the coroner in the Joseph Scholes case.

231  *R (Howard League) v Secretary of State for the Home Department* [2002] EWHC 2497 (Admin).

232  *Strategy for the Secure Estate for Children and Young People*: www.yjb.gov.uk/ Publications/Scripts/prodView.asp?idproduct=270&eP=yjb

# Serving a prison sentence

*continued*

# Recategorisation for adults and young offenders

4.1   As the assessed risk posed by prisoners will change over a sentence, there are procedures for determining a change of security category and if this is altered, for a change in allocation. The reviews for security categories other than category A are not as formal as the category A reviews discussed in chapter 3. Prison Service policy emphasises that recategorisation must be based on:

- evidence of a clear change in the level of risk posed by the prisoner in terms of escape or abscond and/or risk of harm to the public in the event of an escape or abscond; and/or
- new or additional information, which impacts on the original categorisation decision; and/or
- concern that the previous categorisation decision is unsound. There must be corroborative evidence to support that concern; and/or
- control issues which mean that the prisoner poses a threat to the security of the establishment or the safety of staff and prisoners, or that the prisoner's notoriety potentially undermines the security of the prison.[1]

4.2   It is important that prisons address recategorisation by reference to these issues only. Prisons should not have local policies that, for example, state that a prisoner can only be downgraded to category C having spent a set amount of time in a category B prison. Such a consideration may be relevant to risk but cannot be allowed to fetter a proper assessment of whether the prisoner meets the threshold for recategorisation.[2] Similarly, prisons must not take into account issues such as the prisoner's financial position unless this is relevant to the matters referred to above.[3] Assessed risk levels may decrease or increase depending on the circumstances of each individual prisoner and so the categorisation reviews can result in either a reduction or increase in security category. Clearly, given the focus of the policy is risk, it would not be lawful to recategorise a prisoner as a punishment where the alleged misconduct does not impact sufficiently on issues of risk or control.[4]

1   NSF and PSI 45/2004 as updated in by PSI 03/2009 para 8.1.
2   See R (Lowe) v Governor of HMP Liverpool [2008] EWHC 2167 (Admin). See also para 3.49.
3   R (Palmer) v Secretary of State for the Home Department [2004] EWHC 1817 (Admin).
4   R v Governor of HMP Latchmere House ex p Jarvis [1999] EWHC 719 (Admin) at para 23.

4.3    The policy also confirms that it is also essential to consider the particular characteristics and features of the security category for which the prisoner is being assessed (for example the level of supervision available in a prison of a lower security category, or the level of physical security and the type of accommodation provided which may not be suitable for all prisoners), and this is particularly so in considering whether the a prisoner should be categorised as suitable for an open prison. It might be that a prison receiving a prisoner from a prison of a higher security disagrees with the decision that was taken to downgrade that prisoner's security category in the first place. However, it has been held that it would be unlawful for the receiving prison in such circumstances to recategorise the prisoner upwards, purely where there was a difference of opinion:

> A policy has been produced which does emphasise that recategorisations should in all normal circumstances, or indeed in abnormal circumstances, occur when there is significant change in the circumstances of a prisoner. It does not provide, nor would one expect it to provide, that there would be a recategorisation based upon different professional judgments of different governors in different establishments. There is an expectation of prisoners that they will be reviewed annually, or less than annually, if there is a significant change in their circumstances. There is an expectation that they will be dealt with consistently and not dependent upon the differing views of different governors.[5]

## Timing of recategorisation reviews

4.4    All adult prisoners, both men and women, other than those in open and semi-open prisons and those serving less than 12 months, must have their security category reviewed at regular prescribed intervals. The policy states that for prisoners serving fewer than four years[6] this will be no later than six months after initial categorisation and at least six monthly thereafter. For those serving four or more years, the first review should be no later than 12 months after the initial categorisation and then at least every 12 months. For indeterminate and extended sentenced prisoners the timing depends on the length of the custodial period or minimum term.[7]

4.5    Prisoners in open prisons are not subject to routine reviews. In those prisons, recategorisation reviews will only normally be

---

5  *R (Lowe) v Governor of HMP Liverpool* [2008] EWHC 2167 (Admin) – clearly a plain error made by the previous prison could justify a recategorisation.

6  NSF and PSI 3/2009 para 9.1.

7  PSI 3/2009.

prompted either by a significant change in the prisoner's circumstances which impacts on risk levels, or if the prisoner's behaviour gives cause for concern. Common examples of behaviour that would trigger such a review are MDT failures or breaches of the conditions of release on temporary licence.

4.6 Young adult male prisoners will not be subject to routine recategorisation reviews. However, a young adult male prisoner must be risk assessed in the months preceding his attaining adult status so that the transition to the adult estate can proceed seamlessly. It should not be necessary for a young adult prisoner to be transferred from a young offender institution to a local prison for categorisation and allocation but instead he should be allocated direct to an appropriately secure training prison in the adult estate.[8] In some cases maturity assessments on young adult prisoners of any age will indicate that the young adult is 'criminally and behaviourally sophisticated' beyond his years and as such requires the security of the adult estate ('starring up'). In such cases the RC2 must be completed prior to transfer to the adult estate.

## Recategorisation process

4.7 In making the recategorisation assessment, prisons use prescribed forms from the NSF.[9] They are required to obtain input from those prison staff who know the prisoner, are best placed to provide insight into the extent of any change or who have specialist, relevant information. Where there is an OASYs assessment this should be taken into account. Other factors prisons are directed to consider are:[10]

- Security information – any security information reports and any relevant historical information about previous escape or trust failures; information from the police intelligence officer.
- Reports from the personal officer and offender manager which give an insight into the prisoner's attitude to offending and sentence; any involvement in drugs or taxing or bullying of other prisoners which might indicate unsuitability for conditions of lower security or less supervision; similarly any evidence of the prisoner's vulnerability which might make them the target of other

---

8 NSF and PSI 3/2009.

9 And failure to follow the mandatory policies may render a recategorisation decision unlawful – *R v Governor of HMP Latchmere House ex p Jarvis* [1999] EWHC 719 (Admin).

10 PSI 3/2009 para 13.1.

prisoner's bullying and intimidation, particularly if this resulted in a category D prisoner being forced to import drugs or other contraband; notoriety which might attract unwelcome media attention and disruption to the prison.

- Information about any domestic problems which could impact on the prisoner's stability and likelihood of trying to escape or abscond.
- Reports from the medical officer or psychologist indicating concerns about the prisoner's healthcare needs or ability to cope in conditions of lesser supervision.
- The outcome of any offending behaviour programmes undertaken by the prisoner and his willingness to address his offending behaviour. The fact that the prisoner, through no fault of his own, has not yet been able to access a relevant programme should not mean that this source of evidence may be disregarded but rather should be taken as a lack of evidence to support a downgrading to a lesser security category.
- Positions of trust held.
- Successful ROTL application which, from a prisoner in category C, should instigate a review of the prisoner's suitability for category D.
- Behaviour – the prisoner's behaviour is relevant to the assessment only insofar as it may indicate the need for a greater degree of security or supervision. Poor institutional behaviour may pose a threat to the security of the prison or to the safety and well being of staff and other prisoners. In such a case the prisoner may need to be recategorised to a higher security category and reallocated to a suitable prison. Good behaviour does not of itself indicate that a prisoner poses less risk either of escape or risk of harm to the public and is not sufficient justification to downgrade a prisoner. *There must additionally be sound evidence that the prisoner's good behaviour is representative of a change in attitude and an associated reduction in the risks that were evidenced at the last categorisation review.*
- *Victim issues are now also required to be taken into account when assessing a prisoner for open conditions, particularly where the victim of the offence had been specifically targeted by the prisoner.* In all such cases the Offender Manager should be consulted to ensure that the prisoner is not transferred to an open prison in the vicinity of a victim's home.

Different prisons may have different local procedures when making recategorisation decisions. There is no requirement in the Prison Service policy on categorisation decisions, other than category A, that the prisoner should be given disclosure of the categorisation documentation, and an opportunity to make representations, prior to the decision being made.[11]

## Transfers to open prisons

4.8   To address prison overcrowding, the Prison Service has in recent years introduced a number of policies aimed at maximising occupancy of open prisons, traditionally those with greatest capacity. The policy is to ensure that categorisation reviews take place for all determinate sentence prisoners at six monthly intervals in the last 30 months of the sentence to ensure that all eligible prisoners are moved to open conditions.[12]

4.9   For prisoners who are longer away from their release dates the issue is more complex. Governors are also reminded that they 'must keep in mind the particularly challenging management issues associated with the low physical security and supervision levels of the open estate'.[13] Although cases will be decided on their individual merits, long sentence prisoners should not be considered suitable for open conditions until they have served a sufficient proportion of their sentence in a closed prison to enable them to settle into their sentence and access any offending behaviour programmes identified as essential to reducing risk. The policy does not say that the prisoner has to have spent time in a category C prison if they were initially given category B status.

4.10   In particular prisoners should not generally be allocated to an open prison if they have more than two years to serve before their earliest release date (normally the halfway point of the sentence). Where the prisoner is serving a sentence of more than four years imposed before 4 April 2005[14] they must be within five years of the automatic release date at two thirds.[15] Prisoners outside these guidelines can still be considered suitable for open conditions if there are exceptional circumstances.[16]

---

11   An argument that procedural fairness requires such safeguards failed in *R v Secretary of State for the Home Department ex p Peries* [1997] EWHC 712 (Admin).

12   PSI 16/2008 para 5.

13   PSI 3/2009 14.1.

14   And because of the nature of the sentence is not automatically released at the halfway point – see chapter 11.

15   PSI 3/2009 14.6.

16   PSI 3/2009 14.6.

## Transfer of foreign national prisoners to open condition

4.11    There is no blanket prohibition on foreign national prisoners facing deportation from being given category D status. However, Prison Service policy recognises that a prisoner facing deportation from the UK may pose an increased risk of absconding from an open prison.[17] Foreign nationals serving sentences of under 12 months as noted above are eligible to be considered under the streamlined procedure.[18]

4.12    Where the prisoner meets one of the following criteria (which reflect the cases where UK Border Agency's (UKBA) Criminal Casework Directorate will normally seek to enforce deportation), there are particular policy considerations that apply to whether open conditions will be considered suitable:[19]

- recommended for deportation by a court;
- an European Economic Area national sentenced to 24 months or more (except Irish citizens);
- a non-EEA national sentenced to 12 months or more;
- A non-EEA national sentenced to less than 12 months but where the current sentence plus one or two previous sentences within the last five years (taking account of the most significant sentences during the period) total 12 months or more;
- a prisoner who meets the criteria above but whose nationality remains unclear.

4.13    Such prisoners must be risk assessed on the assumption that they are going to be deported which in most cases will be considered to raise the risk of absconding, unless UKBA has already made a decision not to deport.[20] Although the policy reiterates that such cases should be considered on their merits, it states that category D for such prisoners 'will only be appropriate where it is clear that the risk is very low' in order to ensure that the intention to deport is not frustrated.[21] Foreign national prisoners who do not meet these criteria should still be reported to UKBA as they may still be liable to administrative removal from the UK rather than deportation[22] but they can be considered for open conditions in the same way as other prisoners.

17  PSO 4630 para 14.1.
18  PSI 16/2008 para 11.
19  PSO 4630 para 1.10.
20  PSO 4630 para 14.3.
21  PSO 4630 para 14.4.
22  PSO 4630 para 14.7.

## Non-routine reviews

4.14    As noted above, prisoners must have their categorisation reviewed at regular intervals. Reviews can however take place more frequently if there has been a significant change in the prisoner's circumstances impacting on the level of risk, leading to a requirement for reduced or increased security conditions. Sometimes prisoners will need to be transferred at short notice to a prison of a higher security because a change in their circumstances indicates an urgent threat to security. In such cases the prisoner should be transferred to the higher security prison and their categorisation reviewed as soon as possible thereafter, with the opportunity to appeal against the decision using the usual complaints process.[23]

4.15    The policy guidance on urgent recategorisation in the NSF refers to the *Hirst* judgment. In that case the Court of Appeal held that the Prison Service had acted unlawfully in recategorising a lifer whose tariff had expired from category B to category C without giving him an opportunity to make representations as to the proposed reasons.[24] Crucial to the court's decision was the fact that the decision was likely to impact on the lifer's prospects of release. The court also made a distinction between the categorisation decision and the decision to transfer. Whilst it would not necessarily be unlawful to transfer the prisoner to a more secure prison if this was needed for 'operational requirements' this could take place before a categorisation review, which could then take place with the appropriate procedural safeguards. An attempt to argue that determinate sentenced prisoners should also have a right to disclosure and an opportunity to make representations prior to recategorisation was unsuccessful on the basis that the consequences of the decision were not as grave as for lifers.[25] However the reference to the *Hirst* decision in the NSF[26] suggests that policy for determinate sentence prisoners is that in urgent cases the prisoner should be transferred to a higher security prison and that the recategorisation process should then follow.

4.16    Where prisoners in open prisons are refused release on licence by the Parole Board there should be a review of security category on the basis that this change of circumstance may increase the risk of absconding. It may therefore be appropriate for the prisoner to be

---

23   NSF and PSI 3/2009 para 12.

24   *Hirst v Secretary of State for the Home Department* [2001] EWCA Civ 378.

25   *R (McLeod) v Secretary of State for the Home Department* [2002] EWHC 390 (Admin).

26   See also PSI 45/2004.

returned to closed conditions in order to come to terms with the decision and to address any issues raised by the board.[27]

## Recategorisation decisions

4.17    The NSF makes it clear that the recategorisation process is an open one and that prisoners must have the opportunity to see the recategorisation form and evidence on which any decision is based, other than where it has been agreed with the governor that information may be withheld to protect the safety of any third party.[28] This will normally be achieved by disclosure of the recategorisation form itself. The Prison Service has long accepted that prisoners are entitled to reasons for categorisation decisions.[29] If unhappy with such decisions prisoners can use the normal complaints procedure and complain further to the Prisons and Probation Ombudsman.

## Allocation following recategorisation

4.18    In contrast with initial categorisation decisions following conviction and sentence, the NSF does not contain a requirement for a formal interview with the prisoner when deciding upon their allocation. However, it states that it may be useful to speak to the prisoner to see if they have any needs or issues in terms of allocation. Allocation to a particular prison will not necessarily be dependent on the prisoner's agreement. While allocation must primarily be led by the needs of security, account should also be taken of the prisoner's needs in terms of maintenance of family ties, health care and access to offending behaviour work. Often these issues can only be established through talking to the prisoner.[30]

# Particular types of allocation

## The resettlement estate for adult males

4.19    There is separate policy guidance on allocation criteria to the 'resettlement estate': that is resettlement prisons, resettlement regimes in

27  PSI 45/2004.
28  PSI 3/2009 16.1.
29  See *R v Secretary of State for the Home Department ex p Peries* [1997] EWHC 712 (Admin).
30  See for example RC1 form relating to recategorisation of adult males from NSF.

open prisons, and exceptionally discrete resettlement units in closed prisons.[31] Resettlement regimes are designed to 'prepare for release suitable prisoners with identified resettlement needs, ordinarily sentenced to three years or more'.[32] These regimes have two stages. In stage 1, prisoners have the opportunity to undertake unpaid community work and education/training courses outside the prison. In stage 2, prisoners are allowed to undertake full-time paid employment in the community.[33]

4.20    All adult males serving determinate sentences must be considered for a place in the resettlement estate once they are given category C, or if directly categorised to D in light of relevant indicators of resettlement needs identified by an OASys assessment.[34] Eligibility for a place in the resettlement estate will be based on reaching the later of the following dates:

• 24 months before the scheduled release date (the halfway point of the sentence, whether or not release requires Parole Board approval); or
• three months before a prisoner has served half his or her custodial period less half the relevant remand time.[35]

These dates are designed so that prisoners can only be allocated to resettlement units when they will also be eligible for temporary release.[36]

4.21    Although each resettlement unit will have its own published selection criteria there are certain principles that will always apply.[37] Prisoners for whom the risk assessment process indicates a high degree of risk must not be selected for a resettlement place. Low risk prisoners may be selected for a resettlement place. However, prisoners need to demonstrate a 'real need' for a regime which is designed to improve their prospects on release. Prisoners in the low risk category may be selected for a resettlement estate place in order to:

• reduce any institutionalisation which may have occurred;
• stabilise and improve community (including family) ties; and
• improve prospects of employment on release.

The risk assessment process should focus on the prisoner's criminal and prison history and he 'must show evidence of good behaviour

31  See PSO 2300 annex A to chapter 7.
32  PSO 2300 para 7.4.
33  PSO 2300 para 7.6.
34  PSO 2300 para 7.26.
35  PSO 2300 para 7.31.
36  See PSO 6300 and para 7.105.
37  See PSO 2300 annex A to chapter 7.

and demonstrate a capacity and commitment to achieve the maturity and degree of personal responsibility required of prisoners in the resettlement estate'. The guidance states that the following factors might indicate whether a prisoner is suitable:

- freedom from involvement in drugs;
- on enhanced status under the IEP scheme (or be on a waiting list for enhanced status where the IEP scheme is location-based);
- co-operated with the OASys process in terms of identifying issues of risk and/or need, and the means by which these will be addressed; and
- over the preceding six months had no findings of guilt on adjudication for more serious offences.

## Mother and Baby Units (MBUs)

4.22    It has long been the practice of the Prison Service to allow imprisoned women to keep their babies with them in limited circumstances. The Prison and YOI Rules accordingly contain specific provisions allowing the Secretary of State for Justice to permit women to keep their babies with them whilst in custody.[38] A very detailed policy on the criteria and policies for admission to MBUs is contained in PSO 4801. The policy has been regularly reviewed in light of judgments from the Administrative Court. The allocation of women to MBUs is a highly sensitive issue as separation of a baby from the mother will require strong justification and fair procedures to protect the interests of both the baby and the mother, in order to avoid breaching the right to family life under article 8 of the ECHR.

4.23    The policy makes it clear that MBUs 'exist first and foremost for the benefit of the children who are not prisoners and have committed no offence. Their best interests are the primary concern in all matters. If it is considered to be in a child's best interests, he/she should be admitted to the Unit'.[39] The courts have held that the child's best interests must be properly represented by social services departments in the decision making process.[40] MBUs should be 'calm places with a friendly and welcoming atmosphere, which encourages children to thrive' and mothers and babies should not be locked in their rooms.[41]

38  PR rule 12(2), YOIR rule 25.
39  PSO 4801 para 2.2.
40  *R (CD) v Secretary of State for the Home Department* [2003] EWHC 155 (Admin).
41  PSO 4801 paras 3.1–3.2.

## Age limits for children

4.24 Generally babies will be able to stay with their mother in an MBU, subject to meeting the admission criteria, until the age of 18 months. The policy indicates that there is a risk of institutionalisation of a child if s/he remains in prison much beyond that age and none of the Units are properly set up for older children. However, there should be some flexibility, for example, if the mother is due for release within a few weeks of the child reaching the age limit or where it is shown that it is in the best interests of the child, he or she may exceptionally be allowed to stay on for a further period. For the vast majority of cases, however, the child is expected to leave the Unit by the age of 18 months or earlier.[42]

4.25 The policy on flexibility was changed following *R (P and Q) v Secretary of State for the Home Department*.[43] At that time the 18-month policy was rigidly applied. One of the prisoners in that case was serving a short sentence, there was no suitable placement out of the prison and so the potential harm to the child from separation was considerable. The Court of Appeal held that the policy was unlawful and might result in a breach of article 8 if her case was not treated as exceptional. Similarly, it is also wrong to consider that there is a right for the baby to remain with the mother until the age of 18 months. Where women are serving longer sentences, separation much earlier than that may be considered in the best interests of the child. A challenge by a woman serving a sentence of five years arguing that separation at nine months would be unlawful failed in *CF v Secretary of State for the Home Department*.[44]

## Location and management of MBUs

4.26 In January 2008 there were places for 75 children and 82 children in MBUs, located in seven different prisons.[45] Only one of these, HMP Askham Grange, is an open prison.[46] In addition the STC at Rainsbrook can accommodate those under 18-years-old with their babies, the YJB taking responsibility for such placements.

4.27 Day-to-day management of MBUs is the responsibility of the governor of the relevant prison and national operational responsibility

42 PSO 4801 paras 2.9–2.10.
43 [2001] EWCA Civ 1151.
44 [2004] EWHC 111 (Fam).
45 The Prison Service has indicated that the highest number of children held in MBUs has been about 67.
46 PSO 4801 para 5.1.

for the units as a whole rests with the head of women and young people's group (at Prison Service headquarters in the directorate of commissioning and operational policy). The national mother and baby co-ordinator is responsible for the day-to-day discharge of the head of group's responsibilities in this area and provides information and advice as requested, being a central point of contact for all the units.[47]

### Applications to enter MBUs

4.28    Prisons 'must ensure that procedures are in place to identify on re-ception or the earliest opportunity all prisoners who are pregnant or who have children under the age of 18 months'.[48] Such prisoners, or those who discover that they are pregnant after coming to prison, must be provided with information about MBUs and how to apply. Each prison should have a mother and baby liaison officer who is available to assist women in making applications.[49] PSO 4801 con-tains a standard form for making an application. Although women will make an application to the MBU of their choice after discussion with the liaison officer, a refusal from one MBU will be binding on all.[50] In *R v Bloomfield*[51] the Court of Appeal reduced a sentence on a woman whose pregnancy was known to the trial judge to allow her to give birth in the community partly because the MBU at the prison she was held in was full and she faced being moved to another part of the country. The PSO gives detailed guidance on what information should be included with the application, including information from social services and the Probation Service.

4.29    The application will be considered by an admissions board which is chaired independently by experienced social services practition-ers.[52] Except in emergency cases, the boards must consist of as a minimum:

- the independent chair;
- the responsible Governor or MBU manager;
- the mother, with a friend or personal officer if desired; and
- a social services representative and/or probation officer.[53]

---

47   PSO 4801 section 6.
48   PSO 4801 para 8.2.
49   PSO 4801 para 8.5.
50   PSO 4801 para 8.4.
51   [2002] EWCA Crim 1488.
52   PSO 4801 para 6.6.
53   PSO 4801 para 9.2.

There may be other attendees such as drugs workers or nursery nurses if relevant.[54] If the mother is unable to attend the meeting in person, a video link should be arranged. If this is not possible then the mother should be allowed to make a submission to the board in writing and must be assisted by the mother and baby liaison officer.[55]

4.30    Before recommending admission to an MBU the board must be satisfied that:[56]

- It is in the best interests of the child/children to be placed in an MBU.
- The mother is able to demonstrate behaviours and attitudes which are not detrimental to the safety and well-being of other unit residents (or the good order and discipline of the unit).
- The mother has provided a urine sample which tests negative for illicit drugs (and a woman on a detoxification regime prescribed methadone or Subutex must not be excluded from a place on an MBU for that reason alone, also such medications will not be allowed in possession).
- The mother is willing to remain illicit drug-free.
- The mother is willing to sign a standard compact, which may be tailored to her identified individual needs.
- The mother's ability and eligibility to care for her child is not impaired by poor health, or for legal reasons such as the child being in care or on the Child Protection Register as the result of the mother's treatment of that child, or other children being in care.

4.31    PSO 4801 states that although the best interests of the child is the primary consideration, it is not the only one as good order and discipline on the unit may have to take precedence 'where his/her mother's conduct is such that it presents a risk of serious disorder and/or harm to other children and/or their mothers on the unit'.[57] Mothers must also consent to the searching of their babies when considered necessary as a condition of entry to an MBU.[58] The PSO includes advice for boards which reminds them that for women serving long sentences separation at some stage is likely to be inevitable; that later rather than earlier separation may be more damaging to the child; and that boards should not recommend admission to an MBU simply to give

54  PSO 4801 para 9.6.
55  PSO 4801 paras 9.3–9.5.
56  PSO 4801 para 9.8.
57  PSO 4801 para 9.15.
58  PSO 4801 para 17.1.

the mother 'another chance' or yield to pressure from others who may not be representing the child's best interests.[59]

4.32   The policy states that it is good practice for the chair to interview the mother in advance of the meeting.[60] The meeting must be fully and accurately minuted.[61] Each case must be considered on an individual basis and the decision must record the reasons for the recommendation and whether the decision was unanimous.[62] The recommendation, together with the documents considered, are then passed to the governing Governor of the prison within 24 hours for a decision to be made. The governor will make the final decision and this will be given to the prisoner within two working days of the board.[63]

4.33   There are five possible grounds for admission to an MBU and so the board's recommendation will be one of the following:[64]

- *Temporary admission* – where a prisoner is considered suitable for allocation to an MBU but is on remand. Once the sentence is known the matter is reconsidered by the board.
- *Emergency temporary admission* – where a prisoner is admitted to an MBU without a full board having considered the case where the governor considers it is desirable for the baby to be with the mother while the application is being processed. In such cases a full emergency board should be convened as soon as possible.[65]
- *Full admission* – where a sentenced prisoner is considered suitable and it is in the bests interests of the child and there are no identified risks to any others on the unit.
- *Conditional refusal* – where the board is willing to recommend allocation to an MBU as long as the mother can 'successfully address certain issues'. These must be fully explained to the mother with a timeframe set following which a further application can be made.
- *Full refusal* – where the prisoner fails to meet the admissions criteria. Where the recommendation of the admission board is not to allocate a place, the letter and report must give reasons for the decision, make clear whether or not the decision is open to review

59 PSO 4801 section 10.
60 PSO 4801 para 9.9.
61 PSO 4801 para 9.11. The PSO includes a recommended format for the minutes.
62 PSO 4801 para 9.18.
63 PSO 4801 section 12.
64 PSO 4801 para 11.2.
65 PSO 4801 para 11.8.

and, if so, when the mother may apply again. It must also include consideration of a separation plan if the mother is pregnant.

## Appeals against decisions

4.34   If the decision is a second conditional refusal or a full refusal:

- If the prisoner was not present at the board or able to participate by video link, she may request that a further board at which she can be present be convened.
- If she was present or participated by video-link then the refusal must be challenged by way of the request complaint procedure initially by sending the form to head of women and young people's group at Prison Service headquarters.[66]

## Management and regimes in MBUs

4.35   PSO 4801 requires there always to be present on the Units a member of staff who is 'proficient in health and safety; practical parental responsibility; child protection; and first aid and child/adult resuscitation'. Every child living with a prisoner in an MBU must have a child care plan. This should be completed within four weeks of admission to an MBU in consultation with the mother and will set out how the best interests of the child will be maintained and promoted during his or her stay with the mother in prison.[67] The plan should include consideration of separation from the mother as part of the child's development if appropriate, for example, where the mother is serving a long sentence. The plan should be reviewed at least every eight weeks.

4.36   As MBUs should be as calm as possible, the policy notes that the need for discipline is concomitantly greater. However, it also recognises that all options short of expulsion from the unit should be considered before this step is taken. Expulsion should only be considered in consultation with the national MBU co-ordinator and 'there must be clear evidence to demonstrate that the well-being of the child and /or the other occupants of the unit are being seriously threatened by the mother's conduct'.[68]

4.37   Prisoners held in MBUs should be given access to as full as possible range of activities, including offending behaviour courses, and

66   PSO 4801 section 13.
67   PSO 4801 para 15.1.
68   PSO 4801 para 16.2.

a crèche or nursery should be provided to facilitate this.[69] The provision of childcare in MBUs is subject to inspection by Ofsted.

4.38    Babies held in MBUs are not prisoners but the policy in PSO 4801 states that those who are taking children out of the unit, including relatives, must be checked before they are able to take charge of the baby.[70] These checks are carried out by the relevant social services department. In the first instance, prisoners are asked to nominate two people who will be able to look after the child if the mother cannot.

## Separation from children

4.39    The policy recognises that most women with young babies will not enter an MBU and it is therefore important that women prisoners are helped to maintain contact with their families, especially where they were the primary carer, for example through visits and family days.[71] Particular guidance is given on the separation of women from babies who are born in prison.[72]

4.40    Where there has been admission to an MBU, separation must normally be preceded by a separation board which, like admissions boards, have an independent chair. The policy does cater for emergency separations which will only be considered temporary until a separation board can be convened. These will normally occur because of health problems affecting either the mother or baby. However, emergency separation can also take place where social services accept that there is an 'identified, imminent and serious risk of harm'.[73]

4.41    The purpose of the separation board is to consider whether to remove a woman from a MBU bearing in mind:[74]

- The best interests of the child of the woman subject to review and whether those are compatible with the mother's wishes.
- The best interests of the other mothers and babies on the unit, if they are likely to be adversely affected by the continued presence of the mother on the unit.
- Whether or not transfer to another MBU is a possible and preferable option to exclusion.

---

69  PSO 4801 section 19.
70  PSO 4801 section 22.
71  PSO 4801 section 26.
72  PSO 4801 section 27.
73  PSO 4801 section 28.
74  PSO 4801 para 31.2.

4.42    It is important that both proper standards of fairness to the mother are applied, and that the best interests of the child are properly considered by the separation board.[75] Membership of the board should be, as a minimum:[76]

- independent chair;
- responsible governor or MBU manager;
- mother, plus a friend or personal officer if desired; and
- social services representative and/or probation officer.

The mother must be given an opportunity to put her case and must be aware of all the reasons why separation is being considered.[77] If the decision of the board is to proceed with separation, and it is likely to be contested then the documents must be forwarded to the head of the Women and Young Persons' Group for a final decision.[78] Prisoners must be given proper reasons for the decision in writing.[79]

4.43    PSO 4801 gives detailed guidance on the process of separation which will vary depending upon the age and other needs of the individual child. For example for older children the process of spending regular time with the new carer should begin at least two months before separation. Prisons are required to have procedures to provide support to mothers after separation including regular visits and contact where the mother will resume care after sentence, and counselling.[80]

## Protected Witness Units (PWUs)

4.44    These are dedicated units within the prison system for protecting witnesses who are remanded in custody or serving a sentence. As at the beginning of 2009 there were two such units located in HMPs Woodhill and Full Sutton and capable in total of holding 24 prisoners. Prison Service guidance on admission and regimes in PWUs is contained in the NSF and PSI 71/2000. The NSF defines a protected witness as 'a prisoner who is vulnerable to serious harm as a result of providing information to the police or other investigating agency'.

---

75   Earlier versions of PSO 4801 were seriously deficient in this regard and successfully challenged in *R (CD) v Secretary of State for the Home Department* [2003] EWHC 155 (Admin) – where it appeared a decision to separation had been made in light of the mother's behaviour with no proper consideration of the child's best interests, and in an unfair manner.
76   PSO 4801 para 31.5.
77   PSO 4801 para 41.10.
78   PSO 4801 para 31.12.
79   PSO 4801 para 31.13.
80   PSO 4801 section 33.

Not every prisoner who provides information to other agencies will become a protected witness. As a starting point, the NSF states that prisoner should be:

- an active participant in serious crime, which is defined as an offence which:
  - could reasonably be expected to attract a sentence of three years or more for a person who is aged 21 or over with no previous convictions; or
  - involved the use of violence; or
  - results in substantial financial gain; or
  - is conduct by a large number of persons in pursuit of common purpose (for example a riot);
- who elects to identify, provide information, or give evidence against others involved in serious crime; and
- is identified as being at real risk of serious harm after a protected witness assessment has been carried out.

4.45   Clearly the above criteria should not be seen as inflexible or exhaustive. If a prisoner is at risk from others, particularly risk of serious harm or death, then articles 2 (the right to life) and 3 (the prohibition on torture and inhuman or degrading treatment) of the ECHR may be engaged. Article 2 imposes a positive duty on the state to take reasonable steps to protect a prisoner where the authorities know, or ought to know, of the existence of a real and immediate risk to that prisoner's life.[81] If, by application of this test, the reasonable response to an assessed risk is allocation to a PWU then this should take place even where, for example, the CPS decide not to call the prisoner as a witness in the relevant criminal proceedings.[82]

4.46   The PWU team at Prison Service headquarters will consider all applications and carry out a risk assessment on a standard form contained in the NSF. There are four ways that applications can be made and considered:

- By the police or other investigating authority prior to sentence. This is the traditional method where the police (or other agency) and the CPS will recommend placement into a PWU. However if the police give an assurance to a prisoner that they will spend their

---

81   *R (Bloggs 61) v Secretary of State for the Home Department* [2003] EWCA Civ 686, see also the clarification by the House of Lords on when the positive duty under article 2 may be breached in *Chief Constable of Hertfordshire v Van Colle* [2008] UKHL 50.

82   *R (Smith) v Secretary of State for the Home Department* [2003] EWHC 406 (Admin).

sentence in a PWU such an assurance cannot bind the Prison Service if it assesses that there is an insufficient level of risk to warrant such an allocation.[83]

• By the police or other investigating agency after sentence. This can be at any time during the prisoner's sentence and will be as a result of a prisoner making it known that he is willing to give information about a serious crime. The prisoner will be produced into police custody. During this time work must be done assessing the risk and an appropriate secure location must be found if the risk assessment is not completed.

• By the prisoner or his or her legal representative. The NSF states that an application in these circumstances must be taken seriously even where it may appear to be frivolous and forwarded to Prison Service headquarters. The PW assessment team will produce a risk assessment and carry out appropriate follow up action.

• A former PW returns to the prison system. In these circumstances, even though the prisoner may have committed further offences and the protected witness arrangements may have broken down in the community it is incumbent upon the prison authorities properly to consider whether the previously assessed risk is no longer at a level to require admission to a PWU.[84]

4.47 Prison Service headquarters must be advised by the governor or police of this as early as possible so that a risk assessment can be made of the risk in the current location and based on the past history of informing. There is no need for the prisoner to make an application to be put back in the PWU as the assessment must be carried out automatically.

4.48 Any protected witness or potential protected witness (including a former protected witness) must be identified, risk assessed, and allocated to a Protected Witness Unit (PWU), a Vulnerable Prisoner Unit (VPU), or other appropriate accommodation depending on the level of assessed risk. The NSF states that all prisons must be aware that where a potential or former PW comes to light, contact must be made with Prison Service Headquarters immediately. When a prisoner is allocated to a PWU they are given a new name and prison number. These prisoners used to be called 'Bloggs' but this practice has ceased. They will be required to sign a compact relating to the

83  R *(Bloggs 61)* v *Secretary of State for the Home Department* [2003] EWCA Civ 686.
84  R *(DF)* v *Chief Constable of Norfolk* [2002] EWHC 1738 (Admin).

terms of their allocation to the PWU[85] and will be subject to regular reviews of the ongoing risk.

4.49    PWUs must operate separately from the main prison location to ensure that there is no unauthorised contact with protected witnesses and anyone outside the unit. Clearly the restrictions of living in one unit will have a severe impact on the regime provided and available activities and offending behaviour courses. This may therefore limit the opportunity to demonstrate a reduced risk to the public for those, such as lifers, whose release depends on an application to the Parole Board.[86] In 2008 a group of prisoners held in the PWU system obtained permission to bring judicial review proceedings challenging the failure to provide sufficient opportunities to attend offending behaviour courses.

4.50    Every protected witness will have a handler in the agency that is managing the relevant prosecution. The Prison Service guidance contains extra provisions on searching, holding of records and communications specific to PWUs in light of the particular need to protect the prisoners they contain.[87] Prisoners held in PWUs will be subject to the disciplinary and IEP systems like all others.

## Dangerous and Severe Personality Disorder (DSPD) Units

4.51    The DSPD programme is a joint initiative between the Ministry of Justice, Department of Health, the Prison Service and the NHS.[88] There is an inter-departmental DSPD programme board which has overall responsibility for development and management of these services, however the Prison Service is responsible for the individual services provided in prisons. Clinical governance for the assessment and treatment services within the prison units is jointly held by the local NHS trust and the governor of the prison. The programme is still in a pilot phase of developing and evaluating interventions aimed at identifying and reducing the risk to the public posed by those who meet the DSPD criteria. This group of prisoners is seen as the most dangerous, but the least amenable to treatment. Research has indi-

---

85  PSI 71/2000 para 4.3.
86  Although the fact that a prisoner is to be released as a protected witness will be a relevant factor for the Parole Board to consider as this will involve the prisoner being removed from his old home and associates – *R (Tinney) v Parole Board* [2005] EWHC 863 (Admin).
87  PSI 71/2000.
88  Information and materials are available at www.dspdprogramme.gov.uk/

cated that the types of group programmes provided in mainstream prisons are ineffective in reducing the risk to the public posed by this group, and in some instances have been shown to increase risk.

4.52 Detailed guidance on DSPD units for adult males, their aims, the criteria for admission and their day to day running is contained in a planning and delivery guide published jointly by the Ministry of Justice and the Department of Health.[89]

4.53 The aim of the programme is to provide 300 high secure DSPD unit places at the following locations:[90]

- HMP Whitemoor – 70 places
- HMP Frankland – 86 places
- Broadmoor High Secure Hospital – 70 places
- Rampton High Secure Hospital – 70 places

4.54 Prisoners will only be transferred to a high security hospital DHSP unit if the criteria for transfer under the Mental Health Act (MHA) 1983 are met (see chapter 6). This will require there to be an identified mental health treatment need. Prisoners may be admitted to DSPD units within prisons if these three criteria are met:[91]

- They are more likely than not to commit an offence that might be expected to lead to serious physical or psychological harm from which the victim would find it difficult or impossible to recover.
- They have a severe disorder of personality – which is defined as:
  - a score or 30 above on the PCL(R);[92] or
  - a score of 25–29 on the PCL(R) and at least one DSM-IV personality disorder diagnoses other than anti-social personality disorder; or
  - two or more DSM-IV personality disorder diagnoses.
- There is a link between the disorder and the risk of offending.

4.55 Referrals can be made by anyone with regular contact with a prisoner, but it is most likely that referrals will be prisoners in the high security estate (who may also be in the process of being assessed for the CSC system for example). There is a standard referral form which it is anticipated will be completed by the offender manager.[93] Priority for allocation should be given in the first instance, 'to those prisoners who

---

89  Available at www.dspdprogramme.gov.uk/media/pdfs/High_Secure_Services_for_Men.pdf
90  As at October 2008 – see PC 21/2008.
91  Planning and Delivery Guide 4.2.
92  For PCL-R and DSM-IV see below paras 4.100 and 4.103.
93  See appendix E to Probation Circular 21/2008.

present the most serious and immediate threat to public protection'.[94] Prisoners should be given information about the referral and a copy of the form.[95] The prisoner does not have to consent to be transferred to a DSPD unit, either for assessment or longer allocation[96] but in practice, forced entry to a unit is very rare. Whilst there is no upper age for admission to a DSPD unit, the minimum age is 18 and admission of 18- to 21-year-olds should only be on an exceptional basis.[97]

4.56    Prisoners will initially be admitted for an assessment process of around 20 weeks to consider whether the entry criteria set out above are met, to identify treatment needs, to develop a care plan, and to plan appropriate interventions.[98] The report should be disclosed to the prisoner and its implications discussed. If the entry criteria are not met, the prisoner will normally be returned to the referring prison with recommendations for future management. If a prisoner is accepted for treatment, each unit will develop an individualised treatment plan. Although prisoners can be held in the prison based units involuntarily, they cannot of course be compelled to participate in treatment. Units are required to develop strategies to deal with disruptive prisoners. The time that prisoners will spend in DSPD units will vary. However the guidance is that no later than three years after the commencement of treatment there should be a formal meeting where an individual's case and progression plan is discussed. If a prisoner is to remain in a DSPD unit for longer than three years, then a clear case in terms of treatment need must be made out. Optimally, no prisoners should stay longer than five years in a DSPD unit.[99]

4.57    HMP Grendon has a special programme of taking prisoners from the DSPD units on progression and integrating them into the therapeutic community there.[100] The prisoner must meet the normal criteria for admission to a therapeutic community including having at least 18 months to serve and not being a category A prisoner.

4.58    There is a similar, though separate, programme for women prisoners called the Primrose Programme.[101] There are 12 places available for women prisoners who meet the DSPD criteria at HMP Low

94 Planning and Delivery Guide para 4.6.
95 PC 21/2008 para 11.
96 Planning and Delivery Guide para 4.7.
97 Planning and Delivery Guide para 4.8.
98 Planning and Delivery Guide section 5, PC 21/2008 para 16.
99 Planning and Delivery Guide para 5.3.
100 www.dspdprogramme.gov.uk/progression_service4.html
101 Details are contained in the Planning and Delivery Guide at www.dspdprogramme.gov.uk/media/pdfs/Primrose_P&D_Guide_Dec_2006.pdf

Newton. The entry criteria for women are slightly different as they will be considered as having a severe personality disorder where any of the following is met:[102]

- the score on the PCL(R) is 25 or more;[103]
- the score on the PCL(R) is 18–24 and there are two or more personality disorders (under DSM-IV)[104] diagnosed other than antisocial personality disorder;
- there are at least three diagnosed personality disorders.

## Democratic therapeutic communities

4.59    These provide the main alternative to the shorter, cognitive behavioural treatment programmes provided as group work throughout the Prison Service. For many years HMP Grendon was the only prison containing a therapeutic community. As at October 2008[105] there were about 538 places available throughout the Prison Service at HMPs Grendon, Dovegate, Gartree, Blundeston and for women at HMP Send. Therapeutic communities (TC) aim to provide long term, residential, offending behaviour intervention for prisoners who have a range of offending behaviour risk areas, including emotional and psychological needs. The degree of need may prevent them from engaging fully with a shorter programme or may make shorter interventions inadequate.[106]

4.60    Transfer to a TC is voluntary and requires the full consent of the prisoner. The minimum time commitment is 18 months (12 months for women). Prisoners will normally not be accepted if they are appealing against their conviction or have failed an MDT or self-harmed in the past two months. They must have the intellectual capacity to participate in the programme (this usually equates to an IQ of 80) and must not have a current diagnosis of an active mental illness. The TCs at Gartree and Blundeston do not take prisoners convicted of sexual offences. Prisoners considering a transfer to a TC should complete the standard application form.[107] The form together with an up to date OASys assessment will then be sent to the preferred TC by the holding prison and the TC will begin the process of gathering

102  PC 21/2008 annex D.
103  See para 4.100.
104  See para 4.103.
105  See PC 21/2008.
106  PSO 2400 for detailed guidance.
107  PC 21/2008 annex G.

further information and if appropriate, will arrange for the prisoner to be transferred for assessment.

4.61    TCs do require a significant amount of commitment from the prisoner as the regime is significantly different from what is experienced in normal closed prisons. TCs provide 'an open living-learning environment for prisoners and staff. Prisoners and staff teams are empowered to make their own decisions, although they can expect to be questioned by the whole community on any matter eg a decision not to go to work, request for ROTL, a decision to transfer a prisoner, a decision to change the daily timetable'.[108] The core activity at TCs is the therapy group. Prisoners are expected to talk about their offending behaviour and encourage other group members to do the same. Links are drawn between current and past behaviour. Each resident has target areas that they are expected to focus on within the groups. These targets are encapsulated in a therapy plan which is drawn up in parallel with the sentence plan and OASys. All decisions are made in a democratic way with voting by the whole community. In certain areas the staff group retain a veto (for example where the community has voted that an individual should leave therapy) but they must still explain to the whole community the reasons behind their decisions.[109]

4.62    Prisoners who spend a long time in therapy in a TC will normally return to the mainstream prison system before release. They will often then find that, notwithstanding the intensive work on offending that has been carried out in the TC, that they are assessed for and expected to complete normal cognitive behavioural group-work programmes.

## Vulnerable Prisoner Units (VPUs) and Close Supervision Centres (CSCs)

4.63    VPUs and CSCs are units holding prisoners who have been formally segregated under the Prison or YOI Rules for their own protection (VPUs) or because they are considered highly disruptive (CSCs). Accordingly these are dealt with in chapter 8 which deals with segregation.

108  PSO 2400 para 2.4.
109  PSO 2400 para 2.8.

## Mental Health Act transfers

4.64 The transfer of prisoners to psychiatric hospitals and regional secure units under the provisions of the Mental Health Acts are dealt with in chapter 6 on healthcare.

# Transfers to and from other jurisdictions

## Transfers within the UK

4.65 There is statutory power for prisoners serving sentences in England and Wales to be transferred to serve their sentences within the various British Islands jurisdictions.[110] The provisions are used primarily to facilitate family contact, enabling prisoners to transfer to another jurisdiction either to complete their sentences, or for time limited periods, to receive accumulated visits. There is also provision for prisoners to be transferred for judicial purposes.[111] A transfer can be triggered by a prisoner's request. In the case of transfers from the Channel Islands or the Isle of Man, or transfers for judicial purposes the Secretary of State may make an order for a transfer without a request from the prisoner.

4.66 Transfers are made on either an unrestricted or a restricted basis. Where transfers are made on an unrestricted basis the continued administration of the prisoner's sentence becomes a matter entirely for the receiving jurisdiction. Where a prisoner is transferred on a restricted basis the sending jurisdiction continues to administer certain aspects of the sentence, including parole reviews and issuing of licences. Whether the transfer is restricted or unrestricted will depend primarily on its purpose and duration.

4.67 Transfers require the consent of the Secretary of State of both the sending and receiving jurisdictions. Normally, transfer requests will be approved only where the prisoner has at least six months left to serve in the receiving jurisdiction before his or her release date at the time of making the request, and where the prisoner has no outstanding appeal against conviction or sentence, is not charged with further criminal proceedings, and is not liable to any further period of imprisonment in lieu of payment of any outstanding monetary orders made by a court.

110 Crime (Sentences) Act 1997 s41 and Sch 1.
111 PSO 6000 chapter 13.

4.68    Each application will be assessed on its individual merits, taking into consideration:[112]

- the purpose for which the transfer is requested;
- whether the prisoner was ordinarily resident in the jurisdiction to which transfer is sought prior to the imposition of the current sentence; or whether members of the prisoner's close family are resident in that jurisdiction and there are reasonable grounds for believing that the prisoner will receive regular visits from them; or whether the prisoner has demonstrated through preparations that he has made for his life following release from prison that he intends to reside in the receiving jurisdiction upon release and he is in the later stages of his sentence;
- whether there are grounds for believing that the prisoner may disrupt or attempt to disrupt any prison establishment, or pose an unacceptable risk to security; and
- any compelling or compassionate circumstances.

## The Colonial Prisoners Removal Act 1884

4.69    The Colonial Prisoners Removal Act 1884 is still in force. This allows for the compulsory transfer of prisoners. It is mainly used to transfer prisoners given long sentences in territories such as Bermuda or the Cayman Islands, where there are no suitable facilities for long term detention, to the UK to serve sentences.

## Repatriation to serve sentences in the UK or abroad

4.70    Repatriation is the process whereby a prisoner serving a sentence of imprisonment in one country can apply to serve his or her sentence in prison in another.[113] The repatriation of prisoners is governed by the Repatriation of Prisoners Act (RPA) 1984. This states that warrants providing for the transfer of prisoners into or out of the United Kingdom to serve their sentences can only be issued where the UK is a party to international arrangements providing for such transfers.[114] The United Kingdom is party to two multi-party agreements, the Council of Europe Convention on the Transfer of Sentence Persons and the Commonwealth Scheme for the Transfer of Convicted

112   See written answer of Jack Straw on the use of the power: 28 October 1997, col 776.
113   For guidance see PSI 35/2008.
114   RPA 1984 s1(1)(a).

Offenders. In addition the UK has concluded bilateral prisoner transfer agreements with a number of other states. Most transfers are made under the Council of Europe Convention. The states to which prisoners can currently be repatriated to serve their sentence under these agreements are set out in the box on page 143.

4.71    There is no entitlement to repatriation under the Act. As well as there needing to be an international agreement in place with the receiving country:[115]

- the relevant minister in the UK and the 'appropriate authority' of the other state must agree to the transfer; and
- where the international agreement requires the prisoner to be transferred only with consent, the prisoner's consent must be given.

4.72    The requirements of the transfer agreements may vary but generally the conditions will be:[116]

- That the prisoner is a national of the country to which transfer is sought, although if the receiving state is willing to accept a non-national this may be agreed. In *R (Shaheen) v Secretary of State for Justice*[117] a prisoner was accepted in principle for a transfer to The Netherlands, although the transfer was refused on other grounds.
- That the sentence is final and enforceable (there are accordingly no outstanding appeals pending).
- That the offence giving rise to the sentence is an offence in the receiving country.
- That the prisoner has at least six months of the sentence outstanding, or is serving an indeterminate sentence.

## Transfer out of the UK

4.73    PSI 35/2008 states that prisoners cannot be transferred where they have outstanding prosecutions here or before they have satisfied the terms of any confiscation order or term in default. The prisoner makes an application on a specified application form[118] which is then sent to the Cross Border Transfer Section at Prison Service Headquarters. The process of considering the application involves consultation with other states and can take some time. If the responding

115 RPA 1984 s1.
116 See for example article 3 of the Council of Europe Convention.
117 [2008] EWHC 1195 (Admin).
118 Annex B to PSI 35/2008.

state is willing to accept the prisoner then it will provide information to the UK authorities on how it proposes to administer the sentence. If the Cross Border Transfer Section is content with this information, the request will be approved and the prisoner will be asked to sign a form consenting to the transfer in light of the information from the receiving state as to how the sentence is to be administered. The Secretary of State will issue a transfer warrant once a date for transfer has been agreed.[119]

4.74    The receiving state is not required to give reasons for a refusal to agree to a transfer. The UK authorities will most commonly refuse to consent to a transfer where there is concern that the way in which the receiving state will administer the sentence will result in a significant reduction in the sentence (the difference between the 'continued enforcement' and 'conversion of sentence' options under the Council of Europe Convention and the implications for the length of the term to be served are discussed further below). Although such refusals may engage article 8 of the ECHR where prisoners are seeking a transfer to be closer to family, courts will be slow to interfere with such decisions.[120]

## Transfers into the UK

4.75    For a prisoner to be transferred into the United Kingdom RPA 1984 states that the in addition to the requirements set out above:

- the prisoner must be a British Citizen; or
- the transfer appears to be appropriate having regard to any close ties which that person has with the United Kingdom; or
- for the purpose of a temporary return of a prisoner previously transferred out of the UK under the Act.[121]

4.76    Most repatriations are made under the Council of Europe Convention. This gives states the option of 'continued enforcement' or 'conversion' of sentences. The UK has opted for the former[122] which means

---

119  Between 1 January 2002 and July 2006, 392 prisoners were transferred to other countries to continue serving their sentence – written answer of Baroness Ashtal 12 July 2006.

120  In *Shaheen* [2008] EWHC 1195 (Admin) the prisoner was refused a transfer to The Netherlands even though he was resident and had family there because he was a British Citizen and the terms of the transfer would entitle him to return to the UK and potentially re-offend at a time when he would still be serving the sentence were he to remain in the UK. The court held that the decision to refuse the transfer was proportionate in light of these concerns.

121  RPA 1984 s4(1)(b).

122  Article 10 of the Convention and RPA 1984 s3(3).

that it is bound by the 'legal nature and duration of the sentence as determined by the sentencing state'. Sometimes the warrant will need to determine the equivalent domestic sentence – for example a sentence of indefinite preventative detention imposed on psychopath in the Netherlands was specified in the transfer warrant to be a discretionary life sentence in *R (Dillon) v Secretary of State for the Home Department*.[123] So where an English prisoner has received a longer sentence abroad than that which would have been imposed here for a similar offence, this will be enforced if they apply for repatriation.[124]

4.77      The Act states that the transfer warrant should take into account the amount of any remission earned in the transferring state.[125] However, as the prisoner will benefit from early release provisions once transferred, this will impact on how much remission is taken into account when setting the period to be served under the warrant. The release provisions of the CJA 2003 are applied to transferred, determinate sentenced prisoners.[126] The use of the continued enforcement basis for transfer can give rise to apparent unfairness as the early release arrangements are applied to the amount of time specified in the warrant to be served in England and Wales.[127] This means that prisoners serving determinate sentences will serve longer than they would have had the sentence been imposed here, as release is at the halfway point of the balance to serve, not the entire sentence. This effect of the legislation was upheld in *R v Secretary of State for the Home Department ex p Oshin*[128] where the court commented that the legislation's purpose was not to equate the prisoner's position precisely with that of someone sentenced here, but to ameliorate the effects of being sentenced abroad.

123 [2002] EWHC 732 (Admin).
124 Subject to the qualification that if the foreign sentence exceeds the maximum available in England and Wales that it must be reduced to that maximum – *R v Secretary of State for the Home Department ex p Read* [1989] AC 1014. This can have drastic results – the court held it was not open to a prisoner to judicially review a transfer warrant based on a sentence of 29 years 3 months imposed in Thailand for the equivalent offence of possessing class A drugs with intent to supply, even though on similar facts a sentence of about four to five years. The continued enforcement was lawful as it was within the permitted maximum for the equivalent offence in the UK (life imprisonment) and to alter it after transfer would undermine the basis of the agreement between the states: *R (Willcox) v Secretary of State for Justice* [2009] EWHC 1483 (Admin).
125 RPA 1984 s3(3)(b).
126 RPA 1984 Sch 1 para 2(4).
127 RPA 1984 Sch 1 para 1.
128 [2000] 1 WLR 2311.

4.78    For transferred life sentence prisoners the minimum term must be referred to the High Court to be set, whenever the indeterminate sentence was imposed abroad.[129] The court is not bound by the terms of the warrant or any agreement between the states as to the appropriate minimum term.[130]

4.79    There remains a power to pardon prisoners once they have been repatriated which will obviously only be exercised in very rare cases.[131]

4.80    The procedure for applying for repatriation to England and Wales will vary from country to country. Once an application is received by the Cross Border Transfer Section checks will be made to confirm the prisoner's nationality, whether there are outstanding charges in the UK and also that the offence giving rise to the sentence is one which would also be an offence in the UK. If all the requirements are met the authorities will normally agree to the transfer and write to the British embassy in the relevant country in order to obtain the prisoner's consent. The prisoner will be given information as to how the sentence will be administered after transfer.[132]

## Transfer without consent

4.81    The Additional Protocol to the Council of Europe Convention will, once ratified, allow for the transfer of prisoners without consent where they face deportation at the end of the sentence, or where they have fled from another jurisdiction before completing their sentence. The RPA 1984 has been amended to allow ratification of the additional protocol[133] but ratification has not yet taken place. Once it has there will be power to transfer prisoners facing deportation to serve sentences abroad without consent.

129   CJA 2003 s273 – *Re Khan* [2006] EWHC 2826 (QB).
130   See for example *Re Soyege* [2005] EWHC 2648 (QB).
131   Article 12 of the Council of Europe Convention and see *R (Shields) v Secretary of State for Justice* [2008] EWHC 3102.
132   Information on the process was given in the Home Office response to Freedom of Information Act request 209/05 – this also confirmed that in the period between January 2004 and March 2005, 68 prisoners were repatriated to England and Wales to serve their sentences.
133   From 14 July 2008, Police and Justice Act 2006 s44 in relation to prisoners facing deportation, and by CJIA 2008 ss94–95 in relation to prisoners who have fled.

**Countries which have ratified the Council of Europe Convention, the Commonwealth Scheme or which have signed bilateral repatriation agreements with the UK as at October 2008 (updates can be obtained from the cross border transfer section at Prison Service headquarters).**

| | | |
|---|---|---|
| Albania | France | Norway (including |
| America | Georgia | Bouvet Island, Peter I |
| Andorra | Germany | Island and Queen |
| Anguilla | Greece | Maud Land) |
| Antigua & Barbuda | Grenada | Pakistan |
| Armenia | Honduras (ratified | Panama |
| Australia | July 09) | Peru |
| Austria | Hong Kong | Poland |
| Azerbaijan | Hungary | Portugal |
| Bahamas | Iceland | Romania |
| Barbados | India | Samoa |
| Belgium | Ireland | San Marino |
| Bermuda | Israel | Serbia |
| Bolivia | Italy | Slovakia |
| Bosnia Herzegovina | Japan | Slovenia |
| Brazil | Korea | Spain |
| British Virgin Island | Latvia | Sri Lanka |
| Bulgaria | Lesotho | St Lucia |
| Canada | Liechtenstein | Suriname |
| Chile | Lithuania | Sweden |
| Cook Islands | Luxembourg | Switzerland |
| Costa Rica | Macedonia | Thailand |
| Croatia | Malawi | Tonga |
| Cuba | Malta | Trinidad & Tobago |
| Cyprus | Mauritius | Turkey |
| Czech Republic | Mexico | Uganda |
| Denmark | Moldova | Ukraine |
| Ecuador | Montenegro | Venezuela |
| Egypt | Morocco | Vietnam |
| Estonia | Netherlands (including | |
| Finland | Dutch Antilles and | |
| | Aruba) | |

**The Council of Europe Convention has also been extended to include the following UK territories**

| | | |
|---|---|---|
| British Indian Ocean Territories | Gibraltar | Sovereign base areas of Akratri & Dhekelia |
| Cayman Islands | Henderson, Ducie and Oeno Islands | (Cyprus) |
| Falkland Islands | Monserrat | St Helena and |
| Faroe Islands | Pitcairn | dependencies |

# Sentence planning: 'offender management'

## The Offender Management Model (OMM)

4.82   The language of 'offender management' was introduced into the sentence planning of prisoners by *Managing Offenders, Reducing Crime*, Lord Carter's report into what were termed 'correctional services' which was published in 2003 and led to the creation of NOMS. This report recommended a change to the way those sentenced by the courts are dealt with by the prison and probation services with a view to ensuring 'end to end management' in a single process from sentencing to supervision on licence. The OMM was subsequently developed[134] to provide the framework for the anticipated 'end to end management' of those sentenced by the courts. The key elements of the OMM are that a single offender manager should be responsible for the offender for the whole of the sentence, that there should a single sentence plan, that the offender manager should be based in the community, and that resources should follow risk.

4.83   That risk is both risk of re-offending and of harm to the public. The OMM therefore requires that risk assessments are carried out and that prisoners are allocated to the appropriate tier. The four tiers under the OMM are:

- Tier 4 – very high and high risk of harm cases. The primary focus is on public protection with enhanced supervision. These cases require the highest level of skill and resources.
- Tier 3 – medium to high risk of harm cases. The emphasis is on the need for rehabilitation and personal change for prisoners.
- Tier 2 – medium to low risk of harm cases which focus more on re-integration into the community and on practical help.
- Tier 1 – low risk of harm cases. This tier is focused on punishment.

## Roles within the OMM

### The offender manager

4.84   The main consequence of the new approach as set out in the OMM for prisoners is that an offender manager (OM) is appointed to the case as soon as an 'offender first comes into scope' and retains that role until the offender completes their sentence. The OM will be a

---

134   www.noms.justice.gov.uk/news-publications-events/publications/strategy/offender-management-model-1.1

probation officer located in the prisoner's home or resettlement area (who in the absence of the OMM would be known as the home probation officer). The OM takes responsibility for managing the sentence. Prior to the introduction of the OMM such responsibility for serving prisoners lay with the holding prison.

4.85    The OM is responsible for formulating an assessment and a sentence plan. This is done using the OASys (Offender Assessment System – see below) format, which is designed to identify risk factors, identify suitable programmes to address those risks, and determines responsibility for implementation of the plan. The OM is responsible for ensuring that the Parole Board has all relevant information about the identified risks and how they have been addressed. This is dealt with in the PAROM report, which is now the key report for the parole process.

*The offender supervisor and key workers*

4.86    For serving prisoners the OMM also requires the appointment of an offender supervisor (OS) to provide a link between the prison and the OM and who takes primary responsibility for implementing the sentence plan. The OS will be located in the new offender management units in prisons. The sentence plan will identify key workers who are responsible for delivering specific offending behaviour programmes. The OMM also requires the appointment of a case administrator.

## Introduction of the OMM

4.87    The OMM has been phased in by stages. Phase I in the year to March 2006 involved only those serving community sentences. Phase II from November 2006 included adult offenders serving a determinate sentence of 12 months or more who are either assessed as being a high or very high risk of causing serious harm, or have been identified by local crime and disorder reduction partnerships as being prolific and other priority offenders (PPOs). Phase III from January 2008 applied to those serving IPP sentences. The OMM documentation and processes are applied to all life sentenced prisoners, although until OMM is phased in for all sentences an OM will not be appointed in such cases. It is unclear when the OMM will apply to all sentences.

## Assessment of risk

4.88    The two broad methods of assessing risk are actuarial and clinical risk assessment. Actuarial risk assessment looks at the statistical likelihood of populations with similar histories re-offending. It is based on static risk factors: that is those that cannot change, such as number and type of convictions, and age at first conviction. Whilst actuarial risk assessment tools can predict the percentage of prisoners that share certain characteristics that will re-offend within a set time, they cannot predict whether individual prisoners will re-offend.

4.89    The clinical method of risk assessment is intended to consider dynamic risk factors, those that can change over time, such as the response to treatment in custody and changes in attitudes and behaviour. The problem that the Prison Service has identified with this approach is that it can be overly subjective, and lacks an evidential basis.

## The Offender Assessment System (OASys)

4.90    OASys is the key tool used by the prison and probation services to identify the risk to the public posed by prisoners and to identify relevant programmes to address those risks. Although it is core to the processes introduced by the OMM it pre-dates it, and is applied to all prisoners. It aims to embody both the actuarial and clinical approach to risk assessment. It therefore takes into account static factors related to rates of reconviction, but also the clinical judgment of the person completing the assessment. It is designed to be completed at key stages of the sentence to reflect progress made following completion of offending behaviour programmes.

4.91    The offender will have an OASys score (0–168, categorised as low (0–40), medium (41–99) and high (100–168)) which indicates the likelihood of re-conviction. The other assessment is of serious harm to others. The risk of serious harm to others is categorised as:

- Low: current evidence does not indicate likelihood of causing serious harm.
- Medium: there are identifiable indicators of risk of serious harm. Potential to cause harm but unlikely to do so unless there is a change of circumstances.
- High: identifiable indicators of risk of serious harm. Potential event could happen at any time and impact would be serious.
- Very high: imminent risk of serious harm. Potential event is more likely than not to happen imminently. The impact would be serious.

These levels then link to the relevant tier under the OMM (see above).

4.92    The main part of OASys, which is now a computer based system, has 13 sections. The first 12 examine factors which research shows are related to risk of reconviction. At the end of each section, links of risk of serious harm, risks to the individual, other risks and offending behaviour are highlighted. In Section 13 health and other considerations are noted that are relevant to suitability of interventions, but not to risk. OASys also includes sections that deal with sentence planning and indicates suitable treatment programmes with timetables for completion and review.

4.93    OASys has been criticised both by prisoners and probation staff as unwieldy and difficult to understand. Prisoners in particular find it hard to comprehend how reviews of OASys documentation can result in apparently unexplained increases in scores. These concerns have been given support by the Ministry of Justice's own research. In an inter-rater reliability research project looking at how consistently two or more assessors would rate the same offender, it was found that the least reliable sections of OASys (ie where there was poor consensus between the assessors) were financial management, alcohol misuse, thinking and behaviour and risk of serious harm.[135]

### Asset

4.94    The Youth Justice Board uses a similar system as OASys for those under 18 known as Asset.[136] Asset is a structured assessment tool to be used by Youth Offending Teams on all young offenders who come into contact with the criminal justice system. It aims to look at the young person's offence or offences and identify a multitude of factors or circumstances – ranging from lack of educational attainment to mental health problems – which may have contributed to such behaviour. The information gathered from Asset can be used to inform court reports so that appropriate intervention programmes can be drawn up. It should also highlight any particular needs or difficulties the young person has, so that these may also be addressed. Asset is also designed to measure changes in needs and risk of reoffending over time.

### Other risk assessment tools

4.95    The other main risk assessment tools used by the Prison Service are as follows (this is not a complete list as there is a wide variety of tools used by psychologists):

135  Ministry of Justice *Research 1/09*.
136  For guidance see www.yjb.gov.uk/en-gb/practitioners/Assessment/Asset.htm

### Offender Group Reconviction Scale (OGRS)

4.96   This predicts, from a number of criminal history and demographic factors (purely 'static' factors), the probability that an offender will be reconvicted within two years of release from custody or the start of a community sentence. It is often used as a starting point for risk assessment for programmes such as FOCUS (see below) to help guide the level of intervention that will be necessary. The percentage values are converted into specific levels of risk of reconviction. For example 76 per cent and above is a 'high' risk of reconviction, 30 per cent or less 'low'.

### Violent Risk Assessment Guide (VRAG)

4.97   This is the most widely used actuarial tool for assessing violent recidivism and will assign people to one of nine risk categories for future offending. It is limited to the extent that it does not contain any assessment of the nature, severity or frequency of future violence. It involves analysing features ranging from the age at the time of the index offence, performance at school and the history of substance abuse through to existence of psychopathy and personality disorders. There is a more refined version of VRAG designed to address the levels of dangerousness in high risk men called the Violence Prediction Scheme (VPS).

### Violence Risk Scale (VRS)

4.98   The VRS also assesses the risk of violent recidivism. However it uses six static and 20 dynamic risk factors derived from an extensive review of risk assessment and treatment literature that identified factors which are empirically or theoretically linked to violence. The factors are rated on a four-point scale, reflecting the extent of the problem identified by the factors. The VRS adopts a 'stages of change' model, for factors that receive a score of 2 or 3 in order to assess readiness for treatment. Following intervention, the stages of change can be re-assessed to determine progress.

### HCR-20

4.99   The HCR-20 is not an actuarial instrument which seeks to provide a numerical estimate of risk in the form of a probability that a person will reoffend. Instead, the HCR-20 assesses the presence or absence of factors which have been shown by research to have a bearing on future violent offending. These are divided into 20 historical, clinical and risk management factors. The result of the assessment is not numerical, as would be the case with an actuarial method. However, neither does it rely on unstructured clinical judgment. The HCR-20 seeks to guide clinical judgment, so that it depends upon known risk factors rather than the subjective views of the assessor.

### Psychopathy Checklist-Revised (PCL-R)

4.100   The PCL-R is designed to diagnose presence of psychopathy. It was initially developed in the 1970s by Professor Robert Hare. It is used to rate individuals on a three-point scale on each of 20 defining characteristics. The result is a score ranging from 0 to 40. It has become usual to apply the term 'psychopath' to anyone scoring more than 30. The PCL-R is not strictly a predictor of risk, although research has shown that PCL-R scores are related to violent crime, predatory sexual crime, criminal diversity, speed of reconviction, and failure on parole or conditional release. A high score may mean a prisoner is assessed by the Dangerous and Severe Personality Disorder Unit (DSPD).

### Risk Matrix 2000

4.101   This is an actuarial based assessment of future risk of sexual and violent offending which has been developed from the Structured Anchored Clinical Judgement (SACJ) which is based on empirical research into recidivism amongst sex offenders. Whilst the SACJ contained an extensive clinical assessment, the Risk Matrix 2000 was developed from a shortened version concentrating on static risk factors which had been developed to address those situations where the necessary dynamic and clinical data were not available. Although this risk assessment tool can be used for both sexual and violent offenders, it is used far more extensively for sex offenders.

### Structured Assessment of Risk and Need (SARN)

4.102   More akin to clinical assessment, SARN has been developed by the Prison Service and combines the actuarial assessment of risk with the SACJ. This is an instrument that is currently being used within the national prison Sex Offenders Treatment Programme (SOTP), and which is described in the SOTP accreditation documentation. In brief, four 'risk domains' are considered, relating to sexual interests, distorted attitudes, socio-affective functioning, and self-management. It is used to set treatment targets and to determine the level of intervention required. It does have acknowledged limitations as it cannot quantify changes in static risk and is restricted to covering variables that have been identified in research to date, leaving open the possibility that there are further unidentified predictors.

**Personality assessment**

4.103    The most common tool used in the Prison Service for the diagnosis of personality disorder is the International Personality Disorder Examination (IPDE). The purpose of using the IPDE is to determine the identity and relevance of personality traits and the possible presence of personality disorder. The IPDE is a semi-structured clinical interview developed to assess personality disorders defined by the Diagnostic and Statistical Manual of Mental Disorders, 4th Edition (DSM-IV). DSM-IV describes ten personality disorder diagnoses, which are organized into three clusters. The first cluster is labelled odd or eccentric and consists of paranoid, schizotypal and schizoid diagnoses. The second cluster is labeled dramatic and unstable and consists of antisocial, narcissistic, histrionic and borderline diagnoses. The third cluster is labeled anxious and fearful and consists of avoidant, dependent and obsessive-compulsive diagnoses. In prisons and secure hospitals, diagnoses in the dramatic and unstable cluster are most commonly observed.

## Offending behaviour programmes

4.104    The Correctional Services Accreditation Panel (the CSAP) is responsible for advising the Secretary of State on the accreditation of offending behaviour programmes used by the Prison and Probation Services. The CSAP is an advisory non-departmental public body originally established in 1999 and made up of a Chair, independent experts, and representatives of the Prison Service, the National Probation Service, and the Ministry of Justice.[137] Programmes that are not fully accredited but are used within individual prisons must nevertheless be subject to the Prison Service's own validation process to ensure that there is some basis for believing that the intervention is effective.[138] Offending behaviour programmes are managed centrally at the Prison Service by the interventions unit.

4.105    The main core of the accredited offending behaviour programmes that prisoners are now expected to complete are delivered in groups, and are based on the principles of cognitive-behavioural therapy (CBT). The courses based on CBT will normally be made up of a fixed number of sessions and seek to address assessed risk in terms of the relationship between thoughts, feelings and behaviour. CBT developed out of cognitive therapy, which is designed to change people's

137  For fuller details of the workings of the CSAP see PSO 4360.
138  PSO 4350.

thoughts, beliefs, attitudes and expectations, and behavioural therapy, which is designed to change how people act. CBT is based on the assumption that the way people think about a situation affects how they act. In turn, their actions can affect how they both think and feel. It aims to change both the type of thinking and behaviour associated with committing offences.

4.106    Sentence planning will normally involve completion of some offending behaviour programmes. Access to such courses can however be much more crucial for those whose release depends on a Parole Board direction. Prisoners serving indeterminate sentences, if assessed as requiring a specified offending behaviour programme in order to address a key risk factor are highly unlikely to be released by the board until it has been completed. Obtaining access to offending behaviour courses is discussed in chapters 10 and 11 under the early release schemes.

4.107    There remains some controversy over the effectiveness of courses run by the Prison Service but the reliance on its accredited courses can only be challenged on rationality grounds. In these circumstances, where there are two competing bodies of opinion reasonably held as to their effectiveness, the courts will not criticise decisions requiring completion of courses. In a case involving the SARN the judge stated:

> There clearly is a body of professional opinion that has grave reservations about the utility of SARN. On the other hand, there is another body of professional opinion which does not share those reservations, and which considers it to be an useful tool, not of course the be all and end all, but an useful exercise. There is also a respectable body of professional opinion, with which the defendant was entitled to agree, that it would be of advantage for the claimant to undertake the SARN. Against this background, the claimant's challenge comes nowhere near surmounting the irrationality threshold.[139]

## General offending programmes

### Enhanced thinking skills (ETS)

4.108    This is a short course which is the most frequently delivered course provided in prisons. Prisoners will often be required to complete the ETS before being given access to other courses. It does not require prisoners to describe their offences and so can be undertaken by

---

139  *R (Bealey) v Secretary of State for the Home Department* [2005] EWHC 1618 (Admin).

prisoners who maintain their innocence. It is describe by Prison
Service as a cognitive skills course that aims to enable participants
to be less impulsive, more flexible and less rigid in their thinking. It
aims to develop skills for reasoning, perspective taking, self reflec-
tion and inter-personal problem solving. It is made up of 20 sessions
of around two hours and is designed to be completed over a four- to
ten-week period. There is little research evidence that ETS impacts
on reconviction rates.[140] The Probation Service runs a similar community based programme, Think First. For those under 18 there is
the JETS programme, which is a version of ETS specially tailored for
this group of prisoners.

### Cognitive skills booster programme (CSB)

4.109   This programme is run both by the Prison and Probation Services
and is designed to reinforce learning from the ETS. It consists of ten
sessions and can last three to ten weeks.

### FOR

4.110   This is a brief course for those who are within three months of release and are to be supervised in the community. It is a 13-session
programme which aims to increase motivation to change so that
prisoners will be more likely to engage with services on release. It is
designed to be delivered as part of a resettlement programme.

## Programmes for violent offenders

### Controlling anger and learning to manage it (CALM)

4.111   This is a programme which aims to reduce the intensity, frequency and duration of negative emotions associated with offending
including anger, anxiety and jealousy. It is usually used for those
who commit violent offences that are linked to an inability to manage emotions. CALM looks at triggers for anger and teaches skills to
reduce emotional levels of arousal. Whilst it may be appropriate for
those whose violence is emotionally driven, it is not used for people
convicted of instrumental violence for whom the CSCP (see below)

140  See *Findings 226* Home Office RDSD 2003 which found that although
reconviction rates for male adults and young offenders were less at one year
after release as against a control group which had not completed the ETS, this
reduction was not maintained two years after release. Reconviction rates of
women prisoners who completed the ETS have been found to be no different
to those who have not: *Findings 276* Home Office RDSD 2006.

may be appropriate. CALM is made up of 24 sessions and includes up to three individual sessions.

### Cognitive Self-Change Programme (CSCP)

4.112 The CSCP is designed for high-risk violent offenders and is made up of components which runs both in prison and the community. It is run in a rolling format and is made up of about 160 sessions of group work. In addition, every two weeks each prisoner has an individual session. The core part of the course completed in prison will normally take about 12 months. CSCP targets patterns of antisocial thinking and beliefs which support violence. It is primarily aimed at those who use violence to achieve an aim rather than those who use violence because of a loss of emotional control.

### Healthy relationships programme (HRP)

4.113 This programme is designed for men who have committed abusive and violent behaviour in the home and its aim is to reduce the risk of violence towards intimate partners. There are two versions of the HRP – the High Intensity HRP consists of ten modules involving about 68 sessions. The Moderate Intensity HRP consists of six modules and involves about 24 sessions.

### Chromis

4.114 This programme is currently only run at the DSPD in Frankland. It aims to reduce violence in high risk offenders whose level or combination of psychopathic traits disrupts their ability to engage in treatment and change. The programme comprises five core components which take around two years to complete.

## Sex offender treatment programmes (SOTP)

### Core SOTP

4.115 This is the main programme aimed at sex offenders. It is aimed at male medium and high risk offenders. The programme consists of 86 group sessions and lasts about six months. It aims to help prisoners understand how and why they have committed sexual offences and to increase awareness of victim harm.

4.116 The Adapted SOTP covers similar areas to the core SOTP but is adapted for those who have social or learning difficulties. It takes about the same amount of time to complete as the core SOTP.

### Extended SOTP

4.117    This programme is designed for male high and very high risk sexual offenders. It is completed after the Core SOTP and covers three main areas: problematic thinking styles, emotion management and intimacy skills. It lasts for 73 sessions and takes about four months.

### Rolling SOTP

4.118    This is a programme targeted at male low risk sex offenders. It covers similar areas as the core programme but has less emphasis on obtaining an adequate offence account, and more emphasis on relationship skills and attachment deficits. It lasts for 45 to 60 sessions of two to two and a half hours.

### Better Lives Booster Programme (BLB)

4.119    This programme is designed to boost learning from the other SOTP programmes and to provide opportunities to practice relevant skills. It runs for 28 sessions and is suitable only for those who have successfully completed other SOTP programmes. There are two versions, low intensity and high intensity. The latter is designed for those about to be released into the community.

4.120        There is an adapted BLB for those with learning difficulties who have completed the adapted SOTP.

### Healthy Sexual Functioning (HSF)

4.121    This course aims to promote healthy sexual functioning in high risk sexual offenders who are aroused by the thought of sexual offending. It is designed to be completed after the Core and Extended SOTPs. There are four modules to the course: understanding sexuality; patterns in sexual arousal; promoting sexual healthy interest; and relapse prevention.

## Programmes for drug misuse

### Short Duration Programme (SDP)

4.122    This is a programme for male and female prisoners who are serving short sentences, or who are approaching release. It is designed as a stepping stone to further drug treatment both in prison and the community. It comprises of 20 two and a half hour sessions delivered over four weeks.

### Prison Addressing Substance Related Offending (P-ASRO)

4.123 This is a CBT programme which addresses how temperament and socio-economic situations contribute to the development of substance misuse. It is aimed at male prisoners who are 18 or over with a low to medium risk of reconviction. It is made up of 20 sessions delivered over five to six weeks. There is also a version of P-ASRO specifically for women and covers similar areas.

### Substance Treatment and Offending Programme (STOP)

4.124 STOP targets male prisoners who are 21 or older who are medium or high risk dependent offenders. The programme aims to achieve abstinence and consists of 90 one hour sessions.

### 12-Step Programmes

4.125 There are two kinds of 12-Step programmes available in the Prison Service, one delivered by Prison Service staff and one by the Rehabilitation for Addicted Prisoners Trust (RAPt). Both take prisoners through the first five steps of the 12-step process with the further seven steps being completed in the community). It is clearly only suitable for prisoners who can commit to a process that calls in aid a 'higher power'. Both programmes are made up of 60 sessions delivered over 12 weeks. RAPt is developing a programme for women.

### FOCUS

4.126 This is a high intensity programme for adult males with a medium and high risk of reconviction and high or severe drug or alcohol dependence. It comprises 62 sessions delivered over 18 weeks.

### Prison Partnership Therapeutic Community Programme (PPTCP)

4.127 This is a residential programme based on Therapeutic Community Principles that lasts for nine to 12 months. It is suitable for male prisoners aged 21 or over with a medium and high risk of reconviction and level of dependence on drugs. There are three phases: induction; the primary treatment phase of about six months; and the re-entry phase which involves preparation for release. An 18-week version of this programme is being developed for women.

# CHAPTER 5

# Living conditions in prison

*continued*

# Prison cells

5.1 The Prison Act 1952 provides that every prisoner, whether sentenced, on remand or otherwise committed to prison, may be lawfully confined in any prison and that every prisoner shall be deemed to be in the legal custody of the governor of the prison.[1] Within an individual prison, a prisoner can be lawfully kept in any cell provided that the cell is visibly numbered and has been certified by an inspector to confirm that its size, lighting, heating, ventilation and fittings are adequate for health and that it allows the prisoner to communicate at any time with a prison officer.[2] In practice the latter means that each cell must have a functioning cell bell and that it must not be turned off or taped over by prison staff. These provisions reflect the international standards that prisoners' accommodation 'shall meet all requirements of health due to regard being paid to climatic conditions and particularly to the content of air, minimum floor space, lighting, heating and ventilation'.[3] The limited case-law on this issue has suggested that 7–8 square metres for an individual prisoner is adequate.[4]

## Cell sharing

5.2 PR rule 26 and YOIR rule 22 reiterate that no room or cell shall be used as sleeping accommodation unless it has been certified and that the certificate must specify the maximum number of prisoners who may sleep or be confined at one time in the cell to which it relates. That number must not be exceeded without the leave of the Secretary of State. The Rules[5] also stated that every prisoner must be provided with a separate bed and with separate bedding adequate for warmth and health. The STC Rules do not allow for cell-sharing, making it clear that 'every trainee shall be provided with his own room'.[6]

5.3 The final report into the Inquiry chaired by Justice Keith into the death in 2000 in Feltham YOI of remand prisoner Zahid Mubarek[7] recommended that 'the elimination of enforced cell-sharing should

1 PA 1952 ss12–13.
2 PA 1952 s14.
3 European Prison Rule 103; UN Standard Minimum Rules rule 63(1).
4 *Iorgov v Bulgaria* (2005) 40 EHRR 7 at para 80.
5 PR rule 27; YOIR rule 23.
6 Secure Training Centre Rules 1998 rule 18.
7 *Report of the Zahid Mubarek Inquiry* published 29 June 2006.

remain the objective of the Prison Service, and the achievement of this goal should be regarded as a high priority'. Keith J wrote:

> The most obvious and dramatic way of reducing prisoner-on-prisoner in-cell attacks is by eliminating cell-sharing...As we have seen, it has been regarded as desirable for many years that, if possible, prisoners should be accommodated in cells on their own. The reasons for that are obvious, although I do not recall having seen them spelt out any-where. In short, there are countless things prisoners are comfortable about doing in private, but less comfortable about doing if someone else is there. There are some very intimate things, such as mastur-bating or using the lavatory, which many people would be extremely unhappy about doing in the presence of others, and equally unhappy about others doing in their presence. And apart from the lack of priv-acy, sharing a cell with someone has its own particular problems. You may not like your cellmate. They may have habits which in the normal course of things you would be able to put up with, but which you be-come much more aware of in the confines of a prison cell. They may get on your nerves. They may have the sort of habits, such as smoking, which you should not have to put up with. And sharing a confined space with someone will have its own tensions – for example, disa-greements about what television channel to watch, what sort of music to listen to, and about the use being made of the other's possessions.

5.4     Despite these recommendations, enforced cell-sharing remains nor-mal practice, subject to certain constraints and safeguards. The Rules dictate that under no circumstances shall unconvicted prisoners be required to share a cell with a convicted prisoner[8] and all prisoners are subject to a 'cell-sharing risk assessment' (see also chapter 2).[9]

## Cells and smoking

5.5     The smoke-free legislation which came into effect in July 2007[10] ap-plies to prisons. The Prison Service has issued guidance on its appli-cation.[11] This states that all indoor areas in prisons are now to be smoke-free with the exception of cells occupied solely by smokers aged 18 and over, and arrangements should be implemented to mini-mise the dangers of passive smoking.

5.6     Residential units holding persons under 18 must be entirely smoke-free, as must mother and baby units. The PSI states that the

---

8  PR rule 7(2)(b).
9  See PSI 32/2005 and Youth Justice Board guidance at www.yjb.gov.uk/en-gb/ practitioners/Custody/PlacingYoungPeopleinCustody/CellSharing/
10  See the Health Act 2006.
11  PSI 9/2007.

aim is ultimately to ban all smoking in prisons but that the policy in the meantime is that prisoners aged 18 and over are to be permitted to smoke in single cells or cells shared with other smokers. The policy does state that

> [g]overnors may introduce smoke free landings and/or wings where appropriate and feasible, following consultation with staff and prisoners, but this must not undermine the general policy which permits prisoners over 18 to smoke in single cells or cells shared with smokers.

The policy is clear that non-smokers should not be required to share a cell with active smokers.[12]

## Certified Normal Accommodation

5.7　Prison Service Order 1900 on Certified Normal Accommodation sets out arrangements for the certification and management of prisoner accommodation in adult prisons and YOIs and 'introduces measurable standards for the certification of cells that can be applied consistently across the estate'.

5.8　Certified Normal Accommodation (CNA) or 'uncrowded capacity' describes the number of prisoners who can be held in a specific cell or the sum of cells within in establishment in conditions the Prison Service considers to be decent. Any prisoner places provided above CNA are referred to as 'overcrowding places'. Any cell or establishment with an occupancy/population above CNA is referred to as crowded (or overcrowded).

5.9　Baseline CNA is the sum total of all certified accommodation in an establishment except, normally:

- Cells in punishment or segregation units.
- Healthcare cells or rooms in training prisons and YOIs that are not routinely used to accommodate long stay patients.

## Heating, lighting and ventilation

5.10　All accommodation must have heating, lighting and ventilation to recognised technical standards:[13]

- Heating systems should be capable of achieving 19°C in cells and 21°C in wards, hospital rooms, protective rooms and special cells.
- Artificial lighting should provide up to 200 lux at tabletop level.

---

12　PSI 9/2007 para 8.
13　PSO 1900 annex C.

- The requirement for ventilation should be:
  - cells with mechanical extraction: two air changes per hour;
  - cells with integral sanitary annex: six air changes per hour within the annex; (in double cells or rooms containing a WC cubicle, the WC area must be ventilated separately to the living area);
  - cells with natural ventilation: 16,000mm$^2$ of openable area for rapid ventilation, provided in the window; 8,000mm$^2$ of permanent openable area for background (trickle) ventilation.

## Cell furniture

5.11    Each uncrowded place must provide sufficient space for:

- a single bed;
- storage for personal possessions;
- a chair and table area;
- circulation and movement.

Each crowded place must provide sufficient space for:

- a bed, which may be two-tier;
- storage, which may be compacted;
- a chair and table area;
- circulation and movement.

5.12    These minimum space requirements do not apply to single cells. Area managers (who are responsible for cell certification) must be satisfied that smaller single cells provide reasonable space for one prisoner when other relevant factors, such as freedom of movement and time out of cell, are taken into account.

For cells that conform to the space requirements for a CNA of two or more, the establishment may choose between single beds and bunk beds. In 2007 some adverse tabloid publicity was attracted by Bullingdon prisoner Gerry Cooper who began civil proceedings against the Prison Service after injuring himself, falling out of a top bunk. There was less derision later the same year when the High Court awarded compensation to the family of Ryan St George, an epileptic, who suffered massive irreparable brain damage after falling from a top bunk at Brixton prison in 1997, and who now needs lifelong care.

## Overcrowding and environmentally unsafe conditions

5.13    There have been relatively few legal challenges to the physical conditions of imprisonment in Britain. The threshold that needs to be breached for overcrowding to become a breach of article 3 of the

ECHR is extremely high. In *Babushkin v Russia*[14] the court found a violation of article 3. The applicant told the court he had been held for five months in dormitory cells designed for 8–34 prisoners, but which routinely held 50–70, and on occasion 90 inmates, thus meaning there were not enough beds or bedding for everyone to sleep at the same time. The cell had limited access to sanitary facilities, poor levels of hygiene and inadequate levels of daylight. The ECtHR has dealt with a number of similar cases against Russia and the Ukraine.[15] A breach of article 3 was also found in *Peers v Greece*[16] where the detention of a British prisoner in a cell lacking in natural light and ventilation combined with insufficient privacy for toilet facilities was held to be a breach of article 3 on the basis that the conditions were degrading even though there had been no intention to degrade.[17]

5.14    In 2007 prisoners at HMP Norwich took legal action which led to the closure of Gurney wing of the prison. They had complained of leaking soil stacks in cells, mould on walls, broken windows during winter months, pigeons nesting in disused cells and rodent infestation. The wing, described by Her Majesty's Chief Inspector of Prisons as 'among the worst' prison accommodation and by the Independent Monitoring Board as unfit for animals, had been recommended for closure in 2005 and was closed in January 2007 but reopened after just three days due to overcrowding. The prisoners on Gurney wing asked the prison to allow access to an independent environmental health expert. The refusal to allow this expert access was then challenged by judicial review proceedings which were compromised when the prison agreed to jointly approach the local authority and invite it to undertake an environmental health inspection. The inspection found that cells were 50 to 75 times more hazardous to health than normal housing conditions, that the likelihood of harm from infestation had increased from a national average of 1 in 5,585 to 1 in 2, and that of harm in relation to hygiene from a national average of 1 in 7,750 to 1 in 100. The inspectors were most concerned however at the lack of heating in the landings and staircases: blocked vents in every cell which meant that there was no effective heating in the cells and there were strong draughts and excessive damp on the ground floor level.

---

14   Application no 67253/01, 18 October 2007.
15   See also *Novoselov v Russia* (2005) 44 EHRR 11.
16   (2001) 31 EHRR 51.
17   Para 75.

## Sanitation

5.15   One of the 12 key recommendations in Lord Justice Woolf's report into the 1990 protest at Strangeways prison, Manchester, was 'access to sanitation for all inmates ... not later than February 1996'. Pledging to better this, Conservative Party Home Secretary Kenneth Baker gave a commitment to end the practice of 'slopping out' by 1994.[18] The practice did then cease at the majority of prisons in England and Wales; however in Scotland approximately a fifth of prisoners were still slopping out in 2004, when Robert Napier was awarded compensation by the court of sessions for 40 days spent on remand at Barlinnie in 2001.[19] Legal challenges are still ongoing in relation to three prisons in England and Wales (Albany, Long Lartin and Blundeston) where there are no in-cell sanitation facilities on some or all wings. Instead a 'night-bell' system operates, whereby prisoners buzz to be let out, one at a time, and are subject to punishment if they overstay the prescribed time for using the toilet and returning to their cells. In the report of an unannounced follow-up inspection to Blundeston published on 3 February 2009 the Chief Inspector noted that the system's 'defects were evident, not least in the pervasive smell of urine on the exercise yards'.[20]

5.16   PSO 1900 states that prisoners must be able to 'use the WC in private'. This is defined as 'full body visual screening from all points in the cell or room, as would be provided at a minimum by a cubicle'. However the provision is piecemeal: the Prisons Ombudsman has upheld complaints about lack of privacy and the Chief Inspector has reported on prisons where 'modesty screens' have not been provided and in April 2007 the slow progress of providing such privacy in HMP Chelmsford provoked the asking of a parliamentary question by the local MP.[21]

18   At that time most prison cells had no integral sanitation and prisoners were given a bucket for times when they were not allowed out to use the toilet. The subsequent emptying of the buckets in a communal recess area led to the whole process being routinely described as 'slopping out'.

19   *Napier v Scottish Ministers* [2005] 1 SC 307.

20   Report on an unannounced short follow-up inspection of HMP Blundeston by HM Chief Inspector of Prisons, 16–18 June 2008, report compiled November 2008, published Tuesday 3 February 2008.

21   See *Hansard* 29 January 2007: Col 138W.

# Prisoners' property

## General

5.17 Prisoners in adult prisons and YOIs may retain 'a reasonable amount of their personal property' with them while in custody' but the Rules give governors the power to confiscate and hold any item of property in the interests of good order or security, 'to make best use of the limited space available within prisons, to facilitate searching or to support the operation of incentive schemes'.[22] It is a disciplinary offence to borrow or lend, or to give or receive property to another prisoner without the governor's permission, as it is to have in possession 'unauthorised articles'.[23] Along with items which are generally prohibited, such as mobile phones, this can include any property not listed as belonging to the cell's occupant. In 2004 the Prison Service introduced PSO 1250 on Prisoners' Property. This replaced guidance that had been in force for many years on property that could be held in possession, 'volumetric control' and other related matters.[24] It also includes guidance on arrangements for handing in property. Each prison governor retains discretion on the arrangements in each prison, but it is advisable to seek permission in advance if there is any doubt.[25]

5.18 The power to confiscate unauthorised articles does not mean that the confiscated property can be destroyed. It has been held that the Prison Rules provide the only circumstances in which confiscated property can be disposed of, that is, when it has been unclaimed for three years. A policy to destroy confiscated mobile phones where the prisoner could establish ownership has been declared unlawful.[26] In such circumstances the prison must store the property for when the prisoner is released, or allow them to hand the item out. However, in establishing title prisoners may be exposing themselves, and

---

22  PSO 1250 para 1.2.

23  PR rule 51 paras 12–15, YOIR rule 55 paras 13–16. The STC Rules do not contain disciplinary offences but rule 35(3) allows the governor to 'confiscate any unauthorised article found in the possession of a trainee after his reception into a centre, or concealed or deposited within a centre'.

24  PSO 1250 replaces the previous instruction on prisoners' property procedures in Standing Order 1C. It also cancels and replaces other instructions relating to prisoners' property ie CI 48/1992, CI 51/1992, IG 104/1995, IG 87/1996, PSI 23/1997, and part 1 of Standing Order 4.

25  Para 2.10.

26  *R (Coleman) v Governor of HMP Wayland and others* [2009] EWHC 1005 (Admin).

possibly visitors, to criminal sanctions for conveying unauthorised articles into prisons (see further chapter 7).

5.19    The number of items that can be sent or handed in by relatives and friends has been severely reduced over the past 13 years since the introduction of the Incentives and Earned Privileges Scheme (IEPS see below) in 1995 but unconvicted prisoners retain the right to have clean clothes sent in from outside prison[27] and PSO 4550 para 2.31 confirms that religious items essential to the practice of faith can be handed in.

## Reception, property record cards and seals

5.20    All property bag seals must be checked against the Prisoner Escort Record, and all property accompanying a prisoner into prison must be searched and recorded on the property record card,[28] which is created for and accompanies each prisoner, whenever he or she is moved. Prisoners must be allowed access to property authorised to be held in possession as soon as is practical after completion of the reception process. Any action in relation to an item that a prisoner is not allowed to retain in possession must be recorded on the stored property card (form F2056C).

5.21    Any money which a prisoner has in possession on arrival at the prison, or which is later handed or sent in, must be paid into an account credited to the prisoner but under the governor's control.[29] The amount must be recorded and the prisoner asked to confirm in writing that the record is correct.

5.22    Passports or other forms of identification belonging to foreign national prisoners who have been served with a notice of intention to deport should be forwarded to the UK Border Agency. In other cases prisoners must be advised that wherever possible valuable property should be posted or handed out to a relative or friend.

5.23    Prisoners' claims for compensation for valuable property often fail due to the description on their property cards of items as yellow or white metal, rather than gold or silver. This is in accordance with the instructions in PSO 1250 for staff not to take assertions of the value of an item at face value. Valuable items must be placed in sealed bags, with the seal numbers recorded, signed for by the pris-

---

27  PR rule 23(1).

28  See Annex D to PSO 1250.

29  *Duggan v Governor of HMP Full Sutton* [2004] 1 WLR 1010. This means for relatives and friends sending money to prisoners that they must write cheques or postal orders to 'The Governor' but then send the money to the prisoner.

oner, and securely stored. The integrity of the seals must be checked when a prisoner is transferred from another establishment.

5.24   Property records (including old completed cards) must be retained in the prisoner's core record in accordance with PSO 9020 (Data Protection and Freedom of Information). Prisoners who want to see a copy of their property card should be able to do so without needing to make a full request for Data Protection Act disclosure.[30] All property bags into which property has been placed for storage or transfer must be sealed with a uniquely numbered security seal which must be recorded on the property card. The prisoner must be asked to sign the card to confirm that the record is correct and the bags have been properly sealed. Whenever a bag is opened or a seal becomes damaged, a new seal must be attached and its number recorded, ideally in the prisoner's presence. The prisoner must be asked to confirm in writing that a new seal has been applied. If a prisoner refuses to sign the property card, their refusal, and the reason, if known, must be recorded.

## Stored property

5.25   The Prison Service accepts in PSO 1250 that although 'storage of prisoners' excess property, either locally or centrally, is in principle an exceptional or temporary measure', it does not have a power 'to require prisoners to dispose of property which has been accepted, nor to dispose of it without their consent'. If property cannot be handed out, the Prison Service is therefore obliged to store it. Excess property of prisoners with less than six months to serve and those held solely under immigration powers, must be held locally. Other stored property is sent to the National Distribution Centre at Branston, although the governor of whichever prison the prisoner is currently held in remains responsible for it and for any loss or damage incurred.[31] If property remains unclaimed for three years after discharge, then it can be sold and the money obtained donated to NACRO.[32]

## Authorised items

5.26   Prisoners may retain in-possession authorised property appropriate to their privilege level under any locally operating IEP scheme

---

30   PSO 9020 para 4.9 – ad hoc requests.
31   Details of the procedures for storing property at Branston are given in Annex C to PSO 1250.
32   PR rule 44(4): see also *R (Coleman) v Governor of HMP Wayland and Secretary of State for Justice* [2009] EWHC 1005 (Admin).

or facilities list, subject to the limitations of volumetric control. The following items are commonly allowed to be held in possession, but governors have discretion to vary the list as they consider appropriate for local circumstances and can restrict some items on security or other grounds:

- newspapers, magazines and books (excluding any the governor considers offensive or inappropriate)[33]
- a combined sound system, or a radio combined with a record, cassette or compact disc player, with records, cassettes or CDs, and earphones
- a computer, floppy discs, etc (when permitted for legal work or other purposes)[34]
- smoking materials (where smoking is allowed[35]), including up to 62.5 grams of loose tobacco, or 80 cigarettes or cigars or a combination of both for convicted prisoners, or 137.5 grams or 180 cigarettes for unconvicted prisoners
- locally approved games, including approved electronic games and players (only for Standard and Enhanced prisoners – no over-18 games are permitted to prisoners of any age[36])
- materials related to cell hobbies
- one birdcage and one small bird, where birds are allowed
- writing and drawing materials
- a wrist watch
- an electric shaver
- batteries for personal possessions, of an approved type and quantity
- toiletries
- one wedding ring or other plain ring
- one medallion or locket

---

33  Details of the procedures for the 'confiscation or withholding of newspapers, periodicals, magazines and books and other unauthorised items, and offensive displays' are given in chapter 3 of PSO 1250. Unreasonable decisions to withhold publications can be challenged with reference to article 10 of the ECHR. The Ombudsman has upheld several such complaints both in relation to political material and to pornographic publications.

34  Detail on the Prison Service's obligation to provide computers for legal work is given in PSIs 20/2005 and 5/2002 (which was replaced by function 4 of the National Security Framework).

35  Smoking is permitted in cells in adult prisons and within parts of YOIs where all prisoners are over the age of 18. It is not permitted in STCs. The Smoke Free Legislation (Health Act 2006), implemented in prisons by PSI 9/2007, brought in restrictions on where prisoners can smoke.

36  See PSI 32/2008 restricting prisoner access to games consoles and games.

- religious texts and artefacts, and incense (see below)
- photographs and pictures, in unglazed frames (excluding any the governor considers offensive or inappropriate)[37]
- unpadded greetings cards
- a calendar
- a diary or personal organiser
- an address book
- postage stamps and envelopes
- medication (including items used by diabetics), provided that the governor and health care staff are satisfied that the potential risk to the prisoner's health and safety is acceptable, and that arrangements are in place for the appropriate and safe storage of the medication to minimise the risk to other prisoners and maintain the integrity of the medicine. Otherwise, medication, drugs and prescriptions must be retained by healthcare staff
- disability aids.

The existence of local facility lists which vary from prison to prison has given rise to confusion and complaints. In one challenge brought by a prisoner, the Ombudsman upheld a complaint by a prisoner that a stereo system, lawfully purchased at one prison in accordance with the local property list and IEP scheme, should not be confiscated at another prison, even though the item did not meet the specifications on that establishment's facilities list. The complaint was initially rejected by the Prison Service but was eventually accepted in the face of litigation.

## Televisions

5.27    In-cell TV was introduced in 1998 and is now available throughout the prison estate. TV is provided as an incentive to good behaviour, with prisoners on standard and enhanced regimes renting a TV from the Prison Service for £1.00 per week, while those on basic regime are only permitted in-cell TV in exceptional circumstances.[38]

---

37  Guidance on access to photos of children for prisoners convicted of sex offences against minors was contained within the Public Protection Manual, which has recently been withdrawn; however such prisoners are likely to be subject to close scrutiny of pictures including children.

38  See PSO 4000 chapter 3.

## Religious items

5.28   The PSO 4550 on religion states that prisoners must be allowed to have in possession, or have access to such artefacts, texts, and incense, as are required by their religion. A list of approved items is given in that PSO. Any religious books or artefacts held in possession (or in storage) must be treated with appropriate care and respect.

## Volumetric control

5.29   The Woodcock Report into the 1994 escape from Whitemoor recommended that, in the light of concerns about the amount of property that could be accumulated by long-term prisoners in the dispersal estate:

> A volumetric control of all prisoners' possessions should be introduced forthwith to reduce dramatically the amount of property in possession/storage and facilitate effective searching.

5.30   The amount of property held in possession by any prisoner is now limited to that which fits into two standard size, volumetric control boxes. The property need not be kept in the boxes continuously. In addition, prisoners may have in possession the following items:

- one birdcage (in establishments where birds are permitted)
- a sound system or other item which is too large to fit into an empty volumetric control box (eg a guitar or other musical instrument)
- legal papers
- bedding up to the standard cell scale issue. Additional bedding is subject to volumetric control
- one set of clothing (whether prisoner's own clothing or prison issue), including that worn when the volume of property is monitored
- posters etc
- items held by unconvicted prisoners under PR rule 43(1) (ie books, newspapers, writing materials and other means of occupation)[39]
- items held in possession for the care of babies in mother and baby units
- religious texts and artefacts, and incense, essential for the practice of the prisoner's religion.[40]

39  See also PSO 4600 annex B.
40  See PSO 4550 (Religion Manual) paras 1.45 and 2.18–2.31 as well as the faith annexes, which give detailed guidance on each religion in chapter 1 of that PSO.

Governors must consider applications by individual prisoners for additional items to be held in possession outside volumetric control limits, such as outsize medical equipment. Education materials, food, consumables, cooking utensils and cell hobbies items held in possession are subject to volumetric control although some prisons will arrange for such items to be held in the education department or in wing communal freezers or kitchens.

5.31    Once the volumetric control limit is reached prisoners are encouraged to hand or send the excess items out either by post or via visits. Any excess property still remaining may be placed in storage. All actions must be recorded on the appropriate property card.

## Cell clearance

5.32    Cell clearances may take place when a prisoner has died, escaped, absconded, failed to return from release on temporary licence, been segregated, or been transferred to hospital. Vacated cells are to be secured and checked as soon as possible. Governors must ensure that two officers are present at all cell clearances, and arrange for all property left by the prisoner to be recorded on a Cell Clearance Certificate and placed in property bags and sealed.[41]

# Exercise and association

5.33    Prisoners who do not have jobs within the prison often complain of being allowed out of their cells just once per day, for an hour, and spending the remainder of the day within the cell (colloquially known as '23-hour bang-up'). Until 1996 the Prison Rules allowed for a statutory one hour's exercise in the open air once a day. This was then changed by rule 30 (previously rule 27), which states that, 'If the weather permits and subject to the need to maintain good order and discipline, a prisoner shall be given the opportunity to spend time in the open air at least once every day, for such period as may be reasonable in the circumstances'. The rationale was that regimes were improving and prisoners getting exercise and fresh air when moving to workshops, education classes, visits, the gym etc, so the need for a statutory outdoor exercise period no longer existed. The Prison Service was then forced to qualify the change in relation to prisoners on more restricted regimes, leading to the issuing of PSI 50/1998 and

41   PSO 1250 paras 3.5–3.7.

PSO 4725, which state that prisoners in segregation or otherwise on a severely restricted regime *must* be provided with the opportunity to spend a minimum of one hour in the open air each day, as must unconvicted prisoners who exercise their right not to work.[42] The European Prison Rules suggest that the provision of one hour's exercise a day in the open air should be mandatory.[43]

5.34 The YOI and STC rules do not contain specific provisions for periods of exercise in the open air, presumably as the provision for exercise in the form of physical education is greater, with 'physical fitness' being listed as one of the core aims of the YOI regime[44] and 'physical education' listed in the STC Rules as part of the programme.[45]

In addition to the time out of cell specified through the Prison Rules, the Prison Service used to include in its annual business plan an aspiration to provide prisoners with more time out-of-cell. In 1998 Jack Straw told parliament that one of the Prison Service's key performance targets would be:

> To ensure that by 31 March 1998 at least 60 per cent of prisoners are held in establishments which normally unlock all prisoners on the standard or enhanced regime for at least 10 hours per week day.[46]

However, in subsequent years this target, which was never legally enforceable, has vanished from the business plan. Likewise, while earlier versions of PSO 4000 on incentives and earned privileges listed 'association between an establishment's minimum and 12 hours' as a key earnable privilege, the latest version of that PSO, issued in 2006, merely describes the privilege as 'time out of cell for association'.

---

42  See also PSO 4600 para 1.11.

43  EPR rule 27.

44  YOIR rule 3: '(1) The aim of a young offender institution shall be to help offenders to prepare for their return to the outside community. (2) The aim mentioned in paragraph (1) shall be achieved, in particular, by: (a) providing a programme of activities, including education, training and work designed to assist offenders to acquire or develop personal responsibility, self-discipline, physical fitness, interests and skills and to obtain suitable employment after release ...'.

45  STCR rule 27(1): A trainee shall be occupied in education, training, physical education and programmes designed to tackle offending behaviour provided in accordance with rule 3 of these rules.

46  *Hansard* HC Deb 28 October 1997 vol 299 col 774-5W.

# Work, pay, education and other activities

## Work

5.35 Work is compulsory for adult convicted prisoners. PR rule 31(1) requires prisoners to do 'useful work' for a maximum of 10 hours per
day. Work required to be done in the 'ordinary course of detention'
does not count as 'forced or compulsory labour' for the purposes of
Article 4 of the ECHR[47]. It is a disciplinary offence for convicted prisoners to refuse to work or not to work properly.[48] Guidance on work
in prison is still contained in Standing Order 6A (although SO6B on
pay has been replaced by PSO 4460). PR rule 18 and YOIR rule 35
provide that prisoners who are practising Christians should not be
required to do any 'unnecessary' work on Sunday, Christmas Day or
Good Friday, and that prisoners of other religions should not be required to do unnecessary work on their days of religious observance.

5.36 In order to allocate prisoners to suitable types of employment, the
governor and the medical officer have responsibility for classifying
them as No 1 (heavy), No 2 (medium), and No 3 (light) labour, and
they should not be required to do work of a heavier type than their
labour grade.[49] Prisoners who are ill may be completely excused from
work by the medical officer.[50]

5.37 During the past ten years there has been a massive increase in
the number of private contractors now running prison workshops.
Whereas in the past the employer of nearly every prison worker was
the Prison Service, it is now standard practice for outside companies
to run prison industries. It remains the responsibility of the governor
to ensure that safe systems of work are in operation, and delegates
this responsibility to the members of staff who are in charge of each
work area. Health and Safety Executive Inspectors may conduct inspections under the Health and Safety at Work Act 1974.[51]

---

47 ECHR article 4(3). For the purpose of this article the term 'forced or
   compulsory labour' shall not include: (a) any work required to be done in the
   ordinary course of detention imposed according to the provisions of article 5 of
   this Convention or during conditional release from such detention.

48 PR rule 51(21), YOIR rule 55(24). See also PSO 2000 paras 6.106–6.111 for
   detailed guidance, including on distinction between charges under rule 51(21)
   and 55(24) for not working once at a place of work and under rules 51(18) or
   (21) and 54 (20) or (25) for refusing to go to a place of work.

49 Standing Order 6A para 9.

50 PR rule 31(2), YOIR rule 37(3), and in respect of 'regime activities' STCR rule
   27(6).

51 SO 6A paras 14–15.

5.38    The YOI Rules require that prisoners are engaged in education, training courses, work and physical education.[52] If an hour's exercise is provided on that day, they can be required to take part in such activities for up to a total of 11 hours, and if no exercise period is provided, for a total of ten hours, provided they are not required to participate in a single activity for more than eight hours.[53] Work shall 'so far as practicable, be such as will foster personal responsibility and an inmate's interests and skills and help him to prepare for his return to the community'[54] and training courses similarly 'be such as will foster personal responsibility and an inmate's interests and skills and improve his prospects of finding suitable employment after release and 'such as to enable inmates to acquire suitable qualifications'.[55]

## Pay

5.39    PR rule 31(6) makes provision for adult prisoners to be paid for their work, and rule 34(5) of the YOI Rules provides for young offenders to be paid for their work or other participation in regime related activities. Further details on prisoners' pay are contained in PSO 4460, which sets out guidance on rates of pay and the deductions that can be made.

5.40    Mandatory minimum weekly pay rates are:

- Unemployed £2.50
- Employed rate £4.00
- Short-term sick £2.50
- Long-term sick/retired/maternity leave/full-time childcare £3.25
- Outside hospital allowance £4.35 (60p per day)

5.41    There has been no change to these minimum rates since the mid-1990s. A Prison Service proposal to increase the unemployment rate to £4.00 and the employed rate to £5.00 was vetoed by Prime Minister Gordon Brown in April 2008.

5.42    Many prison jobs do in fact pay way above the minimum but access to schemes involving higher rates of pay than the standard rates are linked to which level prisoners are on in the Incentives and Earned Privileges Scheme. Where prisoners are earning significantly higher rates of pay (for example when working outside prison when in a resettlement unit), no deductions from their earnings can be

52  YOIR rule 37(1).
53  YOIR rule 37(4).
54  YOIR rule 40(1).
55  YOIR rule 39.

made for 'board and lodging'. Such deductions were being made until 1998, when the legality of the deductions was challenged in judicial review proceedings.[56]

## Education

5.43    Prisoners of compulsory school age must participate in education or training courses for at least 15 hours per week.[57] Those in Secure Training Centres must do so for at least 25 hours per week.[58] The Prison Service Core Curriculum is set out in PSO 4200.

5.44    Prisoners above compulsory school age are also encouraged to participate in education, both as a core activity and as a hobby, with the Prison Rules stating that educational classes must be arranged at every prison and reasonable facilities shall be afforded to prisoners who wish to do so to improve their education by training by distance learning, private study and recreational classes, in their spare time.[59] Specific provision should be made for prisoners with special educational needs. [60] PSO 4205 on Education in Prisons was introduced in 2000 and describes the purpose of education provision in prison as 'to address the offending behaviour of inmates, by improving employability and thus reduce the likelihood of re-offending upon release'. This led to an increased emphasis on Basic Skills, which some prisoners complained was accompanied by a reduction in the variety of educational opportunities, particularly for higher education. A significant number of long-term prisoners do however take university level qualifications. Arrangements for taking Open University courses are set out in PSO 4201.

## Gym/physical education

5.45    The Prison Rules state that in normal circumstances prisoners over 21 should be given the opportunity to participate in physical education for at least one hour a week and for those under 21 to do so for an average of two hours a week.[61]

---

56  PSI 86/1999 and PSO 4100 Repayment of Deductions for Board and Lodgings.
57  PR rule 32(4), YOIR rule 38(2).
58  STCR rule 28(2).
59  PR rule 32.
60  PR rule 32(3), YOIR rule 38(3).
61  PR rule 29 and YOIR rule 41.

## Library

5.46   All prisons have libraries, the overwhelming majority of which are run by local authorities. All prisoners are entitled to borrow and exchange library books.[62] PSO 6710 on prison libraries contains a list of publications. These include all PSOs and PSIs (which includes both the Prison Discipline Manual and the Lifer Manual as both are now in PSO form), the Race Relations Manual and the Foreign Prisoners' Resource Pack. The European Convention on Human Rights (ECHR) and related international standards such as the European Prison Rules and the UN Minimum Standards must also be available. A selection of legal books on criminal law and prison law are mandatory purchases.

## Incentives and Earned Privileges Scheme (IEPS)

5.47   Access to many of the facilities described so far in this chapter at any level other than the base level set out in the Prison Rules relies heavily on the level a prisoner is at in the IEPS. IEPS was introduced in 1995, several years after the recommendation by Lord Justice Woolf in his 1991 Report into the 1990 Strangeways prison protest that there should be 'incentives' and 'disincentives' towards good and bad behaviour. PR rule 8 and YOIR rule 6 now require every prison and YOI to provide a system of privileges which can be granted to prisoners in addition to the minimum entitlements under the Rules, subject to their reaching and maintaining specified standards of conduct and performance. There is a separate scheme for juveniles that is discussed further below.[63]

5.48   The IEPS has been updated and amended several times since its initial introduction in 1995. The stated aims in the most recent guidance (PSO 4000, issued 2006) are:

- to encourage responsible behaviour by prisoners;
- to encourage effort and achievement in work and other constructive activity by prisoners;
- to encourage sentenced prisoners to engage in OASys[64] and sentence planning and benefit from activities designed to reduce reoffending; and

---

62   PR rule 33, YOIR rule 26, STCR rule 21.
63   See the YJB's *Rewards and Sanctions Systems*.
64   See PSO 2205.

- to create a more disciplined, better-controlled and safer environment for prisoners and staff.

5.49 The IEPS cannot affect prisoners' core statutory entitlements to visits and although additional privileges can be incurred under the scheme, prisoners cannot be deprived of their minimum right for example, to visits or time out of cells.

5.50 There are three IEP regime levels: Basic, Standard and Enhanced[65] and the prison can either be structured around wings offering the different levels of privileges or by simply conferring the privileges to individual prisoners. The level a prisoner is on determines the number of privileges to which he or she has access. The range of privileges available depends upon which establishment a prisoner is in; however local schemes must, unless the nature of the prison renders it irrelevant, include the six key earnable privileges:

- extra and improved visits
- eligibility to earn higher rates of pay
- access to in-cell television
- opportunity to wear own clothes
- access to private cash
- time out of cell for association.[66]

5.51 It is open to individual prisons to add additional earnable privileges. The criteria to bear in mind when deciding what additional privileges to include are:

- Does the privilege meet the requirements of security, control and safety?
- Will it encourage prisoners to behave better in custody?
- Will it encourage prisoners to engage in OASys and sentence planning and therefore discourage further offending and help their rehabilitation?
- Is it likely to be acceptable to reasonable public opinion, to be justifiable if criticised, and not likely to bring NOMS into disrepute?[67]

5.52 The types of privileges that might be included are access to the gym, additional possessions or better access to cooking facilities. Access to educational facilities should not be removed under the IEPS.[68]

---

65  PSO 4000 para 1.8.1.
66  PSO 4000 paras 2.4 and 3.6–3.11.
67  PSO 4000 para 2.6.
68  *R (Cooper) v Governor of HMP Littlehey* [2002] EWCA Civ 632.

## Special groups

5.53    IEPS applies to unconvicted prisoners and immigration detainees, with modifications to take account of their particular position.[69] So, remand prisoners cannot be required to work or take part in other activities and foreign nationals should normally have greater access to telephones rather than visits factored into the scheme. Provision should be made for an appropriate scheme for vulnerable prisoners so that they do not face disadvantage in accessing privileges and prisoners with disabilities cannot be penalised.

## Reviews and warnings

5.54    Decisions about privilege level must be open, fair and consistent.[70] The procedures and the findings must be recorded and involve at least two members of staff. Views must be sought from across the establishment, including education and workshop staff, reports from any relevant treatment programmes and personal officers (if applicable). The decision must be endorsed by a manager at no less than senior officer level or the equivalent in contracted prisons (where operationally possible).

5.55    The determination of a prisoner's privilege level must be based on patterns of behaviour rather than a single incident (unless it is especially serious), be separate from the disciplinary system, and reviewed regularly. The guidance on what type of behaviour should be rewarded under the scheme lists the following:

- Effort and achievement in work and other constructive activities (ie participating fully in sentence planning), constructive attitude and willingness to explore the potential for benefit from relevant treatment programmes.
- Non-violence: no violent or threatening behaviour, no bullying or intimidation, and no aggressive or offensive language.
- Non-discrimination, no racist, obscene or other offensive remarks or gestures.
- Civility: keeping noise down to an acceptable level, no rudeness, appropriate manners.
- Mutual respect: co-operation with staff in the performance of their duties, compliance with staff's reasonable expectations, co-

69  PSO 4000 paras 3.15–3.19.
70  PSO 4000 paras 2.13–2.15.

operation with personal officers, no attempts to deceive or manipulate staff, respect for other prisoners.
- Treating others fairly.
- Supporting the efforts of other prisoners to engage with their sentence plans, address their offending and live more constructive lives.
- Respect for establishment rules and routines: no unauthorised drugs or alcohol, co-operation with mandatory drug tests, no selling, trading, taxing or gambling, following reasonable written and posted procedures, staying within bounds, compliance with rules during visits, compliance with ROTL, due regard for personal hygiene and health.
- Due regard for others' health and safety: cleanliness and tidiness of cells and other areas, proper use of equipment, materials and facilities, compliance with fire safety procedures, including rules on smoking.[71]

5.56 After a review prisoners must be informed of the local appeal process including their right to complain, usually by submitting a complaint form. PR rule 8(4) imposes a statutory duty to give reasons for adverse decisions and details of the appeals process. Reasons for decisions need not be lengthy or detailed, but must be sufficient for the prisoner to understand what criteria he or she has failed to meet, the evidence to support this assertion, and why any representations have been rejected. Automatic reviews of prisoners on the basic IEP level must take place in the first instance within seven days, and at least once a month thereafter (14 days for young offenders). Any representations that are made must be recorded and the decisions notified to the prisoner. The Court of Appeal have accepted that there is an arguable case that prisoners should have a proper chance to make representations before being downgraded to basic[72] but this has never been the subject of a full court decision. Generally, the courts have expressed a reluctance to interfere in IEPS decisions, stating that as the decisions are effectively about matters of judgment in relation to prisoners' behaviour these decisions fall within the administrative sphere and that absent any procedural irregularity in the decision making process, the prisoner would need to establish either bad faith or 'crude irrationality'.[73]

---

71 PSO 4000 para 3.12.
72 *R v Governor of Featherstone and others ex p Bowen* [1997] EWHC 917 (Admin).
73 *R v Secretary of State for Home Department ex p Hepworth, Fenton-Palmer and Baldonzy* and *R v Parole Board ex p Winfield* [1997] EWHC 324 (Admin).

## Transfers between prisons

5.57    PSO 4000 states: that whenever possible, the local scheme must allow prisoners on progressive transfer to retain their privilege level. As a minimum, they must be able to retain the national key privileges wherever these are available. Prisoners who are returned from the resettlement estate without a current IEP level must be treated as new receptions and placed on standard level.

## Private cash allowances

5.58    The IEPS allows prisoners on each level access to different amounts of the money in their private cash account.[74] These are as follows:

| *Unconvicted* | *Convicted* |
| --- | --- |
| basic £22.00 | basic £4.00 |
| standard £47.50 | standard £15.50 |
| enhanced £51.00 | enhanced £25.00 |

## Maintaining innocence

5.59    Since the introduction of IEPS there have been a number of challenges brought by prisoners who, because they maintained their innocence and therefore did not fully participate in sentence planning, were denied access to Enhanced regime and privileges, despite impeccable custodial behaviour. Firstly in 1998 in the case of *Hepworth* five prisoners maintaining their innocence challenged various decisions to do with parole, categorisation and refusal to grant Enhanced status within the IEPS at HMP Wymott on the basis that improper account was taken of their denial of guilt. The IEP policy, which prevented the applicants progressing to Enhanced status because they were not participating in the Sex Offender Treatment Programme, was held to be lawful.[75] Another case along similar lines[76] was unsuccessful in 2001. Part of their argument in that case was based on the fact that prisoners denying their offence are discriminated against in their access to the right to family life under article 8 of the ECHR, as

---

74  See PSI 30/2008.

75  *R v Secretary of State for Home Department ex p Hepworth, Fenton-Palmer and Baldonzy and R v Parole Board ex p Winfield* [1997] EWHC 324 (Admin).

76  *R v Secretary of State for Home Department ex p Potter and others* [2001] EWHC 1041 (Admin).

prisoners on Standard regime receive less or shorter visits than those on Enhanced. Again the courts did not accept this. The same position was restated in 2004 in the case of *Green*.[77]

## IEP systems for children held in YOIs, STCs and SCHs

5.60   YOIs holding under 18-year-olds are required to have a 'rewards and sanctions' scheme in accordance with YJB guidance in the units which hold the under 18-year-olds.[78] STCs are required to have systems of privileges[79] and CHRs may have policies to promote 'appropriate behaviour'.[80] The YJB guidance is called *Rewards and Sanctions Systems*.[81]

5.61   As with the Prison Service guidance it suggests that such systems are based on a number of levels, although it states that institutions may wish to consult on the naming of these levels so that they become, for example 'bronze, silver and gold' rather than basic, standard and enhanced.[82] The difference to the IEP framework is that the YJB guidance includes both rewards for good behaviour and sanctions, beyond being downgraded. The scale of suggested sanctions[83] runs from a verbal reprimand, to criminal prosecution where appropriate. The suggested rewards are similar to the Prison Service scheme and include increased access to possessions, facilities and activities. The guidance states that there should be access to a complaints procedure to appeal decisions under the rewards and sanctions system.[84]

## Food

5.62   PR rule 24 and YOIR rule 20 state that: 'the food provided shall be wholesome, nutritious, well prepared and served, reasonably varied and sufficient in quality'. STCR rule 16 is couched in similar terms and adds that 'so far as practicable the governor shall ensure that

---

77   *R (Green) v Governor of HMP Risley and Secretary of State for the Home Department* [2004] EWHC 596 (Admin).
78   PSO 4950 para 2.13.
79   STCR rule 6.
80   CHR rule 17(2).
81   Available at the YJB website.
82   Rewards and Sanctions Systems paras 6.1–6.2.
83   Rewards and Sanctions Systems Appendix 5.
84   Rewards and Sanctions Systems para 5.26.

meals are provided three times a day at regular intervals and that at each main meal there is a choice for each course, one of which shall be hot at one of those meals'. PSO 4550 in relation to prisons and YOIs provides that 'prisoners must have a diet which accords with the requirements of their religion as agreed between a relevant religious body and Prison Service headquarters'. Each section of the PSO gives specific guidance on the relevant dietary requirement for the particular religion, and detailed guidance on veganism is also included in appendix 3. Despite this, many prisoners complain about the quality of prison food and also find it difficult to obtain meals which fit in with their religious or medical dietary requirements. Bread and water diets as a punishment were abolished in British prisons in 1974[85] and prisoners cannot be punished by withholding food from them.[86]

5.63    PSO 5000 on prison catering services gives detailed guidance to establishments on food hygiene and safety and prisons' compliance with the Food Safety (General Food Hygiene) Regulations 1995. It also provides guidance on menu management and permissible variations in diet, according to religion and other preferences. The Food Safety Act 1990 and Food Hygiene (England) Regulations 2006 are binding in prison establishments.

5.64    Prisoners may complain about the food through the complaints procedure. The Prisons' Ombudsman has on occasion upheld prisoners' complaints concerning food, and made recommendations to the Prison Service for improvement.

## Hygiene

5.65    The Rules of all the institutions require prisoners to be provided with toilet articles necessary for health and cleanliness, which shall be replaced as necessary.[87] This clearly instructs the prison not to charge prisoners for essential items. A wider variety of toiletries can be purchased at prisoners' own expense via the prison canteen system. The Ombudsman has upheld a complaint from a vegan prisoner who was told that he must pay for vegan toiletries. Although the guidance on

---

85  Prison (Amendment) Rules 1974, laid before Parliament 25 April 1974, commencement date 1 June 1974.

86  *R v Governor of HMP Frankland ex p Russell and Wharrie* [2000] 1 WLR 2027.

87  PR rule 28(1), YOIR rule 24(1), STCR rule 20(1).

veganism in PSO 4550 does indicate that vegan toiletries must be stocked in the canteen for purchase, the Ombudsman agreed that to comply with the Prison Rules in the case of a vegan prisoner, basic items must be made available free of charge.

5.66　　The Prison and YOI Rules say that prisoners must wash 'at proper times' and have a hot bath or shower on reception and thereafter at least once a week.[88] The STC Rules say that prisoners may have a bath or shower daily.[89]

## Religion

5.67　　Insofar as religious issues are relevant to matters such as work, food, property or discipline, this book addresses them under the appropriate subject heading. It is a statutory requirement for the governor to record a prisoners' religion[90] and PR rule 13 requires that the 'prisoner is to be treated as belonging to the religious denomination stated in the record'. The requirement is to record the religion declared by the prisoner and does not involve any form of objective assessment. Prisoners may change their registered religion by giving notice in writing to the governor.[91] The faiths that appear on the religious registration card are: Bahai, Buddhism, Chinese, Christianity, Hinduism, Jainism, Judaism, Islam, Sikhism, Zoroastrianism (Parsee) but this is not a definitive list of recognised religions and there is nothing to prevent a prisoner from registering as, for example, a Rastafarian. Although paganism is not included on the registration card, PSO 4550 has detailed guidance about the practice of paganism.

5.68　　The prison chapel is to be used as the place of worship for all Christian denominations and suitable facilities must be provided for all other denominations, such facilities to include adequate amenities for washing or other practices associated with the needs of worship.[92] Provision should also be made for religious education and guidance that is relevant to all faiths, either in groups or in classes.[93]

---

88　PR rule 28(2), YOIR rule 24(2).
89　STCR rule 20(2).
90　PA 1952 s10(5).
91　PSO 4550 para 1.13 – the PSO also has a pro forma that can be sued for this purpose.
92　PSO 4550 paras 1.14–1.15.
93　PSO 4550 para 1.32.

## Race equality

5.69   In 2003 the Commission for Racial Equality (CRE) conducted an investigation into the treatment of ethnic minority prisoners, following the murder of Zahid Mubarak by his racist cell mate at Feltham YOI in March 2000. The CRE's investigation made a number of findings of racial discrimination against the Prison Service and identified 14 failure areas, including prisoner treatment, access to goods, facilities and services, discipline, transfers and allocations, complaints and investigations. Instead of using its power to bring enforcement proceedings against the Prison Service, the CRE worked with the Prison Service to devise a five-year action plan for race equality.

5.70   In December 2008, the Prison Service issued a report reviewing its performance against the CRE five-year action plan.[94] The review concluded that although the Prison Service had made progress tackling overt racism, such as racial abuse, and implementing policies and processes to promote race equality, there had been much less change in terms of the experience of BME prisoners, particularly in areas of prison life that involve the use of discretion by prison officers. The report states, for example, that on average:

- Black prisoners are about 30 per cent more likely than White British prisoners to be on 'basic regime'.
- Black prisoners are about 50 per cent more likely than White British prisoners to be in the segregation unit for reasons of good order or discipline, despite evidence they are not more likely to get into trouble.
- Black prisoners are about 60 per cent more likely than White British prisoners to have force used against them.[95]

5.71   The Race Relations Act (RRA) 1976 as originally enacted offered prisoners a means of seeking legal redress for race discrimination in the provision of goods, services and facilities. The Race Relations (Amendment) Act (RR(A)A) 2000 amended RRA 1976 to extend the protection of the Act to public bodies in carrying out any of their

---

94   *Race Review 2008, Implementing Race Equality in Prisons – Five Years On*, Ministry of Justice (www.hmprisonservice.gov.uk/news/index.asp?id=9355,22,6,22,0,0).The Equality and Human Rights Commission, which has taken over the responsibilities of Commission for Racial Equality, Disability Rights Commission and Equal Opportunities Commission, agreed a new action plan with NOMS, published in April 2009, as part of a broader *NOMS 2009 – 2012 Single Equality Scheme.*

95   *Race Review 2008: Implementing Race Equality – Five Years On* p37.

public functions and RRA 1976 therefore now covers all aspects of prison life.[96] RR(A)A 2000 went further, expanding the existing section 71 to require all public bodies to have due regard to the need to eliminate unlawful racial discrimination and to promote equality of opportunity and good relations between persons of different racial groups.[97] This 'general duty' requires the Prison Service to conduct race equality impact assessments of all policies and practices that may adversely affect different racial groups,[98] and failure to do so may render a policy, practice or decision unlawful.[99] Claims under RRA 1976 must be brought within six months of the act complained of, or if an act extends over a period, six months from the end of that period.[100] The courts have discretion to permit a claim after the six-month limitation period if they consider it just and equitable to do so.[101]

5.72    Under the statutory 'questionnaire procedure' established by RRA 1976[102] prisoners who believe they have been discriminated against can ask the Prison Service questions to obtain information about the facts of their complaint and to enquire into the reasons behind the actions taken by the Prison Service. The purpose of the questionnaire procedure is to help people to bring a claim for discrimination under RRA 1976, but prisoners do not have to be bringing a claim in order to use it. In line with the six-month time limit for bringing a claim under RRA 1976, the questionnaire must be submitted within six months of the act of discrimination complained of.

5.73    PSO 2800[103] sets out the procedures prison establishments should follow to meet their legal obligations under RRA 1976, and the process by which prisoners can make internal complaints about racist incidents. Whilst religion is not a race relations issue, PSO 2800 recognises that religion is an important factor and the policy also covers complaints about religious discrimination. The policy adopts

---

96  RRA 1976 s19B.

97  RRA 1976 s71A.

98  Guidance to public authorities on how to comply with the general duty is set out in the statutory Code of Practice on the Duty to Promote Race Equality (CRE, 2000).

99  See for example *R (C) (a minor) by his litigation friend MS v Secretary of State for Justice* [2008] EWCA Civ 882, and judicial comments in *R (Kaur and Shah) v Ealing LBC* [2008] EWHC 2062 (Admin).

100  RRA 1976 s68(7)(b).

101  RRA 1976 s68(6).

102  RRA 1976 s65. Guidance and sample questionnaire available from: www. equalityhumanrights.com/Documents/CRE/PDF/rr65.pdf

103  Last update issued 25 September 2006.

the definition of a racist incident recommended by The Stephen Lawrence Inquiry, of:

> *any incident which is perceived to be racist by the victim or any other person.*[104]

5.74    PSO 2800 makes it clear, however, that the use of the term 'racist' is not itself racist language. This specified exception to the subjective nature of the definition covers the not infrequent occurrence of officers inappropriately making a racist incident complaint after being accused of racism by a prisoner.[105]

5.75    As set out in PSO 2800, every prison establishment is required to collect and monitor local data on race equality for key aspects of the prison regime such as adjudications, segregation and IEPS levels, and to devise a race equality action plan.[106] Prisons are also obliged to set up race equality action teams (REAT) chaired by a governor or deputy governor which should meet regularly to develop and implement race equality policies. A key member of the REAT is the race equality officer (REO, previously known as the Race Relations Liaison Officer), a trained individual whose duties include acting as a central point of contact for staff and prisoners seeking information on legislation, policy and practice relating to race equality, and maintaining a record of all racist incidents.[107] The REO is the officer who normally investigates racist incident complaints. Some prisons have a diversity manager, who may also carry out the REO role.[108] The REAT must also include prisoner representatives to put forward the general concerns of other prisoners about racial discrimination within the prison.

5.76    Complaints should be submitted on a Racist Incident Report Form (RIRF) which should be readily available on all wings. If not, a standard COMP1 form can be used. Any complaint that raises concerns of racism should be passed to the REO to deal with in the same way as if it had been submitted on a RIRF.[109] A RIRF may also be used to submit a complaint about an incident of religious discrim-

---

104  PSO 2800 para 6.16.
105  PSO 2800 para 6.24.
106  Details of scope of SMART monitoring can be found in the Race Equality Key Performance Targets Manual. See PSO 2800 para 4.7. Further information on SMART monitoring data can be obtained from the race equality action group of the Prison Service at PSHQ.
107  PSO 2800 paras 3.16 and 3.17.
108  PSO 2800 para 3.20.
109  PSO 2800 para 6.7.

ination or abuse. Complaints must be dealt with as confidentially as possible and in a manner that ensures that all parties involved are safeguarded, including the victim and reporter of the incident. As a matter of best practice, boxes for the submission of RIRF complaints should be located in a position on the wing that is not overlooked by the wing office. Access to the RIRF complaint boxes should also be limited to designated staff.[110]

5.77    A racist incident complaint should be acknowledged within three days and the investigation completed within 28 days of the complaint being made. The prisoner should be informed of the outcome within 14 days of the completion of the investigation. If the prison cannot keep to this timetable they must inform the prisoner and explain the reason for the delay.[111] The investigation itself should be conducted in accordance with PSO 1300 on investigations.[112] Complaints should be determined applying the civil standard of proof, 'on the balance of probabilities'. There remains a concern, however, as identified by the CRE review in 2003, that an unreasonably high standard of proof is often applied in practice, particularly when a complaint of racial discrimination is made against a prison officer.[113] As with all other complaints, prisoners may appeal the final decision on their complaint to the Prisons and Probation Ombudsman.

## Disability

5.78    Prisoners over 60 years old are the fastest growing age group in prison.[114] With the majority of these prisoners suffering some form of chronic illness or disability, and the Prison Service faces a growing challenge to meet its obligations towards disabled prisoners. Under the Disability Discrimination Act (DDA) 1995 as amended by DDA 2005, the Prison Service has duties not to discriminate against disabled prisoners in the provision of goods, facilities and services,[115] or in carrying out its functions as a public body,[116] and to make reasonable adjustments where necessary. The available defences and extent

110  PSO 2800 para 6.5.
111  PSO 2800 para 6.11.
112  PSO 2800 para 6.8.
113  *Race Review 2008: Implementing Race Equality in Prisons – Five Years On*, p73.
114  *DOING TIME: the experiences and needs of older people in prison*, Prison Reform Trust report, 10 July 2008.
115  DDA 1995 ss19–21.
116  DDA 1995 ss21B–21E.

of the duty to make reasonable adjustments vary between the 'goods, facilities and services', and 'public function' provisions, with the duties on the Prison Service in its capacity as a service provider being the most onerous. In the prison context, services include the provision of programmes for offending behaviour, skills, employment or drug treatment, and the Prison Service must therefore provide access to these services for disabled prisoners.

5.79    The DDA 1995 also imposes a positive duty on public authorities to eliminate discrimination and promote equality of opportunity for disabled persons.[117] The Commission for Equality and Human Rights (which replaced the Disability Rights Commission) can take legal action against the Prison Service for failure to carry out their responsibilities under the equality duty by issuing compliance notices.[118]

5.80    DDA 1995 defines disability as:

> a physical or mental impairment which has a substantial and long-term adverse effect on [a person's] ability to carry out normal day-to-day activities.[119]

For the purpose of this definition, 'long term' means 12 months or over.

5.81    Guidance on how these legal obligations under DDA 1995 should be met by the Prison Service is contained in PSO 2855.[120] The Prison Service has committed itself to ensuring that:

> ... all prisoners are able, with reasonable adjustment, to participate equally in all aspects of prison life without discrimination.[121]

5.82    Reasonable adjustments are not limited to structural adjustments, and include adjustments to practices, policies and procedures, or the provision of an in-cell fridge for the storage of medication, for example.

5.83    The Prison Service is covered by the Ministry of Justice disability equality scheme, but every prison must also devise a local action plan to identify and address issues affecting the access of disabled prisoners to facilities, programmes and regime activities.[122] All local policies and practices must be impact assessed for disability issues and action should be taken to address any issue that is identified as adversely affecting disabled prisoners.[123] Every prison should have a disability

---

117  DDA 1995 s49A.
118  Equality Act 2006 s32.
119  DDA 1995 s1(1).
120  Last update 3 April 2008.
121  PSO 2800: Prison Service Standard for Disabled Prisoners.
122  PSO 2855 para 1.8.
123  PSO 2855 para 4.11.

liaison officer (DLO), who should be a source of information and contact point for disabled prisoners, and ensure that disabled prisoners' needs are met.[124] Prisoners should be given the opportunity to declare their disability on induction, or at any future point that they choose to do so.[125] Once a prisoner informs the prison that they have a disability, healthcare officers and the DLO should make arrangements to verify their level of disability, consider the prisoner's needs and arrange for those needs to be met.[126] Healthcare staff also have an ongoing responsibility to advise the DLO, wing officer or other staff who can assist a prisoner, of any issues they are aware of relating to the prisoner's disability, and how those issues should be managed.[127] If a prisoner has a need for remedial physical activity, appropriate facilities must be provided.[128]

5.84   As a matter of best practice, officers should not assume they know what the needs of a disabled prisoner are; disabled prisoners should be consulted on how they feel their disability affects them, and given an opportunity to state their needs.[129] Any significant problem that cannot be resolved between the prisoner and the prison within a reasonable period of time should be referred to the area manager to address.[130]

5.85   Prisoners should be allowed to keep in their possession any form of mobility or sensory aid that they need, such as wheelchairs, crutches or sticks, unless there is a good and justifiable reason why they should not be allowed to do so. If there is a concern that a physical aid presents a security risk, a risk assessment must be carried out and a suitable alternative given to the prisoner.[131] Prisoners with disabilities must be searched in a way that considers the prisoner's disability, and maintains their dignity. The searching officers should ask the prisoner what their needs are, and make sure that the prisoner understands how the search will be conducted before the search begins. If an officer has any doubts about how to search a disabled prisoner they should consult a member of the healthcare team.[132]

124  PSO 2855 para 5.3.
125  PSO 2855 para 6.1.
126  PSO 2855 para 1.3.
127  PSO 2855 para 6.4.
128  PR rule 29(3).
129  PSO 2855 para 6.7.
130  PSO 2855 para 4.5.
131  PSO 2855 para 6.8.
132  PSO 2855 para 6.9. Further guidance is set out in NSF Function 3, Searching People with Injuries or Disabilities.

5.86    Prisoners with disabilities must be allocated to accommodation suitable for their needs, and should not be located within healthcare departments on a routine basis.[133] Reasonable adjustments to accommodation and on the wings should be made, and support provided where necessary, to enable prisoners to stay on normal location. A prisoner with a disability should not be prevented from being re-categorised or refused a transfer simply because of their disability. A prison must consider what reasonable adjustments they can make to accommodate any disabled prisoner that applies to move their establishment.[134]

## Facilities for litigants in person

5.87    Standing Order 16(7) describes a litigant in person as, 'a prisoner who refuses to seek or is unable to obtain professional advice and wishes instead to initiate and/or conduct legal proceedings personally'. The Standing Order was amended by PSO 4600[135] and replaced in 2003 by PSO 2600;[136] however the National Security Framework, which was issued in 2004, still refers to SO 16(7), stating that such a prisoner should be provided the necessary facilities in accordance with article 6, and that such facilities may include:

- provision of a laptop computer under the Access to Justice provisions;[137]
- photocopying of legally privileged papers.

Access to computers is usually restricted to Prison Service issue computers and it is very rare for prisoners to be permitted access to their own computer.[138] Prison issue computers are already modified to meet security needs and so the original PSI 5/2001 which set out the detailed specifications for computers has now been withdrawn.

5.88    The leading case on the use of computers is *R (Ponting) v Governor of HMP Whitemoor*[139] where a prisoner litigant in person with

---

133  PSO 2855 para 6.13.
134  PSO 2855 para 6.40.
135  Unconvicted, unsentenced and civil prisoners, issued February 2003. Updates SO 8, SO 12, SO 16, CI 18/85 and CI 30/90.
136  Legal issues relating to prisoners, issued 2003. Replaces SO 12, SO 16, CI 18/1985 and CI35/1989.
137  PSI 20/2005.
138  *Cooper v HM Prison Service* [2005] EWHC 1715 (Admin).
139  [2002] EWHC 215 (Admin).

dyslexia challenged the degree of access he was being allowed to his computer and the conditions imposed upon his use. Although it was confirmed that article 6 was engaged, the Court of Appeal declined to quash the restrictions accepting that the particular limitations in that case were reasonable. Schiemann LJ did envisage that access to these facilities would have to become more common to ensure fairness in the preparation of cases for litigants in person:

> While I would not go so far as to hold that we have advanced to a stage where access to IT facilities is a precondition of having unimpeded access to the courts, it does seem to me that there are likely to be a significant number of prisoners in respect of whom it can properly be said that without such facilities they are at a sufficient disadvantage vis a vis the other party to litigation such that there is inequality of arms between them. It struck me during the course of the argument that there is much to be said for the proposition that a prisoner suing a public authority represented, say, by the Treasury Solicitor, is seriously disadvantaged if he can only use a pencil, biro or pen while his opponent is equipped with a battery of word processors.[140]

## Production at court

5.89    The Crime (Sentences) Act 1997[141] permits the Secretary of State to produce prisoners in civil proceedings in which they are involved. The power is discretionary and is to be exercised where it is desirable in the interests of justice. The current practice has been strongly influenced by the House of Lords decision in *R v Secretary of State for the Home Department ex p Wynne*[142] and by Lord Donaldson's judgment when the case was in the Court of Appeal.[143] The case was actually dismissed because the prisoner had failed to make a formal application for production but general observations about the issue were given both in the Lords and by the Court of Appeal. The system had been that prisoners were required to pay the costs of their production, although those costs were normally limited to the transport costs and subsistence costs of the escorting officers. For prisoners who could not afford those costs, there was a danger that they would not be able to attend court even when their presence was necessary

---

140  At para 74; the 2005 application by Mr Cooper arguing that he needed access to a computer to send coded messages to the SIS was unsuccessful.

141  Sch 1, para 3.

142  [1993] 1 WLR 115.

143  [1992] QB 406.

and in cases where the claim was being brought against the Secretary of State, it may give rise to the perception that he was acting as judge in his own cause if he were to make a decision on the merits of production. Lord Donaldson found it difficult to envisage cases where the prisoner's production would not be in the interests of justice.

5.90    In most cases the power to make a decision on production has been delegated to Governors, with the exception of category A prisoners who require authorisation from the Directorate of High Security Prisons.[144] The policy guiding those decisions is contained in PSO 4625 which confirms that the primary consideration when dealing with prisoners' applications to attend civil court hearings is the statutory test of 'whether it is in the interests of justice that he or she should attend'.[145] The definition of civil court hearings extends to tribunals and appeal panels such as the Criminal Injuries Compensation Authority, Employment Tribunals or Professional Regulatory and Disciplinary hearings.[146] A balancing act has to be performed between the benefit to the prisoner of attending as against the risk to the public of producing the prisoner. The prisoner's ability or willingness to pay for their production must not be a factor in the decision about whether a prisoner should be produced.[147]

5.91    When considering an application to be produced, attention must be paid to article 6 of the Human Rights Act 1998 which protects the right to a fair trial in both criminal and civil cases. PSO 4625 states: 'If it appears that the prisoner's case will suffer detriment if they do not attend, this would be a strong case for allowing the production'.[148] This presumption is strengthened in instances where the prisoner does not have legal representation in the proceedings. Although it would not be unlawful for a governor to refuse to produce a prisoner in cases where the claim is weak, it is unclear how this assessment is to be made. The costs of production are to be charged at a flat rate of £40.00 comprising a £30.00 fee for the call out costs of the vehicle and £10.00 towards the cost of the petrol for the first nine miles. Additional mileage is charged at £1.00 per mile.[149] The governor should investigate whether the prisoner has the means to pay the charge and has the discretion to levy a lower charge if the prisoner has insuffi-

144  PSO 4625 para 4.3.
145  PSO 4625 para 3.1.
146  PSO 4625 para 1.7.
147  PSO 4625 para 5.1.
148  PSO 4625 para 2.2.
149  PSO 4625 para 5.3.

cient means. In cases where the prisoner refuses to pay, the governor must still reach a decision whether production is necessary in the interests of justice.

5.92    Where there is any doubt whether the Governor will arrange for production, it is possible to obtain an order from the High Court under the Rules of the Supreme Court rule 54.9 which provides that:

(1) An application for a writ of habeas corpus ad testificandum or of habeas corpus ad respondendum must be made on witness statement or affidavit to a judge.

(2) An application for an order to bring up a prisoner, otherwise than by writ of habeas corpus, to give evidence in any proceedings, civil or criminal, before any court, tribunal or justice, must be made on witness statement or affidavit to a judge.

5.93    The making of an order for production by the court does not necessarily address the costs issues if a charge is made.

## CHAPTER 6

# Healthcare, suicide prevention and deaths in custody

*continued*

# Healthcare

## Introduction

6.1    Prisoners and young offenders are entitled to the same standard of healthcare as that available in the community.[1] Despite this prisoners frequently experience difficulties gaining access to prompt medical treatment and delays in being taken to external hospital appointments.

6.2    The measures in place to ensure the quality of healthcare provided within prisons and young offender institutions differ for public and private prisons; private prisons must comply with Prison Service standard 22 on healthcare, which is considered in greater detail below. However, this standard is no longer applicable in public sector prisons where healthcare services are the responsibility of the NHS and thus NHS standards apply.

6.3    HM Chief Inspector of Prisons (HMCIP) is responsible for monitoring standards of healthcare in all prisons through her inspections. HMCIP has agreed a memorandum of understanding with the Healthcare Commission in relation to these inspections to ensure that both inspectorates' responsibilities are met.

## Public sector prisons

6.4    Prior to April 2003 the budgetary responsibility for prison health in public sector prisons rested with the Home Office. However, this responsibility has since been transferred to the Secretary of State for Health, who is now responsible for securing a full range of health services for prisoners under section 3 of the National Health Service Act 1977. The Secretary of State for Health has delegated responsibility for commissioning health services to the NHS Primary Care Trusts (PCTs). The respective duties of the PCT/Prison and the Prison Service in relation to the provision of healthcare in prisons are:[2]

- The PCT is responsible for:
  - Commissioning health services for prisoners.

---

1   This requirement is reflected in the European Prison Rules rule 40, and is set out in the Committee for the Prevention of Torture's general standards on medical services, chapter III para 38 and was confirmed in *R (Brooks) v Secretary of State for Justice* [2008] EWHC 2401.

2   National Partnership Agreement between the Department of Health and the Home Office for the accountability and commissioning of health services for prisoners in public sector prisons in England, January 2007.

- Securing resources for the effective delivery of the aims and objectives of the partnership agreement (which include providing prisoners with access to the same quality and range of healthcare services as the general public receives from the NHS and developing appropriate policies for the healthcare of prisoners).
- Monitoring the performance of prison healthcare against the standards set out in service level agreements entered into between the PCT and the prison.
- Buying and maintaining non fixed, freestanding items such as specialist medical equipment.
- The Prison Service is responsible for:
  - The overall duty of care to prisoners.
  - Supporting the effective delivery of health services for prisoners, regardless of the provider.
  - Managing the healthcare facilities in order to deliver the services set out in the service level agreement.
  - Buying new fixed items, such as dental chairs.

6.5    Local PCTs can commission private healthcare companies to provide healthcare facilities in prison and in some prisons private companies will be responsible for the provision of certain facilities, such as mental health, whilst the local PCT retains responsibility for other facilities, such as primary care. In order to establish who is responsible for healthcare within a public sector prison it is advisable to write to the head of healthcare and/or the PCT prison lead and request this information.

## Private sector prisons

6.6    In private sector prisons the director is responsible for employing healthcare staff. The director can chose whether to employ NHS staff or contract healthcare services out to a private healthcare company. In both cases, the Director will enter into agreements as to the services to be provided. Private sector prisons must comply with the Prison Service standard on healthcare,[3] which requires them to provide prisoners with access to the same range and quality of services as the general public receives from the NHS. The standard sets out minimum requirements on matters such as medical records, in-patient care, health assessment on reception and substance misuse services.

3  *Health Services for Prisoners*, May 2004.

## Secure Training Centres and children's homes

6.7     All Secure Training Centres (STC) are privately run and therefore like private prisons, they can choose whether to commission the healthcare services from a private company or the NHS. A medical officer will be responsible for the provision of healthcare within the STC. If the medical officer considers that any trainee's health is likely to be injuriously affected by continued detention or any conditions of detention, they must report this to the governor and the governor must send the report with his or her own recommendations to the Secretary of State who can consider whether to authorise the trainee's release.[4] The medical officer also has a duty to pay special attention to any trainee whose mental health condition appears to require it and make any special arrangements for the trainee's supervision or care.[5] If the medical officer believes that any trainee has suicidal intentions they must inform the governor and the trainee must be placed under special observation.[6]

6.8     There is an obligation on the registered managers of children's homes to ensure that:[7]

- Each child is registered with a general practitioner.
- Each child has access to such medical, dental, nursing, psychological and psychiatric advice, treatment and other services as he or she may require.
- Each child is provided with such individual support, aids, and equipment as he or she may require as a result of any particular health needs or disability he or she may have.
- Each child is provided with guidance, support and advice on health and personal care issues appropriate to his or her needs and wishes.
- At all times, at least one person on duty at the children's home has suitable first aid qualification.
- Any person appointed to the position of nurse at the children's home is a registered nurse.

6.9     The registered manager of children's homes is also required to make suitable arrangements for the recording, handling, safekeeping, safe administration and disposal of any medicines received into the children's home.[8]

4  Secure Training Centre Rules (STCR) rule 24(1).
5  STCR rule 24(2).
6  STCR rule 34(3).
7  Children's Homes Rules (CHR) rule 20.
8  CHR rule 21.

## The role of governors/directors and medical staff in prisons

6.10　The Prison Act (PA) 1952 s7(1) no longer contains a requirement for each prison to have a medical officer, this requirement having been removed by the Offender Management Act (OMA) 2007 s25.[9] This reflects the practice that healthcare in prisons is now provided by the PCT. The professionals employed by the PCT in the prison are responsible for the physical and mental health of all prisoners detained in that prison.[10] Prison governors are responsible for ensuring that there are proper arrangements in place for managing, monitoring and improving healthcare in prisons. Thus they retain responsibility for the overall performance of healthcare in prisons and for ensuring that healthcare is being appropriately delivered, whilst members of the healthcare team are responsible for individual clinical performance.[11] All doctors working in prisons will be subject to clinical appraisals[12] and basic checks must be carried out on doctors and dentists working in prisons.[13] Prison health regional teams are responsible for helping prisons develop 'clinical governance'[14] in accordance with the NHS quality agenda and at national level, the Prison Service Director General, retains responsibility for ensuring that the quality of clinical care in prisons is acceptable.

6.11　The specific duties of doctors working in prisons are set out in Department of Health Guidance issued in 2003. The guidance highlights the particular difficulties of providing healthcare within prisons and some of the challenges faced by prison doctors. It covers matters such as:

- managing security risks without compromising good clinical care;
- balancing the need to protect patient confidentiality with the duty to share information with prison staff for example for adjudica-

---

9　This amendment also repealed sections 17 and 28(5) of the Prison Act 1952 which imposed specific duties on the prison medical officer and the specific duties contained in PR rr20 and 21.

10　PR rule 20(1) and YOIR rule 27(1).

11　PSO 3100 para 2.1.

12　PSI 29/2003.

13　PSI 38/2003.

14　Clinical governance is defined as 'a framework through which NHS organisations are accountable for continuously improving the quality of their services and safeguarding high standards of care, by creating an environment in which excellence in clinical care will flourish': PSO 3100, para 1.1.

tion purposes, after incidents of injury or self-harm or use of force; and

- developing procedures to allow prisoner to access healthcare despite the restrictions of the prison regime.

6.12    Doctors and other healthcare professionals working in prisons have specific responsibilities relating to the prison regime:

- They are required to assess whether prisoners are fit for segregation[15] and either they or another member of healthcare must carry out daily visits of prisoners held in the segregation unit.[16]
- They are required to inspect the food and report any deficiencies to the prison governor.[17]
- They are required to sanction the use of restraints.[18]
- They are required to advise on early release on medical grounds.[19]

## Access to healthcare

6.13    All prisoners should be given a health assessment within 24 hours of their arrival in prison and a new clinical record should be completed for them. In addition, a health screen should be completed before a prisoner's first night in custody to establish their immediate needs and risk of suicide or self-harm.[20] Healthcare staff should attempt to retrieve information from the prisoner's GP and other relevant healthcare professionals involved in the prisoner's care in the community.[21]

6.14    Prison staff must record all prisoners' requests to see a doctor, nurse or other registered healthcare professional and pass those requests promptly to a medical officer.[22] Different prisons have implemented different procedures to grant prisoners access to doctors; some have dedicated healthcare postal boxes whilst others rely on prison staff to communicate prisoners' requests to see a member of healthcare. In the latter case confidentiality issues arise and prisoners can be reluctant to access doctors through prison staff.[23]

15   PR rule 58 and YOIR rule 61.
16   PSO 1700.
17   PR rule 24(1) and YOIR rule 20(3).
18   PR rule 49 and YOIR rule 52.
19   PSO 3050 paras 7.14–7.18.
20   PSO 3050 para 2.6.
21   PSO 3050 paras 2.1–2.2.
22   PR rule 20(2) and YOIR rule 27(2).
23   HMCIP annual report 2007–2008, p28, records that in one prison it took two weeks for prisoners' requests to reach the healthcare service.

6.15    Prisoners will only be entitled to see a doctor of their choice where they are unconvicted and agree to pay any charge incurred; or where they need to see a doctor in connection with legal proceedings.[24] Reasonable facilities out of the hearing of prison staff must be provided for this purpose.

6.16    Prisoners should have access to specific healthcare assistance to meet their needs and the prison must develop polices to ensure health promotion within the prison.[25] In addition national policies have been developed to address specific issues, for example to ensure that prisoners with diabetes can access the same facilities as those available in the community[26] and to ensure smoking cessation schemes are available in prisons.[27]

6.17    Where a prisoner is transferred from one prison to another healthcare staff have a duty to provide continuity of care[28] and further healthcare assessments should be conducted whenever a prisoner is transferred to a new prison prior to their first night of arrival.[29] In certain circumstances, healthcare staff can sanction a prisoner's transfer and place a prisoner on clinical hold, for example where necessary to ensure the prisoner receives external hospital treatment. In addition healthcare staff can impose restrictions on a prisoner's transfer, for example where they must be held in a prison with 24-hour healthcare facilities.[30]

## External medical appointments

6.18    Depending on their security category prisoners can be escorted to external hospital appointments[31] or released on temporary licence to attend hospital appointments.[32] In addition, in exceptional circumstances remand prisoners can be temporarily released to remain in hospital if they are so seriously ill or incapacitated as to be incapable of escaping and where they present no danger of assisted escape[33] Where escorts are necessary, prisoners frequently experience severe

24  PR rules 20(5) and (6) and YOIR rule 27(3).
25  PSO 3200 on health promotion.
26  PSO 07/2002.
27  PSI 44/2001.
28  PSO 3050 paras 5.11–5.13.
29  PSO 3050 para 5.24.
30  PSO 3050 para 5.9.
31  PA 1952 s22(2)(b).
32  PR rule 9 and YOIR rule 6.
33  PA 1952 s22(2)(b).

delays with attending external hospital appointments and escorting arrangements often create difficulties with patient-doctor confidentiality. In an attempt to overcome these difficulties the budgetary responsibility for healthcare escorts and bed watches was transferred from HM Prison Service to PCTs in November 2007. However, governing governors retain responsibility for individual risk assessments and for determining the level of security required for the escort period.[34]

6.19    Prior to escorting a prisoner to hospital from any closed or semi-open prison, staff must complete a risk assessment to establish the appropriate level of escort the restraint. In emergency situations a prisoner can be taken to hospital before the risk assessment is completed. The risk assessment must take into account:

- The prisoner's medical condition (consulting with the prison medical officer if required).
- The prisoner's category.
- The nature of the offence, the risk to the public and hospital staff (including the risk of hostage taking).
- The prisoner's motivation to escape, the likelihood of outside assistance and the prisoner's conduct whilst in custody.
- The physical security of the hospital including the consulting room and where possible, other areas where tests or treatment may take place.
- The particular procedures that must be followed for pregnant prisoner.
- The need for the prisoner to be accompanied during consultation.

6.20    The standard escort arrangements for prisoners from closed prisons will require two officers to accompany the prisoner and the use of restraints, unless there are medical objections. The risk assessment can require either a higher or lower level of escort and restraints. Restraints should normally be removed during medical consultations but they may be left in place the risk assessment shows the risk of escape is too high. The restraints should be reapplied once the treatment or consultation has concluded.

6.21    The NSF contains specific provisions for hospital escorts for pregnant women. Pregnant women attending hospital should have restraints removed on arrival in the waiting room and these should not be reapplied until after the consultation. Where the prisoner

34  NSF 'Hospital Escorts'.

presents an exceptionally high risk of escape the restraints can remain in place. However, the restraints should be removed if a healthcare professional so requests because of: a health risk; or because the prisoner is in pain or discomfort; or if the restraints are impeding examination or treatment. If escorting staff are concerned that the restraints should remain in place despite the request of healthcare staff, they should consult with a prison governor who will make a final decision on the use of restraints or arrange for the treatment to be delayed until alternative security measures can be put in place.

6.22    Where possible, two female officers should escort prisoners to hospital to give birth, and where this is not possible, at least one of the escorts should be a woman. If necessary the number of escorting staff can be increased to address any security risks. Physical restraints should be removed when a prisoner arrives at the hospital and escorting staff should not be present in the delivery room or where an intimate examination is taking place.

## The use of handcuffs

6.23    Strasbourg jurisprudence has established that the use of handcuffs in any circumstances must be necessary and proportionate to the assessed risk in connection with a lawful detention. In two cases concerning two patients who posed low level security risks, the European Court found that the use of handcuffs was disproportionate and could not be justified in the circumstances, amounting to a breach of article 3.[35] Further, it was pointed out in *Henaf* that in its report to the French government on its visit to France from 14 to 26 May 2000, the European Committee for the Prevention of Torture and Inhuman or Degrading Treatment or Punishment (CPT) recommended, among other things, that the practice of attaching prisoners to their hospital beds for security reasons be prohibited (para 57).

6.24    The domestic courts have also held that the routine handcuffing of a prisoner receiving hospital treatment without first assessing the risk of escape in each case is likely to be unlawful and to involve a breach of article 3 in *R (Graham) v Secretary of State for Justice; R (Allen) v Secretary of State for Justice*.[36] The court considered that the decision to handcuff Mr Graham constituted a breach of article 3 as his risk of escaping was low, but the decision to handcuff Mr Allen was not in breach of article 3 as his risk of escaping was

---

35  See *Hénaf v France* (2005) 40 EHRR 44 and *Mouisel v France* (2004) 38 EHRR 34.
36  [2007] EWHC 2910 (Admin).

high. It was relevant that Mr Graham was a terminally ill, low level offender whereas Mr Allen was a triple-murderer with a non-fatal heart condition.

## Preventing communicable diseases

6.25   The spread of HIV and hepatitis in prison is of particular concern due to the ease with which they are transmitted through needle sharing and unprotected sex. Despite this the Prison Service does not provide prisoners with access to needles and only provides limited access to condoms. Prison doctors can prescribe condoms if, in their clinical judgment, there is a known risk of HIV infection. This policy was unsuccessfully challenged in *R v Home Secretary ex p Fielding*.[37] It was argued that the policy was irrational because a request for condoms by a homosexual prisoner meant that he was intent upon otherwise unsafe sexual activity and therefore clinical judgment was irrelevant. However, the court held that the policy was lawful due to the Prison Service's legitimate concern that it should not be seen to encourage homosexual activity within prisons and that condoms could be used for other purposes which made it necessary for the prison staff to exercise a degree of control over their issue. The court highlighted that condoms should be provided where prison medical staff were satisfied that a genuine request was being made by a practising homosexual prisoner who would otherwise participate in unsafe sex.

6.26   The Prison Service aims to reduce the spread of communicable diseases through the use of education programmes[38] and disinfecting tablets. Disinfecting tablets should be made available to all prisoners in all prisons.[39] The use of these tablets was previously withdrawn in 1995 due to concerns about their safety. However, following further clinical tests they were reintroduced in 1998 on a trial basis in 11 prisons, following which it was recommended that they be reintroduced across the prison estate. The aim is that the tablets allow prisoners who continue to inject drugs to clean illicitly held injecting equipment before passing it to others.

6.27   The legality of the Prison Service policy not to provide prisoners with access to clean needles was challenged unsuccessfully in *Shelley v United Kingdom*.[40] Needle exchange programmes exist in nine

37   (1999) *Times* 21 July.
38   PSO 3845 para 6.1.
39   PSI 05/2005.
40   (2008) 46 EHRR SE16.

jurisdictions within the EU, including Scotland, and they are being developed in several other jurisdictions. Evidence suggests that the programmes have been successful and do not produce countervailing effects that outweigh the benefits to prisoners. The court rejected the applicant's arguments that the failure to provide him with access to clean needles violated his rights under articles 2 or 3; he had not specified that he was at real or immediate risk of becoming infected through unclean needle use and a general, unspecified fear of risk of infection was not enough to raise issues under articles 2 or 3. The court went on to reject the applicant's arguments under article 8, which does not oblige contracting states to pursue particular preventative health policies. It noted that matters of healthcare policy fall within the margin of appreciation of domestic authorities given their ability to prioritise the use of resources and social needs. The applicant's arguments under article 14 were also rejected on the basis that the difference in treatment between prisoners and non-prisoners fell within the margin of appreciation and was proportionate.

## Clinical services for substance misusers

6.28   Clinical services for prisoners who abuse drugs or alcohol are provided by members of healthcare staff who should work in conjunction with CARATs[41] drug workers and local NHS specialist drug misuse services. Governing governors are responsible for ensuring that proper procedures are in place to implement the minimum standards for clinical services for substance misusers.[42] These minimum standards provide that:[43]

- All prisoners should be screened on their arrival into prison by a healthcare worker trained to identify those with immediate health needs due to substance misuse.
- All prisoners should have immediate access to detoxification programmes for opiate, alcohol and benzodiazepines in line with the Department of Health Guidelines 1999.
- Information must be available on substance misuse treatment services, health promotion (including details of the effects of drugs and alcohol and how to control its misuse) and harm prevention (including details of overdose risks and relapse prevention).

41   Counselling, Assessment, Referral, Advice and Throughcare services, which should be available in every prison.
42   PSO 3550.
43   PSO 3350 annex A.

- CARATs guidelines and care plans for individual prisoners should provide for the involvement of healthcare where appropriate.
- An NHS consultant in substance misuse should have regular contact with prison healthcare staff.
- The clinical management of substance misusers should be in line with the Department of Health Guidelines 1999.
- Healthcare staff must develop relationships with CARATs drug workers and community drug workers to ensure assistance for substance misusers on their release from prison.

## Complaints about prison healthcare

6.29 All prisoners should be provided with details of how to make a complaint about the healthcare they receive in prison during their induction process, including details of the timescale within which they will receive a response to their complaint. Prisoners have the right to utilise the NHS complaints procedures (which are detailed below) in relation to NHS services they receive outside the prison system. However, when a prisoner wishes to complain about the healthcare they receive within prison the complaints procedure will vary depending on who is providing the healthcare:

- In prisons where healthcare is provided by a PCT complaints will be dealt with in accordance with NHS complaints procedures, which are governed by the Local Authority Social Services and NHS Complaints (England) Regulations 2009.[44] The Regulations provide that complaints must be made within one year of the incident giving rise to the complaint, or as soon as the complainant becomes aware of it. A complaints manager must be appointed and complaints must be properly investigated and appropriate action must be taken. Complaints should be responded to within six months and an interim response should be sent where this is not possible.
- In prisons where healthcare is provided by an independent provider commissioned by the NHS the independent provider must have in place arrangements for the handling and consideration of complaints, which should comply with the Regulations.
- Where a complaint is not resolved at a local level it should be referred to the Parliamentary and Health Service Ombudsman.[45]

44  SI No 309. Separate complaints procedures apply to prisons in Wales.
45  In Wales complaints should be made to the Public Services Ombudsman for Wales.

- In private sector prisons where the healthcare services are provided by a private company, complaints must be dealt with in accordance with the company's complaints procedures, copies of which should be obtained directly from the company. The Ombudsman cannot investigate complaints about private healthcare companies and therefore there is no independent body to which these complaints can be referred.

6.30    If prisoners wish to complain about matters related to healthcare, but which do not concern clinical decisions (such as the escort arrangements for external hospital appointments) they should use the internal complaints procedure and once this has been exhausted they should refer their complaint to the PPO.

6.31    Prisoners can receive assistance with healthcare complaints from the Independent Monitoring Board and, where the healthcare is commissioned or provided by the NHS, the Independent Complaints Advocacy Service and the Patient Advice and Liaison Service.

6.32    Where a prisoner's health is damaged as a result of the failure of prison healthcare staff to provide them with appropriate care or treatment they are entitled to bring civil proceedings and the normal rules of clinical negligence will apply. Prisoners who have suffered as a result of inadequate or inappropriate healthcare may also wish to bring a claim under the Human Rights Act for violations of articles 3 and 8. It has been established that the Secretary of State will be responsible for violations of Convention rights occurring as a result of deficient healthcare even where the healthcare provider is commissioned by a private company.[46]

6.33    In *Keenan v UK*[47] the ECtHR held that there had been a violation of article 3 in the case of a prisoner who committed suicide whilst held in the segregation unit. The court criticised the medical care provided to Mr Keenan, including the lack of medical notes and the failure to refer him to a psychiatrist. The decision was heavily influenced by the fact that disciplinary measures had been utilised to manage Mr Keenan's custodial behaviour rather than seeking a medical solution. In *McGlinchy v UK*[48] the court found there had been a violation of article 3 due to the failure of the Prison Service healthcare staff to provide appropriate treatment to a female prisoner who was suffering from withdrawal symptoms for heroin use and who died in outside hospital.

46  *S v Secretary of State for the Home Department* [2007] EWHC 1654 (Admin).
47  (2001) 33 EHRR 38.
48  29 April 2003.

# Management of prisoners at risk of suicide or self-harm

6.34 Levels of suicide and acts of self-harm in prisons continue to be alarmingly high,[49] highlighting the inadequacy of the procedures in place to assist and protect prisoners with mental health problems. The Prison Service has set an auditable standard on protecting prisoners at risk of suicide or self-harm.[50] This requires 'care and support to be provided to all prisoners to reduce the likelihood of suicide or self-harm'. Staff are required to 'identify prisoners at current risk of suicide or self-harm and implement plans to keep them safe and address the cause of their problems'.

6.35 Prisoners deemed to be at risk of suicide or self-harm are managed through ACCT (Assessment Care in Custody and Teamwork) procedures, and all staff must receive at least foundation stage ACCT training.[51] Whenever a member of staff is worried that a prisoner might be at risk of self-harm or suicide they must open an ACCT plan for that prisoner (escort staff must use a suicide/self-warning form).[52] Guidance on opening and closing ACCT plans is set out in Annex 8G to PSO 2700, and it requires the following actions to be undertaken:

- To open an ACCT plan the member of staff must complete the concern and keep safe form of the ACCT document and must then obtain a log number for the ACCT document and inform the ACCT administrative officer.
- The ACCT plan must then be passed to the unit manager, who must decide whether the prisoner should remain on normal location or be transferred to healthcare.
- An immediate action plan should be completed within one hour of the ACCT document being opened. This should outline matters such as where the prisoner should be located and detail the supervision requirements for the prisoner.
- If the prisoner at risk is aged under 18-years-old, staff should consider whether to contact their next of kin and all prisoners should be offered access to a listener or the Samaritans.

---

49 In 2007–2008, 153 self inflicted deaths occurred in prisons in England and Wales, statistics available on INQUEST website.

50 Prison Service Standard 60, October 2007.

51 PSO 2700 para 1.2.1.

52 PSO 2700 para 1.2.2.

- The immediate action plan should be replaced within 24 hours by a detailed CAREMAP. This document should be completed at the first case review, which must be chaired by the unit manager and to which relevant members of staff (including where appropriate mental health staff and healthcare staff) should be invited to attend. Prisoners should also attend this review. Staff should try to establish the cause of their problems and outline interventions to assist them and assess their level of risk or self-harm as well as identifying events which might increase this risk.
- A case manager should be appointed to update the ACCT form and ensure the CAREMAP requirements are complied with.
- Further case reviews should be held at appropriate intervals and the ACCT plan can be closed at any case review. ACCT plans should only be closed once all actions identified on the CAREMAP have been completed and the review team considers it safe to do so. ACCT plans should not be closed within 72 hours of a prisoner's transfer to a new establishment.
- A post closure interview must be held within seven days of closing an ACCT plan to establish whether the prisoner requires any further assistance. Further post-closure reviews can be held if necessary.

PSO 2700 contains further specific guidance on the management of young people and women at risk of suicide and self-harm.

6.36     ACCT plans were introduced to replace forms known as '2052SH', which were considered to provide inadequate protection to vulnerable prisoners. Unfortunately, many problems remain, and ACCT plans are frequently not completed properly or not complied with. There is no mandatory requirement for case reviews or post closure reviews to be multi-disciplinary with the result that key decisions about whether to continue to implement procedures to protect prisoners with severe mental health problems are taken by prison officers with limited ACCT training.[53]

---

53 These deficiencies are noted in HMCIP annual report 2007–2008 which records recurring mistakes and ineffective use of ACCT procedures and highlights the lack of staff training, the lack of multi-disciplinary case reviews, the lack of involvement of personal officers or key workers in care plans and formulaic entries in care plans which evidenced little engagement by prison staff (p21).

# Transfer to secure hospitals or units

6.37 Research shows that 72 per cent of male prisoners and 70 per cent of female prisoners suffer from two or more mental health disorders.[54] Furthermore, rates of serious disorders such as schizophrenia or delusional behaviour run at 14 per cent for women prisoners and 10 per cent for male prisoners compared with less than one per cent in the wider population.[55] Despite this prisoners experience real difficulties with gaining access to appropriate mental health care within prisons and, where appropriate, in obtaining a transfer to a psychiatric unit. Prisons should have specialist mental health in-reach teams which are responsible for assisting prisoners with mental health problems, and it is recognised that these mental health services should be integrated with other healthcare services.[56]

6.38 The Secretary of State can direct that a prisoner should be transferred to a psychiatric hospital if, on receipt of report from at least two registered medical practitioners, he is satisfied that:

- the prisoner is suffering from mental disorder; and
- the mental disorder from which the person is suffering is of a nature or degree which makes in appropriate for him or her to be detained in a hospital for medical treatment; and
- appropriate medical treatment is available for the prisoner.[57]

6.39 Prisoners are usually transferred under restriction directions pursuant to the power at MHA 1983 s49.[58] Where a restricted transfer has been made, if the Secretary of State is advised that:

- the prisoner no longer requires treatment in hospital for mental disorder;
- that no effective treatment for his or her disorder can be given in the hospital to which the prisoner has been transferred.

The Secretary of State can order either that the prisoner is returned to prison or that the prisoner is released on licence.[59] The restriction direction shall cease to have effect on his release date and if the prisoner remains in hospital it will be as a detained person subject

---

54 The Prison Reform Trust, Bromley Briefings Prison Fact File, June 2008.
55 Ministry of Justice Disability Equality Scheme 2008-11, page 18.
56 PSO 2700 para 6.2.2. Also see PSI 2007/50.
57 Mental Health Act 1983 ss47–48.
58 This makes the prisoner subject to the restrictions contained in MHA 1983 ss40–41 which ensure that the Secretary of State has a continuing role over matters such as temporary releases and discharge.
59 MHA 1983 s50: see also *R v Birch* [1989] 11 Cr App R(S) 202 at para 211.

to a hospital order under section 37.[60] If no restriction order is made because, for example, the prisoner is approaching release at the time of the transfer, the prisoner is treated as having been released from prison custody on licence and the licence conditions will continue to operate allowing for the prisoner to be returned to custody if there is a breach of those conditions.[61]

6.40    Where a transfer direction is made for a prisoner's removal to psychiatric hospital, the direction must be acted upon within 14 days, after which period it is invalid. Difficulties frequently arise with finding appropriate secure hospital beds for prisoners and it is widely recognised that there is a shortage of beds available for prisoners with mental health problems. Thus, an HM Inspectorate report on the mental health problems of prisoners notes 'the lack of NHS secure and acute beds and insufficient community provision continues to be a barrier to successful diversion'.[62] In *Drew v United Kingdom*,[63] a complaint made by a prisoner that a delay of eight days in securing his transfer from prison to a regional secure unit breached article 3 was found to be inadmissible.[64]

6.41    A similar decision was made in respect of article 8 in the case of *R (D) v Secretary of State for the Home Department*[65] where a young offender had his possible transfer to a hospital discussed for eight months and a place eventually only become available on his release and in the face of the litigation. The court accepted that once the Prison Service had reasonable grounds to believe that a prisoner required treatment in a mental hospital, the Secretary of State was under a duty expeditiously to take reasonable steps to obtain appropriate medical advice and, if transfer was advised, to take reasonable steps to effect a transfer. In this case the delay and consequent suffering arose from the lack of agreement as to diagnosis and treatment and was exacerbated by the lack of suitable places available.

---

60  MHA 1983 s50(2).
61  *R (Miah) v Secretary of State for the Home Department* [2004] EWHC 2569 (Admin).
62  HM Inspectorate of Prisons, *The mental health of prisoners: a thematic review of the care and support of prisoners with mental health needs*, October 2007.
63  (2006) 43 EHRR SE2.
64  The section 47 delay had been fairly minimal, the major period of delay occurring between the identification of the need for a hospital order to be made and the subsequent imposition of a prison sentence istead of that hospital order thereby necessitating the section 47 procedure to be implemented.
65  [2004] EWHC 2857 (Admin).

# Deaths in custody

## Introduction

6.42    There continues to be an alarmingly high number of deaths in custody, arising both from homicide and suicide.[66] The statistics illustrate the prison authorities' continuing failure to protect and assist the vulnerable people in their care.

6.43    It is well established that the prison authorities owe a common law duty of care to prisoners to protect them from the criminal acts of third parties and from acts of self-harm and suicide. Furthermore, the authorities have an obligation under article 2 of the ECHR to protect a prisoner's right to life. This requires them to take preventive operational measures to protect prisoners whose life is at risk from the criminal acts of another individual;[67] to protect prisoners who are at risk of suicide[68] and to provide prisoners with proper medical treatment.[69] The positive obligation under article 2 to protect an individual's right to life will arise where it can be established that the authorities knew or ought to have known of a real and immediate risk to life.[70]

6.44    In every case where it is arguable that the state has failed its positive obligations under article 2, it must hold an effective investigation into the circumstances of the death. Recent domestic case-law has established that an article 2 compliant enquiry must also be conducted into near-deaths in custody.[71]

6.45    Article 3 of the ECHR also requires the state to protect vulnerable prisoners under their care, and this may also require them to provide prisoners with access to appropriate medical and psychiatric care and not to place vulnerable prisoners in segregation.[72] The state must provide a plausible account of any injuries sustain in custody and this requires them to carry out an effective investigation into such injuries.[73] This chapter considers the role played by the Prison

---

66  In 2008 there were 166 deaths in custody. Up to date figures can obtained from Inquest: http://inquest.gn.apc.org/data_deaths_in_prison.html
67  *Edwards v UK* (2002) 35 EHRR 19.
68  *Keenan v UK* (2001) 33 EHRR 38.
69  *Keenan v UK* (2001) 33 EHRR 38.
70  *Osman v UK* (1998) 29 EHRR 245.
71  *R (JL) v Secretary of State for Justice* [2008] UKHL 68.
72  *Keenan v UK* (2001) 33 EHRR 38.
73  *R (AM and others) v Secretary of State for the Home Department* [2009] EWCA Civ 219.

Service, the PPO and coroners in carrying out investigations which comply with the requirements of articles 2 and 3.

## The role of the prison staff

6.46  All prisons are required to have contingency plans in place to respond to deaths in custody, and local protocols must be adopted setting out the key roles of staff. As a minimum, on discovering an apparent death the following steps must be taken:[74]

- The first person on the scene must immediately summon help and request local emergency assistance.
- An ambulance should be called and key personnel must be alerted.
- If the incident has taken place in a cell the first person on the scene must enter the cell and carry out emergency first aid procedures. If the incident has taken place elsewhere the area should be cleared of other prisoners and emergency first aid procedures commenced.
- The member of staff must then give a concise report to clinical staff when they arrive and clinical staff will assume responsibility for the casualty.
- The appropriate faith chaplain or other religious leader should attend if possible.
- Once the death has been a member of staff should be posted to remain at the scene and keep a record of the names of all those who enter the cell. All relevant evidence must be preserved before the police arrive.
- If relevant any prisoners should be relocated and a record should be made of prisoners in adjacent and opposite cells, or if the incident occurs outside a cell, the names of other prisoners present.
- The body should be removed from the prison without other prisoners seeing this and the cell should then be sealed until the police authorise staff to reopen it.

## Reporting requirements

6.47  Following a death in custody prison staff must notify:[75]

- the police;
- the coroner;

74  PSO 2710 para 2.
75  PSO 2710 paras 3.1–3.3.

- the area manager or Director of High Security Prisons or the head of prisoner escort custody services or the controller, as appropriate;
- the national operations unit, which must be provided with an initial incidents report;
- the press office, who should not release the news before the next-of-kin have been informed;
- the next-of-kin and any other person the prisoner has reasonably requested to be informed;
- prisoners, especially friends, associates or Listeners;
- relatives or co-defendants in other prisons;
- staff;
- the co-ordinating chaplain and relevant faith chaplain;
- the care team leader;
- the suicide prevention team leader, the suicide prevention co-ordinator (or equivalent), the safer custody co-ordinator (or equivalent) and the area psychologist;
- the IMB;
- the local Samaritans branch;
- the PCT (where relevant);
- the visitors centre;
- the prison switchboard operators, who should also be told to whom they should refer enquiries about the death; and
- the prison's police liaison officer.

6.48    In addition, where the prisoner is a convicted prisoner, staff must inform:[76]

- the police national computer;
- the relevant home probation officer, and if the prisoner is a young offender, their social worker; and
- if appropriate the Parole Board.

Where the prisoner is unconvicted, staff must inform:[77]

- the committing court;
- the prisoner's solicitors; and
- the relevant home probation officer.

Where the prison is a civil prisoner, staff must inform:[78]

- the Official Solicitor.

---

76  PSO 2710 para 3.4.
77  PSO 2710 para 3.5.
78  PSO 2710 para 3.6.

Where the prisoner is a juvenile, staff must inform:[79]

- the appropriate Youth Offending Team;
- the Youth Justice Board;
- the juvenile group; and
- the local and home social services (if there is a care order in place, parental responsibility may be shared by the parent and local authority).

Where the prisoner is a foreign national, staff must also inform:[80]

- consular officials.

## The family liaison officer

6.49    Prisons should appoint a family liaison officer (FLO), whose role is to ensure that the family of a prisoner who dies in custody is treated 'appropriately, professionally and with respect for their needs'.[81] The FLO should receive special training and be supervised by a governor.[82]

6.50    Following a death, the FLO must:

- Notify the next-of-kin and any other reasonably nominated person, giving a factual account of what has happened. This should take place face-to-face where possible and the family liaison officer should visit the family's home, with a chaplain or another member of staff. Where this is not possible due to distance, the police should be asked to inform the family. As a last resort the family should be informed by telephone.[83]
- Offer support, practical help and advice to the family (before and after the inquest), ensuring that the family are given information about bereavement agencies.[84]
- Liaise with other key agencies, particularly the coroner's officer.[85]
- Arrange for the family to visit the establishment to meet staff/prisoners who had known the deceased and to provide them with an opportunity to visit the scene of the incident.[86]
- Offer to help arrange the funeral and offer to pay reasonable

79  PSO 2710 para 3.8.
80  PSO 2710 para 3.10.
81  FLO guidance para 4.1.
82  FLO guidance paras 2.4–2.8.
83  PSO 2710 para 4.2 and FLO guidance paras 4.9–4.13.
84  FLO guidance para 4.31.
85  FLO guidance para 4.4.
86  FLO guidance para 4.22.

funeral expenses. The guidance suggests that a figure of £3,000 was appropriate in 2005–2006.[87]

• Manage the handover of the prisoner's property.[88]

In addition, the governor should send a letter of condolence to the family.[89]

## Support for staff and prisoners

6.51 Prisons must have local protocols which detail the support to be provided to all staff and prisoners after a death in custody.[90] In particular, prisoners should be offered support from the Samaritans, the chaplaincy team and where appropriate, probation staff, psychology staff and the mental health in-reach team. Staff must be alert to the impact of a self-inflicted death on other vulnerable prisoners, particularly those who have been on ACCT.[91]

# The role of prison staff in investigations into deaths in custody and inquests

6.52 All deaths in prison custody are subject to:

• a police investigation (on behalf of the coroner, and if necessary, a criminal investigation);
• an investigation by the PPO; and
• a coroner's inquest before a jury.

6.53 All prison staff, including those not directly employed by the Prison Service and those working in the prison on a contract or locum basis, are required to co-operate fully with these investigations.[92] In particular, governors/directors must:[93]

• Write to the coroner with details of the death. This also applies to deaths that occur outside the prison.
• Liaise with the coroner, coroner's officer, safer custody group, Treasury Solicitor, PPO, police and press office as necessary.

87 FLO guidance paras 4.29–4.30.
88 FLO guidance para 4.24.
89 PSO 2710 para 4.2.
90 PSO 2710 para 5.1.
91 PSO 2710 para 5.5.
92 PSO 2710 para 6.1.
93 PSO 2710 para 6.5.

- Collate documents required by the investigating teams. This should be done as soon as possible after the death to minimise any allegations of interference.
- Provide copies of all documents requested to the investigating teams and keep a record of all those documents handed over.
- Provide contact details of any prisoner the investigating team may wish to interview.
- Liaise and assist the investigating teams in accordance with agreed national and local protocols.
- Ask the safer custody group to arrange legal representation for the prison through the Treasury Solicitor.[94]
- Notify, as appropriate, the trade unions, chair of IMB, staff welfare officer, safer custody group, press office, area manager or controller, care team, chaplain, women's team and juvenile, of the date of the inquest or trial and the verdict.
- Inform staff and prisoners about the inquest process and arrange a meeting with the Treasury Solicitor's representative and counsel.
- Advise the Samaritans if a listener is called as a witness to the inquest, so that the Samaritans can support the listener.
- Ensure a senior member of staff attends any pre-inquest reviews.
- Arrange a post-inquest de-brief meeting for those who attended the inquest.
- Send any letters from the coroner under rule 43 of the Coroner's Rules[95] with the prison's comments to the safer custody group.
- Review the inquest findings with the suicide prevention team, area suicide prevention coordinator, area psychologist and safer custody group outreach team member.

6.54 Prisons are required to implement local protocols which must indicate how lessons will be learnt from a death in custody, with particular regard to any recommendations made following the investigations. Families should be informed of any action taken and area managers should ensure that recommendations are shared with other prisons and agencies (for example PCTs) in their area. On a national level the Safer Custody Group must progress recommendations with national and/or policy implications as necessary with appropriate senior personnel or policy groups. The Safer Custody Group is required to

---

94  The Treasury Solicitor will usually act for all prison officers and separate legal representation will only arise when there is a conflict of interest. In addition, the Prison Officer's Association may provide separate legal representation for prison officers at an inquest.
95  See below.

maintain a national database of reports and analyse recommendations and trends.[96]

# Prison and Probation Ombudsman's investigations into deaths in custody

6.55    Since 1 April 2004 the PPO has been responsible for investigating deaths in prison custody (including YOIs). This includes people temporarily absent from the prison, but still in custody (for example prisoners under escort, at court or in hospital), but does not include prisoners who are on temporary release. However, the PPO has the discretion to investigate any case that raises issues about the care provided by a prison.[97] The PPO will also investigate deaths of residents at approved premises and those held in immigration detention.

6.56    The PPO's investigation is an extremely important part of the investigative procedures available to families to enable them to gain a greater understanding of the circumstances surrounding their relative's death. The quality of PPO investigations varies and is dependent to a certain extent on the approach adopted by the investigator appointed to the case. It is important that families are legally represented during the PPO investigation so that solicitors can engage with the PPO investigation and ensure that all areas of concern, and in particular the family's key areas of concern, are thoroughly investigated.

## Terms of reference of the investigation

6.57    The PPO will commence an investigation on being informed of the death by the relevant detaining service and has the power to decide on the extent of the investigation required depending on the circumstances of the death. His remit will include all relevant matters for which the Prison Service and the National Probation Service are responsible or would be responsible if not contracted from elsewhere; it therefore includes services commissioned by the Home Secretary from outside the public sector[98].

---

96  PSO 2710 para 7.1.
97  *Death in Custody Investigations by the PPO. Joint Working Protocol between NOMS, the Prison Service/Contract Prisons and the PPO.* Annex A terms of reference for investigation of deaths, para 1.
98  *Death in Custody Investigations by the PPO,* para 2.

6.58    The PPO will set terms of reference for each investigation.[99] However, given that the PPO investigation forms part of the investigative
obligation under article 2 of the ECHR, it is clear that the family
should play a part in setting the terms of reference to ensure they
are sufficiently involved in the investigation to safeguard their interests.[100] It is therefore important the family should attend a meeting
with the PPO investigator at an early stage so that the PPO is aware
of the family's key concerns and the matters they would like to be
investigated. The PPO will appoint a family liaison officer to work
with the person carrying out the investigation, and the FLO will act
as the main point of contact for the family. One of the key roles of the
FLO is to identify the family's questions and ensure the draft report
responds to those questions.

6.59    The PPO investigation must aim to:

- Establish the circumstances and events surrounding the death,
  particularly with regard to the management of the individual by
  the relevant service, and including any relevant outside factors.
- Examine whether any change in operational methods, policy, and
  practice or management arrangements would help prevent a recurrence of a similar incident.
- In conjuncture with the NHS where appropriate, examine relevant health issues and assess clinical care.
- Provide explanations and insight for bereaved families.
- Assist the coroner's inquest in fulfilling the investigative obligation arising under article 2 of the ECHR by ensuring as far as possible that the full facts are brought to light and any relevant failing
  is exposed, any commendable action or practice is identified and
  any lessons from the death are learned.

## Gaining access to information

6.60    The PPO has no statutory powers and therefore acts on an administrative basis only. In particular, he has no power to compel prison
staff or other witnesses to provide evidence. Despite this, all prison
staff, including those not directly employed by the Prison Service
and those employed on a contract or temporary basis, are required
to co-operate with the investigation.[101] If a member of staff fails to

99  *Death in Custody Investigations by the PPO*, para 3.
100  *Edwards v UK* (2002) 35 EHRR 19.
101  *Death in Custody Investigations by the PPO. Joint Working Protocol between
NOMS, the Prison Service/Contract Prisons and the PPO*, para 1.2.

co-operate or act in any which undermines a PPO investigation they will be in breach of their standards of conduct and if employed under contract this may lead to the termination of their contract with the Prison Service. The PPO investigator will record their interviews with staff and staff are entitled to be accompanied by a work colleague or trade union representative.[102]

6.61   The PPO must be provided with unfettered access to Prison Service information, documents, establishments and prisoners and this includes classified material and information provided by other services such as the police.[103] Staff should notify the PPO of any information which they consider should not be disclosed to the public.[104] Non-disclosure might be justified where, for example, disclosure of the information would be against the interests of national security or prejudice the security of the prison.

6.62   The information the PPO receives during his investigation can be disclosed to the family. Practice varies between PPO investigators, but generally the family will be provided with copies of all documents obtained by the PPO and copies of transcripts of interviews conducted by the PPO prior to the disclosure of the draft or final report. The documents will be disclosed to third parties only to the extent necessary to fulfil the aims of the investigation.[105] Accordingly, the PPO can share those documents with, amongst others, the NHS and social services.

6.63   The following documents are regarded as essential documents to assist the PPO investigation:[106]

- Statements from staff and prisoners, including, those first on the scene, others attending, the last person to see the prisoner alive, the duty governor, prisoners in adjacent and nearby cells, the doctor, and others with knowledge of the prisoner.
- The prisoner's core record – F2050 (including security file, visits sheets and property cards).
- Clinical record F2169 and F2169a (including care plan, drug treatment programme records and dental records).
- Incident forms and adjudication history.
- Incident log, including a copy of any suicide note.

102 *Death in Custody Investigations by the PPO*, para 4.2.
103 PSO 2520 para 4.3.
104 PSO 2520 para 4.17.
105 *Death in Custody Investigations by the PPO. Joint Working Protocol between NOMS, the Prison Service/Contract Prisons and the PPO*. Annex A terms of reference for investigation of deaths, para 8.
106 *Death in Custody Investigations by the PPO*, annex C.

- Any ACCT documents (current and previous).
- Copy of contingency plans for a death in custody.
- Wing occurrence book or F2060 observation book.
- Copy of local suicide prevention policy and procedures.
- Copies of previous three suicide prevention team minutes.
- Names of prisoners in adjacent cells and current or recent cell-mates.
- Reception register.
- Relevant details of staff duties, including night staffing.
- Movement sheets.
- Details of core day.
- Copies of any other relevant correspondence found in the cell.
- Specifications (map of wing/landing).
- LIDS print-out for the deceased prisoner.
- The Prisoner Escort Record.
- CARAT casework file.
- Form 191a, the medical restriction register.

6.64   In addition the following documents must be provided for juveniles:

- TI:V risk assessment.
- ASSET report.
- Pre sentence report.
- Post court report.

6.65   The following documents are identified as being useful, but not essential to provide to the PPO:

- Relevant governor's order and notices to staff.
- Staff training records.
- Copies of latest HMCIP report.
- Copies of any standards audit reports within the preceding 12 months.
- Action plans of any investigations into previous deaths within the preceding 24 months at the prison.
- Registration procedures for ACCT documentation.
- Roll on day: receptions and discharges.
- Wing application books.
- Request/complaint forms.
- Details of prisoner's referrals to listener schemes.
- Copy of suicide prevention strategies guidance document.
- Copy of PSO 2700.
- Risk assessment for bed-watches.
- Bed-watch log.

- Times of escort arrivals and departures and names of escorting staff.
- Governor journal entries.
- Copy of PSO 2710.
- F1352 movement books.
- For category A prisoners, referrals to HQ.
- Minimum staffing levels breakdown.
- Cell clearance forms.
- Night sheets.
- Duty governor's book.
- Segregation forms.
- Copy of Health Care Standards (these will not be relevant where healthcare is commissioned by the PCT).
- Food refusal book.
- Cell sharing risk assessment.

## Clinical reviews

6.66  A separate clinical review will be conducted into the healthcare the prisoner received and this will form part of the PPO's final report. The body responsible for conducting this review depends upon who is responsible for the provision of healthcare within the prison:[107]

- The PPO will be responsible for investigating clinical issues relevant to the death where the healthcare services are commissioned by a privately run prison. The PPO must obtain clinical advice as necessary and should take steps to involve the local PCT in the investigation.
- Where the healthcare services were commissioned by the NHS, the NHS has the lead responsibility for investigating clinical issues under their procedures for investigating a serious untoward incident. Where the mental health services are provided by the NHS the PCT must involve the relevant mental health trust.

6.67  The clinical review will form an important part of most PPO investigations into deaths in custody and can address matters such as the keeping of medical records, provision of appropriate medical or mental healthcare, communication between internal and external healthcare providers and the systems in place for ensuring prisoners gain access to medication.

---

107 *Death in Custody Investigations by the PPO. Joint Working Protocol between NOMS, the Prison Service/Contract Prisons and the PPO*, para 7.2.

6.68    The independence of clinical reviewers, who are often employed by the PCT which is responsible for the provision of healthcare services within the prison, is a matter of some concern. It is also important to ensure that the clinical reviewer has the necessary expertise to consider the relevant issues and where necessary a second clinical reviewer should be appointed to comment on discrete issues, such as the quality of the psychiatric care provided to a prisoner. Where the family is dissatisfied with a clinical review they should raise their concerns with the PPO investigator and, where appropriate, request that a further review be carried out. The PPO has the authority to require a fuller investigation if necessary.[108]

## Other investigations

6.69    The PPO may decide during the course of his investigation that police or disciplinary investigations are necessary and can require the prison or probation service to take immediate action in relation to any findings he makes. Police investigations take priority over the PPO investigation.[109]

## The PPO report

6.70    Once the PPO has completed his investigation he will prepare a draft report, which may contain recommendations. This must first be sent to the prison or probation service[110] to allow them to:

- respond to recommendations;
- highlight any inaccuracies or omissions;
- identify any material they consider should not be disclosed; and
- allow any staff criticised in the report to respond to those criticisms.

6.71    Any other persons identified by the Coroner as 'properly interested persons'. In practice, the PPO will always send the draft report to the family of the deceased who will be provided with an opportunity to respond to the report. This allows the family to identify any areas which they believe the PPO has not investigated sufficiently and/or address any factually inaccurate information concerning the deceased.

6.72    The PPO can review the report of an investigation and make fur-

---

108 *Death in Custody Investigations by the PPO*, para 7.4.
109 *Death in Custody Investigations by the PPO*, para 6.
110 *Death in Custody Investigations by the PPO*, para 10.

ther enquiries and if necessary issue a further report or recommendations on receipt of further information and in particular following the inquest.[111]

6.73    The final report will be sent to HM Chief Inspector of Prisons and HM Inspector of Probation and the Secretary of State for Justice. An anonymised copy of the report will be published on the PPO website.

6.74    The Prison or Probation Service is required to provide the PPO with a written response indicating the steps to be taken within set timeframes to respond to any recommendations made the PPO.[112]

## Investigations into near-deaths in custody

6.75    Where a prisoner attempts suicide in custody and is left with a serious injury, article 2 requires there to be an investigation into the circumstances of that suicide attempt.[113] The precise definition of the term 'serious injury' remains unclear. In *JL* Lord Roger suggested that independent investigations would only be required where the injury meant that the prisoner was mentally impaired and thus unable to hold the authorities to account for their actions which led to their injuries. By contrast Lord Walker appears to suggest that an investigation would be necessary where the prisoner was a known suicide risk or where, for example, the attempt suggested a failure in the system of cell searches.

6.76    To ensure compliance with article 2 investigation into near-deaths resulting in serious injury must:

- Be held in public.
- Must be capable of compelling the attendance of witnesses.
- Allow victim's representative to attend the enquiry and to make appropriate submissions, including submissions relating to the questioning of witnesses.
- Allow the victim's representative to be given advance access to all relevant evidence.
- Provide adequate funding for the victim's representative.[114]

---

111 *Death in Custody Investigations by the PPO*, annex A terms of reference for investigation of deaths, para 8.

112 *Death in Custody Investigations by the PPO*, para 13.

113 *R (JL) v Secretary of State for Justice* [2008] UKHL 68.

114 *R (D) by the Official Solicitor for his litigation friend v Secretary of State for the Home Department and Inquest (intervener)* [2006] EWCA Civ 143.

6.77   The exact form this investigation must take is not prescribed. However, it is likely that such investigations will be carried out by the PPO as was suggested by the Equality and Human Rights Commission who intervened in *JL*. Difficulties may arise with ensuring PPO investigations meet the above obligations as the PPO has no power to compel the attendance of witnesses or to compel the Prison Service to comply with his investigation. In *D* it was suggested that these difficulties could be overcome by making the investigation subject to the Inquiries Act 2005. It is clear that investigations by Prison Service staff will not satisfy the requirements of article 2 given their lack of independence to the issues under investigation.[115]

# Inquests

6.78   A detailed examination of the inquest system can be found in *Inquests: a practitioner's guide*.[116] This section is intended to do nothing more than provide a very brief and general overview of the inquest system to help understand the relationship between the various investigations following a custodial death. At the time of writing the Coroner's and Justice Bill is progressing through parliament, the Bill includes proposals for key changes to inquests into deaths in custody.

## The purpose of an inquest

6.79   An inquest must be held for every death in prison,[117] and the inquest must always be held with a jury.[118] The purpose of an inquest to establish the facts of the death; under the Coroner's Act and the Coroners Rules 1984 the proceedings and evidence at an inquest must be directed to ascertaining who the deceased was and how, when and where the deceased came by his death.[119]

6.80   Inquests into deaths in custody form a key role in ensuring the state fulfils its obligation to investigate possible violations of article 2. In order to fulfil this obligation an inquest must have the following characteristics:

115  *SP v The Secretary of State for the Home Department* [2004] EWHC 1318 (Admin).

116  Thomas, Straw and Friedman, *Inquests: a practitioner's guide*, 2nd edition, Legal Action Group, 2008.

117  Coroners Act (CA) 1984, s8(1)(c).

118  CA 1984 s8(3)(a).

119  CA 1984 s11(5)(b) and CR rule 36.

- The investigation must be effective; it must be capable of establishing the cause of death and identifying those responsible.
- The investigation must be reasonably prompt and proceed with reasonable expedition.
- The investigation must make enquiries of relevant witnesses and secure relevant evidence.
- The investigation must be independent.
- It must be subject to public scrutiny so as to ensure accountability.
- The investigation must involve the next of kin to the extent necessary to safeguard their interests.[120]

6.81   The role of an article 2 compliant inquest was outlined by Lord Hope in *R (Sacker) v West Yorkshire Coroner*:[121]

> There is a high level of awareness, and much effort has been devoted to improving the system for prevention of suicides. But every time one occurs in prison the effectiveness of the system is called into question. So all the facts surrounding every suicide must be thoroughly, impartially and carefully investigated. The purpose of the investigation is to open up the circumstances of the death to public scrutiny. This ensures that those who were at fault will be made accountable for their actions. But it also has a vital role to play in the correction of mistakes and search for improvements. There must be a rigorous examination in public of the operation at every level of the systems and procedures which are designed to prevent self-harm and to save lives.

6.82   In this case the House of Lords considered held that an inquest into the death by suicide of a woman in prison was deficient and did not meet the requirements of article 2 because it did not identify the cause or causes of the woman's suicide, the preventative steps that could have been taken and the lessons to be learnt to reduce similar risks for other prisoners.

## Opening the inquest

6.83   On being informed of a death in custody a coroner will open the inquest to record the person's identity. The coroner will appoint a legally qualified pathologist to carry out a post-mortem and this must be carried out as soon after the death as is reasonably practicable.[122]

---

120  *R (Amin) v Secretary of State for the Home Department* [2004] 1 AC 653.
121  [2004] UKHL 11.
122  CR 1984 rule 5.

The coroner must inform various people, including the family of the deceased of the date, time and place of the post-mortem.[123] On completion of the post-mortem the body will be released and the coroner will issue an interim death certificate. For deaths in custody, the inquest will then be adjourned pending completion of the PPO's investigation into the death and/or any police investigations.

## Representation at the inquest

6.84   Family members and those who fall within the definition of 'properly interested persons'[124] are entitled to examine witnesses at an inquest. It is advisable for families to be legally represented at inquests and 'exceptional funding' can be obtained from the LSC to cover the costs of representation at the inquest.[125] The LSC guidance confirms that funding will be granted only if:

- representation is necessary to obtain a significant wider public interest; or
- representation is likely to be necessary to enable the coroner to carry out an effective article 2 investigation.

6.85   The LSC has discretion to waive financial eligibility limits where it is not reasonable to expect the family to bear the costs of representation at the inquest. Coroners are sometimes willing to support a family's application by confirming that their representation would aid the coroner's inquiry.

## The pre-inquest review

6.86   On completion of all other investigations the coroner will decide when and where the full inquest hearing will be held and will confirm this information to all relevant people.[126] Prior to the inquest the coroner will consider issues such as the witnesses to call and a provisional timetable for the attendance of those witnesses, the need for expert evidence, the evidence to be provided to the jury, and the length of the inquest. It is likely that the coroner will hold a pre-inquest review at which these issues can be further explored. The family's legal representative should attend this review as will other interested parties' legal representatives.

123  CR 1984 rule 7(1).
124  CR 1984 rule 20(2).
125  Access to Justice Act 1999 s6(8).
126  CR 1984 rule 33(2).

## Documents

6.87 Many of the documents to be relied on at the inquest should have been disclosed to the family during the PPO investigation. The coroner is only obliged to disclose uncontroversial documentary evidence.[127] However, to ensure compliance with article 2, the coroner should disclose copies of all relevant evidence to all parties to the inquest.[128]

## Witnesses

6.88 For deaths in custody it will clearly be important to ensure that all the key individuals responsible for the prisoner's care prior to their death give evidence at the hearing. In addition the PPO investigator will attend to give evidence on the key findings in their report. The coroner has the discretion to decide which witnesses to call.[129] However, interested parties can make an application to the coroner as to who should be called and any failure by the coroner to call relevant witnesses may amount to a violation of article 2. The family will be given the opportunity to question witnesses through their legal representative. Such questions should be limited to relevant questions pertaining to the witnesses' knowledge of the facts of the death.[130]

## The verdict

6.89 The Coroner's Rules provide that no verdict should be framed in a way to appear to determine criminal or civil liability.[131] However, to ensure compliance with article 2, when concluding 'how' a death occurred a jury must be able to express its conclusion on disputed factual issues central to the case by returning a 'narrative verdict' as opposed to a traditional short form verdict.[132] Thus when answering the question of 'how' a death occurred, the jury must be able to describe by what means the deceased died and in what circumstances.[133] This is

---

127 CR 1984 rule 37.
128 *R (D) v Secretary of State for the Home Department* [2006] EWCA Civ 143.
129 CA 1988 s11(2).
130 CA 1988 s11(2).
131 CR 1984 rule 42.
132 Examples of narrative verdict are set out in *Inquests: a practitioner's guide* (2nd edn, Legal Action Group, 2008) at appendix C.
133 *R (Middleton) v HM Coroner for the Western District of Somerset* [2004] UKHL 10.

necessary to ensure that lessons are learned from the death which may save the lives of others.

## Rule 43 reports

6.90   Following the inquest the coroner can send a report to the prison authorities, or other relevant bodies, making recommendations with a view to avoiding similar fatalities in future. The authority is obliged to respond in writing to the report and the coroner must make the report and the response available to all interested parties to the inquest. The Lord Chancellor can publish the report and any response to the report.

# Contact with the outside world

*continued*

# Introduction

7.1 The importance of prisoners maintaining contact with the outside world is reflected in provisions contained in the Prison and YOI Rules and the Secure Training Centre Rules. All highlight the need for prisoners to be encouraged and assisted in establishing and maintaining relations with people and agencies outside prison to promote their best interests, the interests of their family and their rehabilitation.[1] Despite this prisoners' ability to maintain meaningful contact with their families during their imprisonment is subject to many restrictions arising as a result of their place and conditions of detention. Restrictions on prisoners' visits have been subject to legal challenge, particularly since the introduction of the Human Rights Act 1998 under which arguments have been advanced that restrictions violate ECHR article 8. However, as is examined in greater detail below, in many instances the courts have held that restrictions on visits are justified for reasons of security, and that whether they should be considered necessary has to take into account 'the ordinary and reasonable requirements of imprisonment'.[2]

# Visits

## Visits to adult prisoners and young offenders

### Requirements of the Prison and YOI Rules

7.2 Convicted prisoners are entitled to receive two statutory visits every four weeks,[3] from a 'relative or friend'[4] although the Secretary of State can reduce this to one visit every four weeks. A Governor can defer a prisoner's visits during a period of cellular confinement.[5] The domestic courts have held that the minimum statutory visits comply with prisoners' right to respect for private and family life under

---

1 PR rule 4, YOIR rule 42 and STCR rule 29.
2 *Golder v UK* (1975) 1 EHRR 524, in this case, involving restrictions on a prisoner's correspondence, the ECtHR was careful that this did not amount to a doctrine of 'implied limitations' on prisoners' enjoyment of Convention rights, but that the construction of 'necessity' must reflect the prison context.
3 PR rule 35(2)(b) and YOIR rule 10(1)(b).
4 PR rule 35(8) and YOIR rule 10(7) – visits from persons not in this category require leave of the Secretary of State.
5 PR rule 35(5) and YOIR rule 10(4).

article 8.[6] This is in accordance with the jurisprudence of the European Court of Human Rights that restrictions on visits imposed due to the restraints of prison life and discipline do not generally breach article 8.[7]

7.3    In addition to statutory visits, the governor[8] or the IMB[9] can grant 'privilege visits'. The Secretary of State also has the power to authorise additional visits for individual or particular classes of prisoners.[10] The Rules specify that a governor should grant privilege visits where necessary for the welfare of the prisoner or his or her family or as part of incentives and earned privileges schemes. There is no guidance as to when the IMB should use its power to authorise extra visits or to allow a statutory visit to last for longer than normal. In practice this power is exercised rarely.

7.4    Prisoners are also entitled to special visits from legal advisers[11] and other people visiting in a professional capacity, such as probation staff, priests and consular officials. Privilege and special visits do not detract from the number of statutory visits to which prisoners are entitled.

7.5    Unconvicted prisoners are entitled to receive as many visits as they wish 'within such limits and subject to such conditions as the Secretary of State may direct, either generally or in a particular case'.[12] The current policy provides that unconvicted prisoners must be allowed a minimum of hourly visits, on at least three days a week and once a fortnight one of those days should fall on a weekend.[13] Visitors to unconvicted prisoners do not need a visiting order to enter the prison, although it is advisable that they telephone in advance to ensure they are granted access to the prison. Visits to unconvicted prisoners are subject to the same regime as visits to convicted prisoners.

### Prison Service policy on visits

7.6    The Prison Service central policy on visits is contained in PSO 4410. This requires prisons and YOIs to have local visits strategy but which should deal with areas of local discretion such as visiting times. The

6   *R (K) v Home Secretary* [2003] EWCA Civ 744.
7   *Nowicka v Poland* [2003] 1 FLR 417 – although individual decisions, for example to ban a visitor with insufficient justification, may breach article 8 – further see below.
8   PR rule 35(3) and YOIR rule 10(6).
9   PR rule 35(6) and YOIR rule 10(5).
10  PR rule 35(7) and YOIR rule 10(6).
11  PR rule 38 and YOIR rule 16.
12  PR rule 35(1).
13  PSO 4410 paras 1.2 and 1.7.

local visiting strategy should be displayed in the visits area.[14] PSO 4410 gives further detailed guidance on mandatory requirements in relation to visits.

7.7　　The policy, in recognition of the right to family life contained in article 8 of the ECHR, provides particular provisions with regards to visits by 'close relatives', and states that restrictions on visits from them will require greater justification. Close relatives are defined as:[15]

> a spouse/partner (including a person – whether of the same or different sex – with whom the prisoner was living as a couple in an established relationship immediately prior to imprisonment) parent, child, brother, sister (including half- or step-brothers and sisters), civil partner, fiancé or fiancée (provided that the Governor is satisfied that a bona fide engagement to marry exists), or a person who has been acting in loco parentis to a prisoner, or a person to whom the prisoner has been in loco parentis. Grandparents may also be included within this definition of close relative for the purposes of social visits.

## Conditions for social visits

7.8　　All visitors must have a valid visiting order to gain entrance to the prison. Visiting orders are issued to the individual prisoner, who then sends them out to the proposed visitor. Special provisions are made for visitors who do not have a permanent address.[16] The validity period of visiting orders is a local matter, but the local policy must allow a governor the discretion to reissue the visiting order on request.[17]

7.9　　Social visits must take place within sight of a prison officer and can take place within hearing of an officer if it is deemed necessary.[18] In general, up to three adults together with any accompanying children are permitted at any one time. The visits should take place in a visiting room with a table and chairs. Prisoners and visitors should be allowed 'reasonable physical contact' subject to security considerations and public protection measures.[19] Visits may be conducted in any language. However, if considered necessary in the interests of security or to prevent crime, a governor can require a visit to be conducted in English, or monitored by a person who speaks the language used or tape recorded for later translation.[20]

14  PSO 4410 para 1.1.
15  PSO 4410 para 2.6.
16  PSO 4410 para 1.9.
17  PSO 4410 para 1.10.
18  PR rule 34(5)–(6), YOIR rule 9(5)–(6), PSO 4410 para 3.4.
19  PSO 4410 para 3.2.
20  PSO 4410 para 3.16.

7.10    In recognition of possible challenges under disability discrimination legislation, the policy specifically recognises that 'reasonable adjustments' must be made to accommodate disabled prisoners or prisoners with particular requirements.[21]

7.11    In addition, special social visits can be granted at the governor's discretion to allow prisoners to make arrangements for business affairs that remain unresolved on their conviction and to allow for the conduct of legal proceedings.[22] Prisons can adopt local policies to require prisoners to seek permission prior to handing out or receiving documents during visits.[23] Separate provisions apply to legal documents and these are discussed below.

## Prohibited items

7.12    The Rules provide that visitors cannot bring unauthorised articles into prisons and that such items can be confiscated.[24] From 1 April 2008 changes to the Prison Act and the Rules made by the Offender Management Act 2007[25] have created a new framework of offences of conveying unauthorised articles to prisoners.

- 'List A' items are controlled drugs, explosives, firearms or other offensive weapons[26] and their unauthorised conveyance into or out of a prison or supply to a prisoner attracts a maximum ten-year sentence.[27]
- 'List B' items are alcohol, mobile phones, cameras and sound recording devices[28] and similar offences involving them attract a maximum of two years.[29]
- 'List C' items are tobacco, money, clothing, food, drink, letters, paper, books, tools and information technology equipment.[30] Offences involving List C items are summary only with a maximum punishment of a £1,000 fine.[31]

---

21  PSO 4410 paras 2.15.
22  PSO 4410 para 1.12.
23  PSO 4410 para 3.8.
24  PR rule 70, YOIR rule 74.
25  A new rule 70A is inserted by SI 2008 No 597.
26  PA 1952 s40A.
27  PA 1952 s40B.
28  PA 1952 s40A.
29  PA 1952 s40C(5).
30  PR rule 70A, YOIR rule 74.
31  PA 1952 s40C(6).

- Further offences of unauthorised photographing or sound-recording in prisons, and of removing or transmitting restricted documents out of a prison, are also created[32] with maximum punishments of two years' imprisonment.

## Accumulated visits

7.13    Due to overcrowding in the prison system prisoners are frequently held in prisons a long distance from their families and therefore cannot receive visits. To accommodate this problem, prisoners can accumulate a maximum of 26 statutory visits during a 12-month period and then apply for a temporary transfer to a different prison to receive the visits. Such transfers will normally be for a period of one month and can take place every six months.[33] Category A prisoners must make written requests for a transfer for accumulated visits to the High Security Directorate and prisoners who wish to be transferred for accumulated visits to Scotland, Northern Ireland, the Channel Isles or the Isle of Man must apply to the Cross Border Transfer Section of NOMS.[34] Privilege visits can also be accumulated at the governor's discretion.[35]

7.14    Unfortunately, again due to overcrowding, prisoners frequently have to wait for long periods of time before being granted a temporary transfer. Prisoners have no right to choose where they will serve their sentence[36] and the courts have held that separation from their families is an inevitable consequence of their detention. Accordingly, their detention a long way from their home will only exceptionally constitute a violation of article 8.[37]

## Inter-prison visits

7.15    Visits are also allowed between two prisoners at different prisons who fall within the definition of close relatives (see para 7.7 above). Such prisoners can be transferred to another prison for the purposes of the visit. Again, this is subject to security and the availability of transport and accommodation and can take several months to arrange

---

32    PA 1952 s40D.
33    PSO 4410 para 1.19.
34    PSO 4410 para 1.22.
35    PSO 4410 para 1.16.
36    PA 1952 s12 allows for prisoners to be lawfully held in any prison in England and Wales.
37    See, for example, *McCotter v UK* (1993) 15 EHRR CD98. For further discussion of the ECHR's application to issues of where a prisoner is held see para 3.55.

and prisoners have often complained successfully to the PPO about delays with such visits. Prisoners are entitled to inter-prison visits once every three months and each prisoner must surrender one visiting order.[38] Where inter prison visits are exceptionally difficult to organise governors should consider the use of video link facilities as an alternative and with current overcrowding levels in prisons the use of video link is likely to become more common.

7.16    The policy also states that subject to resources, Governors may allow visits between prisoners and close relatives who are in custody outside the Prison Service (for example, in military detention or detained under the Mental Health Act 1983) provided that they are satisfied that the visit would not jeopardise security or control and would nor impede the rehabilitation of either.[39]

## Stopping visits

7.17    Visits will be stopped in extreme circumstances and PSO 4410 lists the following examples:

- an attempt is made to pass an unauthorised article;
- violence occurs or is threatened;
- plans for escape, criminal offences or the obstruction of the course of justice are overheard; or
- an incident occurs which threatens the smooth running of the prison.

In certain circumstances information about the contents of a conversation can be disclosed.[40]

## Restrictions on social visits

7.18    Following the introduction of the Human Rights Act 1998, the Prison Rules and the Young Offender Institution Rules were amended to ensure the restrictions on prison communications including visits were compatible with the Act and in particular the requirements of article 8. Accordingly, the Rules[41] require that any restrictions on visits that interfere with convention rights must be proportionate and must only be imposed for one of the following grounds, which mirror the qualifications set out in article 8(2):

---

38   PSO 4410 paras 12.6–12.8.
39   PSO 4410 para 2.22.
40   PSO 4410 paras 3.6–3.7.
41   PR rule 34(2)–(3), YOIR rule 9(2)–(3).

- the interests of national security;
- the prevention, detection, investigation or prosecution of crime;
- the interests of public safety;
- securing or maintaining prison security or good order and discipline in prison;
- the protection of health or morals;
- the protection of the reputation of others;
- maintaining the authority and impartiality of the judiciary; or
- the protection of the rights and freedoms of any person.

7.19     Visits can be restricted by requiring prisoners to sit at special tables which are more closely monitored than other tables. Alternatively, closed visits can be applied, during which a panel of glass separates a prisoner from his or her visitor in order to prohibit any physical contact. Further details on closed visits are set out below.

7.20     In more extreme circumstances the Secretary of State can ban a visitor from the prison for such period of time as is considered necessary.[42] Again, to ensure compliance with article 8, any decision to ban a visitor must be proportionate to the stated aim and must be necessary on the grounds set out above.

7.21     Visitors who are close relatives should only be banned in exceptional circumstances but other classes of visitors are more vulnerable. Legal visitors and visitors who are members of the Independent Monitoring Board cannot be banned.[43] In considering whether the decision to ban a visitor is a proportionate response to the threat posed by the visitor it is necessary to consider all relevant factors and the strength of the evidence to support the allegations made against the visitor. For example, it will be necessary to consider whether the visitor is the prisoner's only visitor or whether the visitor is a child, if so the infringement of the prisoner's article 8 rights will be greater and a stronger justification will be required for the ban. It will always be necessary for staff to consider whether closed visits would address the security concerns, as this will provide a more proportionate response and should suffice in most circumstances.

7.22     Further guidance on banning visitors is set out in PSO 3610, which deals specifically with visitors who are banned due to allegations that they are smuggling drugs into the prison. Under the guidance visitors, including family members, found smuggling drugs into prisons should normally be banned from visiting for at least three months,

---

42  PR rule 73 and YOIR rule 77.
43  PR rule 73(2) and YOIR rule 77(2).

followed by a period of closed visits for three months.[44] The policy specifies that visitors should only be banned for drug smuggling if they are 'found to be engaging in this activity' and not solely on the basis of intelligence, or on the indication of a drug dog.[45] A ban should be imposed unless there are 'exceptional reasons' for not doing so.[46] The following examples of exceptional reasons are set out in the policy:

- where the ban would cause disproportionate harm to the right to a family life protected under article 8 of the ECHR;
- where the ban would cause disproportionate harm to the rights of a child to access their parent as protected under article 9(3) of the UN Convention on the Rights of the Child;
- where the prisoner is a juvenile and the ban would cause disproportionate harm to his or her right of access to a parent; and
- for exceptional compassionate or other grounds.

7.23    The policy has been carefully worded in an attempt to avoid successful challenges under the Human Rights Act and requires governors to make decisions based on proper evidence and to consider a proportionate response taking into account the prisoner's and the visitor's rights, even where drugs are found. There is however an obvious concern that the policy is framed by reference to a test of 'exceptionality', as a decision is either proportionate or not, and this cannot depend upon such a test.[47]

7.24    Despite the guidance decisions to ban visitors are often made with no proper consideration of the policy and on very slight evidence. An appeal against a decision to ban a visitor should be made using the normal complaints procedure.

7.25    Decisions which engage article 8 and the right to respect for family life can be challenged under the Human Rights Act. As stated above, in the majority of cases any legitimate security concerns, about the passing of unauthorised articles, can be met by the imposition of closed visits, rather than by an outright ban. Accordingly a decision to ban a visitor who was allegedly assisting a category A high escape risk prisoner with an escape plan, was a disproportionate response to any risk posed. Instead, the court accepted that the risk could be appropriately managed through closed visits which would allow staff to monitor the visitor's contact with the prisoner.[48]

---

44  PSO 3610 para 3(ii)–(xiii).
45  PSO 3610 paras 6–7.
46  PSO 3610 para 3(ii).
47  See paras 3.55 and 12.76.
48  *R (Wilkinson) v Home Office* [2002] EWHC 1212 (Admin).

## Closed visits

7.26 The Rules specifically make specific provision for closed visits, that is, where physical contact is prevented, usually by a glass screen.[49] Closed visits are frequently imposed when prisoners are suspected of receiving unauthorised articles during visits or where behaviour during a visit has breached standards of good order and discipline. Closed visits cannot be imposed as a punishment at an adjudication hearing. Instead, the decision must be made on its own merits and closed visits can be imposed even when there has been no formal disciplinary charge against a prisoner, or when the charge has been dismissed. In such circumstances prisoners often feel aggrieved but it can be very difficult to challenge a decision to impose closed visits, which may be based on security intelligence the details of which will not be disclosed to a prisoner.

7.27 PSI 40/2008 sets out specific guidance on the use of closed visits imposed due to concerns over the smuggling of unauthorised articles, and should be read in conjunction with PSO 3610. The PSI confirms that closed visits should only be applied where prisoners are proved or reasonably suspected of involvement in drug smuggling through visits, or are considered to pose a reasonable risk of involvement.[50] In addition, when deciding whether to impose closed visits prisons must take into account all the individual circumstances of the case and ensure that the decision is proportionate. The PSI provides guidance on the factors to be taken into account and examples of when closed visits are likely to be a proportionate response to the risk posed by a prisoner.[51] Failure of a single MDT will not usually justify closed visits.[52] The prisoner must be placed on closed visits for a specific period of time rather than for a set number of visits and the decision must be reviewed monthly to establish whether there is a continuing need for them.[53] Where necessary a further period of closed visits can be applied to run concurrently.[54]

---

49  PR rule 34(4) and YOIR rule 9(4).
50  PSI 40/2008 para 13.
51  PSI 40/2008 para 14.
52  PSI 40/2008 para 16.
53  PSI 40/2008 para 21.
54  PSI 40/2008 paras 22–24.

## Visits from children

7.28    Children will only be allowed to visit where contact with the prisoner is in the child's best interest and a Governor has the discretion to refuse a visit if he or she thinks it could place the child's safety at risk. People aged 16 years or over are allowed to visit a prisoner unaccompanied at the Governor's discretion.[55]

7.29    Prisoners who are assessed as posing a risk to children are required to make a written application for any person under the age of 18 to visit or have any other form of contact. Applications must be considered under the procedures set out in the Prison Service Public Protection Manual.[56]

7.30    Prisoners who are assessed as posing a risk to children will only be allowed contact with their own immediate family and/or the children of their partner with whom they were living prior to imprisonment, unless the Governor agrees that contact with other children will be in the child's best interests. Prior to granting any contact will the views of the child's parent or carer must be sought. If the parent or carer agrees, a multi agency risk assessment, involving the police, social services, the probation service and where appropriate the NSPCC, must be completed.

7.31    The prison must then decide on the level of contact to be allowed:

- Level one: no contact with any child is permitted and all correspondence and telephone calls must be monitored.
- Level two: contact is permitted only by written correspondence and all correspondence and telephone calls must be monitored.
- Level three: contact is permitted via written correspondence and telephone and all correspondence and telephone calls must be monitored.
- Level four: no restrictions are applied and the prisoner can have contact via correspondence, telephone and visits. Routine sampling of telephone calls and correspondence and general observation during visits must be conducted.

7.32    The lawfulness of a decision to ban a child from visiting a prisoner was considered in the case of *R (Banks) v The Governor of HMP Wakefield and the Home Secretary.*[57] The prisoner had been convicted of gross indecency and indecent assault on a boy. He challenged the decision to

---

55  PSO 4410 paras 2.8 and 2.9.
56  *Child Contact Procedures*, chapter 2, section 2.
57  [2001] EWHC 917 (Admin).

ban him from receiving visits from his six-year-old nephew, and the legality of the child protection policy then in force. The court held that there was no violation of article 8(1) because the relationship between the prisoner and his nephew was not sufficiently strong. However, the court also held that, had article 8 been engaged, the decision would have been justified under article 8(2). The policy had the legitimate aim of protecting children. It allowed for a child to visit a prisoner where it was in the child's best interests and achieved a proportionate and fair balance between the rights of the child and the rights of the prisoner.

## Visits by journalists

7.33    A new policy on prisoners' access to journalists was introduced following successful challenges to the previous policy.[58] Under the old policy, prisoners were not generally allowed to receive visits from journalists acting in a professional capacity. Visits from journalists in a personal capacity were allowed, but the governor could require the journalist to give an undertaking that any material obtained would not be used for publication or other professional purposes.[59] Visits from journalists in a professional capacity were only allowed on the provision of a written undertaking that the interview would be conducted in accordance with any conditions imposed by the governor and that the material would only be used for the purposes permitted.

7.34    In *Simms and O'Brien*[60] the Secretary of State contended that his policy only allowed for interviews with journalists if the prisoner was incapable of communicating in another way. The House of Lords held that although the provisions of the policy itself were not ultra vires the Prison Act 1952 or the Prison Rules, the Secretary of State's interpretation of the policy amounted to a blanket ban, which was unlawful and could not be justified. Their Lordships held that prisoners have a fundamental right to have oral interviews with journalists to seek to persuade them to investigate the safety of their conviction and to publish their findings to assist prisoners' efforts to gain access to justice.

7.35    The current policy is set out in PSO 4470, which aims to ensure that prisoners are granted access to journalists in accordance with their rights set out in article 10 of the ECHR. As previously, where

---

58  See *R v Home Secretary ex p Simms and O'Brien* [1999] 3 All ER 400 and *R (Hirst) v Home Secretary* [2002] EWHC 602 (Admin).

59  Standing Order 5A para 37 (no longer in force).

60  *R v Home Secretary ex p Simms and O'Brien* [1999] 3 All ER 400.

a journalist wishes to have a domestic visit they must give a written undertaking that any material received will not be used for professional purposes.

7.36    If a prisoner wishes to see a journalist in a professional capacity they must apply to the Governor. Such visits will only be allowed where:

- The sole purpose of the visit is to highlight an alleged miscarriage of justice.
- The prisoner has exhausted all appeals and no further publicly funded assistance is available.
- The visit is the only suitable method of communication and the prisoner and the journalist have previously communicated in writing which has proved inadequate.
- The journalist intends to make a serious attempt to investigate a prisoner's case and to bring it to the attention of the public.
- Permitting the visit will not cause any threat to security or the good order and discipline of the prison.[61]

7.37    Exceptionally, a visit will be allowed where a prisoner has not exhausted all appeals and where the CCRC has agreed to accept an application from a prisoner or where the CCRC has made the decision to refer a prisoner's case to the crown court or Court of Appeal.[62] There is obvious concern that the revised policy is unlawful insofar as it imposes a blanket ban on journalists visiting in a professional capacity in any circumstances except where a miscarriage of justice is raised. The prisoner may wish to raise serious issues of public interest on matters affecting prisons and prisoners, and there may be reasons why a personal visit is important. For these reasons the amended policy is liable to be challenged as disproportionate.

7.38    There is a detailed application process and before granting a visit a governor must be sure that all relevant criteria are met. The journalist must provide a written undertaking in the form set out at annex B to the PSO.[63]

7.39    The visit should take place in a private and quiet room but within the sight and sound of a prison officer.[64] Governors should try to allow 90 minutes for the visit.[65] The discussion must be 'limited to the prisoner's representations against his/her conviction or sen-

---

61   PSO 4470 para 4.5.
62   PSO 4470 para 4.6.
63   PSO 4470 para 4.14.
64   PSO 4470 paras 4.18 and 4.20.
65   PSO 4470 para 4.17.

tence, and serious comment on the processes of justice or the penal system'.[66] Specific restrictions on the content of the visits are set out at paragraph 4.22 and any breach of these restrictions can cause the visit to be terminated. Visits can be recorded by the journalist at the discretion of the governor and by the Prison Service where the facilities exist.[67] A second visit from the journalist will be granted only in exceptional circumstances.[68]

### Visits by former prisoners and witnesses

7.40    The policy in PSO 4410 also has guidance on visits from former prisoners who are being supervised on licence in the community.[69] The prisoner should apply in writing for permission for such a visit in advance. The Governor should consult the prisoner's offender manager, and can only refuse an application where the visitor is a close relative in exceptional circumstances. Visits to unconvicted prisoners from witnesses in the criminal matter who are relatives or friends should not be refused unless the court has so directed.[70]

### Searching visitors

7.41    The provisions and policies in relation to searching visitors are dealt with in chapter 8. The visits policy does reiterate that when conducting searches prison staff must be aware of the particular needs of visitors with injuries or disabilities and must consult healthcare professionals when necessary. They must also be aware of religious and cultural sensitivities.[71]

### Visits to category A prisoners

7.42    All social visitors to category A prisoners have to be approved (see chapter 3). Visitors to category A prisoners are more likely to be asked to submit to a search and all category A prisoners will be strip searched after open visits. Exceptional risk category A prisoners must have closed visits unless the Director of High Security Prisons consents to open visits. The prison management has the discretion to approve visits to category A prisoners by close relatives under closed

---

66  PSO 4470 para 4.21.
67  PSO 4470 paras 4.25–4.27.
68  PSO 4470 para 4.29.
69  PSO 4410 paras 2.18–2.19.
70  PSO 4410 paras 2.20–2.21.
71  PSO 4410 para 3.1.

visiting conditions pending the outcome of their application to be added to the approved visitors list.

## Visits by legal advisers

7.43    Facilities must be made available for legal advisers to visit prisoners in connection with legal proceedings to which the prisoner is a party[72] and may be made to allow legal advisers to visit the prisoner about any other legal business.[73] In practice prisons will not enquire into the reasons why a legal adviser requests a visit. A 'legal adviser' is defined as a prisoner's counsel or solicitor, including a clerk acting on behalf of a solicitor'.[74] The visiting facilities should allow the prisoner to be interviewed in sight of, but out of the hearing of, a prison officer.

7.44    Legal visits with high security category A prisoners may be subject to more stringent measures, such as observation cameras and closed visits conditions, which can raise concerns about the confidentiality of the legal visit. These measures were challenged unsuccessfully in *R v Home Secretary ex p O'Dhuibhir*.[75] However, this decision pre-dates the Human Rights Act 1998 and the decision in *R v Home Secretary, ex p Daly*[76] following which the courts are required to consider whether any interference with prisoners' Convention rights is limited to that which is necessary to meet legitimate security concerns. Accordingly, in the case of *Cannan v Home Secretary and Governor of HMP Full Sutton*[77] the Court of Appeal held that a policy that only allowed documents to be passed between lawyer and client where prior notice had been given, except in exceptional circumstances, would breach a prisoner's rights under article 6 of the ECHR. The court recognised that situations might arise which were not exceptional where a prison could not justify prohibiting the exchange of documents without prior permission having been granted.

---

72  PR rule 38(1) and YOIR rule 16(1).
73  PR rule 38(2) and YOIR rule 16(2) – these provisions have been amended in light of legal challenges to the definition of 'being party to legal proceedings'. See, for example, *Guilfoyle v Home Office* [1981] QB 309 and *R v Home Secretary ex p Anderson* [1984] QB 778 – a successful challenge to an old policy which prohibited solicitors from visiting prisoners to discuss complaints that had not also been raised with the prison authorities.
74  PR rule 2 and YOIR rule 2. 'Legal adviser' in PR rule 2 includes European lawyers with rights of audience before English courts: *R (Van Hoogstraten) v Governor of Belmarsh* [2003] 1 WLR 263.
75  [1997] COD 315 CA.
76  [2001] UKHL 26.
77  [2003] EWCA Civ 1480.

For example, it might not always be possible for a solicitor to seek permission in time. Therefore, the court held that the policy did not strike the right balance between the right to free communication between lawyer and client and the legitimate security concerns in the high security estate. The judgment stressed the need for policies, and in particular local policies, to make plain that they should be applied flexibly by prison staff.

## Visitors to secure training centres

7.45     Children in secure training centres are entitled to receive a minimum of a one-hour visit each week. Such visits can be supervised so long as any supervision is not unnecessarily intrusive.[78] The STC Rules contain similar provisions as contained in the Prison and YOI Rules as to the right to legal visits out of hearing of an officer.[79]

## Visitors to children's homes

7.46     Children are entitled to receive visits with friends and relations and suitable facilities must be provided to allow these visits to take place in private at any time.[80] In addition children must be allowed to receive official visits from, for example, their solicitor or social worker.[81] Restrictions can be imposed on visits to safeguard and promote the welfare of the child.[82] Any restriction imposed on visits must be approved by the child's placing authority, and where the restriction is imposed in an emergency, full details must be provided to the placing authority within 24 hours.[83] In addition, visits will be subject to the provisions of any relevant court order relating to contact between the child and any person.[84]

## Marriage, conjugal visits and starting a family

7.47     The case of *Hamer v UK*[85] established that the right to marry under article 12 of the ECHR applies to serving prisoners. There is now

78   STCR rule 11.
79   STCR rule 13.
80   CHR rule 15(1)(a) and (b).
81   CHR rule 15(2).
82   CHR rule 15(6).
83   CHR rule 15(7).
84   CHR rule 15(8).
85   (1979) 4 EHHR 139.

detailed Prison Service guidance on prisoners' marriages and civil partnerships.[86] Prisoners are expected to have at least three months to serve to be able to marry or register a civil partnership whilst in prison.[87] Depending on the security category of the prisoner, they may be entitled to release on temporary licence to marry or attend the civil partnership ceremony (see below). Failing this they may be escorted to their marriage or civil partnership registration. It is only if security concerns preclude these options that the ceremony should take place in prison.[88] Category A prisoners are not allowed to attend outside ceremonies even on escort, and category B prisoners will not normally be allowed to. This presumption, subject to an individualised assessment of risk, is reversed for category C and D prisoners.[89]

7.48    Conjugal visits are not permitted in the UK, although they are allowed in certain European countries. Several prisoners have attempted to challenge the ban on conjugal visits in the UK on the basis that this amounts to a violation of a prisoner's article 8 rights. However, the Commission has found that it is within the UK's margin of appreciation to apply a blanket ban on conjugal visits.[90]

7.49    Prisoners are entitled to access artificial insemination (AI) facilities whilst in prison. There have been several challenges to the legality of the policy on access to AI, which is granted only in exceptional circumstances.

7.50    In *R (Mellor) v SSHD*[91] a prisoner argued that the policy amounted to an unjustified interference with his rights under articles 8 (right to respect for private and family life) and 12 (right to found a family). He conceded, however, that there were no exceptional circumstances to justify the provision of AI in his case. The Court of Appeal rejected the challenge and approved the reasons given by the government for the policy which included the need to maintain public confidence in the penal system and the implications of children being disadvantaged by being brought up in single parent families.

7.51    However, the Grand Chamber decision in *Dickson v UK*[92] rejected the government's justifications for the policy and held that the ap-

86  PSO 4450 and PSO 4445 respectively – see also Marriage Act 1983 s1 which permits marriages to be solemnised in prisons if the prisoner cannot be released.

87  PSO 4450 para 2, PSO 4445 para 2.4.

88  PSO 4450 part 4, PSO 4445 part 4.

89  PSO 4450 part 4, PSO 4445 part 4.

90  *ELH and PBH v UK* [1998] EHRLR 231.

91  [2001] 3 WLR 4.

92  Application no 44362/04.

plication of the policy to the applicants amounted to an unlawful interference with their article 8 rights. In considering each of the justifications for the policy the Grand Chamber held:

- The inability to beget a child was not an inevitable consequence of imprisonment. There were no security issues surrounding the granting of AI facilities, nor would this impose significant administrative or financial demands on the State.
- The policy could not be justified solely on the basis of public opinion and the policy failed to consider the importance of the rehabilitation of prisoners, particularly towards the end of a long prison sentence.
- The positive obligation to consider the welfare and protection of children, does not extend to preventing parents from conceiving a child in circumstances where one parent would be in the community and could look after a child before a prisoner's release.

7.52     The Grand Chamber went on to hold that the policy placed an inordinately high 'exceptionality' burden on the applicants when requesting access to AI facilities. It required the applicants to demonstrate that the deprivation of access to AI facilities might prevent conception altogether; and that the circumstances of their case were exceptional within the meaning of the policy. Thus the policy failed to allow a balancing of the competing individual and public interests and a proportionality test by the Secretary of State or the domestic courts. Further, the policy had not been subject to Parliamentary scrutiny to allow for a proper consideration of the various competing interests or an assessment of proportionality.

7.53     At time of writing the Prison Service had not amended its policy on access to AI facilities to reflect the European Court's judgment.

## Correspondence

7.54     Convicted prisoners in prisons and YOIs can send one letter a week at public expense.[93] Additional letters can be sent as a privilege with the permission of the governor or the IMB in special circumstances and under the IEP scheme.[94] Children held in STCs can send three letters a week a public expense and any number of letters at their own expense.[95] Children held in children's homes must be able to send and

---

93  PR rule 35(2)(a) and YOIR rule 10(1)(a).
94  PR rule 34(3)–(7) and YOIR rule 10(2) and 10(5).
95  STCR rule 11(1)(a).

receive any number of letters and, if necessary, emails.[96] The regulations concerning restrictions imposed on visits in children's homes apply equally to restrictions on correspondence (see para 7.46 above).

7.55    The Prison Service policy on prisoners' correspondence that applies in prisons and YOIs is set out in PSO 4411 which specifies that the Prison Service will encourage prisoners to maintain close relationships with family and friends and links with life beyond the prison through letter writing which will 'constructively contribute towards the prisoner's successful resettlement'.

7.56    Prisoners are entitled to send as many privilege letters as they wish each week, except for in prisons where routine reading is in force (see below). Prisoners must meet the costs of such letters from their own funds.[97] Where routine reading is in force, the governor has a discretion to limit the number of privilege letters that may be sent, subject to a minimum of one a week for adults and two a week for young offenders, although prisoners should be able to send as many privilege letters as are practicable bearing in mind the staff resources available for reading correspondence.[98] In general, there is no restriction on the length of letters, but the governor can set a limit of a minimum of four sides of A5 if routine reading is in force.[99]

7.57    Special letters are issued according to a prisoner's needs. The general guidance is that they should be issued in the following circumstances:

- Before a prisoner is transferred to another establishment; or, if the prisoner is not given a special letter before transfer, on reception at the new establishment. The number of letters should correspond to the number of outstanding visiting orders.
- Immediately after conviction to settle business affairs.
- Where necessary for the welfare of the prisoner or his or her family.
- In connection with legal proceedings to which the prisoner is a party (but see legal correspondence below).
- To enable a prisoner to write to a probation officer or to an agency arranging accommodation or employment on release.
- To enable a prisoner to write to the relevant council tax officer on his or her reception into custody.
- On a discretionary basis for additional contact with their MP,

96   CHR rule 16(4)(b).
97   PSO 4411 para 2.2.
98   PSO 4411 para 2.3.
99   PSO 4411 para 6.4.

member of National Assembly for Wales, MEP or consular representative.

- To enable a prisoner to write to the Prisons and Probation Ombudsman.

7.58   The cost of special letters will normally be met from prisoners' own funds, save in the case of transfers, when they should be sent at public expense.[100]

## Restrictions on correspondence

7.59   Correspondence can be restricted on the same basis that visits are restricted as set out in PR rule 34 and YOIR 9 (see para 7.18 above). Therefore the restrictions or conditions on correspondence must not interfere with Convention rights. Any interference must be:

- necessary on the grounds specified in rule 34(3) listed at para 7.18 above;
- compatible with the Convention right being interfered with; and
- proportionate to the aim to be achieved.

7.60   The STCR provide that the Secretary of State can impose restrictions on communications in accordance with the needs of good order and the prevention of crime.[101] Letters to children in STCs can be stopped if their contents are objectionable or of inordinate length.[102] Such provisions featured in both the Prison and YOI Rules before they were amended to ensure that they were compliant with article 8 and the failure to amend the STCR must have been an oversight, which is unfortunate given the particular need for children to stay in contact with their families.

7.61   Although the STCR do not incorporate the language of the Convention, it is clear that they must be read to ensure compatibility with the ECHR.[103] Accordingly any restrictions must be necessary for a legitimate aim and proportionate.

7.62   In prisons and YOIs letters out must include the name of the sender and the address of the prison. The address of the prison can only be omitted on request to the governor.[104] Similarly, people sending letters to the prison must normally display their name and address on the letters.

100   PSO 4411 para 2.4.
101   STCR rule 10(1).
102   STCR rule 10(3).
103   In accordance with HRA 1998 s3.
104   PSO 4411 para 6.1.

7.63    The following restrictions can be imposed on letters:[105]

- Correspondence to minors can be stopped at the request of a person with parental responsibility.
- Prisoners identified as presenting a risk or potential risk to a child must first apply to a member of staff.
- Correspondence between a minor in custody and any person with whom it is thought it would not be in that minor's interests to communicate can be stopped by a governor.
- Correspondence between convicted prisoners is permitted if they are close relatives, or if they were co-defendants and the correspondence relates to their conviction or sentence. In all other cases, the approval of both governors must be obtained.
- Correspondence with ex-prisoners is permitted unless the governor considers that this would impede the rehabilitation of either party or that there would be a threat to good order or security. If the ex-prisoner is under supervision in the community the views of his or her probation officer should be sought.
- Correspondence by a convicted with a victim or a victim's family, will be permitted on application by a governor, unless the victim is a close family member and wishes to receive correspondence or where the victim has already written to the prisoner.
- Any correspondence can be stopped if the governor has reason to believe that the correspondent is engaged in activities or planning which present a genuine and serious threat to the security or good order of that prison or the prison estate.
- Prisoners are only able to advertise for pen friends with approval of the governor and after submitting the text of the advertisement. In prisons where most or all correspondence is monitored the governor has the discretion to withhold replies if the number is excessive.
- Prisoners will only be allowed to write to a PO Box at the governor's discretion if the prisoner does not know the private address of the correspondent.

7.64    Correspondence may also be prohibited on the grounds of its contents.[106] The following material is prohibited:

- Material which is threatening, indecent, grossly offensive or false.
- Plans or material which would assist or encourage the commission of a criminal or disciplinary offence.

---

105  PSO 4411 paras 4.3–4.13.
106  PSO 4411 para 4.6.

- Escape plans or material which jeopardises the security of the prison.
- Material that would jeopardise national security.
- Descriptions of the making or use of any weapon, explosive, poison or other destructive device.
- Obscure or coded messages which are not decipherable.
- Material which is indecent and obscene under the Postal Services Act 2000.
- Material which, if sent to, or received from, a child might place his or her welfare at risk.
- Material which would create a clear threat or present danger of violence or physical harm to any person, including incitement to racial hatred.
- Material intended for publication or broadcast if it:
  - Is for publication in return for payment (unless the prisoner is unconvicted). However, prisoners are permitted to receive payment for pieces of artwork or work of literary merit if they do not contravene any other restrictions on correspondence and if the money is paid to appropriate charitable institutions.
  - Is likely to appear in a publication associated with a person or organisation to which the prisoner may not write as a result of the restriction on correspondence to someone engaged in activities which present a threat to the good order or discipline of the prison.
  - Is about the prisoner's own crime or past offences or those of others except where it consists of serious representations about conviction or sentence or forms part of serious comment about the criminal justice or penal system.[107]
  - Refers to individual prisoners or members of staff in a way that might identify them.
  - Contravenes any of the restrictions applying to letters
- In the case of convicted prisoners, material constituting the conduct of business activity unless it relates to a power of attorney, the winding up of a business following conviction or the sale or transfer of personal funds, or other personal financial transactions within set limits.
- Where a prisoner is subject to a deportation order material constituting or arranging any financial transaction unless the governor is satisfied that there is a need for the transaction.

---

107 *Nilsen v Governor of HM Prison Full Sutton and Home Secretary* [2003] EWHC 3160, see below.

- Where a prisoner is subject to a receiving order or is an undischarged bankrupt material, constituting or arranging any financial transaction except on the advice of the official receiver, to pay a fine or debt to secure the prisoner's earlier release, to defend criminal proceedings, or to pay costs in connection with bankruptcy proceedings.

Prisoners cannot ask another person to correspond on their behalf where the correspondence would contravene the PSO.

7.65    Any interference with or restriction on a prisoner's correspondence must be compliant with the prisoner's right to respect for private and family life and their right to freedom of expression as protected under articles 8 and 10 of the ECHR. In *Nilsen v Governor of HM Prison Full Sutton and Home Secretary*[108] a prisoner challenged the refusal of the prison to return his draft autobiography to him (which had been sent out of the prison). The prison refused to do so on the basis that the material was prohibited under the policy then set out in Standing Order 5B. The court rejected the prisoner's arguments and accepted that the policy was consistent with the prisoner's article 10 rights.

## Interception of correspondence

7.66    Prisoners' non-legal correspondence can be intercepted and disclosed if:

- the interception is necessary on the same grounds as for interference with visits and correspondence (see para 7.18 above); and
- the interception is proportionate to the aim sought to be achieved.[109]

7.67    'Interception' includes 'opening, reading, examining and copying' the written or drawn communication. The governor may not disclose the intercepted material to anyone who is not an employee of the prison or the Prison Service, NOMS or the Ministry of Justice unless he considers that the disclosure is necessary on the specified grounds and proportionate to the aim sought to be achieved by the disclosure. Third parties to whom this material may be disclosed include the police, and other relevant authorities.[110]

---

108  [2004] EWCA Civ 1540.
109  PR rules 35A–35D, YOIR rules 11–13.
110  PSO 4411 para 10.5.

## Routine reading

7.68 Routine reading can be introduced for the following prisoners' correspondence, other than legal and confidential correspondence: [111]

- All correspondence sent or received by prisoners at high security prisons.
- All prisoners from high security prisons temporarily held elsewhere.
- All category A or potential category A prisoners.
- All prisoners held in separate units for category A prisoners.
- All prisoners on the escape list.
- All outgoing mail for prisoners remanded or convicted for an offence of sending or attempting to send obscene correspondence.

7.69 Other prisoners may also be subject to routine reading in exceptional circumstances including where necessary on the grounds set out in PR rule 35(A) and YOIR rule 11, where a prisoner or his or her correspondent may attempt to breach any of the restrictions set out in PSO 4411 or where reading is thought to be in a prisoner's best interests or is required on a prisoner's ACCT care map.[112] Routine reading of the correspondence of named individuals may continue only for as long as is necessary.

7.70 In addition, a maximum of five per cent of correspondence can be subject to random reading. This maximum can be exceeded where necessary and proportionate for security and good order or discipline.[113]

7.71 Furthermore, correspondence can be examined for illicit enclosures. This must be carried out with due respect for the privacy of the letter's contents. Incoming correspondence, other than legal correspondence, should be examined as a matter of routine. Outgoing non-legal correspondence should only be examined:

- where routine reading is in force; or
- there is a special instruction to read the prisoner's correspondence; or
- there is reason to believe unauthorised items are enclosed.[114]

111 PSO 4411 para 9.5.
112 PSO 4411 para 9.6.
113 PSO 4411 para 9.8.
114 PSO 4411 para 9.3.

7.72   At open prisons prisoners can seal outgoing non-legal correspondence, which should only be examined if there is reason to suspect it
contains an illicit enclosure.[115]

*Unconvicted prisoners*

7.73   Under PR rule 35(1) unconvicted prisoners can send and receive
as many letters as they wish, subject to such limits and conditions
directed by the Secretary of State. Such limits and conditions are only
rarely imposed, other than for provisional category A prisoners and
prisoners convicted of specific offences, whose letters will be subject
to routine reading as specified above.[116]

## Legal and confidential correspondence

7.74   There have been a number of cases in which prisoners have challenged prison authorities interference with legal correspondence.
The Prison Rules were amended following the ECtHR's ruling in
*Campbell v United Kingdom*[117] that the prison authority's routine
reading of the applicant prisoner's correspondence with his lawyer
breached his article 8 rights. In reaching its decision the court referred to its judgment in *Campbell and Fell v United Kingdom*[118] and
held that the principle under article 6 which protected a prisoner's
right of access to the court should also be applied to article 8 to allow
a prisoner privileged correspondence with his or her lawyer without
fear of prejudicing any cause of action the prisoner might have.

7.75   The Rules[119] allows prisoners to correspond confidentially with
their legal advisers and the courts[120] and to be provided with writing materials for such correspondence. In *R (Skanes) v Secretary of
State for the Home Department*[121] a prisoner was refused permission
to move for judicial review to challenge the refusal to allow him to
communicate confidentially with an adviser at a citizens advice bureau (CAB). It was held that Rules restricted legal advisers to solicitors, counsel or a solicitor's clerk and that employees of the CAB

---

115  PSO 4411 para 9.4.
116  See Annex B to PSO 4600.
117  (1992) 15 EHRR 137.
118  [1983] 5 EHRR 207.
119  PR rule 39, YOIR rule 17, STCR rule 14.
120  The definition of a court includes the European Commission and Court of
Human Rights and the European Court of Justice.
121  [2006] EWHC 1571 (Admin).

would not automatically fall within that category. However, the Prison Service accepted that any lawyer employed by a non-governmental organisation, including a CAB and charities such as the Prisoners' Advice Service or the Howard League, would be covered by rule 39.

7.76    Prisoners can exercise their right to confidential correspondence with their legal adviser regardless of whether or not they are party to legal proceedings. Legal correspondence can only be opened, examined and read if the governor has reasonable cause to believe that it contains an illicit enclosure or reasonable cause to believe that its contents may endanger prison security, the safety of others or that its contents are otherwise of a criminal nature. A prisoner whose legal correspondence is opened has the right to be present when it is opened and to be informed if the correspondence or any enclosure is to be read or stopped.

7.77    PSO 4411 confirms that rule 39 allows legal mail to be handed in sealed and provides that it should not be read or examined except in special circumstances, as set out in annex A to PSO 4411.[122] Letters from prisoners to legal advisers should be marked 'rule 39' (or 'rule 17' for young offenders, and 'rule 14' for those in STCs) and as long as the recipient is a legal adviser or court (prisons are advised to check the adviser's status) then the letter will be protected by the rule. To ensure that it is also covered by rule 39, incoming legal correspondence should be marked 'rule 39' and marked to identify that it is from a legal adviser (for example by a stamp on the back).

7.78    Despite the clarity of the measures set out in rule 39, prisoners frequently complain that their legal correspondence has been opened. Complaints should be pursued through the internal complaint procedure and continual breaches of the rule should be challenged by way of judicial review. There can be no justification for the routine checking of all prisoners incoming and outgoing legal correspondence in any particular prison and any interference with prisoner's legal correspondence must be justified on a case by case basis. In *R v Home Secretary ex p Daly*[123] the court confirmed that any interference with prisoner's right to confidential correspondence with their legal adviser should be limited to the extent necessary to meet the aim sought by the interference.

7.79    In *Watkins v Secretary of State for the Home Department*[124] a prisoner sought to argue that the wilful opening of his legal correspondence

---

122  PSO 4411 para 5.2–5.3.
123  [2001] UKHL 26.
124  [2006] 2 WLR 807.

amounted to a breach of his right to confidential correspondence with his legal advisers and the courts. He claimed damages for misfeasance in public office. The House of Lords rejected his claim on the basis that there was no proof of special damages[125] – which it held essential ingredient of the tort of misfeasance in public office. This case clarifies that any claims arising from continued breaches of the Rules on legal correspondence, in the absence of such loss, should be made under the Human Rights Act 1998. In *Woodin v Home Office*[126] a prisoner claimed damages under the Human Rights Act for violations of rule 39, as well as claiming damages for misfeasance in public office arising from the psychiatric damage he had suffered as a result of his letters being opened. His claims were rejected as he failed to establish that the officer who opened his correspondence did so in bad faith and there was insufficient evidence to show he had suffered psychiatric damage. Similarly the court did not accept that he was a 'victim' for the purposes of the Human Rights Act as the staff had apologised to him and steps had been taken to prevent further interferences with rule 39.

## Confidential access correspondence

7.80   Prisoners are also entitled to confidential access correspondence with certain organisations, including the Criminal Cases Review Commission (CCRC) and the PPO.[127] Such correspondence is entitled to the same privileged handling arrangements as legal mail but should be marked 'confidential access' and bear the appropriate identifying mark for the organisation.

## Medical correspondence

7.81   In *R (Szuluk) v Governor of HMP Full Sutton*[128] a prisoner successfully argued that his correspondence with his external doctors should be treated on a confidential basis. His case was dependent on the facts that he was suffering from a life-threatening condition and required continual care. Whilst the Court of Appeal allowed the Governor's appeal[129] the European Court of Human Rights confirmed

---

125  That is loss or damage to property, or physical or psychiatric injury.
126  (2006) 31 July, unreported, QBD.
127  PSO 4411 para 5.1.
128  [2004] EWHC 514 (Admin).
129  [2004] EWCA Civ 1426.

that the checking of the correspondence was in breach of article 8[130] holding:

> In light of the severity of the applicant's medical condition, the Court considers that uninhibited correspondence with a medical specialist in the context of a prisoner suffering from a life-threatening condition should be afforded no less protection than the correspondence between a prisoner and an MP.

## Telephone calls

7.82    Prisoners' access to telephones is vital to enable them to maintain meaningful relations with the outside world. There are no restrictions on the calls children can make and receive in STCs and children's homes.[131] However, prisoners and young offenders are subject to strict regulations on their use of telephones.

7.83    A new personal identification number, or 'PIN', system for prisoners was introduced in 2000 to replace the old card phone system. The new system was introduced with a view to improving the control of prisoners' use of telephones. It aims to strike 'a balance between the security and good order of establishments; the need for prisoners to keep in contact with their families and friends; and the protection of the public from unwanted telephone contact from prisoners'.[132]

7.84    It had been proposed that the new system would include a pre-recorded message advising people that the call was from a prisoner. However, the proposal was dropped following legal challenges. Prisoners are given an eight digit personal identification number which they must use before making any calls. If a prisoner discloses their PIN to another prisoner a new PIN must be created for them, and governors are entitled to charge for this.[133] Before being issued with a PIN a prisoner must sign a form agreeing to the terms and conditions of the system. This form confirms that allowing another prisoner to use their PIN or using another prisoner's PIN is an offence against prison discipline.[134]

7.85    Each prisoner has their own account and they will only be able to make calls if they have sufficient credit on their account. A prisoner's credit balance will be displayed on the screen when they make a call.

---

130  *Szuluk v UK* [2009] ECHR 845.
131  STCR rule 11(2), CHR rule 15(4).
132  PSO 4400 para 1.4.
133  PSO 4400 para 2.12.
134  PSO 4400 para 2.8.

Prisoners are allowed a maximum amount of £50.00, although lower limits can be set as part of the IEP scheme. Foreign national prisoners are allowed to have more than £50.00 and this must be funded from their private cash account.[135] Prisoners must be allowed to top up their balance once a week in amounts of £1.00.[136]

7.86    The cost of calls from prison was challenged in *R (RD) v Secretary of State for the Home Department*[137] in which a prisoner sought to argue that the cost violated articles 8 and 14 of the ECHR. The court rejected his arguments and held that article 8 was not engaged relying on *AB v The Netherlands*[138] which held that article 8 did not guarantee a prisoner's right to make phone calls 'particularly where the facilities for contact by way of correspondence are available and adequate'. Accordingly the situation may be different where a prisoner's sole means of contact with family is by phone.

7.87    However following a complaint to Ofcom supported by the Prison Reform Trust amongst others, BT (which retains the contract to deliver the PIN phone system) reduced the cost of calls to prisoners from April 2009. The evidence was that a 30-minute call from a prison to a landline was over seven times more expensive than the equivalent call from a public payphone.[139]

## Call barring and call enabling

7.88    Under the PIN phone system there are two types of telephone service; the call enabling regime and the call barring regime. The call barring system allows prisoners to call any number other than those specifically barred by the prison, this might include the prisoner's victim's telephone numbers or other people's numbers who have asked not to be contacted by the prisoner (see below).

7.89    The call enabling regime is more restrictive. It provides that prisoners can only call those numbers that have been approved by the prison staff. Under this system prisoners are entitled to have a maximum of 35 telephone numbers they can call: 20 personal numbers and 15 legal numbers, although governors have the discretion to allow prisoners 30 legal numbers in exceptional circumstances.[140] These

---

135  PSO 4400 para 2.9.
136  PSO 4400 para 2.10.
137  [2008] EWCA Civ 676.
138  [2003] 37 EHRR 48.
139  see PRT information on the complaint at www.prisonreformtrust.org.uk/
     standard.asp?id=1735
140  PSO 4400 para 2.15.

limits were approved following legal challenges to the draft PSO. Each prison must approve the telephone numbers, and on transfer to a new prison the numbers are not automatically approved.[141] Appellants are entitled to purchase additional credit from their private cash account to speak to their legal advisers.

7.90    The call enabling system must be applied to the following prisoners:

- category A;
- potential category A;
- E List;
- prisoners identified as being subject to harassment procedures (PSO 4400 chapter 2 – The Protection From Harassment Act 1997);
- prisoners identified as being subject to Safeguarding Children Child Contact Measures (see the Public Protection Manual);
- prisoners subject to IG 54/94 (as amended by PSO 22/2005) – release of prisoners convicted of offences against children under the age of 18;
- prisoners who the police and/or probation service have identified as presenting a risk against witnesses and/or victims;
- anyone who is detained in a prison establishment following certification as a suspected international terrorist under Part 4 of the Anti-terrorism, Crime and Security Act 2001; and
- those detained under Immigration Act powers in the interests of national security.[142]

7.91    In addition, governors can apply the call barring system to an entire establishment or parts of an establishment with the consent of the area manager. In *R (Taylor) v Governor of Risley Prison*[143] a prisoner at HMP Risley unsuccessfully challenged the decision to impose a call barring system to the entirety of that prison. He argued that the decision amounted to an unlawful interference with his article 8 rights as it required him to pay 20 pence each time he wished to add a new telephone number to his list; he had to pay the charge regularly as he had many relations who moved frequently. The court rejected his challenge. It accepted that the call barring regime was necessary due to the extensive drug problem in the prison. It also accepted that it was not practicable for the prison to operate a dual system as the

---

141  PSO 4400 para 2.21.
142  PSO 4400 para 2.16.
143  [2004] 2 PL 198.

262 Prisoners: law and practice / chapter 7

prison held both sex offenders and other offenders; the introduction of a dual telephone system could result in bullying. Furthermore, the court held that the 20 pence charge was justifiable and that on the evidence the prisoner had extensive contact with his family, so no violation of article 8 arose.

7.92 Governors are required to review the type of regime in force on an annual basis or where there is a major regime change[144] and in *Taylor* the court was keen to emphasise that the decision to impose the call barring regime must be justified on a case by case basis with due regard to the Prison Rules and the European Convention on Human Rights.

7.93 Certain telephone numbers are globally approved; this means that all prisoners can automatically access them. Such numbers include the Samaritans and the Prisoners' Advice Service. Individual establishments can also agree a list of locally approved numbers.

## Special telephone calls

7.94 Prisoners are allowed to use official telephones in exceptional circumstances and where there are urgent legal or compassionate circumstances calls can be made at public expense. Inter-prison phone calls can be authorised between close relatives held at different prisons.[145] The definition of close relative is that set out in para 7.7 above. Foreign national prisoners or those with close family living abroad must be granted a free five minute call once a month where the prisoner has had no domestic visits during the preceding month and governors must consider allowing such prisoners to access phones outside normal hours to allow them to make calls to their country of origin.[146]

## Barring telephone numbers

7.95 If a member of the public requests that a prisoner should not be allowed to contact them, the prisoner's telephone account must be amended to bar him from contacting that person.[147] Prisoners will also be barred from telephoning a particular individual or organisation where there are grounds for believing that the person or organisation is planning activities which present a threat to the security or good order and discipline of the prison.[148] In addition, prisoners are

144 PSO 4400 para 2.17.
145 PSO 4400 para 2.45.
146 PSO 4400 para 6.7.
147 PSO 4400 para 3.1.
148 PSO 4400 para 3.2.

not allowed to telephone a victim of their offence unless he or she is a close relative, the victim has first approached the prisoner, or the governor considers that the call would not cause undue distress to the victim. Governors must consult with their area manager before ordering any prisoner not to telephone a close relative.[149]

7.96    Prisoners can be barred from calling minors where the person with parental responsibility so requests. Similarly, a child prisoner's phone account can be amended to bar him or her from calling someone where it is considered to be in their best interests, although the person with parental responsibility must be consulted.[150]

### Restrictions on telephone calls

7.97    Telephone calls are restricted in the same way as visits and correspondence[151] and the NSF provides that prisoners must be informed that telephone calls which include any of the following are prohibited:

- Plans or material which would assist any disciplinary or criminal offence.
- Escape plans or material which might jeopardise the security of the prison.
- Material which might jeopardise national security.
- Material associated with the making of any weapon or explosive.
- Obscure or coded messages.
- Material which would create a threat or present a danger of violence or harm to any person, including incitement to racial hatred, or which might place a child's welfare at risk.

### Recording telephone calls

7.98    The NSF provides that all telephone calls made by prisoners are recorded. Legal calls are excluded from routine recording. However, in 2008 it emerged that a prisoner's telephone calls to his solicitor had been unlawfully recorded at HMP Channings Wood in 2004 and 2005 following the accidental disclosure of transcripts of the telephone calls to the solicitor. The Prison Service alleged that the mistake occurred due to the failure of the prisoner to inform them of his solicitor's number. As a result of this incident the Justice Secretary announced that new rules will be introduced to require the chief operating officer of NOMS to authorise the interception of legal calls.

---

149  PSO 4400 para 3.3.
150  PSO 4400 para 3.4.
151  As set out in PR rule 34 and YOIR rule 9 – see above.

## Routine listening

7.99    The following prisoners will be subject to routine listening:

- Category A prisoners held in category A units.
- Prisoners who pose a threat to children.
- Prisoners held for an offence of harassment or convicted of sex offences.

Routine listening for such prisoners must be reviewed on a six monthly basis and must continue for no longer than necessary.

7.100    Routine listening for other prisoners can take place where necessary for one or more of the purposes set out in PR rule 35A or YOIR rule 11(4) (see para 7.66 above), and where the information required could not be obtained by less intrusive means. Routine listening for such prisoners should continue for no longer than necessary and must be reviewed every three months.

## Random listening

7.101    In addition, telephone calls, other than calls to legal advisers, may be subject to random listening. The National Security Framework suggests this should be no more than five per cent. Provisions for random listening must be agreed with the area manager and notified to prisoners.

## Category A prisoners

7.102    Category A and E List prisoners must be subject to the call enabling telephone system and if they wish to call people other than their approved visitors or close relatives they must apply to the area or operational manager or to the Director of High Security Prisons. For high and exceptional risk category A prisoners and E List prisoners legal telephone calls must be listened to only to the extent necessary to ensure that the call is genuinely to a legal adviser. Once this has been established, monitoring staff must stop listening and the centrally held recording must not be listened to. Accordingly, there is a high risk that privileged conversations will be monitored.

## Calls to the media

7.103    Section 3 of PSO 4400 sets out details of the circumstances in which prisoners will be granted access to the media by telephone. The policy was revised following the case of *R (Hirst) v Secretary of State for the Home Department*[152] in which a serving prisoner who campaigned for

---

152 [2002] EWHC 602 (Admin).

prisoners' rights argued that the previous policy which only allowed prisoners to access the media in exceptional circumstances breached his rights under article 10 of the European Convention on Human Rights. Whilst the court held that the policy contained in the PSO was not unlawful, it did find that it was applied in an insufficiently flexible way by the Secretary of State; there was an assumption that a prisoner's need to contact the media would almost always be met by the prisoner writing, rather than speaking to the media. On the facts of the case the court held that the imposition of what amounted to a blanket ban was unlawful.

7.104   Under the amended policy a governor may grant a prisoner's written application for access to the media by telephone where:

- A telephone conversation is the only suitable method of communication (for example for reasons of urgency).
- The sole purpose of the conversation is to comment on matters of legitimate public interest concerning prisoners or prisons (including alleged miscarriages of justice).
- The broadcast will not cause distress to victims or public outrage.
- There will be no threat to security or good order and discipline or disruption to staff duties and no ill-feeling among prisoners.
- There is no reason to doubt that those involved will disrespect any reasonable conditions imposed.[153]

Interviews must be pre-recorded and will be vetted by the Prison Service prior to being broadcast.

# Temporary release

## Introduction

7.105   Under the Prison, YOI and STC Rules prisoners and those in YOIs are entitled to temporary release for certain specified purposes and for limited periods of time.[154]

7.106   Temporary release for prisoners and young offenders is seen as important to ensure prisoner's rehabilitation and to enable them to prepare for release back into the community from prison. In particular, life sentenced prisoners or prisoners with long sentences will generally be required to demonstrate their trustworthiness through

153  PSO 4470 para 3.2.
154  PR rule 9, YOIR rule 5, STCR rule 5.

compliance with release on temporary licence before being granted release on life licence or parole licence. Against the need to aid prisoners' rehabilitation the Prison Service must balance the public's concerns about the risks posed by prisoners and the need to maintain public confidence in the punitive element of prison sentences. Thus before granting a period of temporary release the Secretary of State must be satisfied that the person will not present an unacceptable risk of committing further offences or that the frequency of release will not undermine public confidence in the administration of justice.[155]

## Grounds for temporary release

7.107    Prisoners in adult prisons or YOIs can be granted release on temporary licence (ROTL) for the following reasons:[156]

- On compassionate grounds or to receive medical treatment.
- To engage in employment or voluntary work.
- To receive instruction or training not generally available in prison.
- To participate in proceedings before any court or tribunal.
- To consult with a legal adviser where the consultation cannot take place in the prison.
- To assist the police in their enquiries.
- To facilitate a transfer between prisons.
- To assist in the maintenance of family ties or the transition from prison life to freedom.

7.108    To facilitate temporary release for these reasons there are four types of licence:

- Resettlement day release.
- Resettlement overnight release.
- Childcare resettlement .
- Special purpose.

Details of the policy on temporary release for each of these types of licence are set out in PSO 6300.

7.109       Under 18-year-olds held in YOIs are eligible for all types of ROTL although there is a requirement to give consideration to the particular types of activity that will be appropriate due to age.[157]

---

155  PR rule 9(4) and 9(5) and YOIR rule 5(5) and 5(6).
156  PR rule 9(3) and YOIR rule 5(3).
157  PSO 6300 chapter 3.

## Eligibility for temporary release

7.110   Certain prisoners are excluded from release on temporary licence.[158] These include:

- Category A prisoners.
- Prisoners on the escape list.
- Prisoners who are subject to extradition proceedings.
- Remand and convicted unsentenced prisoners.
- Sentenced prisoners who are remanded for further charges or further sentencing.
- Prisoners held on behalf of the International Criminal Tribunal for the Former Yugoslavia.
- Prisoners with consecutive default terms for confiscation orders during their original sentence.[159]

7.111   In *R (Adelana) v (1) The Governor of HMP Downview and (2) Secretary of State for Justice*[160] a female prisoner challenged the exclusion of release on temporary licence for prisoners with consecutive default terms for confiscation orders during their original sentence and argued that this policy was being rigidly applied and therefore offended against the principle that all policies should not fetter a statutory discretion. The court accepted her arguments and held that the policy was insufficiently flexible. At the time of writing the policy has not been amended in response to the judgment.

7.112   Prior to being granted release on temporary licence all prisoners must be risk assessed. OASys is used for prisoners aged 18 or over, and for prisoners in the under18 units the ASSET risk assessment will be used.[161] Where such assessments are not available or are not up to date the prison must conduct a separate risk assessment which should consider various matters including: previous compliance with temporary release, criminal history behaviour in custody police information and specific areas of concern. The assessment must be conducted by the offender manager and police information should be obtained.

---

158  PSO 6300 para vii.
159  Such prisoners are eligible during their default confiscation term of their sentence.
160  [2008] EWHC 2621.
161  PSO 6300.

## Resettlement day release

7.113    Resettlement day release (RDR) can granted for the following activities: unpaid employment, training or education, maintaining family ties, housing, probation interviews, job searches and interviews and opening bank accounts. In addition, for prisoners in a designated resettlement prison, RDR will be granted for paid employment, driving lessons and car maintenance.[162]

7.114    RDR can also be used to allow prisoners to take their statutory visits outside the prison where there are insufficient visiting facilities to allow statutory visits to take place within the prison. In addition, governors can allow prisoners in open or semi-open conditions to use RDR to attend religious worship where this will restore links between the prisoner and the wider community.[163]

### Eligibility for RDR

7.115    Depending on which is the later date, prisoners will be eligible for RDR either:

- 24 months before their release date; or
- once they have served half the custodial period less half the remand time.[164]

7.116    Where a prisoner has been assessed as eligible for release on HDC before their RDR eligibility date they are entitled to one period of RDR to undertake pre-arranged interviews for work or college.[165]

7.117    Where a prisoner has been recalled following conditional release on licence eligibility for RDR will be immediate, but the prisoner must be subject to a risk assessment.[166]

### Frequency and duration of RDR

7.118    The Governor must decide on the frequency and duration of RDR, but this should be increased in line with the prisoner's sentence plan and personal development. Where a category C prisoner is assessed as suitable for regular RDR they should ordinarily be recategorised to category D and transferred to open conditions.[167]

---

162  PSO 6300 para 2.1.
163  PSO 6300 paras 2.1.2 and 2.1.3.
164  PSO 6300 para 2.1.4.
165  PSO 6300 para 2.1.8.
166  PSO 6300 para 2.1.9.
167  PSO 6300 paras 2.1.10 and 2.1.11.

## Resettlement Overnight Release

7.119 Resettlement Overnight Release (ROR) allows prisoners to spend time at their release address or an approved hostel to enable them to re-establish links with the community and their family. ROR can also be used to facilitate interviews for work, training or accommodation.[168] ROR will usually be granted for a maximum of four nights.[169]

7.120 ROR can be granted to allow prisoners to complete placements with community service volunteers. In all cases where prisoners will be working with children or young adults staff must complete the appropriate Criminal Record Bureau checks and consider other public protection issues in accordance with the guidance in the Public Protection Manual.

### Eligibility for ROR

7.121 Depending on which is the later date, prisoners will be eligible for ROR either:

- 24 months before their release date; or
- once they have served half the custodial period less half the remand time.[170]

7.122 Separate eligibility provisions exist for prisoners in particular circumstances:

7.123 For men, women and young adult prisoners held in open/semi-open conditions or assessed as suitable for open conditions and those held in resettlement regimes with parole eligibility dates (PED):[171]

- A prisoner with a PED can apply for one period of ROR three months before their PED.
- If the prisoner is granted parole they can apply for one further period of ROR if time allows before release. If a prisoner is refused parole they can apply for a maximum of six ROR's in the twelve months following the PED. ROR will only be granted following a risk assessment.
- Prisoners who have withdrawn from the parole process can apply for ROR three months after their PED.

---

168 PSO 6300 para 2.2.
169 PSO 6300 para 2.2.4.
170 PSO 6300 para 2.1.4.
171 PSO 6300 2.2.2 – those with PED dates are now prisoners serving extended sentences for public protection under the CJA 2003 imposed before 14 July 2008 and prisoners serving sentences of four years or more under the CJA 1991 where the offence is contained in CJA 2003 Sch 15A.

- All prisoners who are recalled following conditional release and held in open conditions:
  - If immediate release is refused but the Parole Board sets a future date for release then ROR may be taken once every four weeks on receipt of the decision.
  - Where the Secretary of State sets a future review date that will be treated in the same way as an initial PED for the purposes of eligibility for ROR (see above).[172]

7.124 Adult males in category C training prisons, adult women in closed conditions and young adult prisoners in closed conditions:

- Where a category D prisoner is held in closed conditions they will be eligible for ROR under the same arrangements for prisoners in category D conditions.
- Category C prisoners who do not have a PED will be eligible for two periods of ROR in the last six months before their release date.
- Prisoners with a PED can apply for ROR in the three months prior to their PED and if they complete this period successfully they should be considered for re-categorisation and transfer to open conditions.
- Prisoners with a PED who:
  a) are unsuccessful on a period of release on temporary licence prior to their PED; or
  b) are not recategorised to category D; or
  c) withdraw from the parole process
  are not eligible for ROR until three months before any further parole reviews, when they can apply for one period of ROR.
- If a category C prisoner is successful at their first parole review, they can apply for one period of ROR before release if time allows.
- If a category C prisoner is refused parole they can apply for a maximum of three ROR's in the twelve months following the PED. ROR will only be granted following a risk assessment.
- All prisoners who are recalled following conditional release and held in category C conditions:
- Where the Parole Board recommends release at a later date a prisoner can take a maximum of two periods of ROR in the last six months before re-release.

---

172 PSO 6300 has not been amended to take into account the fact that the Parole Board is no longer responsible for setting further dates for the review of recalled prisoners.

- Where the Secretary of State sets a future review date that will be treated in the same way as an initial PED for the purposes of eligibility for ROR for prisoners in category C (see above).[173]

## Childcare resettlement leave

7.125　Childcare resettlement leave will be considered for prisoners who establish that they have sole caring responsibility for a child under 16 and who are:

- resident in open or semi-open conditions; or
- categorised as suitable for such conditions; or
- resident in a mother and baby unit and have other children being cared for outside the prison; and
- are not excluded from release on temporary licence.[174]

There is no minimum eligibility date for childcare resettlement leave which can be granted to prisoners who are not yet eligible for RDR or ROR. It should be granted no more than once every two months and for a maximum period of three nights.[175]

## Special purpose licence

7.126　This is granted to prisoners to prisoners in exceptional, personal circumstances. All prisoners, other than those excluded from release on temporary licence, can apply for temporary release on special purpose licence. The licence will normally be granted for the period of time necessary to achieve the stated purpose and can be extended to cover overnight absences at the discretion of the governor.[176]

7.127　Special purpose licence may be granted for the following reasons:[177]

- On compassionate grounds for:
  - Visits to dying relatives, funerals or other tragic circumstances.
  - For prisoners who have general parental responsibility for a child under 16 to deal with emergencies relating to their parental duties.

173　Again the policy is in PSO 6300 does not reflect the changes in recall arrangement.
174　PSO 6300 para 2.5.1.
175　PSO 6300 paras 2.5.4–2.5.6.
176　PSO 6300 para 2.6.
177　PSO 6300 para 2.7.

- For prisoners who will have the sole caring responsibility of an elderly or disabled relative on release to deal with emergencies relating to their caring duties.
- To allow prisoners to attend medical out-patient or in-patient appointments.
- To attend their own marriage ceremony.
- To allow prisoners (other than life sentence prisoners) to transfer from a closed to an open prison.
- To attend court, tribunal or inquiry proceedings.
- To attend conferences with legal advisers where absolutely necessary and in exceptional circumstances.
- To assist the police with their enquiries.

## Temporary release for life sentenced prisoners

7.128    Life sentenced prisoners are entitled to release on all four types of temporary licence.[178] However, they will normally only be eligible if they are held in semi-open or open conditions. In all cases life sentenced prisoners will be subject to a rigorous risk assessment and the probation service must be consulted to ensure that any victim issues are addressed.[179] Life sentenced prisoners can only be granted temporary release from category C conditions if they have been assessed as suitable for open conditions but remain in closed conditions for medical reasons.[180]

7.129    The length of time a lifer must spend in open conditions before becoming eligible for release on temporary licence will depend upon the length of time until their next parole review from the date of their arrival in open conditions:[181]

- Lifers with more than 12 months until their next parole review will be eligible to apply for:
  - supervised activities outside the prison boundary after two months in open conditions;
  - RDR after six months in open conditions;
  - ROR (other than for paid work) and childcare resettlement leave after nine months in open conditions; and
  - ROR for paid work and for five days a week after 12 months in open conditions.

178  PSO 6300 para 4.2.
179  PSO 6300 para 4.3.
180  PSO 6300 para 4.3.1.
181  PSO 6300 para 4.3.3.

- Lifers with up to 12 months until their next parole review will be eligible to apply for:
  - supervised activities outside the prison boundary after one month in open conditions;
  - RDR after four months in open conditions;
  - ROR (other than for paid work) and childcare resettlement leave after six months in open conditions; and
  - ROR for paid work and for five days a week after eight months in open conditions.
- Lifers with up to nine months until their next parole review will be eligible to apply for:
  - supervised activities outside the prison boundary after one month in open conditions;
  - RDR after three months in open conditions;
  - ROR (other than for paid work) and childcare resettlement leave after five months in open conditions; and
  - ROR for paid work and for five days a week after six months in open conditions.
- Lifers with up to six months until their next parole review will be eligible to apply for:
  - supervised activities outside the prison boundary after two weeks in open conditions;
  - RDR after one month in open conditions;
  - ROR (other than for paid work) and childcare resettlement leave after three months in open conditions; and
  - ROR for paid work and for five days a week after four months in open conditions.

## Temporary release for foreign national prisoners and immigration detainees

7.130  Foreign national prisoners are eligible to apply for ROTL. However where the prisoner is subject to a court recommendation for deportation, a decision to deport or a deportation order[182] the views of the Criminal Casework Directorate of the UKBA must be sought. The Governor retains the final discretion as to whether to allow ROTL.[183] In other cases where the prisoner meets the criteria for referral to the CCD (see para 4.12) the risk assessment must proceed on the

---

182  That is, liable to be dealt with under Immigration Act 1971 Sch 3.
183  PSO 6300 para 5.5.2.

basis that the prisoner is to be deported, unless UKBA has made a decision that this is not to happen.[184] This presumption will therefore be a very significant factor in determining the risk of the prisoner absconding (although clearly it should not be determinative and the policy stresses the need to consider each case on its facts).

7.131    Irish nationals are treated differently under the policy. The risk assessment only operates on a presumption that deportation will be enforced (as opposed to clear information that it will be) where there is a court recommendation that has not been processed by the CCD.[185]

7.132    In relation to paid work or study only EU nationals with valid passports/identity cards and non-EU nationals with leave to remain from IND with no conditions attached preventing them from doing so can be granted temporary release for these purposes.[186]

7.133    Those detained solely under the Immigration Act cannot be granted ROTL[187] but where there are compassionate reasons prisons should refer the case to UKBA so that it can give consideration as to whether the Immigration Act detention should be maintained.

7.134    Prisoners transferred to England and Wales on a restricted basis under the provisions of Crime (Sentences) Act 1997 will be eligible for temporary release, however, the views of the sending jurisdiction must be sought before a prisoner is transferred.[188]

## Temporary release for other classes of prisoners

7.135    Some additional guidance on eligibility for temporary release is given for other classes of prisoners:

- Civil prisoners and fine defaulters are eligible to be considered for temporary release if they have a sufficiently long period of time to serve to fall within the timeframes for temporary release specified above.[189]
- Prisoners who are serving a term for contempt of court cannot be granted temporary release without the permission of the clerk of the court concerned.[190]

---

184  PSO 6300 paras 5.5.3–5.3.4.
185  PSO 6300 para 5.5.6.
186  PSO 6300 para 5.5.1.
187  PSO 6300 para 5.5.9.
188  PSO 6300 para 5.6.2.
189  PSO 6300 para 5.1.
190  PSO 6300 para 5.2.

- Prisoners who are detained in default of a confiscation order can be considered for temporary release if they have a sufficiently long period of time to serve to fall within the timeframes for temporary release specified above.[191]
- Appellants can be granted temporary release where the court has confirmed that their attendance is required.[192]
- US servicemen can be granted temporary release in exceptional circumstances where they have close family living in this country.[193]

## Refusal of release on temporary licence

7.136 Prisoners are entitled to receive written reasons where they are refused release on temporary licence and all information used for the risk assessment process must be disclosed to them other than in the following circumstances[194]:

- In the interests of national security.
- For the prevention of disorder or crime, including information relevant to prison security.
- For the protection of a third party who may be put at risk if the information is disclosed.
- If, on medical or psychiatric grounds, it is felt necessary to withhold information where the mental and/or physical health of the prisoner could be impaired.
- Where the source of the information is a victim and disclosure without their consent would breach any duty of confidence owed to that victim or would generally prejudice the future supply of information.

7.137 In all cases governors must consider disclosing the information either in summary or in an edited form that protects the anonymity of the person providing the information. If victims do not want their views to be disclosed to a prisoner they must make representations to the governor in support of the non-disclosure of their views. However, if the governor decides against the representations the victim cannot prevent their views being disclosed, although they can resubmit the information in an anonymous form or gist.[195]

191  PSO 6300 para 5.3.
192  PSO 6300 para 5.4.
193  PSO 6300 para 5.7.
194  PSO 6300 para 6.1.
195  PR rule 9(8), YOIR rule 5(8), PSO 6300 para 6.2.

## Breach of temporary licence

7.138   A prisoner who is released on temporary licence can be recalled at any time whether or not the conditions of his or her release have been broken.[196] Where a prisoner is found to have breached his or her licence conditions, they must be recalled if it is not considered safe or appropriate for them to remain out on licence.[197] Once a decision has been made to recall a prisoner the governor must ask the police to take the prisoner into police custody before returning him or her to the nearest appropriate prison or YOI[198]. A prisoner will be 'unlawfully at large' once the temporary licence has been revoked until they have returned to custody.[199]

7.139   Where a prisoner is arrested on suspicion of a criminal offence he or she must be charged under the prison rules on returning to the prison. The adjudication hearing must be suspended pending the outcome of the police investigation. If the criminal charges are dropped the governor must decide whether or not to proceed with the disciplinary charge in accordance with the guidance set out in PSO 2000 (see chapter 9). Other breaches of temporary licence conditions should be dealt with as disciplinary offences.[200] Both the Prison Rules 1999 and the Young Offender Rules specify the offence of failing to comply with any condition upon which a prisoner was temporarily released, as well as allowing for prisoners to be charged with taking a controlled drug whilst outside the prison.[201]

## The right to vote

7.140   At the time of writing all convicted and sentenced prisoners are banned from voting in elections other than:

- those convicted for contempt of court and otherwise classified under PR7(3); and
- those serving a term of imprisonment in default of payment of a sum of money adjudged to be paid on conviction.[202]

---

196  PR rule 9(8), YOIR rule 5(8).
197  PSO 6300 para 7.1.1.
198  PSO 6300 para 7.1.3.
199  See chapter 2.
200  PSO 6300 para 7.2.
201  PR rule 51(8) and (9), YOIR rule 55(9) and (10).
202  Representation of the People Act 1983 s3 and PSO 4650 para 1.3.

7.141   However, the Grand Chamber of the European Court of Human Rights has held that this ban violates article 3, protocol 1 of the EHCR which requires Contracting States to the Convention to hold free elections under conditions which will ensure the free expression of the opinion of the people in the choice of the legislature.[203]

7.142   In its judgment the ECtHR highlights that the severe measure of disenfranchisement must not be taken lightly and that the principle of proportionality requires a discernable and sufficient link between the sanction imposed and the conduct and circumstances of the individual concerned. The court accepted that the ban on prisoners voting pursued the aims of preventing crime and of enhancing civic responsibility and respect for the rule of law as well as conferring an additional punishment on prisoners. However, the court considered that the ban on voting was disproportionate to the aims it sought to achieve. The ban applies to a large number of people who have been convicted of a wide range of offences and are serving a range of sentences. The sentencing courts make no reference to disenfranchisement when passing a sentence. Furthermore, there was no evidence that parliament or the courts had ever sought to weigh the competing interests or assess the proportionality of a blanket ban on prisoners' right to vote.

7.143   The court declined to give any guidance on how Convention restrictions could be imposed on the right of prisoners to vote. It is noteworthy that several contracting states do have total bans on prisoners voting which have not been held to violate Convention rights.

7.144   In October 2008 the Parliamentary Joint Committee on Human Rights warned that 'there is a significant risk that the next general election will take place in a way that fails to comply with the Convention and at least part of the prison population will be unlawfully disenfranchised'.[204] On 2 February 2009 Lord Lester of Herne Hill asked in the House of Lords whether the government had taken account of decisions in the South African and Australian courts[205] in considering how to comply with the judgment of the in *Hirst v UK*.[206] The Parliamentary Under-Secretary of State, Ministry of Justice

---

203   *Hirst v UK* (2004) 38 EHRR 40.

204   Joint Committee on Human Rights, *Monitoring the Government's Response to Human Rights Judgments: Annual Report 2008*, p 31. Available at: www.publications.parliament.uk/pa/jt200708/jtselect/jtrights/173/173.pdf

205   *South African Constitutional Court in Minister of Home Affairs v NICRO* (2005 (3) SA 280 (CC)) and *High Court of Australia in Roach v Electoral Commissioner and Commonwealth of Australia* (2007 HCA 43).

206   *Hirst v UK* (2004) 38 EHRR 40.

(Lord Bach) replied that the government was 'mindful' of these and other cases but 'remains committed to carrying out a second public consultation'.[207] It is uncertain when this public consultation will be completed.

207  Human Rights / House of Lords / 2 Feb 2009 : Col WA91. See www. publications.parliament.uk/pa/ld200809/ldhansrd/text/90202w0001. htm#09020211000376

## CHAPTER 8

# Security, intelligence, searching and control

*continued*

# The National Security Framework

8.1   In the Prison Service, the centrally issued policy on prison security is contained in PSO 1000: the National Security Framework (NSF). This replaced the earlier security manual which was paper based. The NSF is accessed by prisons through the Prison Service intranet. It is not available on the Prison Service website. The introduction of the NSF reflected a general shift in the way that central policy is issued by the Prison Service in that it is less prescriptive and detailed than the earlier versions of the security manual. Aside from core requirements which prisons are required to adhere to the policy states that local prisons are largely responsible for defining how expected outcomes are to be achieved. Accordingly at the heart of the NSF is the requirement for prisons, within its core framework, to devise their own local security strategy (LSS). Clearly the content of a prison's LSS will vary depending on the category and profile of the prisoners it holds.

8.2   The four 'functions' covered by the NSF are categorisation and assessment, accounting and control, searching and communications and surveillance. The NSF requires all Prison Service establishments to have a security department with a security manager, a duty governor available 24 hours a day, and a security committee that meets at least monthly. This will be responsible for reviewing the prison's security measures, such as the levels of searching and the use of intelligence.

# Intelligence

8.3   The NSF requires all prisons to have an intelligence system with objectives set which must:

- Contribute to the overall security aims of the prison.
- Take account of known deficiencies in security, good order or discipline.
- Take account of existing intelligence to identify deficiencies in knowledge, and opportunities for further development.
- Carry a detailed strategy proposed by the security department of how the information is to be gathered.
- Be supported by an intelligence assessment.
- Be communicated by the security manager to staff who are in a position to gather any relevant information. Depending on the intelligence objectives, this may range from only a few staff to all staff.

8.4    The NSF requires intelligence objectives to be reviewed at least monthly by senior prison management. All prisons must also produce intelligence assessments, monthly or more frequently if required. These are written statements of the conclusions drawn from the analysis of strategic and operational intelligence, and which lead to agreed intelligence objectives and a counteracting strategy. The NSF also states that prison management must introduce a system of identifying prisoners who present a risk to the security of the establishment. Each identified prisoner must be listed as one of the four types of target:

- *Prominent nominals*: individual prisoners who pose a high risk to the security objectives and priorities of the prison.
- *Development nominals*: individual prisoners who, because of their current or increasing level of activity, should be monitored and intelligence gathered on them to establish the degree of threat they pose to the security objectives and priorities of the prison.
- *Agency nominals*: individual prisoners who are prominent nominals of another prison or agency, and who have declared their interest.
- *Security threats groups*: a group of prisoners which intelligence suggests may act against the security or control of the prison. Membership need not be formal, but there should be evidence of a common purpose, a degree of leadership and an implied bond of confidentiality.

8.5    It is recognised that heightened surveillance or monitoring of prisoners may raise issues under article 8 of the ECHR. Accordingly a clear security justification is required before more intrusive measures are applied. The basic structure of evaluating, collating and disseminating security intelligence required by the NSF is a system based upon the following elements or their equivalent in a computer-based approach:

- Security intelligence reports (SIRs).
- Inmate intelligence cards (F2185 and F2185A) for named prisoners.
- Special index cards (F2184) for specific categories or types of incident.
- The security file (F2058) which forms part of a prisoner's record.

## Security intelligence reports

8.6    SIRs are one of the most important tools used by Prison Service establishments in gathering intelligence relevant to security. The use of SIRs in prisons can be a source of great resentment. Prisoners may lose certain types of employment or be subjected to more drastic forms of administrative action such as being placed in segregation due to information recorded on a SIR. As the information will normally not be fully disclosed as exempt from disclosure under the Data Protection Act (DPA) 1998 the prisoner will not be able to make any meaningful representations as they will not know the precise nature of the allegations against them. SIRs also remain on the prisoner's security file which will travel with them and their contents may appear and re-appear in future reports.

8.7    The NSF states that SIRs may contain details of intelligence sources or methods which need to be protected. All security information relating to the prisoner, however received, must be recorded on an SIR of a design approved by the Security Group at Prison Service headquarters. The NSF recognises that the type of information may include unusual associations on exercise, conversations with prisoners, or overheard between prisoners, unusual occurrences on an escort, hoarding of goods from the prison shop or clothing, a prisoner's actions which are out of character, and any other information which may affect order and control in the prison.

8.8    SIRs should be processed using what the NSF terms either a '4 x 4' or '5 x 5 x 5' system. Both these rate firstly the quality of the source of information (ranging from 'always or highly reliable' to 'untested or unreliable') and then of the information itself (ranging from 'true with no reservations' to 'not known to be true, or untrue'. The 5 x 5 x 5 system also then adds a handling code confirming to which agencies the information may be disseminated. Both systems include a consequence code which sets the security implications against the likelihood of any consequences arising from the information. Even if a prisoner is not given any more than an unsourced gist of security information arising from a SIR, it is difficult to understand why rating of a SIR under these systems should not be disclosed.

## Prisoner informants

8.9    The NSF also includes guidance on managing prisoners who provide intelligence. All prisoner sources of intelligence must be registered if any one or more of the following applies:

- They seek a reward (whether or not one is actually given).
- They seek total anonymity, even from staff.
- The risk assessment of the information they have provided, or

their actions in providing it, suggests that they are at risk, or if it is judged for any other reason that they need the support system which is available to registered sources.

* Their conduct falls within the definition of the conduct of a covert human intelligence source (within the meaning of Part 2 of the Regulation of Investigatory Powers Act (RIPA) 2000).
* They are to be tasked to find out information.

The NSF states that it is not Prison Service policy to recruit a source under 18 years of age.

8.10    Every source must have a secure file held by a designated system manager who deals with human intelligence sources. A register of all sources must be maintained by the manager and kept secure. The manager must also select appropriate handlers (the source's contact point) and controllers (who manage the handlers) for the sources. The NSF specifies the rewards that may be given to prisoner sources which are limited to:

* A commitment to report directly on the source's work to third parties, such as the Parole Board.
* An acknowledgement that the prisoner's approach to criminal behaviour has improved, justifying progress to better regimes.
* A sympathetic consideration of transfer requests where security factors permit.
* Additional facilities, for example: longer visits, favourable job allocations (which must, however be risk assessed in the usual way), and access to other discretionary facilities available within the prison.
* Payments of incentive bonuses within the provisions of the prisoners' pay scheme.
* In particularly worthy cases, a recommendation that the use of the Royal Prerogative of Mercy be considered to remit part of the sentence as a reward for meritorious act (see chapter 11).

8.11    The NSF recognises that almost all use of prisoner informants will come within the definition of a 'covert human intelligence source' within the meaning of the Regulation of Investigatory Powers Act 2000.[1] Where this does apply there are statutory requirements for the proper authorisation for their use.[2] The NSF states that the author-

---

1   RIPA 2000 s26 – the Act was introduced in order to ensure that surveillance had a proper lawful basis as required by article 8 of the ECHR.
2   RIPA 2000 s29.

ising officer in most cases will be the system manager (in private prisons the controller should be the authorising officer as the legislation requires a public official to fulfil this function) although the use of specially vulnerable sources should be authorised by the regional DOM, or the Director of High Security Prisons as appropriate.

## Surveillance

8.12 The interception of correspondence and telephone calls is dealt with in chapter 7. However, there are also legal powers for the Prison Service and other agencies to obtain intelligence using covert surveillance methods.

### Covert surveillance

8.13 This is also covered by RIPA 2000 and requires proper authorisation[3]. The scheme of RIPA 2000 is designed to ensure that covert surveillance is only used when necessary and proportionate to do so, and in a way that interferes as little as possible with the rights of those likely to be affected by it. The use of covert surveillance is subject to monitoring by statutory surveillance commissioners. RIPA 2000 distinguishes between directed and intrusive surveillance (the latter which involves surveillance in private residential premises or vehicles).[4] Intrusive covert surveillance can be authorised on narrower grounds than directed surveillance and requires a higher level of authorisation.

### Covert surveillance in cells

8.14 The NSF treats covert surveillance in cells as intrusive under RIPA 2000. It states that intrusive covert surveillance is only permitted where necessary for the purpose of preventing or detecting serious crime during a major incident in a prison cell or other living accommodation. For in-cell hostage incidents, the application for authorisation will be made to the Prison Service duty director. In all other cases the authorising officer is the Secretary of State for Justice, or

3 RIPA 2000 s32.
4 RIPA 2000 s26(3).

in his absence another Secretary of State. The application must show that the operation is technically feasible and that:

- A serious crime is being committed (or likely to be) and that the surveillance is necessary to assist.
- The information could not be obtained through other less intrusive means.

## Covert surveillance of a 'public' area in a prison

8.15    Directed surveillance by the Prison Service for its own purposes may be authorised when this is necessary for one of the following purposes:

- Preventing and detecting crime or preventing disorder.
- In the interests of public safety.

The authorising officer must be the Director of High Security Prisons or the relevant regional DOM who must be satisfied that the information sought could not reasonably be obtained by less intrusive means, taking into account not only the interference with the article 8 rights of the target but also those of others who may be observed during the surveillance operation. All authorisations must either be renewed after three months or cancelled when the operation is no longer necessary.

## Surveillance by other agencies

8.16    Clearly other agencies may have interest in setting up covert surveillance in prisons, most notably the police. The NSF confirms that the police must seek authorisation from the Prison Service. An application signed by a senior police officer will be considered by the police advisers' section at the Prison Service which will consider the necessity for the information sought and the proportionality of the proposed surveillance. Concerns about police covert surveillance in prisons were raised by the case of Babar Ahmad, a prisoner at HMP Woodhill, whose visits from Sadiq Khan MP were recorded by Thames Valley police.[5]

---

5   The report into these incidents by the Chief Surveillance Commissioner: Report on two visits by Sadiq Khan MP to Babar Ahmad at HMP Woodhill (Feb 2008 Cm 7336), found that the surveillance was properly authorised for counter terrorism purposes and that his visits were monitored as he visited as a social visitor rather than as an MP.

## Confidential material

8.17    The NSF sets out specific requirements where 'confidential material' is likely to be obtained by covert surveillance or use of a covert human intelligence source. Confidential information is defined as:

- Legally privileged material.
- Confidential personal information relating to physical or mental health – this situation may arise where the source or the target is a Listener, or works in healthcare.
- Confidential journalistic material – that is information provided to a journalist subject to an undertaking to hold it in confidence.

In such circumstances the NSF states that the authorising officer for RIPA 2000 purposes must be the Director General or Deputy Director General of the Prison Service.

8.18    The House of Lords has recently held that the broad words of RIPA 2000, namely that covert surveillance, if carried out in accordance with the Act, 'shall be lawful for all purposes',[6] mean that authorisation may be given to monitor legal visits notwithstanding the right to consult privately with a lawyer contained in the Rules.[7] This is subject to the Code issued under RIPA 2000 being amended to require such authorisations only to be made exceptionally and with the applicable safeguards relating to intrusive rather then directed surveillance.[8]

## Overt observation by CCTV

8.19    The Rules[9] permit governors to make arrangements for prisoners to be placed under constant observation by means of an overt CCTV system where it is considered necessary and proportionate in the interests of the prisoner's health and safety or that of another person, for the prevention or detection of crime, or for securing security or good order and discipline.

---

6   RIPA 2000 s27(1).
7   PR rule 38, YOIR rule 16.
8   *In re McE and others* [2009] UKHL 15 – the report into Babar Ahmed's visits stated that enquiries had established that 'since 2005 at least, there have been no authorities for directed surveillance of legal visits in prisons in England and Wales to prisoners in custody in relation to terrorist or other criminal matters'. The Court of Appeal stayed a prosecution as an abuse of process where the police recorded conversations between a suspect and his lawyer in the exercise yard of a police station even where there was no evidence of prejudice: *R v Grant* [2006] QB 60.
9   PR rule 50A, YOIR rule 54.

# Searching

## The legal authority to search: public sector prisons and YOIs

### Search of prisoners

8.20   The Prison Act 1952 s8 states that prison officers while acting as such 'shall have all the powers, authority, protection and privileges of a constable'. In relation to prisoners there is specific authority in the Rules to allow the search of prisoners on reception and subsequently as the 'governor thinks necessary or as the Secretary of State may direct'. This power must be exercised 'in as seemly a manner as is consistent with discovering anything concealed' and prisoners must not be strip-searched in the sight of another prisoner, or in the sight of a person of the opposite sex.[10] Reasonable force may be used when subjecting prisoners to searches.[11]

8.21      There is also provision in the Prison Act to allow 'authorised persons', defined to mean a person working at the prison of a description authorised by the governor to exercise such powers, a limited power of search. This enables the authorised person to conduct a search for unauthorised property, but not to require the prisoner to remove any clothing other than outer coat, jacket, headwear, gloves and footwear. The power carries with it a right to use reasonable force where necessary to effect the search and to seize any unauthorised property.[12] Accordingly only prison officers have the power to strip search prisoners although other staff have the power to conduct less intrusive searches such as pat down searches.

### Search of visitors or vehicles entering prisons

8.22   The Rules also provide that any person or vehicle entering or leaving a prison may be stopped, examined and searched. Visitors may also be photographed, fingerprinted or required to submit to other measurement, this power is to allow security measures to identify visitors on entry and exit. Any search, as with prisoners must be carried out in as seemly as manner consistent with discovering any concealed item.[13]

---

10   PR rule 41, YOIR rule 46.
11   PR rule 47, YOIR rule 43.
12   PA 1952 s8A.
13   PR rule 71, YOIR rule 75.

# The legal authority to search: private prisons and YOIs

8.23 PCOs in private prisons are given statutory power to search, in accordance with the Rules, any prisoner and any other person who is in or is seeking to enter the prison. These powers include the right to use reasonable force where necessary.[14] PCOs are therefore subject to the same requirements under the Prison and YOI Rules as officers in public prisons. However, PCOs in private prisons do not have the constabulary powers of prison officers[15] which give them the specific statutory powers to search visitors without consent in certain circumstances (see below). The Offender Management Act (OMA) 2007 provided PCOs with the power to detain visitors for specific offences for up to two hours pending the arrival of the police. Power has recently been given to workers at private prisons who are not PCOs to carry out searches 'upon the instruction and supervision of a prisoner custody officer or the director'.[16]

# The legal authority to search: secure training centres

8.24 Custody Officers at STCs have similar statutory powers to search those detained in, and visiting STCs, as given to PCOs in private prisons.[17] These powers are further defined in the Secure Training Centre Rules which largely reflect the Rules relating to adults. However the STC Rules specify that prisoners should not be strip searched without the authority of the governor, in the presence of more than two officers, or in the presence of any other prisoner or an officer not of the same sex.[18] The Rules also provide for the stopping, examination and searching of any person or vehicle entering or leaving the centre.[19]

# The legal authority to search: secure children's homes

8.25 SCHs are required to have a 'behaviour management policy' which sets out the measures of 'control, restraint and discipline' to be used

---

14  CJA 1991 s86 – amendments to the legislation made by OMA 2007 removed the previous restriction on prison custody officers which meant that they could only perform rub-down searches on visitors.

15  CJA 1991 s87(3).

16  CJA 1991 s86B(2) and The Contracted-Out Prisons (Specification of Restricted Activities) Order 2009 SI No 576 in force from 6 April 2009.

17  Criminal Justice and Public Order Act (CJPOA) 1994 s9.

18  STCR rule 33.

19  STCR rule 41.

– such measures must not be 'excessive or unreasonable'.[20] The statutory regulations do not contain any specific powers in relation to use of searching except to say that there is no authority to conduct any intimate search.

## Limits on the power to search

8.26    Under the common law, use of excessive force during a search, or a search conducted in breach of the Rules will constitute the tort of battery, although the recoverable compensation will be small in the absence of significant physical or psychiatric injury. There is also a tort of intentionally inflicting harm, but this requires intent or recklessness and either physical or psychiatric injury. There is no tort of invasion of privacy that can be invoked in relation to searches (although article 8 may be breached, see below).[21]

8.27    Where searches (of persons, property or correspondence) are carried out in breach of the Rules with at least reckless disregard of the consequences, the tort of misfeasance in public office may be made out – although there must be special damage (loss of property, personal or psychiatric injury) before a claim can be made.[22]

8.28    Under the ECHR – searches which are carried out in a manner which is debasing and which significantly aggravates the humiliation inherent in the procedure can in principle breach article 3, subject to the minimum degree of severity threshold being met (and routine strip searches without proper security justification may in themselves breach article 3[23]). Searches, including searches of correspondence, may breach article 8 as disproportionate if not carried out in line with agreed procedures and policies.[24] If the prison has adopted a policy or

---

20  CHR 17.
21  *Wainwright v Home Office* [2004] 2 AC 406 – in this case a visitor with physical and learning disabilities who had been strip searched in breach of the Rules and who suffered post-traumatic stress disorder following the experience was awarded £3,750 compensation for the battery.
22  *Watkins v Secretary of State for the Home Department* [2006] 2 AC 395.
23  See for example *Van de Ver v The Netherlands* (2004) 38 EHRR 46.
24  *Wainwright v UK* (2007) 44 EHRR 40 – the visitors in this case (the same as in footnote 21 above) established a breach of article 8 and were each awarded 3000 Euros – the court commented '[w]here procedures are laid down for the proper conduct of searches on outsiders to the prison who may very well be innocent of any wrongdoing, it behoves the prison authorities to comply strictly with those safeguards and by rigorous precautions protect the dignity of those being searched from being assailed any further than is necessary'. However the threshold for a breach of article 3 was not made out.

practice of searching that is unlawful then this may be challenged in judicial review proceedings.[25]

# Searching policy

## Prisons and YOIs

8.29 The NSF requires Prison Service establishments to have a local searching policy or strategy which must be agreed between the governor and the relevant regional director of offender management or director of high security.

It should define, drawing on risk assessments where available:

i *Context.* The different areas of the prison or situations in which searching is required (eg prisoners, visitors, staff, contractors, vehicles, equipment, goods, stores, mail, property, workshops, sportsfields, cell searches, escorts, at night etc). All parts of the prison, including the perimeter, storm drains, underground services and communal areas must be included in the strategy.

ii *Object.* What is being sought in each situation? (eg weapons, drugs, prisoners, keys, etc).

iii *Technique.* Resource and regime implications, the search technique or techniques to be used to maximise the chance of finding the object, and the technical aids, if any, needed to conduct the search.

iv *Staffing.* The staff or group of staff (including dogs teams) needed to carry out the search in each context (eg wing staff, gate staff, dedicated search team, etc). This will need to take into account who has the legal authority to conduct particular searches, the structure of any teams, and the arrangements for managing searches.

v *Frequency targets.* How often, in each context, routine, or random searches will be conducted. Management should ensure that the strategy is implemented fairly and without bias against any group.

vi *Non-routine searches.* Procedures for non-routine (ie intelligence-led) searches, including planning procedures for large-scale searches, such as lock down searches.

vii *Action on a find.* Procedures for preservation and continuity of evidence and avoidance of contamination, action to take with the prisoner or other person involved (including powers of arrest where appropriate).

---

25 For example the unlawful cell searching policy examined in *R (Daly) v Secretary of State for the Home Department* [2001] 2 AC 532.

viii *Training needs*. The training needed for each technique, the staff or groups of staff to be trained in each technique, and the targets for training any staff who need it any ongoing training and testing.

ix *Procedures for audit*. A clear strategy should be in place for self audits of searching and this should be communicated to staff.

8.30 The NSF states that extracts from the strategy should be made available to prisoners and visitors where relevant. It recognises that is particularly important that visitors have as much information as possible in areas such as searching techniques and procedures. It should highlight policies on religious and cultural issues. Such information should be sent with visiting orders and displayed prominently in visits rooms.

8.31 These policy requirements on disclosure of policies on searching are in keeping with the principle that any interference with the right to private life under article 8 of the ECHR (which includes the right to bodily integrity) must be 'in accordance with the law'. This means that any policy that forms the basis of the restriction with that right must, amongst other things, be adequately accessible. If such policies are not accessible then this may constitute a breach of article 8.[26] Although the NSF requires the drafting of local policies, where it expressly provides for the appropriate level of interference with a Convention right a prison would have to have cogent reasons for imposing greater restrictions.[27] The rest of this chapter refers to the NSF as disclosed in 2004, but the Prison Service has refused to disclose a more up to date version.

## Staff authorised to carry out searches

8.32 The NSF authorises a wide range of staff to carry out rub-down searches, or a metal scan. However civilian staff can only carry out such searches only if this forms part of their contracted duties, they are directly employed or seconded, and they have been authorised to do so by prison management. Full or strip searches are different

---

26 For example in *Silver v UK* (1983) EHRR 347 the then non-availability of policies on prison correspondence then contained in Standing Order 5 breached this requirement.

27 See by analogy *R (Munjaz) v Mersey Care NHS Trust* [2006] 2 AC 148 where a special hospital had such reasons for departing from a centrally issued Code of Practice on segregation.

and the NSF only authorises prison officers, operational managers or prison custody officers to carry these out.

8.33    Only medical staff have power to carry out intimate searches of prisoners, and only the police have the power to carry out intimate searches of visitors or members of staff.

## Types of authorised search

8.34    Detailed guidance on the use of the statutory powers of search is contained in the NSF. Essentially there are three kinds of search:

- a rub down search for prisoners and personal visitors;
- a less intrusive rub down search for official visitors and staff; and,
- a 'full search' – this is more commonly called a strip search.

## Rub down searches

8.35    The NSF states that rub down searches can be carried out on staff, visitors and contractors on entry or exit of the prison and may be carried out by a single officer. Women should only be rub down searched by a female officer. The rub down search must be undertaken using open hands with fingers spread out. If the officer conducting the rub down search finds nothing, but suspects that an unauthorised article is being concealed, then he or she should make the necessary arrangements to move to a more detailed search.

## Full or strip searches

8.36    The NSF states that all E List prisoners should have a full search at reception, after visits and after work activities. Other prisoners should have a full search at reception upon arrival or departure from the prison. Once searched at reception prisoners should be kept apart from other prisoners who have not been searched. In closed prisons, prisoners should have a strip search during routine cell searches. Full searches should be conducted in accordance with the training provided. Medical advice should be readily available. If anything unauthorised is found, officers must ask the subject for an explanation and include the answer in a written report. Headwear, including wigs, should only be removed by the person being searched. Religious headwear should be searched in accordance with PSO 4550 on religion.

## Level A rub down (for routine searches of domestic visitors and prisoners, those entering closed supervision centres (CSU), special secure units (SSU) and for all targeted searches)

**Male subject**

| i | Stand facing the subject |
|---|---|

↓

| ii | Ask him if he has anything on him that he is not authorised to have |
|---|---|

↓

| iii | Ask him to empty his pockets and remove any jewellery including wristwatch |
|---|---|

↓

| iv | Search the contents of pockets; jewellery and any other items, including bags he is carrying then place them to one side |
|---|---|

↓

| v | Ask him to remove any headwear and pass it to you for searching |
|---|---|

↓

| vi | Search the head by running your fingers through his hair and round the back of his ears, or asking him to shake out his hair and run his fingers through it. Untie long hair if necessary |
|---|---|

↓

| vii | Look around and inside his ears, nose and mouth. You may ask him to raise his tongue so that you can look under it |
|---|---|

↓

| viii | Lift his collar, feel behind and around it and across the top of his shoulders (search any tie and ask him to remove it if necessary) |
|---|---|

↓

| ix | Ask him to raise his arms level with his shoulders. His fingers must be apart with palms facing downwards. Search each arm by running your hands along the upper and lower sides |
|---|---|

↓

| x | Check between his fingers and look at the palms and back of his hands |
|---|---|

↓

| xi | Check the front of his body from neck to waist, the sides, from armpits to waist and the front of the waistband |
|---|---|

↓

| xii | Check his back from collar to waist, back of the waistband and seat of the trouser. You may need to ask him to turn around |
|---|---|

↓

| xiii | Check the back and sides of each leg from the crotch to the ankle |

↓

| xiv | Check the front of his abdomen and front and side of each leg |

↓

| xv | Ask him to remove footwear and search thoroughly. Check the soles of the feet |

↓

| xvi | Look at the area around him for anything he may have dropped before or during the search |

↓

| xvii | Ask him to step to one side to ensure he is not standing on anything he has dropped before or during the search. |

**Female subject**

| i | Stand facing the subject |

↓

| ii | Ask her if she has anything on her that she is not authorised to have |

↓

| iii | Ask her to empty her pockets and remove any jewellery including wristwatch |

↓

| iv | Search the contents of pockets; jewellery and any other items, including bags she is carrying, then place them to one side |

↓

| v | Ask her to remove any headwear and pass it to you for searching |

↓

| vi | Search the head by running your fingers through her hair and round the back of her ears, or asking her to shake out her hair and run her fingers through it. Unpin long hair if necessary |

↓

| vii | Look around and inside her ears, nose and mouth. You may ask her to raise her tongue so that you can look under it |

↓

| viii | Lift her collar; feel behind and around it and across the top of her shoulders (search any scarf or tie and ask her to remove it if necessary) |

↓

| ix | Ask her to raise her arms level with her shoulders. Her fingers must be apart with palms facing downwards. Search each arm by running your hands along the upper and lower sides |
|---|---|

↓

| x | Check between her fingers and look at the palms and back of her hands |
|---|---|

↓

| xi | Run the flat of your hand underneath and from the shoulders to the top of the bra. At no time touch her breast |
|---|---|

↓

| xii | Check her sides and front of abdomen from underneath breasts to and including the waistband |
|---|---|

↓

| xiii | Check her back from collar to waist, back of the waistband and seat of the trouser or skirt. You may need to ask her to turn around |
|---|---|

↓

| xiv | Check the back and sides of each leg from the crotch to the ankle |
|---|---|

↓

| xv | Check the front and sides of each leg. (If she is wearing a skirt, it is more difficult to search the top of the legs. Run hands down both sides of each leg outside the skirt. (Use a metal detector) |
|---|---|

↓

| xvi | Ask her to remove footwear and search thoroughly. Check the soles of the feet |
|---|---|

↓

| xvii | Look at the area around her for anything she may have dropped before or during the search |
|---|---|

↓

| xviii | Ask her to step to one side to ensure she is not standing on anything he has dropped before or during the search |
|---|---|

## Level B rub down (for prisoners, official/professional visitors and members of staff)

**Male subject**

| i | Stand facing the subject |
|---|---|

↓

| ii | Ask him if he has anything on him that he is not authorised to have |
|---|---|

↓

| iii | Ask him to empty his pockets and remove any jewellery including wristwatch |
|---|---|

↓

| iv | Search the contents of pockets; jewellery and any other items, including bags he is carrying then place them to one side |
|---|---|

↓

| v | Ask him to remove any headwear and pass it to you for searching |
|---|---|

↓

| vi | Lift his collar, feel behind and around it and across the top of his shoulders (search any tie and ask him to remove it if necessary) |
|---|---|

↓

| vii | Ask him to raise his arms level with his shoulders. His fingers must be apart with palms facing downwards. Search each arm by running your hands along the upper and lower sides |
|---|---|

↓

| viii | Check between his fingers and look at the palms and back of his hands |
|---|---|

↓

| ix | Check the front of his body from neck to waist, the sides, from armpits to waist and the front of the waistband |
|---|---|

↓

| x | Check his back from collar to waist, back of the waistband and seat of the trouser. You may need to ask him to turn around |
|---|---|

↓

| xi | Check the back and sides of each leg from the crotch to the ankle |
|---|---|

↓

| xii | Check the front of his abdomen and front and side of each leg |
|---|---|

↓

| xiii | Look at the area around him for anything he may have dropped before or during the search |
|---|---|

↓

| xiv | Ask him to step to one side to ensure he is not standing on anything he has dropped before or during the search |
|---|---|

**Female subject**

| i | Stand facing the subject |
|---|---|

↓

| ii | Ask her if she has anything on her that she is not authorised to have |
|---|---|

↓

| iii | Ask her to empty her pockets and remove any jewellery including wristwatch |
|---|---|

↓

| iv | Search the contents of pockets, jewellery and any other items, including bags she is carrying, then place them to one side |
|---|---|

↓

| v | Ask her to remove any headwear and pass it to you for searching |
|---|---|

↓

| vi | Lift her collar; feel behind and around it and across the top of her shoulders (search any scarf or tie and ask her to remove it if necessary) |
|---|---|

↓

| vii | Ask her to raise her arms level with her shoulders. Her fingers must be apart with palms facing downwards. Search each arm by running your hands along the upper and lower sides |
|---|---|

↓

| viii | Check between her fingers and look at the palms and back of her hands |
|---|---|

↓

| ix | Run the flat of your hand underneath and from the shoulders to the top of the bra. At no time touch her breast |
|---|---|

↓

| x | Check her sides and front of abdomen from underneath breasts to and including the waistband |
|---|---|

↓

| xi | Check her back from collar to waist, back of the waistband and seat of the trouser or skirt. You may need to ask her to turn around |
|---|---|

↓

| xii | Check the back and sides of each leg from the crotch to the ankle |
|---|---|

↓

| xiii | Check the front and sides of each leg. (If she is wearing a skirt, it is more difficult to search the top of the legs. Run hands down both sides of each leg outside the skirt. (Use a metal detector) |
|---|---|

↓

| xiv | Look at the area around her for anything she may have dropped before or during the search |
|---|---|

↓

| xv | Ask her to step to one side to ensure she is not standing on anything he has dropped before or during the search |
|---|---|

8.37 Men can be asked to squat during a strip search (so that officers can examine whether anything has been inserted into the anal area), but the NSF states that under no circumstances should women be asked to squat. Such squat searches have been described as 'extreme and intrusive'.[28] The searching officer must have reasonable suspicion that an unauthorised article may be concealed in the anal or genital area before a prisoner is required to submit such a search. If a prisoner refuses to bend or squat in such circumstances, they are disobeying a lawful order and, if appropriate, reasonable force can be used to make them bend or squat, or alternatively mirrors or other visual aids can be used.

8.38 If no item is visible, the NSF states that there are no further grounds to continue this procedure, and the full search should be completed in the normal manner, including an update of the relevant searching records. However, if an item becomes visible during the squat search the officers conducting the search must ask the prisoner to remove it. If the prisoner refuses, then the guidance states that action taken should be proportionate to the threat posed by the item, so:

- Where an item is clearly visible it may be removed without consent only where there is a serious risk to prison security if the prisoner retains possession (eg a weapon), and removal can be undertaken without undue risk of causing the prisoner any internal injuries.

- Where the suspected item does not pose immediate or serious danger to prison security, eg a small quantity of drugs, or forced removal is not justified under the first bullet point, then less intrusive measures may be undertaken within the prison's disciplinary procedures.[29]

8.39 If a prisoner does not obey an order to remove a visible item, and it cannot be forcibly removed in line with the above guidelines, the NSF requires an intimate search to remove the item to be offered to the prisoner. These searches can only be carried out with the consent of the prisoner and by a medical practitioner. This also applies if leaving

---

28 *R (Carroll and Al-Hasan) v Secretary of State for the Home Department* [2005] UKHL 13, [2005] 1 WLR 688.

29 *In R (Black) v Secretary of State for the Home Department* [1999] EWHC 578 (Admin) a finding of guilt against a prisoner who refused an order to remove an item from this anus as he stated it was not possible for him to do so was upheld. The judge held that the adjudicating governor did not have to investigate the defence, that the item was a suppository, if he found that the prisoner was lying.

the item raises health concerns for the prisoner. Where an item can be more easily removed, but still involves a large degree of intrusion (for example a drugs package visible under the foreskin), the NSF authorises officers to use force to remove the item, as a last resort, if consent is not given. However in all cases careful consideration must be given to the risk of internal injuries to the prisoner by removing the item.

8.40    The NSF applies the same guidance to physical searches of the mouth, as this also amounts to an intimate search. However searching staff can visually inspect the mouth during a rub down or full search in line with standard procedures.

8.41    The position of prisoners undergoing gender re-assignment raises particular issues. The NSF states that post-operative prisoners will be treated as their post-operative gender for the purposes of searching whether or not they have been transferred to an appropriate prison. Pre-operative prisoners will be searched according to their birth gender, unless the medical practitioner reports in writing that it would be in the prisoner's best interest to be treated differently. In such cases rub down searches of those undergoing gender re-assignment from male to female must only be carried out by a female member of staff. Prisoners who have commenced or completed gender reassignment surgery will normally be searched in accordance with the procedures set out in the local strategy for prisoners of their gender choice, unless it is appropriate to depart from this general principle. The particular arrangements for searching in such cases will therefore be for the governor to decide, after consultation with the medical officer. The wishes of both the prisoner concerned and individual members of staff who may be asked to conduct the search should be taken into account.

8.42    The detailed guidance on how to conduct a strip search states that at no time must a person be completely naked during a strip search. They can only be carried out by two officers of the same sex as the person being searched and away from the view of any other person.

## Strip search: male

The correct procedure to use when conducting a full search is as follows:

| Officer 1 | Officer 2 |
|---|---|
| 1 **The officer in charge of the search. He is responsible for controlling the search. He will normally observe the subject from the front.** | **Responsible for receiving clothing and other items from the subject and searching them. He should return the clothing and other items back to the subject at the direction of officer 1. Normally observes from back or side.** |
| 2 Ask the subject if he has anything on him he is not authorised to have. Ask him to empty his pockets and remove any jewellery, including wristwatch, and hand over any bags or other items being carried. | Search the contents of the pockets and the jewellery and place them to one side. Search any bags or other items. |
| 3 Ask him to remove any headwear and pass it to officer 2 for searching. | Search headwear. |
| 4 Search his head either by running your fingers through his hair and around the back of his ears, or ask him to shake out his hair and run his fingers through it. | |
| 5 Look around and inside his ears, nose and mouth. You may ask him to raise his tongue so that you can look under it. | |
| 6 Ask him to remove the clothing from the top half of his body and pass it to officer 2. | Search the clothing. |
| 7 Ask him to hold his arms up and turn around whilst you observe his upper body. Check his hands. | Return the clothing. |
| 8 Allow him time to put on clothing. | |

| | | |
|---|---|---|
| 9 | Ask him to remove his shoes and socks and pass to officer 2. | Search the shoes and socks and then place them to one side. |
| 10 | Ask him to lift each foot so the soles can be checked. | |
| 11 | Ask him to remove his trousers and underpants and pass to officer 2. | Search trousers and underpants and place to one side. |
| 12 | Once the clothing has been searched ask him to raise the upper body clothing to his waist and observe the lower half of his body. | |
| 13 | He must stand with his legs apart while the lower half of his body is observed. | |
| 14 | Look at the area around him for anything he may have dropped before or during the search. | |
| 15 | Ask him to step to one side to ensure he is not standing on anything he has dropped before or during the search. | Return the clothing. |
| 16 | Allow the prisoner time to put on his clothing. | |

## Strip search: female

The correct procedure to use when conducting the WOMEN'S FULL SEARCH is as follows:

| WOMEN'S FULL SEARCH LEVEL 1 | Officer 1 | Officer 2 |
|---|---|---|
| *Note* an appropriate manager needs to authorise the search in the case of a 'target' or 'special search' (ie not following reception or a visit, or a cell search) | The officer in charge of the search. She is responsible for controlling the search. She will normally observe the subject from the front. She should explain the need for the search and each step, taking into account any cultural or religious sensitivity. | Responsible for receiving clothing and other items from the subject and searching them. She must return the clothing and other items back to the subject at the direction of officer 1. Normally observes from back or side. |
| | 1  Ask the subject if she has anything on her she is not authorised to have. Ask her to empty her pockets and remove any jewellery, including wristwatch, and hand over any bags or other items being carried. | Search the contents of the pockets and the jewellery and place them to one side. Search any bags or other items. Scan her body slowly with a metal detector (wand). |
| | 2  Ask her to remove any headwear and pass it to officer 2 for searching. | Search headwear. |
| | 3  Search her head either by running your fingers through her hair and around the back of her ears, or ask her to shake out her hair and run her fingers through it. | |
| | 4  Look around and inside her ears, nose and mouth. You may ask her to raise her tongue so that you can look under it. | |

Women may be wearing particular underwear in order to help them feel better about how they look eg bras with foam or gel padding or inserts. These items should generally be allowed unless there is reasonable suspicion that they have been or are being used to conceal illicit items. If there is suspicion that this may be the case Level 2 of this search should be proceeded with. If illicit articles are discovered, the article of clothing may be placed into property.

5   Ask her to remove the clothing from the top half of her body except for her bra and pass it to officer 2.

Search the clothing.

If she is not wearing a bra continue the search. Offer a towel, new bra or crop top to put on if she wishes one.

Particular sensitivity should be shown if the woman is wearing a mastectomy bra.

6   Ask her to hold her arms up and turn around whilst you observe her upper body. Check her hands.

Return the clothing.

7   Provide a dressing-gown (pre-searched). Allow her time to put it on for the rest of the search.

8   Ask her to remove her shoes, socks, tights etc and pass to officer 2.

Search the shoes, socks, tights etc and then place them to one side.

9   Ask her to lift each foot so the soles can be checked.

10   Ask her to remove all clothing from the lower part of her body except for her briefs and pass to officer 2.

Search all clothing and place to one side.

11   Once the clothing has been searched ask her to raise the dressing-gown to her waist and observe the lower half of her body.

Do not ask the woman to remove any sanitary towel at this point.

12 Look at the area around her for anything she may have dropped before or during the search.

13 Ask her to step to one side to ensure she is not standing on anything she has dropped before or during the search. | Return the clothing and search the dressing-gown again.

14 Allow the prisoner time to put on her clothing.

| **WOMEN'S FULL SEARCH LEVEL 2** | **If there is any suspicion or intelligence that the woman has concealed any item in her underwear, or any illicit articles have been discovered concealed, during level 1 of the search, proceed as follows:** | |

15 Ask the woman to lower her dressing gown to her waist and remove her bra. | Search the bra.

16 Ask her to hold her arms up and turn around whilst you observe her upper body. Check her hands. Ask her to put her bra back on and the dressing gown | Return the bra.

17 Ask her to remove her briefs and pass to officer 2. | Search the briefs.

18   Once the briefs have been searched ask her to raise the dressing-gown to her waist and observe the lower half of her body.

*Note* if necessary the woman 18 or over, can be required to expose part of her body where items are thought to be concealed i.e. under breasts or stomach area.

19   She must stand with her legs apart while the lower half of her body is observed.

Staff must be aware of the policy applying to the removal and disposal of sanitary wear. Externally applied sanitary towels will be removed and placed in an appropriate container and disposed of. A replacement must be provided. Staff must not remove, or ask the subject to remove, internally fitted tampons.

20   Look at the area around her for anything she may have dropped before or during the search.

*Note* in no circumstances can a woman prisoner be asked to squat

21   Ask her to step to one side to ensure she is not standing on anything she has dropped before or during the search.

Return the clothing and search the dressing-gown again.

22   Allow the prisoner time to put on her clothing.

*Note* do not record names of sources – include number of SIR if appropriate.

23   Sign record to state why level 2 search indicated.

Sign record to state why level 2 search indicated.

## The 'BOSS' chair

8.43   The Prison Service has introduced the Body Orifice Security Scanner (BOSS). This is a 'non-intrusive scanning system within a moulded chair, designed to detect small metallic objects, such as mobile phones and their component parts or weapons, concealed within anal or vaginal cavities and the abdominal area'.[30] The Prison Service guidance indicates that it can be used both on prisoners and visitors as

> a searching aid to complement a rubdown search when carrying out routine searches. For example, on entry to establishments, before and after visits and as part of targeted, intelligence-led searches. It may also be used following a full search in instances where suspicion remains that a metallic illicit item is concealed internally, and, in the case of male prisoners, a squat search has failed to reveal the item.[31]

If prisoners give a positive indication and have been strip searched and nothing found, they may be segregated until they either hand over the item or give a negative reading.[32] A visitor who refuses to comply with a BOSS search may be refused entry. A positive reading may give rise to criminal proceedings if an item is surrendered which is prohibited under the Prison Act 1952. It may also result in a ban or closed visits being imposed.[33]

## Searching and activities

8.44   The NSF requires that items under construction by prisoners (including, for example, models) should be subjected to careful physical examination, and X-rayed where the equipment is available if they are still believed to present a security risk. In relation to work and activities the standard of search to be applied to a prisoner leaving the session early for any reason should be agreed between the governor and regional director of offender management or director of high security, and included in the searching strategy. Staff should search prisoners leaving together at the end of a session according to the instructions set out in the prison's searching strategy. The searching strategy must also include provision for occasional full rub

---

30   PSI 5/2009 para 10 – gives detailed guidance on the use of the 'BOSS chair' and requires prisons to incorporate the device into local searching policies.
31   PSI 5/2009 para 18.
32   PSI 5/2009 para 31.
33   PSI 5/2009 paras 33–35.

down searches of all prisoners coming out of any workshop, either at random, or based on intelligence. Where prisoners are allowed to carry personal possessions to and from activities these should be thoroughly searched. Before any large-scale gathering of prisoners (such as concerts or religious services), the area in which the activity is to take place should be searched in accordance with the local searching strategy.

## Outside working parties

8.45    For outside working parties, there must be a searching programme for all prisoners leaving or entering a prison. In particular the NSF specifies that all prisoners returning from outside work should be strip searched and checked using a metal detector, though this may be based on local risk assessments if applicable. In order to reduce the scope for smuggling illicit items, prisoners leaving and entering the prison in connection with outside work should carry the absolute minimum of personal possessions. These should be stipulated by the governor.

## Cell searches

8.46    The NSF states that all residential units, including all prisoner areas, should be searched in accordance with the local strategy. The fabric of all prisoner accommodation areas, including cells, rooms and dormitories, should be checked daily. These fabric checks are not designed to discover unauthorised items but to detect any evidence of an attempt to break out of the cell. So window frames and bars, walls, floors and ceilings are checked. Such searches are completed by wing staff, and do not take more than a minute or two to complete.

8.47    Full cell searches including searches of the prisoner's property take much longer and will be accompanied by a strip search of the prisoner themselves. Legally privileged material held in cells should be searched in the prisoner's presence, and then sealed whilst the prisoner is required to leave the cell.

8.48    The NSF confirms that dogs should not come into contact with individual clothing or religious artefacts during cell searches. The prisoner should be allowed to point out such items before the search is carried out.

8.49    Cell searching procedures were significantly overhauled following the recommendations of the Woodcock report into the escapes from HMP Whitemoor in 1994.[34] This report was concerned that prisoners

34  1994 Cm 2741.

had been able to condition staff into accepting living conditions and searching levels that enabled the accumulation of unauthorised articles. The changes led to the introduction of dedicated search teams in high security prisons and a policy that cells should be searched in the absence of the prisoner. When the policy was first introduced it stated that such privileged material in cells should be searched in the absence of the prisoner as with other in-cell possessions. The House of Lords subsequently held that the policy was disproportionate resulting in the current system.[35]

## Searching and visits

8.50    The NSF states that visitors, as a condition of entry to the prison, must consent to be searched and, where applicable, to deposit property. Staff should be aware of items not allowed in the prison. The NSF also specifies the level of searching that should be used on visitors. Visitors may be given a routine rub-down search although those entering an SSU or those searched on suspicion should be given a full rub-down search. Prisons' local security strategies must determine the percentage of visitors to be to be searched and this will clearly depend upon the security category of the prison concerned. Only female staff must search female visitors, prisoners and staff. Male visitors, prisoners and staff may be rubbed down searched by male or female staff, but must only be strip searched (see below) by male prison officers. However the NSF states that refusal by a man to be routinely searched by a woman will not be grounds to refuse entry.

8.51    A visitor should have their religious headwear searched using a hand held metal detector. Its removal is only authorised by the NSF if there is an alarm that cannot be accounted for, or there is reasonable suspicion that an unauthorised item is being concealed. If there is a need to search the headwear, it should be done in private by staff of the same sex and removed only by the wearer.

8.52    Individual prisons are required by the NSF to determine the levels of searching of prisoners and visitors following visits, including the use of metal scans, and percentages of prisoners to be full searched, but, as a minimum, staff should:

- Strip search all E List prisoners following visits.
- Strip search a percentage of other prisoners at random following visits, at a level agreed between the governor and regional director of offender management.

35  *R (Daly) v Secretary of State for the Home Department* [2001] 2 AC 532.

- Strip search prisoners following visits if there is sufficient reason to believe they are smuggling contraband.

8.53    Prisons holding high and exceptional risk prisoners should ensure that staff:

- Strip search prisoners before visits and provide them with sterile clothing (these may be the prisoner's own clothes if he or she is entitled to wear them) to wear during the visit.
- Strip search all category A prisoners following an open visit.
- Are aware that, following open visits, visitors should be metal scanned and rub down searched on leaving the SSU visits room, and their property should be searched by X-ray and by hand.

8.54    Once visitors are inside the prison there are certain circumstances where they can be searched without consent. At any point, a visitor may decide to terminate the visit and should be allowed to leave, except where other legislation allows a search without consent or the visitor has been arrested. Certain statutory powers allow those with the powers of a constable (that is prison officers only) to conduct searches (up to and including strip searches) within the context of their duties as prison officers, without consent, in the following circumstances:

- If there is reasonable cause to suspect the subject is carrying a firearm (with or without ammunition) in a public place, or (in public or private) for the purpose of committing an indictable offence.[36]
- If there is reasonable cause to suspect the subject is carrying a class A, B or C controlled drug.[37]
- If an officer of the prison has arrested the subject, a search may be conducted if there is reasonable cause to suspect they are a danger to self or others, or to search for anything which might be used to escape from arrest or which might be evidence relating to an offence. But, there should be reasonable cause to suspect they have such an item on them. They should not be required to remove more than a coat, jacket or gloves in public, and the search should only be to the extent that is reasonably required to find the object.[38]

---

36  Firearms Act 1968 s47.
37  Misuse of Drugs Act 1971 s23.
38  Police and Criminal Evidence Act 1984 s32.

8.55 Prison custody officers at private prisons do not have these powers but do have the power to use reasonable force to detain those suspected of certain offences for up to two hours to allow for the arrival of the police.[39] Only the police have the power to conduct an intimate search •of visitors or staff, and then only with the consent of the subject, or where there are serious health or security issues.

## Use of dogs and searches

8.56 Prisons may use three different types of dog. The NSF states that patrol dogs should not be used for searching people, but may be used as a visual deterrent. Proactive search dogs should never be used to search people. They are to be used only searching for arms, explosives, or drugs, or for cell-searching prior to a prisoner occupying the cell. Passive search dogs are the only dogs that should be used when dealing with people. They should not be used in the same way as patrol or proactive search dogs, but only for:

- preventing drugs being smuggled into prison;
- detecting drugs that have been smuggled into the prison; and
- as a deterrent against drug smuggling.

8.57 Every prison is required by the NSF to have procedures in place following a dog indication so that if any action is deemed necessary then it can be defended as being lawful. It states that a positive indication from a passive drug dog is not conclusive evidence of anything and amounts to no more than the potential presence of drugs. If drugs are present, the indication will not provide an explanation as to why drugs are present. For example there may be innocent contamination. The NSF specifies that a visitor can only be strip searched where there is reasonable cause (see para 8.54) and a passive dog indication on its own cannot amount to reasonable cause and should never lead directly to a strip search. Similarly such an indication without more should never lead directly to the imposition of ban of a visitor.[40] However, the NSF does suggest that records should be kept on visitors who have been indicated by a dog and that consistent positive indications over the course of a number of visits is likely to raise sufficient reasonable cause to conduct a strip search. It also states that a passive dog indication on its own can lead to a closed visit.

39 CJA 1991 s86A.
40 Under the policy in PSO 3610.

# Segregation

## Introduction

8.58   Prisoners are restricted in their movements and in their contact with the outside world but they are generally allowed to associate with each other in their cells, and on wings or in other common areas, albeit for limited periods. The negative effects of imprisonment are massively compounded when prisoners are segregated and held separately from other prisoners. There are various legal grounds for such segregation of prisoners, and the practical impact will vary (segregation as punishment may amount to 'solitary confinement', whereas a group of prisoners segregated for their own protection may have extensive association with each other). Segregation for whatever purpose in prisons and YOIs will most often be associated with allocation to a dedicated unit within the prison.

8.59   The case of *R v Deputy Governor of HMP Parkhurst ex p Hague*[41] held that a wrongful segregation decision does not amount to false imprisonment and that challenges to segregation decision will normally be made through judicial review. The issue as to whether segregation in breach of law or policy could amount to unlawful detention was revisited after the coming into force of the Human Rights Act 1998 in *R (Munjaz) v Mersey NHS Care Trust*[42] where it was held that unlawful seclusion (the special hospital equivalent of segregation) would not breach article 5 of the ECHR. Other articles of the ECHR might be engaged in segregation decisions. *Munjaz* confirmed that, subject to the facts, breaches of either article 8 or 3 of the ECHR may be breached. The circumstances of segregation that might breach article 3 would obviously have to be extreme, although the vulnerability of the prisoner will be relevant as to whether there is a breach.[43]

### The legal basis for segregation

8.60   **Adults and young offenders**

- These prisoners can be removed from association for the 'maintenance of good order or discipline' or in their 'own interests'.[44] The

---

41   [1992] 1 AC 58.

42   [2006] 2 AC 148.

43   A breach of article 3 in *Keenan v UK* (2001) 33 EHRR 38 was contributed to by the imposition of cellular confinement as punishment against a mentally ill prisoner.

44   PR rule 45(1) and YOIR rule 49(1).

power to segregate contained in the Rules is subject to detailed guidance in PSO 1700.

- The Rules also contain a power to order that 'refractory[45] or violent' prisoners are confined temporarily in a special cell.[46] Again detailed policy guidance on this power is included in PSO 1700.
- Prisoners in adult prisoners who are assessed as posing heightened control problems can be removed from association in order to be placed in a close supervision centre (CSC).[47] The policy on selection for, and regimes in, CSCs is contained in the CSC Operating Standards, and Referral Manual.

8.61   Cellular confinement can be imposed as a punishment by governors or Independent Adjudicators following a disciplinary hearing.[48] As this is a punishment it is dealt with in chapter 9 on discipline below.

### 8.62   Children in STCs

- Prisoners in STCs can be removed from association in order to prevent them harming themselves or others, or causing significant damage to property.[49] As noted below, the STC Rules do not include a power to segregate for purposes of 'good order and discipline'. The policy guidance on the power to segregate in STCs is contained in a Code of Practice issued by the YJB – *Managing the Behaviour of Children and Young People in the Secure Estate.*

### 8.63   Children in secure children's homes

- Secure children's homes are required to have a 'behaviour management policy' which sets out the measures of 'control, restraint and discipline' to be used.[50] Guidance on use of segregation in secure children's homes is issued by the Secure Accommodation Network.[51]

## Segregation in prisons and YOIs

8.64   The segregation of adult prisoners and those held in YOIs under the Prison and YOI Rules is subject to detailed policy guidance set out

---

45  Defined in the Oxford English Dictionary as 'stubborn, obstinate, perverse; unmanageable, rebellious'.
46  PR rule 48(1) and YOIR rule 51(1).
47  PR rule 46(1).
48  PR rules 55(1)(e) and 55A(1) and YOIR rules 60(1)(f) and 60A(1).
49  STCR rule 36(1).
50  CHR 17 issued under the Care Standards Act 2000.
51  www.secureaccommodation.org.uk/practiceguidelines.htm

in PSO 1700. The PSO requires all closed prisons and YOIs to set up monitoring arrangements to ensure compliance with the policy, and states that best practice is for institutions to set up a segregation monitoring and review group, which should report quarterly to the governor and regional DOM.

8.65    The power to segregate for the 'maintenance of good order or discipline' should only be used 'when there are reasonable grounds for believing that the prisoner's behaviour is likely to be so disruptive or cause disruption that keeping the prisoner on ordinary location is unsafe'. The use of segregation for reasons of good order or discipline as a punishment is not permitted and PSO 1700 gives examples of the types of conduct that might be considered sufficient to justify segregation for this purpose, such as:

- situations where there is evidence of a planned or imminent breach of security;
- a prisoner incites others to breach security or prison discipline;
- there is a risk to the safety of staff or other prisoners or a risk of damage to prison property;
- it is believed on reasonable grounds (such as CCTV evidence) that the prisoner is holding drugs internally that they intend to take themselves or distribute to other prisoners;
- where a governor's initial adjudication hearing is inconclusive, but the need for segregation is still felt to exist;
- a prisoner consistently fails to co-operate with anti-bullying strategies;
- prisoners who embark on *dirty protests* (to protect others);
- where the prisoner is subject to police or internal investigations into serious offences that occurred while in prison custody, particularly when the offence was committed against another prisoner.

8.66    The policy on segregation in the prisoners own interests states that the power should only be used, 'when there are good and sufficient reasons for believing that the prisoner's safety and well being cannot reasonably be assured by other means'. The policy makes it clear that the power is primarily aimed at protecting prisoners from the risk of assault from other prisoners. Generally, prisoners should not be segregated on request without reasons to believe that the prisoner is at risk. If a prisoner's fear of assault appears unfounded but is so great as to cause concern about their mental state on normal location, this may sufficient to justify considering segregation. The prisoner may also exceptionally request 'own interest' segregation for reasons other than a fear of assault by other prisoners (such as genuine inability to cope on normal location for a specific time period because of, for example, stress or bereavement).

## Segregation procedures

8.67 An overview of the procedures to be followed when making a segregation decision is:

- the initial decision must be made by the governor or an operational manager;
- this authority can last for up to 72 hours;
- reasons should be given to the prison for the decision;
- after 72 hours, further segregation must be authorised by a review board on behalf of the Secretary of State;
- further authorisations can be for periods of up to 14 days at a time;
- there is no limit on the period of time that a prisoner can be segregated providing it is properly authorised.

## The initial decision to segregate

8.68 The Prison and YOI Rules require the initial decision to segregate to be made by the governor[52] or by the director or Controller in a private prison.[53] PSO 1700 states that the initial decision can be delegated to an operational manager of Grade F or above, or to a deputy Controller in a private prison. The initial decision to segregate made by the governor (or director/controller) only authorises segregation for the first 72 hours.[54] In *Hague*,[55] it was held that the requirements of procedural fairness did not require adult prisoners to be given the opportunity to make representations before the decision to segregate was taken. This has been modified in relation to those under 18 years old held in YOIs where it has been held that there should be an opportunity to make representations before the decision to segregate distinguishing *Hague*[56] at least to the extent of being able to comment upon the 'tentative' reasons for segregation. The impact on a child of being segregated was seen as being sufficiently grave to enhance the requirements of fairness when considering whether to

52  PR rule 45(1) and YOIR rule 49(1).
53  PR rule 82(1)(b)(iii) and YOIR rule 86(1)(b)(iii).
54  PR rule 45(2) and YOIR rule 49(2).
55  [1992] 1 AC 58.
56  *R(SP) v Secretary of State for the Home Department* [2004] EWCA Civ 1750.

segregate, at least to the extent of commenting on the factual basis for the decision.

8.69    In consequence, PSO 1700 requires the YOI authorities to consider whether the prisoner who is either under 18 or serving a DTO should be given an opportunity to make representations before the decision to segregate is made. Factors to be taken into account when deciding whether representations should be sought include the risks to the prisoner and others, the availability of staff and the behaviour and competence of the prisoner to make representations prior to the decision. The policy also requires the prison authorities to consider the help any advocacy service may be able to provide in helping to make representations.

8.70    Within two hours of the prisoner being located in the segregation unit PSO 1700 requires the completion of an initial segregation safety screen form. This form is in two parts. The first requires an algorithm to be completed to determine whether there might be healthcare reasons not to segregate (this looks at issues of self-harm, vulnerability and mental health). Any concerns raised by the algorithm should be discussed with the healthcare team. The second part of the form is completed by a doctor or registered nurse so that advice can be provided as to whether there are any clinical reasons not to segregate. The form states that it is meant to provide a 'snapshot' and is 'not intended to be a comprehensive mental or physical health assessment'. If the form raises healthcare issues against segregation the duty governor can only decide to segregate for operational reasons on the basis that an initial case review will be held within two hours.

8.71    Prisoners on an open ACCT should only remain in segregation in exceptional circumstances and a self-harm case review should take place within 24 hours. PSO 1700 also suggests that in these circumstances the prisoner should be located in a 'safer cell' and the use of overt CCTV surveillance should also be considered.[57] If no doctor or registered nurse is on duty, then if the segregated prisoner is on an open ACCT then they should be observed at least five times an hour at irregular intervals, and other prisoners at least every 30 minutes until the safety screen can be completed.

8.72    The decision to segregate should be recorded on an 'authority for initial segregation' form. This sets out the reasons for segregation, including why the decision has been taken in the face of any healthcare concerns. There is a separate form used for those under 18 or serving DTOs which requires confirmation that an opportunity

---

57   Under PR rule 50A or YOIR rule 54.

to make representations has been provided before the decision has been taken (see para 8.69 above). Both forms also require confirmation that the prisoner has been provided with reasons for the decision to segregate.

8.73 The reasons should be provided to the prisoner on 'reasons for initial segregation' form. The policy states that reasons should be given both orally and in writing. Where the decision is recording a decision to segregate for good order or discipline the reasons will often be extremely vague if reliance is placed on third party, or security information which is not disclosable to the prisoner. In these circumstances, the giving of reasons does not assist the prisoner in making meaningful representations against the decision. The prisoner should also be told of when the segregation will be reviewed.

8.74 Once a decision to segregate has been made, a 'segregation history form' must be opened which is used to monitor the prisoner, and will include daily comments on behaviour and attitude, and will also be used to record any visits. PSO 1700 also requires 'all relevant people' to be informed of the decision to segregate. As well as healthcare, the policy requires that the IMB are informed within 24 hours of the decision to segregate. If a prisoner is on an open ACCT then the suicide prevention co-ordinator should be informed, and if the prisoner is under 18 so should the relevant YOT.

## Segregation after 72 hours

8.75 The Prison and YOI Rules state that prisoners should not be removed from association for reasons of good order or discipline, or in their own interests, for more than 72 hours without the authority of the Secretary of State. In practice, this decision is delegated to Segregation Review Boards (see below). Once a further decision to segregate is made it must be renewed on behalf of the Secretary of State every 14 days.[58] However, the Rules also make it clear that these decisions to segregate do not prevent the governor (or controller/director in private prisons) from deciding at any time in his or her discretion that the prisoner should resume association. In exercising this discretion the governor is required to consider any recommendation made by a doctor or registered nurse.[59] These provisions therefore ensure that segregation should not continue for any longer than necessary.

8.76 The policy guidance in PSO 1700 states that the decisions authorise segregation beyond the first 72 hours must be taken on behalf of

---

58 PR rule 45(2) and YOIR rule 49(2).
59 PR rule 45(3) and YOIR rule 49(3).

the Secretary of State by a Segregation Review Board which is chaired by an operational manager. The policy states '[t]he aim is to return a prisoner to normal location as soon as it is practicable to do so. The safety of the prisoner whilst in segregation is of paramount importance'. Although recent changes to the Rules clarified that both directors and controllers in private prisons have authority to make the same decisions in relation to segregation as governors,[60] the fact that the Rules require the Secretary of State to take the decision as further segregation will mean that a Controller must be responsible for the final decision in private prisons.

8.77    Up until 2006, the Independent Monitoring Boards (IMB) had a role in deciding whether segregation should continue. There were obvious concerns about the boards being concerned both with protecting the interests of prisoners and also having a formal role in disciplinary matters. Now the decision is taken by Segregation Review Boards to be chaired by an operational manager of at least grade F. The first review board is to take place within 72 hours of the decision to segregate and must consist of at least a chairperson and a healthcare representative. Boards that then continue to authorise segregation every at least 14 days must include:

- chairperson (mandatory);
- healthcare representative (mandatory);
- segregation personal officer;
- chaplain;
- psychologist; and
- prisoner (for at least part of the board).

8.78    The policy does state that a member of the IMB should be present at the board 'whenever possible'. This is purely an observational role and the IMB member will play no part in the decision making process. Where an IMB member is present, however, the policy states that it will be good practice to ask them to comment on the decision and their agreement or otherwise should be on the form recording the decision. If the IMB member has serious concerns about the decision to maintain segregation, PSO 1700 states that these objections should be raised with the governor, and if the IMB remain dissatisfied the concerns can be raised successively with the regional director of offender management, Deputy Director General and ultimately the minister or Director General.

60  Prison (Amendment No 2) Rules 2007 SI No 3149 in force from 2 November 2007.

8.79     The matters that PSO 1700 requires Segregation Review Boards
to consider are:

- *The initial reasons for segregation.* These will be an important element
  of defining what behaviour and/or attitudes need to be addressed
  before the prisoner may return to normal accommodation.

- *Behaviour and attitude of the prisoner since the last review.* At the previous review the prisoner should have been set certain behaviour
  and/or attitude targets in order to start to work towards returning
  to normal accommodation. The extent to which the prisoner has
  met these targets should be considered.

- *Any concerns that may have come to light about how the prisoner is
  coping with segregation.* The policy recognises that research indicates that a person's mental health is very likely to decline when
  they are kept in segregation. The board must consider any observations or concerns raised by a member of staff or the prisoner
  about their ability to cope in segregation. The board must consider
  additional steps to safeguard the mental health of prisoners whilst
  in segregation. Particular care should be given to authorising continued segregation of a prisoner on an open ACCT – continued
  segregation should occur only in exceptional circumstances and
  an ACCT case review must take place at the same time as the segregation review board. If a prisoner needs to be segregated from
  others, but is considered to be at a high risk of suicide then the
  board should decide whether to locate the prisoner in healthcare
  or allocated a member of the healthcare team to be based in the
  segregation unit.

- *What the prisoner needs to demonstrate in order to be considered for
  a return to normal location or alternative accommodation.* The prisoner should be set some targets that the board feels will start to
  demonstrate a willingness and ability to change the behaviour
  that led to segregation in the first place. The targets should be
  reasonable, specific, relevant and time bound (achievable before
  the next review).

- *Privileges or incentives to be awarded or removed.* The review board
  assesses the extent to which the prisoner has met or been willing to meet some or all of the targets set at the last review board.
  The board may then allow access to greater facilities, or remove
  them (subject to the comments on what constitutes an acceptable
  regime above).

- *Transfer to another establishment.* The review board should consider whether they think that the prisoner needs to be transferred

to another establishment. The policy states that this may be inevitable if the prisoner has become so disruptive, dangerous or notorious that they will be unable to return to normal location in their current establishment or if they have been unwilling to make any progress whilst in segregation. Prisoners are normally told if they are being considered for transfer to another establishment (except category A and E List prisoners). After transfer the new prison will have to consider whether to make a fresh decision to segregate the prisoner.

8.80   After consideration of these factors, the review board decides whether to authorise segregation for up to a maximum of 14 days. The board chair has the authority to make the decision and should sign the relevant section of the review board form. The policy in PSO 1700 does not state that a copy of the form should be given to the prisoner. However the reasons for continued segregation should be set out on a separate form given to the prisoner which also sets behaviour targets, and the date for the next review.

8.81   If the decision of the board is that segregation is no longer necessary, review boards are required to consider whether the prisoner can go directly back to normal location, or via a phased return to ordinary location (normally where the prisoner has been segregated for over a month – the phased return involves the prisoner remaining in the segregation unit, except for specific periods of activities out of the unit. Such a phased return requires the agreement of the prisoner), or a return through a high supervision unit (usually only available in large local prisons – for prisoners not suitable for segregation but needing greater supervision).

8.82   PSO 1700 also includes detailed guidance on the treatment of prisoners on dirty protest who will normally be in segregation. A dirty protest is defined as 'is where a prisoner has chosen to either defecate or urinate in a cell or a room without using the facilities provided'. Most of the policy largely focuses on the health and safety of both the prisoner and the staff dealing with him or her.

8.83   There is no long stop time limit as to how long prisoners may remain in segregation and it is of concern that sometimes prisoners can spend months or even years in segregation units. The reality is that those prisoners who spend a long continuous period in segregation are likely to eventually be transferred to one of the CSCs (see below).

8.84   The policy states that there is no separate Prison Service appeal process for segregation decisions but prisoners can make use of the normal complaints procedure and take their cases to the Prisons and Probation Ombudsman where appropriate. Segregation decisions may also be challenged by judicial review.

## Regimes in segregation

8.85   The form that notifies the prisoner of the decision to segregate should also clarify what regime facilities will be available pending the first review (see below). In keeping with the principle that segregation either for good order or discipline, or in the prisoner's own interests, is not punitive, PSO 1700 states that the regime 'should be as full as possible and only those activities that involve associating with mainstream prisoners should be curtailed'. Work or education that can be done in the segregation unit should be encouraged and access to activities such as domestic visits, legal visits, use of the telephone, canteen, exercise and showers should be comparable to those for a prisoner held on normal location. Any restriction of normal facilities (for example substituting cell furniture with cardboard furniture, or not allowing the prisoner a lighter or matches for cigarettes) must be supported by a risk assessment that clearly states why the restriction is being placed on that prisoner and how often the assessment will be reviewed. The policy states that certain facilities such as television, association within the unit, or access to the gym may be used as incentives in the context of targets set by the Segregation Review Boards (see below).

8.86   The Prison Rules include provision that that 'if weather permits and subject to the need to maintain good order and discipline, a prisoner shall be given the opportunity to spend time in the open air at least once every day, for such period as may be reasonable in the circumstances'.[61] For those in segregation this power is subject to mandatory policy which states that

> governors and directors must ensure that ... prisoners subjected to a severely restricted regime (e.g. those held in the segregation unit as a punishment or under Rule [45] in the interests of good order and discipline) are provided with the opportunity to spend a minimum of one hour in the open air each day.[62]

---

61   PR rule 30.
62   PSO 4275.

### Regimes for children held in YOIs

8.87    The policy in PSO 1700 includes special provision for those under 18 held in YOIs. For these prisoners a separate assessment must be made to identify the regime activities in which they can participate safely with others. This assessment will be carried out before the first segregation review board and should be reviewed at each board. This policy was amended following a case in which a segregated 17-year-old challenged the conditions in which he was held in a YOI. The judge held 'there was a clear breach in failing to provide education, training and physical education, contrary both to those Rules and to the Prison Order. It is not permitted to deprive a trainee, even when he is removed from a unit, of such facilities, or the facilities of a daily shower'.[63]

8.88    Although the provisions of PSO 1700 outlined above do apply to those under 18 years old held in YOIs, the Prison Service has issued additional guidance on the treatment of this particularly vulnerable group, in the interests of 'safeguarding the welfare and distinguishing the individual needs of the young person'.[64] With regard to the use of segregation, this guidance requires governors to draw up a 'behaviour management policy' which takes into account relevant YJB guidance (see below) and must be agreed with the regional director of offender management.[65] In relation to the use of segregation the guidance states:

> Governors must strictly control the use of separation (segregating of young people), whether by reason of good order or discipline (GOOD), own protection, or prior to an adjudication in a serious case or removal from unit. Segregation must only be used when necessary and must always be accompanied by a strategy of intervention through advice and counselling, the objective of which is to return the young person to ordinary accommodation as soon as possible. Governors must also ensure that, while in segregation, every young person is given the opportunity to engage in education, vocational training, work and PE. All such activities must be documented. The Process of Segregation and the Principles of the Segregation Unit outlined in PSO 1700 must be followed at all times. Local policies must be approved by the Regional director of Offender Management.[66]

63    *R (BP) v Secretary of State for the Home Department* [2003] EWHC 1963 (Admin).

64    PSO 4950 para 1.2.

65    PSO 4950 para 2.13.

66    PSO 4950 para 2.17.

# Use of special cells in adult prisons and YOIs

## The legal authority to confine to a special cell

8.89 The Prison Act 1952 s14(6) requires every prison to have 'special cells' (including 'special rooms') in the case of young offenders, for the temporary confinement of 'refractory or violent prisoners'.[67] The Prison and YOI Rules accordingly give the governor (or a controller or director in a private prison) power to order such temporary confinement. This power is specifically not to be used as punishment and can only continue for as long as the prisoner is 'refractory or violent'.[68] Confinement in a special cell (or room for young offenders) must not exceed 24 hours without a direction in writing given by an officer of the Secretary of State which should state the grounds for the confinement, and the time for which it can continue.[69]

## Policy on use of the power

8.90 Guidance on these powers is contained in PSO 1700. This requires the use of special accommodation to be monitored together with the use of segregation. The policy defines special accommodation as:

> a dedicated cell, or improvised normal accommodation with any one (or more than one) of the following items removed in the interests of safety: furniture, bedding, sanitation. Special Accommodation can be located anywhere in a prison, including Healthcare and is not only found in Segregation Units or Care and Separation Units.

It is further stated that special accommodation 'must only be used to manage prisoners who cannot be located safely in normal accommodation'. In particular those identified as at risk of suicide or self-harm must not be placed in special accommodation unless they are in addition 'refractory or violent'.

## The initial decision to place the prisoner in special accommodation

8.91 In line with the policy on segregation, there is a requirement to give prisoners under 18 an opportunity to make representations before a decision is taken to place them in special accommodation. Further there is a requirement to inform the relevant YOT and head of placements of the YJB when such a decision is taken. If a child is placed in a room to 'calm down' then the policy makes it clear that the proper

67 PA 1952 s14(6).
68 PR rule 48(1), YOIR rule 51(1).
69 PR rule 48(2), YOIR rule 51(4).

special accommodation procedures should be followed where any of the items referred to in para 8.87 are removed.

8.92    The decision has to be taken by the duty governor (controller or director in private prisons), or where they are not available the 'person in charge of the prison' must make the decision and inform the duty governor at the earliest opportunity. The initial decision relates to the first 24 hours and must be recorded on form OT013. The policy states that '[t]he reason for placing the prisoner in Special Accommodation must be explained to him or her at the earliest opportunity, making it clear that it is not a form of punishment'.

8.93    If the prisoner is on self-harm measures the ACCT co-ordinator should be consulted, if not before the decision to place the prisoner in special accommodation, then as soon as possible afterwards. The decision maker is directed by the form OT013 to consider that the alternatives to the use of special accommodation have been considered. A case review should then be held within two hours. Unless the case review specifically rules it out a mental health assessment should also be carried out.

8.94    Prisons and YOIs are required to have a designated manager who must be of at least senior officer grade (or the equivalent in private prisons) who is then required to assess the suitability of the continued location of the prisoner in special accommodation at a frequency set out on form OT013. This has to be at least hourly. The Duty governor must also specify on the form the frequency with which the prisoner should be observed, which must be at least five times an hour at irregular intervals (these should take into account the ACCT form for those at risk of self-harm). During these assessments and observations, which must be recorded on the form OT013, staff 'must make every effort to talk to the prisoner and de-escalate the situation to minimise the prisoner's time in special accommodation'.

8.95    The healthcare department must be informed of the decision and a doctor or registered nurse should attend immediately and complete the same kind of safety screen as that used in relation to decisions to segregate (para 8.67). If the safety screen indicates clinical reasons not to use special accommodation, but the duty governor considers that operational reasons make such use necessary, then there should be case review within two hours. A doctor or registered nurse is required to visit the prisoner at least twice in any 24-hour period and record the visit in the clinical record. The IMB of the prison must also be informed of the decision and invited to attend as soon as possible and in any event, within 24 hours of the decision. The visits of the IMB must be recorded on form OT013.

8.96　　PSO 1700 makes it clear that '[e]very effort must be made to keep the time a prisoner is held in special accommodation to a minimum, ie minutes rather than hours or days'.[70] Accordingly a review does not need to take place for a prisoner to be removed. An operational manager grade has authority under the policy to decide that special accommodation is no longer necessary.

## Use of special accommodation for more than 24 hours

8.97　　A review of the use of special accommodation must take place within 24 hours. The review board should consist of:

- an operational manager grade or controller as chair;
- a doctor or registered nurse;
- the designated manager;
- the ACCT case manager for a prisoner on self-harm measures; and
- staff from where the special accommodation is located.

8.98　　Consideration should be given as to whether the attendance of other staff (such as from psychology or the prisoner's personal officer) would be helpful. The review board has delegated responsibility under the policy to provide Secretary of State's further authorisation as required by the Rules.[71] Further reviews if necessary must take place at intervals of no more than 24 hours.

8.99　　A member of the IMB should be invited to attend the review and note any concerns on form and if these are not resolved at local level such concerns will be referred, as in segregation decisions, ultimately to Deputy Director General level. The policy states the IMB role is important in ensuring compliance with the policy as set out in PSO 1700. The operational manager or controller[72] has final authority to decide whether use of special accommodation beyond 24 hours is necessary. The decision must be recorded on form OY013 and the decision must be communicated to the prisoner as soon as possible. The intervals for continued assessments and observations must be re-stated, with similar minimums as apply for the first 24 hours (see para 8.94 above).

70　In the five high security prisons in a nine-month period from January to September 2005 special cells were used on 88 occasions with an average length of time in the special cell of about seven hours – see *Extreme Custody* HMCIP 2006 para 4.17.

71　PR rule 48(2), YOIR rule 51(2).

72　As the decision to retain in a special cell beyond 24 hours must be taken by the Secretary of State, staff of a private prison could not be responsible for the final decision.

8.100    Decisions to use cardboard furniture must be recorded and justified on form OT013. A decision to deprive a prisoner of normal clothing should not be made unless their behaviour is life threatening. In
such circumstances the prisoner should be provided with 'protective
clothing' (most commonly a paper suit). The aim must be for the prisoner to remain in protective clothing for the 'shortest time possible'.

### Ending use of the special accommodation

8.101    Once the reasons for ending the use of special accommodation no
longer exist, the Duty governor or Controller should be contacted and
if they are in agreement the relevant part of form OT013 is completed
(although as noted above the policy states that an operational manager grade has authority to remove the prisoner). This records the
reasons for the decision. The IMB and healthcare should then be informed and the prisoner placed in appropriate alternative accommodation. The completed form OT013 must be placed on the prisoner's
core record and a copy given to IMB and healthcare. In addition, a
copy should be sent to the Ministry of Justice's data collection unit.

## 'Managing Challenging Behaviour' and close supervision centres

### Background to the CSC system

8.102    CSCs were introduced into the adult prison system (the YOI Rules
contain no power to transfer prisoners to a CSC) by amendments to
the Rules introduced in 1998. They are intended to deal with those
prisoners assessed as the most disruptive or dangerous in custody. It
is important to note that this is a system for dealing with those who
are considered to pose a risk to others in custody. Those prisoners
who are assessed as posing the highest risk to the public may pose
no control problems at all. Where prisoners meet both criteria for the
CSC system and a DSPD unit, the guidance suggests that initially
they should be referred to the CSC system. Once they are no longer
posing 'daily control problems' consideration can be given to transfer
to a DSPD unit (chapter 4).

8.103    Prior to the CSC system, the Prison Service had in the 1970s held
this class of prisoner in control units which were highly controversial in light of the poor conditions some prisoners were subjected to
over periods of years.[73] This was the followed by the special units.

---

73   See *Williams v Home Office (No 2)* [1981] All ER 1211.

The ethos behind these units aimed to move away from the punitive nature of the control units, with more open regimes and voluntary involvement. Those too disruptive for the special units, however, were subject to the 'continuous assessment scheme', whereby prisoners could end up being transferred from segregation block to segregation block for years.[74] Following the Parkhurst and Whitemoor escapes in the mid 1990s, the Prison Service commissioned a report[75] that recommended that the special unit and CAS system be replaced with a system of small units that which would re-impose a strict regime, designed to both contain and change disruptive prisoners. Crucially the system was to be compulsory. This was effectively what was implemented in 1998 with the introduction of the CSCs.[76]

### Treatment of disruptive prisoners prior to referral to a CSC

8.104    Prison Service policy contains a number of measures for dealing with those assessed as disruptive short of referral to a CSC.[77] At the lowest level these can include what are commonly known as 'anti-bullying' measures or sanctions under the IEP scheme. The relevant policies that apply short of referral to a CSC are as follows:

### PSO 2750 (violence reduction) and PSO 1810

8.105    Every prison is now required to have a local strategy that 'promotes the safety of prisoners, staff and others and minimises the use of violence' through measures that include behaviour management for particular individual prisoners.[78] PSO 2750 replaced previous centrally issued guidance on anti-bullying measures to be adopted in prisons. The Violence Reduction strategy must require that 'prisoners involved in unacceptable behaviour towards others must be appropriately and consistently challenged and given support to improve their behaviour'.

8.106    In 2005 the long-standing policy on 'Management Strategy for Disruptive Inmates' contained in Instruction to Governors (IG)

---

74  Sometimes known in its earlier incarnations as the 'ghost-train'. HMCIP has raised concerns that the use of designated cells within the CSC system has replicated some of the concerns of this approach. See below.

75  The Spurr report – Prison Service 1996.

76  For some background to the creation of the CSCs see *Evaluation of CSCs*, Home Office Research Study 219.

77  In August 2005 when HMCIP conducted research for *Extreme Custody* (HMCIP 2006) there were only 30 prisoners in the CSC system.

78  PSO 2750 para 2.4.

28/1993 was eventually replaced with PSO 1810. This requires prisons to 'develop a local strategy for the management of prisoners whose behaviour is difficult or disruptive'[79] and also for regional DOMs to implement 'population protocols' which include instructions agreed with headquarters on management of 'difficult' prisoners and on disciplinary and security transfers.[80] The guidance in PSOs 2750 and 1810 suggests that responses to disruptive behaviour should include:

- Staff intervention to resolve conflict in its early stages.
- Use of compacts.
- Sanctions through the IEPS scheme which 'must be part of a package of measures which address the causes and contributory factors', or through the use of the prison disciplinary process.
- Use of segregation where appropriate.
- Relocation within the prison.
- Referral to the criminal justice system in response to assaults occasioning serious injury.
- Use of sentence planning to incorporate appropriate objectives
- Transfer from the prison on a permanent basis which, if it is out of the area, needs to be arranged through the Population Management Section at Prison Service Headquarters.[81]

8.107    The PSO requires incidents of unacceptable behaviour to be properly recorded on the prisoner's history sheet.[82] It may be appropriate to encourage dialogue between any two parties involved but such restorative processes must be entered into voluntarily.[83]

8.108    The PSO also deals with the processes for assessing the safety of cell sharing arrangements and was introduced in the wake of the inquiries into the death of Zahid Mubarek who was killed by a racist prisoner, who was assigned to share his cell at HMYOI Feltham, despite obvious concerns about the risks he posed. This requires completion of a Cell Sharing Risk Assessment (CSRA) in closed prisons and YOIs whenever it is proposed to place a prisoner in a cell with others.

8.109    The policies also state that where prisoners are assessed as particularly difficult or disruptive, so that an acceptable level of behaviour cannot be maintained in the holding prison, any transfer should

79  PSO 1810 para 2.5.
80  PSO 1810 para 3.2.
81  PSO 2750 paras 3.4 and 7.3, PSO 1810.
82  PSO 2750 para 4.1.
83  PSO 2750 para 4.4.

be on a permanent basis. The reasons for transfer must be formally recorded and accompany the prisoner on transfer along with any relevant CSRA documents. The prisoner's offender manager should be informed.[84] Transfers can be arranged between the two prisons except for those involving category A prisoners, those in PWUs, young prisoners whose location is decided by the YJB, and those held in the CSC system.[85]

### 'Managing Challenging Behaviour Strategy' in high security prisons

8.110   In January 2009 the Prison Service issued a policy (not in the form of a PSO and not therefore available on the internet) dealing with the Managing Challenging Behaviour Strategy (MCBS) in the high security prisons. The stated purpose of the policy is to 'provide a framework for the care and case management of prisoners whose behaviour is dangerous, disruptive, and particularly challenging to manage, whilst in custody'. The policy's aims are said to include the progression and safe return of such prisoners to normal location, a reduction in the number and length of stay of prisoners held in segregation units in high security prisons, and the creation of a 'more permeable management system' between segregation units, CSCs and other discrete units such as DSPD units.

8.111      Responsibility for management of identified prisoners is given firstly to Local Establishment Panels (LEPs) in the individual high security prisons, and secondly to a Case Management Group (CMG) centrally at the Prison Service which provides central case management of complex cases, and support and advice to LEPs. Such co-ordination between the LEPs and the CMG is designed to prevent prisoners ending up moving between high security segregation units for periods of months or years with no effective steps being taken to facilitate a return to normal location.[86] Both LEPs and the CMG are multi-disciplinary teams. Effectively, the policy states that the MCBS is a bridge between segregation units and the CSC system. Accordingly the CMG plays an important role in the decision as to which prisoners are eventually transferred into the CSC system (see below).

---

84   PSO 2750 para 7.1.

85   PSO 2750 para 7.4.

86   The HMCIP in *Extreme Custody* criticised the practice of 'merry go round' or 'sale or return' transfers, processes which merely targeted prisoners identified as 'difficult' and then moved them around the system with no individual management or care.

8.112    The policy gives guidance on the prisoners suitable for management under the MCBS. A distinction is made between those who cause 'daily challenges for staff' and the small minority whose behaviour has a 'significant impact' on staff, other prisoners and the regime. Criteria for inclusion (not exclusive) include those who:

- would benefit from a multi-disciplinary approach;
- have been in segregation for over three months;
- have multiple disciplinary offences;
- have frequent occurrences of violence, bullying, intimidation or threats;
- have extreme levels of self-harming behaviour;
- have failed the segregation unit algorithm;
- are disrupting the regime;
- have been referred to the CSC (for interim management);
- have not been selected for the CSC (and who have been given a care plan as an alternative by the CMG).

The CMG will also manage for an initial period those who are deselected from the CSC system.

8.113    The process begins with a local referral being prepared and sent to the Challenging Behaviour Manager (CBM) at the local high security prison. The CBM then requests a set of reports prior to an LEP meeting. The reports will include contributions from security, mental health, psychology, probation and other relevant sources. The policy does not suggest that the documentation should be disclosed to the prisoner in advance of the LEP meeting. However there is clearly an argument that fairness would require disclosure to the prisoner of the reports[87] and an opportunity to make representations to the LEP and it is difficult to see why this process should be distinguished from the CSC selection system (see below) in this regard.

8.114    When the LEP considers the case there are three possible outcomes under the policy:

- Further documentation is requested.
- The LEP considers that the prisoner does not require full multi-disciplinary case management. The LEP will give advice on the future management of the prisoner where appropriate.
- The LEP decides that multi-disciplinary case management is necessary or appropriate. An initial care and management plan is agreed by the LEP and sent to the residential manager.

---

87 Which except for sensitive security information will be obtainable under the DPA 1998 in any event.

8.115 The prisoner will be informed of the outcome if the decision is to manage them under the MCBS. There will then be monitoring of the prisoner's case and the care and management plan at monthly LEP meetings. The prisoner will continue to be managed under the local LEP until *either* the CBM, in consultation with the LEP, decides that multi-disciplinary management is no longer needed, *or* there is a deterioration in behaviour necessitating a referral to the CMG or to a CSC (in which case the LEP will continue to manage the prisoner pending the result of any referral). Referral to the CMG can take place if the CBM considers that:

- there has been an escalation in the difficult behaviour;
- all local management options have been exhausted with no or little progress;
- staff require respite from a difficult prison; or
- the case requires central management due to its complexity.

8.116 The CBM must complete a prescribed form and forward it to the MCBS/CSC Support Manager at HMP Woodhill. Again the policy is silent on disclosure of the referral to the prisoner but it is difficult to understand any basis for it being withheld subject to sensitive security material being removed or redacted. The CMG will then in consultation with the holding prison (either by attendance at a LEP, or via video conferencing) provide advice and a recommendation on a management strategy. The options will be that the LEP should continue to manage locally, that the prisoner be transferred to give respite to staff or the prisoner or for specific treatment programmes, that a CSC referral should be made, that a referral to a DSPD or special hospital should be made, or that further reports should be commissioned. If the advice is that a CSC referral should be made then reports for the LEP may be used for this purpose if sufficiently complete and up to date.

8.117 If the recommendation is for a transfer, for whatever reason, then the CMG will co-ordinate the move with the CBMs at both prisons. This is to ensure that all essential information is communicated between prisons.[88] If the CMG decides to centrally manage the case a care and management plan will be drawn up and a member of the CMG will attend LEP meetings. CMG maintains a central database of those being managed under the MCBS 'maintaining strategic oversight of the number, location, and distribution of prisoners moving

---

88 In March 2005 an inquest jury examining the death of Paul Day who died in HMP Frankland in October 2002 severely criticised the inadequate transfer of information between the segregation units in which he was held.

around the estate'. Referrals into the high security estate will also be referred to the CMG to offer advice on the suitability of location and management options prior to transfer. CMG also liaises with the category A review team, the high security Counter Terrorism Intelligence Unit, regarding the reviews of prisoners within their remit. The policy states that Offender Supervisors must be informed when prisoners are managed under the LEP arrangements and that MCBS reports should be included in parole reports.

### Transfer to a CSC

8.118    The Prison Rules provide for a specific type of removal from association for the purpose of locating a prisoner in a close supervision centre. PR rule 46(1) states that the Secretary of State may direct a prisoner's removal from association and transfer to a CSC where it 'appears desirable, for the maintenance of good order or discipline or to ensure the safety of officers, prisoners or any other person, that [the] prisoner should not associate with other prisoners, either generally of for particular purposes'. A CSC is either part of a prison used for holding such prisoners, or a single cell.[89] Such a direction can only last one month at a time (although the Secretary of State can terminate it at any time), but can be renewed, and also remains in force notwithstanding the transfer of a prisoner from one CSC to another.[90] The Secretary of State has to take into account any medical considerations before making such a direction.[91]

8.119    The guidance on the circumstances in which prisoners will be transferred to CSCs, and the regimes they will be subjected to are contained the Operating Standards for CSCs, and the CSC Referral Manual.[92] The CSC Referral Manual was most recently revised in January 2009. At the time of writing the Operating Standards, the last available version of which date from 2005, were also due to be updated. These policies contained many changes from the first versions

---

89  PR rule 46(5) – this rule was amended in 2000 to allow the transfer of prisoners to single cells in prisons without a proper CSC.

90  PR rule 46 (2)–(3): the provision that preserves the direction on transfer was also introduced in 2000 in response to concerns that prisoners were being transferred from CSC to CSC without a proper renewal of a direction. Location in a CSC is therefore different to segregation following a governor's decision, the authority for which ceases once the prisoner is transferred – see para 8.79 above.

91  PR rule 46(4).

92  These are not on the Prison Service website.

that accompanied the introduction of the CSC system in 1998, following criticisms from HMCIP and others that initially the system was too focussed on containment and punishment.[93]

8.120 The body that makes decisions on transferring prisoners into the CSC system on behalf of the Secretary of State is the CSC management committee (CSC MC). Its decisions under the policy need to be ratified by the Director of High Security Prisons. The power to ratify does mean that the director is able to reject decisions of the committee and refer issues back to it for reconsideration.[94] This body conducts the monthly reviews of every prisoner in the CSC system and makes the decision as to whether segregation for CSC purposes should continue for another month. The Operating Standards state that although the process does not require the consent of the prisoner such consent will be sought where possible.[95] The Operating Standards require that referrals to the CSC will normally follow the guidance set out in the Referral Manual. This in turn states that a prisoner may be considered suitable for referral to the CSC if any one or more of the following criteria are evident:

- Demonstrating violence towards others on a regular basis.
- Carriedout, or orchestrated, a single yet extreme or significant act of violence or disorder, eg hostage taking, murder, serious assault, concerted indiscipline etc.
- Causingsignificant day-to-day management difficulties by undermining the good order of the establishment ie through bullying, coercion, regime disruption. Involvement in such activities may not always be visible but be supported by significant intelligence indicating that individual's involvement.
- Threateningand/or intimidating behaviour, directed at staff and/or prisoners.
- A long history of disciplinary offences.
- Repeatedperiods of segregation under Prison Rule 45 (good order or discipline).
- A continuous period of segregation exceeding six months.[96]

8.121 Prisons are also instructed that before consideration is given to referral to a CSC that 'all attempts to manage the prisoner must have been made using existing management tools' including compliance with

93 See *Extreme Custody* (HMCIP 2006) – a thematic report into the CSC system and segregation in high security prisons, the original Inspectorate thematic review was issued in 1999.

94 *R (Nelson) v Secretary of State for Justice* [2009] EWHC 1124 (Admin).

95 CSC OS 2.1.

96 CSC Referral Manual 2009 section 1 part 2.

a local strategy as required by PSO 1810 (see above). Prisons must ensure that any referral demonstrates:

1) that the individual has sufficiently exhausted all appropriate options with regard to his management and control under the managing challenging behaviour strategy, both locally and centrally, and that the CSC is the final remaining option to reduce the level of risk he poses;

2) the extent of his dangerous behaviour and risk towards himself, staff and/or other prisoners is clearly documented; and

3) using recent evidence, demonstrate how and why current management and control strategies are insufficient to protect the individual and others from harm.

8.122    As set out above, the referral to the CSC may also follow on from management under the MCBS in the high security estate. The Referral Manual sets out the assessment process, which it states should take about 12 weeks. There are five separate stages:

### Stage 1: CSC initial referral

8.123    The holding prison completes the Initial Referral Form. This will set out the reason for the referral, will include details of the prisoner's disciplinary and segregation record and reports from the prison. The form has a dual purpose – for the prison to determine whether a prisoner should be referred to the CSC system, and to bring the prisoner to the attention of the CSC management team if a referral is made. The Case Management Group (CMG) at HMP Woodhill will then review the referral, and seek any necessary clarification arising from the referral form and associated reports. The CMG will draft recommendations for the CSC MC to consider.

8.124    Following the review of the referral by the CMG the reports must be disclosed to the prisoner by the holding prison so that he will have an opportunity to make representations for consideration by the CSC MC. The guidance states that any security reports must be 'sanitised' either by removing references to sources of information, and information that may identify sources, or by redaction. The right to reasons for decisions in the CSC process, and to disclosure of full reports and an opportunity to make representations are included in the Prison Service policies. This is a marked improvement from when the CSC system was introduced in 1998 when prisoners were initially transferred into the system without being given either disclosure or reasons for decisions. In an early challenge to the process two prisoners argued that this breached the requirements of procedural fairness. Before the case reached a full hearing the Prison Service disclosed the first version of the Operating Standards, which introduced entitlement to disclosure of a gist of the reports.[97]

8.125    The case will then be considered at the next scheduled CSC MC meeting which will consider the recommendations made by the CMG. If the prisoner is considered suitable for the CSC system arrangements will be made to transfer them to either Woodhill or Long Lartin for the assessment process. The CSC MC decision has to be ratified by the Director of High Security Prisons. From this point Rule 46 will apply to the prisoner and so for continued segregation to be lawful there must be monthly reviews carried out on behalf of the Secretary of State by the CSC MC. The prisoner will be told of the decision and given details of the assessment process. The prisoner is invited to consent to the assessment process but warned that if consent is withheld that the assessments may be completed on the basis of file information and reports from staff. The IMB at the holding prison should also be informed within 24 hours of the decision.

8.126    If the prisoner is not considered suitable for the CSC then the CSCMC will make recommendations to the holding prison regarding an appropriate management plan.

## Stage 2: assessment period

8.127    There follows a four-month period of observation and assessment at either Woodhill or Long Lartin. This is made up of a three-month period of assessment with a further month to write reports. A variety of reports are completed at the end of this process. The process encompasses reports on wing behaviour, psychological assessments, mental health assessments, security and intelligence information, and other contributions from those involved in dealing with the prisoner. Detailed guidance is contained in the CSC Referral Manual on completing these reports. The assessment will include use of

---

97    *R v Secretary of State for the Home Department ex p Mehmet and O'Connor* [1999] EWHC 123 (Admin): surprisingly the judge decided that although the Prison Service had acknowledged the need for at least limited disclosure and reasons for decisions, such basic elements of fairness were not required by the common law in this context. He reasoned that, unlike with category A decisions, there was no knock on effect on liberty, and he also accepted that the CSC system offered the prisoner a benefit rather than a detriment – due to its stated aim of challenging disruptive behaviour. This was notwithstanding the punitive regimes associated with the early CSCs which were criticised both by HMCIP and the Ombudsman. It is difficult to imagine such a case being decided in this way now.

the following tools: the VRS, the HCR 20, the PCL-R (see chapter 4) and a functional analysis of the prisoner's violent and/or disruptive behaviour.

8.128    Again, once the reports are completed the Referral Manual states that they should be disclosed to the prisoner although security reports may be anonymised or redacted as set out above. The prisoner will therefore have an opportunity to make representations in response to them. The reports from the prison will also be forwarded to the CSC support manager by then end of the fourteenth week from the date of the letter confirming the prisoner's selection for assessment.

## Stage 3: local assessment case conference

8.129    When the reports have been completed a case conference will be held at the prison, chaired by the CSC Operational Manager, to review the contents of the reports and decide on a recommendation to the CSC MC. The CSC MC should consider the recommendation of the case conference by the end of the four-month period. The case conference should be convened two weeks prior to the end of the four-month assessment period. Members of the CMG will attend the meeting with representatives of the local prison. The writers of the assessment reports should attend the meeting together with other staff who may have a bearing on the case. The meeting may recommend further assessments that should form part of the prisoner's care and management plan should he be selected for the CSC.

## Stage 4: selection into the CSC system

8.130    The CSC MC will either decide that the prisoner should be selected for the CSC, that the prisoner should not be selected for the CSC but referred for central case management under the Managing Challenging Behaviour Strategy (see PSO 1810), or that the prisoner should be referred to an alternative regime such as a DSPD unit or special hospital. If, exceptionally, the CSC MC is unable to come to a decision within the four-month period then the director of High Security will authorise continued detention under rule 46 pending the completion of the assessment process (which will of course have to be renewed on a monthly basis). The CSC MC decisions have to be ratified by the Director for High Security Prisons. If the CSC MC decides that the prisoner should remain in the CSC system, he will be moved to one of the main units at either Woodhill, Whitemoor or Wakefield. However it may be considered necessary to transfer the prisoner into one of the designated CSC cells in one of the other high security prisons if the criteria for such a move contained in the Operating Standards are met (see below).

8.131    The CSC Referral Manual states that the aim of the CSC system is to reduce the risk that the prisoner presents in order to be able to safely return him to normal location. In the CSCs prisoners will undergo regular monitoring and reviews including weekly behaviour monitoring, the completion of monthly reports for the CSC MC meeting which decides whether segregation under rule 46 should continue, quarterly reviews of the care and management plan, and annual care and management plan reviews. Although there is no formal policy, prisoners will normally be allowed to attend the quarterly care and management plan meetings and will be permitted to have a representative present at two of these meetings each year. Prisoners who have been held in the CSC system for more than two years will be reviewed more fully by the CSC MC to consider their long-term management arrangements. Prisons should try to avoid moving prisoners while care and management plans are being reviewed.

8.132    The monthly reports prepared for the CSC MC should be disclosed to the prisoner who has an opportunity to make written representations, which will be considered by the CSC MC. As with category A decisions, in rare cases fairness may require that the prisoner is given an opportunity to attend such meetings. By analogy with the situations where the courts have held that category A decisions require an oral hearing, this may arise where there is a significant difference of opinion as to the appropriate management of the prisoner, or disputed facts relating to behaviour said to be relevant to risk, which can only be fairly resolved at an oral hearing (chapter 3).

## Stage 5: deselection from the CSC

8.133    The CSC Referral Manual states that the threshold for consideration for return to normal location from a CSC is that the prisoner 'no longer requires the enhanced interventions and supervision of Prison Rule 46'. It further states that a prisoner will only be deselected where 'the risk he presents to others can be assessed, as far as is possible, to have reduced to a point where he can be managed within a mainstream prison environment'.

8.134    The local multi-disciplinary team at the holding CSC will raise the prospect of de-selection at the CSC MC meeting. If the CSC MC considers that the case is appropriate for consideration it will commission a set of de-selection reports, which essentially mirror the reports that are commissioned for the assessment process. The holding CSC

will then convene a de-selection case conference to decide whether
a recommendation for de-selection should be made to the CSC MC.
The case conference's recommendation will then be considered by
the CSC MC at the next monthly meeting. Although the Referral
Manual does not specify this, the de-selection reports should be disclosed to the prisoner as with other reports so that he can submit
representations to the CSC MC on this issue. If de-selected the prisoner will be monitored and managed centrally for an initial period as
agreed at the de-selection case conference.

## Regimes in the CSC

8.135    As noted above, the CSC MC must review a prisoner's selection on
a monthly basis in order to comply with the Rules. The CSC Operating standards (last updated in 2005 and due to be replaced during
2009) confirm that prisoners are entitled to reasons for all decisions
confirming placement in the CSC[98] and for decisions to move them
to more restricted regimes within the CSC.[99] They will also be given
disclosure of the monthly reports to the CSCC and an opportunity to
comment in writing on them.[100]

8.136    All CSC units must be capable in security terms of holding high
risk category A prisoners, although only prisoners who are actually
high risk category A should have procedures relevant to that class of
prisoner applied to them.[101]

8.137    The Operating Standards state that IMB members should have
unrestricted access to all parts of CSC units subject to restrictions
on the grounds of security or personal safety. Board members must
be invited to observe the handling of serious incidents in CSCs may
raise concerns with prison management up to and including the
ministerial level.[102] Each CSC unit should have a published regime
approved and certified by the Deputy Director General and prisoners
should be provided with written information about regimes within
24 hours of arrival on a unit.[103]

8.138    The 2005 Operating Standard set out the following roles of the
various CSCs:

98  CSC OS 2.4.
99  CSC OS 3.8.
100  CSC OS 5.1.
101  CSC OS 7.1.
102  CSC OS 9.5–9.7.
103  CSC OS 6.1–6.4.

- Woodhill CSC – this is the core management centre for the CSC system. There are three distinct units, a 'progressive' regime (this is for those undertaking CSC selection, on induction or assessed as making progress), a 'structured intervention' regime (aimed at managing and reducing risk of disruptive behaviour to a level that will facilitate transfer back to a mainstream location) and a 'violence reduction' programme.
- Whitemoor – the purpose of this unit is to provide a consistent and supportive environment that encourages prisoners who have a history of highly disturbed behaviour to take part in a structured and meaningful regime.
- Wakefield – has the exceptional risk unit for those 'assessed as presenting so great a threat to the safety of staff and other prisoners that containment in a secure and isolated accommodation is the only option'. This unit only accepts referrals from other CSCs. The unit can be used for CSC prisoners who do not meet this criterion, for example for accumulated visits or for reasonable management purposes.
- Long Lartin – holds a CSC assessment centre where prisoners can be held in designated cells, there is no unit proper, for the purposes of assessment, to manage prisoners who refuse to co-operate with the assessment process, or for prisoners who are refusing to comply with regimes in other CSC units.[104]

8.139  Movement between various parts of the CSC system will be approved by the CSC MC either in advance, or if the decision is taken urgently by the Operational Manager at the next CSC MC meeting.[105]

## Use of the designated cells

8.140  The Rules were amended in 2000 to provide that single cells could constitute a CSC. Such designated cells in high security prisons (other than those where there are CSC units) are used for temporary transfer of prisoners who:

- Present exceptionally difficult control problems.
- For whom such a transfer is in the interests of their physical and/ or mental health.
- Or to facilitate the 'reasonable management of prisoners within the system'.[106]

104  CSC OS 6.5–6.15.
105  CSC OS 4.1–4.2.
106  CSC OS 4.4 and 6.16.

8.141   The CSC Operational Manager can authorise the removal of a CSC prisoner to a designated cell for the following reasons;

- adjudication;
- punishment;
- good order or discipline;
- own protection; or
- to facilitate the reasonable management of CSC prisoners.

As noted above, the CSC MC must then approve the transfer at the next meeting.

8.142   The Operating Standards state that the designated cells 'will provide an environment in which prisoners can reflect upon their refusal to co-operate, their behaviour or seek temporary respite from cycles of disruptive and/or violent behaviour'[107] which makes fairly clear the punitive intent in locating prisoners in the designated cells, in what amounts to segregation upon segregation.

8.143   There is no upper time limit for the time prisoners may be held in such designated cells[108] accordingly staff are required to actively encourage prisoners to participate with management plans or assessment so as to enable a return to a mainstream CSC location.[109] The CSC MC will review on a monthly basis the appropriateness of location in a designated cell.

8.144   HMCIP was critical of the use of designated cells within the CSC system in the thematic review completed following inspections in 2005:

> We considered that there were dangers associated with the use of designated cells as a control mechanism for open-ended periods, without any apparent consultation with clinical staff, little local ownership of their management, and limited independent oversight. In practice this aspect of their use replicated the merry-go-round system which was now otherwise discontinued in the segregation system, and did not fit well into a system of holistic management and care.[110]

## Segregation in secure training centres

8.145   As STCs will only be holding child prisoners the relevant rules contain more specific safeguards. The only purposes for which for which a prisoner in an STC may be segregated are:

107  CSC OS 6.17.
108  CSC OS 4.4–4.5.
109  CSC Operating Standard 6.18.
110  *Extreme Custody* HMCIP 2006.

- to prevent them causing significant harm to themselves or others; or
- to prevent them from causing significant damage to property.[111]

8.146    The power to segregate is given to the director (all STCs are contracted out). Changes were made to the STC Rules in 2007 to include a power to segregate in the interests of good order and discipline. A legal challenge was successful in quashing these amendments[112] and so segregation may only be used specifically for the purposes set out above.

8.147    The STC Rules require 'all appropriate methods of control' to be applied without success before recourse to the power to segregate is made.[113] Where a decision to segregate is made a proper record must be kept[114] and the child must:

- be observed at least every 15 minutes;
- not be left unaccompanied during normal waking hours for more than three hours continuously, or for a total of more than three hours in any period of 24 hours;
- be released from segregation as soon as it is no longer necessary for the purposes referred to above; and
- be given the reasons for segregation both orally and in writing.[115]

8.148    Given the age and vulnerability of children held in STCs fairness will require the director to give the opportunity to make representations before the decision to segregate is made, in accordance with the position for children held in YOIs. (See para 8.69.)

8.149    A Code of Practice on the use of segregation in STCs has been issued by the YJB.[116] This states that the decision to remove a child or young person because of problematic behaviour must be made only on the basis of an assessment that:

- the continued presence of the child or young person in the normal location threatens the good order of the establishment, or

---

111 STCR rule 36(1).
112 The Secure Training Centre (Amendment) Rules 2007 SI No 1709 were quashed by the Court of Appeal in *R (C) v Secretary of State for Justice* [2008] EWCA Civ 882 – this case is discussed in more detail below in relation to use of force in STCs.
113 STCR rule 36(2).
114 STCR rule 36(4).
115 STCR rule 36(3).
116 *Managing the Behaviour of Children and Young People in the Secure Estate (YJB, 2006): available at* www.yjb.gov.uk/Publications/Scripts/prodView. asp?idproduct=280&eP=PP

- the child or young person will benefit from a period of separation to assist him or her in bringing his or her behaviour under control.[117]

8.150    The Code of Practice further states that:

- The decision to remove the child or young person must be taken by a senior member of staff.
- It must not be used as a punishment.
- The reasons for the decision must be made clear to the child or young person.
- Every effort must be made to assist the child or young person in addressing the behaviour that led to the removal, so that he or she may be restored to the normal location as soon as possible.
- While the child or young person is separated, he or she must continue to have access to regime activities, particularly education.
- The separation arrangement must be reviewed frequently to ensure that it is still justified.
- When the period of separation is over, the child or young person must be given the opportunity to debrief with a suitable member of staff.

## Segregation in secure children's homes

8.151    The use of segregation in secure children's homes is subject to a different statutory and policy framework to that which applies in STCs. As noted above SCHs are required to have a 'behaviour management policy' which sets out the measures of 'control, restraint and discipline' to be used – such measures must not be 'excessive or unreasonable'.[118] The statutory regulations do not contain any specific powers in relation to use of segregation. Further guidance on use of segregation in secure children's homes is issued by the Secure Accommodation Network ('SAN')[119] *The Use of Single Separation in Secure Children's Homes*. It was common ground in the C case (referred to above) that nothing in the statutory or policy framework relating to the use of segregation in SCHs permits its use for reasons of 'good order or discipline'.

8.152    The SAN policy on what it calls 'single separation' states that:

---

117  However this guidance must be read compatibly with the Rules, and so references these grounds for segregation must relate to a risk of significant harm or of damage to property.

118  CHR rule 17.

119  www.secureaccommodation.org.uk/practiceguidelines.htm

Single separation is considered as a last resort and all other efforts should be made to prevent this extreme action. Staff will endeavour, at all times, to attempt to resolve any situation with a young person without the use of single separation.[120]

8.153 The definition of single separation is:

the confining of a young person in his/her bedroom or another room or area as a means of control and without the young persons permission or agreement, without a member of staff being present and with the door locked in order to prevent exit or to further restrict their liberty in excess of that permission already granted by a court under section 25 of the Children Act 1989, section 100 of the Powers of Criminal Courts (Sentencing) Act 2000 or sections 90–92 of the Powers of Criminal Courts (Sentencing) Act 2000.[121]

8.154 The policy envisages three types of separation:

- enforced separation – where the child is locked in their bedroom or another area to deal with behaviour that has become unsafe, threatening or violent;
- directed separation – where a child is asked to take 'time out' alone and the door is not locked;
- elected separation – where the door is locked at the request of the child.

8.155 Further the use of single separation should only be for the following purposes:

- Where a young person is likely to cause significant harm to her/himself or others.
- Where a young person is likely to cause significant damage to property.
- During full security checks in order to ensure that the check is thorough and can be completed without interference or obstruction.
- Where a detainee is refusing to comply with a personal search. Allowing the young person free access around the home may pose a risk to her/himself or others, eg from being in the possession of a prohibited or restricted item.
- Where the young person has elected (chosen) to remain in their room. Elected separation cannot be suggested by staff but must be requested by young people (and staff must consider whether the child is electing separation in order to commit an act of self-harm.

120 Para 1.3.
121 In the SAN Policy.

8.156    As with STCs, segregation without the consent of the prisoner depends on a risk of significant harm to the detainee or others, or of a risk of significant damage to property. In particular the policy specifies that single separation must not be used to protect the child from others, or for the administrative convenience of staff.

8.157    The policy contains further provisions on who should make the decision, and provides that detainees should be observed every 10 minutes at least and a 'single separation log' maintained. The initial decision to separate for 30 minutes can be taken by the shift leader, but beyond that the duty manager should authorise the continuation. If separation continues beyond five hours then the assistant director of children's services at the local authority should be contacted. Parents, social workers and YOT workers should be informed of the situation, and staff should consider any request by the child for access to an advocacy service or a solicitor (although the policy suggests such access may be denied in certain circumstances, where for example the child is not calm or rational enough to make phone contact without the likelihood of further harm or damage being caused).

# Use of force

## Limits on the use of force and restraints

8.158    Use of force or restraint by prison officers can constitute an assault if there is not lawful justification or where the degree of force is unreasonable or excessive. Where it is unnecessary or disproportionate, it may also breach article 3 of the ECHR. There are detailed criteria and procedures for all detaining institutions on use of force due to the sensitivity of this issue. Compliance with both the statutory framework and the published policies is very important in this area as what might consider a reasonable or proportionate use of force might rely on strict adherence with guidelines.

8.159    In recent years the most controversial issue in this area has been the use of force and restraint on children following the deaths of two young boys in STCs. Clearly, the question of whether force is necessary and what level of force is proportionate is highly contextual. The courts have recognised, in declaring unlawful an attempt to widen the circumstances of when force can be used in STCs, that there should be tighter restrictions on when such techniques can be used on children. There are, therefore, significant differences on the statutory and policy frameworks depending on the type of institution under consideration. YOIs present a specific problem due to the fact that they will hold both children and adults.

## Limits on the use of force and restraints: adult prisons and YOIs

### Statutory powers

8.160   There is no primary statutory authority for prison officers to use force in the Prison Act 1952 itself. Prison Service policy makes reference to the general statutory power applicable to everyone, namely a 'person may use such force as is reasonable in the circumstances in the prevention of a crime, or in the effecting or assisting in the lawful arrest of offenders or suspected offenders unlawfully at large'.[122] This would clearly not cover the use of force for all purposes in prisons.

8.161      The Prison and YOI Rules do contain further provisions on the use of force. These provide that officers 'in dealing with a prisoner shall not use force unnecessarily and, when the application of force to a prisoner is necessary, no more force than is necessary shall be used'.[123] The Rules also state that officers must not act deliberately in a manner likely to provoke a prisoner.[124] The Rules also contain more detailed provisions on when prisoners can be 'put under restraint'.[125] These restrict the circumstances as to when mechanical restraints may be used to situations where they are 'necessary to prevent the prisoner from injuring himself or others, damaging property or creating a disturbance'. The Rules also provide for further procedures to be adopted when prisoners are under restraint (see para 8.164).

### Private prisons

8.162   In private prisons prison custody officers have the statutory power to use reasonable force where necessary to:

- to prevent prisoners escaping;
- to prevent, or detect and report on, the commission or attempted commission by prisoners of other unlawful acts;
- to ensure good order and discipline; and
- to attend to prisoners' wellbeing.[126]

122  Criminal Law Act 1967 s3(1).
123  PR rule 47(1), YOIR rule 50(1).
124  PR rule 47(2), YOIR rule 50(2).
125  PR rule 49, YOIR rule 52.
126  Criminal Justice Act 1991 s86(3) and (4).

## Escorts

8.163    Prisoners' remain in lawful custody whilst being transferred and so prison officers or prison custody officers retain their powers to use force when driving escorts.[127] Private contractors escorting prisoners between prisons or to and from court have similar statutory powers to use force as those given to prison custody officers in private prisons. The only distinction is an additional power to use reasonable force when necessary to 'to give effect to any directions as to their treatment which are given by a court'.[128]

## Policy on use of force and restraints

8.164    Detailed policy guidance is contained in PSO 1600 and PSO 1700 on the use of force and restraint in adult prisons and YOIs. This policy confirms the general legal position that non-consensual use of force is unlawful unless legally justified. Justification in the policy is summarised as depending on the use of force being:

- *reasonable in all the circumstances* – this will take into account factors such as the size and age of the prisoner, and the seriousness of any threat;
- *necessary* – an example given of where force would not be necessary is to enforce an order to stop swearing at a teacher (force would only be justified according to the policy if there was a persistent failure to comply and all other alternatives of de-escalation had failed);
- *no more than is necessary*;
- *proportionate* – this is a recognition that excessive use of force may give rise to breaches of article 3 of the ECHR, the prohibition on torture and inhuman or degrading treatment. The key aspects of proportionality in this context are that policies on use of force must be adhered to, and that the degree of force used must be no more than strictly required.

8.165    PSO 1600 requires prisons and YOIs to monitor their use of force and report to headquarters on the incidence of use of force on a monthly basis.

---

127  PA 1952 s13(2).
128  CJA 1991 s82(3) and (5).

## Types of use of force under PSO 1600

8.166   PSO 1600 sets out five categories of use of force namely:
- personal safety techniques;
- use of batons;
- control and restraint (C & R);
- advanced C & R;
- mechanical restraints.

The policy guidance also makes reference to other policy guidance on the use of these techniques. Firstly the Use of Force Training Manual which is issued to all prisons and is not a restricted document. Secondly the C & R Advanced Manual which is restricted to national C & R instructors and those in the 'Gold Command' suite.

## Medical issues

8.167   Officers are required to consider the medical implications of the use of force whichever technique is used and specific guidance is given on this. For example, officers are warned of the dangers of asphyxiation whenever pressure or blows are directed to the neck or throat area, and details of how to recognise the warning signs of positional asphyxia when prisoners are under restraint are also set out. The policy also requires a healthcare presence whenever there is a planned use of C & R techniques, to monitor the prisoner's health (clearly healthcare staff should play no role in restraining the prisoner). PSO 1600 stipulates that an appropriately qualified healthcare professional (doctor or registered nurse) must be informed whenever force has been used to restrain a prisoner. He or she must examine the prisoner as soon as possible and must complete a form F213 in all cases, even if the prisoner appears not to have sustained any injuries. The prisoner must see an appropriately qualified healthcare professional within 24 hours of the incident occurring.

## The use of force form

8.168   Whenever force is used, PSO 1600 requires the completion of a 'Use of Force' form. This sets out the time and location of the incident, the technique used, the officers present, the purported justification for the use of force and should record any injuries sustained by the prisoner. The first part of the form must be completed by the supervising officer (or the officer who used force if it was a single person use of force). The second part (annex) must be completed and signed by every officer who used force in any way (for example, every member of a C & R team). The supervisor must also complete an annex A. Officers are reminded that copies of the use of force form may be produced for internal or external investigations and so it is important that when a written statement is given it creates as full a picture as possible in order to justify the actions that have been taken.

## Personal safety

8.169    PSO 1600 mandates that officers should only use personal safety techniques in the correct circumstances, when it is lawful and necessary, 'to prevent harm to themselves or a third party'. The policy suggests these techniques can be used by any member of staff (which reflects that such circumstances would give rise to the common law right to use force to protect oneself or others from harm). The policy makes it clear that the techniques should only be used when all other alternatives for trying to control or evade a violent situation have failed, where C & R is impractical, and specifies that a 'defensive strike' must be seen as an exceptional measure. Personal safety techniques are contained in the training manual and should be taught by qualified C & R instructors.

## Use of batons

8.170    It is a requirement of PSO 1600 that 'batons are used by officers in extreme circumstances as a defensive implement only with due regard to relevant medical implications'. Staff must not carry batons unless they have been trained in their use, and must only carry approved batons. Use must be regarded as an exceptional measure and must never be regarded as anything other than a defensive implement.  It may be drawn or used only when:

- it is necessary for an officer to defend themselves or a third party from an attack threatening serious injury; and
- there is no other option open to the member of staff to save themselves or another person but to employ this defensive technique.

8.171    The baton must be directed at the prisoner's arms and legs, where serious injury is less likely to result. Further batons must not:

- be carried in dedicated juvenile units inside a YOI or adult prison;
- be carried in women's' prisons;
- be carried in open prisons; or
- by hospital or nursing staff.

## Control and restraint techniques

8.172   Control and restraint (C & R) techniques are to be used as a last resort in order to bring a violent or refractory prisoner under control. The techniques are applied for as short a time as is possible. C & R techniques were first introduced into the Prison Service in 1983 and are based on the martial art aikido. The techniques are set out in the training manual. C & R techniques use arm and wrist locks which mean pain can be applied if deemed necessary. There are also a series of manoeuvres, the use of which will depend on the circumstances and prisoner's response, including the use of prone restraint where the prisoner is taken to the floor in a face down position. Although pain is obviously part of the technique, it should not be inflicted when not necessary and the prisoner is compliant. The basic C & R techniques are to be used by teams of three officers, with an option of an additional officer when needed to control the legs. Officers must continue to attempt to de-escalate the situation throughout any incident with the aim of releasing holds and locks.

8.173      Planned incidents involving C & R are used when there is no urgency or immediate danger. In these situations, a supervisor should prepare officers for the incident and will notify a member of healthcare in advance who will attend and observe the planned intervention (if there is any member of healthcare staff on duty). Unplanned incidents may occur when there is an 'immediate threat to someone's life or limb or to the security of an establishment and staff need to intervene straight away'. In these situations a member of healthcare and a supervising officer should attend as soon as possible.

8.174      PSO 1600 requires a full risk assessment to be carried out before C & R techniques are used on pregnant women prisoners.

## Use of handcuffs within C & R

8.175   The policy accepts that the application of handcuffs to a person is an assault and unlawful unless it can be justified. Justification is achieved through establishing not only a legal right to use handcuffs, but also good objective grounds for doing so in order to show that what the officer did was a reasonable use of force. PSO 1600 authorises the use of ratchet handcuffs during a C & R incident which must be authorised by the supervising officer. The test set out in the policy is that ratchet handcuffs may be applied temporarily if it is necessary to remove a prisoner from one part of the establishment to another (eg relocation to a cell or the segregation unit). The following factors need be taken into account when making an objective decision regarding their use:

- the distance involved;
- whether the prisoner is continuing to be violent/aggressive and handcuffs are deemed preferable to using C & R locks during movement and relocation; and
- whether the prisoner is reasonably compliant but it is not judged safe enough to permit the prisoner to walk completely independently to the relocation venue.

8.176   The policy states that factors such as age, gender, respective size and apparent strength and fitness may or may not support the justification of handcuffs, taking into account all the accompanying circumstances at the time. The physical condition of the prisoner is another consideration in deciding whether or not handcuffs should be applied or their application continued. For example, a prisoner with an arm or wrist injury may be prone to particular risk of further injury or pain if handcuffed; this might make the use of handcuffs unreasonable.

8.177   Ratchet handcuffs should not be used as an alternative to a body belt and must never be left on an unsupervised prisoner. After the use of C & R techniques prisoners should cuffed with their hands behind them. The use of handcuffs must be recorded on a use of force report form.

## Advanced Control & Restraint

8.178   In what are described as, 'serious incidents of concerted indiscipline', use of force may be used by specially trained and equipped staff who are issued with personal protective equipment (effectively riot gear such as helmets and shields). The techniques used by such staff are contained in the restricted manual referred to above. The units are known as 'Tornado Response' and each prison is required to have sufficient numbers of trained officers to meet their assessed need.

## Mechanical restraints

8.179   The policy on use of mechanical restraints is now contained in PSO 1700 (the policy on the use of segregation). Handcuffs are not mechanical restraints within the meaning of Prison Service policy. The policy states that the only form of authorised mechanical restraint to be used in prisons and YOIs is a 'body belt' (however see use of handcuffs in relation to escorts below). The Rules provide for specific safeguards when such extreme measures are used:

- the power is only exercisable to prevent self-harm, harm to others, damage to property or to stop the prisoner 'creating a disturbance';
- the IMB and healthcare staff must be notified without delay, and the latter must inform the governor of any medical reasons that restraint should not be used;
- restraint must be for no longer than necessary and beyond 24 hours must be authorised by a member of the IMB or an officer of the Secretary of State.[129]

8.180 The policy in PSO 1700 states that body belts are:

only used in extreme circumstances when all other options have failed or are considered unsafe, to prevent a violent or refractory prisoner engaging in life-threatening behaviour, either towards another person or him or herself. A body belt **is not** used as a punishment. A body belt **is not** used for prisoners under the age of 18.[130]

8.181 Every effort must be made to avoid the use of a body belt and all other alternatives, including the use of special accommodation must be attempted. In very extreme situations the policy accepts that body belts may be used together with special accommodation. The governor (director or controller in a private prison) must give authority before a prisoner is put in a body belt. In an emergency, the duty governor can give this authority. The authority will be valid for a maximum of 24 hours and must be recorded on form OT012. The policy states that the reason for placing a prisoner in a body belt must be explained to them at the earliest opportunity, making it clear that it is not a form of punishment.

8.182 If a body belt is used for a prisoner at risk of self-harm, the ACCT documents must be consulted. The governor must chair a case review within 60 minutes of the decision being made. A mental health assessment must be carried out for every at-risk prisoner in a body belt unless the case review specifically rules one out. As with use of special accommodation, the duty governor must nominate a designated manager who must be at least of senior officer rank or equivalent. The designated manager must assess the prisoner's continued

129 PR rule 49, YOIR rule 52.
130 YOIR rule 52(2) specifies that prisoners under 17 years old must not be put under restraint, unless handcuffs are used to prevent the prisoner from injuring themselves or others, damaging property or creating a disturbance. The policy now more specifically excludes all children.

location in a body belt at a frequency specified on the form OT012. These assessments must take place at least once every hour. The designated manager must also oversee the completion of form OT012.

8.183    In accordance with the Rules, PSO 1700 requires that healthcare staff must be notified immediately. A doctor or registered nurse must attend, and the time that healthcare were notified and the time that a doctor or registered nurse attended must both be recorded on the form OT012. The doctor or registered nurse must assess the prisoner to determine if there are any apparent clinical reasons to advise against the use of a body belt. This assessment should be made using the initial segregation safety screen (see above para 8.70). The duty governor must fully consider healthcare advice before deciding the most appropriate course of action. At this stage or at any subsequent stage, the prisoner must be released from the body belt if a doctor or registered nurse considers that there are clinical reasons why the prisoner should not be restrained.

8.184    The regional DOM must be informed if any prisoner is placed in a body belt. An IMB member must be notified and invited to attend as soon as possible and in any case within 24 hours of the prisoner being placed in a body belt. The time that the IMB were notified and the name of the IMB member must also be recorded on form OT012. The IMB member must record his or her visit on form OT012.

8.185    PSO 1700 states that a prisoner in a body belt must at no time be left alone. The officer must talk to the prisoner and attempt to calmly de-escalate the situation to minimise the prisoner's time in a body belt. A prisoner restrained in a body belt must be provided with refreshments, particularly water, regularly. A record of refreshments offered and taken must be made on form OT012. The governor must visit any prisoner held in a body belt at least twice in any 24-hour period. A doctor or registered nurse must also visit the prisoner at least twice in any 24-hour period. A note of each visit must be made in the prisoner's clinical record.

8.186    In keeping with the requirement that restraint is for no longer than absolutely necessary it is not necessary for a review to be held in order for a prisoner to be removed from a body belt. A prisoner may be removed from a body belt at any time on the authority of an operational manager. The prisoner must be reassessed at a case review within four hours of being placed in a body belt. The four-hour case review must be chaired by the governor in charge as chair, and must include a doctor or registered nurse, the designated manager, the ACCT case manager if applicable, and staff from the segregation unit or wherever the prisoner is located. Further reviews must take place at least every four hours. The IMB must be informed about the four-hour case review and invited to attend as quickly as possible. If present, the IMB member must complete the relevant section of form OT012. Other staff, such as the prisoner's personal officer, psychologist or a member of the chaplaincy team, could also attend, if considered helpful.

8.187    If the case review considers that the use of a body belt needs to exceed 24 hours, a recommendation must be sent to the regional director of offender management on form OT010 along with OT015 (location in body belt 24-hour case review). The regional DOM must give written authority on form OT010 to allow the use of a body belt to exceed 24 hours. This reflects the requirement in the Rules that the authorisation beyond 24 hours cannot be made by an officer of the prison.[131] If the prisoner remains in a body belt following the case review, the review must set out the frequency at which the designated manager must assess the prisoner's continued location in a body belt. As a minimum there will be an hourly assessment by the designated manager.

8.188    The IMB member does not play any part in authorising the use of a body belt under the policy in PSO 1700, but the Rules still state that the IMB do have the power to authorise restraint beyond 24 hours. However, he or she plays an important role in overseeing the prisoner's welfare. Although their presence is not mandatory, an IMB member should aim to attend the review to oversee the decision-making process and satisfy him or herself that the use of a body belt is reasonable and consistent with PSO 1700. An IMB member should express any concerns over continued use of a body belt to the duty governor. If this fails to resolve the matter, the policy provides for the IMB member to raise concerns with Prison Service hierarchy in the same way as in the segregation process.

8.189    Once the reasons for using a body belt no longer exist, the duty governor must be contacted as soon as possible. If the duty governor agrees, he or she must complete the relevant section of form OT012, inform healthcare and notify the IMB. The duty governor must ensure that the prisoner is relocated to the appropriate accommodation following a period of time in a body belt. This is likely to be segregation or healthcare.

131  PR rule 49(4), YOIR rule 52(5).

### Children held in YOIs

8.190    As noted below, there has been serious concern over the circumstances in which children held in STCs are restrained, and about the techniques used. A significant number of prisoners who are under 18 are held in Prison Service establishments and this means that, unlike for those in STCs and SCHs, force can be used against these prisoners to ensure 'good order or discipline'. In light of this it is alarming that specific guidance on use of force and restraint on children held in YOIs is fairly limited, apart from specific requirements such as that body belts must never be used on under 18-year-olds. The only general guidance states that '*[f]orce must only be used as a last resort and no more force than is necessary may be used ... Staff must be competent in C & R techniques* and should be sensitive to their use on young people'.[132]

8.191    The review commissioned into the use of restraint on detained children commissioned by the Ministry of Justice which was published in December 2008 recommended that restraint techniques specific to young people should be introduced to YOIs, together with new behaviour management policies to improve officers' conflict resolution and de-escalation skills. The review also recommended that batons should not be routinely deployed in units holding children, and that the nose control technique in C & R, similar to the 'nose distraction' technique in PCC used in STCs (see below) should be withdrawn. These recommendations have been accepted.

## Use of handcuffs and restraints on escorts

### Types of restraint

8.192    The NSF authorises three kinds of restraints for use on escorts:

- *Handcuffs.*
  - Standard handcuffs for use on male prisoners, both adult and aged under 21.
  - Ratchet handcuffs for use on male prisoners in situations where standard handcuffs and inserts do not provide a sufficiently secure fit.
  - Ratchet handcuffs for use on thin-wristed and female prisoners.
  - Hyatt handcuffs for escort contractors.

---

132 PSO 4950 para 2.16.

- *Escort Chain.* This must be carried on all escorts for use whenever the use of handcuffs would be inappropriate, for example, if the prisoner needs to use the toilet. If the escort chain is used in public it must be kept as short as possible to make its use inconspicuous.
- *A body belt.* PSO 1700 states that a prisoner should only ever be escorted in a body belt in extreme circumstances if considered absolutely necessary. In such rare cases, the Prison Service, not a private contractor, must undertake the escort. Calming and de-escalation techniques must be used whilst the escort is underway. If the officer in charge of the escort considers that the reasons for using the body belt no longer exist, he or she must contact the duty governor. If the duty governor/controller authorises the removal of the body belt, then normal cuffing procedures will be applied before the body belt is removed. A doctor or registered nurse must assess a prisoner being held in a body belt before he or she is transferred. A member of healthcare staff must accompany any prisoner being transferred in a body belt. At the receiving prison, a copy of form OT012, and form OT010 where appropriate, must be made, showing the handover of the prisoner, to return to the sending prison.

### The risk assessment

8.193    Prisons are required by the NSF to undertake a local risk assessment to decide whether restraints should be used on an escort, including those conducted under in emergency situations such as a prisoner being taken to hospital. The NSF states that under normal circumstances, an escort of a prisoner who is categorised in any group other than category D should be escorted with at least two officers and have restraints applied. If it is necessary to escort a category D prisoner, rather than using the temporary licence provisions, the escort should consist of one officer with no restraints. Particular arrangements regarding strength of escort and use of restraints must be put in place for category A and E List prisoners.

8.194    The local risk assessment should indicate whether double or single cuffing is required. Double cuffing is where the prisoner's wrists are cuffed together and then cuffed to the escorting officer. Normal practice is for male category B, remand prisoners and E List prisoners to be double cuffed while on escort and other groups of prisoners to be single cuffed. Double-cuffing is mandatory for all category A prisoners.

8.195    The NSF states that handcuffs will not normally be used in the following circumstances, although the officer in charge of the escort may authorise the use of handcuffs if the prisoner becomes violent or tries to escape. In these cases the officer must make a written report to the governor on return to prison:

• When prisoners are being moved to an open prison.
• When prisoners from open prisons are being escorted unless being returned to closed conditions.
• On a mentally disordered prisoner who is subject to an order or direction for compulsory detention under the Mental Health Acts, unless the governor, with the agreement of Healthcare staff, directs that handcuffs must be used because the prisoner poses a security problem.
• On prisoners attending for medical treatment outside the prison, if the prisoner's medical condition renders restraints inappropriate or a risk assessment demonstrates they are unnecessary in all the circumstances. Restraints will not normally be necessary when the prisoner's mobility is severely limited, eg when he or she is on crutches. There are particular arrangements for escorting pregnant women and mothers and babies.
• On a category C life sentence prisoner on escorted absence. A prisoner who is ineligible or considered unsuitable for release on temporary licence may be permitted to leave the prison in the custody of an officer. The prisoner remains in legal custody and the escorting officer has the power to physically detain them in the event of an escape attempt.

8.196    Perhaps the issue where the use of handcuffs is most sensitive is when prisoners are handcuffed during medical treatment. The ECtHR has held that handcuffing does not normally give rise to an issue under article 3 where the measure has been imposed in connection with lawful detention and does not entail the use of force or public exposure exceeding what is reasonably considered necessary in relation to risks of absconding or risk to the public (of injury or damage).[133] Further the risk assessment is seen by the courts as very much a matter for prison officials and judges will be slow to criticise such assessments.[134]

8.197    However, the fact that a prisoner is receiving health treatment

---

133  *Raninen v Finland* (1988) EHRR 563.

134  *R (Faizovas) v Secretary of State for Justice* [2008] EWCA Civ 373 – a challenge to the risk assessment in judicial review proceedings would necessitate an application to cross examine the person who made the assessment (para 27).

may be relevant to the issue as to the use of handcuffs is disproportionate to the needs of security.[135] Moreover even if an initial risk
assessment does justify the use of handcuffs, the position might
change over time and prison authorities should keep the issue under
review especially where there has been a deterioration in health.[136] In
particular the Prison Service has been seriously criticised for handcuffing women during labour and it is to be noted that the NSF specifies that this is one of the circumstances in which restraints should
normally be removed (see para 8.203). This issue is discussed further
in chapter 6.

### Escort vehicles

8.198    The NSF states that escorting officers must not use public transport.
Prisoners' property and personal prison records must be loaded by
staff into the escort vehicle and never by the prisoners themselves.
When a car or coach is used for an escort, property and records will
be stored in the boot, or a separate lockable storage compartment.
When a minibus is used, or if no lockable compartment is available,
every effort must be made to keep the property and records out of the
prisoners' reach and to prevent them knowing their whereabouts.
Prisoners must not carry with them any items of property. The policy
also notes that whilst current legislation includes an exemption for
prison officers from wearing seatbelts whilst escorting prisoners, it
is Prison Service policy that staff must wear seatbelts for their own
personal safety where they are provided. All prisoners (including
pregnant women) must also wear seatbelts where they are fitted to
the escort vehicle, unless a certificate of exemption has been issued
by a registered medical practitioner on medical grounds.

8.199    Prison management and escort contractors are obliged to ensure
that the transport for escorts is secure, properly searched and fit for
use (especially if the vehicle has been hired). The vehicle must be
operated in such a way so as to minimise the risks associated with
escorting prisoners outside of a prison. During the planning stage
consideration should be given as to the suitability of the vehicle in relation to any special needs that the prisoner's may have. These needs
should be clearly marked on the PER form.

135  *Mouisel v France* (2004) 38 EHRR 34, *Uyan v Turkey*, application no 7496/003,
8 January 2009.
136  *R (Graham and Allen) v Secretary of State for Justice* [2007] EWHC 2940
(Admin) – one of the claimants was awarded £500 for breaches of article 3 in
respect of unnecessary use of handcuffs over a three day period in hospital,
and on five subsequent short periods during out-patient appointments.

8.200       The NSF authorises the following options:

- Cellular vehicle – these are designed to hold prisoners securely in individual cells. When in use a member of the escorting staff should sit in the rear accommodation to observe the prisoners, maintain security, and deal with any emergency and possible evacuation.
- People carrier – subject to a satisfactory risk assessment, these vehicles are suitable for long distance escorts involving a mother and baby where a degree of parental care is required.
- Coach or mini bus – subject to a satisfactory risk assessment, they may be used to transfer groups of lower category prisoners.
- Taxis and hire cars – subject to a satisfactory risk assessment taxis may be used for short distance movements like hospital outpatient visits. Vehicles like black cabs, with central locking and a partition to protect the driver, are recommended for use where possible. Establishments may also set up local contracts for the provision taxis and other vehicles. These should include a criminal records check of the drivers to be used.

## Application of restraints

8.201   The NSF also provides guidance on how escort restraints should be applied. It states that whenever restraints are applied they must be frequently checked for efficacy in keeping the prisoner secure. Escorting officers must apply handcuffs between the elbow and the wrist bone, but as near as possible to the wrist bone. Handcuffs must not be applied to any other part of the body. Officers are required to apply handcuffs as tightly as possible, without pinching the flesh or affecting the circulation and if necessary, officers should use inserts with standard handcuffs to ensure a close fit. Officers are also require to make sure that a prisoner does not attempt to reduce the effectiveness of handcuffs by pumping up his or her wrist, or applying cream or grease before handcuffs are applied. If an officer observes a prisoner attempting to reduce the efficacy of handcuffs in such ways, prison staff should consider what additional security precautions need to be taken for that particular escort.

8.202       Escorting officers should prevent a prisoner from draping clothing or any other item over the handcuffs in order to conceal them. When a prisoner is handcuffed to an officer, the officer's stronger arm should be left free if possible. If prisoners are not handcuffed to an officer, they must be handcuffed to one another. Restraints must not be used to attach prisoners to furniture or any other fixtures and fittings. If the escort for a single prisoner is of such high risk that three officers are required, restraints will be applied to the level indicated by the local risk assessment. The use of a cellular vehicle should be considered.

### Removal of restraints

8.203  Restraints during an escort will be removed only in the specific circumstances specified in the NSF. These are:

- When a prisoner (whatever their category) is inside the cubicle of a cellular vehicle, the cell door restraining chain is in place, and the outer door is locked. At the end of the journey, restraints must be reapplied and checked before the outer doors are unlocked. If, however, there is strong reason to believe that a prisoner has secreted a weapon, the prisoner may be required to wear restraints while locked in the vehicle.
- On arrival in the courtroom, unless the judge permits them to remain on the prisoner.
- In the court custody cells, but only after the area has been thoroughly checked. Even then restraints must be used in any part of the custody suite which is insecure, particularly a toilet.
- In certain circumstances at marriage ceremonies.
- In certain circumstances at funeral services or during visits to dying relatives.
- In certain circumstances during hospital treatment.
- In an emergency where life is being threatened.
- When a female prisoner is attending an antenatal check, or giving birth.
- On board an aircraft.
- When a medical professional requests their removal on health grounds. If necessary, escorting officers must seek permission from the duty governor in such instances.

8.204  Escorting officers must never remove handcuffs from a prisoner to allow him or her to use the toilet in an insecure area without first applying the escort chain and the toilet area must be searched before the prisoner uses it. Particular attention must be paid to any windows in the toilet area. The chain must be positioned to prevent the prisoner from locking the toilet door.

### Dispensing with handcuffs altogether

8.205  The NSF states that under no circumstances will a tetraplegic or paraplegic prisoner be handcuffed. This instruction must not be overridden without the formal and personal approval of the Director General, the Deputy Director General, or the Director of High Security Prisons.

## Use of force and restraint in secure training centres

8.206   The use of force and restraint in STCs has been extremely controversial. General concern over both the frequency with which force is used in STCs, and over the specific techniques used, was given focus by two deaths in 2004. On 19 April 2004 Gareth Myatt, a prisoner in Rainsbrook STC, died whilst being restrained by officers. On 8 August 2004, Adam Rickwood, a prisoner in Hassockfield STC, was found hanging in his room after he had been subjected to restraint by staff. At the inquest into the death of Adam Rickwood it became clear that it had become routine for the use of force in STCs to be used in circumstances not authorised by the statutory and policy framework.

### Statutory framework

8.207   All STCs are contracted out and the statutory framework governing the powers of officers working within them are somewhat complicated. The Criminal Justice and Public Order Act 1994 contains a general power for officers in private STCs to use reasonable force when necessary to:

- prevent escape;
- prevent, or detect and report upon, the commission or commission of other unlawful acts;
- ensure good order and discipline; and
- to attend prisoners' well-being.

8.208   These powers reflect those applicable to those that exist in adult prisons and YOI. In particular included is the possible use of force in order to ensure 'good order and discipline'. However the Secure Training Centre Rules are more specific in limiting the circumstances when use of force or restraint may be employed. These state firstly that officers shall not use force unnecessarily, and no more force than is necessary, and that officers must not deliberately provoke prisoners.[137]

8.209   In relation to use of physical restraint (and it is clear from the statutory and policy context that this is any use of restraining force, not the use of mechanical restraints as in the adult prison and YOI context) the Rules are more specific. They state that no prisoner

137   STCR rule 37.

should be physically restrained except where necessary to prevent them (and only when alternative methods of preventing the relevant event have failed):

- escaping from custody;
- injuring themselves or others;
- damaging property; or
- inciting another prisoner to do any of these acts.

It is therefore clear from the Rules that prisoners in STCs should not be restrained for general reasons of ensuring 'good order or discipline', for example to enforce compliance with staff instructions.

## Policy on use of force in STCs

8.210   The authorised restraining techniques for children held in secure custodial settings are known as Physical Control in Care (PCC) and were subject to extensive consultation before being developed.

> PCC comprises two elements, what we might call restraint proper; and 'distraction techniques'. So far as restraint is concerned, a number of specific 'holds' are permitted. These are used to prevent damage or injury by the person held ... Distraction techniques are different. The YJB in its evidence to the House of Lords and House of Commons Joint Committee on Human Rights [the JCHR] in 2008 described them as relying on techniques that create pain, for instance by a blow to the nose or by pulling back the trainee's thumb. The YJB said in its evidence that the techniques '... are designed for use in dangerous or violent situations where a person is at serious risk of injury. Distraction techniques inflict a momentary burst of pain to the nose, rib or thumb to distract a young person who presents a danger to him/herself or others.' After criticism of its effectiveness, the nose distraction technique was withdrawn by the Secretary of State in December 2007.[138]

8.211   The use of force and restraint is also the subject of detailed guidance issued by the YJB.[139] This guidance sets out, as would be expected, among other considerations that:

- officers in STCs need to be trained to carry out restrictive physical interventions;
- they should be used as a last resort when all alternatives have been exhausted;

138  *R (C) v Secretary of State for Justice* [2008] EWCA Civ 882.
139  *Managing Children and Young People's Behaviour in the Secure Estate: a Code of Practice* (YJB, 2006) available at www.yjb.gov.uk/Publications/Scripts/prodView.asp?idproduct=280&eP=PP

- that techniques that cause pain must only be used in exceptional circumstances;
- the minimum of force for the shortest possible time should be used;
- records must be kept of incidents where force is used and institutions should prepare an annual report on use of PCC; and
- prisoners should be medically examined on request or if there is any sign of injury.

Crucially, with regard to the use of such techniques for general 'good order or discipline' purposes, the guidance states '[r]estrictive physical interventions must not be used as a punishment, or merely to secure compliance with staff instructions'.

8.212    It was clear from evidence given at the Inquest into the death of Adam Rickwood that the use of the 'nose distraction' technique prior to his death was not necessary to prevent any of the specific circumstances set out in the STC Rules. Somewhat surprisingly, in the face of this case and other evidence that there was widespread abuse of the Rules in STCs, the Government's response was not to ensure compliance with the law, but to seek to legalise the practice by amending the STC Rules to allow for the use of physical restraint and segregation for the very broad purpose of ensuring 'good order and discipline'.[140] These amendments to the Rules were subsequently declared unlawful and quashed by the Court of Appeal as there was inadequate consultation (with the Children's Commissioner) and a failure to carry out a race relations impact assessment. Moreover, the court noted article 3 of the ECHR when applied to children in custody had to be interpreted consistently with the provisions of the UN Convention on the Rights of the Child 1989 in particular article 37[141] and the views of the Committee on the Rights of the Child as the expert monitoring body charged with the implementation of the state's obligations under the Convention. It further noted that in General Comment 8 of the UN Committee on the Rights of the Child it was indicated that deliberate infliction of pain is not permitted as a form

---

140   STC (Amendment) Rules 2007 SI No 1709.
141   UN CRC article 37 provides in part as follows: 'States parties shall ensure that: (a) no child shall be subjected to torture or other cruel, inhuman or degrading treatment or punishment ... (c) every child derived of liberty shall be treated with humanity and respect for the inherent dignity of the human person, and in particular in a manner which tales into account the needs of person or his or her age'. The court however did not consider that 'good order or discipline' in itself was too vague a criterion to justify the lawful use of force under the ECHR.

of control of juveniles. The Court held that as there was no proper evidence that the use of the PCC techniques for general 'good order or discipline' purposes was necessary in STCs (the Ministry of Justice filed no evidence with court to support the assertion), the amendments also breached both articles 3 and 8 of the ECHR.

8.213    After the Court of Appeal judgment the Ministry of Justice published a review commissioned into use of force, and the Government's response. The review[142] was not focussed on whether restraint was necessary for 'good order and discipline' purposes but on the restraint techniques used on children, whether in YOIs, STCs or secure children's homes run by local authorities. The report made a large number of recommendations most of which have been accepted by the Ministry of Justice. Notably the techniques of 'nose distraction' and the 'double basket hold' (the latter used on Gareth Myatt prior to his death) are to be permanently removed from authorisation and safer alternatives brought in.

8.214    It remains of great concern that the report did not recommend that uses of other types of restraint designed to cause pain should be prohibited from use on children. The inadequacy of the report in this respect was quickly highlighted by a further judgment of the Administrative Court ordering a fresh inquest into Adam Rickwood's death because of the original coroner's failure to rule on the lawfulness of the force used prior to his death. The judge commented:

> Moreover, it should have been clear to all properly self-directing public authorities that the limits on the use of force on children in custody was driven by the core principles set out in the UN Convention on the Rights of the Child, to which effect was designed to be given in UK law by the Children Act 1989, and which informs any detailed elaboration of human rights relating to children set out in the Human Rights Act 1998. Deliberate infliction of pain and force on children as young as 14 could only be justified by very compelling reasons such as those contemplated by the STC Rules, rather than generally to support staff orders. The authors of the Smallridge and Williamson report to the Ministers were very much mistaken if they believed that the requirements of the UN CRC were irrelevant to the limits of restraint that could be used in the UK.[143]

8.215    It is therefore clear that there will be further developments in the types of approved techniques for use on detained children. Such techniques

---

142    Smallridge and Williamson, *Independent Review of the use of Restraint in Juvenile Secure Settings*, Ministry of Justice, 15 December 2008.

143    *R (Pounder) v HM Coroner for North and South Districts of Durham and Darlington* [2009] EWHC 76 (Admin).

as are used must only be used in accordance with the STC Rules which do not permit their use for general 'good order or discipline' reasons. The Government has accepted the Review's recommendations that a 'new, simpler and safer' method of PCC should be devised for STCs, as well as the removal of the two specific holds referred to above.

## Use of force in secure children's homes

8.216   Use of force in SCHs is authorised by the Children's Home Regulations 2001. Secure children's homes are required to have a 'behaviour management policy' which sets out the measures of 'control, restraint and discipline' to be used.[144] Guidance on use of segregation in secure children's homes is issued by the Secure Accommodation Network.[145]

8.217   There is policy guidance given by SAN on the use of restrictive physical interventions in SCHs.[146] This clarifies that in SCHs, as in STCs, such techniques should not be used in order to enforce compliance with instructions but only where to prevent detainees:

- harming themselves or others;
- causing significant damage to property;
- inciting other young people to cause physical harm or damage to property; or
- absconding both from within and outside of the unit.

8.218   In particular the policy states that techniques should not involve the child being deliberately taken to the floor. Where this does occur during the course of an incident or where holds other than approved holds have been used, the reapplication of approved techniques should be achieved as soon as possible. Similarly with any use of pain compliance techniques it must be demonstrated that no reasonable alternative existed and that only force that was reasonable in the circumstances was applied. The guidance strongly recommends that the use of pain compliant techniques should be avoided wherever and whenever possible.

8.219   The policy guidance states that records should be kept of all incidents when restrictive physical interventions are used. Records should contain:

144   CHR rule 17 issued under the Care Standards Act 2000.
145   www.secureaccommodation.org.uk/practiceguidelines.htm
146   *The Use of Restrictive Physical Interventions (RPI) in Secure Children's Homes (England and Wales)*, Secure Accommodation Network. See www.secureaccommodation.org.uk/practiceguidelines.htm

- the child's details;
- staff involved;
- description of build-up, incident and resolution;
- description of hold;
- record of any injury to the child; and
- confirmation of debriefing for staff and young person.

8.220   As a minimum, the parents and the YOT and social workers should be informed in all cases where restraint results in an injury to the young person. The Youth Justice Board need to be informed where restraint has resulted in a serious injury to the young person or a complaint investigated under child protection procedures.

8.221   The methods of restraint used in SCHs are not exactly the same as in STCs as PCC is not used. Instead a variety of commercially developed systems are used. This lack of consistency is obviously of some concern. the Smallridge and Willliamson review recommended mandatory accreditation of all techniques. Specifically it also recommended removal of the nose distraction technique and the double-basket hold where this was included in the techniques used in SCHs.

# Prison discipline

• *Escapes or absconds from prison or from prison or from legal custody* • *Fails to comply with any condition upon which he is temporarily released* • *Has in his possession any unauthorised article or a greater quantity of any article than he is authorised to have* • *Sells or delivers to any person any unauthorised article* • *Sells or, without permission delivers to any person any article which he is allowed to have only for his own use* • *Takes improperly any article belonging to another person or to a prison or YOI* • *Intentionally or recklessly sets fire to any part of a prison or YOI or any other property, whether or not his own* • *Destroys or damages any part of a prison or YOI or any other property, other than his own* • *Causes racially aggravated damage to any part of a prison or YOI or any other property, other than his own* • *Absents himself from any place where he is required to be or is present at any place where he is not authorised to be* • *Is disrespectful to any officer, or any person (other than a prisoner) who is at the prison for the purpose of working there, or any person visiting a prison* • *Uses threatening, abusive or insulting words or behaviour* • *Uses threatening, abusive or insulting racist words or behaviour* • *Intentionally fails to work properly or, being required to work, refuses to do so* • *Disobeys any lawful order* • *Disobeys or fails to comply with any rule or regulation applying to him* • *Receives any controlled drug, or, without the consent of an officer, any other article, during the course of a visit (not being a legal visit)* • *Displays, attaches to or draws on any part of a prison threatening, abusive or insulting racist words, drawings, symbols or other material* • *Attempts to commit; incites another prisoner to commit; or assists another prisoner to commit any of the foregoing offences*

**9.119   Offences relating to drug and alcohol misuse**

*Is intoxicated as a consequence of consuming any alcoholic beverage* • *Consumes any alcoholic beverage whether or not provided to him by another person*

# The prison disciplinary system

## Introduction

9.1    The Prison and YOI Rules set out a comprehensive code of formal disciplinary procedures. There is no formal disciplinary system in either secure training centres or in local authority secure care homes. The Ministry of Justice statistics show that a there were a total of 109,117 prison disciplinary charges found proved in 2007.[1] This figure has remained fairly constant over the last 10 years. This means, in light of the increasing prison population, there has been a reduction in the average number of offences proved for each prisoner in the system. In 2007 there were 136 proven offences against prison discipline for every 100 prisoners, about 23 per cent lower than in 1997. Women prisoners had a higher offence rate in 2007 than male prisoners (189 compared with 133 proven offences per 100 population in prison). Additional days were given as punishment in 13,640 of the proven charges.

9.2    The most frequently used punishment in 2007 was forfeiture of privileges accounting for 47 per cent of all punishments. This was followed by stoppage or reduction of earnings, and confinement to cell or room. This has changed since 1997 when imposition of additional days was the most frequently used punishment. The Ministry of Justice suggests that the fall in use of additional days is for two main reasons. From 1 April 2001, additional days were no longer available as a punishment for prisoners serving DTOs. Secondly, the *Ezeh and Connors* judgment[2] led to the withdrawal of the governor's power to impose additional days. This power passed to independent adjudicators, and from 2002 district judges began conducting adjudications in prisons, imposing additional days where appropriate.

## Origins and development of the current system

9.3    In order to fully understand the current system it is necessary to look back at the development of prison discipline. This is because many of the decisions made in the context of earlier systems still have relevance, although their terminology and context are different. The prison disciplinary system originated in the late nineteenth century and was based on the arrangements for military discipline. The

---

1    www.justice.gov.uk/docs/omcs2007.pdf
2    *Ezeh and Connors v UK* (2002) 35 EHRR 28.

system was structured around providing a swift hearing in order to preserve order. The tension between the harshness of some of the punishments available and the perceived need for speed has been at the heart of how the courts have interpreted the requirements of fairness in this area. For example in an early case in which a prisoner attempted to establish a right to legal representation the Court of Appeal held:

> We all know that, when a man is brought up before his commanding officer for a breach of discipline, whether in the armed forces or in ships at sea, it never has been the practice to allow legal representation. It is of the first importance that the cases should be decided quickly. If legal representation were allowed, it would mean considerable delay. So also with breaches of prison discipline. They must be heard and decided speedily.[3]

9.4    In the 1970s the disciplinary system had two tiers. The Boards of Visitors (now IMBs) were responsible for hearing the more serious charges and could impose very severe punishments including unlimited 'loss of remission'. Governors heard the less serious charges and could only impose a maximum of 28 days loss of remission. Following the riots at HMP Hull in 1976 there were a number of challenges to hearings where the BoV had imposed very severe punishments. The courts decided that the rules of natural justice did apply to hearings before the boards, that their findings could be challenged by way of judicial review, that prisoners had a right to request the attendance of witnesses which should not be denied purely on administrative convenience and that contested hearsay evidence could not be used as the sole or primary basis for a finding of guilt.[4] The House of Lords later confirmed that findings of guilt made by governors were also amenable to judicial review.[5]

9.5    The ECtHR also looked at the BoV's disciplinary function when handing out large periods of lost remission as punishment. A prisoner who received a punishment of 570 days loss of remission for prison mutiny and assaulting an officer succeeded in establishing that the scale of this punishment rendered the charges criminal

---

3   *Fraser v Mudge* [1975] 1 WLR 1132. Since the 1970s there has been a parallel development of jurisprudence dealing with fair procedure in the military and prison contexts.

4   See *R v Board of Visitors of HMP Hull ex p St Germain (No 1)* [1979] QB 425 and *R v Board of Visitors of HMP Hull ex p St Germain and others (No 2)* [1979] 1 WLR 1401.

5   *Leech v Deputy governor of HMP Parkhurst* [1988] AC 533.

within the meaning therefore of article 6 of the ECHR. The failure to allow legal representation breached article 6.[6]

9.6   Following the recommendations of the Woolf Report, the BoV lost their disciplinary function by changes to the Prison Rules made in April 1992.[7] The change to the early release regimes in the CJA 1991 also meant that prisoners no longer lost remission but had 'additional days' added to their release and licence dates. Further changes limited governors' punishments to a maximum of 42 additional days[8] and ensured that the most serious allegations were referred to the police. This limit on the number of additional days was intended to prevent disciplinary charges being considered criminal within the meaning of article 6 (the right to a fair trial), the rationale being that article 6 had applied only where the effective loss of liberty was for many months, rather then weeks.

9.7   In 2002 two prisoners successfully argued in the ECtHR that prison disciplinary charges were criminal within the meaning of article 6 whenever additional days were given as punishment.[9] One of the prisoners had only been given seven additional days. In applying the criteria for determining whether the charges were purely disciplinary or criminal in nature[10] the court held that:

- the domestic classification of the charges as disciplinary was not determinative;
- a charge could be criminal for the purposes of article 6 either because of its nature, or because of the severity of the punishment – these considerations were not necessarily cumulative; and
- the imposition of additional days as punishment amounted to deprivation of liberty the seriousness of which raised a presumption that the charges were criminal.

9.8   As the charges engaged article 6, there were obvious breaches as prison governors were not independent, and there was no right to legal representation for the prisoners. The government's response to the judgment was to amend the Prison Rules in 2002 so that

---

6   *Campbell and Fell v UK* [1983] 5 EHRR 207 – however despite concerns over the boards' close links with prison management it held that they were sufficiently independent.

7   Prison (Amendment) Rules 1992 SI No 518.

8   The equivalent to lost remission brought in by the Criminal Justice Act 1991.

9   *Ezeh and Connors v UK* (2002) 35 EHRR 28, judgment of the Third Section upheld by the Grand Chamber at (2004) 39 EHRR 3.

10   The Engel criteria – from *Engel v Netherlands* (1979–80) 1 EHRR 647, namely, the charge's classification under domestic law; the nature of the charge; and the severity of the penalty.

governors no longer had the power to award additional days and a system of independent adjudicators was created to hear those cases where additional days might be awarded. The government also remitted all additional days imposed as punishment by prison governors since the coming into force of the Human Rights Act (HRA)1998 on 2 October 2000, but not before. The rationale for this was that as the HRA 1998 was not retrospective prisoners could have no complaint domestically that punishments given before that date breached article 6.[11] Although the punishments were remitted, the findings of guilt were not actually quashed.[12] It was also held by the House of Lords that a quashing of the finding of guilt where there is a breach of article 6 constitutes just satisfaction for the purposes of the HRA 1998 and there will not generally be a right to compensation for such breaches in the context of prison discipline.[13]

## The current system

9.9    Disciplinary charges are heard by:

- Governors (directors or controllers in private prisons)[14] where the charge is insufficiently serious to justify a punishment of additional days (references to governors in the rest of this chapter should be taken to also refer to directors and controllers in private prisons). Those hearing charges are commonly called 'adjudicators'.
- Where the charge is serious enough potentially to warrant an award of additional days, it is referred to an Independent Adjudicator (IA) for hearing. IAs are district judges from the magistrates' court system appointed by the Secretary of State for Justice.
- Prisoners can be advised under the CDS advice and assistance scheme where there is no legal representation, and represented under the CDS advocacy assistance scheme when a charge is referred to an IA, or where a governor allows legal representation as a matter of discretion.

11  *R (Rogers) v Secretary of State for the Home Department* [2002] EWHC 2078 (Admin) upheld this approach.

12  *R (Napier) v Secretary of State for the Home Department* [2004] 1 WLR 3056. The court accepted that, once the additional days were remitted, article 6 did not require quashing of the finding of guilt.

13  *R (Greenfield) v Secretary of State for the Home Department* [2005] 1 WLR 673.

14  Governors can delegate this power to a suitably trained operational manager F, and directors to an officer senior enough to be in charge of the prison in the director's absence. While controllers retain statutory power to conduct adjudications it is anticipated they will no longer routinely do so once directors and their staff are suitably trained: PSO 2000 para 1.4.

## The statutory framework

9.10    The Prison Act 1952 s47(2) requires that Rules made under it must 'make provision for ensuring that a person who is charged with any offence under the rules shall be given a proper opportunity of presenting his case'. Both the prison and YOI Rules have detailed provisions relating the hearing of charges[15] and specific rules to confirm the prisoner's right to the essentials of procedural fairness (that a prisoner 'shall be given a full opportunity of hearing what is alleged against him and of presenting his own case'[16]). The Rules that apply depend on the prisoner's location so, for example, an adult female held in a YOI must be charged under the YOI Rules.[17]

9.11    All those held in prisons and YOIs can be placed on report as they are subject to the Rules. Therefore those detained solely under the Immigration Act can be placed on report, although they cannot be given additional days as punishment. Remand prisoners can be given prospective additional days as a punishment which then become activated if they are given a custodial sentence.

9.12    There is also very detailed policy guidance on the conduct of prison disciplinary hearings, commonly known as adjudications, set out in PSO 2000. This states that the purposes of the disciplinary procedure are:

- to help maintain order, control, discipline and a safe environment by investigating offences and punishing those responsible; and
- to ensure that the use of authority in the prison is lawful, reasonable and fair.[18]

9.13    The PSO provides invaluable information to prisoners and their advisers when contesting charges, and failure to follow its provisions will often lead to successful challenges to findings of guilt.[19] However the policy, unlike the statutory provisions, is not binding on Independent Adjudicators as they cannot be directed as to their functions by the Prison Service[20] as this would compromise the need for an article 6 compliant body to be independent of the parties to the hearing.

---

15  PR rules 51–61, YOIR rules 55–66.
16  PR rule 54, YOIR rule 59.
17  PSO 2000 para 2.8.
18  PSO 2000 para 1.1.
19  Copies should be kept on every wing, the prison library and wherever adjudications take place PSO 2000 introduction para 9.
20  PSO 2000 para 13.14.

9.14    The offences that can give rise to disciplinary charges in prisons
and YOIs[21] are a combination of matters that could give rise to criminal charges outside prison (such as assault, taking property without
consent, damaging property or using threatening behaviour) and
matters specific to the prison context (such as disobeying a lawful
orders or failing a mandatory drug test). Changes are periodically
made to the Rules, most recently in 2005 to facilitate the punishment
of those who fail mandatory alcohol tests.

9.15    Children under the age of 18 who are held in YOIs can face disciplinary charges but guidance states that 'due regard' to the prisoner's
age and maturity should be given, and further that:

> [e]very young person must be allowed access to the advocacy service (if
> they so wish), where available, and/or to the Independent Monitoring
> Board (IMB), as appropriate. governors must give due consideration
> to the benefits of using the minor report procedure [see below] with
> this age group in order to expedite the disciplinary sanction.[22]

## Laying the charge

9.16    Disciplinary proceedings are commenced when the prisoner is given
a charge sheet on form F1127[23] (commonly referred to by prisoners
as a 'nicking sheet', or as being 'put on report'). The Rules require
the charge to be 'laid as soon as possible and, save in exceptional
circumstances, within 48 hours of the discovery of the offence'.[24]
This is a mandatory requirement and so a failure to promptly lay
the charge will make any subsequent proceedings unlawful.[25] PSO
2000 confirms that matters such as the unavailability of staff will not
constitute 'exceptional circumstances' to justify a delay in laying the
charge beyond 48 hours.

9.17    Normally the charge sheet will be completed by the officer who
witnessed the incident and will contain a brief account of their
evidence. The charge should include sufficient explanatory detail to
ensure that there is no doubt as to the substance of the allegation.[26] It

21   See PR rule 51, YOIR rule 51.
22   PSO 4950 para 2.19.
23   PSO 2000 para 2.3.
24   PR rule 53(1), YOIR rule 58(1).
25   *R v Board of Visitors of Dartmoor Prison ex p Smith* [1986] 3 WLR 61.
26   PSO 2000 para 2.12. In *R (Haase) v Independent Adjudicator* [2008] EWCA Civ
     1089 the Court of Appeal decided that article 6 does not require an independent
     prosecutor in the context of prison discipline.

will not be sufficient merely to rehearse the wording of the relevant rule without any detail of the actual alleged misconduct. The charge sheet will then form the basis of the case to be considered by the adjudicator.[27]

9.18    The officer who lays the charge is known as the 'reporting officer'. The reporting officer is required to consult the Adjudication Liaison Officer (the 'ALO' – who must be appointed by the governor and trained in the interpretation of offences) or their line manager before laying the charge.[28]

9.19    Once a charge has been laid, it cannot be amended if, for example, after hearing evidence the adjudicator considers that the prisoner may be guilty of a different or lesser charge. If the prisoner has been charged with an incorrect offence, a fresh charge can only be laid if it is still within 48 hours of the discovery of the offence.[29] Where a single incident properly gives rise to a number of separate charges (for example both an assault and damage to property) then the prisoner may be charged with both and potentially found guilty of each of them.[30] If it is unclear whether the alleged behaviour amounts to one or more alternative offences, more than one charge may be laid (for example, an assault and a racially aggravated assault). They can then be heard together and the adjudicator can determine which of the charges is correct.[31]

9.20    Prisoners under escort are deemed to be in the custody of the governor and the escorting officers can lay charges for any alleged misconduct that amounts to an offence under the Rules. The charge will then be dealt with by the receiving prison.[32] Charges cannot be laid in respect of behaviour which takes place when the prisoner is in court as they are in the custody of the court, or which the court has already punished as that would amount to double punishment.[33]

9.21    Allegations of serious criminal misconduct should be reported immediately to the governor or director so that consideration may be given as to whether to refer the matter to the police. If this occurs,

---

27  And so where the charge sheet alleges unauthorised possession of a 'sharpened stabbing implement' then the adjudicator must be satisfied that this was what the object was, rather than just a sharp object: *R (Shreeve) v Secretary of State for Justice* [2007] EWHC 2431 (Admin).

28  PSO 2000 para 2.2.

29  PSO 2000 para 2.6.

30  PSO 2000 para 2.13.

31  PSO 2000 para 2.7.

32  Criminal Justice Act 1991 s83.

33  PSO 2000 para 2.9.

the prison disciplinary charge should still be laid within the 48 hour time limit and the matter adjourned pending the police investigation[34] (see further below).

9.22     PSO 2000 makes clear that disciplinary charges should not be brought in respect of behaviour relating to incidents of self-harm. The policy recognises that the threat of punishment is not an appropriate part of the strategy for dealing with such behaviour.[35]

## Timing of the first hearing

9.23     The governor – or the director or controller in private prisons[36] – is required to hold the first hearing the day after the laying of the charge not taking into account Sunday or public holidays, save in exceptional circumstances.[37] There is no policy or statutory guidance on what will constitute exceptional circumstances but this is likely to refer to highly unusual occurrences such as major disturbances rather than routine administrative or staffing problems. The prisoner may be segregated in between the laying of the charge and this first hearing[38] but the guidance in PSO 2000 states that this *'must not be an automatic measure but be used where there is a real need, such as the risk of collusion or intimidation relating to the alleged offence which segregation of the accused may prevent'*. Any segregation beyond the first hearing must be authorised in accordance with the normal procedures.

## Referring charges to the police

9.24     If the charge is criminal in character (such as a serious assault) and the governor or director 'believes it is sufficiently serious to be reported to the police, the hearing must be opened and adjourned until the outcome of the police investigation or subsequent prosecution is known'.[39] Detailed guidance is given in annex C to PSO

---

34  PSO 2000 para 11.1.
35  PSO 2000 para 2.19, and see also *Keenan v UK* (2001) 33 EHRR 38 where use of disciplinary measures against a vulnerable mentally ill prisoner contributed to a finding of a breach of article 3.
36  From November 2007 directors in private prisons were given the same power to conduct adjudications as controllers: Prison (Amendment No 2) Rules 2007 SI No 3149, YOI (Amendment No 2) Rules 2007 SI No 3220 – made under Offender Management Act 2007 s26 which removed the prohibition on directors carrying out functions relating to discipline and segregation.
37  PR rule 53(3), YOIR rule 58(3).
38  PR rule 53(4), YOIR rule 58(4).
39  PSO 2000 para 4.28.

2000 as to when such referrals should take place and this guidance
is referred to in the description of the charges below. The guidance
on referral was agreed with the police, the CPS and the Ministry of
Justice.

9.25   The policy also states that if the victim, and this will include prisoner victims, of any alleged criminal act wishes the matter to be referred to the police then this must be done.[40] It also confirms that
racial aggravation will strengthen the case for referral.[41] The guidance also gives specific guidance as to the kinds of alleged offence
that should be referred, and on issues such as preservation of the
crime scene.

9.26   If the prisoner is prosecuted and evidence presented in court, or
is cautioned, for the offence then the prison disciplinary charge must
be dismissed.[42] If no prosecution or caution results from the referral
then the governor or director may continue to hear the disciplinary
charge. The policy states that:

> [i]f it is clear that the police or CPS have decided that a prosecution
> cannot be brought because the available evidence is insufficient, and
> the disciplinary charge is similar to and relies on the same evidence
> as the potential prosecution, the adjudicator must dismiss the discip-
> linary charge.[43]

However where, for example, witnesses are willing to co-operate with
the prison hearing, but not the police, or where the criminal matter is
discontinued before the hearing of evidence, then the policy suggests
it would be possible to continue to hear the charge.

9.27   Particular considerations that apply when prisoners face criminal
prosecution are dealt with below (see para 9.206 onwards).

## Referring charges to an independent adjudicator

9.28   The Prison Rules require the governor to 'determine whether [the
charge] is so serious that additional days should be awarded for the
offence, if the prisoner is found guilty' and if so, it must be referred to
an Independent Adjudicator.[44] Referrals '*must be reserved for offences
which pose the most serious risk to the order and control of the establish-*

40  PSO 2000 C.6.
41  PSO 2000 C.7.
42  PSO 2000 paras 11.8 and 11.10.
43  PSO 2000 para 11.6.
44  PR rule 53A(1), YOIR rule 58A(1).

*ment or to the safety of those in it*'.[45] More detailed guidance on which offences to refer is contained in annex N of PSO 2000 which outlines aggravating factors in relation to disciplinary offences which will warrant referral (see below when the individual charges are examined).

9.29　　Before making a decision to refer a charge the governor 'must ensure that they have considered whether other punishment available to them would be more appropriate, given all the circumstances of the offence'.[46]

9.30　　The PSO confirms that the decision to refer a case to an IA will only be made where there is the possibility of additional days as punishment. As such, prisoners serving life sentences who cannot receive additional days on their sentences will ordinarily never have their cases referred to an IA. The only circumstance where the PSO envisages this arising is if a lifer is one of a number of defendants, at least one of whom is serving a determinate sentence[47] and the determinate prisoner has the case referred to the IA. The PSO is founded on an interpretation that article 6 only applies where there is a possible deprivation of liberty as the punishment. The Court of Appeal has considered that there might potentially be cases where lifers could face charges so serious that article 6 was engaged.[48] This has subsequently been applied to a life sentence prisoner, who faced with a charge of assaulting a prison officer successfully argued in the Administrative Court that article 6 was engaged purely due to the seriousness of charge.[49]

9.31　　In light of this, notwithstanding the contents of the PSO, consideration should still be given by the governor whether the charge itself is seriousness enough to justify a referral to the IA. The same principle will apply to other prisoners who cannot receive additional days as punishment (those serving DTOs, civil prisoners, those detained in prison solely under the Immigration Act, and prisoners recalled to custody who cannot have their release date extended beyond the sentence expiry date).[50]

9.32　　Whilst the referral to an IA will normally take place at the first hearing, the governor has the power to make a referral at any time

---

45　PSO 2000 para 13.5.
46　PSO 2000 para 7.40.
47　PR rule 53A(2)(b), YOIR rule 58A(2)(b) and PSO 2000 para 13.3.
48　*R (Tangney) v Governor of HMP Elmley* [2005] EWCA Civ 1009.
49　*R (Smith) v Governor of HMP Belmarsh and another* [2009] EWHC 109 (Admin).
50　PSO 2000 para 7.38.

afterwards, including after a finding of guilt.[51] If the referral takes place after the hearing of evidence then the IA must hear the matter afresh without reference to the record of hearing before the governor to ensure that the hearing fully complies with the necessity for the charge to be considered by an independent tribunal in accordance with article 6.

9.33    Once the matter has been referred, the first hearing before the IA must take place within 28 days[52] unless there are exceptional circumstances. The IAs who hear charges in prisons are either district or deputy district judges from the magistrates' court system, who have been appointed by the Minister of Justice for the purpose of hearing charges referred by governors.[53] The Chief Magistrate's Office at the City of Westminster Magistrates' Court at Horseferry Road London is responsible for administrating and allocating IAs and queries about hearings by IAs and requests for adjournments should be addressed there.

9.34    Once a charge has been referred to an IA, the prisoner has a right to legal representation at the hearing[54] in keeping with the requirements of article 6. The CDS Advocacy Assistance Scheme provides public funding for such hearings (see chapter 12). When the referral to an IA has been made, the prisoner should be informed straight away and given the opportunity to consult a solicitor, and if they do not have one should be referred to the Legal Services Officer.[55]

9.35    The Rules do not include any provision for a case to be referred back to a governor or director once it has been referred to the IA. It would seem that if an IA believes a case was wrongly referred, then there is no power for the governor to then hear the charge. This is confirmed in PSO 2000 which states that

> If a charge has been referred to the Independent Adjudicator, the governor or controller cannot proceed with the hearing under any circumstances, nor can the Independent Adjudicator refer it back to a Prison Service adjudicator.[56]

---

51  PR rule 53A(3), YOIR rule 58A(3).
52  PR rule 53A(3), YOIR rule 58A(3).
53  PR rule 2(1), YOIR rule 2(1).
54  PR rule 54(3), YOIR rule 59(3).
55  PSO 2000 para 13.7.
56  PSO 2000 para 13.4.

## Minor reports for young offenders

9.36   Although not specifically provided for in the Rules, PSO 2000 allows
for a system of 'Minor Reports' for certain charges for young offenders held in either YOIs or in prisons.[57] The punishments are limited
(to cautions, forfeiture of privileges for three days, stoppage of earnings for three days, and extra work of two hours a day for three days).
These charges can be heard by senior officers who have had authorised training.[58] The Minor Report system is designed to provide for
'swift punishment for minor lapses of discipline' and so procedures
need to provide for the speedy hearing of the report and 'certainly
within 48 hours of the alleged offence'.[59] It is difficult to see how
such systems with such tight timescales could properly accommodate the need for the young offenders to either access legal advice or
obtain evidence in support of their defence where this is needed. It is
up to governors or directors to decide whether to establish a system
of minor reports in their prison.

## Preparation for the hearing

9.37   PSO 2000 states that prisoners must be given at least two hours to
prepare for a hearing.[60] In all but the simplest cases where the prisoner is pleading not guilty this will clearly be insufficient. The policy
also states that if the prisoner, or a legal representative 'asks for a
copy of all statements to be submitted in evidence so as to prepare a
defence or mitigation these must be supplied at public expense'.[61] As
soon as a legal adviser is contacted by a prisoner regarding a disciplinary charge, it is good practice to immediately request all documentation citing this provision, and to ask the prison to confirm that the
hearing will not proceed before disclosure has taken place and there
has been an opportunity to provide advice.

9.38        There is also guidance on the prisoner's right to interview potentially relevant witnesses prior to the hearing and to consult PSO 2000
itself and other reference books.[62] If the prisoner has legal representation the solicitor may request access to the prison in order to inspect
the scene relating to the allegation or to interview witnesses. The

57   PSO 2000 para 4.41–4.50.
58   PSO 2000 para 1.4.
59   PSO 2000 para 4.41.
60   PSO 2000 para 2.10.
61   PSO 2000 para 2.20.
62   PSO 2000 paras 2.21–2.22.

request must be dealt with by a member of staff that is not involved in the disciplinary process.[63]

## The first hearing

9.39    Both governors and IAs will normally record the hearing on form F256. This 'need not be a verbatim transcript but it must indicate the way in which the adjudicator pursued the inquiry. If the charge is proved it must be clear from the record why the adjudicator rejected any defence put forward'.[64]

9.40    The requirement for prisoners to be declared medically fit to face adjudications was removed when PSO 2000 was introduced in 2006. It is now a matter for the governor or IA to consider, although a list of those facing hearings should be passed to the healthcare department sufficiently in advance of any hearing to allow any concerns to be passed back. If there are concerns the governor should adjourn to obtain a health assessment before proceeding.[65]

9.41    At the first (and subsequent hearings) form 256 prompts the governor or IA to consider certain matters, namely whether the prisoner:

- has received notice of, and understands the charge;
- has had enough time to prepare;
- wants to call any witnesses;
- wants legal advice, legal representation or the assistance of a McKenzie friend; and
- wants to plead guilty, not guilty or refuses to plead.

## Witness issues

9.42    If the prisoner requests the attendance of witnesses, a governor

has the discretion to refuse to call witnesses named by the prisoner or by the reporting officer but this must be done reasonably and on proper grounds and not, for example, for reasons of administrative convenience or because the adjudicator considers the case against the prisoner has already been established.[66]

The reasons for any refusal must be recorded on the record of hearing. The policy states that the prisoner should indicate what evidence

---

63  PSO 2000 paras 3.19–3.23.
64  PSO 2000 para 4.31 – this also sets out the key issues the F256 should cover, for example responses to witness requests and reasons for adjournments.
65  PSO 2000 paras 2.25–2.26.
66  PSO 2000 para 5.14.

the witness will provide, and then the governor will consider whether the witness should be called.

9.43 Examples of acceptable reasons for refusing to call a witness are:

- where it is clear that the witness does not have any relevant evidence to provide;
- where the governor believes the request is part of an attempt to make the hearing unmanageable; and
- if the governor accepts as true the evidence the prisoner hopes the witness will confirm (this is not the same as the governor believing the witness will say what the accused prisoner says he or she will).

9.44 Prison disciplinary hearings remain inquisitorial, therefore, the governor or IA is under a duty to call relevant evidence even where this is not requested by the prisoner. If, unknown to the prisoner, a member of staff knows of a relevant witness to an incident then this must be brought to the attention of the governor hearing the charge.[67] However, this inquisitorial role does not mean that where a prisoner has chosen not to call a potentially relevant witness, perhaps for tactical reasons, any resultant finding of guilt will be unfair.[68]

9.45 There is no power to compel the attendance of witnesses at prison disciplinary hearings. Any reasons for witnesses refusing to attend should be recorded on the record of hearing. Prisoners can call other prisoners, members of staff, or members of the public (for example if an incident takes place in the visits room). PSO 2000 states that if a member of the public has relevant evidence, but for security reasons they cannot be admitted to the prison, then the charge may have to be dismissed. If witnesses do attend the costs of attendance must be borne by the prison.[69]

## Legal advice and representation

9.46 Governors are required to ask the prisoner at each hearing of a charge whether they require assistance and if so explain about the possibilities of legal representation, assistance from a McKenzie friend, or legal advice.[70] Even if requests are refused at the first hearing circumstances may change and so they must be considered afresh at

---

67 PSO 2000 para 5.16 and see *R v Blundeston Board of Visitors ex p Fox Taylor* [1982] 1 All ER 646.

68 *R (Lake) v Governor of Highdown Prison* [2007] EWHC 3080 (Admin).

69 PSO 2000 para 5.13.

70 PSO 2000 para 3.4.

each hearing, and issues may even arise during a hearing that necessitate the consideration of assistance for the prisoner.

9.47    Legal representation involves an advocate appearing for the prisoner in person at the hearing. Legal advice will normally require an adjournment for a prisoner to contact a lawyer for guidance on how they should conduct their defence themselves. A McKenzie friend is someone to attend the hearing not formally to represent them but to assist by taking notes, giving advice and making suggestions as to how to challenge evidence.

9.48    Where a charge is referred to an IA, then there is a right to legal representation. This does not mean that the prisoner will never have a right to representation in cases heard by a governor and there remains discretion to allow representation at governors' hearings. The courts have set down guidelines on what governors should take into account in making such a decision[71] and governors must consider the following factors which are known as the *Tarrant* criteria:

1) the seriousness of the charge;
2) whether any points of law are likely to arise;
3) the capacity of the prisoner to present his or her own case;
4) whether or not there are likely to be any procedural difficulties;
5) the need for reasonable speed in hearing the charge; and
6) the need for fairness as between prisoners and between prisoners and prison staff.

9.49    PSO 2000 has included an additional catch-all consideration: any other matter that the prisoner raises that might be relevant as to the grant of legal representation[72] which reflects that the *Tarrant* criteria should not be seen as exhaustive. In practice, it is very rare for governor's to grant representation especially as the more serious charges are referred to an IA.

9.50    The governor is required to ask the prisoner whether he or she wants legal representation and to record this request and reasons for refusal on the record of the hearing.[73] Perhaps the most important category of prisoners to whom this decision will remain important is those serving indeterminate sentences. As explained above (paras 9.30–9.31), these prisoners cannot be given additional days as punishment and so on the face of the Rules cannot have their cases referred to an IA. The grant of representation under the *Tarrant* criteria therefore remains important for lifers whose charges are not so serious as

71  *R v Secretary of State for the Home Department ex p Tarrant* [1984] 1 All ER 799.
72  PSO 2000 para 3.12.
73  PSO 2000 para 3.11.

to engage article 6. Representation should be sought where either the charge itself is serious, or where a finding of guilt will have severe consequences (for example if an allegation relevant to the lifer's risk factors arises which may jeopardise a parole hearing), or where the prisoner is particularly vulnerable. If legal representation is granted under the *Tarrant* criteria for a hearing before a governor then, as with hearings before an IA, public funding in the form of advocacy assistance is available.

9.51     Exceptionally, where legal representation is permitted before a governor, the Prison Service may also choose to be represented. This will normally be reserved for cases where there are complex points of law or procedural difficulties. In such circumstances the prison will contact Treasury Solicitors to arrange representation.[74]

9.52     If a request for a McKenzie friend is made then such requests should also be made by reference to the *Tarrant* criteria above. Any refusal should be recorded with reasons on the record of hearing. Governors are required to consider whether a McKenzie friend is 'suitable' (but the guidance is clear that there is nothing in principle to stop another prisoner, or a member of the public taking such a role).[75]

9.53     As a minimum, a prisoner should normally be allowed an adjournment at the first hearing of a charge to obtain legal advice where this is requested, or where a request for legal representation or a McKenzie friend has been refused. The hearing should not resume until the prisoner has had a reasonable opportunity to seek legal advice.[76] Where an adjournment is given for a solicitor to provide legal advice it will be important to request disclosure of all evidence to be used in the hearing.

## Adjournments

9.54     Adjournments of disciplinary hearings are very common. This might be necessary to enable a prisoner to seek legal advice. In many cases where the prisoner pleads not guilty, an adjournment may be necessary in order to secure the attendance of witnesses, to obtain further evidence or to arrange for an interpreter for to be present. PSO 2000 confirms that adjudicators 'must always offer an adjournment to the accused if it has been necessary to amend the detail of the charge or if the accused has misunderstood its nature'.[77]

74  PSO 2000 para 3.18.
75  PSO 2000 para 3.12.
76  PSO 2000 para 3.2.
77  PSO 2000 para 4.26.

9.55    If a number of adjournments are necessary, for example, where the reporting officer is sick or unavailable and the prisoner requires their attendance for cross examination then the governor must consider whether a prolonged adjournment 'endangers the requirement of being fair to the accused'.[78] In contrast with the statutory requirements as to when charges must be laid, and hearings commenced, there is no specific limit in the Rules on how long charges can be hanging over prisoners and sometimes it can be months before a charge is concluded. However, PSO 2000 does state that adjudicators must consider whether fairness has been compromised if a charge is adjourned for more than six weeks and if after that time the charge is proceeded with, a note must be made as to why the governor does consider that 'natural justice has not been compromised'.[79] The PSO also states that if a necessary witness is not available 'in a reasonable time' the charge should be dismissed.

9.56    Where legal representation is granted before the governor under the *Tarrant* criteria, it is acknowledged that there will be some delays and the PSO suggests that the hearing should be resumed no later than six weeks after the grant of representation and if the representatives are not ready then a further three weeks should be given. This guidance is subject to the requirement for governors to ensure that prisoners are given a proper opportunity to prepare their case.[80] This might mean that a prisoner is released before a charge is heard if it has not been possible to hold a fair hearing before that date.

9.57    Requests for adjournments in cases which have been referred to an IA must be made either at the hearing or to the Chief Magistrate's Office at Westminster Magistrate's Court.[81] There are dangers in assuming that an adjournment will be granted as due to the inquisitorial nature of the prison disciplinary system, IAs may decide that the interests of summary disposal outweigh concerns over fairness to the prisoner.[82]

9.58    Between adjournments, it can be difficult to ascertain any infor-

---

78  PSO 2000 para 4.26.
79  PSO 2000 para 4.39.
80  PSO 2000 para 4.27.
81  PSO 2000 para 13.9.
82  And similarly the judicial review court will look at whether the facts of the case really required an adjournment in deciding whether a decision to refuse one is flawed – in *R (Lashley) v Independent Adjudicator* [2008] EWHC 1853 (Admin) a trainee solicitor was refused an adjournment as the case 'did not require the skills of a Marshall-Hall' – the prisoner was given 25 additional days after a finding of guilt and the High Court did not interfere with this outcome.

mation from the prison or obtain responses to requests for disclosure. PSO 2000 suggests that where legal representation has not been granted that concerns raised by solicitors should be brought up by the prisoner at the hearing.[83] However, it is good practice to write to the prison (addressed to the governor) with disclosure requests promptly, and with any legal submissions where the client is not represented. These should also be copied to the prisoner so that they can present them at the hearing.

## Standard and burden of proof

9.59 Prison disciplinary charges must be proved to the criminal standard, that is, 'an adjudicator must be satisfied beyond reasonable doubt that the prisoner has committed the offence with which he or she is charged. Otherwise the charge must be dismissed, *regardless of how the prisoner has pleaded*'.[84] This reflects the long understanding that prison disciplinary charges, even before the courts considered that article 6 could apply to them, bear a 'close similarity' to criminal offences.[85] Despite prison disciplinary hearings retaining an inquisitorial character, it is not for the prisoner to prove his innocence and a finding of guilt can only be made when evidence sufficient to prove the charge is produced at the hearing (whether by the reporting officer or at the instigation of the adjudicator).

## Elements of the charges

9.60 Part 6 of PSO 2000 contains very detailed guidance on the elements of each charge that need to be established before guilt can be established to the requisite standard. This is summarised below. However, the guidance does have to be considered with caution. As the Rules are statutory their construction is for the courts and the policy as set out in PSO 2000 cannot determine their meaning.

9.61 When PSO 2000 was introduced in 2006, the executive summary stated that 'the prisoner's intent to commit an offence or recklessness are no longer among the criteria adjudicators must use to decide on guilt or innocence, except when these factors are included in the

83 PSO 2000 para 3.25.
84 PSO 2000 para 7.1.
85 See *R v Secretary of State for the Home Department and another ex p McConkey* (QBD, 20 September 1982, unreported), and in *Tarrant* (see above) the court commented that it had rightly been conceded that the criminal standard of proof applied.

wording of the relevant Prison or YOI Rules'. Previous guidance issued by the Prison Service[86] had suggested that intent or recklessness was a necessary element of charges, even where this was not included in the wording of the Rules. This does not impact on many charges where a mental element is either specified or is inherent due to the nature of the charge (such as assault). Other charges do raise problems – for example the charge of damaging property does not refer to intent or recklessness, whilst that relating to setting fire to property does. Certainly where charges have been referred to an IA it would appear to breach the presumption that criminal sanctions are not imposed without a mental element[87] for the Rules to be construed in accordance with PSO 2000 in this way.

9.62    Even where governors are hearing charges there is a strong argument that it is not lawful for sanctions to be applied under the disciplinary system when it is accepted that there was no intent to break to Rules or recklessness. There is authority that 'the rules which create these offences should ... be construed no more harshly against a prisoner than would be appropriate were the offences criminal'.[88] Prisoners and those advising them should always submit that, for example, a prisoner cannot be found guilty of disobeying a lawful order unless intention or recklessness as suggested by the Prison Service guidance that was in existence for more than ten years, even though this is not now set out in PSO 2000.

# The specific charges

9.63    The full list of disciplinary offences contained in the Rules[89] is as follows:

> A prisoner is guilty of an offence against discipline if he or she:
> *   commits any assault (PR rule 51(1)/YOIR rule 55(1));
> *   commits any racially aggravated assault (PR rule 51(1A)/YOIR rule 55(2));
> *   detains any person against his will (PR rule 51(2)/YOIR rule 55(3));

---

86  In the *Prison Discipline Manual* – first issued by the Prison Service in 1995.
87  *Sweet v Parsley* [1970] AC 132 – where a statutory provision creating a criminal offence is silent as to whether a mental element is required, this presumption requires the reading in of one.
88  *R v Secretary of State for the Home Department and another ex p McConkey* (QBD, 20 September 1982, unreported).
89  PR rules 51 and 55.

- deniesaccess to any part of the prison to any officer or any person (other than a prisoner) who is at the prison/young offender institution for the purpose of working there (PR rule 51(3)/YOIR rule 55(4));
- fights with any person (PR rule 51(4)/YOIR rule 55(5));
- intentionallyendangers the health or personal safety of others or, by his conduct, is reckless whether such health or personal safety is endangered (PR rule 51(5)/YOIR rule 55(6));
- intentionallyobstructs an officer in the execution of his duty, or any person (other than a prisoner) who is at the prison/young offender institution for the purpose of working there, in the performance of his work (PR rule 51(6)/YOIR rule 55(7));
- escapesor absconds from prison/a young offender institution or from legal custody (PR rule 51(7)/YOIR rule 55(8));
- failsto comply with any condition upon which he is temporarily released under PR rule 9/YOIR rule 5 (PR rule 51(8)/YOIR rule 55(9));
- isfound with any substance in his urine which demonstrates that a controlled drug has, whether in prison or while on temporary release under rule 9/rule 5, been administered to him by himself or by another person (but subject to rule PR rule 52/YOIR rule 56) (PR rule 51(9)/YOIR rule 55(10));
- isintoxicated as a consequence of consuming any alcoholic beverage (but subject to rule PR rule 52A/YOIR rule 56) (PR rule 51(10)/YOIR rule 55(11));
- consumesany alcoholic beverage whether or not provided to him by another person (but subject to rule PR rule 52A/YOIR rule 56A) (PR rule 51(11)/YOIR rule 55(12));
- has in his possession:
    (a) any unauthorised article, or
    (b) a greater quantity of any article than he is authorised to have (PR rule 51(12)/YOIR rule 55(13));
- sellsor delivers to any person any unauthorised article (PR rule 51(13)/YOIR rule 55(14));
- sells or, without permission, delivers to any person any article which he is allowed to have only for his own use (PR rule 51(14)/YOIR rule 55(15));
- takesimproperly any article belonging to another person or to a prison/young offender institution (PR rule 51(15)/YOIR rule 55(16));
- intentionallyor recklessly sets fire to any part of a prison/young offender insitution or any other property, whether or not his own (PR rule 51(16)/YOIR rule 55(17));
- destroysor damages any part of a prison/young offender institution or any other property, other than his own (PR rule 51(17)/YOIR rule 55(18));

- causesracially aggravated damage to, or destruction of, any part of a prison/young offender institution or any other property, other than his own (PR rule 51(17A)/YOIR rule 55(19));
- absentshimself from any place he is required to be or is present at any place where he is not authorised to be (PR rule 51(18)/YOIR rule 55(20));
- isdisrespectful to any officer, or any person (other than a prisoner) who is at the prison/young offender institution for the purpose of working there, or any person visiting a prison/young offender institution (PR rule 51(19)/YOIR rule 55(21));
- usesthreatening, abusive or insulting words or behaviour (PR rule 51(20)/YOIR rule 55(22));
- uses threatening, abusive or insulting racist words or behaviour (PR rule 51(20A)/YOIR rule 55(23));
- intentionally fails to work properly or, being required to work, refuses to do so (PR rule 51(21)/YOIR rule 55(24));
- disobeys any lawful order (PR rule 51(22)/YOIR rule 55(25));
- disobeysor fails to comply with any rule or regulation applying to him (PR rule 51(23)/YOIR rule 55(26));
- receivesany controlled drug, or, without the consent of an officer, any other article, during the course of a visit (not being an interview such as is mentioned in PR rule 38/YOIR rule 16) (PR rule 51(24)/YOIR rule 55(27));
- displays,attaches or draws on any part of a prison/young offender institution, or on any other property, threatening, abusive or insulting racist words, drawings, symbols or other material (PR rule 51(24A)/YOIR rule 55(28));
- (a) attempts to commit,
  (b) incites another prisoner to commit, or
  (c) assists another prisoner to commit or to attempt to commit, any of the foregoing offences (PR rule 51(25)/YOIR rule 55(29)).

9.64   Details of the individual charges, save for mandatory drug testing and use of alcohol which are dealt with separately are as follows.

### Commits an assault[90]

9.65   PSO 2000 states that alleged offences of murder, manslaughter, non-consensual buggery or rape, and threats to kill with apparent genuine intent should all be referred to the police. So should allegations:

- Involving use of a weapon causing, or likely to cause, serious injury.
- Where serious injury is caused.
- Where serious violence is used.

90  PR rule 51(1), YOIR rule 55(1).

- Involving sexual violation where there is use or threat of violence or the victim is especially vulnerable.[91]

9.66 The policy states that the kinds of assaults that should be referred to an IA are 'serious assaults'. Indicators of seriousness are the level of injury (such as fractures, breaking of skin and serious bruising), premeditation, a history of violence and the circumstances of the alleged assault.

9.67 Where the charge is heard by an adjudicator under the Rules, PSO 2000 states that a prisoner will be guilty of an assault is he or she applies unlawful force to another person, or – as under the criminal law – he or she causes another person to fear the application of immediate unlawful force. PSO 2000 states that this may be the correct charge where a prisoner spits on an officer, although where there is no physical contact the more appropriate charge would be use of threatening behaviour (see para 9.104 below). The adjudicator must be satisfied on the evidence that:

- Unlawful force was applied – or an act that led another person to fear immediate application of unlawful force was committed. Consent is not a defence.
- The force was unlawful – that is not reasonable force used in self-defence or to prevent the commission of serious crime. What is reasonable will vary according to the circumstances as the accused honestly believed them to be.[92]

## Commits any racially aggravated assault[93]

9.68 This charge requires the same elements as assault to be proved with the additional elements that:

- At the time of committing the offence, or immediately before or after doing so, the prisoner demonstrated towards the victim hostility based upon the victim's membership (or presumed membership) of a racial group (which means a group of persons defined by reference to race, colour, nationality (including citizenship) or ethnic or national origins).

---

91  PSO 2000 C12.
92  PSO 2000 para 6.16.
93  PR rules 51(1A) and 51A, YOIR rules 55(2) and 57 – the Rules state that 'racial group' and 'racially aggravated' have the same meaning as given by section 28 of the Crime and Disorder Act 1998 – definitions which are reflected in the PSO 2000 guidance.

- The offence is motivated (wholly or partly) by hostility towards members of a racial group based on their membership of that group.
- Membership of a racial group includes association with members of that group and 'presumed' membership means presumed by the accused.[94]

9.69   The guidance in PSO 2000 also states that where this charge is laid a charge should also be laid for plain assault on the assumption that if racial aggravation is not proved the prisoner could still be punished if assault is made out. The guidance on referral of this charge to the police or an IA is the same as for assault, although the guidance suggests generally that racial motivation will be a factor in favour of referral to an IA in relation to all charges.[95]

*Detains any person against his will[96]*

9.70   This charge is designed to deal with prisoners who take a hostage. The guidance states that this is a charge that will normally be referred to an IA.[97] The adjudicator must be satisfied that:

- The victim was detained (including in the open). This means freedom of movement must have been curtailed in some way by force or threat of force.
- The detention was against the victim's will. Collusion is therefore a defence (in which case the charge of denying access may be appropriate on the facts). However adjudicator's are advised to investigate whether there has been an attempt to pressurise the victim into saying they were colluding, and to recognise that initial collusion may develop into a situation where the victim is detained against their will.[98]
- This is a charge where previous Prison Service guidance suggested that intention to detain, or recklessness as to whether this would happen also needed to be proved. PSO 2000 has removed this requirement but for the reasons set out above this mental element should still be established before guilt can be established.

94   PSO 2000 paras 6.18–6.19.
95   PSO 2000 C.7.
96   PR rule 51(2), YOIR rule 55(3).
97   PSO 2000 N5.
98   PSO 2000 para 6.24.

### Denies access to any part of the prison to any officer or any person (other than a prisoner) who is at the prison for the purpose of working there[99]

9.71 This charge is designed to deal with barricades but is also appropriate, for instance, where the prisoner denies access without constructing a physical barrier. PSO 2000 suggests that this charge should be referred to an IA where denial of access goes beyond 'simple obstruction' (to conceal a larger offence such as drug exchange for example).

9.72 The adjudicator must be satisfied that:

- Access was denied.
- The site was part of a prison or YOI.
- The person denied access was an officer (which in this context means a prison governor, prison officer, chaplain, medical officer, controller, prison director or prisoner custody officer) or anyone else (other than a prisoner) who was at the establishment for the purpose of working there.[100]
- Again PSO 2000, contrary to previous guidance, states that intent or recklessness is not required to establish guilt but for the reasons set out above prisoners and their advisers should argue that this is still required.

### Fights with any person[101]

9.73 Governors are advised to consider referral of this charge to an IA in light of factors including where the fight took place, how many people were involved and the extent of any injuries.[102]

9.74 For this charge to be established the adjudicator must be satisfied

- The prisoner intentionally committed an assault by inflicting unlawful force on another person. Fighting is similar to assault or any other like charge in that self-defence is a complete defence. Similarly consent is not a defence.
- The assault must have been committed in the context of a fight with the other person. It is for the adjudicator to decide whether the conduct did or did not amount to a fight in the ordinary sense of that word. It is implicit in the idea of a fight that another person must also have been involved in events. This does not mean that

99 PR rule 51(3), YOIR rule 55(4).
100 PSO 2000.
101 PR rule 51(4), YOIR rule 55(5).
102 PSO 2000 N5.

the accused can be found guilty only if the other person is also found guilty. The other person may have a defence, for example acting in self-defence. But it does mean that the other person must have applied force, whether by one or more blows or forceful resistance, to the accused.[103]

*Intentionally endangers the health or personal safety of others or, by his conduct, is reckless whether such health or personal safety is endangered*[104]

9.75 Governors should consider referral of this charge to an IA where there is evidence of intent rather than recklessness, or where there was serious risk to others.[105]

9.76 The PSO suggests this charge may be suitable where a prisoner tampers with the electricity supply to wire up an appliance, but only where the criteria below are met. The guidance suggests that offences arising out of dirty protests may more appropriately be dealt with in the charge relating to damage to property (see para 9.99 below).

9.77 The adjudicator must be satisfied that:

- The health or personal safety of at least one person other than the accused was endangered. In other words there was a definite risk of harm to the health and safety of at least one specific person.
- The danger was caused by the accused's conduct.
- The accused intended this to occur, or was reckless as to whether it would.[106]

*Intentionally obstructs an officer in the execution of his duty, or any other person (other than a prisoner) who is at the prison for the purpose of working there, in the performance of his work*[107]

9.78 PSO 2000 suggests that this charge can cover both physical obstruction, but also situations where, for example, a prisoner provides false information. The PSO does not suggest that this is a charge that would normally be referred to an IA. The adjudicator must be satisfied:

- There was an obstruction of some sort, physical or otherwise.
- The person obstructed was an officer (defined in the same way as in the charge relating to denial of access above) or anyone else

103  PSO 2000 para 6.29.
104  PR rule 51(5), YOIR rule 55(6).
105  PSO 2000 N5.
106  PSO 2000 para 6.32.
107  PR rule 51(6), YOIR rule 55(7).

(other than a prisoner) who was at the prison for the purpose of working there.

- The officer was attempting to carry out his or her duty, or the person was attempting to perform his or her work.
- The accused intended such a person to be obstructed in such a way.[108] Due to the wording of the charge recklessness is insufficient to prove guilt for this charge.

## Escapes or absconds from prison or from prison or from legal custody[109]

9.79    The policy states that the following should be referred to the police:

- Alleged escapes, or attempted escapes from closed prisons or secure escort.
- Any other serious case where the means of escape have been found and referral is needed to discover how they were obtained and to prosecute those responsible.
- Escapes or absconds from open prison where the prisoner has been absent for a substantial period (normally over eight weeks), or where there have been determined efforts to avoid recapture.
- Where further offences are committed.
- Premeditation, deception of staff or previous escapes are aggravating factors which may justify referral.[110]

9.80    If the police decide to take no action in deciding whether to refer to an IA the governor should consider the level of physical security overcome in order to escape, and whether any injury or damage to property has been caused.[111]

9.81    This charge relates to getting 'clean away' from the prison. If the prisoner did not get beyond the boundary of the prison an attempt charge (see para 9.116 below) can be laid. If a prisoner in an open prison absents themselves with every intention of returning (the PSO gives the example of a prisoner buying something from a nearby shop) it is suggested that the charge of absenting themselves (see para 9.102 below) would be appropriate. The elements of the charge to be proved are that:

- The prisoner was held in prison or in legal custody including on escort or on a working party.

---

108  PSO 2000 para 6.35.
109  PR rule 51(7), YOIR rule 55(8).
110  PSO 2000 C13-15.
111  PSO 2000 N5.

- The prisoner escaped or absconded. The charge should detail how it is alleged that the prisoner did this, not just rehearse the words of the charge.
- The prisoner had no lawful authority to do what he or she did. The governor's authorisation to leave the prison, or the control of an officer, will be a defence.
- The prisoner intended to escape. It must be shown that the prisoner knew they were leaving lawful custody without lawful authority. It is a defence if the prisoner genuinely believed that they had authority to go where they did.[112]

### Fails to comply with any condition upon which he is temporarily released[113]

9.82    Charges under this rule must relate to specific conditions in the licence granting temporary release. It is therefore important that the licence makes clear what is expected of the prisoner, and that any alleged misconduct was a breach of the conditions before a charge is laid.[114]

9.83    Remaining unlawfully at large after a period of release on temporary licence is a specific criminal offence.[115] PSO 2000 suggests that such cases should be referred to the police where the prisoner has been unlawfully at large for a substantial amount of time (normally over eight weeks), where there have been 'significant efforts' to avoid capture or where further offences have been committed.

9.84    Temporary licences should include a statement to be completed by a doctor if the prisoner states they were not fit to travel. This will provide a defence. A prisoner who is physically prevented from returning due to circumstances that were genuinely beyond their control will also have a defence.

9.85    All misconduct amounting to breaches of licence should be charged under this rule except allegations relating to consumption drugs or alcohol (see paras 9.124–9.156 below).

9.86    Before a prisoner can be found guilty the adjudicator must be satisfied that:

- A valid temporary release licence had been issued, its terms were clear and unambiguous and the prisoner was made aware of them. A copy of the licence, preferably the original, should be produced in evidence.

112  PSO 2000 para 6.38.
113  PR rule 51(8), YOIR rule 55(9).
114  PSO 2000 para 6.43.
115  Prisoners (Return to Custody) Act 1995 s1.

- The prisoner failed to comply with any one of the conditions. This includes the condition as to time of return.
- There was no justification for the failure to comply with any condition.[116]
- This is another charge where PSO 2000 has removed a reference to the need for intent or recklessness to be proved for a finding of guilt to be made.

### Has in his possession any unauthorised article or a greater quantity of any article than he is authorised to have[117]

9.87 PSO 2000 states that the possession of the following items should be referred to the police:

- Firearms, imitation firearms or explosives (manufactured or locally produced).
- Other offensive weapons if there is evidence to suggest that it was intended for use in the commission of a further serious offence (such as a serious assault or escape).[118]
- Where there is possession of Class A drugs with or without intent to supply. In relation to Class B drugs possession with intent to supply unless this is small scale for no payment. Possession of small quantities of Class B drugs or possession or supply of Class C drugs should not normally be referred.

9.88 In other cases governors are advised to consider the nature of the article in deciding whether to refer the case to an IA.[119]

9.89 This charge is designed to deal both with items which are by their nature unauthorised (such as weapons or drugs), and with items which, although not prohibited are not authorised to be in the possession of the particular prisoner. A prisoner's property will be all recorded on their property card.

9.90 The following elements of the charge must be proved:

- *Presence*: the article exists, it is what it is alleged to be and is found where it is so alleged.[120] If the charge is of possession a controlled drug and the prisoner pleads not guilty on the basis that the item is something else then the adjudicator may need to send it off for

---

116 PSO 2000 para 6.45.
117 PR rule 51(12), YOIR rule 55(13).
118 PSO 2000 C16.
119 PSO 2000 N5.
120 Although PSO 2000 states the item should be produced in evidence see para 9.159 below.

forensic analysis.[121] However in other circumstances an adjudicator may not require expert evidence to determine the nature of the article.[122]

- *Knowledge*: the prisoner knew of the presence of the article and its nature. Knowledge of its nature can be properly inferred from all the circumstances. The guidance states that it is good practice for a reporting officer to question the prisoner as soon as an article is found so that the immediate reaction to its presence can be presented in evidence.
- *Control*: the accused exercised sole or joint control over the article. A prisoner who drops or throws away an article simply because they believe that it is about to be discovered may still be guilty of possession at an earlier stage if there is sufficient evidence that it was in their control before it was abandoned.[123]

9.91    A genuine belief that the article was authorised or that there were no restrictions on quantity allowed in possession will be a defence. The reasonableness of such a belief may go to the prisoner's credibility.

### Sells or delivers to any person any unauthorised article[124]

9.92    The guidance on referral of charges under this rule to an IA is the same as for possession of unauthorised articles.

9.93    The adjudicator must be satisfied:

- The article was sold or delivered by the accused to another person. The person to whom the article was sold or delivered does not have to be a prisoner.
- The item was unauthorised.
- A genuine belief, the reasonableness of which may go to credibility, that the accused was authorised to dispose of the item in that way would be a defence.[125] Again reference to a requirement of intent or recklessness in relation to this charge was removed from the guidance when PSO 2000 was introduced.

---

121  PSO 2000 para 6.6.
122  In *R (Gibson) v Governor of HMP Garth* [2002] EWHC 1429 (Admin) – the court held that a governor was entitled to conclude that a bottle contained fermenting liquid by smelling it on the basis that this was analysing, rather than providing, evidence.
123  PSO 2000 para 6.70 – the requirement for control over the item was established in *R v Deputy Governor of Camphill ex p King* [1985] QB 735 which confirmed that a prisoner in a shared cell should not be found guilty of possession merely due to knowledge of the item's presence.
124  PR rule 51(13), YOIR rule 55(14).
125  PSO 2000 para 6.75.

### Sells or, without permission delivers to any person any article which he is allowed to have only for his own use[126]

9.94 Governors are advised by PSO 2000 to refer charges under this Rule to an IA where the article is sold or delivered under duress.[127] The adjudicator must be satisfied:

- The item was sold or delivered to another.
- The item was allowed only for the prisoner's own use.
- In the case of delivering, that the prisoner did not have permission.
- A genuine belief, the reasonableness of which may go to credibility, that the item was not only for their own use, or that they had permission to deliver it, would be a defence.[128] Again the need to establish intent or recklessness for this charge was removed from the guidance when PSO 2000 was introduced.

### Takes improperly any article belonging to another person or to a prison or YOI[129]

9.95 This charge is analogous to theft. PSO 2000 states that where a theft is accompanied by the use or threat of serious violence or of a weapon (thereby amounting to a robbery) that this should be referred to the police.[130] The guidance on referral to an IA states that this should normally occur if the article was taken under duress.[131]

9.96 The adjudicator if considering the charge must be satisfied:

- There was an article.
- The article belonged to another person or to a prison.
- The accused assumed physical control of the article.
- The article was taken improperly. This means that the accused did not have permission to take it.
- It will be a defence to a charge under this paragraph that the accused genuinely believed, the reasonableness of which belief may go to credibility, they owned the article or had permission to take it.[132] Again the need to establish intent or recklessness for

---

126 PR rule 51(14), YOIR rule 55(15).
127 PSO 2000 N5.
128 PSO 2000.
129 PR rule 51(15), YOIR rule 55(16).
130 PSO 2000 C21.
131 PSO 2000 N5.
132 PSO 2000 para 6.81.

this charge was removed from the guidance when PSO 2000 was introduced.

### Intentionally or recklessly sets fire to any part of a prison or YOI or any other property, whether or not his own[133]

9.97   The PSO states that allegations that amount to arson should normally be referred to the police unless it is clear that there was little or no risk of the fire taking hold.[134] If not referred to the police the governor should consider in deciding whether to refer to an IA the seriousness of the fire, the level of damage and the history of the prisoner.[135] However the guidance also reminds governors that cell fires may be evidence of a prisoner in a vulnerable or suicidal state of mind, and so may be examples of conduct that should not be punished under the disciplinary system (see para 9.22 above).

9.98   The adjudicator must be satisfied:

- The prisoner set fire to a part of an establishment or other property.
- The prisoner intended to set fire to the property, or was reckless as to whether this would happen.

### Destroys or damages any part of a prison or YOI or any other property, other than his own[136]

9.99   This charge is obviously analogous to the offence of criminal damage. The guidance states that allegations should be referred to the police only in very serious cases, normally to a value of in excess of £2,000. Evidence of concerted action by a group of prisoners strengthens the case for referral.[137] In other cases the governor is advised to consider the seriousness of the damage in deciding whether to refer the charge to an IA.[138]

9.100  The guidance does suggest that this may be an appropriate charge in relation to a dirty protest (as cleaning the cell will take time and incur expenditure). In all cases the adjudicator must be satisfied:

- Part of the prison/YOI or other property was destroyed or damaged.

133  PR rule 51(16), YOIR rule 55(17).
134  PSO 2000 C19.
135  PSO 2000 N5.
136  PR rule 51(17), YOIR rule 55(18).
137  PSO 2000 C19.
138  PSO 2000 N5.

- The property did not belong to the prisoner.
- There was no lawful excuse to damage the property.
- That the article was damaged by the prisoner and that guilt is not determined merely on the basis of being in possession of a damaged article or is in occupation of a damaged cell.
- A genuine belief that the prisoner owned the property or was entitled to damage it (the reasonableness of which may go to credibility) will be a defence.[139] Again the need to establish intent or recklessness for this charge was removed from the guidance when PSO 2000 was introduced.

### Causes racially aggravated damage to any part of a prison or YOI or any other property, other than his own[140]

9.101   The elements of this charge and guidance on referral to the police or an IA are the same as for the previous charge, although clearly the level of racial aggravation will be a relevant factor. Racial aggravation is defined in the same way as for the charge of racially aggravated assault (see para 9.68 above). As with that charge the guidance states that the non-racially aggravated version of this charge should be laid at the same time.[141]

### Absents himself from any place where he is required to be or is present at any place where he is not authorised to be[142]

9.102   The guidance suggests that this charge can relate to conduct both inside and outside the prison (if for example a prisoner in an open prison goes without permission to a local shop with every intention of returning). The adjudicator must be satisfied:

- The accused was required to be in a particular place or was not authorised to be in the place where they was found. It will be important to be able to show that any local instructions to prisoners have been communicated.
- The prisoner was absent from the place they were required to be in, or were present at the place they were not authorised to be in.
- The prisoner had no justification for their actions.
- Genuine belief of justification will be a defence although the reasonableness of that belief may go to credibility.[143] Again references

139  PSO 2000 para 6.86.
140  PR rule 51(17A), YOIR rule 55(19).
141  PSO 2000 para 6.91.
142  PR rule 51(18), YOIR rule 55(20).
143  PSO 2000 para 6.94.

to the need to establish intent or recklessness were removed from the guidance on the issuing of PSO 2000.

### Is disrespectful to any officer, or any person (other than a prisoner) who is at the prison for the purpose of working there, or any person visiting a prison[144]

9.103    The guidance states that this charge can cover verbal, written or physical acts, although clearly such conduct of any seriousness will more likely be charged under the charge below. The adjudicator must be satisfied:

- There was an act.
- The disrespect was directed towards a specific individual or group.
- The act was disrespectful in the ordinary meaning of the term.
- The person to whom the act was disrespectful was an officer (see para 9.72 above) or anyone else (other than a prisoner) who was at the prison for the purpose of working there, or a visitor to the prison.
- A genuine belief that, for example, the conduct was not disrespectful will be a defence.[145] This is another charge where PSO 2000 removed any reference to the need to establish intent or recklessness.

### Uses threatening, abusive or insulting words or behaviour[146]

9.104    Unlike the charge above, it is not necessary with this charge to determine whether the conduct was directed at anyone in particular. Governors are advised to consider referral to an IA where words and/or behaviour are threatening, and all conduct which is racially aggravated.

9.105    The adjudicator must be satisfied:

- The prisoner performed a specific act or adopted a general pattern of behaviour or said specific words. This need not be a single incident as in the above specimen but may have continued over a period of time.
- The act, pattern of behaviour or words was either threatening, abusive or insulting. These terms should be given their ordinary meanings, taking account of the circumstances of the case. It

144  PR rule 51(19), YOIR rule 55(21).
145  PSO 2000 para 6.97.
146  PR rule 51(20), YOIR rule 55(22).

should be borne in mind that words or behaviour might be annoying or rude without necessarily being abusive or insulting. To find guilt it is only necessary to be satisfied that a reasonable person at the scene would consider the words or behaviour threatening, abusive or insulting.[147]

- Again the need to establish intent or recklessness for this charge was removed from the guidance when PSO 2000 was introduced.

### Uses threatening, abusive or insulting racist words or behaviour[148]

9.106 This rule creates a racially aggravated version of the above charge. In addition to the above elements the words and behaviour must be racist, which means racially aggravated (see the definition of racially aggravated assault above). As with the other racially aggravated charges staff are advised to also charge the prisoner with the non-aggravated version.

### Intentionally fails to work properly or, being required to work, refuses to do so[149]

9.107 The elements of the charge of failing to work properly that need to be proved are that:

- The prisoner was lawfully required to work (for example remand prisoners cannot be made to work) at the time and in the circumstances specified.
- The prisoner failed to work properly as measured against a standard.
- A genuine belief, the reasonableness of which may go to credibility, that the work was adequate would be a defence to this charge.[150]

9.108 The elements of the charge relating to refusal to work are that:

- The prisoner was lawfully required to work as above.
- The prisoner refused to work.
- A genuine belief that the prisoner was not required to work there and then would be a defence to this charge.[151]

---

147  PSO 2000 para 6.100.
148  PR rule 51(20A), YOIR rule 55(23).
149  PR rule 51(21), YOIR rule 55(24).
150  PSO 2000 para 6.108.
151  PSO 2000 para 6.109.

9.109   If the prisoner claims to have been medically certified unfit to carry out the work he or she is required to do, care must be taken to investigate fully such a defence. If the prisoner claims to have been unfit to carry out such work but has not been medically certified as unfit the adjudicator is still advised to seek evidence on the point. Again PSO 2000 has removed reference to intent and recklessness from the guidance in relation to this charge. If the prisoner refuses to attend the place of work the correct charge is that relating to absenting themselves from where they are required to be (see above).

### Disobeys any lawful order[152]

9.110   PSO 2000 advises governors to consider referring charges under this Rule to an IA where the refusal relates to searching or other control issues. For refusals to provide a urine sample for a mandatory drug test see below.

9.111   The guidance states that a lawful order is one which is reasonable and which a member of staff has authority to give in the execution of their duties. The adjudicator must be satisfied:

- The action of a member of staff amounted to an order. An order is a clear indication by word and/or action given in the course of their duties by a member of prison staff requiring a specific prisoner to do or refrain from doing something. It will normally, but does not have to be, issued verbally.
- The order was lawful. The adjudicator should establish the lawful basis for the order (for example whether there was in fact good reason to require the prisoner to submit to a squat search,[153] or whether a random MDT was genuinely random[154]).
- The prisoner did not comply with the order. Even if a prisoner eventually complies with an order, there may nevertheless be sufficient evidence to find them guilty where the adjudicator can be satisfied that the prisoner deliberately delayed compliance.
- The prisoner must have understood what was being required of them.[155]
- Again the need to establish intent or recklessness for this charge was removed from the guidance when PSO 2000 was introduced.

152  PR rule 51(22), YOIR rule 55(25).
153  See the facts of *R (Carroll and another) v Secretary of State for the Home Department* [2005] 1 WLR 688.
154  *R v Secretary of State for the Home Department ex p Russell* [2000] EWHC 366 (Admin).
155  PSO 2000 para 6.114.

## *Disobeys or fails to comply with any rule or regulation applying to him*[156]

9.112   This charge can cover breaches of the Prison Rules, but is more particularly designed to enforce local rules that might be issued by a prison, such as one stating that prisoners must not tamper with electric fittings by wiring up an appliance to the mains supply. The adjudicator must be satisfied:

- The rule or regulation applied to the prisoner. They must have been aware of the rule or regulation or reasonable steps must have been taken to make them aware. A genuine belief, reasonably held, that the rule or regulation did not apply to the prisoner in question would be a defence to this charge. A breach of compact is not, in itself, a breach of a rule.
- The rule or regulation was lawful. Lawful has the same meaning as it does in relation to orders.
- The prisoner did not comply with the rule or regulation.[157]
- Again the need to establish intent or recklessness for this charge was removed from the guidance when PSO 2000 was introduced.

## *Receives any controlled drug, or, without the consent of an officer, any other article, during the course of a visit (not being a legal visit)*[158]

9.113   PSO 2000 states that charges under this rule involving large quantities of drugs, or small quantities of Class A drugs, or lethal weapons should normally be referred to the IA.[159] Where the drug or article is discovered after the visit but not in the visits or searching areas, or there is some doubt the article was received during the visit then the charge of possession of an unauthorised article will be used. CCTV evidence may however that the drug or article was received during the visit. The charge can cover articles being passed from prisoner to prisoner as long as this takes place during the course of the visit.

9.114   The adjudicator must be satisfied:

- That the prisoner received a controlled drug or other article during the course of the visit.
- That the prisoner knew the controlled drug or article existed.

156  PR rule 51(23), YOIR rule 55(26).
157  PSO 2000 para 6.117.
158  PR rule 51(24), YOIR rule 55(27).
159  PSO 2000 N5.

- That the prisoner knew they did not have permission to have that article.
- It must be established that the prisoner knew they did not have permission to accept such an article from their visitor. A genuine belief by the prisoner that permission had been granted to have that article (not being a controlled drug) would be a defence to the charge.

### Displays, attaches to or draws on any part of a prison threatening, abusive or insulting racist words, drawings, symbols or other material[160]

9.115  This charge is primarily directed at racist graffiti. The definition of racist is the same as elsewhere in the Rules. The adjudicator must be satisfied:

- The prisoner either drew, displayed, circulated or attached the material (or words) set out in the charge.
- The displayed, or circulated material was threatening, abusive or insulting (which have the same meaning as when referring to behaviour) and racist (as defined in para 9.68 above).
- A genuine belief, the reasonableness of which may go to credibility, that the behaviour was not racially insulting or abusive would be a defence to this charge.[161]

### Attempts to commit; incites another prisoner to commit; or assists another prisoner to commit any of the foregoing offences[162]

9.116  This rule must be used in conjunction with one of the primary offences under the rules. The elements of attempting are that:

- The prisoner did an act, which was more than merely preparatory to the commission of the intended offence.
- The prisoner intended to commit the full offence.[163]

9.117  The elements of inciting are that:

- The prisoner's action was communicated to other prisoners. It is necessary to show that other prisoners were sufficiently near to be able to react to the incitement.

---

160  PR rule 51(24A), YOIR rule 55(28).
161  PSO 2000 para 6.126.
162  PR rule 51(25), YOIR rule 55(29).
163  PSO 2000 para 6.130.

- The act was capable of inciting other prisoners to commit the full offence. Incitement in this context means seeking to persuade another prisoner to commit a disciplinary offence.
- The full offence was either the subject of the incitement or the consequence of it.[164]
- PSO has removed guidance which states that the prisoner must have intended to incite or was reckless.

9.118 The elements of assisting are that:

- Another prisoner committed an offence. This may include an attempt. However it will be a defence that the other prisoner was found not guilty of the substantive offence.
- The prisoner actively assisted in the commission of the offence.
- The prisoner intended to assist the other prisoner.

# Offences relating to drug and alcohol misuse

## Mandatory drug testing (MDT)

9.119 There are a number of different circumstances in which prisoners can be tested for drugs:

- Testing for clinical purposes – this can only be undertaken by healthcare staff with the informed consent of the prisoner. The purpose of such testing is to determine appropriate treatment and the results should be confidential. Such testing cannot of course give rise to any disciplinary charge.
- Voluntary drug tests – these may be undertaken as part of a compact. The prisoner's informed consent is required. The results of voluntary testing cannot form the basis of a disciplinary charge,[165] the sanction for positive tests may be exclusion from the compact and/or other administrative measures specified in the compact.
- Mandatory drug tests (MDTs) carried out under the provisions of the Prison Act and the Rules which allow for them are the only tests the outcome of which can form the basis of disciplinary charges.[166]

---

164 PSO 2000 para 6.132.
165 PSO 2000 para 6.48, PSO 3601 para 8.10.
166 PSO 3601 para 2.1.

## Legal authority for MDT tests

9.120    Mandatory drug tests were introduced to the prison system in 1995.[167] The Prison Act 1952 was amended to include a provision to require prisoners to submit to tests. The Act states that where an authorisation, issued by the governor, is in force any officer 'may, at the prison, in accordance with prison rules, require any prisoner who is confined in the prison to provide a sample of urine for the purpose of ascertaining whether he has any drug in his body'.[168] The Act also allows samples other than urine specified in the authorisation to be required, but not intimate samples apart from urine (so saliva, hair and sweat can be taken, but not blood). In practice prisons and YOIs generally only use urine sampling for MDT purposes.

9.121    The requirement in the Prison Act for a governor's authorisation to be in place before MDTs are introduced means that a formal notice must be signed by the governor and published – a copy should be displayed in the MDT suite and a copy may be placed in the library.[169]

## MDT procedures

9.122    The prison and young offender institution rules contain further provisions on the procedures to be adopted.[170] These provisions state that the officer taking the sample should:

- So far as is reasonably practicable to inform the prisoner that they are required to provide a sample and that a refusal to provide a sample may lead to disciplinary proceedings.[171]
- Require the prisoner to provide a fresh, unadulterated sample.

9.123    The Rules allow for prisoners to be kept apart from other prisoners for up to an hour for provision of the sample to be facilitated, or up to a maximum of five hours if the prisoner is unable to provide a sample. The Rules specify that prisoners should be afforded a level of privacy compatible with the need to 'detect any adulteration or falsification of the sample' and that they should not be required to provide a sample within the sight of an officer of the opposite sex.

---

167 An early challenge asserting that MDT procedures in themselves breached either articles 3 or 8 of the ECHR fell at the admissibility stage – *Galloway v UK* Application no 34199/96, 9 September 1998.

168 PA 1952 s16A.

169 PSO 3601 paras 5.14–5.15.

170 PR rule 50, YOIR rule 53.

171 The appropriate charge in these circumstances is of refusing a lawful order.

## The charge

9.124   The Rules contain a specific disciplinary charge of:

> *Is found with any substance in his urine which demonstrates that a controlled drug has, whether in prison or while on temporary release under rule 9, been administered to him by himself or by another person.*[172]

This charge is subject to specific statutory defences (see below). PSO 2000 suggests that this charge will normally be referred to an IA.[173]

9.125   Detailed policy guidance is contained in PSO 3601 on how MDT procedures should be implemented in practice. This states that prisons or YOIs with populations of 400 or more must randomly test at least five per cent of their population each month, and those with populations of less at least 10 per cent. Prisoners must be given information about MDTs on reception. All prisoners may required to provide an MDT unless medically unfit, including remand prisoners and those detained solely under the Immigration Act.

## Types of mandatory drug testing

9.126   The PSO sets out five circumstances in which the power to test under the Rules should be exercised:

- *Random testing*: prisoners should be selected randomly using lists generated by the LIDS[174] computer. The system runs once a month to generate a set percentage of prisoners to be tested.[175]
- *Testing on reasonable suspicion*: the guidance states that care must be taken to prevent abuse of authority, and that past drug misuse cannot give rise to reasonable suspicion of current misuse. Examples of valid reasons for requiring a prisoner to provide a sample under this head include recent unexplained or unpredictable behaviour, intelligence, discovery of drugs in an area over which the prisoner has some access or control and discovery of

---

172  PR rule 51(9), YOIR rule 55(10) – these Rules were amended in 2005 to include the reference to release on temporary licence. Prior to this if prisoners tested positive for drugs on return to the prison from a period on temporary licence it would not be possible to determine whether the drug was taken in prison, or on licence in the community. This meant that if the prisoner pleaded not guilty that guilt could not be established of either taking drugs in prison or of breaching licence conditions. The changes to the Rules removed this loophole.

173  PSO 2000 N5.

174  The Local Inmate Database System.

175  PSO 3601 paras 4.4–4.21.

drug contaminants or urine intended for use in falsifying tests. A prisoner must not be targeted for an test under this head purely as a result of approaching a member of staff for help for a drug problem, or as a result of a positive voluntary test (unless there is perceived to be a significant risk to the health or safety of the prisoner or public, for example where a prisoner is due to be temporarily released to operate machinery). Voluntary testing compacts should indicate the circumstances in which failure of a voluntary test might give rise to an MDT on suspicion.[176]

- *Risk assessment*: this includes testing before prisoners are given access to release on temporary licence, before allocation to outside working parties, as part of the recategorisation process, or before being given employment involving the operation of machinery.[177]
- *Frequent testing programme*: the guidance states that prisoners who test positively and have a finding of guilt for a class A drug, and those who have been found guilty more than once for a drug offence may be considered for frequent testing. Decisions to subject prisoners to frequent testing must be reviewed at regular intervals and at least every month.[178]
- *Testing on reception*: the guidance suggests this is a way of reinforcing the message that use of drugs will not be tolerated by the prison, and may also be used to assist the design of local strategies to combat drug use. Women prisoners cannot be located in a mother and baby unit without providing a negative MDT.[179]

## When are prisoners not required to provide MDTs?

9.127 PSO 2000 recognises that on health grounds prisoners may be excluded from testing if they are unfit to attend the drug testing area.[180] Other reasons prisoners may have for objecting to being tested raise more complicated issues. Prisons are advised to be pragmatic about prisoners assessed as dangerous – in some circumstances they may be too dangerous to themselves or staff to be included.

9.128 Pregnant women will not automatically be excluded from testing although those who have problems in providing a sample in later stages of pregnancy must not be held in confinement cells for

176 PSO 3601 paras 4.22–4.27.
177 PSO 3601 paras 4.33–4.36.
178 PSO 3601 paras 4.33–4.46.
179 PSO 3601 paras 4.47–4.59.
180 PSO 3601 para 4.62.

extended periods.[181] Similarly menstruation will not be considered as a reason not to provide a sample. As the procedures for taking a sample do not involve staff viewing of genitalia Prison Service advice is that there is no reason for exempting prisoners on religious grounds from testing. However such cases will need to be considered on an individual basis if a prisoner does refuse to provide a sample on religious grounds.[182] Observance of Ramadan does raise issues as Muslim prisoners cannot drink water if they are unable to provide a sample. Advice is that such prisoners should be scheduled for testing first in the day, and that if they cannot provide a sample after four hours that they should be released from the requirement to produce a sample.[183]

## Taking the sample

9.129 MDTs must only be taken at a designated collection site with sufficient space and facilities for the key stages of the process. These include an area for holding prisoners prior to testing, an area for searching, an area for provision of samples and a place for maintenance and storage of records.[184] Prisoners should be given a clear order to go to the collection site to provide a sample and have the reason for testing explained to them before being escorted there.[185] The order to provide a sample is a single order comprising both the requirement to attend the collection site and when there, to provide a sample.[186]

9.130 When prisoners arrive at the collection site they should be provided with the mandatory drug authorisation form. This formally informs the prisoner of the legal authority for the test, who authorised the test, which of the five grounds for taking a sample applies and the consequences of failing to provide a sample. The form also asks the prisoner to consent to disclosure of medical records for so that positive results due to prescribed medication can be identified.[187]

9.131 Prisoners will be searched before being required to provide a sample. The type of search will depend on what is considered

---

181  PSO 3601 para 4.62.
182  PSO 3601 paras 4.64–4.69.
183  PSO 3601 paras 4.70–4.74.
184  PSO 3601 chapter 5.
185  PSO 3601 para 6.9.
186  *R (Russell) v Secretary of State for the Home Department and others* [2000] EWHC 366 (Admin) – in this case the Prison Service sought to argue that there were two distinct orders involved.
187  PSO 3601 appendix 2.

necessary in the particular prison to prevent adulteration of samples, but strip searches are usual.[188] If there is reasonable suspicion that a male prisoner has secreted an item in the anal or genital area, he may be required to squat as part of a search. Women prisoners must not be asked to squat.[189] The prisoner will then be asked to wash their hands to remove any potential contaminants.[190]

9.132      The prisoner is asked to provide a sample and should be shown the collection cup. The sample should be at least 35 millitres of urine[191] although where the prisoner has problems in providing a sample as long as there is sufficient urine to place the minimum 15 millilitres in the two containers then this may be accepted.[192] The Rules require prisoners to be given such privacy as is compatible with the process. PSO 3601 suggests that officers should not directly observe prisoners providing a sample.[193]

9.133      Where prisoners cannot immediately provide a sample they can be confined for up to five hours. Four hours should be allowed initially and if a sample still cannot be provided, that the fifth hour should be allowed unless the prisoner is 'blatantly uncooperative'.[194] They should be provided with a third of a pint of water at the beginning of each hour. Prisoners should be asked if they wish to discuss their inability to provide a sample with the healthcare department.[195]

9.134      If a prisoner refuses to attend the collection site or refuses to provide a sample or, where the officers are satisfied that the prisoner is being blatantly uncooperative, a charge of disobeying a lawful order can be laid even if the four-hour time period has not elapsed.

9.135      Immediately after the sample is provided, the prisoner should be asked to wash their hands again. The sample should then be checked for adulteration or dilution. The temperature of the sample should be checked immediately using the temperature strip on the sample container to confirm that the sample was freshly provided as required by the Rules. The sample should be within the range of 32–38 degrees Centigrade.[196] Staff are also advised to take account of the smell and

188  PSO 3601 para 6.15.
189  PSO 3601 para 6.17.
190  PSO 3601 para 6.20.
191  PSO 3601 para 6.22 although there is discretion where the prisoner has difficulty in providing a sample.
192  PSO 3601 para 6.41.
193  PSO 3601 para 6.27.
194  PSO 3601 para 6.65.
195  PSO 3601 paras 6.51–6.54.
196  PSO 3601 para 6.99.

appearance of the sample in order to check for adulteration. Samples should only be rejected outright by staff when the temperature check has failed. In other circumstances, even where staff strongly believe that the sample has been adulterated or diluted, it should still be sent to the laboratory.[197]

9.136　　The sample is split into two tubes which are then sealed and marked with a bar code that matches that on the chain of custody form. The code will then be referred to on the results given by the laboratory. The prisoner is asked to sign the chain of custody form to confirm that they have witnessed that the procedures have been properly followed. One of the samples is forwarded to the testing laboratory and one remains available for the prisoner to obtain and independent test.

## The screening test

9.137　The analysis of samples is a two stage process. The screening test is an initial test using a process called enzyme immunoassay. The laboratory will provide a screening certificate where the test is positive. Tests will be negative if the levels detected are less than the cut-offs set out in the table below. There are standard wordings for samples that are assessed as adulterated or so dilute as to be inconsistent with human urine (the latter relying upon analysis of specific gravity and creatinine levels).[198]

9.138　　The screening test result will be either faxed or emailed to the prison within 48 hours of receipt by the laboratory. Prisoners should be informed of the result. If the test is positive, the receipt by the prison of the faxed screening certificate is treated as the discovery of the offence for the purposes of the charge having a controlled drug in a urine sample. Prisoners should therefore be charged within 48 hours of receipt.[199] The only exception to this is if the test is positive for opiates or amphetamines.

9.139　　This test is not sufficiently reliable to allow prisoners to be found guilty where they have pleaded not guilty. Even in cases where the prisoner has pleaded guilty, confirmation tests should be sought where opiates, amphetamines or other class A drugs have been detected, or where the case has been referred to an IA.[200]

197　PSO 3601 para 6.110.
198　PSO 3601 para 7.3.
199　PSO 2000 para 6.49 and PSO 3601 para 7.26.
200　PSO 3601 paras 7.1–7.17.

| Drug | Screening test nanograms per mililitre | Confirmation test nanograms per mililitre |
|---|---|---|
| Amphetamine | 1,000 | 250 |
| Barbiturates | 200 | 200 |
| Benzodiazepines | 200 | 200 |
| Buprenorphine | 10 | 2 |
| Cannabinoids | 50 | 15 |
| Cocaine metabolite | 300 | 150 |
| LSD | 0.5 | 0.3 |
| Methadone | 300 | 300 |
| Opiates | 300 | 300 |
| 6-Monoacetylmorphine | 2 | 1 |

9.140   Commonly prescribed drugs can result in positive tests for these drugs. If a screening test is positive and the prisoner has not been receiving prescribed medication, they should be charged immediately as normal. If prisoner has been receiving medication that may have affected the test result, the charge can be laid immediately, or alternatively the prison can await the outcome of the confirmation test.[201] If the medication the prisoner is receiving is clearly consistent with the positive test result then the prisoner should not be charged.[202] The guidance in PSO 3601 contains very detailed provisions on precise responses to positive tests depending on the drug or combination of drugs detected.[203]

9.141   On receipt of the result the prison should also conduct a LIDS check to ascertain that the prisoner was in custody or on temporary licence at the time the drug was taken. This of course depends on how long particular drugs stay in the system. The Prison Service applies the following waiting periods and the charge will refer to the offence having been committed during this period.[204]

9.142   The waiting times are important for two main reasons. Firstly, if the drug could have been taken at a time when the prisoner was not either in prison custody or on temporary release then the prisoner

201  PSO 3601 para 7.29.
202  PSO 3601 para 7.37.
203  PSO 3601 Table 7.4.
204  PSO 3601 Table 8.1.

| Drug | Comment | Min waiting period (days) |
|---|---|---|
| Amphetamines | including ecstasy | 4 |
| Barbiturates | except Phenobarbital | 5 |
| | Phenobarbital | 30 |
| Benzodiazepines | | 30 |
| Buprenorphine | Temgesic/Subutex | 14 |
| Cannabis | | 30 |
| Cocaine | | 4 |
| Methadone | | 5 |
| LSD | | 3 |
| Opiates | morphine, codeine and Dihydrocodeine | 5 |
| | 6-MAM (consistent only with heroin) | 3 |

cannot be found guilty of the charge (for example the prisoner tests positive for cannabis seven days after arriving in prison from the community). Secondly a charge cannot be laid in respect of a positive test obtained during the waiting period following a previous positive test that has resulted in punishment as this risks punishing the prisoner twice for the same act (unless there has been an intervening negative test).

9.143    Where the prisoner has been in police custody or the custody of the court during the waiting period before the positive test, the guidance suggests that they may be charged even though these periods are not in prison custody on the basis that it may be evidentially possible to establish that the prisoner could not have taken a drug outside of prison custody (for example by obtaining the evidence of police officers).[205]

9.144    If the screening test suggests that the sample was adulterated or so dilute to be inconsistent with human urine then the prisoner should be charged with failing to obey a lawful order to provide a fresh, unadulterated sample of urine for the purposes of testing. This should be laid within 48 hours of the report being received. These samples will not be sent for a confirmation test.

205  PSO 3601 paras 8.11–8.12.

## The confirmation test

9.145    Where the prisoner at the first hearing of the charge pleads not guilty, or if the screening test is positive for Class A drugs,[206] a confirmation test will be obtained from the laboratory by faxing back the screening report. The Prison Service treats the confirmation test as 'definitive' as it uses more sophisticated technology than the screening test.[207] The confirmation test will normally take six days to be returned to the prison. The confirmation test will generate a report from the laboratory which will confirm whether the drug has been detected above the cut-off levels referred to above and whether the drug is consistent with any prescribed medication.

9.146    The confirmation certificate is documentary hearsay. However, when MDTs were first introduced it was held that it can form the basis of a finding of guilt, even if contested, without the laboratory scientist attending to give evidence on the basis that it is expert scientific evidence and so is an exception to the general rule prohibiting findings of guilt being based on hearsay evidence alone.[208] This does not mean that the adjudicator should always reject requests for the laboratory scientist to attend to give evidence, however, as there may be circumstances where fairness requires this, although the prisoner will need to explain exactly why the scientist needs to attend and what aspects of the evidence are contested.

## Findings of guilt

9.147    PSO 2000 states that before the adjudicator can make a finding of guilt the following must be established:

- A controlled drug was administered. There must have been no significant irregularities in the chain of custody procedures so that it can be confirmed that the sample provided by the accused was the one tested and is the one referred to in the test report presented to the adjudicator. It is for the adjudicator to decide what would amount to a significant irregularity.
- The controlled drug must have been taken at a time when the prisoner was subject to Prison or YOI Rules, including on temporary release. Correct dates entered in the particulars of the charge are therefore essential. The later date should be the date of collecting

---

206  PSO 2000 para 6.50.
207  The technique is either Gas Chromatography Mass Spectrometry, or Liquid Chromatography Mass Spectrometry.
208  *R v governor of HMP Swaleside ex p Wynter* [1998] EWHC 535 (Admin).

the sample and the former date should be the date of collection minus the minimum waiting period for the drug which tested positive.

- The prisoner has not been charged previously for misusing the same drug within a period of time which might mean that the current charge could have arisen from the same act of administration as the earlier charge.[209]

## Independent tests

9.148 The MDT sample is split into two so the prisoner can obtain an independent analysis of the sample. Procedures on obtaining an independent analysis are set out in Prison Service guidance and this also contains details of laboratories which can carry out independent tests (which cost about £100 and can be paid for under the CDS scheme as a disbursement if there are reasonable grounds for obtaining one).[210] Practically, there is little recorded and little anecdotal evidence to suggest that the Prison Service laboratory tests have ever been found to be inaccurate.

- Prisoners and their legal representatives should be sent a copy of the procedures within three days of request.
- The prisoner or their solicitor should ask the prison to release the sample to the laboratory within four weeks of the first adjournment for the purpose of independent testing.
- The independent test should be completed within 14 days of the release of the sample after which the hearing will proceed.
- Accordingly the maximum time that should elapse for the purpose of an independent test is about six weeks. Where a prisoner or their solicitor does not provide any valid reason for delay the hearing will proceed on the basis of the available evidence.

9.149 The charge following a positive MDT is subject to specific statutory defences[211] which avoid the need for any additional finding of intention or recklessness:

- the controlled drug had been, prior to its administration, lawfully in the accused's possession for his or her use or was administered to the accused in the course of a lawful supply of the drug to him or her by another person;

209 PSO 2000 para 6.54.
210 PSO 2000 annex G and PSO 3601 appendix 17.
211 PR rule 52, YOIR rule 56.

- the controlled drug was administered by or to him or her in circumstances in which he or she did not know and had no reason to suspect that such a drug was being administered; or
- the controlled drug was administered by or to the accused under duress or to him or her without consent in circumstances where it was not reasonable for the accused to have resisted.

9.150    PSO 2000 suggests that there is no need to enquire into a statutory defence raised by a prisoner unless 'credible evidence' is presented which casts doubt on any of the elements of the charge.[212] It is also suggested that where the prisoner relies on one of the statutory defences, that the burden of proof is on them to establish the defence on the balance of probabilities.[213] The statutory defences might arise where the prisoner states that he was unknowingly given drugs (for example in a cigarette or drink) and this advice was issued to assist adjudicators in situations where prisoners claimed that they must have been 'spiked' by other prisoners putting drugs in their food or drink without their knowledge.

9.151    It is unclear whether this is the proper approach. Certainly where a case is referred to an IA and there is therefore no doubt that article 6 of the ECHR applies, there is a respectable argument that the prisoner has only an evidential rather than a legal burden in this situation. That is, once they submit sufficient evidence to raise a real issue as to the defence it is for the adjudicator to find that the statutory defence does not apply beyond reasonable doubt. To proceed otherwise may arguably breach the presumption of innocence in article 6(2).[214]

## Offences relating to alcohol use

9.152    Although the Prison Act has contained a provision which permits mandatory testing for alcohol since 1997[215] (the wording of the provision is similar to that relating to drug testing), the Rules were only amended to permit such testing until April 2005[216] (again the wording of the Rules very closely mirrors the provisions for mandatory drug testing). As with MDTs, the statutory framework requires a governor's authorisation to be in place before mandatory alcohol testing can be implemented. A prisoner cannot be put on report for refusing

212  PSO 2000 para 6.56.
213  PSO 3601 para 8.46.
214  See by analogy *R v Lambert* [2001] UKHL 37.
215  PA 1952 s16B.
216  PR rule 50B, YOIR rule 54A.

a lawful order to provide a sample unless there is such an authorisation in place. Although the Rules allow for alcohol testing by the taking of urine samples, Prison Service policy is that breath testing is the primary means of taking such samples.[217] The policy set out in the Prison Service Manual on Alcohol Testing[218] allows testing on reasonable suspicion, for a risk assessment (for example for outside employment) and randomly (although unlike with MDTs random testing should not be routine).

9.153    There is no equivalent disciplinary charge to the MDT charge of having a controlled drug in a sample of urine. Instead, the Rules contain two specific charges in relation to which positive alcohol tests may be admitted as evidence. PSO 2000 does not suggest that these charges would normally be referred to an IA. The charges are:

### Is intoxicated as a consequence of consuming any alcoholic beverage[219]

9.154    This is the more serious of the alcohol charges as it involves intoxication. However any positive test will not be conclusive evidence of this charge as the adjudicator will need to be satisfied:

- The prisoner was intoxicated – this will depend on the evidence which must go beyond establishing mere 'exuberance'.
- The intoxication was as a result of consuming alcohol.

The charge has similar statutory defences as those relating to MDTs.[220]

### Consumes any alcoholic beverage whether or not provided to him by another person[221]

9.155    This requires merely proving that the prisoner has consumed alcohol and does not require intoxication to be established. A positive breath test properly required and obtained from the prisoner will be sufficient to prove the charge subject to the same statutory defences.

---

217  See PSI 15/2005 annex C – an approved breath testing device should be used – the cut off for levels of alcohol above which samples can be used as evidence of drinking is 9 μg of ethanol per 100 millilitres of breath.

218  *Manual of Policy and Procedures*, December 2004: www.hmprisonservice.gov. uk/assets/documents/100008CBalcohol_testing_for prisoners_doc

219  PR rule 51(10), YOIR rule 55(11).

220  PR rule 52A, YOIR rule 56A.

221  PR rule 51(11), YOIR rule 55(12).

## Alcohol charges and temporary licence

9.156    PSO 2000 states that when a prisoner is released on temporary licence and has an additional licence requirement not to consume alcohol, he or she should be charged with failing to comply with a temporary release condition and/or the charge relating to intoxication above. When a prisoner returns from a period of temporary licence which does not contain an additional licence requirement not to consume alcohol, he or she should be charged with the offence relating to intoxication providing that there is clear evidence through impairment testing to warrant this.[222]

# Evidence in disciplinary hearings

9.157    In keeping with the general requirements of natural justice and of the Rules themselves which require prisoners to fully know the case they have to answer, PSO 2000 confirms that prisoners and their representatives 'must hear, and have the opportunity to challenge, all the evidence. The adjudicator must not consider anything relevant to the alleged offence not brought out in the course of the hearing'.[223]

### Hearsay evidence

9.158    A finding of guilt cannot be founded on the basis of contested hearsay evidence.[224] Any written evidence or reports that the prisoner does not accept must not be admitted, or should be disregarded unless the maker of the statement attends to give evidence orally and to be cross examined. The exception to this rule is the confirmation certificate obtained in MDT cases (see above). Hearsay evidence may be admitted if it is accepted by the prisoner.

### Physical evidence

9.159    PSO 2000 notes that: '[i]t is important that physical evidence, including photographs, is retained and produced at the hearing. The accused must be allowed to ask questions about it in the same way as other evidence'.[225] This mandatory requirement will refer to, for example,

222  PSO 2000 para 6.42.
223  PSO 3601 para 5.3.
224  PSO 2000 para 5.9.
225  PSO 2000 para 5.7.

allegedly unauthorised articles that are found on searches. However, the failure to produce the physical evidence – despite the mandatory nature of the guidance in the PSO – will not always be fatal to a finding of guilt. In one case an IA found a prisoner guilty of possession of an unauthorised article notwithstanding the fact that the article (a mobile phone aerial) could not be found at the time of the hearing. The IA took into account the fact that the officer described finding the article, was able to describe its appearance and his attempts to preserve it as evidence. When the court considered whether the finding of guilt should be quashed it rejected the prisoner's claim, although the judge confirmed that the adjudicator 'must look with some care as to why the evidence has not been retained and produced'. In this case the IA had sufficient evidence to find that the item was a mobile phone aerial.[226]

9.160    While at first sight it is alarming that prison officers can lose physical evidence and still successfully prosecute disciplinary charges, the case makes it clear that IAs and governors must take proper care to establish the existence of the item in such cases. The same approach applies when the item is never found, for example, where CCTV conclusively shows an unauthorised article being passed on a visit, but the subsequent strip search finds nothing, a prisoner may still be found guilty.[227] There will be times when the officer's evidence in circumstances where the alleged unauthorised item is either never found or lost is inadequate to prove the charge to the criminal standard.

9.161    If electronically recorded evidence (including CCTV footage) is used at an adjudication then the prisoner must be given an opportunity to consider it and it must be preserved for at least three months after the hearing, a further nine months from the date of a response to a complaint to Prison Service headquarters (see below) and subsequently for as long as the charge remains under review (by the courts or the PPO).[228]

## Conduct of disciplinary hearings

9.162    Chapter 10 of PSO 2000 contains a model procedure as to how disciplinary hearings should be conducted. The PSO is not binding on

---

226  *R (O'Neil) v Independent Adjudicator* [2008] EWHC 1371 (Admin).
227  See *R (Lashley) v Independent Adjudicator and another* [2008] EWHC 1853 (Admin).
228  PSO 2000 para 5.8.

IAs but its requirements are informed by principles of natural justice and good administration of hearings and so in practice IAs will normally adopt them.

## Bias and the need to hear the charge impartially

9.163    Even where charges are not heard by IAs issues of independence can arise. Specifically the PSO recognises that there will be circumstances in which a governor should not hear a charge.

9.164    In the leading case on this issue a charge of disobeying an order to submit to a squat search was heard by a deputy governor who had been present when the governor approved the decision to require the search. The House of Lords quashed the finding of guilt confirming that the test to consider when deciding whether an adjudicator should decline to hear a charge because of concern over bias is 'whether the fair-minded and informed observer, having considered the relevant facts, would conclude that there was a real possibility of bias'. In this case the Lords considered that the fair-minded observer might infer that the deputy governor had tacitly accepted that the order was lawful, so that, when it was disobeyed and the he subsequently came to rule upon its lawfulness, there was a real possibility that he might be predisposed to find it lawful.[229] What the Lords were also clear about however was that just because the deputy governor was aware of the background to the charges this would not have been enough to justify quashing the finding of guilt. This kind of knowledge will often be inevitable where governors hear charges. It was specifically presence when the searches were authorised which tipped the balance in the prisoners' favour.

9.165    The PSO also notes that it is not only knowledge of factual circumstances given rise to the charge that may raise issues of bias. For example, if in hearing and considering applications for legal representation or advice the governor has heard prejudicial evidence or information (such as details of the defence or relevant incriminating admissions), perhaps at earlier hearings of the charge, then the same governor will not be able to fairly hear the charge and must adjourn so that another adjudicator can hear it.[230] The governor should not have access to the prisoner's core record during the hearing.[231]

---

229  *R(Carroll and Al-Hasan) v Secretary of State for the Home Department* [2005] UKHL 13.
230  PSO 2000 paras 3.15 and 3.17.
231  PSO 2000 para 4.21.

## Opening procedure

9.166   Prison Disciplinary charges will be held in the segregation unit of the prison. The hearings are not therefore held in public. However, although article 6(1) states that the hearing of a criminal charge should be at 'a fair and public' hearing it has been held that even where charges are referred to an IA that the hearing can be held in private.[232] This was on the basis that to allow public access to prisons would raise security and public order concerns. The more realistic alternative of holding hearings outside prisons it was held would impose a disproportionate burden on the resources of the state.

9.167   The officer in charge of managing the hearing, normally a segregation unit senior officer, must ensure that the reporting officer and witnesses enter the adjudication room after the prisoner facing the charge, and that they leave the room before the prisoner. This is to ensure that there is no complaint that evidence may have been heard in the absence of the prisoner.[233] There should be two escorting officers whenever the charge is heard by an IA, otherwise the governor decides whether an escort is necessary.[234]

9.168   Governors are instructed to ensure that the general atmosphere in the hearing is as relaxed as possible 'whilst maintaining sufficient formality to emphasise the importance of the proceedings'.[235] The prisoner must be allowed to sit and be offered writing materials. Further the prisoner must not be subjected to any intimidating behaviour, in particular escorts should not sit facing the prisoner or attempt to maintain eye contact.[236]

9.169   PSO 2000 states that at the beginning of the hearing the governor should:

- Identify the prisoner.
- Ascertain that they have received the charge sheet at least two hours before the hearing.
- Ascertain that the prisoner understands the procedure.
- Read out the charge.
- Ascertain that the prisoner understands the charge and has had sufficient time to prepare a defence.

---

232  *R (Bannatyne) v Secretary of State for the Home Department* [2004] EWHC 1921 (Admin) which held that there was no reason to depart from a similar approach adopted by the ECtHR in *Campbell and Fell v UK* (1984) 7 EHRR 165.

233  PSO 2000 para 4.18.

234  PSO 2000 para 4.20.

235  PSO 2000 para 4.16.

236  PSO 2000 para 4.20 – commonly known as 'eyeballing'.

- Ask whether the prisoner has prepared a written answer.
- Ask whether the prisoner wishes to make an application for legal representation, legal advice or a McKenzie friend.
- Ask whether the prisoner wishes to call any witnesses.[237]

9.170  If the adjudicator considers that the prisoner requires further time to prepare a defence or legal advice or representation then an adjournment will be necessary. Similarly if relevant witnesses are unavailable (although the adjudicator may hear some evidence and adjourn for other witnesses).

9.171  Where multiple charges arise out of one incident PSO 2000 suggests that the evidence for all charges should be heard before reaching findings of any of them. This is in order to avoid the finding on one charge prejudicing consideration of any others. If one charge arising from an incident is referred to an IA, then so should all the charges.[238]

9.172  If there is more than one prisoner charged with an offence arising out of an incident then the guidance states that best practice is for the charges to be heard together, which will enable all parties to hear all the evidence. If the charges are not heard together adjudicators must ensure that evidence heard atone adjudication is not taken into account in reaching a decision at another unless the evidence is also presented at the other hearing.[239]

## Hearing the evidence

9.173  PSO 2000 suggests that the adjudicator should hear the evidence of the reporting officer and then invite the prisoner to question them. Historically, the practice was to allow the prisoner only to question witnesses, including the reporting officer, through the governor. PSO 2000 now makes clear that this is improper and prisoners should be able to directly question witnesses unless they abuse this right.[240] Adjudicators are of course entitled to prevent questions which are legally irrelevant from being put to witnesses[241] (although if the governor gets this wrong then any finding of guilt may be quashed – for example where a governor refuses a prisoner to ask questions which go to the elements of the charge such as the lawfulness of an order).[242]

237  PSO 2000 para 10.7.
238  PSO 2000 para 4.10.
239  PSO 2000 paras 4.12–4.14.
240  PSO 2000 para 5.26.
241  PSO 2000 para 5.28.
242  *R (Russell) v Secretary of State for the Home Department* [2000] Prison LR 145.

9.174    Once the reporting officer and any supporting witnesses have given evidence and been questioned then the adjudicator should invite the prisoner to offer their defence, by adducing and affirming a written statement, by giving oral evidence and by calling witnesses if appropriate. These witnesses in turn may be questioned by the reporting officer and the adjudicator. Where facilities are available witnesses may give evidence by video link. Once witnesses have given evidence they should not remain in the adjudication room.[243]

9.175    If allegations are made against staff during the hearing, such as an assault during the incident giving rise to the charge, then the adjudicator should consider whether the allegation is relevant to the charge. If it is not the prisoner should be advised that a complaint can be made in writing and the hearing can proceed. If it is relevant (an alleged assault might establish self-defence) then the adjudicator should either investigate the matter as part of the hearing, or where the allegation is too 'weighty or complicated' the adjudicator should adjourn the hearing for an investigation to take place.[244] Any evidence arising from an investigation which is subsequently to be used in the hearing of the charge must be disclosed to the prisoner.

## The decision

9.176    Once all the evidence has been heard the adjudicator should ask the prisoner whether they have anything to say about the case by way of closing submissions before a decision is made as to guilt. This is separate from the opportunity to offer mitigation if guilt is established.[245] The adjudicator will then consider whether the charge is proved to the necessary criminal standard of proof. The decision must be announced and recorded on the record of hearing F256. The PSO confirms that so that prisoners have a proper opportunity to challenge decisions the adjudicator must give reasons for decisions.[246] However there is authority that as there is not a statutory duty to give reasons in the Rules that the failure to do so does not render a decision unlawful in itself.[247]

243  PSO 2000 paras 10.13–10.20.
244  PSO 2000 paras 5.29–5.30.
245  PSO 2000 para 10.21.
246  PSO 2000 paras 10.22 and 7.4.
247  *R (Gleaves) v Secretary of State for the Home Department* [2004] EWHC 2522 – in this case although the adjudicator did not indicate how a defence had been investigated this defect was cured by the adjudicator explaining how this was done in a statement put before the court.

9.177     If a charge is proved the prisoner should be asked if they have
anything to say in mitigation or whether they wish to call any witnesses in support of mitigation. Before deciding on any punishment
the adjudicator should ask for a conduct report which is completed
on a standard form and includes comments on the prisoner's recent
behaviour in prison. The prisoner, if they want to, should be able to
question the author of the conduct report.[248]

## Hearings in the prisoner's absence

9.178    PSO 2000 envisages three circumstances in which a disciplinary
hearing may proceed in a prisoner's absence:[249]

- Where the prisoner is unable to attend (for health reasons, or due
  to prolonged court appearances for example). In such circumstances even though the open the adjudication may be opened in
  the prisoner's absence, it cannot be concluded until the prisoner
  can attend. This may mean that the charge may have to be dismissed if the inability to attend is prolonged.
- Where the prisoner refuses to attend. The adjudicator must
  record that the prisoner is considered fit for adjudication, that
  they have been informed that the hearing will proceed in their
  absence, the name of the person who spoke to the prisoner and
  what the prisoner said in response. If the hearing does proceed
  in the prisoner's absence it will be important that the adjudicator conducts as full an investigation into the charge as possible
  by questioning witnesses. The prisoner must be informed of the
  result and any punishment as soon as possible after the hearing's
  conclusion.
- The adjudicator refuses to allow the prisoner to attend. This may
  occur where, for example the prisoner is on dirty protest or is in-
  decently dressed. The prisoner should be warned that the hearing
  will proceed in their absence unless they present themselves in a
  decent state. The prisoner should be informed of key stages of the
  proceedings.
- If a prisoner is legally represented the representative should be
  present at hearings where the prisoner is absent.
- If the prisoner is disruptive during a hearing they should be
  warned that if they continue to be disruptive that they will be
  removed from the hearing which will continue in their absence.

248  PSO 2000 paras 10.25–10.26.
249  PSO 2000 paras 4.1–4.9.

# Punishments

## Punishments other than additional days

9.179 The Rules set out a different range of punishments available to governors and IAs. The governor can impose one or more of the following (although a caution cannot be combined with any other punishment):[250]

(a) caution;
(b) forfeiture for a period not exceeding 42 days of any of the privileges under rule 8 (21 days if the prisoner is under 21);
(c) exclusion from associated work for a period not exceeding 21 days;
(d) stoppage of or deduction from earnings for a period not exceeding 84 days (42 days if the prisoner is under 21) ;
(e) cellular confinement for a period not exceeding 21 days (10 days if the prisoner is under 21);
(f) removal from his wing or living unit for a period of 28 days (21 days if the prisoner is under 21);
(g) in the case of a prisoner otherwise entitled to them, forfeiture for any period of the right, under rule 43(h), to have the articles there mentioned.

9.180 The punishments for prisoners in YOIs are slightly different.[251] They do not include (c) and (g) above, but include removal from activities (other than education, work, training courses and physical education) for up to 21 days, two hours extra work a day for up to 21 days, and removal from the wing or living unit for up to 21 days. Maximum periods of cellular confinement, forfeiture of privileges, and stoppage of earnings are 10, 21 and 42 days respectively for young offenders.

9.181 In April 2000 the power to punish those under 18 with cellular confinement was removed from the Rules.[252] Where consecutive punishments are imposed the total period of cellular confinement must still not exceed 10 days.[253]

9.182 Although the Prison Rules 1999 do provide for central guidelines on what punishments should be handed out by governors, none have been published except in relation to smuggling in drugs.[254] However, PSO 2000 introduced a mandatory requirement for prisons to

---

250 PR rules 55 and 57.
251 YOIR rule 53.
252 See also PSO 2000 para 7.28.
253 YOIR rule 60(2).
254 PR rule 55(4): for the charges relating to smuggling in drugs – guidelines are contained in annex C to PSI 22/1999.

establish local punishment guidelines and where punishments differ from the local guidelines the reason for this should be recorded.[255]

9.183 Further guidance on punishments is included in PSO 2000. This confirms that the adjudicator 'must be aware of the physical and mental state of the prisoner when deciding punishment' and 'no particular punishment must be imposed if the adjudicator has any doubts about the ability of the prisoner to undergo the punishment'.[256] Punishments should take into account the seriousness of the offence, previous custodial behaviour, good order and discipline within the prison, whether the offence had any impact on the general running of the regime and the need for a deterrent effect on other prisoners.[257] Governors are also instructed that punishments should be proportionate[258] and consistent between prisoners who are equally culpable and charged out of the same incident.[259] Punishments can be suspended for up to six months or imposed to run concurrently with punishments awarded at the same time. If the punishment is suspended then it can be activated if a further finding of guilt is made during the suspension period, although this should not be automatic.[260] A governor cannot activate a suspended punishment of additional days and so these should be referred to the IA.[261] All punishments will take effect immediately unless suspended.

9.184 The imposition of a punishment under the disciplinary process does not prevent the prison also taking steps to impose sanctions in the IEP system.[262]

## Punishments of cellular confinement

9.185 The imposition of cellular confinement is subject to specific statutory limitations and guidance given that this amounts to a period of enforced segregation, in dedicated accommodation usually in the segregation unit. As set out above the maximum period is 21 days per offence (ten for young offenders aged 18 or over). Before deciding whether to impose a punishment of cellular confinement the governor or IA must first enquire of a registered medical practitioner

255  PSO 2000 para 7.8.
256  PSO 2000 paras 7.11–7.12.
257  PSO 2000 para 7.7.
258  PSO 2000 para 7.6.
259  PSO 2000 para 7.9.
260  PSO 2000 paras 7.46–7.47.
261  PSO 2000 para 7.47.
262  PSO 2000 para 7.55 and see chapter 5.

or registered nurse as to whether there are any medical reasons why the punishment is unsuitable and this advice must be taken into account.[263] Adjudicators must also consider whether the use of cellular confinement is proportionate.[264] Prison Service guidance states that prisoners at risk of suicide or self-harm should only be punished with cellular confinement 'exceptionally'.[265] In all cases alternative punishments should be considered and local protocols should ensure that prisoners awarded this punishment are given access to diversionary material, so additional punishments of removal of privileges may be inappropriate.

9.186    Governors must ensure that the healthcare unit and chaplaincy are informed on a daily basis of the prisoners who are segregated and when serving a punishment of cellular confinement prisoners should be subject to the same observational and monitoring requirements as prisoners segregated for other reasons.[266]

9.187    Prisoners should be allowed all normal privileges except those that are incompatible with cellular confinement and those which been removed as part of the punishment.[267]

9.188    PSO 2000 now contains guidance on the maximum number of days of cellular confinement that can be imposed when the prisoner is already serving such a punishment. Consecutive punishments of cellular confinement now have a maximum of 35 days (16 for young offenders) following a pattern of three adjudications.[268]

## Additional days

9.189    The punishments available to IAs[269] are same as those available to governors but include the power to impose a punishment of up to 42 additional days both for adults and young offenders. Additional days are added to the prisoner's release dates including HDC and eligibility for early removal, and also extend the length of the licence

---

263  PR rule 58, YOIR rule 61 – this medical advice should be provided in the form of an initial segregation safety screen in the same way as for segregation under rule 45 – PSO 2000 para 7.27A.

264  PSO 2000 para 7.27.

265  PSO 2000 para 7.27 and PSO 2700 – although why this class of prisoner should ever face such punishment is not explained. The imposition of segregation as punishment against a mentally ill prisoner contributed to a finding of breach of article 3 in *Keenan v UK* (2001) 33 EHRR 38.

266  PSO 2000 paras 7.33–7.34.

267  PSO 2000 paras 7.31–7.32.

268  PSO 2000 paras 7.27–7.27H.

269  PR rule 55A, YOIR rule 60A.

by the number of days given (although they cannot delay the eventual sentence expiry date) and are served in full. It is therefore important to seek legal advice where the prisoner is facing the possibility of such a punishment. Remand prisoners can be awarded prospective additional days which come into operation if they are convicted and receive a prison sentence.[270] As noted above additional days cannot be given to those serving DTOs, civil prisoners, those detained only under immigration powers and recalled prisoners whose release date is already the date of sentence expiry.[271]

9.190   PSO 2000 states that two or more punishments of additional days will be treated as consecutive unless the adjudicator ordered them to run concurrently, but that punishments for related offences arising from a single incident should not exceed 42 days in total as required by the Rules.[272]

9.191   The Chief Magistrate's office has recently issue guidelines to IAs on the punishment of additional days. These set out starting points for each charge, together with a guideline range. The guidelines state that IAs should adopt the following approach:

1) Adjudicators should first decide the starting point for the punishment. This starting point will normally be within the guideline range. The starting point suggested is for a prisoner (i) with no previous findings of guilt on adjudications and (ii) following a not guilty plea.

2) The starting point should be increased to reflect any aggravating features of the offence itself and of the offender (such as previous findings of guilt) to ascertain the provisional punishment.

3) The starting point may exceed the range if the aggravating features justify this in which case the Adjudicator should make the appropriate entry on the punishment sheet.

4) The provisional punishment should then be adjusted to reflect any personal mitigating factors.

5) Having thus ascertained the provisional punishment that takes into account all aggravating and mitigating factors the punishment should then be reduced by a third to reflect a discount for a TIMELY plea of guilty if that has been entered.

6) Punishment may be suspended for a period not exceeding six months.

The starting points and guideline ranges for each offence are as follows:

---

270  CJA 2003 s257, CJA 1991 s42.
271  PSO 2000 para 7.38.
272  PR rule 55A(3), YOIR rule 60A(3) and PSO 2000 para 7.36.

| Rule | Disciplinary offence | Starting point (days) | Range of added days |
|------|---------------------|----------------------|---------------------|
| 51(1) | Commits any assault: | | |
| | (a) Upon staff: | | |
| | Push | 8 | 5–15 |
| | Deliberate blow | 28 | 21–42 |
| | Spitting | 28 | 21–42 |
| | Weapon used | 32 | 28–42 |
| | Sustained attack | 32 | 28–42 |
| | (b) Upon inmate: | | |
| | Push | 5 | 3–10 |
| | Deliberate blow | 16 | 10–30 |
| | Weapon used | 32 | 28–42 |
| | Sustained attack | 32 | 28–42 |
| 51(1A) | Racially aggravated assault – add to above days | + 7 | + 7 |
| 51(2) | Detains any person against his will | 28 | 21–42 |
| 51(3) | Denies access to any part of the prison to any officer or other person (other than a prisoner) who is at the prison for the purpose of working there. [Dependent on duration] | 20 | 10–42 |
| 51(4) | Fights with any person. [If sustained treat as a sustained attack as in (1) above] | 14 | 7–28 |
| 51(5) | Intentionally endangers the health or personal safety of others or, by his conduct, is reckless whether such health or personal safety is endangered. | | |
| | Intentional: | 32 | 28–42 |
| | Reckless: | 20 | 14–35 |
| 51(6) | Intentionally obstructs an officer in the execution of his duty, or any person (other than a prisoner) who is at the prison for the purpose of working there, in the performance of his work. | 14 | 6–30 |
| 51(7) | Escapes or absconds from any prison or legal custody. | | |
| | Escapes: | 32 | 28–42 |
| | Absconds: | 22 | 14–42 |
| 51(8) | Fails to comply with any conditions upon which he is temporarily released under rule 9. | 16 | 10–30 |

| Rule | Disciplinary offence | Starting point (days) | Range of added days |
|------|----------------------|:---------------------:|:-------------------:|
| 51(9) | Administers a controlled drug to himself or fails to prevent the administration of a controlled drug to him by another. | | |
| | Class A: | 32 | 28–42 |
| | Class B/C: | 12 | 7–21 |
| | Non-prescribed medication: | 12 | 7–21 |
| 51(10) | Is intoxicated as a consequence of knowingly consuming any alcoholic beverage. | 20 | 14–30 |
| 51(11) | Knowingly consumes any alcoholic beverage other than that provided to him pursuant to a written order under rule 25(1). | 15 | 10–30 |
| 51(12) | Has in his possession: (a) any unauthorised articles, or (b) a greater quantity of any articles that he is authorised to have. | | |
| | Weapons: | 32 | 28–42 |
| | Class A drugs: | 32 | 28–42 |
| | Class B/C drugs: | 12 | 7–21 |
| | Item to cheat MDT: | 32 | 28–42 |
| | Camera phone: | 38 | 35–42 |
| | Mobile phone and/or accessory: | 32 | 28–42 |
| | Alcohol: | 22 | 14–42 |
| | Other item: | 13 | 5–30 |
| 51(13) | Sells or delivers to any unauthorised person any unauthorised article. | 18 | 10–35 |
| 51(14) | Sells or, without permission, delivers to any person any article which he is allowed to have only for his own use. | 10 | 6–21 |
| 51(15) | Takes improperly any article belonging to another person or to a prisoner. | 18 | 10–35 |
| 51(16) | Intentionally or recklessly sets fire to any part of a prison or any other property, whether or not his own. | | |
| | Intentionally: | 32 | 30–42 |
| | Recklessly: | 20 | 14–35 |

| Rule | Disciplinary offence | Starting point (days) | Range of added days |
|---|---|---|---|
| 51(17) | Destroys or damages any part of a prison or any other property, other than his own.<br>Intentionally:<br>Recklessly: | <br><br><br>28<br>12 | <br><br><br>21–42<br>7–21 |
| 51(17A) | Destroys or damages any part of a prison or any other property, other than his own, when racially aggravated. Add to above days: | + 7 | + 7 |
| 51(18) | Absents himself from any place he is required to be or is present in any place where he is not authorised to be. | 16 | 10–42 |
| 51(19) | Is disrespectful to any officer or other person (other than a prisoner) who is at the prison for the purpose of working there, or any person visiting a prison. | 10 | 6–21 |
| 51(20) | Uses threatening, abusive or insulting words or behaviour. | 14 | 5–30 |
| 51(20A) | Uses threatening, abusive or insulting racist words or behaviour. Add to above days: | + 7 | + 7 |
| 51(21) | Intentionally fails to work properly or, being required to work, refuses to do so. | 10 | 5–21 |
| 51(22) | Disobeys any lawful order:<br>MDT:<br>Other: | <br>32<br>16 | <br>28–42<br>10–30 |
| 51(23) | Disobeys or fails to comply with any rule or regulation applying to him | 6 | 3–14 |
| 51(24) | Receives any controlled drug, or without the consent of an officer, any other article during the course of a visit (not being an interview such as is mentioned in rule 38). | 32 | 28–42 |
| 51(24A) | Displays, attacks or draws on any part of a prison or on any other property, threatening, abusive or insulting racist words, drawings, symbols or other material. | 22 | 15–36 |

# Challenging findings of guilt and punishments

9.192   The Secretary of State has the power to quash any finding of guilt and to remit any punishment awarded made by a governors or directors.[273] There is a separate review procedure for the decisions of IAs.[274]

## Governors' decisions

### Review by the BCU

9.193   The statutory power to review governors' and directors' decisions is delegated to the Briefing and Casework Unit[275] (BCU) at Prison Service headquarters which will 'review' adjudications on the basis of the record of hearing (form F256 and any other evidence relied on).[276] The BCU will then make a recommendation to the DOM for the prison who has the delegated authority to make the decision.

9.194   The review procedure is commenced either by the prisoner submitting an ADJ 1 form or at the written request of the prisoner's solicitor. The application should be sent to BCU within six weeks of the decision. If the prisoner is serving a punishment of cellular confinement the request for a review should be faxed to the BCU or ONC and should be dealt with by way of a fast-track process.[277]

9.195   PSO 2000 introduced a new procedure in relation to governor's adjudications so that where a governor or director becomes aware that an adjudication is flawed (as illegal or procedurally unfair) they may remit the punishment or set aside the finding.[278] This power of the governor or director is in addition to the prisoner's right to seek a review of the adjudication referred to above.

---

273   PR rule 61(1), YOIR rule 64(1).

274   PR rule 55B, YOIR rule 60B.

275   Although PSO 2000 suggests directors' decisions should be sent to the Office for National Commissioning the BCU has in fact dealt with decisions from private prisons from 1 June 2008. BCU is at room 615 Cleland House, Page Street London SW1P 4LN.

276   When conducting the review it is not open to the BCU to uphold a finding of guilt on the basis of reasoning not adopted by the adjudicator: *R (Shreeve) v Secretary of State for Justice* [2007] 2431 (Admin).

277   PSO 2000 para 9.1: this was a recommendation contained in *Keenan v UK* (2001) 33 EHRR 38 which raised the concern that prisoners had no realistic way of challenging a punishment of cellular confinement before it had been served at least in part.

278   PSO 2000 para 8.5.

### Review by the PPO

9.196 If the BCU upholds the finding of guilt in a governor's adjudication, there are two options available. The first is through a complaint to the Prisons and Probation Ombudsman. The complaint must be made by the prisoner or the prisoner's solicitor within one month of the BCU's decision to uphold the adjudication, and the Ombudsman will aim to complete his investigation within 12 weeks. The complaint can be made through confidential access and the address is The Prisons Ombudsman, Ashley House, 2 Monck Street, London SW1P 2BQ. Complaints to the Ombudsman that are made outside the time limit will only be considered if there are exceptional circumstances. If the PPO upholds the complaint a recommendation can be made to the Chief Operating Officer of the Prison Service that the finding of guilt be quashed or the punishment remitted. Such recommendations are only exceptionally rejected.

## Challenging independent adjudicators' hearings

9.197 The changes to the Rules introduced in 2005 removed the power of the Secretary of State to review IA's hearings. Instead a procedure was introduced whereby a prisoner may within 14 days request a review of the adjudication.[279] The reviewer will be a senior district judge (SDJ) who will have power to reduce, substitute or quash the punishment entirely where it appears that the punishment was 'manifestly unreasonable'. There is no set form for requesting a review but the prisoner must make his application in writing to the governor or director (who will forward it to the senior district judge) within 14 days. There is a fast-track procedure for dealing with punishments of additional days for prisoners who are close to their release date.[280]

9.198 It may appear anomalous that the Rules now contain no power to quash the finding of guilt in IA cases. This may be due to the fact that the courts have held that article 6 is only engaged in the prison disciplinary system where additional days are awarded and there is no breach of the article in refusing to quash a finding of guilt where the punishment of additional days has been remitted.[281] The limiting of the procedure to a review concerned solely with punishment may therefore be an attempt to avoid any characterisation of it as an appeal process that would in itself have to meet article 6 safeguards.

279 PR rule 55B, YOIR rule 60B.
280 PSO 2000 para 13.19.
281 *Napier v Home Secretary* [2004] EWHC 936 (Admin).

The concern that, as prisoners cannot have findings of guilt quashed, there would be a massive increase in judicial reviews of decisions does not appear to have happened. Presumably it will be open to prisoners to request the senior district judge to quash punishments on the basis that the punishment is 'unreasonable' because the finding of guilt was improperly made but this is clearly inadequate if it leaves on the prisoner's record a finding of guilt.

9.199    Where there has been an IA hearing no complaint can be made to the Ombudsman following the Rule changes that took effect from 18 April 2005. This is because it was only the fact that under the old Rules that IA hearings could be reviewed by the Secretary of State that meant complaints could be made to the PPO.

9.200    If a governor or director believes that an IA adjudication is flawed then this must be referred back to the IA at the Chief Magistrate's Office[282] as neither the governor nor the Secretary of State has any power to interfere with the decisions of the IA (subject to the power to remit additional days to recognise good behaviour – see below).

## Grounds for challenging findings of guilt

9.201    Whether or not prisoners are represented it will be important to promptly obtain the record of hearing and other documents presented at the hearing in order to prepare representations to challenge the finding of guilt. The prison has to provide free copies of the papers relating to the adjudication to prisoners or their advisers.[283] If the prison delays in providing copies of the paperwork it will be necessary to put in a holding application to the BCU or the SDJ to avoid missing time limits.

9.202    Where legal representation was not granted it will be necessary for legal advisers to seek detailed instructions on the adjudication paperwork and on the conduct of the hearing. Common issues that arise at prison disciplinary hearings that may provide grounds for challenging decisions are set out in the table opposite.

## Judicial review

9.203    Whether the adjudication was conducted by a governor or by an IA the final remedy is judicial review. Generally speaking the judicial review court will not quash findings of guilt on the basis of minor

282  PSO 2000 para 8.5.
283  PSO 2000 para 9.5.

- Was the charge laid as soon as possible and in any event within 48 hours? Prisoners will be given a new charge sheet to inform them of each adjourned hearing and so it is important to obtain the first form F1127 which should state when it was given to the prisoner.
- Was the prisoner medically fit for the hearing?
- Did the person hearing the charge have any involvement in the incidents giving rise to the charge, or any other knowledge which might raise issues of bias?
- If the charge was referred to an IA did the first hearing take place within 28 days?
- Was the prisoner given at least two hours between the laying of the charge and the hearing?
- Was the prisoner given enough time to prepare their defence, including an opportunity to obtain relevant evidence or contact relevant witnesses?
- Were any requests for an adjournment improperly refused?
- Was the charge sufficiently particularised to enable the prisoner to understand the allegation?
- Did the adjudicator properly consider any request for legal representation, legal advice or for the assistance of a McKenzie friend, and properly record the decision?
- Were requests for witnesses properly considered and adequate reasons given for any refusal to allow witnesses?
- Did the adjudicator fail to properly inquire into any defence put forward by the prisoner?
- Did the adjudicator or anyone else at the hearing by their conduct or attitude prevent the prisoner from being able to put forward their case?
- Was there evidence to prove each element of the charge?
- Was contested hearsay evidence improperly admitted?
- In MDT cases was there proper compliance with the prescribed procedures and were there any defects in the chain of custody?
- Did the adjudicator give reasons for finding the prisoner guilty, including why any defence was rejected?
- Did the adjudicator apply the correct standard and burden of proof?
- Was the punishment excessive, in excess of statutory maximums, or disproportionate?

technical breaches of procedure (such as spelling the prisoner's name incorrectly on a charge sheet), but will examine whether such breaches have actually resulted in unfairness. However breach of statutory requirements will result in findings being quashed. Judicial review is discussed further in chapter 12.

## Remission of additional days

9.204    The Rules contain further power for governors and directors to remit punishments imposed *either* by governors or IAs on the grounds of good behaviour in accordance with directions given by the Secretary of State. [284] The relevant directions are contained in PSO 2000.[285] This is an extremely important power as if prisoners have accrued a large amount of additional days early in a sentence then a successful application later may significantly bring forward their release date.

9.205    Applications will be considered provided that within the previous six months (four months for young offenders) the prisoner has not had a finding of guilt or submitted any other application for remission for which they were eligible. This period runs from the date of commission of the offence, not the imposition of the punishment. Once the application is submitted a report will be prepared on the prisoner's conduct. Governors are then required to take into account (the decision can be delegated to operational grades F or above):

- That the power should be used to reward prisoners who take a 'constructive approach' towards their imprisonment.
- Remission of additional days should also be used to acknowledge 'a genuine change of attitude' which may for some prisoners be shown merely by keeping out of trouble.
- Full account of the offences for which the days were added must be taken. Remission under the power should be limited to a maximum of 50 per cent of the additional days for each offence except in the most exceptional circumstances where more than 50 per cent may be remitted.[286]

284  PR rule 61(2), YOIR rule 64(2).
285  PSO 2000 paras 8.6–8.22.
286  PSO 2000 para 8.20.

# Prosecution of criminal offences committed by prisoners

9.206   It is now the intention that serious offences committed in prison, whether or not they could also give rise to a prison disciplinary charge, should be referred to the police for prosecution and Annex C to PSO 2000 provides guidance on this decision. Where the possible criminal offences also relate to potential disciplinary charges the relevant guidance is included in the analysis of those charges above. Otherwise the guidance states that where there has been a major disturbance offences amounting to prison mutiny, or violent disorder should be referred.[287] Where a victim wishes an alleged breach of a restraining order to be referred the governor should agree to this.[288]

## Preserving and gathering evidence by the prison

9.207   Prisons are advised that good practice in prisons can increase the likelihood of successful prosecution of a serious offence and of the need to:

- Notify the police immediately in appropriate cases.
- Make a comprehensive note as soon as possible after an incident has occurred, using form F2147.
- Preserve the scene of the incident.
- Preserve the evidence.
- Avoid contaminating physical evidence if at all possible.
- Leave the taking of statements to the police.[289]

9.208   The notes which staff take immediately after an incident and any other papers, such as interview notes, which are relevant must be carefully preserved and a copy placed with the record of the prisoners involved. The original should be handed to the police. If they are required to give evidence in court, staff may be permitted to refresh their memories by reference to any written notes made or verified by them, and made contemporaneously with the facts to which to which they can testify. Moreover, if a prosecution results, the Crown Prosecution Service is under a duty to disclose relevant unused material. Whilst

287  PSO 2000 C.22.
288  PSO 2000 C.25.
289  PSO 2000 para 11.5.

there is discretion to withhold certain types of material, it is vital that the Crown Prosecution Service has easy access to everything.[290]

9.209    Until the police arrive on the scene, the prison officer first on the scene should take charge until he is provided with full assistance. The identity of any witnesses, prisoners or prison officers must be noted. The police should be left to interview the alleged perpetrator and witnesses should be interviewed by the police. As soon as is reasonably practicable the officer first on the scene and other staff witnesses must make written notes. These will form the basis of witness statements to the police and form F1127 in relation to internal proceedings. Each note should be recorded on form F2147, which should be available on every wing. The note must record details of:

- How the officer became aware of the incident.
- What the officer observed, for example injuries or damage.
- Potential exhibits left at the scene of the incident.
- What those involved said initially.
- The date and time the note is made.[291]

9.210    The scene of an alleged crime must be sealed and nothing disturbed, unless it is unavoidable while awaiting the arrival of the police investigating officer.[292] Items at the scene must not be handled unless this is essential. In this event there must be minimum contact to reduce damage to marks or other evidence. Covering the hands before touching objects does not preserve such evidence.[293] The police may seize items of a prisoner's clothing which could be evidence if this is necessary to prevent concealment, loss or damage.[294] Guidance on giving evidence in court is contained in PSO 2600.

## Prisoner witnesses

9.211    Any prisoner who makes a formal statement to police following an incident is a potential prosecution witness in a criminal trial. The Prison Service has a policy which confirms that it has a duty to offer as much protection as possible to these prisoner witnesses.[295] Prisoners should be advised not to discuss their involvement in the case with anyone else. Any letter from the police or Witness Order from the Crown

290  PSO 2000 C.9.
291  PSO 2000 C.38.
292  PSO 2000 C.39.
293  PSO 2000 C.40.
294  PSO 2000 C.41.
295  PSO 2600 paras 5.7–5.12.

Prosecution Service which arrives at the establishment for a prisoner witness should be issued by a senior member of staff, Operational Manager F or above, in a private interview and the prisoner should be advised that the defendants in the case will be made aware of the identity of those whose statements are to be used in evidence. They should be advised to approach the governor if they are concerned about this disclosure, or have any other problems, and he or she will be able to put them in touch with the police officer in the case.

9.212 The establishment should open a register, kept securely in the governor's office, for prisoner witnesses to sign to acknowledge that they have read or have had read to them, letters from the police or Crown Prosecution Service. Letters should be stored with the prisoners' valuable property to ensure they are not left where other prisoners may see them. Prisoners should be advised that, if they are released and subsequently committed to prison, they should on reception identify themselves as a potential witness in a forthcoming trial.

9.213 Prisoners should be advised that all efforts will be made to give them the protection necessary before, during and after the trial. If any problems are experienced, governors should contact the Incident Management Support Unit number in cases involving large numbers of witnesses, or the police officer in charge of the case.

9.214 In cases where there is a high risk to a prisoner because of their witness status they can be transferred to a Protected Witness Unit (see chapter 4).

## Offences specific to the prison context

9.215 There are relatively few criminal offences that are specific to the prison context. Offences relating to the unlawful conveyance of prohibited articles into prison are dealt with in the section on visits (see chapter 7).

### Prison mutiny

9.216 The crime of prison mutiny was introduced following the riots at HMP Strangeways.[296] The offence arises where:

> (1) Any prisoner who takes part in a prison mutiny shall be guilty of an offence and liable, on conviction on indictment, to imprisonment for a term not exceeding ten years or to a fine or both.

296 Prison Security Act 1992 s1.

(2) For the purposes of this section there is a prison mutiny where two or more prisoners, while on the premises of any prison, engage in conduct which is intended to further a common purpose of overthrowing lawful authority in that prison.

(3) For the purposes of this section the intentions and the common purpose of prisoners may be inferred from the form and circumstances of their conduct and it shall be immaterial that conduct falling within subsection (2) above takes a different form in the case of different prisoners.

(4) Where there is a prison mutiny, a prisoner who has or is given a reasonable opportunity of submitting to lawful authority and fails, without reasonable excuse, to do so shall be regarded for the purpose of this section as taking part in the mutiny.

(5) Proceedings for an offence under this section shall not be brought except by or with the consent of the director of Public Prosecutions.

9.217    It is clear from the structure of the section that it creates a single offence of prison mutiny which can be committed either by conduct with the requisite purpose as defined in subsection (2), or on a deemed basis pursuant to subsection (4). The former is more serious than the latter. An indictment should make clear upon which basis a person is charged. Where a prisoner is charged in the alternative, he or she should be charged under two separate counts. It is apparent from subsections (3) and (4) of the section that conduct of a wide kind and participation in a variety of ways will constitute the offence providing the requisite intention is proved. The required intention of subsection (1) is an intention to further a common purpose of overthrowing lawful authority in the prison. The word, 'overthrowing' was chosen deliberately to confine the offence of prison mutiny to serious disturbances, and would appear not to cover a mere defiance of or challenge to lawful authority of the prison.[297]

9.218    The deeming provision in subsection (4) whilst it is parasitic upon at least two prisoners being engaged in a prison mutiny with the purposes required by subsection (2), does not require proof that the person failing to submit to the lawful authority shared that purpose. However, if the disturbance only became a mutiny after a failure to submit to lawful authority, the failure will not be caught by subsection (4).

9.219    Substantial sentences of imprisonment have been imposed in cases of Prison Mutiny. In *R v Lambert*[298] sentences of nine years'

297 *R v Mason and Cummings* [2005] 1 Cr App R 11, CA.
298 [2006] 2 Cr App R(S) 107.

imprisonment, to run consecutively to sentences that the offenders were serving were upheld for the instigators of a prison mutiny at HMP Lincoln. The disturbance at the prison was the worst prison mutiny since the riot at HMP Strangeways in Manchester in 1991. The Lincoln mutiny involved serious injury to both prison officers and prisoners and the total cost to the Prison Service was over two million pounds.

## Escape from lawful custody

9.220   It is an indictable offence at common law, punishable by fine and imprisonment, for a prisoner to escape without the use of force from lawful custody on a criminal charge. The Court of Appeal in *R v Dhillon*[299] set out the four essential factors that the prosecution must prove to establish the offence of escape from lawful custody:

- that the defendant was in custody;
- that the defendant knew that he or she was in custody (or at least was reckless as to whether he or she was or not);
- that the custody was lawful; and
- that the defendant intentionally escaped from that lawful custody.

9.221   A person may be in custody notwithstanding that he or she is not physically confined, provided that the person is nevertheless under the direct control of a representative of authority. In *Rumble*[300] the prisoner immediately after being sentenced to a custodial term, simply left the court, which had at that time no usher or security staff present. On appeal he took the point that since at the moment he walked out no one had yet sought to subject him to any restraint, there being no one in the court to do so, he could not be said to be in custody. The court rejected that submission and held that he was in the custody of the court from the moment that he had surrendered to his bail, whether or not any officer or member of the court staff had actually sought to restrain his movements.

9.222   There has been some confusion about the status of prisoners who remain unlawfully at large. In some cases prisoners have pleaded guilty to escape from lawful custody in circumstances amounting to a prisoner being unlawfully at large. In *R v Montgomery*[301] the court stated that a prisoner who failed to return to prison after the expiry

299  [2006] 1 Cr App R 15, CA.
300  [2003] EWCA Crim 770; 167 JP 205, CA.
301  [2007] EWCA Crim 2157; (2007) *Times* September 6, CA.

of the period of his temporary release could not be found guilty of the common law offence of escaping from lawful custody, as he was neither in prison nor under the immediate control of members of the prison authority whilst on temporary release. The court stated that as a matter of common sense and ordinary language Montgomery had not escaped from custody but had failed to return to it. In such a case it is likely that the offender would have committed the summary offence under section 1 of the Prisoners (Return to Custody) Act 1995 (the offence specifically designed for this situation).

9.223    In *R v Sutcliffe*[302] the court held that escape from lawful custody was always a serious offence, which the courts had to mark with an immediate sentence of imprisonment.

### Breaking prison

9.224    This is an indictable offence at common law, which involves the escape from lawful custody by the use of any force. The breaking proved must be an actual breaking; merely climbing over the walls will not suffice. The breaking need not be intentional, an accidental break will be sufficient. The offence is treated as a serious offence by the courts that will attract a substantial sentence of imprisonment to be served consecutively to that already being served.[303]

### Other offences

9.225    Other offences include assisting prisoners to escape,[304] which attracts a maximum sentence of ten years. Likewise harbouring escaped prisoners[305] carries a maximum sentence of ten years' imprisonment. In this context 'harbour' means to shelter a person.

## Interviews with the police

9.226    An interview with a prisoner is governed by Code of Practice C issued under the Police and Criminal Evidence Act 1984.[306] HM Chief Inspector of Constabulary has provided guidance to Chief Constables and Commissioners of Police that interviews conducted with convicted prisoners must be conducted in accordance with the Police

---

302  (1992) 13 Cr App R (S) 538.
303  *R v Coughtrey* [1997] 2 Cr App R(S) 269.
304  PA 1952 s39.
305  CJA 1961 s22.
306  http://police.homeoffice.gov.uk/operational-policing/powers-pace-codes/pace-code-intro/

and Criminal Evidence Act 1984 and the Codes of Practice. In *R v Rowe*[307] while the appellant was serving a sentence of imprisonment for other offences, he was seen by police officers on three separate occasions in relation to offences of attempted obtaining by deception. According to the police, he made admissions in the third interview. The officers made notes in their pocket books later, in the prison car park. The appellant denied the admissions. The court found that the third meeting was an interview and the failure by the police to make a contemporaneous record of that interview was a breach of Code of Practice C.

9.227    PSO 1801 deals with the production of prisoners at the request of the police. There is statutory power for the Secretary of State to direct that any prisoner is taken to any place out of the prison in the interests of justice or for the purposes of any public inquiry.[308] Prisoners remain in custody under such a direction. This provision allows for prisoners to be produced at court, but also for them to be taken to police stations or other places to assist investigations. The policy guidance suggests that governors and directors have devolved power to make such a direction which can only be used for the statutory purpose. Police must make an application to the prison on a prescribed form set out in an annex to PSO 1801. Examples of when its use might be appropriate in relation to production to the police are:

- To answer another charge.
- To be dealt with for an offence for which they are placed on probation or conditionally discharged, or for which a suspended sentence was passed.
- To appear as a prosecution witness.
- To help recover stolen property or hidden firearms or explosives.
- To identify premises in connection with criminal investigations.
- To be interviewed in connection with the investigation of a serious arrestable offence.
- To take part in an identification parade.[309]

9.228    Governors and directors must ensure that production is for the shortest period of time necessary in the interests of justice or of any public enquiry and must review any production which exceeds 24 hours (at least every 28 days).[310] Prisoners must be held at an accredited police

307 [1994] Crim LR 837.
308 Crime (Sentences) Act 1997 Sch 1 para 3.
309 PSO 1801 para 3.2.
310 PSO 1801 para 4.1.

station and should retain the rights and entitlements they had whilst in prison custody and the prisoner must be visited regularly where production is for more than a day (after three days, then 14 days then at least every 28 days).[311]

## Prison cell confessions

9.229   The courts have long recognised the dangers of cell confessions. *R v Hickey and Molloy*[312] was a case which centred on alleged confession evidence in two different contexts: alleged confessions to the police in interview and prison cell/wing confessions. It was the former which ultimately led to the convictions being quashed. In the context of cell confessions Roch LJ stated:

> Before it is decided by the prosecution to call a fellow prisoner to give evidence of alleged incriminating remarks by an accused who has been remanded pending his trial in prison, we consider that it is necessary for the prosecution to research fully the character and antecedents of that prisoner with the Criminal Records Office and the Prison Authorities, and if it is decided to call the fellow prisoner as a prosecution witness, to make the results of that research available to the defence.

9.230   The point has more recently been re-emphasised in *R v McCartney and Hamlett*[313] which stated that when pivotal evidence comes from a man with a known prison record, the prosecution should at an early stage in its preparation equip itself with his prison records. The authorities in this area of the law have repeatedly echoed the need for great caution when a cell confession is used as part of a prosecution case. The judge will generally need to point out to the jury that such confessions are easy to concoct and difficult to prove and that experience has shown that prisoners might have many motives to lie by making up a confession against their cell mate. The prison informer may think that providing such information to the authorities might assist him or her in securing a reduced prison sentence or in obtaining early release.

9.231   In *R v Stone*[314] the court held that not every case requires a warning to the jury; such cases would be where there was no evidence of improper motive or where the confession would have been difficult to invent because the information provided to the police by the

311  PSO 1901 para 5.2.
312  [1997] EWCA Crim 2028.
313  [2003] EWCA Crim 1372.
314  [2005] Crim LR 569.

prison informer could only have come from the offender and was information not in the public domain.

9.232 In *Allan v UK*[315] and subsequently *R v Allan*[316] a detained suspect had been subjected to repeated questioning by the police and had remained silent during his police interview. The police officers then placed him in a cell with a known registered police informant and gave instructions to the informant to elicit information from the suspect. The court held that the use of the confession evidence at trial had impinged on the applicant's right to silence and privilege against self incrimination.

9.233 *Allan v UK* can be distinguished from the general cell confession cases, which tend to involve two people who just happen to be sharing a cell together, because *Allan v UK* was a case which focused on the use of a 'state agent' to subvert the normal protections available to a suspect in a police interview and involved the functional equivalent of interrogation. The necessary protections that were bypassed included the caution, which makes clear that what a suspect says may be used in evidence; the presence of a solicitor should additionally ensure that the suspect understands the questions, knows the importance of his or her answers and the seriousness of the occasion; the requirements of audio recordings introduced to overcome problems associated with actual (or unfounded allegations of) 'verballing' by police officers now ensure an accurate record of questions and answers.

## Issues of disclosure in criminal cases involving prisoners

9.234 According to the Attorney-General's Guidelines of 2005 where the prosecution believes that a third party agency, in this case, a prison, has material or information which might be relevant to the prosecution case, reasonable steps should be taken to obtain the material. If the material is not voluntarily forthcoming by the agency a witness summons should be served in order to produce the material.

9.235 In *R v McCartney and Hamlett*[317] the defence had sought disclosure of a prosecution witness prison file, the prosecution passed the request on to the prison authorities, who declined to disclose it until relevance and particularity had been established. This was conveyed

315 (2003) 36 EHRR 12.
316 [2005] Crim LR 716.
317 [2003] EWCA Crim 1372.

to the defence, the prosecution took the view that the ball was in their court, and the matter was not further pursued by any party. In such circumstances, where the Home Office refuse to disclose material, the parties ought to subpoena the Home Office so as to secure production of the relevant material.

9.236    In the course of preparing the defence case, it may be helpful to request the following items from the prosecution:

- Forms relating to the charging of a prisoner for an internal disciplinary offence arising from the same incident and the transcript of any adjudication proceedings. These can be requested for the defendants and suspects that have been eliminated.
- Records of segregation of the defendants, or prisoner witnesses/ victims.
- Medical records of the victims or the defendant if he or she was injured in the incident (it is common for prison staff to be attended by a prison doctor in the first instance, and so it is worth asking for the records of prison officer victims as well as prisoners).
- Prison history sheets.
- Reports of injury to inmate/prison staff.
- Serious Incident Reports completed by prison officers who are prosecution witnesses.
- Security Intelligence Reports completed by prison officers who are prosecution witnesses.
- Disciplinary findings against prison officer witnesses.
- Records of sick leave taken by prison officer victims.
- CICA (Criminal Injuries Compensation Authority) claims completed by victims.
- Reports of any internal enquiries conducted by the Prison Service in the aftermath of the incident (the presence of these will depend on the seriousness of the incident).
- Requests/complaints forms relating to the incident (eg where a defendant has complained to a governor that he or she was assaulted by staff).
- Control and Restraint (use of force) records.
- Use of Special Cell Forms (if it is not clear whether a prisoner was held in a special cell, the cell Certificate, indicating type of cell, can be requested).
- Fifteen minute watch forms.
- Audio tapes of relevant phone calls made by prisoners.
- Video tapes from any CCTV cameras in the vicinity of the incident.

- A list of all prisoners who were in the prison or on the wing at the time of the incident, and an up-to-date list of their locations. This information is held on computer at each prison and can be invaluable in tracking down witnesses.
- Prison disciplinary findings against prisoner victims/prisoner prosecution witnesses.
- Criminal convictions of prisoner and prisoner officer witnesses.
- Emergency Control Room Logs. These are created in the course of more serious incidents or where incidents last for a protracted period of time, and should provide a contemporaneous record of the actions of prison staff involved in managing the incident, and information coming into the control room from other sources.
- Photographs/plans of the area of the prison in which the incident took place.

## Visits to the crime scene

9.237    The Prison Service is usually amenable to allowing defence lawyers to attend a prison to view the scene of the incident and to take photographs of it. Whilst it is generally appropriate to liaise with the police in relation to this, security governors at establishments can also be approached in order to arrange access. If it is important to see any area of the prison other than the one in which the incident took place (eg the segregation block, any sterile areas, sight lines from cells or from the grounds of the prison into the prison) it is advisable to make a written request to the governor beforehand in order that any security arrangements can be made.

9.238    Juries are sometimes taken to view the prison during the course of the trial. In such cases it can be invaluable to have advance knowledge of the layout of the jail, as this will enable informed discussion with the prosecution as to which areas of the prison it would be useful for the jury to see.

## Issues arising at court

9.239    The National Security Framework deals with all issues relating to security at court. Court escorts are often contracted out, and so the policy applies equally to private contractors and prison staff on escort duty. In practice, prison staff are generally used to escort category A prisoners to court; the lower security categories are normally escorted by private security companies.

9.240   As to whether or how a defendant is to be restrained during his or her trial is a matter which falls within the judge's discretion, but the principle in general must be that unless there is a danger of violence or escape, a defendant ought not to be handcuffed or otherwise restrained in the dock, or, more clearly, in the witness box. In *R v Mullen*[318] applying *R v Vratsides*[319] the court stated that, usually there are other means of protecting the public and preventing escape, which involves less risk of prejudice to the defendant. In an appropriate case and with proper authority it may be sufficient to have covertly armed police officers on duty in the court building or in a court room where there is a specially protected dock. If a defendant is to be handcuffed during a trial, the judge must give an appropriate warning to the jury to minimise the risk of prejudice.

9.241   As it is for the court to decide whether handcuffs should be worn in court itself the NSF requires prisons in their local security strategy to include risk assessment procedures to flag up and consider whether an application for handcuffs in court needs to be submitted. The NSF states that applications should routinely be made for high and exceptional risk category A prisoners.

9.242   For all other prisoners, the NSF states consideration should be given to completing a handcuff application where the risk assessment has indicated warnings of violent behaviour, escape risk, concealed weapons, or other areas of concern. Applications may be made regardless of age, gender or legal status.

9.243   Applications for handcuffing in court may only should be submitted on a prescribed form contained in the NSF which requires supporting information about the assessed risks of violence and/or escape and must be signed by an operational manager F or above.

9.244   The NSF states that if the escort contractor becomes aware of additional information that would support a handcuff application both during the escort, or whilst in the court custody unit, through either intelligence received or observing the prisoners behaviour, they should record the information on part C of the handcuff application form, or part B of the Prisoner Escort Record. Prison Custody Officers at court may only raise handcuff application forms themselves if they believe they have strong supporting evidence that a handcuff application is necessary because they consider the prisoner poses a threat to the safety of others in the court, or where there is evidence that the prisoner may attempt to escape. Any such application must be re-

318 [2000] Crim LR 873.
319 [1988] Crim LR 251.

corded in the 'Record of events' section of the PER. Custody officers may also submit applications for prisoners received directly from the police where no formal application has been made, but the prisoner's behaviour, whilst in their custody, causes concern. Such applications should be noted on the PER form if the prisoner is subsequently remanded in custody.

9.245    If the prosecution decline to make an application for handcuffs to be worn in court, they have been requested to return the application form to the issuing prison, clearly stating their reasons. If the application is declined and returned to court custody staff, they may return it to the prison attached to the prisoner's PER form. The same applies if magistrates or judges refuse to allow the application. A court should not accede to a request for handcuffing in the dock merely on the basis of a tick box risk assessment on the PER in light of the importance of the decision. The court should only make such a decision where there is full supporting information.[320]

## Video link evidence for criminal trials

9.246    Prisoners appearing at preliminary hearings in the criminal courts can remain in the prison during the course of the court hearing. The Crime and Disorder Act 1998, ss57A–57E allows for the court to conduct proceedings through live link. The accused is to be treated as present in court when, by virtue of a live link direction, he attends a hearing through a live link.

9.247    It is a procedure which has been well received by prisoners who often prefer to stay at their existing prisons rather than run the risk of going to court and not returning to the same prison at the conclusion of the day's hearing. Prison Service Order 1030 focuses on video links between magistrates' courts and local prisons. Defendants will have been notified by the court on remand to custody from their first appearance that their next hearing is listed for a video links appearance. Defendants must be offered an opportunity to view the training video, provided by Security Group, before their first hearing. Defendants must be escorted to the video court in good time for their allocated timed hearing. When the court is ready to hear a case, the defendant shall be shown into the prison video court. A member of staff will remain with the defendant throughout the hearing, to operate the equipment, and to answer any procedural questions which the defendant may have. Defendants must be escorted to the video

320  *R v Horden* [2009] EWCA Crim 388.

booth in good time for their pre-court conference. Once the legal conference starts, the staff member must leave the booth, so that the confidentiality of the hearing is respected. The defendant will be kept within sight, but out of hearing of prison staff.

9.248    The video link is predominantly used for preliminary hearings; however, it can continue to be used for sentencing hearings too. If at the preliminary hearing, the defendant pleads guilty to a charge, the court can proceed to sentence the accused if the accused consents to the procedure and the court is satisfied that it is not contrary to the interests of justice for him to do so.

# Release: indeterminate sentences

*continued*

# Introduction

10.1    The question of how prisoners come to be released from custody has grown increasingly complex. It is surprising that such a basic and fundamental principle as liberty should be so difficult to negotiate. The roots of these difficulties lie in the constant overhauls of sentencing practice and policy over the last 20 years and the interplay of principles established in English law with the requirements of the European Convention on Human Rights (ECHR). The result is a series of different release arrangements provided for in domestic statues which have then been interpreted through the prism of the rights protected by article 5. Unfortunately, the only way to resolve the problem of how individuals are affected is through a careful analysis of very complex legislation. This chapter will seek to provide an overview of the procedures and processes that must be followed for a prisoner serving a life or indeterminate sentence to be released from prison. A more detailed exploration of the parole process can be found in the companion guide to this book, *Parole Board Hearings: law and practice*[1] which contains a practical guide to all aspects of a parole review and the hearing itself.

10.2    The theory underlying all release arrangements is that prisoners will not serve the sentences imposed by the courts in their entirety but instead have the prospect of release at an earlier stage. The purpose of 'early' release is to provide an incentive for reform and good behaviour whilst in custody and to allow for further supervision and control of the prisoner in the community after release. Early release can take two forms: either as a statutory right which will result in false imprisonment if it is not complied with,[2] or discretionary release where the right at stake is simply to be considered for release.

10.3    The early release schemes are extraordinarily and, arguably, unnecessarily complex. The problem has arisen partly because domestic law has been gradually evolving since the concept of parole was first codified in the Criminal Justice Act 1967. This has resulted in a number of different early release schemes existing side by side, creating confusion for prisoners and prison administrators. The second complicating issue has been the interplay of the ECHR with domestic law and in particular, the relevance of article 5 to early release schemes.

---

1 Arnott & Creighton, 2006, Legal Action Group. Second edition publishing December 2009: see www.lag.org.uk
2 *R v Governor of HMP Brockhill ex p Evans* [2001] 2 AC 19.

10.4    The aim of the Criminal Justice Act (CJA) 2003 (as amended by the Criminal Justice and Immigration Act (CJIA) 2008) has been to try to rationalise the system so that prisoners are effectively divided into two categories: those who are not considered to be dangerous at the time of their conviction and who will qualify for automatic early release subject to the sanction of recall and those who are considered to pose a risk to public safety at the time of sentencing and for whom release will be discretionary. The Carter Report on the criminal justice system, 'Managing Offenders, Reducing Crime: a new approach', which was produced contemporaneously to the Act, noted that although the increased use of imprisonment does not reduce crime:

> Estimates suggest that of the 100,000 persistent offenders who commit 50 per cent of all crime, around 15,000 are held in prison at any one time. If we could identify and incapacitate the 100,000 persistent offenders, crime could fall dramatically.[3]

10.5    The theory underpinning this approach to imprisonment and sentencing would therefore appear to be an attempt to refine incapacitation into one of the main the planks of criminal justice policy. The direct impact of this approach to sentencing has been to place the parole system at the forefront of penal policy. The aim of this chapter will be to provide an explanation of how the parole scheme operates for those who have received life and indeterminate sentences, those being the group of prisoners who can never regain their liberty without the intervention of the Parole Board.

# The historical background

10.6    It is now 40 years since the Parole Board was first established by the CJA 1967. The 1965 white paper, *The Adult Offender* had envisaged a system where:

> prisoners who do not of necessity have to be detained for the protection of the public are in some cases more likely to be made into decent citizens if, before completing the whole of their sentence, they are released under supervision with a liability to recall if they do not behave.[4]

10.7    This aim of conducting risk assessments upon prisoners has re-

---

3  HMSO, 2003, p 5.
4  See Livingstone, Owen & Macdonald, *Prison Law* (Oxford 2008), 4th edn at p502 for a detailed discussion of the history.

mained the principle of the early release system since that time and it is simply the mechanism for conducting this assessment that has changed over the years.

10.8    When the Parole Board was created, it was intended to simply be an administrative arm of the Home Office. It was a body wholly sponsored by the Home Office, its members appointed on behalf of the Secretary of State and its staff were nearly all drawn as seconded placements from the Home Office's prisons department. Most importantly, the board had a purely advisory function making recommendations to the Secretary of State but with virtually no powers to reach binding decisions. The statute was simply an expression of the theory that parole was no more than an executive act of mercy. This theory was expressed judicially by Lord Denning who stated in 1981, when deciding that a mandatory life sentence prisoner was not even entitled to the reasons as to why release had been refused,

> But, so far as I can judge of the matter, I should think that in the interests of the man himself, as a human being facing indefinite detention, it would be better for him to be told the reasons. But, in the interests of society at large, including the due administration of the parole system, it would be best not to give them.[5]

10.9    Over the last twenty years the position has changed following a series of legal challenges brought by prisoners relying on both the requirements of procedural fairness under common law and article 5 of the ECHR. It is important to note that even where article 5 is not engaged, the Parole Board has statutory discretion to hold an oral hearing to determine any issue it has to decide.[6]

## Article 5 and parole

10.10   Now all indeterminate sentences are administered in the same way – the sentence is divided up into two parts – the punitive term set by the sentencing court, following which detention can only be justified where the Parole Board has decided that the offender poses a risk to the public. The reason why the question of whether article 5 applies has been so important is because it requires decisions on detention to be made by a court-like body. The removal of the decision from the executive and turning it into a formal court process ensures higher

---

5   *Payne v Lord Harris of Greenwich and another* [1981] 2 All ER 842.
6   *R v Parole Board ex p Davies*, 25 November 1996, unreported. See now CJA 2003 s239(3).

standards of procedural fairness, such as disclosure, oral hearings and legal representation. The orthodoxy for the past 20 years has been that where article 5(4) applies, it carries a right to an oral hearing.[7] However, the Parole Board is now asserting the view that the decision does not need to be made at an oral hearing and that decisions on the need for an oral hearing will be made on a case by case basis. The amendments made by statutory instrument in the Parole Board (Amendment) Rules 2009 have put this onto a statutory footing.

10.11   In relation to determinate sentences it has been established that article 5(4) does not apply to initial release decisions.[8] However, when a prisoner has already been released and is subsequently recalled to custody, it has been held that there is a new basis for detention and so article 5(4) does apply.[9] The manner in which article 5(4) has been analysed in these cases accepts the view that release before a statutory release date is simply a matter of administration of a lawful sentence imposed by the criminal courts and that the sentencing process safeguards article 5 rights. However, the physical act of release represents a break with the original authority for detention and so a recall to custody raises fresh issues that need to be determined by a court-like body.

10.12   It can be seen that there is a fundamental conceptual difference between determinate and indeterminate sentences in this analysis. Article 5 prevents arbitrary detention and so provides a limited set of lawful purposes of detention. The relevant sections of the article when considering when an oral hearing is required in the parole context are 5(1) – detention 'after conviction by a competent court' and 5(4) – the requirement for the lawfulness of detention to be reviewed by a court like body. The starting point is that where a person is given a custodial sentence as punishment, article 5 is satisfied by the sentence of the court. There is no need for any further proceedings in order to comply with article 5. As the European Court of Human Rights (ECtHR) put it in *De Wilde, Ooms and Versyp v Belgium (No 1)*,[10] where a decision is taken by a court at the close of judicial proceedings, 'the supervision required by article 5(4) is incorporated into the decision'. No fresh issues regarding the lawfulness under article 5 arise because at any point during the sentence the justification for detention remains the sentencing court's decision as to what is

---

7   *Hussain v UK* (1996) 22 EHRR 1.
8   *R (Black) v Secretary of State for Justice* [2009] UKHL 1.
9   *R (Smith) v Parole Board* [2005] UKHL 1.
10  (1971) 1 EHRR 373.

appropriate as punishment. However if domestic law provides for a statutory entitlement to early release on licence, then article 5(1) will be breached by a failure to release a prisoner in accordance with that entitlement.[11] This is not because the nature of the basis of detention has changed, but because of the need in Convention terms for detention to be lawful domestically.

10.13    By contrast, where there may have been a break in the 'causal link' between the detention and the objectives of the sentencing court, article 5(4) may require a court-like body to examine whether detention remains lawful (whatever the domestic arrangements) and to direct release if it is not.[12] This was first applied to life sentences in *Weeks v UK*[13] and was addressed in the case of *Thynne, Wilson & Gunnell v UK*[14] where the ECtHR analysed the nature of the discretionary life sentence. The court considered that as the sentence is imposed on persons who are considered to be unstable or dangerous at the time of sentencing, that it contains a fixed punitive element that is referable to a determinate prison sentence followed by an indefinite protective element where release can be ordered if the prisoner no longer poses a danger to the public. Although the dividing line may be difficult to draw in particular cases, the principles underlying such sentences at that time were that they were composed of a punitive element and subsequently of a security element designed to confer on the Secretary of State the responsibility for determining when the public interest permits the prisoner's release. However, the court's concusion was that:

> ... the detention of the applicants after the expiry of the punitive periods of their sentences is comparable to that at issue in the *Van Droogenbroeck* and *Weeks* cases: the factors of mental instability and dangerousness are susceptible to change over the passage of time and

11  *R v Governor of Brockhill Prison ex p Evans* [1997] QB 443, *Grava v Italy*, Application no 43522/98, 10 July 2003, ECtHR, the principle also applies where conditional release has to be granted by a court: *Gebura v Poland*, Application no 63131/00, 6 March 2007.

12  See *Winterwerp v The Netherlands* (1979) 2 EHRR 387 at p408, para 55 where the European Court held that the *De Wilde* principle could not be sustained in the case of confinement of persons of unsound mind, at any rate when the confinement was for an indefinite period as the reasons initially warranting confinement of persons on the ground of unsound mind might cease to exist and so the very nature of the deprivation of liberty under consideration appeared to require a review of lawfulness to be available at reasonable intervals.

13  (1987) 10 EHRR 293.

14  (1990) 13 EHRR 666.

new issues of lawfulness may thus arise in the course of detention. It follows that at this phase in the execution of their sentences, the applicants are entitled under article 5(4) to take proceedings to have the lawfulness of their continued detention decided by a court at reasonable intervals and to have the lawfulness of any re-detention determined by a court.[15]

10.14   At this stage, the discretionary life sentence was distinguished from the mandatory life sentence on the basis that a conviction for murder actually resulted in a sentence authorising lifelong punitive detention and so release from that sentence was purely a matter of executive discretion.[16] The ECtHR accepted that even though the domestic practice was to set a punitive term, this formal analysis of the sentence was correct.[17]

10.15   The position of prisoners sentence to detention at Her Majesty's Pleasure following a conviction for murder committed when under the age of 18 was distinguished from adult lifers on the basis that the due to the age of the person at the time the offence was committed, the sentence had to allow for maturity and development and so contains a protective as well as a punitive element.[18] When the automatic life sentence was introduced by the Crime (Sentences) Act 1997 (see below), as the sentence required a finding of dangerousness to be made, albeit one where there was a statutory presumption of dangerousness,[19] this line of jurisprudence meant that the domestic statutory regime recognised that article 5(4) was engaged by the release process from the outset.

10.16   For adults convicted of murder, the theory that their punishment consisted of lifelong punitive detention was not displaced until 2002 when the ECtHR examined the case of a mandatory lifer who had been released and then recalled to custody for non-violent offences.[20] The Secretary of State contended that he had the power to keep the

15  (1990) 13 EHRR 666 at para 76.
16  Angela Rumbold's Parliamentary statement of 16 July 1991 analysed the sentence in those terms and was accepted *R v Secretary of State for the Home Department ex p Doody* [1993] 1 AC 531, albeit that the Lords considered that highest standards of procedural fairness applied to decisions affecting the length of the sentence.
17  *Wynne v UK* (1994) 19 EHRR 333.
18  This was first explored in *R v Secretary of State for the Home Department ex p Prem Singh* [1993] COD 501 in the domestic courts before the ECtHR held that article 5(4) does apply to the release and recall of such prisoners in *Hussain & Singh v United Kingdom* (1996) 22 EHRR 1.
19  *R v Offen* [2001] 1 WLR 253.
20  *Stafford v United Kingdom* (2002) 35 EHRR 32.

prisoner in custody pursuant to the original life sentence where there was any risk of the commission of further offences, whether violent or not as otherwise public confidence in the criminal justice system might be undermined. The ECtHR finally rejected this approach on the grounds that once the person had been released, it was clear that the punitive element of the original sentence had been served and that any decision to re-detain had to have a causal link to that sentence otherwise detention would become arbitrary and in breach of article 5(1).[21] The consequent failure to allow for the decision on release to be taken by a court-like body therefore breached article 5(4). This decision effectively ended a ten-year period of divergence between the various types of life sentence and resulted in a unified set of release procedures being introduced.

10.17    The question of whether article 5 has any role to play beyond the provision of a formal hearing before a court-like body on the expiry of the tariff and at regular intervals thereafter was explored in a series of cases concerning the arrangements put in place by the Secretary of State following the introduction of sentences of indeterminate detention for public protection (IPP) which culminated in the House of Lords decision in *R (James (formerly Walker), Lee and James v Secretary of State for Justice.*[22] The various cases had arisen from the chaos that engulfed the lifer system when large numbers of prisoners received IPP sentences but the government had not made sufficient preparation. This was a particular problem as so many of these prisoners had very short tariffs and the result was that many IPP prisoners came to their first parole hearings without any sentence planning having been carried out, with no offending behaviour work completed or with inadequate reports having been written about them. These problems also lead to the Parole Board having to delay hearings until the information they felt that they needed to make a proper and informed risk assessment was available. In the lower courts, judicial opinion had varied as to whether these failings amounted to a breach of article 5(4), or a breach of article 5(1) or both and if so, whether the prisoners continued detention in the absence of an effective parole hearing was unlawful. When the case reached the Lords the Secretary of State accepted that the system had failed to meet the demands placed upon it and this was described by the Lords' as a 'systemic failure'. Having accepted that there was a

---

21  (2002) 35 EHRR 32 at para 81.
22  [2009] UKHL 22.

systemic failure, the Lords then had to answer three questions about the consequences that would follow:

1) Was the post-tariff detention of all or any of the appellants unlawful at common law?
2) Was the post-tariff detention of all or any of the appellants in breach of article 5(1) of the ECHR?
3) Has there been delay in determining their safety for release such as to breach article 5(4) of the Convention?

10.18  The Lords held that the detention after the tariff had expired was not a breach of common law. Lifers can only be released if the Parole Board directs this to happen and the Crime (Sentences) Act 1997 s28 only permits the board to make that direction if the prisoner no longer poses a risk to the public. The Secretary of State's failures could not require the Parole Board to act in a way that might be unlawful. In response to the second question, the prisoners in this case argued that if no treatment was available to them by the time their tariffs had expired, their detention became arbitrary and in breach of article 5(1)(a) as no one could know if there was still good reason for them to remain in prison. The Lords rejected this argument on the grounds that as the IPP sentence is imposed because the sentencing court considers the person to be dangerous at the time of sentencing, there would have to be a very long period of detention with no effective parole review before this could amount to a breach of article 5(1).

10.19  The final challenge was based on article 5(4) and the argument that a review where the parole reports are inadequate does not allow for an effective review of detention and so is in breach of the right. The Lords were troubled by this argument and Lord Simon Brown in the main speech said:

> The appellants' argument is a strong one. What is the point of having a Parole Board review of the prisoner's dangerousness once his tariff period expires unless the board is going to be in a position then to assess his safety for release?

10.20  Ultimately, however, he decided that all that the board required to have a meaningful review that met the obligations of article 5(4) was the basic parole dossier. If the board was unable to order release without receiving further information, this would mean that there was enough evidence for the prisoner to remain detained and so article 5(4) would not be breached. All of the Law Lords who gave opinions were however very critical of the Ministry of Justice. Lord Simon Brown finished his judgment by saying that:

It is a most regrettable thing that the Secretary of State has been found to be – has indeed now admitted being – in systemic breach of his public law duty with regard to the operation of the regime, at least for the first two or three years.

10.21 Lord Hope used even stronger language when he said that: 'There is no doubt that the Secretary of State failed deplorably in [his] public law duty'. However, despite the trenchant criticism, the unanimous rejection of the argument that article 5 could be breached in these circumstances indicated a return to the more procedural view of the application of article 5 to indeterminate prison sentences. That is once the sentence has been lawfully imposed, the guarantee is little more than a formal one requiring a review to be conducted, and it will need truly exceptional circumstances for a substantive breach to occur simply as a result of the conditions that exist within the prison system.

# The different life and indeterminate sentences

10.22 Although the release from these sentences follows the same procedures, the manner in which risk is assessed before release can take place is referable back to the reasons why the sentence was imposed in the first instance. It is therefore necessary to have some understanding of the various types of life and indeterminate sentence to place the progression through the sentence towards release into context.

## Murder

10.23 It is a statutory requirement to impose a life sentence following a conviction for murder and so the sentence is often referred to as the mandatory life sentence. There are three possible mandatory life sentences and the decision about which one applies is dependent upon the age of the prisoner at the time the offence was committed:

- The life sentence which is imposed automatically on persons convicted of murder who are aged 21 or over when the offence is committed (Murder (Abolition of Death Penalty) Act 1965 s1).
- Custody for life which is imposed automatically on people convicted of murder who are aged 18 or over but under 21 when the offence was committed (Powers of Criminal Courts (Sentencing) Act (PCC(S)A) 2000 s93).

- Detention at Her Majesty's Pleasure (HMP detention) is imposed on people convicted of murder who were under the age of 18 when the offence was committed (PCC(S)A 2000 s90). This sentence has a complex history, originally being introduced at the start of the twentieth century to replace the death penalty for minors with indefinite detention. When the death penalty was abolished for adults, the sentence effectively became subsumed into the adult mandatory life sentence but a series of cases over the past 15 years have allowed the courts have allowed the courts to reaffirm the distinctive nature of HMP detention. HMP detention provides an additional safeguard in relation to the review of the minimum term for this class of prisoner as the sentence contains an intrinsic welfare element as well as the normal punitive and protective elements in sentences imposed on adults.

## Discretionary life sentences

10.24    The discretionary life sentence can be imposed where life is the maximum sentence (eg for a range of offences such as attempted murder, manslaughter, arson with intent to endanger life or where there is recklessness, rape, buggery where the victim is under 16, armed robbery or other serious offences of violence). The statutory authority for the sentence to be imposed for offences committed after 4 April 2005 is CJA 2003 s225 which requires the imposition of a life sentence where the offence attracts a maximum of life imprisonment and the court considers that the seriousness of the offence is such to justify the imposition of a life sentence. Prior to the enactment of CJA 2003, the statutory authority for the sentence was found in PCC(S)A 2000 s80) and prior to that it was an offence allowed by the common law.

10.25    The justification for the imposition of a discretionary life sentence arises where the sentencing court believes the offender is dangerous. It is therefore meant to be reserved for offenders whose mental state makes it difficult to predict future risk or where the offences or so serious that there may be ongoing risk. The classic analysis of the criteria required for the imposition of the sentence is contained in *R v Hodgson*:[23]

- where the offence or offences in themselves are grave enough to require a very long sentence;

23  [1968] 15 Cr App R 13.

- when it appears from the nature of the offences or from the defendant's history that he or she is a person of unstable character likely to commit such offences in the future;
- where, if further offences are committed, the consequences to others may be especially injurious, as in the case of sexual offences or cases of violence.

10.26   The second of these criteria, the requirement for mental instability, helped shape the case-law relating to the review and release of this category of lifer due to the overlap between this class of prisoner and persons detained under the Mental Health Acts. However, subsequent case-law has indicated that the sentence is also available in cases where the severity of the offence justifies it, even if there is no direct evidence of mental instability. This development seems to have been particularly concentrated on sexual offending.[24]

## Automatic lifers

10.27   The automatic life sentence had a short lived history having been introduced in 1997 and then removed from 4 April 2005 when it was replaced by the sentence of imprisonment for public protection (see below). However, the sentence was so prevalent for while that there are large numbers of automatic lifers serving the sentence in custody and on licence.

10.28      The sentence was originally introduced by the Crime (Sentences) Act 1997 s2 (subsequently replaced by PCC(S)A 2000 s109). It required the courts to impose a life sentence on anyone convicted for the second time of the following offences:

(1) attempted murder, incitement or conspiracy or soliciting to commit murder;
(2) manslaughter;
(3) wounding or committing GBH with intent;
(4) rape or attempted rape;
(5) sexual intercourse with a girl under 13;
(6) possession of a firearm with intent to injure;
(7) use of a firearm with intent to resist arrest;
(8) carrying as firearm with criminal intent; or
(9) armed robbery.

10.29   Although the second conviction must have been after the 1997 Act came into force, the first conviction can have occurred at any time. The

24  See for example *R v Billam* (1986) 82 Cr App R 347.

statute sought to constrain the discretion available to the judiciary to impose the sentence, hence its description as an 'automatic sentence'. It was also commonly referred to as the 'two strike' sentence.[25]

10.30 The automatic life sentence, after an uncertain start, eventually came to have close parallels with the discretionary life sentence. The rationale for the sentence was founded on the premise that persons convicted of a second serious offence were presumed to be dangerous, unless exceptional circumstances displaced that presumption. In the early days of the sentence, the Court of Appeal created a very narrow test of exceptional circumstances. However, following the application of the Convention to the sentence in *R v Offen*,[26] the Court of Appeal accepted that this construction breached article 5(1) in that it had the potential to render the sentence arbitrary. As a consequence, the Court of Appeal stated that if offenders could establish that they did not pose a continuing danger to the public, the exceptional circumstances criterion would be met. The result was that the sentencing court had to make a finding that persons who had committed a second serious offence presented a potential for continuing danger to the public at the outset before it could be imposed. The statutory framework that presumed the existence of risk following the commission of a second serious offence did mean that the risk posed needed to be somewhat less than that required for a discretionary life sentence.

## Imprisonment for Public Protection (IPP)

10.31 This has replaced the automatic life sentence and has been one of the most contentious sentences of modern times. To qualify for one of the new sentences, the offender must be convicted of a 'specified offence', that is one of the 153 categories of violent or sexual offences listed in CJA 2003, Schedule 15, Parts 1 or 2. Violent offences range from murder to affray and threats of various kinds and sexual offences from rape to indecent exposure.

10.32 A specified offence may or may not be serious (section 224). It will be serious if it is punishable, in the case of a person aged 18 or over, with ten years' imprisonment or more (section 224(2)(b)). If serious, it may attract life imprisonment or imprisonment for public protection for an adult (section 225) or detention for life or detention

25 A reference to the notorious 'three strikes and you're out' legislation introduced in California in the 1990s.
26 [2001] 1 WLR 253.

for public protection for those under 18 on the day of conviction (section 225). It will attract such a sentence if the court is of opinion that there is a significant risk to members of the public of serious harm by the commission of further specified offences and if the minimum term to be imposed for the offence would be two years or more.[27]

10.33 Significant risk must be shown in relation to two matters: first, the commission of further specified, but not necessarily serious, offences; and, secondly, the causing thereby of serious harm to members of the public. If there is a significant risk of both, either a life sentence or indeterminate imprisonment for public protection must be imposed on an adult (section 225(2) and (3)). It must be a life sentence if the offence is one for which the offender is liable to life imprisonment and the seriousness of the offence, or of the offence and one or more offences associated with it, is such as to justify imprisonment for life (section 225(2)); otherwise it must be imprisonment for public protection. For sentences passed on or after 14 July 2008 it is a requirement that the offence is serious enough to justify a minimum term of at least two years (section 225(3)).

10.34 The requirement for a two year minimum term was as a qualifying feature was introduced by the CJIA 2008 to try to halt the explosion in the numbers of prisoners serving IPP and was a response to the Home Affairs' Justice Committee critical report on the sentence and the lack of thought and planning that had preceded its introduction.[28]

10.35 In relation to those under 18, there are similar provisions in relation to detention for life and detention for public protection subject, in the latter case, to an additional criterion by reference to the adequacy of an extended sentence under section 228 (section 226(2) and (3)). By section 229(3), where an offender aged 18 or over has previously been convicted of a specified offence, the court must assume there is a significant risk under sections 225 and 227 unless this would be unreasonable after taking into account information about the nature and circumstance of each offence, any pattern of behaviour of which any offence forms part and the offender.

10.36 The Court of Appeal has, notwithstanding the complexity of the new provisions, held that essentially the sentencing court, as with the old sentences, will really be making a decision as to whether the offender is 'dangerous'.[29] The only key difference between the life

---

27  Sections 225(1), 225(3) and 226(1).
28  'Towards Effective Sentencing' HC-184-1, 22 July 2008.
29  *R v Lang and others* [2005] EWCA Crim 2864 para 8.

and indeterminate sentence is that IPP detainees can apply for their licence to be terminated after ten years in the community[30] whereas a life licence continues indefinitely even after the reporting requirements have ended.

# Fixing the length of the sentence

10.37   The period of time that a lifer must spend in custody before the Parole Board can consider suitability for release is known as the minimum term or relevant part. This is the punitive part of the sentence that is imposed for the purposes of retribution and deterrence. Historically, this part of the sentence was referred to as the 'tariff' but was changed on the advice of the Sentencing Advisory Panel as it was felt that minimum term would help convey more clearly that release at the end of this period is not automatic but dependent on risk being reduced sufficiently. The terms 'tariff' and 'minimum term' are now used interchangeably, although minimum term is the correct expression.

## Minimum terms for murder

10.38   Since 18 December 2003, the Criminal Justice Act 2003 s 269 has required the court which imposes a mandatory life sentence to set the minimum term. Very strict statutory guidelines are contained in Schedule 21 to the CJA 2003. There are three statutory starting points for the length of the term, and aggravating and mitigating features are then considered.

10.39   The sentencing court is also required to specify whether allowance is being given for time spent on remand and if so, how time has been allowed.[31] The term that is imposed is subject to the normal provisions for an appeal against sentence to the Court of Appeal, either by the prisoner or on an Attorney-General's reference.[32]

---

30  CJA 2003 Sch 18.
31  CJA 2003 s269(3).
32  CJA 2003 ss270–271 which also amends section 9(1) of the Criminal Appeal Act 1968.

## Whole life sentences

10.40 Lifers can received a whole life sentence, meaning they will never be eligible for release if they were over 21 at the time the offence was committed and the offence involved:

(a) the murder of two or more persons, where each murder involves any of the following –
(i) a substantial degree of premeditation or planning,
(ii) the abduction of the victim, or
(iii) sexual or sadistic conduct,
(b) the murder of a child if involving the abduction of the child or sexual or sadistic motivation,
(c) a murder done for the purpose of advancing a political, religious or ideological cause, or
(d) a murder by an offender previously convicted of murder.[33]

## 30 years

10.41 A minimum term of 30 years is considered to be the correct starting point for people aged 18 years or over convicted of the following types of murder:

(a) the murder of a police officer or prison officer in the course of his duty,
(b) a murder involving the use of a firearm or explosive,
(c) a murder done for gain (such as a murder done in the course or furtherance of robbery or burglary, done for payment or done in the expectation of gain as a result of the death),
(d) a murder intended to obstruct or interfere with the course of justice,
(e) a murder involving sexual or sadistic conduct,
(f) the murder of two or more persons,
(g) a murder that is racially or religiously aggravated or aggravated by sexual orientation, or
(h) a murder falling within paragraph 4(2) committed by an offender who was aged under 21 when he committed the offence.[34]

## 15-year starting point

10.42 For all other cases where the prisoner is 18 years or older at the time the offence was committed, the starting point is 15 years.[35]

---

33 CJA 2003 Sch 21 para 4.
34 CJA 2003 Sch 21 para 5(2).
35 CJA 2003 Sch 21 para 6.

## Aggravating features

10.43    The factors which will justify a higher sentence being imposed are:

(a) a significant degree of planning or premeditation,
(b) the fact that the victim was particularly vulnerable because of age or disability,
(c) mental or physical suffering inflicted on the victim before death,
(d) the abuse of a position of trust,
(e) the use of duress or threats against another person to facilitate the commission of the offence,
(f) the fact that the victim was providing a public service or performing a public duty, and
(g) concealment, destruction or dismemberment of the body.[36]

## Mitigating factors

10.44    The relevant factors which mitigate the length of the sentence are:

(a) an intention to cause serious bodily harm rather than to kill,
(b) lack of premeditation,
(c) the fact that the offender suffered from any mental disorder or mental disability which (although not falling within section 2(1) of the Homicide Act 1957), lowered his degree of culpability,
(d) the fact that the offender was provoked (for example, by prolonged stress) in a way not amounting to a defence of provocation,
(e) the fact that the offender acted to any extent in self-defence,
(f) a belief by the offender that the murder was an act of mercy, and
(g) the age of the offender.[37]

10.45    These statutory provisions require far more severe sentences to be imposed than those received when 'tariffs' were fixed by the Secretary of State. It is debateable whether this increase would have happened in any event as a result of overall inflation in sentencing, or whether they were a direct response to the loss of executive control over the mandatory life sentence. The outcome remains that the old starting points which varied between 12 and 15 years for most murders[38] and 20 years for the murder of state officials or murders committed with a firearm for gain[39] have been massively inflated.

---

36  CJA 2003 Sch 21 para 10.
37  CJA 2003 Sch 21 para 11.
38  See the discussion of the various Practice Statements concerning life sentences in *R v Sullivan* [2004] EWCA Crim 1762.
39  The infamous Brittan Policy from 1983 which was analysed by the House of Lords in *Re Findlay* [1985] AC 318.

10.46     There have been two particularly significant issues discussed in relation to the current tariff setting procedures. The first was the appropriate reduction for a guilty plea. The longstanding sentencing principle had been that a plea of guilty could result in a reduction of sentence by up to 30 per cent.[40] In the case of murder, this was reviewed by the Sentencing Guidelines Council (SGC) in 2005 and the recommendation was made that:

> 6.5 ... the special characteristic of the offence of murder and the unique statutory provision of starting points, careful consideration will need to be given to the extent of any reduction and to the need to ensure that the minimum term properly reflect the seriousness of the offence. Whilst the general principles continue to apply (both that a guilty plea should be encouraged and that the extent of any reduction should reduce if the indication of plea is later than the first reasonable opportunity), the process of determining the level of reduction will be different.[41]

10.47   The SGC went on to recommend that:

- There will be no reduction for a guilty plea in whole life cases.
- In other cases, the court must avoid imposing 'inappropriately short sentences'.
- The maximum reduction will be one sixth and should never exceed five years.

10.48   In *R v Last and others*[42] the Court of Appeal upheld these guidelines while confirming that there remains a residual discretion for all sentencing courts to depart from them. It has also been confirmed that there should be no reduction to a whole life term following a guilty plea.[43]

10.49     Prior to the introduction of the statutory regime, there had been only a very small band of 'whole lifers'. The legality of the sentence had been challenged by Myra Hindley and it was upheld on the grounds that the Secretary of State retained a discretion to review and reduce the sentence if appropriate.[44] Now that the sentence is imposed by the judiciary and so does not carry the right to be reviewed,

---

40  The requirement for a reduction in sentence to be made following a guilty plea is now contained in the Powers of Criminal Courts (Sentencing) Act 2000 s152.

41  The original report was prepared in 2005 and was updated in 2007 – the reports can be found at the SGCs website: www.sentencing-guidelines.gov.uk/guidelines/council/quick.html

42  [2005] EWCA Crim 106.

43  *R v Jones* [2005] EWCA Crim 3115.

44  *R v Secretary of State for the Home Department ex p Hindley* [2000] 1 QB 152.

there has been renewed judicial consideration of whether it is lawful or whether it carries the risk of breaching article 3. In *Kafkaris v Cyprus*[45] the European Court of Human Rights held that a prisoner who received a whole life sentence in Cyprus retained some prospect, albeit limited, of release and as such, the imposition of the sentence did not constitute inhuman or degrading treatment.

10.50    This was followed domestically in *R v Bieber*[46] where a lifer who had been convicted of the murder of one police officer and the attempted murder of two others a well as various firearms offences appealed against the trial judge's decision to impose a whole life tariff. The trial judge had accepted that the statutory starting point for the offence was a 30-year tariff, but he considered that the aggravating features of the case where one injured officer had then been shot in the head justified a departure from that starting point and the imposition of a whole life order. The appellant argued that, as a matter of principle, the whole life term was objectionable as it breached article 3 and that on the facts of his case, the departure from the starting point was unjustified. The Court of Appeal decided to quash the sentence accepting that even though the offence was horrific, it was difficult to suggest that the nature of the killing took it from one statutory starting point to the next. The judgment went on to explore whether a whole life sentence is compatible with article 3 and followed *Kafkaris* which had established the following general points of principle:

(a) The imposition of a sentence of life imprisonment will not involve a violation of article 3 if the sentence is reducible.
(b) The fact that the offender may be detained for the whole of his life does not involve a violation of article 3.
(c) The imposition of a life sentence that is irreducible may raise an issue under article 3.[47]

10.51    As domestic law provides the Secretary of State with the power to release any prisoner on compassionate grounds pursuant to Crime (Sentences) Act 1997 s30), the sentence of whole life imprisonment could not be classified as irreducible and so did not breach article 3.

10.52    The Court of Appeal has confirmed that it is inappropriate to impose life sentences consecutive to each other[48] and instead the overall sentence should reflect the fact that there have been two offences

---

45   Application no 21906/04, 12 February 2008, ECtHR Grand Chamber.
46   [2008] EWCA Crim 1601.
47   At para 27.
48   *R v O'Brien* [2006] EWCA Crim 1714 involving sentences of IPP.

committed.[49] However, it is possible to order determinate sentences to run concurrently to life sentences.[50]

## Transitional cases

10.53   There are very large numbers of prisoners serving life sentences for murder that were imposed prior to 18 December 2003. These comprise one group who had minimum terms set by the Secretary of State when he still retained this power and a smaller group who never had a minimum term set by the Secretary of State as their convictions occurred after it was decided it was in breach of article 6 for him to fix these sentences.[51] Both of these groups of lifers are entitled to have a judicially set minimum term. Those who never had a minimum term fixed had cases considered by a High Court judge as a result of an automatic referral by the Secretary of State whereas those who did have a tariff or minimum term set by the Secretary of State obtained the right apply to the court if they wish to have their term reset by a High Court judge, providing the existing term had not already expired.[52]

10.54   Prior to the enactment of CJA 2003, the decision on how long a mandatory lifer should serve before being released was solely a matter for the executive. The power to set the 'tariff' was regarded as ancillary to the power to release lifers.[53] As noted above in the *Payne* decision, the parole and tariff setting procedures carried no procedural rights for 30 years. It was not until the case of *R v Secretary of State for the Home Department ex p Doody*[54] that the House of Lords recognised that as the mandatory life sentence as a matter of substance contained a penal term followed by a protective term, that certain procedural safeguards were put in place. Lord Mustill formulated six principles of fairness in the administrative decision making process and where, as here, the issue at stake was the length of imprisonment, it was held that fairness required the disclosure

49   *R v Malasi* [2008] EWCA Crim 2505 at para 23 where this was approved in a case where there was a conviction for two separate murders.

50   *R v Hills and others* [2008] EWCA Crim 1871.

51   This occurred in November 2002 when the House of Lords ruled in *R (Anderson) v Secretary of State for the Home Department* [2003] AC 837.

52   CJA 2003 Sch 22 paras 6 and 3(1)–(2).

53   A power first contained in the Murder (Abolition of Death Penalty) Act 1952 s2 and subsequently enacted in CJA 1967 s61(1) and CJA 1991 s39.

54   [1994] 1 AC 531.

of the gist of material to be considered by the Secretary of State, the right to make representations and the right to be informed of the decision reached. The practice at the time was for the trial judge to complete a report following a conviction for murder setting out the facts of the case and recommendations for the appropriate tariff. The Lord Chief Justice would then add his view and these would be considered before a final decision was made by the Secretary of State. These reports will often still form part of the parole dossiers for lifers sentenced under this regime.[55] When an application is made pursuant to CJA 2003 for a tariff set by the Secretary of State to be reset by a High Court judge as a minimum term, these papers will form part of the material to be considered.

10.55    The legislation states that when the court sets the term for these transitional groups, it is prohibited from setting a minimum term greater than the previously notified tariff or the term that would have been set by the Secretary of State at the time. This provision was presumably introduced as it was considered that a decision to increase the old tariff might breach article 7 of the ECHR, although subsequent cases would seem to indicate that a decision to increase a sentence providing it does not exceed the maximum available at the time would not amount to a breach.[56] Leaving aside the Convention, as a matter of common law the House of Lords had already decided that a decision to increase a tariff under the old scheme would breach the longstanding principle of non-aggravation of penalties.[57] It is possible, therefore, that the legislative provision is in recognition of this common law principle.

10.56    In reaching a decision, the legislation requires the High Court to have regard to:

- the term previously set;
- the judicial recommendations; and
- the guidance contained in CJA 2003 Sch 21 for current sentences.[58]

The procedure for setting the minimum terms was originally intended to be conducted solely in writing, although the final decision

55  For a detailed discussion of the history of mandatory life sentences see Livingstone, Owen and Macdonald, *Prison Law* (fourth edition, 2008, OUP) at pp566–576.
56  See for example *Flynn v Lord Advocate* (2004) *Times* 18 March; *R (Uttley) v Secretary of State for the Home Department* [2004] UKHL 38 and *Kafkaris v Cyprus* Application no 21906/04, 12 February 2008, ECtHR Grand Chamber.
57  *R v Secretary of State for the Home Department ex p Pierson* [1998] AC 539.
58  CJA 2003 Sch 22 para 4.

is given in open court. However, the House of Lords established that the court does retain the power to convene an oral hearing where it is necessary.[59] The High Court has a specific department, the life imprisonment minimum terms section (or LIMIT) responsible for processing these application. A pro forma has to be completed requiring details of the original conviction and tariff set by the executive to be entered and inviting written representations. Public funding is available to advise and draft representations under the Criminal Defence Service's advice and assistance scheme. Any request for an oral hearing should be made in this application. It is now practice for the application to be notified to the CPS office responsible for the case to ensure that any additional material that might be needed by the court for the application to be determined is available. Inquiries will also be made to see if any of the victim's family wish to make impact statements and these will be disclosed. The final decisions are available on the Court Service's website.[60] A right of appeal exists against the decision, either by the prisoner or on a reference by the Attorney-General.[61]

10.57 The legislative scheme that requires the court to have regard to the various recommendations and decisions does not resolve the issue of which should prevail where there is a discrepancy. There were, for example, a significant number of tariffs set by the Secretary of State at a higher level than the judicial recommendations. In *R v Riaz*,[62] a case where the trial judge had recommended a ten-year term, the Lord Chief Justice 15 years, and the tariff was actually set by the Secretary of State at 20 years, Hooper J commented:

> 48 ... Unaided as I am by any representations from the Secretary of State as to how I should approach paragraph 4 and unaided by submissions in an oral hearing, I confess that I find paragraph 4 very difficult if not impossible to apply. In crude mathematical terms, there are now three views of the seriousness of the offence to which I must have regard as reflected in the terms recommended or notified or laid down in Schedule 21: 16 years, 20 years, and whole life. It is not possible to reconcile the views and I must therefore make a choice.

10.58 In the event, the choice made in that case was to prefer the views expressed by the Lord Chief Justice of the day on the basis that he had oversight of the terms recommended for all mandatory lifers and so

59  *R (Hammond) v Secretary of State for the Home Department* [2005] UKHL 69.
60  www.hmcourts-service.gov.uk/cms/minterms.htm
61  CJA 2003 Sch 22 paras 14–15.
62  [2004] EWHC 74(QB).

was in the best position to distil the judicial view. These decisions do not appear to be made with strict reference to the principle of precedent and so it does not appear that this is necessarily an approach that has to be followed. Certainly, the inflation brought about in the length of minimum terms by the CJA 2003 seems to be increasingly influential in High Court decisions on resetting tariffs.

10.59    The other factor that still has to be taken into account is whether there is any exceptional progress that should serve to reduce the term. It was a requirement of the old scheme that tariffs had to be kept under review by the Secretary of State and that the tariff could be reduced if there had been exceptional progress by the prisoner.[63] When the process was judicialised, there was some debate as to whether this could remain as other criminal sentences do not attract the possibility of a reduction for progress made in custody.

10.60    However, in *Cole, Rowland and Hawkes*[64] the Divisional Court confirmed that this class of lifer had an ongoing expectation and right that exceptional progress would continue to be taken into account. The evidence of the Secretary of State about what would constitute exceptional progress rather than the normal expected progress was quoted in full by the Court of Appeal and remains the basis for making these decisions:

> The Home Secretary has never issued a definition of what constitutes progress in prison. Cases are considered on an individual basis and exceptional progress has to stand out clearly from the good progress in prison that is expected of all mandatory life sentence prisoners. In broad terms the Home Secretary would look for an exemplary work and disciplinary record in prison, genuine remorse, and successful engagement in work (including offence-related courses) that has resulted in substantial reduction in areas of risk. All these would have to have been sustained over a lengthy period and in at least two different prisons. To reach the threshold of exceptional progress there would also need to be some extra element to show that the lifer had done good works for the benefit of others. Examples would be acting as a Listener (helping vulnerable prisoners), helping disabled people use prison facilities, raising money for charities, and helping to deter young people from crime. Again there would need to be evidence of sustained involvement in at least two prisons over a lengthy period.

10.61    The Court of Appeal has subsequently held that the progress must be 'outstanding', and that where it does warrant a reduction in mini-

---

63  See *R v Secretary of State for the Home Department ex p Hindley* [2000] 1 QB 152.
64  [2003] EWHC 1789 (Admin).

mum term this will be 'very modest'.[65] Accordingly decisions of the High Court have confirmed that exceptional progress would justify a reduction in the minimum term of no more than two years.[66]

## HMP detainees

10.62 The minimum term for this group is set by the trial judge pursuant to the Powers of Criminal Courts (Sentencing) Act 2000 s90 and the relevant principles to be taken into account when setting the term are contained in CJA 2003 Sch 21 para 7. This specifies that the starting point will be 12 years. The normal aggravating and mitigating factors specified in the Act (see paras 10.43–10.44 above) should then be applied to the sentence. Although the statutory regime specifically excludes people under the age of 21-years-old from the whole life orders and people under 18 years from the 30 years staring points, this does not mean that very lengthy sentences are precluded for under 18-year-olds.

10.63 In one case, a 16-year-old was convicted of one murder and pleaded guilty to another separate murder and fell to be sentenced for both at the same time. The trial judge's approach which was to accept that the starting point was 12 years but to treat the circumstances of the murder and second murder as aggravating features justifying a longer minimum term. He also considered it preferable to have one minimum term to reflect the gravity of the offences rather than two separate terms for each offence. The appropriate term for the first murder was considered to be 24 years and for the second 12 years. The trial judge decided to aggregate these terms making a total of 36 years and then reduce the period to take account of the totality of the sentence arriving at a term of 30 years which would be imposed for each murder. The Court of Appeal upheld this approach, notwithstanding the very strong mitigating factors advanced on behalf of defendant, and in doing so making a comparison as to a likely sentence of 35 years that would have been imposed under the statutory regime for adult lifers just 18 months older.[67] The Court of Appeal's comparator with an adult sentence is somewhat disturbing in the context of the sentencing of children. It is the very nature of the

---

65  *In Re Caines, In Re Roberts* [2006] EWCA Crim 2915.

66  See for example *R v Cadman* [2006] EWHC 586 (Admin), *R v Miller* [2008] EWHC 719 (QB).

67  *R v Malasi* [2008] EWCA Crim 2505.

mandatory indeterminate sentence for children, with the incorporation of a welfare element, that has required there to be such a firm distinction between the lengths of the minimum terms imposed upon children and adults. As this distinction has been preserved by parliament it is perhaps unhelpful for the Court of Appeal to suggest that 18 months is a short period of time as this actually represents a significant period time in the life span of a minor.

10.64    As with adult mandatory lifers, there was a significant period of time where this class of prisoner had a tariff set by the Secretary of State. This practice was found to breach article 6 in the case of *V & T v United Kingdom*.[68] Prior to the introduction of new legislation, a decision was taken to all HMP detainees serving tariffs set by the Secretary of State to apply to the Lord Chief Justice for a minimum term to be set judicially. That process has now been completed[69] and would be an historical footnote except for the fact that the House of Lords held that as a result of welfare element of the sentence, there remains a duty on the Secretary of State to keep these sentences under review to ascertain whether the detainee's progress warrants a reduction in the minimum term even where it has been set or reset judicially.[70] The Lords' decision only required the tariffs set before 30 November 2000 to be the subject of ongoing review. This was the appropriate cut off date as the changes brought in by the Powers of Courts Criminal (Sentencing) Act 2000 s90 required minimum terms to be set by the trial judge as from that date. The Secretary of State decided, notwithstanding the limits to this judgment, to extend the review process to all HMP detainees, whenever sentenced.

10.65    The Secretary of State's policy is to allow the detainee to apply for a review after serving one half of the minimum term. The process is administered by a tariff department at PPU. If an application is made, the prison will prepare a set of reports and these will be compiled into a dossier together with the original tariff papers, information about the offence, previous convictions and progress in prison and, if a parole review has taken place, the parole reports. This process should take 12 weeks and the prisoner then has 30 days to make written representations. If it is not sent on for judicial consideration,

---

68    (2000) 30 EHRR 121. See also *R v Secretary of State for the Home Department ex p V & T* [1998] AC 407 where the House of Lords had previously found that the decisions on the individual cases were irrational but that there had been no breach of article 6.

69    The decisions can be found at www.hmcourts-service.gov.uk/cms/145.htm

70    *R (Smith )v Secretary of State for the Home Department* [2006] 1 AC 159; [2005] UKHL 51.

then the prisoner will be informed of the reasons and given a further 30 days to respond. If PPU consider that the criteria for a reduction may be met, the application will be forwarded onto a High Court judge for a decision to be made and the Secretary of State has agreed to be bound by the judicial advice.

10.66   The most significant matters that will be looked into are whether there has been a significant change in maturity and outlook since the offence was committed, whether there are risks to the detainee's development that cannot be sufficiently mitigated in custody and any information that might cast doubt on the correctness of the original tariff. There is no case-law dealing with the application of these criteria at present, but the history of this procedure seems to suggest that critical points in the sentence might include a move from an STC to a YOI, or from there onto an adult prison. In *Venables and Thompson*[71] Lord Woolf explained that this was a highly relevant factor in his decision:

> They are both now 18 years of age. Being 18 they would be due to be transferred to young offenders' institutions. The reports make clear that the transfer would be likely to undo much of the good work to which I have referred. Having been living in an unnaturally protected environment, they are unprepared for the very different circumstances in which they would be detained in a young offenders' institution. They are unlikely to be able to cope, at least at first, with the corrosive atmosphere with which they could be faced if transferred. There is also the danger of their being exposed to drugs, of which they are at present free. [para 13]

10.67   In addition to these criteria, the exceptional progress reduction that can apply to transitional adult mandatory lifers is also relevant for all HMP detainees. A reduction in the minimum term may be authorised if such progress can be demonstrated (see para 10.59 above).

10.68   There is no right to an oral hearing in this procedure. When the original case came before the Lords, they also heard a co-joined appeal from another HMP detainee who argued that the failure to afford him an oral hearing when his tariff was reset by the Lord Chief Justice had breached article 6(1). He had further argued that in order for the minimum term to properly take account of the welfare principle, it should be reduced and this would allow the need for continuing review to be discharged by the Parole Board rather than by the executive.[72] The appeal was dismissed and the new procedures appear to

---

71  www.hmcourts-service.gov.uk/legalprof/tariffs/tariff_t_v.htm
72  *R (Dudson) v Secretary of State for the Home Department* [2005] UKHL 52.

address the concerns raised about the need for continuing review to be independent of the executive. A decision about the lack of an oral hearing is pending in the European Court of Human Rights.[73]

## Discretionary lifers, automatic lifers and IPP detainees

10.69   These categories of lifer all have their minimum terms set by the trial judge according to the procedures contained in PCC(S)A 2000 s82A. The executive has no input to the sentence and it is subject to the normal appeal procedures. Once a minimum term has been fixed, the prisoner cannot be considered for release until that period has been served in full.[74] The court should normally deduct the time spent on remand when calculating the term.[75]

10.70   As with mandatory lifers, a whole life order is available to the court should the offences be serious enough.[76] It is difficult to imagine a case where a whole life order would appropriate for such these categories of lifers bearing in mind the principles that must be applied. The Court of Appeal has established that the normal approach is to specify the appropriate determinate sentence that would apply and then to set the minimum term at one half of that period to reflect the parole eligibility dates for determinate prisoners.[77] The minimum term must be imposed taking account solely with reference to the requirements of retribution and deterrence and must not take account of the need to protect the public which is a decision to be made by the Parole Board on the expiry of the term.[78] As noted above, for sentences of IPP imposed since 14 July 2008, the equivalent determinate sentence has to be four years or more to meet the threshold of seriousness.[79] Whilst the norm has been for the sentence to be one

---

73   The article 6(1) application being founded on the ECtHR decision in *Easterbrook v United Kingdom*, Application no 48015/99, 12 June 2003 where a similar transitional arrangement that allowed the Lord Chief Justice to reset tariffs for discretionary lifers after that process was judicialised by CJA 1991 was found to be in breach.

74   PCC(S)A 2000 s82A(2).

75   *R v Marklew* [1999] 1 WLR 485.

76   PCC(S)A 2000 s82A(4).

77   *R v Secretary of State for the Home Department ex p Furber* [1998] 1 All ER 23; *R v Marklew* [1999] 1 Cr App R (S) 6; *R v Szczerba* [2002] 2 Cr App R (S) 387.

78   *R v Wheaton* [2005] 1 Cr App R (S) 425.

79   CJIA 2008 s13.

half of the determinate sentence, the Court of Appeal has refused to be too prescriptive allowing leeway up to the two thirds point in more serious cases. This was reflected in the legislation which made specific reference to the early release provisions of the Criminal Justice Acts as a basis for determining the minimum term.[80]

10.71 Until the inflation in sentencing that occurred with CJA 2003 and the increase in the use of whole life terms for mandatory lifers, it was difficult to imagine any determinate sentence that could be so long that it could result in a whole life term for other lifers once the appropriate adjustments had been made. However, in addition to this general inflation in sentences, CJIA 2008 s19 has amended the statutory framework so that in serious cases, minimum terms can be set with reductions of just one third or less from the notional determinate by inserting new provisions into section 82A of PCC(S)A 2000 (although as at 31 January 2009, no commencement date for these provisions had been announced). The prospect of whole life terms for non-mandatory lifers is therefore more likely in the future.

## Serving the life sentence

10.72 The introduction of the automatic life sentence and IPP has resulted in an explosion in the lifer population. In 1992 there were less than 3,000 lifers. This had risen to just under 4,000 in 1998 but by September 2008, the figure stood at 11,659. IPP prisoners represented nearly 5,000 of this total, a figure that had doubled since February 2007.[81] The average length of the IPP minimum term before the legislative move to restrict the IPP sentence to cases where the minimum term must be two years or more, was 38 months with half of those being less than 20 months. While the changes are therefore likely to slow the rate of increase in the lifer population,[82] the absolute numbers of lifers looks likely to increase for many years to come, not least because of the bottlenecks caused to the system by the sheer weight of numbers.[83]

10.73 This increase in numbers and the relatively short length of the

---

80  PCC(S)A 2000 s82A(3)(c).

81  These figures are summarised in the Prison Reform Trust's *Bromley Briefing; Prison Factfile, December 2008* p12. The Ministry of Justice publishes regular statistics on the prison population and sentencing trends.

82  It is predicted that this will result in a decrease of approximately 305 in the numbers of people receiving IPP sentences: *Bromley Briefing: Prison Factfile, December 2008*, Prison Reform Trust, p13.

83  The Prison Reform Trust record that by July 2008 only 31 IPP prisoners had been released and that 880 had served beyond their tariffs: *Bromley Briefing: Prison Factfile, December 2008*, Prison Reform Trust p12.

terms to be served compared to discretionary and mandatory life sentences has forced NOMS to radically rethink the manner in which lifers are managed. When the system was designed to cope with prisoners serving tariffs of ten years or more, there was room for a slow and measured approach to the sentence. This involved progression through prison categories from high security or category B prisons, through to category C and then onto open conditions to prepare for release. Whilst this system is still in place for prisoners serving minimum terms of five years or more, the for those with shorter terms the system has had to become more flexible to accommodate the different offending behaviour requirements and the lesser need for people to spend time in an open prison after a short sentence than is needed after a lengthy time in prison.

10.74   The key document issued by NOMS to guide progress through the life sentence is Prison Service Order 4700 or 'The Lifer Manual'. This is a comprehensive document providing guidance on every aspect of the management of persons serving life sentences. It was originally prepared when the numbers of lifers was relatively small and as the sentence has been extended, it is planned to gradually replace it with an Indeterminate Sentence Manual. It is likely that the various chapters of the Lifer Manual will be replaced by the new Indeterminate Sentence Manual gradually (the first chapters of the Indeterminate Sentence Manual were in fact issued in July 2009).

10.75   The overarching policy statement in relation to lifers is that:

> The Prison Service, working in accordance with its statement of purpose, vision, goals and values, and jointly with the Probation Service, aims to work constructively with life sentence prisoners by:
> - keeping them in custody and ensuring the safety and protection of the public;
> - allocating them to prisons whose regimes best meet individual needs;
> - helping them come to terms with their offence;
> - assisting them to identify, address and modify their problem behaviour and attitudes; and
> - ensuring their suitability for release is objectively assessed by staff in a range of settings.[84]

10.76   Historically, lifers have always posed a particular organisational problem due to the tension between the desire of the Ministry of Justice (formerly the Home Office) to maintain control over the life sentence and the practicalities of the sentence which require individual prisons

---

84   PSO 4700 para 1.8.

to assess lifers and prepare reports upon them. It is important to have a little understanding of this history in order to make sense of parole dossiers for lifers who have served along time in prison. Originally, all decisions on the progress and allocation of lifers were made centrally by two departments at the Home Office:[85] the Lifer Management Unit and Lifer Review Unit. Eventually, the functions of these two departments were merged into a consolidated Lifer Unit. In 2004, this department was replaced by the Lifer Review and Recall Section (LRRS) which retained responsibility for the parole review process but decisions on categorisation and allocation were devolved to the prisons holding the individual lifers. In late 2008, LRRS was replaced by the Public Protection Unit (PPU) whose responsibility is:

- to monitor the whole parole review process for all lifers;
- to consider individual recommendations in those cases where the Parole Board has recommended the transfer of a lifer from closed to open conditions;
- to consider and where appropriate, to refer cases to the Parole Board for advice on a lifer's continued suitability for open conditions;
- to monitor the progress of life licensees in the community, including recall to custody and the cancellation of supervision;
- to oversee and develop policy in respect of lifers in the above areas
- to liaise with the Prison Service on operational lifer policy development.[86]

10.77    It is important to note that decision pertaining to category A lifers, both in relation to their categorisation and allocation are still dealt with centrally by the Director of High Security Prisons acting on behalf of the Secretary of State.

## The remand stage

10.78    Remand and local prisons are instructed to identify those on remand who may face a life sentence, those who are newly convicted and have received a life sentence and recalled lifers. The reasoning behind this is because lifers are considered to require closer support than those serving determinate sentences with particular concerns at hopelessness and the prospect of self-harm. A lifer management team is required to be in place at all prisons (now within the

---

85  This was prior to the movement of NOMS to the Ministry of Justice.
86  PSI 8/2004 amending PSO 4700 para 3.

offender management units) holding potential lifers including a lifer manager, a lifer trained wing manager and a multi-disciplinary team that must include a seconded probation officer. The guidance suggests that potential lifers should be offered this special support on the first night it is identified that they fall within this category and for newly sentenced lifers, within 24 hours of reception. Information should be made available to the prisoner about the life sentence and staff should be prepared to meet with family members to explain what a life sentence means. Voluntary measures suggest establishing a prisoner lifer group for mutual support and family days to involve families more closely.[87]

10.79    Identifying potential lifers is necessarily a difficult task for all charges other than murder. The guidance has been that charges of arson, rape, manslaughter and buggery would alert staff to the possibility of a life sentence being imposed, as would the presence of serious previous convictions. Interestingly, this advice has not been updated since the implementation of IPP sentences which has massively increased the range of offences for which an indeterminate sentence might be imposed. Once identified a form LSP 0 should be completed to act as a record for future reference. Regimes will not be any different for potential lifers than for anyone else on remand.

## Male young offenders

10.80    Young offenders do not have formal security classifications beyond Category A and an assessment for suitability for closed or open prisons. Once a life sentence has been imposed they will ordinarily be allocated to one of the four long-term closed YOIs at Aylesbury, Castington, Moorland and Swinfen Hall. On reception an immediate review should be held to determine whether the young offender should be allocated to education or employment and this is followed by a more comprehensive review after six months that is intended to address personal and training and remedial needs as well as identifying areas of concern and risk that need to be addressed (PSO 4700 para 10.5). It is usual practice to transfer young offenders to the adult prison between the ages of 21 and 22, although for those serving long sentences this can often occur earlier. Transfer can be to any category of prison depending on the length of the sentence left and the progress made. On transfer, responsibility for management reverts to the normal adult system.

87   PSO 4700 paras 4.3.9–4.3.10.

## Female lifers

10.81  The number of women in prison has increased rapidly in the past ten years with the overall female population standing at nearly 4,500 in 2008 compared with just over 2,500 in 1997.[88] As at 31 October 2008, there were a total of 366 women serving life sentences.[89] The number of female establishments has also risen to 15 and this has allowed for women lifers to have a structure for sentence planning and release that more closely follows male lifers and so the procedures set for male lifers below can now be applied to women as well.

10.82  Women's prisons are formally allocated as first and second stage lifer establishments, the first stage prisons usually being Buckley Hall, Bullwood Hall, Durham and Holloway. The second stage prisons are Buckley Hall, Cookham Wood, Durham, Foston Hall, Holloway and Styal. As there is an overlap between the prisons holding first and second stage lifers, it is important for female lifers to ensure that it is noted on their sentence plans when they have moved onto the second stage, as there is a greater chance that they will remain in the same establishment despite the progression.

## Adult male lifers

10.83  It is a requirement that all life sentenced prisoners have a life sentence plan, the purpose of which is to structure the sentence from remand to release. The implementation of a single sentence planning framework allows for all information on risk assessment and progress to be integrated and properly monitored. This requires all of the different assessment systems to be considered and summarised. In addition, it allows the individual to understand what objectives have been set. There are currently two overlapping systems in place with the Offender Management Model (OMM)[90] covering IPP prisoners convicted after 7 January 2008 gradually being rolled back to include all IPP prisoners and other lifers. It is therefore necessary to look at both models.

10.84  The new OMM requires that the offender manager (OM) completes an OASys prior to the pre-sentence report and that these documents are provided to the prison for the first sentence planning review

---

88  NOMS, *Prison Population and Accommodation Briefing*, 21 November 2008.

89  Ministry of Justice, Lifer News, Winter 2008/2009, p8.

90  Available at http://noms.justice.gov.uk/news-publications-events/publications/ guidance/phase_III_implementation_guide/Phase_III_Specification_ doc?view=Binary

following sentence. This review should take place within either eight weeks or 16 weeks of the sentence depending on the length of the tariff. If the tariff is two years or under the shorter time scale is applied. If the OASys was not completed before sentencing, a post sentence report and OASys should be provided within that time. Additionally, as part of the induction process and within ten days of the sentence a 'promoting protective factors' (accommodation, employment, family ties, healthcare) assessment should be completed by Prison Service staff and an interview conducted by the offender supervisor (OS) and feedback from that interview should be conveyed to back to the OM.

10.85   The OASys therefore becomes the primary tool for sentence planning within the prison and the OS then has responsibility for assisting the OM in obtaining Sentence Planning and Review (SPR) Reports for sentence planning review meetings to aid the sentence planning process. The OS is tasked with 'driving forward' the plan during the custodial period. The OM, following consultation with the OS, reviews and revises the OASys risk of re-conviction, risk of serious harm and sentence plan no more than 12 months after the last review while the offender is in custody. A review meeting is chaired by the OM, either in person or by video link and involves the offender, OS and any relevant key workers or specialist staff working with the offender. This review meeting must be held at a minimum once every year. Early experiences of this system have indicated that it can cause considerable delay in starting the sentence planning process and that the OM often does not have access to the information needed to keep the OASys up to date, particularly when the prisoner has been undertaking substantial work on offending behaviour issues in custody.

10.86   For those IPP prisoners already in custody on 7 January 2008 and for other lifers, transition to this new scheme is determined on a case by case basis. Until then, the existing sentence planning scheme remains in place for this group. This required that following conviction, the following forms were to be completed by the local prison:[91]

LSP 1A   Post conviction immediate needs assessment
LSP 1B   Initial allocation to first stage prison
LSP 1C   Post conviction induction report
LSP 1D   Local prison lifer profile
LSP 1E   Multi-agency lifer risk assessment panel report
LSP 1F   Pre-transfer report to first stage prison
LSP 1G   Pre-first stage report

91  PSO 4700, para 8.3.

10.87   The forms LSP 1B and LSP 1G must be sent to PPU. For all lifers other than IPP prisoners, the prison should then identify three potential options for allocation and notify these options to the Population Management Section – a department at NOMS that organises the physical movement of prisoners. The special arrangements for IPP prisoners are set out below. PMS then make arrangements for the move to take place. Adult male lifers are expected to pass through three stages in their sentence: first stage being the initial allocation where the core sentence planning and offending behaviour work is completed; second stage which can include a mixture of time in category B training prisons and category C prisons where the focus gradually shifts to rehabilitation; and third stage which is reached when a move to open conditions to commence resettlement work. The first stage prisons are normally either the one of the five high security prisons (Frankland, Full Sutton, Long Lartin, Wakefield, Whitemoor) or the following category B training prisons: Cardiff, Bristol, Dovegate, Gartree, Liverpool, Manchester, Swaleside and Wormwood Scrubs. All category A prisoners will be allocated to a high security prison, of which there are currently five. Non-category A prisoners can also be allocated to a high security prison if it felt that the offence or the lifer's history justifies these conditions. For category A prisoners, the LSP 1B form should be used and marked 'high security allocation'.

10.88   The police will also be asked to supply information about each convicted lifer and this usually consists of a summary of the evidence in a case and permits the senior investigating officer to attend a meeting at the prison to discuss the case if necessary. It is intended that the written document will be received at the prison within two months of the sentence and rather worryingly, it is treated as a confidential document. The document should then be considered by a multi-agency lifer risk assessment panel (MALRAP) that is convened by the lifer manager and should include the following staff as a minimum: the lifer manager, the wing lifer officer or personal officer, the home probation officer and the police investigating officer(s). This panel is intended to inform the home probation officers post sentence report (LSP 1F) and will also generate a confidential document to be placed on the individual's file with risk factors entered into the life sentence plan. This procedure is potentially quite worrying for lifers as it does involve a mechanism for the police to feed concerns into the sentence planning process without any check or balance in the system. Police reports that have routinely appeared in determinate parole dossiers (police forms MG5) have tended to contain an account of the police investigation including reference to police suspicions and unconvicted allegations. The prospect of sentence planning and risk factors being based on undisclosed material does have the potential to undermine the general principle of openness in the reporting process and may in some cases breach basic standards of administrative fairness.

10.89   A life sentence plan (LSP) will produced after conviction at the prison to which the lifer is allocated immediately after conviction (the first stage) – see PSI 26/2006. After an OASys assessment (currently not mandatory) and completion of the core life sentence plan document (LSP2) the lifer should progress to the second stage (either a category B or C prison). This is where the majority of the work on addressing the risk factors identified in the LSP will be carried out. From 1 October 2007 initial risk factors will be set by using the OASys 2 report supplemented by the form OASys 7A instead of the LSP 2.[92]

10.90   There should be an annual reviews of the life sentence plan (with reports known as LSP 3B reports) and more intense reviews at significant points of the sentence, such as the completion of a relevant piece of offending behaviour work and at least every five years. The more intensive reviews are completed on forms LSP 3E reports and are the same as the format used for compiling reports for Parole Board reviews. During their time in category B or high security prisons, male lifers will usually carry out the bulk of the offending behaviour work identified on the life sentence plan. It is quite common, particularly for those serving longer sentences, to spend time in a number of different category B prisons.

10.91   Once a lifer is considered suitable for the second stage, they can be moved to either another category B prison (the second stage ones are: Albany, Bristol, Cardiff, Dovegate, Dovegate Therapeutic Community, Garth, Gartree, Grendon, Kingston main, Parkhurst, Rye Hill, Swaleside) or, if their categorisation is reduced to category C, onto a category C prison.[93]

10.92   Guidance on the factors to be taken into account on the allocation decision are set out in PSI 26/2006, annex A. These encompass security issues, control issues, life sentence issues, risk assessment and regime issues. The areas will require consideration is given to the nature of the offence, any history of escape planning, custodial behaviour, the location of co-defendants, OASys assessments, family

92  PSI 13/2007.
93  As at February 2009, 26 category C prisons accepted lifers – a full list can be found in PSO 4700 at appendix 4.

and resettlement matters. The proximity of the prisoner's Parole Board review is also of importance and more controversially, ministerial public or media interest may be taken into account. The PSI recognises the general public law duty to give proper and reasoned decisions in relation to allocation and categorisation (para 17).

10.93　The LSP 3E reports follow the same pro forma as the reports used for full parole reviews except they will obviously not comment on release or a transfer to open conditions as the prisoner will be too early in the sentence for this to take place. They will usually comprise of reports prepared by the lifer manager, personal officer, seconded and home probation officers and the prison psychologist. The purpose of the LSP3E review is to:

- Enable the prisoner's progress and life sentence plan to be monitored.
- Provide an opportunity for staff to comment on progress or other circumstances that might justify a transfer or change in security categorisation.
- Provide information on any reduction of risk that has been achieved.[94]

10.94　LSP 3 E reports will be disclosed to the prisoner and a period of seven days should be allowed for any comments to be made. Lifers may take legal advice on this and representations may be made by a solicitor on their behalf.

10.95　The movement of adult lifers to category C conditions is of particular significance as it represents the stage at which the majority of offending behaviour work has been completed and represents the opportunity for further testing. The Prison Service state that there is a significantly higher degree of trust in category C prisons and as such, a 'proper assessment of a lifer's trustworthiness and escape potential must remain a key factor in the recategorisation decision'.[95] Transfer will not take place until there are no outstanding or security concerns to justify retention in category B conditions.

## Special provisions for IPPs and short tariff lifers

10.96　As the categorisation of all male lifers was premised upon placement in category B conditions, it was considered that this might be inappropriate for those serving IPP sentences where the average tariff in

94　PSO 4700, para 5.4.1.
95　PSI 26/2006 para 20.

2008 was under four years. The Prison Service recognised that this group of lifers would previously have been likely to receive determinate sentences and may have been eligible for category C conditions at the outset. To address the problem, an amended form ICA1 was introduced in February 2008 (PSI 07/2008) which identifies those with tariffs of under three years so that they can be assessed for suitability to be moved directly to category C conditions. NOMS have also been working on replacing the staged approach to progression and release with the concept of new pathways to release for IPP and short tariff prisoners. Any such changes will be incorporated into PSO 4700 in due course.

## Accessing offending behaviour courses

10.97    The question of whether prisoners have a right to be allowed to attend relevant offending behaviour programmes became a major problem with the rapid increase in the number of lifers that followed the introduction of the automatic life sentence in 1997 and then reached crisis point when the IPP sentence was introduced in 2005. It had been thought that there was no public law duty arising in relation to making places on courses available to prisoners, on the basis that this was actually an issue about the allocation of resources with which the courts could not interfere. In the case of *R (Cawser) v Secretary of State for the Home Department*[96] an automatic lifer who was significantly over tariff and had been told that he would have to wait several years for a place on a sex offender's course sought to challenge the delay. The Secretary of State conceded that there was a public law duty to provide courses that were needed to reduce risk and allow for release, although he argued that it was a rational policy to target resources at prisoners who were serving determinate sentences and so would be released anyway as this would place the public at less risk. An argument that the failure to provide courses could also breach article 5(1) on the grounds that the purpose of the detention was being defeated was rejected by the Court of Appeal, with one dissenting opinion from Arden LJ:

> ... in a very exceptional case the failure by the Secretary of State to provide a particular prisoner with an appropriate treatment course, which in practice is a condition of release, may, if sufficiently prolonged, break that causal link and render the detention unlawful.'
> (para 47)

96 [2003] EWCA Civ 1522.

10.98 The issue was revisited for IPP prisoners in 2008 and following a first instance decision that the failure to provide courses was unlawful and breached articles 5(1) and 5(4) thus rendering the detention unlawful. The Court of Appeal in *Secretary of State v Walker and James*[97] considered that the failure to provide courses was unlawful and resulted in a breach of article 5(4) but that did not necessarily render the detention itself unlawful. The simple finding of dangerousness at the time the sentence was imposed did not mean that the prisoner would remain dangerous indefinitely and so it could not be assumed that there remained a danger. If the Parole Board was unable to make that assessment because relevant course work had not been provided, then this is where there might be a breach of article 5(1). Although that position had not been reached in those two cases, the Lord Chief Justice was highly critical of the situation that had developed:

> This appeal has demonstrated an unhappy state of affairs. There has been a systemic failure on the part of the Secretary of State to put in place the resources necessary to implement the scheme of rehabilitation necessary to enable the relevant provisions of the 2003 Act to function as intended.[98]

10.99 Appeals on these cases and the joined case of another prisoner were subsequently heard by the House of Lords in *R (James (formerly Walker), Lee and Wells v Secretary of State for Justice*[99] and a far more restrictive approach to the application of article 5 was taken. The Lords were very critical of the 'systemic failures' to provide the necessary facilities and resources for these prisoners but considered that this had not resulted in a breach of either article 5(1) or 5(4). The decision is discussed at some length in the introduction to this chapter and the worrying aspect of the ruling is that is appears to reduce the parole review to a matter of form rather than substance.

## Escorted absences

10.100 Once in category C conditions, lifers are also eligible to apply for escorted absences or town visits. Eligibility arises if the prisoner is within 12 months of the first parole review (ie within four years of tariff expiry). In July 2009 PSI 22/2009 amended PSO 4700 so that lifers must have also served ten years continuously in custody in order to be eligible for town visits. If the first parole review has been

97 [2008] EWCA Civ 30.
98 [2008] EWCA Civ 30 at para 72.
99 [2009] UKHL 22.

brought forward by six months (see below), eligibility for town visits is also brought forward by the same period. For post tariff lifers, they must simply be within 12 months of their next parole review. Foreign nationals and prisoners with deportation orders are eligible to be considered for town visits although extra consideration must be given to the possibility of an abscond and advice sought from the UKBA (for many years the Prison Service maintained that prisoners facing deportation were not eligible for escorted absences but following a challenge in 1998, this policy was abandoned).

10.101   The lifer must have been in the prison for six months before consideration can be given to an application to allow staff to make a reasoned assessment and the normal practice is to allow for a maximum of three escorted absences in any 12-month period. They will not normally be permitted over the Christmas or New Year period due to the increased risk of failure at that time of year. The purposes of escorted absences are stated to be:

- to enable prisoners to familiarise themselves with aspects of community life after a long period in custody;
- to assist them to make appropriate resettlement arrangements;
- to allow them to engage in selected community projects;
- to observe their ability to behave responsibly whilst in contact with members of the public;
- to test their ability to avoid absconding or in any other way abusing a position of trust, thereby measuring their readiness for open conditions;
- to enable them, where possible, to visit an open prison.[100]

10.102   All escorted absences require a full risk assessment to be conducted with a board including the lifer manager, a seconded probation officer and the personal officer with the final recommendation subject to approval by the governing governor. The police must also be consulted by the holding establishment. Victim's Code of Practice enquiries must be completed, usually through the home probation service and the police also have to be consulted, although their objections should only prevent an escorted absence if they are 'insuperable' (para 4.17.7). For Schedule One offenders, agreement must also be obtained from the social services department. As with other aspects of decision making for lifers, open reporting procedures are followed and reports will normally only be withheld if they raise victim's code of practice issues or security information (para 4.7.27).

---

100 PSO 4700 para 4.7.5; see also PSI 22/2009.

10.103     A review of the applicability of these procedures for IPP lifers with short tariffs was commenced in January 2009. The escorted absence programme was introduced to aid rehabilitation after lengthy periods of imprisonment and so has less importance for those who have only been in custody for a short period of time, hence the decision in July 2009 to restrict eligibility to those who have served ten years continuously in custody.

## Regressive moves within closed prisons

10.104   It is possible for lifers to be subjected to regressive moves within closed prisons (eg from C to B or from a category B training to a high security prison). The procedures followed are the same as for determinate prisoners (see chapter 3). The evidence and reasons for the decision must be given to the prisoner on a form LSP 4D, subject to the normal power to withhold for security reasons and the opportunity must be given for representations to be made in respect of such decisions. If an urgent decision is taken before the opportunity is given to make representations, an opportunity must be given to do so as soon as possible after the move.[101]

# Movement to open conditions and the first parole review

10.105   The Secretary of State has a policy that lifers can only be moved to an open prison (or the 'third stage') once advice has been sought from the Parole Board. It is not a statutory requirement to obtain advice from the board but simply a policy decision and so can be circumvented in exceptional circumstances. The decision to allow lifers the opportunity to move to open conditions before the minimum term has been served was introduced to reflect the requirement that most *mandatory* lifers will need to spend time in open conditions before they will be released. This period of time is considered necessary to establish a release plan and to demonstrate that they can be trusted to comply with supervision on life licence in the community.[102] PSO 4700 explains the rationale of the policy as follows:

101  PSI 26/2006 paras 30–33. See also chapter 3.
102  Ministerial statement of 7 November 1994: this policy was affirmed by the Court of Appeal in *R v Secretary of State for the Home Department ex p Stafford* [1998] 1 WLR 503 and this part of the judgment was not criticised by either the House of Lords or the European Court of Human Rights.

A period in open conditions is essential for most life sentenced prisoners ('lifers'). It allows the testing of areas of concern in conditions
which are nearer to those in the community than can be found in
closed prisons. Lifers have the opportunity to take home leave from
open prisons and, more generally, open conditions require them to
take more responsibility for their actions.[103]

10.106 As the rationale for this practice is twofold – to allow for institution-
alised prisoners to re-adjust to life in the community and to allow for
testing of an individual and a release plan before release is approved
– even though lifers with short tariffs might not require a period of
time in open conditions to counter the effects of institutionalisation,
such a move might be necessary to test trustworthiness or to establish
a viable release plan. For short tariff lifers, it will often not be possible
to allow for a parole review before the end of the minimum term. It
is arguable that in a case where there would not normally be time
to schedule a parole review but where the lifer meets the criteria for
open conditions and is likely to require open conditions to establish a
case for release, the Secretary of State is obliged to consider the case
as an exception to the general policy, either by referring the case to
the Parole Board for an expedited hearing or by considering the case
outside of that normal policy.

## Timing

10.107 The first formal review of a lifer's case by the Parole Board takes place
three years before the expiry of the minimum term. The purpose this
review is to enable consideration to be given as to whether the lifer
has made sufficient progress to be moved to open conditions. The review time is set at three years before the earliest release test in order
to allow for the lifer to spend some time in open conditions before
the minimum term expires.

10.108    The date of this review can be brought forward by six months
in cases where the prisoner has been in a category C prison – or
a second stage female prison – for at least one year before (ie for
12 months before the three and half years prior to the expiry of the
minimum term).[104] There has been one reported challenge to this
policy with a lifer arguing that she had completed all necessary work
in closed conditions and would benefit from a longer period of time
in open conditions was rejected by the High Court, although clearly

---

103 Appendix 7, p4.
104 See *R v Secretary of State for the Home Department ex p Roberts*, 8 July 1998,
   unreported and the ministerial statement of 9 July 1998.

there must remain a residual discretion to authorise such a move in exceptional cases.[105]

10.109    The statutory basis for the referral of these cases to the Parole Board is contained in CJA 2003 s239(2) which requires the board to advise the Secretary of State 'with respect to any matter referred to it by him which is to do with the early release or recall of prisoners'. This review does not engage article 5(4) as it takes place before the expiry of the minimum term and the referral is solely for the purposes of the board advising on the prisoner's suitability for open conditions and not release.[106] The board has the inherent power to manage its own proceedings and to adopt such procedures as are necessary to fulfill its statutory duty. This power extends to convening oral hearings if it considers such a hearing is necessary to fairly determine the case.[107]

## The review process

10.110   The review, as with oral hearings, is fixed to take place on a six-month timetable. The first stage is the disclosure of the parole dossier. The dossier will be identical in form to the dossier prepared for an oral review on the expiry of the minimum term (see below). A skeleton dossier is compiled by the Public Protection Unit (PPU) at NOMS containing historical information about the prisoner such as details of the conviction, progress in custody and any previous parole reviews.[108] The prison then add the reports from the lifer manager, personal officer, the wing manager, the prison and field probation officer, the prison medical officer and usually a psychologist or psychiatrist.[109]

105   *R (Payne) v Secretary of State for the Home Department* [2004] EWHC 581 (Admin).

106   There is a long history of cases on this issue that are examined in more detailed below. Two of the more recent cases to affirm this position are *R (Hill) v Secretary of State for the Home Department* [2007] EWHC 2164 (Admin) and *R (Day) v Secretary of State for the Home Department* [2004] EWHC 1742 (Admin). Also, in *Davies v Secretary of State for Justice* [2008] EWHC 397 (Admin), damages were refused in a claim for false imprisonment and/or pursuant to article 5(5) in relation to the removal of a life sentenced prison from open conditions.

107   *R v Parole Board ex p Davies*, 27 November 1996, unreported.

108   Although the Parole Board Rules (PBR) do not apply to pre-tariff reviews, the contents of the dossier are the same as for tariff expiry reviews and so the full details of what is included in the skeleton dossier can be found in the PBR 2004, Sch 2 part A.

109   PBR 2004, Sch 2 part B.

10.111    Following disclosure of the dossier, the prisoner will be given one month in which to make representations in writing. Prisoners are entitled to obtain legal advice and representatives will commonly draft representations on behalf of their clients. Close attention needs to be paid to the directions issued by the Secretary of State to the Parole Board in relation to movement to open conditions. Once written representations have been made, a panel of the Parole Board will consider the case on the papers alone. If the panel considers that the prisoner is likely to meet the test for open conditions, in accordance with the policy of only moving lifers to an open prison after an oral hearing, the case will be referred for such a hearing. If that should happen, the case will then proceed as a normal oral hearing case and the PBR will be followed. If the board do not consider that the prisoner meets the criteria for open conditions, a refusal letter will be sent. This will normally be the last opportunity the prisoner has to be moved to open conditions before the end of the minimum term, although if there is major progression in the case it is still possible to ask the Secretary of State to refer the case for a second time before the end of the punitive part of the sentence.

## The Secretary of State's directions

10.112   The Secretary of State has issued directions to the Parole Board setting out the matters they should take into account when deciding whether to authorise a transfer to open conditions. It had been argued held that the practice of the Secretary of State issuing directions to the Parole Board breached the concept of judicial independence and so impinged on article 5(4) and although this argument was successful at first instance, it was partially overturned on appeal.[110] The current position is that the Secretary of State may give directions to the Parole Board, 'so as to provide guidance to the board as to the matters to be taken into account'[111] but not to give directions purporting to restate the statutory test for release. As the movement of life sentenced prisoners to open conditions does not engage article 5, the directions made by the Secretary of State in relation to the move to open conditions still apply.

10.113    The board is required to 'balance the risks against the benefits to be gained by such a move' and following specific factors which in-

110  R *(Girling) v Parole Board and Secretary of State for the Home Department* [2006] EWCA Civ 1779.

111  R *(Girling) v Parole Board and Secretary of State for the Home Department* [2006] EWCA Civ 1779 at para 23.

form that assessment. They require the board to assess whether the prison has made sufficient progress in tackling offending behaviour to minimise risk and to assess whether he or she is trustworthy enough not to escape. The board is also specifically instructed that advice is only sought on the suitability of a move to an open prison – or for lifers at the end of their minimum term, release – and is not required to comment on the timing of the next review or moves to other categories of prison.[112] Thus, if the board does recommend that a prisoner is suitable for open conditions, the Secretary of State still retains the final decision.[113]

## Reviews on and after tariff expiry

10.114 It is a statutory requirement for all lifers to have their cases referred to the Parole Board by the Secretary of State on the expiry of the tariff or minimum term and at least every two years thereafter.[114] Although the statutory language expresses this as a right to require the Secretary of State to make the referral, in practice this is done automatically. The article 5(4) requirement for release to be determined by a court like body is satisfied by the referral of cases to the Parole Board. Concerns that the Parole Board was not sufficiently independent from the Secretary of State were upheld by the Court of Appeal in *R (Brooke and others) v Parole Board and Secretary of State for the Home Department*.[115] The Parole Board is a corporate body now constituted by section 239 of CJA 2003 and since this decision, its sponsorship arrangements and system of appointments have been changed to provide it with the necessary independence from the executive. It is a non-departmental public body sponsored by the Access to Justice group[116] in the Ministry of Justice since 9 May 2007. The precise future status of the board is under review with the proposals being that it should either become part of the Tribunal Service or join the Court Service.

112  *R (Spence) v Secretary of State for the Home Department* [2003] EWCA Civ 732.
113  See for example *R (Hill) v Secretary of State for the Home Department* [2007] EWHC 2164 which also contains an examination of a period when the Secretary of State began to reject increasing numbers of these recommendations.
114  Crime (Sentences) Act 1997 s28(7).
115  [2008] EWCA Civ 29.
116  Rather than by a NOMS body.

10.115    The referral is timed to take place six months before the review concludes. The review will take approximately six months to completion and it is therefore necessary for the review to finish in time to allow the prisoner to be released at the conclusion of the punitive part of the sentence.[117] The obligation to ensure that a parole decision could be made by the time other tariff expires was also held to extend to the Parole Board. The board had sought to defend a practice of listing cases in quarters of the year on the basis of administrative convenience, even though this might mean a prisoner being detained for up to three months beyond the end of the minimum term. The Court of Appeal found that this breached article 5(4) and noted that administrative convenience did not provide a defence.[118]

10.116    The Secretary of State has the power to make Rules for the procedure to be followed by the Parole Board,[119] the current version being the Parole Board Rules 2004.[120] The current Rules are not laid by statutory instrument although future versions will be subject to the negative resolution procedure.[121] It is the PBR that provide the structure and framework for the review process.

10.117    The review commences with the referral of the case to the board by the Secretary of State. In order to meet the concerns about the review needing to conclude in sufficient time, this will normally take place eight months before date when the review must be completed. The prisoner will normally be given a slip to sign at the prison confirming that he or she wishes to participate in the review. PPU will then disclose the skeleton dossier to the prison containing historical information about the prisoner's offences and progress in custody.[122]

10.118    Following the referral, the board are to notify the parties that the case has been listed within five working days[123] and within eight weeks, the Secretary of State is required to disclose the parole dossier.[124] The prison will have added to the skeleton dossier the docu-

---

117    The rationale behind this can be found in the decision in *R v Secretary of State for the Home Department & Parole Board ex p Norney* [1995] 7 ALR 861 where the practice of referring cases on the last day of the tariff was found to be unlawful as it meant that the lifer could spend an additional six months in prison even in cases where he or she was safe to be released.

118    *R (Noorkoiv) v Parole Board* [2002] EWCA Civ 770.

119    See CJA 2003 s239(5), previously a power contained in CJA 1991 s32(5).

120    At the time of writing the most recent amendments had come into force on 1 April 2009.

121    CJA 2003 s239(5).

122    Parole Board Rules 2004 Sch 2 Part A. See footnote 108 above.

123    PBR rule 4.

124    PBR rule 6(1).

ments relating to the prisoner's behaviour and progress since the last review[125] and normally comprises of reports containing details of the offence, behaviour in custody, previous parole decisions and a series of current reports prepared by prison and probation staff together with psychiatric and psychologists' reports. It is very often the case that these reports are not prepared by the deadline, and all subsequent actions should only be undertaken once the dossier has been disclosed.

10.119   Once the dossier has been disclosed, the prisoner is allowed four weeks in which to submit written representations and any other evidence that he or she wishes the board to consider at that stage.[126] The case is then referred to a single member for a preliminary decision and for intensive case management, or ICM.[127] The ICM process was originally introduced to try and cut down on the number of cases that had to be deferred on the day they were due to be heard as it turned out that material had been omitted or witnesses were unavailable. The amendments to the Rules do not make it clear whether the ICM process and consideration of cases on the papers by a single member of the board are a single process but it appears that they must be. The ICM member who considers each case therefore has a dual task of making a decision on the papers and then going onto identify whether any material is missing and what witnesses might be needed and will set a deadline for this to be provided and the witnesses to be notified. This may mean that some cases will need to be considered on the papers twice, once to make sure that all the material is present and if not, to then await its receipt before reaching a decision. Similarly, if a paper decision is made and representations are submitted after that decision, it may be necessary for the case to be reconsidered on the papers.

10.120   When making a decision on the papers, the single member has two options. The first is to decide that the case should be referred for an oral hearing. This is the decision that will be reached in any case where there is a realistic argument to be made for open conditions or release as the board will now only make recommendations or directions for these options following an oral hearing.[128] If the prisoner is not considered suitable for release, a written notification must be sent to the prisoner with reasons for the decision within one week.[129]

125  PBR Sch 2 Part B.
126  PBR rule 7.
127  PBR rule 8(1).
128  PBR rule 11(2)(a).
129  PBR rule 11(3).

On receipt of this decision, the prisoner has four weeks in which to request an oral hearing, giving full reasons for that request.[130] Where an oral hearing is to take place, the single member will fulfil the ICM function of making directions for any further material to be provided and to identify relevant witnesses to attend the hearing. Interestingly, the Administrative Court has held that a failure by the Parole Board to properly case manage a case after directions have been given can give rise to a breach of article 5(4).[131]

10.121    This change to the Rules replaces the opportunity to require an oral hearing to be held with the possibility of requesting such a hearing. It ends the long held assumption that article 5(4) required an oral hearing to take place, an assumption that also seems to have been shared by the European Court of Human Rights. In the context of finding that there had been a violation of article 5(4) by failing to have a system for the release of HMP detainees that allowed for an independent court like body to determine release, it was stated that:

> 59. The Court recalls in this context that, in matters of such crucial importance as the deprivation of liberty and where questions arise which involve, for example, as assessment of the applicant's character or mental state, it has held that it may be essential to the fairness of the proceedings that the applicant be present at an oral hearing.

> 60. The Court is of the view that, in a situation such as that of the applicant, where a substantial term of imprisonment may be at stake and where characteristics pertaining to his personality and level of maturity are of importance in deciding on his dangerousness, article 5(4) requires an oral hearing in the context of an adversarial procedure involving legal representation and the possibility of calling and questioning witnesses.[132]

10.122    The extent to which matters have moved on since that judgment in relation to the need for oral hearings in parole proceedings will no doubt be tested both domestically at the ECtHR.

10.123    The Secretary of State has issued guidance to the Parole Board on how they should consider the cases of life sentence prisoners. As noted above, the Court of Appeal's decision in *Girling* indicated that the decision to issue directions does not of itself compromise of judicial independence. Moreover, the factors to be taken into account as outlined in the directions were considered to be common sense in

---

130  PBR rule 12.
131  *Craig Smith v Secretary of State for Justice and Parole Board* [2008] EWHC 2998 (Admin).
132  *Hussain v UK* [1996] 22 EHRR 1.

terms of the board's deliberations and the only objectionable one was that which purported to explain the statutory test for release.

## Procedure and evidence at oral parole hearings

10.124 Oral parole panels are appointed by the chairman of the Parole Board and for mandatory lifers, HMP detainees, automatic lifers and discretionary lifers, the panel must be chaired by a sitting or retired judge. For IPP prisoners, there is no longer a requirement for the panel to be chaired by someone with a legal qualification at all.[133] The PBR also no longer prescribe the number of members who have to hear a case and while in the past all panels had three members, this is no longer a mandatory requirement. Prisoners have the right to be represented at hearings but serving prisoners, people who have been released from prison but are on licence, people with unspent criminal convictions or people who are liable to be detained under the Mental Health Act 1983 cannot be appointed.[134]

10.125    The normal procedure is that all material will be disclosed to the prisoner but there is a power to withhold information from the prisoner if the Secretary of State considers that disclosure would be adverse to the health and welfare of that prisoner or others.[135] Where the Secretary of State wishes to withhold material from the prisoner, it must be served on the chair of the panel with reasons for the request. If the chair upholds the request, an order can be made permitting disclosure to the prisoner's representative with a direction that it cannot be disclosed onto the prisoner.[136] As a matter of good practice, lawyers should always notify their clients if the board propose to utilise this rule and seek permission to receive the material on those terms.

10.126    In extreme cases, there remains a power to withhold information from both the prisoner and the legal representative. In *R (Roberts) v Parole Board*[137] the board decided that it could not authorise disclosure of material to either the prison or the lawyer on the grounds that the safety of the sources of the evidence was at risk. The board appointed a special advocate to receive the material and to represent the prisoner's interests in his absence. The Lords, by a 3–2 majority, decide that the Parole Board did have the inherent power to appoint

---

133  PBR rule 3.
134  PBR rule 1997 r 5.
135  PBR rule 6(2).
136  PBR rule 6(3).
137  [2005] UKHL 45

a special advocate. The ratio of the judgment is less clear on how far this procedure can go and whether it permits a final decision to be made on the basis of material that has been withheld or whether it is more limited. Following decisions of the Court of Appeal in relation to control orders, the Administrative Court held that the standards of fairness are flexible and that this means that there is no right to disclosure, even if this renders the proceedings less fair to the prisoner, if disclosure would pose an unacceptable risk to the safety of others involved in the process such as witnesses.[138]

10.127   Where a case proceeds to an oral hearing, it will be held in the prison where the prisoner is located unless the Secretary of State consents to a different venue.[139] Proceedings remain private and attempts to argue that article 6 applies and requires a public hearing have been rejected by the ECtHR.[140] Although hearings will often follow a similar format with witnesses being questioned by the prisoner's representative, the panel and the Secretary of State's representative in that order, the procedure is intended to avoid formality and there are no rigid procedural rules. Save for cases where there are contested facts to determine, witnesses will usually be present for all of the evidence and the panel will conduct the hearing as it sees fit for the individual circumstances of the case. Where cases cannot be concluded the panel can either defer or adjourn proceedings.[141] An adjournment will usually take place where evidence has been received and the same panel must then reconstitute to resume the case. Deferrals are far more common and will be ordered before formal evidence is received if it is decided that the hearing cannot proceed. A deferral allows for greater flexibility as a fresh panel can hear the case when it resumes. In the case of *R v Parole Board ex p Robinson*,[142] the panel heard evidence and determined that the prison was safe to be released but were not happy with the release plan that had been proposed. The panel adjourned with directions for the probation service to provide a release plan but as the chief probation officer opposed release, this was not done and instead, at the resumed hearing the panel were persuaded to rescind their earlier finding on risk and re-

---

138  *R (Roberts) v Parole Board* [2008] EWHC 2714 (Admin) but this decision is probably no longer good law since the House of Lords overruled the Court of Appeal's decision on control orders in *AF, AM, AN and AE v Secretary of State for the Home Department* [2009] UKHL 28.

139  PBR rule 18.

140  *Hirst v UK* [2001] Crim LR 919.

141  PBR rule 9.

142  [1999] Prison LR 118 and (1999) *The Independent*, 8 November.

lease was not directed. This decision was quashed on the grounds that having already made a finding on risk, in the absence of any material change of circumstances, the board's funding on risk was final and could not be reopened. The board are generally very careful not to make any final findings on risk when adjourning cases to avoid this problem.[143]

10.128   The informality of the proceedings is reflected in the nature of the evidence that can be received. There are no formal evidential rules at parole hearings and so hearsay is admissible, although it has been held that there are circumstances where evidence might be so fundamental that it would be unfair for the panel to rely on this decisively.[144] The practical application of this principle was illustrated in a case where a prisoner had been on licence for over 20 years and was recalled because of allegations made by his ex-wife which in some ways mirrored his index offence. The board relied upon her written statement even though the allegations were denied and the court held that this was an exceptional case where the evidence needed to be tested orally in order to ensure fairness.[145]

10.129   In *R (Brooks) v Parole Board and Secretary of State for the Home Department*[146] the Court of Appeal upheld a decision of a panel to rely on hearsay evidence from probation officers and social workers of a reported rape even though it was denied by the prisoner and the complainant refused to give evidence to either the police or the panel. The *Brooks* case also explored the issue of securing the attendance of reluctant witnesses, a problem which will often arise at hearings. The board has no power to compel witnesses and any witness summons must be obtained from either the county court or High Court.[147] In cases where the witness whose attendance was required was a witness for the Secretary of State, the chairman of the panel hearing the case should be asked to issue a direction requiring the Secretary of State to obtain a witness summons to secure their attendance.

---

143   it is also important to note that the Probation Service do not have a statutory duty to find accommodation for a life sentenced prisoner seeking release: *R (Irving) v London Probation Board* [2005] EWHC 605 (Admin); *R (Churchman) v West Midlands Probation Board* [2007] EWHC 1521 (Admin).

144   See for example *R (Sim) v Parole Board and Secretary of State for the Home Department* [2003] EWCA Civ 1854.

145   *R (Headley) v Parole Board* [2009] EWHC 663 (Admin). It is arguable that the decision in this case actually went slightly too far by suggesting that the board could not rely upon the material at all in the absence of oral evidence rather than addressing the weight that the material should have been given.

146   [2004] EWCA Civ 80.

147   Using the inherent power of the court pursuant to the CPR rule 34.4.

10.130    The flexibility that a panel has when receiving evidence was illustrated in the case of *R (Gardner) v Parole Board*[148] where it was held that the board did not act unlawfully when excluding the prisoner from part of a hearing when his wife was giving evidence in support of allegations against him, and in circumstances where she expressed herself as unwilling to give evidence if he was in the same room, even though the Rules did not include any express provision for this to happen. The prisoner's advocate was able to be present, and was allowed time to take instructions on the evidence given so the witness could be cross-examined. Following the House of Lords decision in *Roberts* (see para 10.126 above), it was held that the board has inherent power to adopt such a procedure, and moreover there was no breach of article 5(4) of the Convention in doing so, the court citing the flexibility allowed by the ECtHR in article 6 cases.[149]

10.131    The standard of proof at parole hearings is the civil standard, being the balance of probabilities, although the more serious the allegation, the more cogent the evidence needed to prove it.[150] In *Re: D v Life Sentence Commissioners for Northern Ireland*[151] the evidential issues were explored in the context of a prisoner who had been recalled in Northern Ireland under a system largely analogous to the system in England and Wales. The Lords held considered that greater cogency of evidence was needed in cases where the allegations are more serious, an analysis that they thought properly applied the principles established in *Re H (Minors Sexual Abuse: Standard of Proof)*.[152] They went on to confirm that there is a single standard of proof in civil matters (ie the balance of probabilities) and it is the application of that standard that is flexible. Thus for a more serious allegation, the standard of proof does not change but the strength or quality of the evidence needed to prove the allegation.[153]

---

148 [2006] EWCA 122 (Admin).

149 For example *Doorson v Netherlands* (1996) 22 EHRR 330.

150 *R (Brooks) v Parole Board and Secretary of State for the Home Department* [2004] EWCA Civ 80.

151 [2008] UKHL 33.

152 [1996] AC 563.

153 The discussion on the standard of proof in the speech of Lord Brown is particularly interesting as he explores the practical difficulties that arise from trying to separate out the need for 'more cogent evidence' from actually applying a different standard of proof. He suggested that in certain civil cases it might be more appropriate to apply the criminal standard, although interestingly, he seems quite content to exclude parole from the category that requires the criminal standard, even when dealing with disputed factual allegations amounting to criminal behaviour.

10.132 These cases also go some way to determining the issue of whether there is a *burden* of proof, the answer seeming to be that as the board are required to make an assessment of risk on the material before them, it is not especially helpful to try and reduce this to a specific burden falling on either party. In *R v Lichniak & Pyrah*[154] Lord Bingham expressed doubt as to whether the concept of a 'burden of proof' really had a place in the context of risk assessment in parole reviews:

> I doubt whether there is in truth a burden on the prisoner to persuade the Parole Board that it is safe to recommend release, since this is an administrative process requiring the board to consider all the available material and form a judgment. There is, inevitably, a balance to be struck between the interest of the individual and the interest of society, and I do not think it objectionable, in the case of someone who has once taken life with the intent necessary for murder, to prefer the latter in case of doubt. (at para 16)[155]

## The test for release

10.133 Section 28(6)(b) of the Crime (Sentences) Act 1997 contains the statutory test for release, requiring the board to direct release where it 'is satisfied that it is no longer necessary for the protection of the public that the prisoner should be confined'. This confirms that detention after the minimum term has expired can only be authorised on the basis of risk. The next question is 'what risk is being assessed?' The classic analysis is contained in the case of *R v Parole Board ex p Bradley*[156] where the court held that the prisoner can only be detained if there remains a risk of committing further offences that would result in serious harm, or the 'life and limb' test.[157] It is important to

154 [2002] UKHL 47.
155 In *R (Hirst) v Secretary of State for the Home Department and Parole Board* [2002] EWHC 1592 (Admin) the Administrative Court refused to make a finding on this issue in an application made in advance of a parole hearing on the basis that it was academic. The court indicated that the position was somewhat different from those detained under the Mental Health Acts – see *R (H) v North London and East Region Mental Health Review Tribunal* [2001] 3 WLR 512 – and suggested that the obiter views of Lord Bingham are probably correct. The one situation where the courts have held that the board must be positively satisfied as to the existence of a sufficient level of risk to justify detention, because of a presumption of liberty, is where those serving extended sentences are recalled – *R (Sim) v Parole Board* [2004] 2 WLR 1170.
156 [1991] 1 WLR 134.
157 In *R (Bayliss) v Parole Board and another* the Secretary of State agreed that the test for release for IPP sentence prisoners had to relate to the basis upon which the sentence was imposed, that is a significant risk of committing offences occasioning serious harm.

distinguish the risk of committing further serious violent offences from the risk of committing offences that would not result in serious harm.[158] In practical application this was articulated by Leggatt LJ in the following terms:

> the Board must be satisfied that it is not necessary that he should be kept in prison and not that there would be a substantial risk if he were released. In other words it must be shown that the risk is low enough to release him, not high enough to keep him in prison.[159]

10.134 Although there is one uniform test for release, this does not necessarily result in a uniform approach to different classes of lifers (and different individuals). For example, discretionary and automatic lifers are sentenced on the basis of a finding that the prisoner posed a danger to the public in order to justify the sentence. In contrast, HMP detainees and mandatory lifers have their sentence imposed as a matter of law and so there is not necessarily a pre-existing finding of dangerousness. It is therefore wrong for the Parole Board to make any assumptions as to the 'pathology' of these prisoners. This was accepted in a judicial review application made by one such recalled HMP prisoner (although the application failed on other grounds) by Dyson, J:

> It is quite wrong to make any assumptions about the dangerousness of an HMP detainee. When considering whether the prisoner poses a risk to life and limb that is more than minimal, the board must apply the most careful scrutiny since a fundamental human right, the right to liberty is at stake. I am prepared to accept the submission [of the applicant] that the board require cogent evidence before being satisfied that a prisoner poses more than a minimal risk of danger to life and limb.[160]

10.135 Some further assistance on risk assessment can be found from the decisions made by the Court of Appeal in relation to the test that must be made out in order to impose a life sentence in the first instance. In *R v Lang*[161] which looked at the circumstances in which a sentence of IPP should be imposed, Rose LJ explained that it was necessary to look at the risk of further offences being committed and then the risk that if further offences were committed, they would pose a significant risk of harm. In many ways, the analysis of the risk of harm

---

158 See for example *R v Secretary of State for the Home Department ex P Cox* [1992] COD 72 and *Stafford v UK* (2002) 35 EHRR 32.

159 *R v Parole Board ex p Lodomez*, unreported, 4 May 1994, p18 of transcript.

160 *R v Parole Board ex p Curley* unreported, 22 October 1999, HC.

161 [2005] EWCA Crim 2864.

in this judgment is more lucid than the cases seeking to identify the correct approach in the parole context. The approach to risk taken in the criminal context appears to be far more robust:

> ... repetitive violent or sexual offending at a relatively low level without serious harm does not of itself give rise to a significant risk of serious harm in the future. There may, in such cases, be some risk of future victims being more adversely affected than past victims but this, of itself, does not give rise to significant risk of serious harm. (at para 17(iv))

10.136 The risk that must be established does not need to be specific to one type of offending. As the statutory test requires the risk of harm to be assessed, this can arise in relation to risk of a different kind than that for which the prisoner is convicted. A discretionary lifer convicted of arson challenged a recall decision relating to his risk of sexual offending on the grounds that there was insufficient causal link between the original sentence and the recall and that continued detention would be arbitrary and in breach of article 5(1). This was rejected by Stanley Burnton J with the following explanation:

> I conclude that where both the original sentence and the continued detention of a life prisoner are based on the risk of serious harm to the public, there is no inconsistency between the original objectives of the sentencing court and the decision not to release or the decision to re-detain notwithstanding that the sentencing court had in mind a different kind of offence from that subsequently feared.[162]

10.137 The final aspect of the test is that the risk that needs to be assessed on release is not confined to the United Kingdom. Arguments from lifers who are to be deported that any continuing risk will be in a foreign jurisdiction have been dismissed as the risk to the public test is not specific to one country.[163] It is important for lifers who are to be deported at the end of the sentence to be aware that deportation will not be automatic and that they will still have to satisfy the board that they no longer pose a risk of harm. Indeed, this can often be more onerous given that a move to open conditions will be far more difficult to achieve and because there is unlikely to be a release plan or any supervision available in the country to which the lifer will be deported.

---

162  *R (Green) v Parole Board* [2005] EWHC 548 (Admin). Also see *R (Wyles) v Parole Board and Secretary of State for the Home Department* [2006] EWHC 493 (Admin).

163  *R v Parole Board ex p White* (1994) *Times* 30 December.

## Lifers facing deportation

10.138   In cases where the lifer is to be deported, the board can direct release from the life sentence but do not have jurisdiction to interfere with any decision made by the immigration authorities to detain. In the majority of cases, lifers being deported will be released from closed prison conditions. In those cases, it will be normal for the immigration authorities to seek to continue the detention pending the physical deportation. In the rarer cases where the lifer has already been to open conditions and is released from there, it may be far more difficult for detention on immigration grounds to be justified.

10.139   The physical process for arranging deportation can be lengthy, even where the deportation is not contested. Arrangements are dealt with by the Criminal Casework Team of IND. They will require proof of citizenship such as a passport or birth certificate to enable the receiving state to agree to accept the return of the prisoner. The physical arrangements will involve making a booking with an airline which will nearly always required the prisoner to be escorted and then finding a date on which escorts are available. Even in cases where it has been possible to arrange for the documentation issues confirming nationality to be resolved promptly, it can still take several weeks for the physical flight arrangements to be resolved.

## The decision

10.140   Following an oral hearing, the panel are required to send decisions in writing to prisoners within 14 days,[164] the period of time having been increased from the seven days permitted prior to April 2009. The decision must be unanimous, a change from the old position when majority decisions were acceptable (rule 10(1)). In accordance with the article 5(4) obligation that release must be decided by a court like body, the *statute* provides that a direction for release is binding upon the Secretary of State.[165] As noted above in relation to the pre-tariff parole reviews, there have been a long line of cases exploring whether article 5 requires the board to have the power to direct moves to open conditions on the basis that this is intimately tied to release. These have always been unsuccessful and it remains the case that the move to open conditions remains outwith article 5.[166] Similarly, the board

164  PBR rule 20.
165  Crime (Sentences) Act (C(S)A) 1997 s28(3).
166  The ECtHR has consistently held that article 5 applies only to release decisions: see *Blackstock v UK* (2006) 42 EHRR 2.

has no jurisdiction to determine the timing between reviews or to make recommendations on movement within close conditions.[167]

10.141 The statutory duty to provide reasons for decision contained at rule 15(2) is also required by the common law, the reasons needing to be intelligible and dealing with the substantial points that have been raised.[168] In *R (Gordon) v Parole Board*[169] Smith J explained that the appropriate standard was to assess, 'whether the reasons for the decision are proper, sufficient and intelligible'. She expanded on this duty in the following terms:

> I acknowledge of course that it is not incumbent upon the board to set out its thought processes in detail or to mention every factor they have taken into account. However, in my judgement the balancing exercise they are required to carry out is so fundamental to the decision making process that they should make it plain that this has been done and to state broadly which factors they have taken into account. (at para 38).

10.142 A direction for release will be forwarded to PPU where the licence will be drawn up. This requires the caseworker to liaise with the probation service to ensure that the release address is available and to fix a date for the lifer to report to the officer. It usually takes around a week for the licence to be completed and the release date notified, although if release is dependent upon a hostel bed being available, this may take longer. If release is not directed, then PPU will issue a notification informing the prisoner of the next review date. In a case where open conditions have been recommended, this notification will also inform the prisoner whether that recommendation has been accepted on behalf of the Secretary of State and if not, the reasons for the refusal.

## Further reviews

10.143 If release is not directed, then the prisoner will face a further parole review. The statute provides that this must take place at least every two years.[170] The two years period is the maximum interval between

167 *R (Spence) v Secretary of State for the Home Department* [2003] EWCA Civ 732 and *R (Day) v Secretary of State for the Home Department* [2004] EWHC 1742 (Admin) where it was held that although it would make sense for the board to have the power to set the period between reviews, it was not a requirement of article 5.
168 See for example: *R v Parole Board ex p Telling* [1993] COD 500; *R v Parole Board ex p Lodomez* [1994] COD 525.
169 [2000] EWHC 414 (Admin).
170 C(S)A 1997 s28(7).

reviews, however, and the precise period must be set with reference to the needs of the individual.[171]

10.144    There have been a number of cases decided by the ECtHR in relation to the interval between reviews for lifers and many of these are summarized in the leading domestic case of *R (MacNeil) v Discretionary Lifer Panel*.[172] An argument was made that the statutory two year interval breaches of article 5(4) but this argument was rejected. Instead, the Court of Appeal considered that an individual assessment was needed on the facts of the individual case to determine whether an earlier review was needed. In *McNeill*, it was held that the two-year review ordered was lawful in light of the prisoner's history of absconding and drug failure and his subsequent poor behaviour following the parole decision.

10.145    The ECtHR appears to be slightly more purposive in determining the appropriate interval between reviews and in *Oldham v UK*[173] a two-year review period was held to be unlawful as all of the relevant coursework had been completed in eight months. The manner in which the issue should be approached was explained by the ECtHR in *Hirst v UK*[174] where it was explained that the very nature of the life sentence is such that the prisoner is liable to change and so reviews have to be set with the possibility of maturity, development and change in mind.[175] The decision goes onto note that the Secretary of State sought to defend the action on the grounds that if there had been further development that had not been expected, an earlier review could be ordered at that stage. This principle has subsequently been accepted as the correct approach in domestic law meaning that it is possible to as prisoner to ask the Secretary of State to advance a review if there are developments justifying an earlier hearing.[176]

10.146    The appropriate method for the courts to adopt when determining these issues is to reach a primary decision on what is required

---

171  For a general background on the ECtHR view of the requirements of article 5(4) see *Herczegalvy v Austria* (Series A, no 244) and *Sanchez-Reisse v Switzerland* (Series A, no 107).

172  [2001] EWCA Civ 448.

173  (2001) 31 EHRR 813.

174  [2001] Crim LR 919.

175  Further ECtHR cases relating to domestic decisions can be found in *Blackstock v UK* (2006) 42 EHRR 2, *AT v UK* 20 EHRR CD 50; *Curley v UK* [2001] 31 EHRR 14; and *Waite v UK* (2003) 36 EHRR 54.

176  See *R (Ashford) v Secretary of State for Justice* [2008] EWHC 2734 (Admin) where the court held that the appropriate question to be determined was whether the prisoner's progress justified an earlier consideration of his case, before proceeding to dismiss the claim on the merits.

in the case rather than to simply make a reasonableness assessment. This duty arises partly because the initial decision is being taken by the executive and partly because it is a Convention right that is at stake.[177] Furthermore, in keeping with the cases addressing the provision of relevant offending behaviour programmes and the mechanisms for hearing cases, the decision on the appropriate timing is an objective question to be answered without reference to resources as per *R (Loch) v Secretary of State for Justice.*[178]

## Article 6 and parole hearings

10.147 The question of whether a parole review for a prisoner serving a life sentence involves the determination of an article 6 right, whether civil or criminal, has never been conclusively determined. For prisoners serving determinate sentences, the House of Lords rejected arguments that either criminal or civil rights within the meaning of article 6 were engaged in *R (Smith) v Parole Board.*[179] Lord Bingham stated that the recall of prisoners serving determinate sentences was not a criminal matter as it results in detention designed to protect the public and not to a fresh punishment. In relation to the engagement of the civil limb of article 6, Lord Bingham chose not to determine the issue as he did not feel that it added anything in terms of the fairness of procedure or the protection of rights that could be obtained through the Parole Board's common law duty of procedural fairness.[180] Lord Slynn and Lord Hope who gave the other speeches in that case both agreed that parole proceedings did not involve the determination of a criminal charge and went further than Lord Bingham to suggest that article 6 civil rights were not engaged.

## Victims' Code of Practice

10.148 The role and status of victims within the parole process came under scrutiny in the 2006 when the Secretary of State intimated an intention to increase the representation of victims on the Parole Board itself and at parole hearings.[181] In fact, the Secretary of State appears

---

177 See *R (MacNeil) v Discretionary Lifer Panel* [2001] EWCA Civ 448.
178 [208] EWHC 2278.
179 [2005] UKHL 1.
180 [2005] UKHL 1 at paras 40–44.
181 Discussed in the *R (Brooke and others) v Parole Board and Secretary of State for the Home Department* [2008] EWCA Civ 29 concerning the independence of the board.

to have given little consideration to the statutory regime when making these comments and the extent to which victims do have a formal role to play within the parole system. The important point to be made at the outset is that there is no mandate, either in common law or statute, for the views of victims to be permitted to have any influence on release decisions.

10.149    There is a statutory requirement (contained in the Domestic Violence, Crime and Victims Act 2004) for the Probation Service to enquire of victims whether they wish to make representations to the Parole Board or other bodies responsible for the release of prisoners as to particular licence conditions that may be imposed (see chapter 2). Under the Code of Practice issued under the legislation the Parole Board is required to take victims' representations into account in deciding which licence conditions to impose.

10.150    The Parole Board has now begun to adapt its procedures to try and allow for a more formal role in the proceedings for victims and they explain to victims how to submit a victim's impact statement through the probation service. The statement is invited to cover they impact of the original offence and any concerns about release. In some instances the board will allow victims to present their cases in person but there are no procedural guidelines issued and the board appear to determine this on an ad hoc basis.[182] The written views of victims will often remain confidential under the rule 6 procedure and the recommendations in terms of licence conditions that flow from the views will simply be summarised in the licence conditions set for the prisoner. In cases where licence conditions are in issue, this may be problematic in terms of a full examination of the evidence (see the section on licence conditions below). Anecdotal evidence would suggest that on the few occasions where oral evidence from victims has been allowed, there has been little thought given to an appropriate system for the presentation of the evidence.

10.151    On a more principled level, it is clear that the views of the victims cannot have a direct impact on the decision as to whether the prisoner should be released and this is reflected in the statutory provisions concerning the ambit of the views that are sought. In the criminal sphere, it has been confirmed that victims' views should not alter the sentences that are imposed[183] and it was made clear that in the area of tariff setting, the invitation to victims to make representations is

---

182  See the statement of the board at www.paroleboard.gov.uk/victims_and_families/making_a_victim_personal_statement/

183  See for example *R v Nunn* [1996] Cr App R (S) 136.

limited to the impact of the offence on the individual and does not extend to the appropriate length of the tariff itself.[184] This approach is consistent with the views of the ECtHR on release where the complaint made by a relative of a victim that she had been refused the opportunity to have a formal role in the release process was considered to be inadmissible.[185]

## Multi-Agency Public Protection Arrangements (MAPPA) and release

10.152 Multi-Agency Public Protection Panels (MAPPP) are constituted to discharge MAPPA duties.[186] MAPPA requires the responsible authority consisting of the police, prison and probation services to assess the risk posed by serious sexual and violent offenders.[187] Detailed guidance has been issued by the Secretary of State explaining the role played by the various bodies in the process[188] and the Prison Service has issued a Public Protection Manual.[189]

10.153    MAPPPs will be convened for three categories of offender:[190]

- Category 1 offenders – registered sexual offenders. This group are those who have been convicted or cautioned of a sexual offence and have therefore become subject to the statutory registration requirements under Part 2 of the Sexual Offences Act 2003.
- Category 2 offenders – violent and other sexual offenders. In short this category includes violent offenders and other sexual offenders who receive a sentence of imprisonment of 12 months or more (including extended and indeterminate sentences) for specified offences.[191]
- Category 3 offenders – other dangerous offenders. This category comprises offenders, not in either category 1 or 2 but who are considered by the responsible authority to pose a risk of serious harm to the public which requires active inter-agency management.

---

184 *R (Bulger) v Secretary of State for the Home Department and Lord Chief Justice* [2001] EWHC (Admin) 119.
185 *McCourt v United Kingdom* (1993) 15 EHRR CD 110.
186 See chapter 2 for an overview of the statutory basis for MAPPA.
187 CJA 2003 s 325(1).
188 www.probation.homeoffice.gov.uk/files/pdf/MAPPA Guidance 2009 Version 3.0.pdf
189 Which has replaced PSO 4745.
190 MAPPA Guidance section 4.
191 Those contained in CJA 2003 Sch 15.

10.154   Each MAPPA area then applies three levels of management of relevant offenders:[192]

- Level 1 – ordinary agency management. This is the level used in cases where the risks posed by the offender can be managed by the agency responsible for supervision/case management of the offender (such as the Probation Service). Category 3 cases cannot by their nature be managed at this level. Other agencies might be involved but referral to a MAPPP meeting is not required.
- Level 2 – active multi-agency management. Cases should be managed at level 2 where the offender:
  - is assessed under OASys (or ASSET) as being high risk of causing serious harm;
  - requires active involvement and co-ordination of interventions from other agencies to manage the presenting risks of harm; or
  - has been previously managed at level 3 and the seriousness of risk has diminished, and/or the complexity of the multi-agency management of the risks have been brokered, and a RMP for level 2 has been firmly established.
- Level 3 – active multi-agency management. The criteria for referring a case to a level 3 MAPPP meeting are where the offender:
  - is assessed under OASys (or ASSET) as being a high or very high risk of causing serious harm; and
  - presents risks that can only be managed by a plan which requires close co-operation at a senior level due to the complexity of the case and/or because of the unusual resource commitments it requires; or
  - although not assessed as a high or very high risk, there is a high likelihood of media scrutiny and/or public interest in the management of the case and there is a need to ensure that public confidence in the criminal justice system is maintained.

10.155   Accordingly it is only for Level 2 and 3 cases that regular MAPPP meetings are held in order to make decisions as to risk, and the content of any RMP. For serving prisoners the guidance states that the appropriate MAPPA level should be set six months before the anticipated release date, or immediately if the release date is less than six months ahead.[193] It will be for the offender manager initially to determine the prisoner's level in consultation with other relevant agencies.

---

192  Section 10 of the MAPPA guidance and section 2 of the Prison Service Public Protection Manual.
193  Para 3.1 of the Public Protection Manual (PC 15/2006).

10.156    The Prison Service Public Protection Manual requires individual prisons to set up Interdepartmental Risk Management Teams (IRMTs) to provide regular monitoring of prisoners who pose the greatest risk to the public. These will have different depending on the type of prison. For example local prisons will focus on monitoring issues and collation of initial information, whereas open prisons will have a focus on temporary licence considerations. Closed training prisons will be focused on the preparation for release.[194] Prisons are required to ensure that police and probation services are informed of the release of MAPPA managed offenders.[195]

10.157    The existence of MAPPA does pose some issues of fairness for serving prisoners. The guidance clearly states that one of the purposes of MAPPP meetings will be to inform decisions relating to release on temporary licence, the licence conditions that prisoners will be subject to on release, and the decision of the Parole Board.[196] Whilst the MAPPP meeting cannot decide any of these matters it is of concern that its recommendations are made in a process that affords very little in the way of procedural fairness for prisoners.

10.158    MAPPP meetings are not open to the prisoner or legal representatives:[197]

> As a general principle, it is important to be clear that the human rights of offenders should *never* take priority over public protection. In particular, it is considered that the presence of an offender at a MAPP meeting could significantly hinder the core business of sharing and analysing information objectively and making decisions accordingly. *Offenders (and their representatives) should therefore be excluded from MAPP meetings.* The offender should, however, be allowed the opportunity to present written information to the MAPP meeting through their offender/case manager or for this person to provide information on their behalf.

10.159    However the guidance gives no specific guidance on what level of disclosure may be given to offenders to assist them in making representations. In these circumstances the right to make such representations may be meaningless as the offender may be unaware of the matters to be considered, and whether the information before the meeting contains any significant factual errors. It is arguable that fairness does require a basic level of disclosure to an offender prior

---

194  Chapter 1, annex C to the Prison Service Public Protection Manual.
195  Chapter 1, section 7.10 of the Public Protection Manual.
196  Section 14 of the MAPPA guidance.
197  Section 4.8 of the MAPPA guidance.

to a meeting should be required to enable proper representations to be made to address the issues to be considered. After a MAPPP meeting the guidance states that requests by offenders for disclosure of the minutes must be referred to the meeting chair.[198] An executive summary of the minutes can be prepared and this should be supplied to the Parole Board or to an offender if they request it.[199] In practice the executive summary can be an unhelpful and anodyne document and it may be that prisoners who are challenging the recommendations of MAPPP meetings need to make further requests for disclosure.

10.160    The MAPPP meeting decisions are increasingly having an impact upon licence conditions set by the prison or the Parole Board. The practical reality is that MAPPP meetings will make recommendations matters that are adopted by the Offender Manager and in turn by the board. In some cases the MAPPP meeting minutes are submitted to the board as material that is relevant for them to see but which should be withheld from the prisoner. It is arguable therefore that MAPPP meetings and recommendations can engage article 8 of the ECHR.[200] Whilst the guidance recognises the need for recommendations to be proportionate where Convention rights are at stake, it fails to consider the procedural rights that the Convention requires which would necessitate a basic level of prior disclosure to assist in making representations.

## Licence conditions

10.161    A life sentence remains a life sentence even after release – except for prisoners serving IPP – as licence conditions will remain in force until death.[201] IPP prisoners are technically serving indeterminate rather than life sentences as they can make an application to the Parole Board for the licence to cease to have effect after the qualifying period of ten years has elapsed.[202]

10.162    The licence conditions will be set by the Parole Board when directing release pursuant to C(S)A 1997 s31(3) and will usually include the following standard conditions:

198  Section 11.18 of the MAPPA guidance.
199  Sections 6.11 and 14.1 of the MAPPA guidance.
200  See *R (Craven) v Secretary of State for the Home Department and Parole Board* [2001] EWHC 850 (Admin) discussed further at para 10.163.
201  C(S)A 1997 s31.
202  C(S)A 1997 s31A.

- He or she shall place himself or herself under the supervision of whichever supervising officer is nominated for this purpose from time to time.
- He or she shall on release report to the supervising office so nominated, and shall keep in touch with that officer in accordance with that officer's instructions.
- He or she shall, if his or her supervising officer so requires, receive visits from that officer where the licence holder is living.
- He or she will reside only where approved by his or her supervising officer.
- He or she shall undertake work, including voluntary work, only where approved by his or her supervising officer and shall inform that officer of any change in or loss of such employment.
- He or she shall not travel outside the United Kingdom (including the Isle of Man and Channel Islands) without the prior permission of his or her supervising officer.
- He or she shall be well behaved and not do anything which could undermine the purposes of supervision on licence which are to protect the public, by ensuring that their safety would not be placed at risk, and to secure his or her successful integration into the community.

10.163 Licences will often include additional conditions such as exclusion areas designed to protect the interests of victims and victims' families who may not want to come into contact with the lifer. Licence conditions can engage article 8[203] and so must be necessary and proportionate. Guidance on the setting of such licence conditions taking into account article 8 considerations is contained in Probation Circular 28/2003 and chapter 13 of PSO 4700. In *R (Carman) v Secretary of State for the Home Department*[204] a licence condition requiring a determinate prisoner to reside in a hostel was quashed, but Moses J made it clear that it would be an exceptional case where the courts would interfere with conditions and other cases have suggested that not all licence conditions will actually engage article 8 in any event.[205] The reporting restrictions on a life licence will normally remain in force for around four years (although this can be up to ten years for people

203 *R (Craven) v Secretary of State for the Home Department* [2001] EWHC 850 (Admin).
204 [2004] EWHC 2400 (Admin).
205 In *R (Mehmet) v London Probation Board* [2007] EWHC 2223 (Admin) a licence condition prohibiting a determinate sentenced prisoner from travelling abroad was held not to engage article 8.

convicted of sexual offences).[206] Reporting generally starts with week-ly meetings with the supervising probation officer and will gradually reduce over time. During the reporting period, lifers are not permit-ted to travel abroad without express permission of the supervising officer. Permission is generally given only for unforeseen compas-sionate reasons or occasionally for short holidays. However, there are increasing instances of permission being given for travel abroad for work related activities.

# Recall

10.164   The power to recall life sentenced prisoners is contained in C(S)A 1997 s32 (as amended by CJA 2003 and CJIA 2008). The procedure for initial recall used to allow for a dual procedure where the Sec-retary of State either acting on the recommendation of the Parole Board or, where it was expedient in the public interest, by the Sec-retary of State acting alone. CJIA 2008 s31 amended this procedure so that all recalls now taken place on the direction of the Secretary of State alone (s2(1)) and the case must then be referred to the Parole Board (s32(4)).

10.165   Following recall, the prisoner must be given reasons for the deci-sion, 'on his return to prison' (s32(3)(b)) and can then make written representations to the Parole Board (s 33(3)(a)). The Parole Board Rules do not require a paper decision to be made in recall cases and so although they do not expressly provide that there is a right to an oral hearing for thus class of prisoner, the assumption must be that all recall cases will proceed to an oral hearing. As section 32(3) makes a distinction between 'recall' and 'return' to prison (the right to make representations arising with the former, but to reasons only with the latter) there is a right to submit representations before returning to custody where the licence is revoked.[207] It will be much more likely that the first time that the prisoner knows why the licence has been revoked will on the return to custody.

10.166   The speed with which these reasons must be provided was ex-amined in *R (Hirst) v Secretary of State for the Home Department and Parole Board*[208] where the prisoner was returned to custody on 3

---

206  See PC 5/2009.
207  *Brett Roberts v Parole Board* [2005] EWCA Civ 1663 – where the Secretary of State also confirmed that there might be exceptional circumstances where the revocation could be overturned without referral to the board.
208  [2005] EWHC 1480 (Admin).

August 2004 but received no information about the reasons for that decision for eight days and did not receive his recall papers until 26 August. His request for an oral hearing was received on 31 August, the hearing took place on 9 November, and a direction for release was made in writing on 14 November. The court confirmed that the prisoner's right to be informed of the reasons for his arrest under article 5(2) had been breached and that there had been a delay in providing the parole dossier so that the review process began 14 days late as it took 17 days to send out the dossier to rather than the target period of three days.[209] The court rejected a submission by the claimant that as the executive took the decision to effect the recall, this breached articles 5(1)(c) and 5(3). A similar decision on the power of the executive to direct the initial recall was also upheld in *R (Motylski) v Secretary of State for the Home Department and South Yorkshire Probation*[210] where the court considered that the prisoner's Convention rights to a judicial determination of the necessity for recall were protected by the referral of the case to the Parole Board.

10.167    Once the case has been referred to the Parole Board, the board is also under a duty to consider the case as quickly as possible. The board has generally operated to a target date of 11 weeks to hear a case following recall but it has been held that listing of cases is a judicial function and that article 5(4) may require a speedier hearing in some cases.[211] The ambit of the referral to the board is a matter for the Secretary of State. As the statute only requires the board to have the issue of immediate re-release referred, it is solely within the discretion of the Secretary of State to decide whether to refer the question of suitability for open conditions as well and the board, as a creature of statute, does not have any inherent jurisdiction to consider other issues.[212]

10.168    When assessing the suitability for recall, the board is required to assess the level of dangerousness that is posed by the prisoner. Disobedience is only relevant where it is indicative of risk.[213] Where risk is

209  Damages of £1,500 were awarded based on the view that as he was released when the hearing did take place, his release had been delayed by that period of time. Further claims relating to delay in processing the decision and effecting the release itself were rejected.

210  [2004] EWHC 2166 (Admin).

211  In *R (Cooper) v Parole Board* [2007] EWHC 1292 (Admin) the recalled prisoner's mental health was a relevant factor that justified an urgent hearing.

212  *R (Mills) v Secretary of State for the Home Department and Parole Board* [2005] EWHC 2508 (Admin).

213  *R v Parole Board ex p Watson* [1996] 1 WLR 906; *R v Secretary of State for the Home Department ex p Cox* (1992) 5 Admin LR 17.

not considered sufficient to merit recall, the board's power is to direct immediate release.[214] There is some significance in the use of the word immediate in this context as the release cannot be contingent on some future event rather than being capable taking place straight away.[215] The practical implications are that a release address must be available at the time of the hearing and any matters that might interfere with release, such as outstanding criminal charges, should normally be dealt with before the recall hearing takes place.[216]

10.169    There may be cases where there might have been sufficient prima facie evidence to justify a recall at the time the original decision was taken, but the evidence subsequently shows that recall is not necessary. In such situations, the board can reach a finding that the decision to recall was justified but that the prisoner's continued detention is no longer necessary for the protection of the public. Approaching hearings in this manner can sometimes help defuse the need for confrontation, particularly between the prisoner and the probation officer, and allow the panel to concentrate on the risk as it presents itself at the time of the hearing.

10.170    Recall hearings are often amongst the most complex of parole cases as they will very often involve the need to reach a determination of disputed facts. Careful attention needs to be given to the evidence that needs to be adduced at such hearings, the cogency and strength of that evidence and the extent to which the hearing should more closely follow a criminal trial with witnesses only being present to give their own evidence rather than automatically being present for the entire hearing. It is important to bear in mind that as the board operates to the civil standard of proof, it is still possible for the board to reach adverse findings on matters that have been the subject of an acquittal in criminal proceedings.

214  C(S)A 1997 s32(5).

215  In the past this was more of a problem as it was the only occasion when the board had the power to direct the release of a lifer rather than to make a recommendation to the Secretary of State: see for example *R v Secretary of State for the Home Department ex p Gunnell* [1998] Crim LR 170 and *R v Secretary of State for the Home Department ex p De Lara*, 2 March 1995, unreported, where an order for release on the conclusion of a short concurrent determinate sentence was held not to be binding.

216  It should be noted that the mere fact of a criminal charge is not sufficient to justify a recall and that the board has to reach its own assessment of risk: *R (Broadbent) v Parole Board* [2005] EWHC 1207 (Admin) but that similarly, an acquittal of the criminal charges triggering the recall does not prevent the board reexamining the facts or deciding that recall is appropriate on other grounds: *R (Wyles) v Parole Board and Secretary of State for the Home Department* [2006] EWHC 493 (Admin).

10.171    The impact of a recall being upheld is that the prisoner falls to continue serving the original life sentence.[217] Any future reviews and release are dealt with in the same manner as parole reviews for lifers who have never been released.

## Compassionate release

10.172    The Secretary of State retains the power to release prisoners serving life sentences on compassionate grounds at any time of the life sentence[218] and it is the existence of this power that has led the Court of Appeal provisionally to find that the whole life sentence is lawful.[219] The purpose of compassionate release for lifers is ordinarily restricted to medical grounds and is usually applied in the following circumstances:

- the prisoner is suffering from a terminal illness and death is likely to occur very shortly (although there are no set time limits three months may be considered to be an appropriate period for an application to be made to the Public Protection Unit), or the lifer is bedridden or similarly incapacitated, for example, those paralysed or suffering from a severe stoke; *and*
- the risk of re-offending (particularly of a sexual or violent nature) is minimal; *and*
- further imprisonment would reduce the prisoner's life expectancy; *and*
- there are adequate arrangements for the prisoner's care and treatment outside prison; *and*
- early release will bring some significant benefit to the prisoner or his or her family.[220]

10.173    The power is therefore somewhat narrower than for prisoners serving determinate sentences where release on compassionate grounds is permitted where there are tragic family circumstances as well as on medical grounds. In the case of lifers it is usually authorised to allow the prisoner to die outside of prison.

10.174    The power is one which falls entirely within the discretion of the Secretary of State and while he is required to consult the Parole Board, where practicable, before authorising release (s30(2)), the

217  C(S)A 1997 s 32(6).
218  C(S)A 1997 s30
219  See *R v Bieber (aka Coleman)* [2008] EWCA Crim 1601.
220  PSO 4700 para 12.2.1.

discretion remains with the executive. The requirement to consult the board if release is being contemplated does not carry with it a requirement to seek the advice of the board of the Secretary of State does not consider that release is appropriate.[221]

221  *R (Spinks) v Secretary of State for the Home Department* [2005] EWCA Civ 275.

# Release: fixed term sentences

*continued*

# Introduction

11.1  Prisoners serving determinate sentences are subject to a variety of schemes that allow them to be released from their sentence before it has been served in full. Throughout the history of modern imprisonment there have been various ad hoc schemes for allowing prisoners to be released from prison before the very end of their sentences, these practices ranging from transportation through to special remission, but it was not until the introduction of the Criminal Justice Act (CJA) 1967 that the Parole Board was established and the modern concept of parole began to develop.[1]

11.2  The CJA 1967 introduced a two-fold scheme which provided for all prisoners to be released after serving two thirds of their sentences subject to good behaviour. This early release from the sentence was known as remission and could only be delayed if the prisoner had received awards of lost remission at prison disciplinary hearings (see chapter 9 on prison discipline above). In addition to this statutory right to release at a particular point in their sentence, prisoners could also be considered for conditional early release on a parole licence after serving one third of their sentence. The rationale for this scheme was set out in the white paper, 'The Adult Offender' 1965 which envisaged that an early release scheme of this type would promote the rehabilitative aim of imprisonment, provide an incentive for prisoners to reform, and assist the management of prisons. Although there have been many modifications and alterations to the system of parole in the intervening 40 years, this basic model remains in place leading Lord Bingham to observe that:

> ... the sentence passed is not (as it has not within living memory been) a simple statement of the period the defendant must spend in prison. The sentence is in reality a composite package, the legal implications of which are in large measure governed by the sentence passed.[2]

11.3  Since 1967, each new CJA has introduced both amendments to existing release arrangements and new release schemes to run in parallel creating a situation of such complexity that it has caused confusion

---

1 For a more detailed discussion of the historical development of parole schemes and the legislative rationale for change see Livingstone, Owen and Macdonald, *Prison Law* (fourth edition, OUP 2008) chapter 13.

2 *R (Smith) v Secretary of State for the Home Department* [2005] UKHL 1 at 24.

and dismay to prison administrators and the courts.[3] However, the basic premise that all prisoners serving determinate sentences have two release dates has remained intact. The two release dates are the date when there is a statutory right to release and a date when there is a conditional or discretionary entitlement to be considered for release. There have subsequently been a number of other early release provisions layered over these core entitlements, such as end of custody licence and home detention curfew and those entitlements are discussed later in this chapter.

11.4   A basic overview of the entitlement of prisoners to parole and liability to recall is contained in the table on pp531–532.

## Article 5 and determinate release schemes

11.5   The complexity of the domestic statutory release schemes has been further complicated by the application of article 5 to parole. In relation to life and indeterminate sentences, the jurisprudence of the European Court of Human Rights (ECtHR) has gradually established that article 5(4) applies to all forms of indeterminate sentencing (see chapter 10). The basic premise is that indeterminate sentences are explicitly comprised of two parts, a fixed punitive period that is set with reference to equivalent determinate sentences followed by a protective period where further detention is authorised only for the protection of the public. Once a prisoner has entered the protective period, article 5(4) requires a fresh determination of the need for detention by a court-like body that has the power to order release. The failure to make provision for a fresh review of detention at this point and at regular intervals thereafter carries the risk that continued detention might no longer meet the aims of the original sentence and so become arbitrary and in breach of article 5(1).

11.6   The question of whether article 5(1) or article 5(4) have direct application to parole for prisoners serving determinate sentences has been far more complicated and until the decision in *R (Black) v Secretary of State for Justice*[4] there was not a definitive judicial determination of the problem. The approach of the ECtHR has been that for

---

3   In *R(Stellato) v Secretary of State for the Home Department* [2006] EWCA Civ 1639. Longmore LJ commented that: 'One can only sympathise with Prison governors, the Parole Board and indeed Home Office officials and judges in having to interpret these almost intractable provisions'.

4   [2009] UKHL 1.

determinate prison sentences, the guarantees of article 5 are met by
the initial sentencing exercise and that this provides lawful authority
for detention until the very last day of the sentence. This basic
premise applies not only to normal determinate sentences but also to
less usual situations such as the imposition of an extended sentence
where the extension period is imposed specifically because of risk[5]
and to the recall of determinate sentenced prisoners.[6]

11.7    The only time when the ECtHR acknowledged that a fresh article
5 right accrued during the currency of a determinate sentence was
after a crystallised right to release had arisen. This might occur when
a prisoner reached the statutory release date or after a binding decision to release the prisoner on a conditional release scheme had been
made.[7] Once that point had been reached, the further detention could
not be considered to be in accordance with the law and so becomes
arbitrary and so in breach of article 5(1)(a). This view was in keeping
with the domestic courts' interpretations of the tort of false imprisonment and its relationship with article 5(1).[8]

11.8    The ECtHR interpretation of parole and the Convention had been
largely mirrored in domestic law. In the case of *R (Giles) v Parole
Board*,[9] the Lords rejected a claim by a prisoner serving an extended
sentence that once the custodial part of his sentence had been served,
he was entitled to the protection of article 5(4) as he had entered the
punitive phase of the sentence. This was rejected with Lord Hope
giving the following analysis:

> It is plain from this summary that the basic rule which the European
> court laid down in *De Wilde, Ooms and Versyp v Belgium (No 1)*[10] con-
> tinues to apply. Where the prisoner has been lawfully detained within
> the meaning of article 5(1)(a) following the imposition of a determi-
> nate sentence after his conviction by a competent court, the review
> which article 5(4) requires is incorporated in the original sentence
> passed by the sentencing court. Once the appeal process has been
> exhausted there is no right to have the lawfulness of the detention
> under that sentence reviewed by another court. The principle which
> underlies these propositions is that detention in accordance with a

5  *Mansell v United Kingdom* (Application no 32072/96) unreported 2 July 1997.
6  *Ganusauskas v Lithuania* (Application no 47922/99) unreported 7 September
   1999; and the admissibility decision in *Brown v United Kingdom* (Application no
   968/04) unreported 26 October 2004.
7  See eg *Gebura v Poland* (Application no 63131/00) unreported 6 March 2007.
8  *R v Governor of Brockhill Prison ex p Evans (No 2)* [2001] 2 AC 19.
9  [2003] UKHL 42.
10  (1979–80) 1 EHRR 373.

lawful sentence passed after conviction by a competent court cannot be described as arbitrary.[11]

11.9    This orthodoxy continued until the House of Lords decision in *R (Smith) v Parole Board*[12] when the recall system for determinate prisoners fell to be examined. Whilst it was confirmed that the original criminal sentence provided sufficient protection to satisfy the requirements of article 5(1) until the very end of the sentence, Lord Bingham in the lead judgment considered that the routine failure of the Parole Board to convene oral hearings for recalled prisoners, even where there were disputed facts involved, breached the common law duty of fairness. He further considered that article 5(4) was re-engaged by the recall procedure as the Convention requires judicial review of the lawfulness of detention to be wide enough to bear on those conditions which are essential for lawful detention.[13] It was clear that the fact that the prisoners had been released at a statutory release date and had then been subject to re-detention was influential in this decision as it was a major departure from Convention analysis of parole. Whilst the decision appears to more properly reflect the domestic release and recall procedure than the analysis of the ECtHR, the actual reasoning in relation to article 5(4) is far from clear and it appears to confuse the procedural rights arising from the identity of the decision maker with the engagement of the substantive right.

11.10    The Lords looked at the correlation of article 5 and parole in the context of discrimination and article 14 in the cases of *R (Clift, Headley & Hindawi) v Secretary of State for the Home Department.*[14] The case involved two situations where the Secretary of State reserved the right to decide whether the prisoner should be released, rather than giving this power to the Parole Board.

11.11    It was not argued that article 5 was directly engaged but the prisoners contended that parole schemes fell within the ambit of article 5 and so had to be applied in a manner that was not discriminatory in order to comply with article 14. Two of the prisoners were foreign nationals and successfully obtained a declaration that the legislation prohibiting their cases from being referred to the Parole Board was in breach of article 14.[15] The third prisoner failed to establish that the length of sentence was a 'personal characteristic' within the meaning

11   (1979–80) 1 EHRR 373 at para 51.
12   [2005] UKHL 1.
13   [2005] UKHL 1 at para 37.
14   [2006] UKHL 54.
15   Resulting in a change to the legislation – see below.

of article 14 and so was unable to succeed in his argument that the different release arrangements for prisoners serving over 15 years were discriminatory. Lord Bingham explained that even though parole schemes did not directly engage article 5, they still fell within the ambit of the article:

> During the currency of a lawful sentence, article 5(4) has no part to play. But the Secretary of State's argument founders, in my opinion, on a failure to recognise both the importance, in our system, of the statutory rules providing for early release and the close relationship between those rules and the core value which article 5 exists to protect.[16]

11.12    Following this decision and building on these observations, the Court of Appeal held that that article 5(4) did in fact have direct application to all determinate parole decisions. In *R (Johnson) v Parole Board*[17] the Court of Appeal considered that as lifers had their tariffs set to expire on the same date as the first parole review for prisoners serving determinate sentences of the same length, it could not be right that a remedy for delay on parole proceedings was only available to lifers and so, article 5(4) did allow proceedings to be taken to ensure that the review of detention was conducted speedily. *Giles* was distinguished on the basis that the application had actually been concerned with an attempt to seek a review of detention prior to the expiry of the period where the statutory entitlement to parole arises. The conclusion that new issues concerning the lawfulness of detention could also arise in relation to the initial release of prisoners serving extended sentences (that is, during the custodial period of such a sentence) was also accepted in the case of *R (O'Connell) v Parole Board*.[18]

11.13    In the *Black* case, however, the Lords rejected this interpretation and returned to a more limited reading of the Strasbourg authorities. Lord Brown rejected the view that there was a risk of arbitrary detention arising from the parole scheme and stated that there was no Convention duty to involve the Parole Board in the process at all as initial release from a determinate sentence is a purely administrative action. He explained that:

> The essential contrast struck by the ECtHR is between on the one hand 'the administrative implementation of the sentence of the court', for example decisions regarding 'early or conditional release from a determinate term of imprisonment' (para 87 of the court's

---

16  [2006] UKHL 54 at para 16. See also *R (Giles) v Parole Board* [2003] UKHL 32.
17  [2007] 1 WLR 1990. See also *R (Giles) v Parole Board* [2003] UKHL 32.
18  [2008] 1 WLR 979.

judgment in *Stafford* (2002) 35 EHRR 32 set out at para 67 above), and on the other hand 'fixing the tariff' and later determining the length of post-tariff detention in life sentence cases. The administrative implementation of determinate sentences does not engage article 5(4); the decision when to release a prisoner subject to an indeterminate sentence does.[19]

11.14    The decision did not alter the position with the recall of determinate sentenced prisoners. It was accepted that the fact of release, particularly in cases where the prisoner has served up to the statutory release date, means that re-detention can re-engage article 5 rights and so the *Smith* decision remains intact. This conclusion is, however, somewhat inconsistent with the thrust of the reasoning. The dissenting opinion of Lord Phillips in *Black* attempted to marry domestic law with ECtHR decisions and may provide a possible avenue of future argument on this issue. It is sometimes difficult to translate ECtHR decisions about the early release arrangements from other European jurisdictions to the domestic parole scheme as the civil codes that prevail in most of those countries means that there is no Parole Board and early release decisions remain the responsibility of the criminal courts. The absence of such a formal system of judicial oversight in England and Wales may mean that the domestic interpretation of the nature of the right provided by Lord Phillips adheres more strongly to the substance of the right at stake.

## Can changes to parole entitlement be retrospective?

11.15    This is a further preliminary issue that requires some explanation bearing in mind the number of different and overlapping parole schemes in force. The question was first examined through the prism of article 7 in the case of *R (Uttley) v Secretary of State for the Home Department*[20] involving a prisoner who had been convicted of an historic sexual offence. The offence had been committed prior to the coming into force of CJA 1991 but he was tried and convicted afterwards. The sentence he received fell to be administered under the provisions of CJA 1991 meaning that his licence period expired at the three quarter point of the sentence instead of the two thirds point as had previously applied.

19  Para 83.
20  [2004] UKHL 38.

## Parole schemes

| Length of sentence | Relevant legislation | Automatic release date | Parole eligibility date | Licence expiry date |
|---|---|---|---|---|
| *Offences for which sentence was imposed before 1 October 1992* | | | | |
| Any | CJA 1967 | ⅔ | ⅓ | ⅔ |
| *Sentence imposed on or after 1.10.92 and offence committed before 30 September 1998* | | | | |
| < 12 months | CJA 1991 | ½ | n/a | n/a |
| 12 months but < 4 years | CJA 1991 | ½ | n/a | ¾* |
| 4 yrs + | CJA 1991 | ⅔ (unless the offence is not a specified offence *and* the PED falls on or after 09.07.08 in which case the 2003 Act applies) | ½ | ¾* unless recalled on or after 14.07.08 in which case SED |
| *Offence committed on or after 30 September 1998 but before 4 May 2005* | | | | |
| < 12 months | CJA 1991 | ½ | n/a | n/a |
| >12 months but < 4 years | CJA 1991 (as amended by CDA 1998) | ½ | n/a | ¾* |
| 4 yrs + | CJA 1991 (as amended by CDA 1998) | ⅔ (unless the offence is not a specified offence *and* the PED falls on or after 09.07.08 in which case the 2003 Act applies) | ½ | ¾* unless recalled, in which case SED |
| Extended sentence – custodial period under 12 months | CJA 1991 (as amended CDA 1998) | ½ of custodial term | n/a | Specified extension period commencing from ¾ point of custodial term. |

| Length of sentence | Relevant legislation | Automatic release date | Parole eligibility date | Licence expiry date |
|---|---|---|---|---|
| Extended sentence – custodial period 12 months & < 4 yrs | CJA 1991 (as amended by CDA 1998) | ½ of custodial term | n/a | Specified extension period commencing from ¾ point of custodial term. |
| Extended sentence – custodial period 4 yrs + | CJA 1991 (as amended by CDA 1998) | ½ of custodial term | ½ of custodial term | Specified extension period commencing from ¾ point of custodial term. |
| *Offence committed on or after 4 May 2005* | | | | |
| Any determinate sentence of 12 months or more (except extended sentences) | CJA 2003 | ½ | n/a | SED |
| Determinate sentence < 12 months | CJA 1991 | ½ | n/a | n/a |
| Extended Sentence | CJA 2003 | ½ of custodial term | End of custodial term | Specified extension period |
| *Sentence imposed on or after 14 July 2008* | | | | |
| Extended sentence | CJA 2003 (as amended by CIJA 2008) | n/a | ½ of custodial term | Specified extension period |

\* The power always existed for the court to impose an extended licence period up until to SED under CJA 1991 s44 for those convicted of sexual offences.

11.16 Although it was accepted that the additional licence period could be characterised as a penalty within the meaning of article 7, the Lords considered that, providing the sentence imposed did not exceed the maximum available penalty available at the time the offence was committed, article 7 was not breached.[21]

11.17 It is noteworthy that when the Crime and Disorder Act (CDA) 1998 amended CJA 1991 and when CJA 2003 was introduced, the amendments specifically only applied to offences committed after their enactment. This was presumably due to a belief that a retrospective amendment would have breached article 7. Once this had been dispelled by the *Uttley* decision, the commencement provisions for CJA 2003 purported to replace the recall provisions of CJA 1991 with those contained at section 254 of the CJA 2003. This was a significant change as it meant that all CJA 1991 prisoners became subject to a licence that extended to the very end of their sentence if they were recalled, replacing previous provisions that generally restricted the licence period to three quarters of the sentence. An initial attempt to exploit an apparent lacuna in the commencement order[22] to provide an earlier licence expiry date for short term prisoners sentenced after 30 September 2008 was rejected[23] but a subsequent application made by a long term prisoner who was made subject to a longer period of detention as a result of the change proved successful. In *R (Stellato) v Secretary of State for the Home Department*[24] the prisoner had been convicted of offences committed prior to the amendments made to the CJA 1991 by CDA 1998 and the effect of the commencement order was that after his recall, he was liable to be re-detained until his SED rather than having an automatic entitlement to release at the three quarter point of the sentence. The Lords approved the Court of Ap-

---

21 It has been noted that the effect of this change means that Parliament effectively has the power to cancel all prisoners' release dates and impose harsher sentences: 'The upshot of this approach is startling; if Mr Uttley's sentence had been changed the day before his release to a sentence of 30 years imprisonment, this would still have been acceptable on the basis that 30 years imprisonment is still less than the maximum sentence applicable of life imprisonment. This severely curtails the protections afforded by article 7 ECHR, and has several noteworthy effects. It provides least protection to criminals convicted of serious offences who arguably are at most risk of a populist Home Secretary'. Simon Atrill: *Nulla Poene Sine Lege in Comparative Perspective*, Public Law Spring 2005 p127.

22 Criminal Justice Act (Commencement No 8 Transitional and Savings Provisions) Order 2005 SI No 950.

23 *R (Buddington) v Secretary of State for the Home Department* [2006] 2 Cr App R (S).

24 [2007] UKHL 5.

peal's view that there is a 'longstanding principle that existing prisoners should not be adversely affected by changes in the sentencing regime after their conviction'[25] unless there is clear parliamentary approval for the change.

11.18    The response to this judgment has been to introduce subsequent changes to parole schemes through primary legislation. The Criminal Justice and Immigration Act (CJIA) 2008 has effectively made retrospective changes to the previous Criminal Justice Acts applying the early release and recall provisions of CJA 2003 to all prisoners. There is no prospect of challenging these changes through articles 5 and 7 as a result of the *Uttley* and *Black* decisions. The question of whether this amounts to an unlawful change to the sentence imposed by the criminal courts in breach of article 6 remains under debate.

# Criminal Justice Act 2003

11.19    The CJA 2003 provides for three core prison sentences: determinate prison sentences known as the standard determinate sentence (SDS) for people who have not been convicted of a specified offence or who are not deemed to be dangerous at the time of conviction; extended sentences for prisoners convicted of an offence specified by Schedule 15 to the Act[26] but here the maximum penalty is less than 10 years; and sentence of IPP for persons convicted of a serious specified offence.[27] IPP sentences are indeterminate and are dealt with in the previous chapter and extended sentences are examined in detail below.

## Standard determinate sentences

11.20    For SDS prisoners serving sentences of 12 months or more, the longstanding system of discretionary parole has been abolished and all such prisoners are automatically released on licence after having served one half of the sentence (section 244). The licence upon which SDS prisoners are released then lasts until the sentence expiry date (or SED). Those SDS prisoners serving sentences of less than

25  At para 44
26  CJA 2003 s227.
27  CJA 2003 s225.

12 months are excluded from these release provisions and remain subject to the CJA 1991 so that they are released automatically at the halfway point of the sentence and instead of being on licence, are simply at risk of being returned to custody by the criminal courts of they commit further criminal offences.[28]

11.21    It is important to note that all SDS prisoners are eligible for earlier release on Home Detention Curfew (HDC). If not released on HDC, either because they are on the presumed unsuitable list or because they have do not meet the criteria for other reasons, then release on licence at the halfway point – conditional release – is automatic and can only be delayed if additional days have been awarded for disciplinary offences (s257). This provision applies to any SDS prisoner in custody at the halfway point of the sentence including those who have been released on HDC and recalled. PSO 6000, chapter 14, Annex A contains a standard licence[29] that will be issued to all SDS prisoners:

STANDARD CONDITIONS

(i)   To be well behaved, not to commit any offence and not to do anything which could undermine the purposes of your supervision, which are to protect the public, prevent you from re-offending and help you to re-settle successfully into the community.

(ii)  To keep in touch with your supervising officer in accordance with any instructions that you may be given;

(iii) If required, to receive visits from your supervising officer at your home/place of residence (e.g. approved premises);

(iii) Permanently to reside at an address approved by your supervising officer and notify him or her in advance of any proposed change of address or any proposed stay (even for one night) away from that approved address;

(iv)  Undertake only such work (including voluntary work) approved by your supervising officer and notify him or her in advance of any proposed change;

(v)   Not to travel outside the 'United Kingdom' (for the purposes of this licence 'United Kingdom' includes the Channel Islands and the Isle of Man) without prior permission of your supervising officer (which will be given in **exceptional** circumstances only) or for the purposes of immigration deportation/removal.

11.22    In addition to the standard conditions, the sentencing court may have specified additional licence conditions and these must also be included on the licence[30] or the Secretary of State may order

28  CJA 2003 s244(3)(a).
29  CJA 2003 s250(4)(a).
30  CJA 2003 s250(4(b)(i).

additional conditions to be added[31] for the purpose of protecting the public, preventing re-offending and securing reintegration into the community.[32] The additional licence conditions will normally have been recommended by the Probation Service. Where additional conditions are being considered, the Offender Manager is required to contact the local police force for information in accordance with the 'Joint Protocol on Supervision, Revocation and Recall for Prisoners Released on Licence'.[33] A guide to the additional licence conditions that may be imposed is contained in PSO 6000 and these include:

- Additional reporting requirements
- Contact with a psychologist or psychiatrist
- Prohibiting computer use
- Preventing certain activities/employment involving contact with children
- A residency requirement (rather than a simpler notification of address)
- Requirements to attend particular offending behaviour programmes
- Prohibition on contact with victims of their family members
- Exclusion areas
- Non-association with named individuals
- In the case of prolific or priority offenders, drug or alcohol testing

11.23    The Offender Management Act (OMA) 2007 s28 now also permits the Secretary of State to include a polygraph condition as part of the licence conditions for prisoners who have been convicted of a sexual offence specified in Schedule 15 to CJA 2003 and is released on licence. The provision applies to a conviction under any enactment and so can apply to all licences. The polygraph condition can require licensees to participate in polygraph testing for the purposes of monitoring their progress on licence or generally improving their management on licence.[34]

11.24    Multi-Agency Public Protection Panels (MAPPPs) may also have input into the licence conditions for prisoners convicted of sexual or violent offences or who are considered dangerous by the offender manager. MAPPA requirements are discussed in detail in chapter 10 on lifers above.

11.25    The Parole Board is not involved in the imposition of licence con-

31  CJA 2003 s250(4)(b)(ii).
32  PSO 6000 para 14.6.1.
33  Initially introduced by PC 3/2005, and relaunched by PC 5/2007.
34  OMA 2007 s29.

ditions at this stage. Governors, who have responsibility for including any additional conditions on behalf of the Secretary of State are reminded that they must be taken from this approved list and that they must have been recommended by the Probation Service.[35] There may be exceptional cases where the Probation Service believes a condition not listed should be added and in such cases, they are required to seek advice from PPU before notifying the governor. If the governor is concerned that any additional condition is unnecessary or disproportionate, the matter should also be referred the PPU for a decision and in cases where the governor feels additional conditions may be needed but have not been recommended, he or she is required to contact the Probation Service to notify them of the concerns to see if an additional condition is appropriate.

11.26    The licence will be prepared by Custody/Discipline office and explained to the prisoner at least one week before release together with an explanatory note. If the prisoner refuses to sign it, the governor will sign it to confirm that the conditions have been read out and explained to the prisoner. One copy of the is given the prisoner on discharge and further copies kept on the prisoners prison records and sent to the police (both the National Identification Service at New Scotland Yard and to the Chief Constable of the area to which the prisoner is being released).

11.27    Although the SDS originally only applied to persons convicted of offences committed on or after 4 April 2005, CJIA 2008 s36 has been gradually extending its reach back to CJA 1991 prisoners. However, there remain significant numbers of these existing prisoners who are still subject to the original release arrangements, either because the nature of their offences excludes them from automatic release or because their first PED fell before 9 June 2008 when the changes were introduced. It is therefore also necessary to look at the other historical release schemes.

## Criminal Justice Act 1967

11.28    The early release provisions contained in CJA 1967 apply to all prisoners sentenced prior to the coming into force of CJA 1991 on 1 October 1992 which preserved the release arrangements for these prisoners.[36] The entitlement to parole is as follows:

35   PSO 6000 para 14.6.2.
36   CJA 1991 Sch 12 para 8.

- All prisoners sentenced whilst the 1967 Act was in force are eligible to be considered for parole after serving one third of the sentence.
- If refused parole, there is an entitlement to be considered annually, providing the prisoner has 13 months or more to serve until the automatic release date.
- Release is on a licence that lasts until the two thirds point of the sentence.
- After serving two thirds of the sentence, the prisoner is entitled to automatic release.
- After two thirds of the sentence has been served, whether in custody or on licence, there is no power to recall the prisoner to prison.

11.29    There remains a very small number of prisoners subject to this release scheme. This small pool will eventually disappear altogether as the release provisions of CJA 1967 only apply to people sentenced while the Act was in force and not to offences committed at the time but only prosecuted or sentenced at a later date.[37]

## Criminal Justice Act 1991

11.30    The CJA 1991 introduced an early release scheme for prisoners based on the length of their sentence. Although it has been largely repealed by CJA 2003, it still applies to those sentenced to under 12 months, and transitional arrangements have also preserved in part this scheme for those convicted of offences committed before 4 April 2005.[38] The scheme is further complicated as it was amended by CDA 1998 on 30 September 1998 for prisoners convicted of offences committed after that date and has since been partially subsumed into the arrangements contained in the 2003 Act. In order to properly understand how it operates in practice, it is necessary to set out the original statutory arrangements and then to explain the modifications made by subsequent legislation.

11.31    Entitlement to early release under CJA 1991 was dependent upon the length of the sentence imposed by the courts. A summary of the arrangements is:

---

37  See *R (Uttley) v Secretary of State for the Home Department* [2004] UKHL 38.
38  Criminal Justice Act 2003 (Commencement No 8 and Transitional and Saving Provisions) Order 2005 SI No 950.

| Sentence | ½ | ⅔ | ¾ |
|---|---|---|---|
| AUTOMATIC UNCONDITIONAL RELEASE (AUR) Adults serving under 12 months* (+ HDC eligibility if 3 months or more) | AT RISK | | |
| AUTOMATIC CONDITIONAL RELEASE (ACR) Adults and YOIs serving 12 months to Under 4 years (+ HDC eligibility) | SUPERVISION | | AT RISK |
| DISCRETIONARY CONDITIONAL RELEASE (DCR) Adults and YOIs serving 4 years or more | PAROLE ELIGIBILITY | SUPERVISION | AT RISK |

\* Young offenders serving less than 12 months are also subject to supervision.

## Sentences of less than 12 months (automatic unconditional release)

11.32 This remains the way that all sentences of under 12 months, even for offences committed after 4 April 2005, are administered as the CJA 2003 provisions in relation to sentences of this length have yet to be brought into force.[39] Sentences of less than 12 months carry an entitlement to automatic unconditional release after one half of the sentence has been served (CJA 1991 s33(1)(a)). Once released the prisoner is not subject to any licence but remains at risk of being returned to custody if any further offences are committed.[40] The 'at risk' notice will be issued one week before discharge. These provisions apply to all prisoners who are convicted of a further criminal offence after release but before the sentence expiry date and are discussed in more detail below.

39 Except for the 'intermittent custody' sentence pilot schemes.
40 Section 116 of the Powers of Criminal Courts (Sentencing) Act (PCC(S)A) 2000.

## Sentences of 12 months but less than four years (automatic conditional release)

11.33    Prisoners sentenced to 12 months or more but less than four years for offences committed before 4 April 2005 are also entitled to automatic release after having served one half of the sentence but release is subject to a licence. This scheme is known as automatic conditional release. This is not a discretionary scheme as there is an entitlement to release (CJA 1991 s33(1)(b)). The licence continues until the three quarter point of the sentence[41] and the prisoner remains supervised until that point. The implications of recall on the length of the licence are discussed below.

11.34    Prisoners subject to the automatic conditional release scheme will have their release date notified to them by their holding prison and that they will be subject to a licence requiring supervision by the Probation Service after release (PSO 6000, para 3.3.1). These prisoners are:

- Normally eligible to be placed on Home Detention Curfew (HDC).
- If not placed on HDC, are released automatically on licence at the halfway point of their sentence on their Conditional Release Date (CRD).
- Subject to compulsory supervision normally until the licence expiry date (LED).
- If they who breach their licence conditions, they are liable to be recalled by the Secretary of State, or, depending on the date of the original offence, by the magistrates' courts.
- At risk of being returned to custody by the magistrate's court if they commit a further imprisonable offence before the expiry of their sentence.

11.35    In addition, those convicted of sexual offences committed before 30 September 1998 can be subject to supervision up until the SED providing an order to that effect was made by the sentencing court.[42]

11.36    The governor must sign and issue the licence to the prisoner and the conditions.[43] The prisoner is asked to sign the licence and if he or she refuses, the governor must certify on it that the conditions have been explained and that the prisoner has refused to sign. The prisoner cannot be refused release simply because he or she has not

41    Known as the licence expiry date of LED.
42    PCC(S)A 2000 s86.
43    See PSO 6000 para 3.10.

signed the licence as the entitlement to release is statutory and so this procedure is followed to ensure hat the conditions are known to the prisoner and therefore enforceable by the Probation Service. The licence will be prepared by Custody/Discipline office and explained to the prisoner no less than one week before release. ACR prisoners are generally given a standard licence, whether placed on HDC or not but at the request of the Probation Service the governor, acting on behalf of the Secretary of State, may approve additional conditions. One copy of the licence is given to the prisoner on discharge and another sent to the offender manager (formerly referred to as the home or supervising probation officer). Further copies are sent to the National Identification Service (NIS) at New Scotland Yard and to the Chief Constable of the area to which the prisoner is being released.

## Sentences of four years or more (discretionary conditional release)

11.37 Prisoners sentenced to four years or more under CJA 1991 are subject to the discretionary conditional release (DCR) scheme, the scheme that is most commonly understood to be 'parole' in the classic sense.

## The impact of the Criminal Justice Act 2003

11.38 It is important to note that CJA 2003 has restricted the number of 1991 Act prisoners who remain subject to the DCR scheme. As a result of amendments introduced by CJIA 2008 s26, DCR prisoners may be made subject to the release provisions for SDS prisoners under CJA 2003 s244 which provides for automatic release at the halfway point of the sentence without consideration of the case by the Parole Board, although the prisoner then remains on licence until the very end of the sentence and is therefore liable to recall and re-detention until the SED. CJA 2003 excludes from the SDS scheme those prisoners who are serving extended sentences which are generally imposed for violent or sexual offences. In order to achieve symmetry, DCR prisoners sentenced under CJA 1991 are excluded from the SDS automatic release scheme if they are convicted of a specified violent or sexual offence.[44]

---

44 The list of specified offences is contained at CJA 2003 Sch 15 and includes offences ranging from manslaughter to affray and rape through to voyeurism. The Coroners and Justice Bill 2009 proposes extending this to include other offences where the conviction is related to terrorist activity.

11.39    Finally, the commencement order enacting these provisions also restricted the automatic release provisions of CJA 2003 to those prisoners who had not reached their Parole Eligibility Date (PED) prior to 9 June 2008. The legislative intent behind this provision was presumably to ensure that prisoners who had recently been assessed as too dangerous for release were not then automatically released shortly thereafter. Although the DCR release provisions will gradually apply to an ever decreasing group of prisoners, they remain relevant not just for prisoners already serving sentences when the law was changed but also for all people convicted of offences committed before 4 April 2005. The development of parole generally has also been largely guided by this scheme and so many of the principles relating to recall draw on the operation of DCR parole.[45]

## The DCR scheme in practice

11.40    The basic elements of this scheme are:

- Eligibility to be considered for parole at the halfway point of the sentence (the PED ).
- A parole dossier is compiled by the prison and this must include the prisoner's offence and sentence details, record of previous convictions, reports from the offender supervisor and offender manager, a prison medical assessment, the security manager's report and the prison parole assessment.
- The dossier is sent to the Parole Board at least 12 weeks before PED and it is then considered by a panel of the Parole Board on the papers. Even though article 5(4) is not re-engaged by the Parole Board consideration (see above) fairness may require an oral hearing (for example where a hearing is needed to resolve disputed facts – see further below).
- The outcome of the parole review will normally be notified to the prisoner two weeks before PED.
- If not released early on parole, DCR prisoners are released automatically at the two-thirds point of sentence (the Non-Parole Release Date or NPRD).
- The normal review timetable is provides for the review to commence 26 weeks before the PED or anniversary.
- If the prisoner does not wish to be considered for parole, or refuses

45   These amendments have also had an impact on the recall regime that applies to all CJA 1991 prisoners and these are explained in the section addressing recall below.

to sign the application form which is treated as opting out, the governor should also sign the application form.

11.41 The final decision as to release depends upon the length of the sentence being served. For prisoner serving over four years but less than 15 years, the Parole Board's recommendation is binding upon the Secretary of State.[46] However, for DCR prisoners serving 15 years or more, the board only has the power to make recommendations to the Secretary of State who retains the final discretion as to whether release should be authorised.[47]

11.42 There have been two attempts to challenge the lawfulness of this power. In *R (Clift) v Secretary of State for the Home Department*[48] it was argued that as parole falls within the ambit of article 5, the difference in treatment between prisoners serving under and over 15 years was discriminatory under article 14. Although the Lords were sympathetic to the argument and accepted that parole does fall within the ambit of article 5, they did not accept that the sentence length could be considered a personal characteristic capable of being subject to discriminatory treatment.[49]

11.43 In a subsequent case a prisoner in the same position unsuccessfully argued that the retention of the power by the executive was a direct breach of article 5(4), the Lords holding that release on licence for a prisoner serving a determinate sentence does not engage a convention right.[50] However, the Coroners and Justice Bill 2009 proposes an amendment to CJA 1991 s35 giving the board directive power even for this group of prisoner.[51]

## Disclosure

11.44 The presumption is that all the reports in parole dossiers will be disclosed[52] and the prisoner must be given access to one of the copies of the dossier so that there is an opportunity to make written representations to the Parole Board. Access to the dossier must be allowed in

---

46 Parole Board (Transfer of Functions) Order 1998 SI No 3218.
47 CJA 1991 s35.
48 [2007] 1 AC 484.
49 Although the Lords were extremely critical of the decision made by the Secretary of State to retain the power, Lord Bingham describing it as an 'indefensible anomaly' as '[t]he decision in question is not a political decision, appropriate to be made by a minister'. Para 38.
50 *R (Black) v Secretary of State for Justice* [2009] UKHL 1.
51 Clause 126 of the draft Bill published in March 2009.
52 PSO 6000 para 5.15.1.

secure and confidential conditions whenever the prisoner reasonably asks to see it. The prisoner or the prisoner's representative should also be provided with a copy to keep, although a fee to cover administrative and photocopying expenses can be charged. The dossier will contain a disclosure and representations form (appendix E) and this must be handed to the prisoner at the time the dossier is disclosed and before the dossier is sent to the Parole Board.

11.45    At this stage, the prisoner has the opportunity to submit written comments on the dossier and any other relevant information. Where a prisoner intends to instruct a solicitor to draft the representations, it is advisable to note this on the disclosure form so the Parole Board are aware of the situation. Any documents, which arrive after the main dossier has been disclosed to the prisoner should also be subject to the same procedure.

11.46    If the prisoner is unhappy with any document in the dossier a complaint may be made through the request/complaint procedure to the governor, in addition to making representations on the disclosure form. If the dossier has been sent to the Parole Board, the board must be advised that a complaint has been made and kept informed of the progress in resolving it, which must normally be within six weeks. Consideration of the case by the board will not normally be deferred while the complaint is being investigated, although if new information which might have affected the decision comes to light after it has been made the board may need to review the case again.

11.47    Whilst the presumption must be that all reports are disclosed, the governor retains a power to withhold information from disclosure in exceptional cases. The five grounds for withholding information are:[53]

1   in the interests of national security in which case the documents must be sent to PPU;
2   for the prevention of disorder or crime including prison security;
3   for the protection of information which may put a third party at risk;
4   on medical and/or psychiatric grounds to protect the mental and/ or physical health of the prisoner; and
5   where the source of the information is a victim, and disclosure without their consent would breach any duty of confidence owed to that victim.

---

53   PSO 6000 para 5.16.2.

11.48   In cases where consideration is being given to withholding the information, the governor needs to decide whether the material truly is material to the decision in question, whether it is possible to re-write it in a manner that will allow for disclosure or whether it can be reduced to a gist without lessening its impact.[54] If the decision reached is that the material does not qualify for non-disclosure but is relevant to the decision the board must reach, the governor can reach a decision about material generated within the prison but for material supplied by the police or probation, the source of the information must be consulted to obtain permission. Generally, information about the victim can only be disclosed with their consent.

11.49   In cases where a no-disclosure decision has been reached, the normal practice is to disclose it to the prisoner's legal representative, providing an undertaking has been given by the representative not to disclose it to the prisoner. In such cases disclosure will normally be limited to a qualified legal representative such as a solicitor or barrister and not to a lay adviser or McKenzie friend. Where it is not considered possible to disclose it to a solicitor for because of national security or witness protection issues, following the case of *R (Roberts) v Parole Board*[55] it is arguable that consideration should be given to the appointment of a Special Advocate.

11.50   Although the review in *Roberts* was for a life sentenced prisoner and so engaged article 5(4), common law standards of fairness would require the board to take reasonable steps to ensure a fair consideration of the case and this may extend to the appointment of a Special Advocate.

11.51   Once disclosed, the dossier must contain the following information:[56]

Front cover sheet and index
(A) Summary of offence from one of the following sources:
   • police report
   • pre-sentence report (probation)
   • pre-sentence psychiatric report
   • Court transcript of sentencing remarks
(B) Court papers (if applicable, Court of Appeal must be included)
(C) Court Transcript of Sentencing Remarks
(D) Previous Convictions
(F) Pre-sentence medical, or psychiatric reports (if applicable)

54  PSO para 5.16.3.
55  [2005] UKHL 45.
56  PSO 6000, chapter 5, appendix C.

(G) Copy of previous parole dossiers (if applicable)
(H) Copy of previous parole decisions (if applicable)
(J) Sentence Planning and OASys reports
(M) Adjudications and ADAs
(N) Prison parole assessment
(P) Offender supervisor's report
(Q) Report(s) on offence related work
(R) Prison medical and psychiatric reports (if applicable)
(K) Post sentence psychology report
(L) Category A review report (If applicable)
(Y) Security report
(Z) Victim personal statement
(T) Offender manager's report (PAROM 1)
(V) Prisoner's representations disclosure form

11.52    It is not unusual for parole dossiers to contain information that the prisoner feels is inaccurate. If the concern is a question of emphasis or comment, then this is a matter for representations. If the concern is more fundamental that the information is simply inaccurate an application has to be made to the prison parole clerk or PPU for this to be removed. The application has to be made to the Prison Service/NOMS and not the Parole Board as the board has a statutory duty to consider all material referred to it by the Secretary of State.[57] If the board rejects an application for release on licence having considered information that is inaccurate, particularly with reference to the description of the offence, this can provide grounds for the decision to be challenged.[58]

## Oral hearings

11.53    The Parole Board has a discretion under its statutory framework to hold an oral hearing to determine the issue before it whether or not article 5(4) of the Convention applies. In some circumstances the requirements of fairness will only be met by providing an oral hearing. Domestic courts have in fact held that the question as to when an oral hearing is required is the same under the common law as under article 5(4).[59] In the context of the release of an extended sentence

---

57    *R v Parole Board ex p Harris* [1998] COD 223 and CJA 1991 s32(3), now CJA 2003 s239(3).
58    *R v Parole Board ex p Higgins* [1999] PLR 45.
59    *R (O'Connell) v Parole Board and another* [2008] 1 WLR 979 para 21 – although the Court of Appeal in this case held that article 5(4) was not re-engaged it did not overrule the Divisional Court's findings as to the test for an oral hearing under common law.

applying for parole at the halfway point of the custodial term the Latham LJ stated:

> It seems to me that the Parole Board should be predisposed to holding an oral hearing in such cases. That would certainly be the case where there is any dispute of fact, or any need to examine the applicant's motives or state of mind.[60]

11.54 This test was subsequently applied when the Administrative Court considered that fairness required a prisoner serving a six-year determinate sentence for attempted murder[61] to an oral hearing when the Parole Board considered his case at the halfway point. The judge noted that although there were a number of factors pointing against parole (and it is worth quoting at length to demonstrate the factors that may weigh in favour of an oral hearing):

> ... [B]oth probation officers, while conscious of all of the above factors, recommended parole and considered that the risk could be managed satisfactorily in the community. It is apparent that the Parole Board reached a different conclusion from those reached by the probation officers, as they were perfectly entitled to do. However I am not satisfied that it was fair to deprive [the Claimant] of the opportunity of persuading the panel at an oral hearing that the views of the probation officers were correct. [The Claimant] had on the papers and in the reports a very good record on the whole in custody. He appeared highly motivated to reform himself and make a positive start on release. He had the active support of his father and step-mother. He was very young when the offence was committed and appeared to have matured significantly in the 4 years that had elapsed since then. Critically there was no up-to-date formal risk assessment. In my judgment this is one of those cases where it cannot be said that it is fanciful to suppose that the panel might have reached a different conclusion if they had been exposed to [the Claimant] and/or the authors of the various reports. It may be that there were particular concerns which might have been capable of being allayed at such a hearing. I should add that there were also on the evidence facts which were in dispute and which it appears either did or may have influenced the panel in its conclusion.[62]

11.55 Both these cases were decided at a time when it was thought that article 5(4) was re-engaged in the consideration by the Parole Board of

---

60  *R (O'Connell) v Parole Board and another* [2008] 1 WLR 979 at para 24 – applying the principles set out in *R (Smith and West) v Parole Board* – the case which established the basis upon which recalled determinate sentenced prisoners may be entitled to an oral hearing – see further below).

61  Administered under CJA 1991.

62  *R (Hopkins) v Parole Board* [2008] EWHC 2312 (Admin).

the initial release of determinate sentenced prisoners.[63] However, as the courts do not consider that the test as to when such a hearing is required under domestic law is different, the principles they establish remain valid. Accordingly prisoners and their advisers must consider whether there are issues that can only be fairly dealt with by the board by way of direct evidence, whilst appreciating that asserting the right to a hearing may result in delay before the board convenes one.

11.56    The board must be especially careful as to the fairness of the procedures it adopts when dealing with under-18-year-old prisoners. In a case involving a 15-year old serving an extended sentence with a two-year custodial term the court decided that the board had acted unlawfully in failing to consider whether an oral hearing was necessary to fairly consider whether release was granted, and also in failing to ensure that he had appropriate adult assistance in making written representations.[64] Children in the dedicated units in YOIs should have access to the advocacy services located within them for help in making representations and for referrals to solicitors where necessary.

## Amendments made by the Crime and Disorder Act 1998

11.57    CDA 1998 introduced two important changes to the CJA 1991 parole regime.

(i) short-term prisoners released on licence became subject to the recall regime (rather than the criminal penalty for breach of licence);

(ii) a recalled prisoner had to be released on licence at the three-quarter period of the sentence, and so was subject to recall during the remainder of the licence and not merely 'at risk' if he committed a further offence.

The extension of the licence period was not made retrospective.[65]

---

63  That is, before the House of Lords decision in *Black*, see above.

64  *R (K) v Parole Board* [2006] EWHC 2413 (Admin) – and see the Howard League (who brought the case) publication *Parole 4 Kids* (Howard League, 2007) reviewing parole processes for children.

65  The relevant commencement order (Crime and Disorder Act 1998 (Commencement No 2) SI No 237) indicated that the changes came into effect on 30 September 1998: however, the statute indicated (in Schedule 9) that various amendments being made to licence provisions were not retrospective.

## Reasons for parole decisions

11.58  Following on from the standards of procedural fairness that have
been applied to prisoners serving life sentences, it is now accepted
that the board has a duty to give adequate reasons for all its decisions, including for those serving determinate sentences and this
is reflected in PSO 6000, para 5.18.3 which makes this a mandatory requirement. Thus duty has often been explored in the cases of
prisoners who maintain their innocence for the offence. It is well
established that maintaining innocence cannot be the sole basis for
refusing parole. In *R v Secretary of State for the Home Department ex p
Zulfikar*[66] a decision refusing parole on this ground was quashed although a subsequent negative decision in the same case was upheld
for being better reasoned.[67] This duty was explored in *R v Secretary of
State for the Home Department ex p Hepworth and others*[68] where Laws
J put forward the following principles:

- The Parole Board must assume the prisoner's guilt of the offence
  or offences of which he has been convicted.
- The Board's first duty is to assess the risk to the public that the
  prisoner might commit further offences if he is paroled.
- It is therefore unlawful for the board to deny a recommendation
  for parole *on the ground only* that the prisoner continues to deny
  his guilt.
- But in some cases, particularly cases of serious persistent violent
  of sexual crime, a continued denial of guilt will almost inevitably
  mean that the risk posed by the prisoner to the public or a section of the public if he is paroled either remains high or, at least,
  cannot be objectively assessed. In such cases the board is entitled
  (perhaps obliged) to deny a recommendation.

11.59  In the case of *R v Parole Board ex p Oyston*,[69] the Court of Appeal
quashed a decision to refuse parole for a prisoner convicted of sexual
offences. The court considered that the board appeared to find that
an admission of guilt was determinative of the reduction and management of risk and commented that the decision had not been adequately reasoned:

---

66  [1996] COD 256.
67  *R v Secretary of State for the Home Department ex p Zulfikar (No 2)* unreported,
    May 1996.
68  [2007] EWHC 324 (Admin).
69  (2000) *Independent* 17 April, CA.

There is upon the board a duty to give reasons and it is submitted that, even if the substance of the matter was considered, the reasoning was inadequate.[70]

# Recall

## Recall on or after 14 July 2008

11.60    CJA 2003 has a unified recall regime for all prisoners whenever sentenced. The regime it sets out applies to anyone recalled on or after 14 July 2008[71] and provides that:

1. Section 254 provides that the Secretary of State may recall a prisoner released on licence and that the Parole Board must consider representations against recall and to direct the release of a recalled prisoner.
2. Section 256 provides that the board may, if it does not release the recalled prisoner immediately, fix a date for future release. If it does not section 256A provides that the Secretary of State must set a date for a further review no more than 12 months later.
3. Sections 255A–D introduced a scheme for fixed term recall for a period of 28 days.[72]

11.61    After CJA 2003 was initially enacted on 4 April 2005, the Secretary of State decided that to implement the recall scheme retrospectively to provide one single set of arrangements for all prisoners, whenever sentenced. *Stellato* (see above) established that such changes could only be made retrospective through primary legislation and so CIJA 2008 made provision for the recall scheme to have retrospective effect from 14 July 2008.

11.62    The original recall scheme allowed for the initial recall decision to be made either at the instigation of the Parole Board itself or, in emergencies, the Secretary of State. Now, the Secretary of State has sole responsibility for all initial recall decisions.

---

70  Para 28: see also *R (Tinney) v Parole Board* [2005] EWHC 863 (Admin) where a parole refusal was quashed for failing 'to identify in broad terms the matters judged by the board as pointing towards and against a continuing risk of reoffending ...'.

71  CJA 1991 s50A(2) is applicable to any person who has been released on licence under the provisions of the 1991 Act and recalled to prison under section 254 of the 2003 Act and dis-applies CJA 1991 s33. See also PSI 29/2008.

72  Introduced on 14 June 2008 by CJIA 2008 s30.

## Automatic re-release

11.63 Prisoners who are not serving a specified offence and whom the Secretary of State does not consider poses a risk of serious harm will have their re-release on licence authorised automatically by the Secretary of State after 28 days back in custody.[73] This power is only exercised in cases where the Secretary of State is satisfied that the prisoner does not pose a continuing risk of harm to the public.[74] It is interesting to note that the power to recall is based on any risk of reoffending but the decision to authorise automatic release is only restricted in cases where the risk of harm test is met. The prisoner must be notified of this decision on return to custody.[75] The prisoner retains the right to make representations against the decision to recall and if these are made within the 28-day period, the Secretary of State is under a duty to refer the case to the Parole Board. Any recommendation made by the board for release is binding.[76]

11.64 The purpose of this power appears to be to limit the number of cases that need to be referred to the Parole Board and to provide a mechanism for giving prisoners on licence a forceful reminder of the need to abide by their licence conditions and the requirements of supervision. It is difficult to anticipate how widely used this power will be and how the system can operate efficiently enough to allow those who feel they have been wrongly recalled under this power to 'appeal' the decision to the Parole Board within the 28-day period. It is also unclear what impact a short recall might have on resettlement issues, such as the availability of accommodation and how this in turn might make re-release after 28 days problematic.

## Recalls with no automatic re-release

11.65 If the prisoner is serving a specified offence or if the Secretary of State considers that release at the end of the 28-day period would pose a threat to public safety, the prisoner will be notified of this decision when returned to custody. The prisoner then has 28 days in which to make representations and on receipt of the recommendations, the case will be referred to the board by the Secretary of State. If the board recommend release, this is binding (CJA 2003 s255C).

11.66 The number of prisoners recalled has been steadily rising over the

73  CJA 2003 s255A.
74  CJA 2003 s255A(3).
75  CJA 2003 s255A(3).
76  CJA 2003 s255B(4)–(5).

past decade. In a thematic review of the recall system, Her Majesty's Chief Inspector of Prisons noted that in the five years to December 2005 there had been a 350 per cent increase in the number of prisoners recalled.[77] The report was also highly critical of the system for dealing with recalled prisoners noting that they posed an increased suicide risk and that they very often did not receive information about the reasons for the decision or the official paperwork informing them of how to make representations against the decision. Although steps have since been taken to try and provide a clearer framework for providing information to recalled prisoners, there is a continuing concern about the rise in recall rates. The Public Accounts Committee noted in 2009 that recall rates for the commission of further criminal offences had remained constant at around seven per cent for the five-year period from 2003 to 2008.[78] Given that overall recall rates had increased dramatically during this period it demonstrates that 'preventative' recalls in cases where there had been no further criminal behaviour had been responsible for this rise.

11.67    In practice, the Probation Service is usually the instigator of the recall with the Offender Manager making a request for recall to the PPU. The PPU will consider all requests for recall within 24 hours of receipt although in very urgent cases PPU will consider the case within two hours.[79] The Probation Service National Standards 2005[80] stated that 'breach action' may be initiated where there has been 'one unacceptable failure' to comply with licence conditions where appropriate, and if such action is not initiated a formal written warning should be given. This approach clearly drove the increase in recalls. The most recent available guidance to the Probation Service is now contained in the Offender Management National Standards (OMNS) 2007 and makes it clear that recall action in urgent cases must be based on a greater risk to the public.[81]

11.68    In non-urgent cases a failure to comply with licence supervision should only precipitate recall action where the failure is indicative of:[82]

• a serious, gross, wilful or fundamental refusal to comply or breakdown of the licence; or

77  http://inspectorates.homeoffice.gov.uk/hmiprisons/thematicreports1/recalledprisoners.pdf?view=Binary p 5
78  Para 8. See www.publications.parliament.uk/pa/cm200809/cmselect/cmpubacc/251/25105.htm
79  PSO 6000 para 7.6.2.
80  See PC 15/2005.
81  OMNS 2007 2f.3.
82  OMNS 2007 2f.4.

- a significant rise in the risk of serious harm or likelihood of re-offending presented by the offender; or
- in relation to a post-release licence there have already been two written warnings issued in the preceding 12 months.

11.69 The current guidance on recall requires that once the recalled prisoner has been informed of the reasons for the revocation of licence, if they exercise the right to make representations to the Parole Board a formalised timetable should be followed. PSO 6000 contains the model timetable for the initial consideration of recall cases:[83]

- Day 1 – return to custody of recalled prisoner. Notification to PPU by establishment of receipt of recalled prisoner. PPU issues recall dossier to establishment. The PPU notifies supervising probation officer of retrun to custody ofprisoner, and gives provisional panel date for review by the Parole Board. *The parole clerk must ensure the dossier is served on the prisoner immediately and that they understand that they have the right to make representations to the Parole Board.* The establishment has five working days in which to confirm to PPU whether the prisoner intends to make representations, and to advise of legal representative details.
- Day 5 – Annex A [prisoner's intent to make representations] to be returned to PPU.
- Day 14 – prisoner's representations submitted to PPU. Report for review submitted to PPU by the Probation Service, and simultaneously to the establishment, for disclosure to the prisoner. Report for Review and representations to be added to the recall dossier by the PPU and the complete dossier is sent to the Parole Board.
- Day 19 – any additional/late representations to be made by the prisoner in response to the Report for Review must be submitted to PPU by no later than 10.00 am on day 19.
- Day 20 – Parole Board panel sits. PPU notified of the outcome and result notified to Establishment and Probation Service. Establishment notifies the prisoner; where the board recommends release, the establishment must put arrangements in place to give effect to the recommendation.

11.70 Where on a referral the board recommends immediate release on licence, the Secretary of State must give effect to the recommendation.[84] If the Parole Board does not direct immediate release on consideration of written representations, then the effect of the Lords'

---

83   Para 7.14.3 as amended by PSI 29/2008.
84   CJA 2003 s254(4).

decision in *Smith v Parole Board*[85] is that the board must give very careful consideration to the need for an oral hearing to determine the issues that lead to the recall decision.

11.71　　Where an oral hearing is held the Parole Board Rules (PBR) 2004 as amended do not apply – but the board has indicated that the procedure adopted will mirror that utilised for lifer recalls under the Rules save for the fact that the hearing will be before a single member of the board. When considering the recall of normal determinate sentence prisoners the board considers whether to release the offender in light of directions issued under CJA 2003 s239(6). If the board does not direct release, the Secretary of State is under a duty to refer the case back for further consideration within the next 12 months.[86] No date needs to be set if the prisoner is to be released unconditionally (ie at the expiry of the whole sentence) within that year. At subsequent reviews the board retains power to either recommend release or fix future dates for release.[87]

11.72　　Not all licence breaches will justify a recall to custody, even for those serving determinate sentences. However there is a distinction between indeterminate and extended sentences where the grounds for recall must have a 'causal link' with the purpose of the sentence to be lawful,[88] and the position with determinate sentence prisoners where the appropriate test for recall is the likelihood of the commission of *any* further offences, even where they do not necessarily pose a risk of harm to the public. It has been confirmed, however, that those on licence may be recalled if their behaviour suggests that supervision has fundamentally broken down thus making the risk unmanageable in the community.[89]

11.73　　Where the licensee has been charged with further offences, the Probation Service guidance suggests that supervising officers should:

> ... explain the behaviour surrounding the charge, and other behaviour/concerns which lead to your assessment and recommendation for recall. It is not enough to state that the good behaviour condition in the licence has been breached by the further charges, which may be dropped at a later stage. Arrest need not always lead to a request for

85　See above.
86　CJA 2003 s256A: this amended the previous version of the Act where the duty to fix further review dates fell to the board.
87　CJA 2003 s256A(4).
88　*Stafford v UK* (2002) 35 EHRR 32, *R (Sim) v Parole Board* [2003] EWCA Civ 1845.
89　*R (Sim) v Parole Board* [2003] EWHC 152 (Admin) para 44.

recall. An offender may be arrested, having been in a place at a time when an offence has been committed by others, and there may not be any evidence on which to charge the offender.[90]

11.74 Further alleged offences can create difficulties in advising prisoners as the Parole Board does assume that even if criminal proceedings in respect of fresh allegations have not concluded, it is nevertheless usually possible to consider whether recall is appropriate in light of evidence of the offender's behaviour, short of that relating to the new charges themselves. It has been held that the mere fact of a further charge and pending prosecution cannot on its own justify recall on the basis of a risk of re-offending[91] but it is likely to be the case that the board will need to consider the evidence upon which the new charges are based in order to properly come to an assessment of risk.[92] Where the new charge does have a bearing on the risk assessment it is difficult to see how the board can fairly deal with it in advance of the criminal trial without prejudicing the prosecution. Although agreeing to a deferral of the Parole Board hearing pending the outcome of the prosecution will inevitably lead to delay, this course may be advisable where a decision of the board upholding the recall will potentially result in long periods of further detention.

11.75 If the board does uphold recall in advance of the hearing of any further charges by the criminal courts, and the prisoner is subsequently found not guilty, then the Secretary of State retains the discretion to re-refer the original recall decision back to the board where he considers that there is a realistic prospect that a different view may be taken by the board.[93]

11.76 The Prison and Probation Services, the Police and the Home Office have agreed a joint protocol relating to the supervision and recall of offenders[94] which states that prosecutions should not be discontinued purely because an offender has been recalled to custody and in fact the commission of an offence whilst on licence 'is a significant public interest factor in support of a charge'.[95]

11.77 Once the revocation has been issued, if the licensee is not already in custody (for example having been recalled following arrest for a

---

90  Annex F to PC 14/2008.

91  *R (Broadbent) v Parole Board* [2005] EWHC 1207 (Admin) at para 26.

92  *R (Broadbent) v Parole Board* [2005] EWHC 1207 (Admin) at para 29, *R (Brooks) v Parole Board* [2004] EWCA Civ 80.

93  *R (Francis and Clarke) v Secretary of State for the Home Department* [2004] EWHC 2143 (Admin) at para 49.

94  PC 3/2005 and PC 5/2007.

95  Paragraph 8.7 of the National Protocol.

new offence) he or she is deemed to be 'unlawfully at large' until returned to custody.[96] The licensee can then be arrested without warrant.[97] The National Protocol (see above) states that the police shall 'take steps to ensure the speedy arrest of the individual'.[98] Time spent unlawfully at large is not then taken into account when calculating release dates and the eventual sentence expiry date.[99] The offender does not need to be aware of the revocation of licence to be unlawfully at large.[100] However, it has been established that if a mistake is made about the length of the licence and the prisoner is told that the licence has ended when as a matter of law it has not, the Secretary of State cannot recall the prisoner for breaching the licence, although recall can still take place if the prisoner poses an unacceptable risk to the public. In *R (Rodgers) v Governor of HMP Brixton and Secretary of State for the Home Department*[101] the Court of Appeal noted that once the mistake had been made, the Secretary of State should have notified the prisoner of the mistake and required the licence to be re-imposed.[102]

11.78    Following arrest, recalled offenders will be taken to the nearest remand prison.[103] Although the licensee will be unlawfully at large from the time the revocation decision is taken, in cases where there may be evidence to suggest that the decision was unlawful, the Secretary of State remains under a duty to reconsider the decision even if the licensee remains at large.[104] These cases will be relatively rare and confined to serious mistakes of fact given that the normal procedure is for the decision to be subject to the scrutiny of the Parole Board.[105]

---

96  CJA 2003 s254(6).
97  Prison Act (PA) 1952 s49(1).
98  Para 9.3.
99  PA 1952 s49(2) – see guidance in PSO 6650 chapter 7.
100  *R (S) v Secretary of State for the Home Department* [2003] EWCA Civ 426.
101  [2003] EWHC 1923 (Admin).
102  But contrast with the decision of the High Court in *R (Jackson) v Parole Board & Secretary of State for the Home Department* [2003] EWHC 1923 (Admin) where a recall was upheld on the basis of reasons given the home probation officer to the Secretary of State even though the reasons given to the prisoner were different and referred to a condition that was not in his licence. No reference was made in that judgment to the *Rodgers* decision.
103  PSO 6000 para 7.8.1.
104  *R (Brett Roberts) v Secretary of State for the Home Department* [2005] EWCA Civ 1663.
105  *R (Biggs) v Secretary of State for the Home Department* [2002] EWHC 1012 (Admin); *R (Hare) v Parole Board & Secretary of State for the Home Department* [2003] EWHC 3336 (Admin).

11.79 The directions issued to the Parole Board for recalls on or after July 2008 by the Secretary of State pursuant to CJA 2003 s239(6)[106] require the board to determine in particular:

(a) Any current risk assessments prepared by prison and probation staff, including whether the offender is assessed as presenting a high or very risk of serious harm.

(b) Whether the risk management plan, prepared by the Probation Service is adequate to manage effectively any potential risk of serious harm or of imminent re-offending.

(c) Whether, in light of the offender's previous response to supervision, the offender is likely to comply in future with the requirements of probation supervision for the duration of the licence period.

(d) The availability of suitable accommodation, as well as the availability and timing of any offending behaviour work either in or outside of custody or the date on which the outcome of any pending prosecution will be known.

(e) Whether the interests of public protection and the prisoner's long term rehabilitation would be better served if the offender were re-released whilst subject to probation supervision.

(f) Any representations on behalf of the victim in respect of licence conditions.

11.80 These directions do have a slightly different emphasis to those in force previously which indicated that the type of re-offending that might justify recall did need to involve a risk to public safety, and which also suggested that any licence breaches could justify recall. This change of emphasis in the new directions arguably means that cases involving challenges to recalls under the old regime[107] should be treated with caution. In *R (Morecock) v Parole Board*[108] the court accepted that recall could be justified where there was no risk to public safety and in *R (Buxton) v Parole Board*[109] it was held that when deciding whether there is an 'unacceptable' risk the board was not required to balance compassionate factors in the prisoner's favour, if these were not relevant to the level of assessed risk. However, in *R (Gulliver) v Parole Board*[110] a recall decision was upheld in a case where the Parole Board found that the licence breaches alleged at the time of the recall had

106 See appendix K to chapter 7 of PSO 6000 as amended by PSI 29/2008.
107 Prior to the more recent directions coming into force in 2005.
108 [2004] EWHC 2521 (Admin).
109 [2004] EWHC 1930 (Admin).
110 [2007] EWCA Civ 1386.

not actually occurred but nevertheless decided that the prisoner had posed a risk to public safety whilst in the community. This decision does raise the possibility that a prisoner who is automatically released may be liable to a lawful recall even if the licence conditions have not been breached.

## Extended sentences

11.81   The power to impose an extended sentence (a sentence with a distinct custodial term, together with an extended licence period) was originally contained in the Crime and Disorder Act (CDA) 1998 for offences committed on or after 30 September 1998.[111]

11.82   For offences committed on or after 4 April 2005 extended sentences are imposed under CJA 2003 s 227 (s228 for under 18-year-olds).[112] The sentence was originally available to anyone convicted of a violent or sexual offence and permitted the sentencing court to impose an extended licence in addition to the normal licence period. The custodial term and the extension period cannot exceed the total length of the sentence available for the offence and the extension period must not exceed five years for a violent offence or ten years for a sexual offence in any event.

11.83   CJA 2003 s227 as originally enacted required the court to impose the sentence following a conviction for an offence specified in Schedule 15 to the Act where the court considered that the prisoner posed a significant risk of committing further offences that would cause serious harm to the public. This was amended by CJIA 2008 and as from 14 July 2008, the sentence is no longer mandatory and the court has discretion whether to impose it.[113] In addition, the extended sentence should only be imposed in cases where the custodial term would be four years or more.[114] Whatever version of the sentence has been imposed, it is important to note that the sentencing court is required to make some form of assessment of dangerousness.

---

111   Now in PCC(S)A 2000 s85 for offences committed up to 4 April 2005.
112   The other form of sentenced sentence where a longer than commensurate custodial term could be imposed pursuant to PCC(S)A 2000 s80(2)(b) did not survive CJA 2003 having been repealed by the Criminal Justice Act (Commencement No 8 and Transitional and Savings Provisions) Order 2005 SI No 905.
113   CJA 2003 s227(2).
114   CJA 2003 s227(2B).

## CJA 1991 extended sentences

11.84 Prisoners who receive(d) an extended sentence for offences committed before 4 April 2005 will almost inevitably be excluded from the retrospective automatic release provisions of the CJA 2003 as the sentences will have been imposed for violent or sexual offences that are specified by 2003 Act. Therefore, those sentenced to an extended sentence for an offence committed from 30 September 1998 to 3 April 2005, where the custodial term is four or more years, are eligible for discretionary release at the halfway point of the custodial term.[115] As the custodial term will be the same as the sentence commensurate with the seriousness of the offence, release at the halfway point follows the same procedure as for normal DCR cases. For those who received custodial terms of less than four years, release is automatic at the halfway point as for ACR cases.

## CJA 2003 extended sentences

11.85 This comprises two distinct groups, those sentenced prior to 14 July 2008 and those after that date when CJIA 2008 amended the sentence. For those sentenced under the original provisions, release during the custodial period could only take place at the direction of the Parole Board where it is satisfied that the prisoner no longer poses a risk to the public. The requirement for dangerousness to be assessed both at the time of sentence and on release resulted in the Administrative Court holding that article 5(4) was engaged for these prisoners, although this did not extend to a requirement for oral hearings to be convened.[116]

11.86 The correctness of this decision was called into question by the House of Lords in *R (Black) v Secretary of State for Justice*[117] and the Court of Appeal subsequently held that the release at the halfway point of the CJA 2003 extended sentence could not be distinguished from release during the currency of a normal determinate sentence and so article 5(4) is not re-engaged.[118] Once released from the sen-

---

115 CJA 1991 ss44(2) and 35(1).
116 *R (O'Connell) v Parole Board and Secretary of State for Justice* [2007] EWHC 2593 (Admin).
117 [2009] UKHL 1.
118 The Court of Appeal gave judgment on 23 April 2009, the transcript is not available at the time of writing. It is still arguable that the test for initial release of this class of prisoner is dangerousness, although as it arises during the custodial term this does not re-engage article 5(4) safeguards.

tence, either on parole or at the end of the custodial period, the prisoner remains on licence and liable to recall until the end of the extension period.

11.87   For those who receive the extended sentence on or after 14 July 2008, release at the halfway point of the custodial term is automatic and does not require the involvement of the Parole Board. Again the licence lasts until the end of the extension period.

## Recall of extended sentence prisoners

11.88   Since 4 April 2005, all extended sentence offenders (under both CJA 1991 and CJA 2003) are subject to the same statutory framework of recall as other determinate sentence prisoners.[119] However there are important differences in how the board has to approach these recalls. This is because the extended sentence is not like a normal determinate sentence, but is rather a hybrid between a determinate and indeterminate sentence.

11.89   The extension period that follows the custodial term is not imposed as punishment, and the statutory presumption is that it will be served in the community (as the extension period begins at what would otherwise be the LED for CJA 1991 cases, and at the end of the custodial period in CJA 2003 cases). As the extension period is purely preventative, the legality of detention during it requires the supervision of a court-like body under article 5(4) of the Convention, as the degree to which an offender poses a risk to the public is clearly susceptible to change. Without such supervision there is a risk of arbitrary detention, as whether custody is actually necessary to protect the public during the extension period cannot be anticipated by the sentencing court.[120] It does not appear that this position has been displaced by the *Black* decision given that the Lords' decision in *Smith* that article 5(4) does apply to the recall of determinate sentenced prisoner's remains undisturbed.

11.90   As article 5 appears to continue to apply to the recall of extended sentence prisoners during the extension period, there must be a causal link between the grounds for recall and the imposition of the sentence. This gives rise to differing tests the board must apply when considering CJA 1991 cases as against CJA 2003 cases. Extended sentences imposed for offences committed on or after 30 September 1998 but before 4 April 2005 can be imposed for sexual and violent

---

119  CJA 2003 s254.
120  *R (Sim) v Parole Board* [2004] 2 WLR 1170.

offences where the court is satisfied that the licence period applicable to what would be the commensurate sentence is inadequate to prevent the commission of further offences and to secure rehabilitation.[121] Accordingly, a CJA 1991 extended sentence prisoner's recall can only be in accordance with article 5 by reference to a risk that further sexual or violent offences may be committed.[122]

11.91    By contrast, the CJA 2003 extended sentence is only imposed where the sentencing court makes a finding that the offender poses a risk of 'serious harm' and so in these cases the test on recall is therefore a 'serious harm' one as with the indeterminate sentences. Further, recall may be justified where the risk has become unmanageable in the community. Despite this apparent mirroring of the extended and indeterminate sentences, the former are released automatically at the end of the custodial period. This means that the board must also approach these recalls on the basis that the 'default position' is the offender's liberty, and so must be positively satisfied that detention is necessary to protect the public.[123]

11.92    The procedure for instigating recalls will be the same as for normal determinate sentence recalls although the Parole Board have generally adopted a policy of granting oral hearings to all extended sentence recalls. The Parole Board Rules 2004 do not formally apply to extended sentences and since the Rules were amended in April 2009 to do away with the requirement for oral hearings as a matter of right, it is likely that the decision as to whether an oral hearing will be convened will come to be determined on a case by case basis. If the Parole Board do not direct release there is an entitlement to further annual reviews if there is sufficient time before the automatic release date (at the end of the extension period for CJA 1991 cases, and at sentence expiry for CJA 2003 cases). The prisoner has been entitled to oral hearings at the annual reviews[124] although this is also likely to become a discretionary decision. The process begins 26 weeks after the board's confirmation of the recall[125] and the prisoner has been given a choice of paper review or oral hearing.[126]

---

121  PCC(S)A 2000 s85.
122  *R (Sim) v Parole Board* [2004] 2 WLR 1170 at para 44.
123  *R (Sim) v Parole Board* [2004] 2 WLR 1170 at para 51 where the Court of Appeal upheld a Human Rights Act 1998 s3 construction of the statutory test to give this effect.
124  For the applicable process see PSO 6000 part 8.12.
125  PSO 6000 para 8.9.1.
126  PSO 6000 para 8.11.

## 'Return to custody' orders

11.93    Those subject to the provisions of CJA 1991 (including those serving sentences of less than 12 months for offences committed on or after 4 April 2005)[127] remain 'at risk' of being ordered to return to prison on sentencing for a new offence committed before the sentence expiry date of the first sentence, to a maximum of the period between the commission of the new offence and the sentence expiry of the first.[128] This is a separate power from the recall provisions and the use of one does not preclude the other. However, because of the possible severity of the impact on the prisoner it has been held that where a prisoner has been recalled, the sentencing court should take this into account when deciding whether and for how long to order a return to prison, and similarly that any order to return should be a relevant factor in deciding whether to recall.[129] It is important to remember that the return to custody order is a fresh criminal sentence in its own right.[130]

## Home Detention Curfew

11.94    Home Detention Curfew (HDC) was first introduced in January 1999[131] and was extensively amended by CJA 2003. As with parole, this means that there are two schemes running in parallel for CJA 1991 and CJA 2003 prisoners respectively, although the two schemes are very similar in practice.

### HDC and the CJA 1991

11.95    CJA 1991 s34A permits prisoners serving sentences of more than three months but less than four years to be released on HDC (or 'electronic tagging') prior to the halfway point of the sentence. There have been a number of alterations to the original or standard scheme, with a presumptive scheme being introduced in 2002[132] and a list of

---

127    Criminal Justice Act 2003 (Commencement No 8 and Transitional and Saving Provisions) Order 2005 para 29.
128    PCC(S)A 2000 s116.
129    *R (Akhtar) v Secretary of State for the Home Department* [2001] EWHC 38 (Admin).
130    *R (Gilbert) v Secretary of State for the Home Department* [2005] EWHC 1991 (Admin).
131    CDA 1998 ss99 and 100 which introduced section 34A of the CJA 1991.
132    PSI 19/2002.

offences excluded from HDC in July 2003.[133] At the same time that offences were excluded from eligibility, the length of time a prisoner could spend on HDC was increased from 60 to 135 days.[134] It should be noted that the prisoner can only be considered under the scheme in operation at the time of their eligibility, even if the original sentence was imposed before the changes were made.[135]

11.96     There are a number of statutory exclusions from HDC and these include the following prisoners:

(i)    prisoners subject to an extended sentence;

(ii)    prisoners serving a sentence for an offence under section 1 of the Prisoners (Return to Custody) Act 1995 for failing to return to custody following a period of temporary release;

(iii)    prisoners currently subject to a hospital order, hospital direction or transfer direction under sections 37, 45A or 47 of the Mental Health Act 1983;

(iv)    prisoners serving a sentence imposed under paragraph 3(1)(d) or 4(1)(d) of Schedule 2 to CJA 1991 for failing to comply with a requirement of a curfew order;

(v)    prisoners who have *at any time* been recalled to prison from HDC under section 38A(1)(a) of the 1991 Act for breaching the terms of their HDC licence, unless the prisoner successfully appealed against the recall;[136]

(vi)    prisoners liable to removal from the United Kingdom;

(vii)    prisoners who have, during the current sentence, been released on Home Detention Curfew or given early compassionate release under section 36 of CJA 1991 and have been recalled to prison under section 39(1) or (2) of the Act after the HDC period has expired;

(viii)    prisoners who have *at any time* received an order to return to prison for committing an offence before the at risk period of a sentence has expired);

133 PSI 31/2003.

134 The maximum period prisoners liable to removal can be released early under ERS (see below) is by contrast 270 days – however it has been held that this does not unlawfully discriminate against prisoners applying for HDC – see *R (Brooke) v Secretary of State for Justice* [2009] EWHC 1396 (Admin).

135 *R (O'Rourke) v Secretary of State for the Home Department* [2004] EWHC 157 (Admin) applying the principle that the only expectation a prisoner has in relation to executive policies is to be considered under the scheme in operation at the time eligibility arises: see *Re Findlay* [1985] AC 318.

136 Recalls under section 38A(1) subsections (b) or (c) do not exclude the prisoner.

(ix)  prisoners who become eligible for HDC less than 14 days before the halfway point of their sentence;[137]

(x)  prisoners convicted of a sexual offence who are subject to notification requirements (Part II of the Sexual Offences Act 2003).[138]

11.97  As the statutory provisions only apply to those serving sentences of imprisonment, those in custody for contempt of court or defaulting on fines cannot apply.[139]

11.98  The original exclusions also included those under 18 but this age restriction was removed in July 2003.[140] As a matter of policy, prisoners who have outstanding confiscation orders with default terms are not eligible.[141]

## Presumed unsuitable offences

11.99  In addition to the statutory exclusions, there are a range of offences for which prisoners will be presumed unsuitable.[142] The presumed unsuitable offences are:[143]

- Homicide including attempted murder, threats to kill, conspiring, aiding or inciting murder and death by reckless driving
- Causing explosions, placing explosives, possessing explosives
- Possession of offensive weapons
- Possession of firearms with intent
- Cruelty to children
- Racially aggravated offences
- Any sexual offence save for prostitution, soliciting and consensual adult homosexual behaviour not in a public place[144]
- Terrorism related offences were added to the list of presumed unsuitable offences from 25 February 2008[145]

137 Prisoners on remand or in police custody are not considered to have served the requisite period until the day on which they are sentenced – if the halfway point of sentence is then less than 14 days away, they are therefore ineligible.

138 Originally these prisoners were eligible in exceptional circumstances but were removed from eligibility altogether in March 2001: Criminal Justice and Court Services Act 2000 s65.

139 PSO 6700 para 2.3.1.

140 Release of Short term Prisoners on Licence (Repeal of Age Restriction) Order 2003 SI No 1691.

141 PSO 6700 para 2.6.1.

142 PSI 31/2003.

143 PSI 31/2003 para 23.

144 PSI 31/2003 para 25.

145 See PSI 8/2008.

11.100 Prisoners serving a combination of offences including those that are presumed unsuitable will still be considered to be presumed unsuitable for the entire sentence, even if the offence that excludes them has already been served by the time they become eligible.[146] There must be exceptional circumstances to displace the presumption of unsuitability and these exceptional circumstances should not relate to risk but to other factors.

11.101 Where a prisoner is presumed unsuitable, notification should be given at the start of the sentence so that representations can be made to the governor and any decision is subject to the normal appeal routes.[147] If the governor decides to make an exception and grant HDC, where the prisoner has a history of sexual offending the HDC policy team at PPU must be notified.[148]

11.102 There will be a small number of category A prisoners serving sentences of under four years, in which case the prisoner is not automatically excluded from HDC either by statute or policy. However as these prisoners have already been assessed as presenting a serious risk to the public prisons will not normally automatically embark upon an HDC risk assessment and instead, preparations will be made for release at the conditional or automatic release date. The prisoner can appeal and request consideration for HDC and the governor will then consider whether there are exceptional circumstances to justify commencing a risk assessment.[149]

## The presumptive HDC scheme

11.103 Presumptive HDC applies to prisoners serving less than 12 months (and more than three months) providing they have not been convicted of an excluded offence within three years of the date of the sentence for the current offence. The list of excluded offences is set out at Annex A of PSO 6700 and these include almost all violent offences from assault or possession of an offensive weapon through to infanticide, manslaughter and murder. Any prisoner who does not meet the criteria for the presumptive scheme must still be considered for the normal HDC and should not be prejudiced by exclusion from this category. For prisoners who are within the scheme, on receipt of a satisfactory home circumstances assessment, governors

---

146  *R (Cross) v Governor of HMYOI Thorn Cross* [2004] EWHC 149 (Admin).
147  PSI 31/2003 para 34.
148  PSI 31/2003 para 31.
149  PSO 6700 para 2.5.1.

must release an eligible prisoner on HDC unless they are aware of exceptional and compelling reasons to refuse release. Examples of the kinds of issues which might provide exceptional and compelling reasons for refusal are:

• clear evidence that the prisoner is planning further crime whilst in custody
• evidence of violence or threats of violence, in prison, on a number of occasions
• dealing in class A drugs in custody
• other matters of similar gravity relating to public safety.[150]

## Standard HDC

11.104   In all cases where the prisoner is not in an excluded category or has not been granted presumptive HDC, eligibility dates to apply for release must be notified to them. PSI 31/2003 contains the following table to assist in the calculation of eligibility:[151]

| Sentence length | Requisite period to be served before the HDC eligibility date | Approximate range of minimum and maximum curfew periods |
| --- | --- | --- |
| 3 months or more but less than 4 months | 30 days | Between two weeks and one month depending on length of sentence |
| 4 months or more but less than 12 months | One quarter of the sentence | Between one month and 3 months depending on length of sentence |
| Between 12 months and under 18 months | One quarter of the sentence | Between 3 months and 4½ months depending on length of sentence |
| Between 18 months and under 4 years | 135 days less than half the sentence | 135 days |

As with all other forms of early release, any award of additional days defers eligibility.

150  PSI 19/2002 para 4.8.
151  PSI 31/2003 para 6.

# HDC and the CJA 2003

11.105 The HDC scheme for prisoners convicted of offences committed on or after 4 April 2005 is identical in terms of procedure but has some differences in respect of eligibility and licence conditions. Section 246 allows for any prisoner serving a standard determinate sentence, even if longer than four years, to apply for HDC. However, prisoners serving four years or more fall into the presumed unsuitable category and will therefore have to be notified of their position at the outset of their sentence. The formal statutory exclusions are contained at section 246(4):

(i) violent and sexual offenders currently serving an extended sentence imposed under section 227 or 228 of the Criminal Justice Act 2003.

(ii) prisoners currently serving a sentence for an offence under section 1 of the Prisoners (Return to Custody) Act 1995 (for failure to return to custody following a period of temporary release).

(iii) prisoners currently subject to a hospital order, hospital direction or transfer direction under section 37, 45A or 47 of the Mental Health Act 1983.

(iv) prisoners currently serving a sentence imposed under paragraph 9(1)(b) or (c) or 10(1)(b) or (c) of Schedule 8 of the Criminal Justice Act 2003 in a case where the prisoner has failed to comply with a curfew requirement of a community order.

(v) prisoners subject to the notification requirements of Part 2 of the Sexual Offences Act 2003.

(vi) prisoners currently liable to removal from the United Kingdom.

(vii) prisoners who have been released on licence under this section during the currency of the sentence, and have been recalled to prison under section 255(1)(a) (breach of the HDC curfew condition).

(viii) prisoners who have been released on licence under section 248 (compassionate early release from custody) during the currency of the sentence, and have been recalled to prison under section 254 (equivalent to a section 39 recall).

(ix) prisoners who have less than 14 days remaining between the date of sentence and the date on which the prisoner will have served the requisite period.

11.106 The prisoners who are eligible under CJA 2003 who were not eligible under the CJA 1991 are those serving an order for return to custody[152] and prisoners who have breached the HDC curfew condition on a

---

152 Powers of Criminal Courts (Sentencing) Act 2000 s116.

previous sentence.[153] These two groups do, however, join the list of those presumed unsuitable for HDC.

## Transitional provisions

11.107   Eligibility for HDC can be further confused by the interrelationship between sentences imposed under CJA 1991 and CJA 2003, a position that has not been uncommon as the earlier Act still applies to all offences committed before 4 April 2005 but critically, also to offences committed after that date where the sentence is less than 12 months. In *R (Noone) v Governor of HMP Drake Hall*,[154] a prisoner had received a number of consecutive sentences including terms of less than 12 months. The prisoner's eligibility for HDC depended upon which sentence was calculated to run first and after having initially been given one HDC release date, this was subsequently changed after the Secretary of State applied a policy whereby the sentences would be calculated in the order in which they had been imposed by the sentencing court. The prisoner argued that the sentences should be calculated with the shortest to be served first, this calculation giving her a longer period of eligibility for HDC as it would mean that eligibility would be calculated with reference to a far longer sentence. Although this argument succeeded at first instance, the Court of Appeal held that the transitional arrangements[155] meant that the correct calculation did require the sentence calculation to proceed on the basis of the order in which the court had actually imposed the sentences, even if this meant that the first sentence was longer and therefore governed by CJA 2003 and the final sentence was under 12 months and governed by CJA 1991. The Court of Appeal also held that although it was unlawful for the Secretary of State to adopt a policy that purported to interfere with the sentence of the court, the policy simply reflected the legislative requirements.

11.108   This decision approved a finding in an earlier case where a similar miscalculation of release dates had resulted in a prisoner being released too early under HDC. When his licence was revoked and he was returned to custody, the period for which he had been released

---

153   Although those who have breached the curfew on the current sentence remain excluded.

154   [2008] EWCA Civ 1097.

155   Criminal Justice Act 2003 (Commencement No 8 Transitional and Savings Provisions) Order 2005 (Supplementary Provisions) Order 2005 Sch 2 para 14.

too early was treated as time spent unlawfully at large.[156] These cases also demonstrate the continuing inability of the Secretary of State to introduce legislation that is clear and transparent, a problem trenchantly criticised by Mitting J when he dealt with the *Noone* case at first instance:

> The position at which I have arrived and which I will explain in detail in a moment is one of which I despair. It is simply unacceptable in a society governed by the rule of law for it to be well nigh impossible to discern from statutory provisions what a sentence means in practice.[157]

## The process of applying for HDC

11.109　After calculation of the eligibility date following reception, all prisoners must be given a copy of the form HDC 9 and are invited to complete a form HDC 2 giving details of their proposed accommodation ten weeks before the eligibility date.[158] The prison then decide whether a standard risk assessment is appropriate, in which case a form HDC 1 is completed, or whether an enhanced assessment is necessary requiring form HDC 4. The enhanced procedure is considered appropriate in cases where prisoners are serving a sentence of more than 12 months, have not had a successful temporary release and are considered to be a potential high risk of committing violent or sexual offences.[159] An enhanced risk assessment is conducted by a board at the prison.

11.110　　　Information about the prisoner must be obtained from the supervising Probation Service and a prison officer in regular contact with the prisoner before the form HDC 1 is completed at the prison, usually by the offender supervisor. If it appears that the prisoner is suitable, a form HDC 3 is sent to the Probation Service where the release address is situated to report on the suitability of the address.[160] Release on HDC is considered to be part of the normal progression through the sentence.[161]

---

156　*R (Highton) v Governor of HMYOI Lancaster Farm* [2007] EWHC 1085 (Admin): an application to have the time classified as UAL remitted as special remission had been refused on the grounds of the prisoner's misconduct on licence.

157　[2008] EWHC 207 (Admin) at para 2.

158　Prisoners without accommodation may be able to be released on HDC to accommodation provided by Clearsprings, a private company – see PSI 49/2007.

159　PSI 49/2007 para 5.3.3.

160　PSI 49/2007 para 5.3.2.

161　Para 1.4.

11.111    From 20 October 2008 prisoners may be released on HDC to an address in Scotland.[162]

11.112    Where release on HDC is authorised, form HDC 7 is sent to the offender manager, the Police National Identity Service and the contractor for the tagging 14 days before the proposed release address and the prisoner is given form HDC 5. The decision to release can be postponed and reconsidered if subsequent custodial behaviour is poor or further information comes to light. It is a requirement that the release address has a working phone line and so the consent of the resident at the property may be required. The prisoner must agree to the conditions of the curfew, including payment of the electricity costs of the monitoring device. The normal curfew period will be 12 hours but this can be reduced to nine hours if there are issues concerning, for example, night work, childcare requirements or medical issues.[163] As release on HDC is considered to be the norm, a refusal must only be made in circumstances where:

- there is an unacceptable risk to the victim of the public
- there is a likelihood of reoffending
- there is no suitable address
- it is not considered that the prisoner will abide by the curfew conditions
- there is less than 14 days for the curfew to run.[164]

11.113   A refusal decision is given to the prisoner on a form HDC 6 with reasons for the decision. The prisoner is entitled to obtain disclosure of the relevant material,[165] subject to being notified that material has been withheld under the normal provisos, including national security, the prevention of crime and disorder, where third parties would be put at risk or for the protection of the prisoner on medical or psychiatric grounds.[166] As with parole decisions, consideration has to be given as to whether this material can be summarised or gisted. In *R (Price) v Governor of HMP Kirkham*[167] a decision was quashed for

162  See PSI 41/2008 – these arrangements were introduced even though a previous legal challenge claiming that it was discriminatory for prisoners to be refused release on HDC to Scotland failed in *R (Primrose) v Secretary of State for Justice* [2008] EWHC 1625 (Admin).

163  PSI 41/2008 para 6.2.5.

164  PSI 41/2008 para 5.13.3.

165  *R v Secretary of State for the Home Department ex p Allen* [2000] COD 179 was a successful challenge to the original scheme which did not make provision for disclosure.

166  PSI 41/2008 para 7.6.

167  [2004] EWHC 461 (Admin).

inadequate disclosure, the court confirming that there is a legitimate expectation that the policy on disclosure in the PSO will be followed. Unlike parole decisions, applications to challenge refusals are made through the complaints system as the decision maker is the governor acting on behalf of the Secretary of State. HDC initial release decisions do not engage article 5(4).[168]

## Recall from HDC

11.114   For prisoners released on HDC under CJA 1991, recall can be requested under section 38A(1) if:

(i)     they fail to comply with the curfew conditions of their licence (s38A(1)(a));

(ii)    it is no longer possible to monitor the curfew at the specified address (s38A(1)(b)); or

(iii)   the offender is considered to represent a threat to public safety (s38A(1)(c)).

11.115   For prisoners released on HDC under CJA 2003, recall is governed by section 255 and is authorised if:

(i)     there is a failure to comply with any condition included in the licence (s255(1)(a)); or

(ii)    their whereabouts can no longer be electronically monitored at the address specified in the curfew condition (s255(1)(b)).

11.116   These recall powers relate specifically to the terms of the HDC and if recall is initiated under these powers the prisoner retains an entitlement to release at the statutory release date (the halfway point of the sentence). However recall under the standard licence conditions can also be initiated during the tagging period if the concerns are more to do with risk to the public, rather than inability to maintain the tagging arrangements. In these circumstances the prisoner will not have an entitlement to release at the halfway point of the sentence but will be treated as if recalled under the normal provisions of CJA 2003 s254 (see above).[169]

---

168  *Mason v Ministry of Justice* [2008] EWHC 1787 (Admin).

169  *R (Ramsden and Naylor) v Secretary of State for the Home Department* [2006] EWHC 3502 (Admin) – where the prisoners argued that the regimes for recall from HDC and normal release licence were mutually exclusive, so that recall for whatever reason during the HDC period would not affect the right to automatic release at the halfway point of the sentence.

11.117    Recall decisions are made by PPU. Once returned to custody, the prisoner should be given a representations pack within 48 hours that includes a letter to the prisoner explaining the reasons for the decision and the procedures for appealing. This is done in writing and is considered by PPU.[170] If the appeal against recall is successful, the case is treated as if the recall had not occurred[171] thus ensuring that there is no continuing prejudice in relation to future HDC eligibility. If the prisoner has been recalled because the address could not be monitored re-release on HDC can be approved if a new address can be found or if the original address becomes suitable for monitoring. Before authorising re-release, the governor has to consider the behaviour on curfew and PPU must be consulted. If the appeal is rejected, the prisoner will be released at the normal release date (ie the halfway point of the sentence).

## End of custody licence

11.118    In a further attempt to ease prison overcrowding, an additional form of early release was introduced by the Lord Chancellor on 19 June 2007. End of custody licence (ECL) authorises release up to 18 days before the end of the sentence for prisoners serving sentences of four weeks or more but less than four years. ECL is actually a type of release on temporary licence.[172] Prisoners who are not granted HDC are eligible for ECL but the following are excluded:[173]

(a)    Prisoners serving a sentence for a serious violent offence (annex A of the PSI)

(b)    Prisoners subject to the registration requirements of the Sex Offenders Act 1997/Sexual Offences Act 2003

(c)    Prisoners who have previously escaped from custody

(d)    Prisoners who have breached temporary release conditions

(e)    Prisoners who have offended at any time during a period of temporary release

(f)    Prisoners currently serving a sentence for failing to return from temporary release

---

170  PSO 6700 para 7.4.2.

171  CJA 2003 s255(3).

172  Issued under PR rule 9 and YOIR rule 5. For other types of ROTL see chapter 7.

173  PSI 42/2007 para 4.4.

(g) Prisoners who report that they do not have a release address
(h) Foreign prisoners who meet the criteria for referral for consideration for removal/deportation (as set out in PSO 4630) unless the UKBA has notified the prisoner of a decision not to deport
(i) Prisoners who are subject to extradition proceedings
(j) Sentenced prisoners who are remanded into custody on further charges, or who are awaiting sentence following further convictions
(k) Prisoners who have, on the current sentence, been recalled to custody either for breaching HDC conditions or breach of general licence conditions
(l) Prisoners under the age of 18
(m) Prisoners serving DTO sentences
(n) Prisoners required to undertake a treatment programme as a condition of their supervision licence unless that programme can be arranged to commence during the ECL period or the Offender Manager agrees it can commence later

Unlike HDC, ECL does extend to prisoners serving civil and fine default sentences.

11.119   There is no application to be made for ECL and the assumption is that it will apply to all eligible prisoners. In cases where the prisoner will be subject to probation supervision on release, the probation office which covers the proposed release address must be notified at least seven days before release. The licence issued is for temporary release[174] and so only covers the period of ECL. The licence must state clearly the specific days that the offender is subject to ECL. The prisoner must sign the licence issued before being released on ECL. Normal supervision licences (and the 'at risk notice') commence from the normal release date but as a mater of practice are issued together with the ECL licence.

11.120   As with other forms of temporary release, the prisoner is required to be of good behaviour whilst under the ECL licence and, if subject to supervision, will be required to report to their offender manager as instructed on the licence. Those who fail to report to their offender manager will be liable to recall to custody. Any additional conditions that will apply to the subsequent supervision licence are also included in the ECL licence. Prisoners can be returned to custody before the normal statutory release dates if they breach the ECL licence or commit a new offence during the ECL period but will then fall to

174 Under the general temporary release powers contained at PR rule 9 and YOIR rule 5.

be released under the normal arrangements. As ECL is a form of ROTL the decision to recall is made by the governor of the releasing prison.[175]

## Foreign nationals and early release

11.121  For the purposes of early release arrangements, prisoners who are liable to removal are defined by CJA 2003 s259[176] in the following terms:

- those liable to deportation under section 3(5) of the Immigration Act 1971 and have been notified of a decision to make a deportation order against him or her;[177]
- those liable to deportation under section 3(6) of that Act (a person who has been convicted of an imprisonable offence after the age of 17 and who is recommended for deportation by the court);
- anyone who has been notified of a decision to refuse him or her leave to enter the United Kingdom;
- an illegal entrant within the meaning of section 33(1) of that Act; or
- persons liable to removal under section 10 of the Immigration and Asylum Act 1999.

Irish prisoners will only rarely be considered for deportation in cases involving serious sexual or violent offences or terrorist offences.[178]

### Discretionary release

11.122  Foreign nationals are now subject to the same arrangements for parole under the CJA 1991 as UK citizens. Originally, following a recommendation from the Carlisle Committee that foreign nation-

---

175  PSI 42/2007 section 9.
176  Replacing identical provisions in CJA 2001.
177  Section 3(5) of the Immigration Act 1971 defines a person as liable to deportation from the UK under administrative powers if, having only a limited leave to enter or remain, he or she does not observe a condition attached to the leave or remains beyond the time limited by the leave; or if the Secretary of State deems deportation to be conducive to the public good; or if another person to whose family he or she belongs is or has been ordered to be deported.
178  PSI 21/2007, annex L.

als should be excluded from the DCR scheme,[179] CJA 1991 s50(2) provided that prisoners liable to removal from the UK would not have their cases referred to the Parole Board. Instead, the Secretary of State retained the sole power to determine suitability for release.

11.123    These arrangements were challenged in the co-joined appeals of *R (Clift, Headley & Hindawi) v Secretary of State for the Home Department*[180] where two foreign national prisoners successfully argued that as parole schemes fall within the ambit of article 5, the differential treatment was discriminatory and therefore in breach of article 14. A declaration of incompatibility was made by the Lord in relation to the legislation. In response, to this declaration, CJIA 2008 s27 extended automatic release (and deportation) at the halfway point of the sentence for foreign nationals serving CJA 1991 sentences of four years or more where their parole eligibility date falls after 8 July 2008, save for those serving those sexual or violent offences specified by the CJA 2003.[181]

11.124    For those foreign nationals who are still subject to discretionary release, their cases are now referred to the Parole Board in the same manner as for UK citizens. The major practical difference is be that foreign nationals are far less likely to be permitted to move to open conditions, a policy that was considerably tightened in May 2006 when the Secretary of State, in response to the media spotlighting the issue, decided that the normal policy would be for foreign national prisoners to be deported at the end of their sentences.[182] However, as noted in relation to lifers, the board is still required to conduct a risk assessment and release at the parole eligibility date is not a formality.

11.125    If parole is granted, the prisoner will not be released from custody pending deportation but instead, a decision will be made by the Secretary of State for the Home Department whether to exercise the powers of detention under the Immigration Acts pending removal. Although a decision has to be taken on each individual case, the default position tends very strongly towards detention. For the policy

---

179  The committee recommended that 'those sentenced to more than four years should be statutorily excluded from parole eligibility if they ... have had a deportation order signed against them. Instead the Home Secretary should be empowered to release them and deport them once they have reached what would have been their parole eligibility date at the 50% point of the sentence' (para 473).

180  [2006] UKHL 54.

181  See also PSI 14/2009.

182  See PSO 4360 and *R (Chindamo) v Secretary of State for the Home Department* [2006] EWHC 3340 (Admin) and further see chapter 4.

on when those detained solely under the Immigration Act should be held in prisons, rather than immigration detention centres see chapter 2.

## Early Removal Scheme

11.126   In a mirror of HDC, the Early Removal Scheme (ERS) was introduced by CJA 2003 to allow any fixed term prisoner who is liable to deportation to be removed before the statutory release date.[183] It was subsequently extended from prisoners facing deportation to any person who can demonstrate to the Secretary of State that they have a settled intention to permanently settle abroad.[184] The period was initially for 135 days but was also extended to 270 days. The more generous entitlement to early removal may arguably amount to discrimination against prisoners who are not liable to removal.[185] As with HDC there were initially a number of statutory exclusions from ERS. However these were removed by amendments to the statutory scheme brought in by CJIA 2008 from 3 November 2008.[186] This means that '*all* foreign national determinate sentence prisoners who are subject to deportation or administrative removal from the United Kingdom are now liable to removal under the scheme, subject to refusal by the prison governor if there are 'exceptional or compelling' reasons to refuse.[187]

11.127   The ERS scheme is somewhat wider than HDC and applies to CJA 1991 prisoners serving four years or more who have not been granted automatic release. However those serving sentences of four or more years for an offence committed before 4 April 2005 for an offence contained in Schedule 15 to the CJA 2003[188] are subject to an 'enhanced risk assessment'.[189]

11.128   Otherwise, as noted above, there is a strong presumption that

---

183  CJA 2003 s260(1).

184  CJIA 2008 s27.

185  See *R (Thompson) v Secretary of State for Justice* [2008] EWHC 3305 (Admin) where a British prisoner complained that the discrepancy was discriminatory but was released before his case was heard and did not proceed. Collins J noted that he had granted permission to another prisoner on the same issue and hoped that the matter could be resolved shortly.

186  CJA 2003 s260 as amended.

187  PSI 45/2008 para 3.

188  That is the same class of DCR prisoners whose earliest release date is still subject to a decision by the Parole Board.

189  PSI 45/2008 para 9.

ERS will be granted.[190] It will normally only be refused where there is clear evidence of the prisoner planning further criminal behaviour, evidence of repeated threats or acts of violence or drug dealing class A drugs in custody. Cases considered to be notorious require special consideration and must be referred to the Director General of NOMS.[191]

11.129    Eligibility dates for ERS are:

| Sentence | Period to be served before early removal date | Length of early removal period |
|---|---|---|
| Less than 4 months | ¼ of the sentence | Up to one month depending on the length of sentence |
| 4 months or more but less than 18 months | ¼ of the sentence | Between one month and 4½ months depending on the length of sentence |
| 18 months or more but less than 3 years | ¼ of the sentence | Between 4½ months and 9 months depending on the length of sentence |
| 3 years and over | 270 days less than half of the sentence | 270 days |

(PSI 19/2008, para 7)

11.130   Those subject to the presumptive scheme will be checked to ensure that they are not subject to a statutory exclusion, there are no barriers to their removal and there are no further outstanding charges of confiscation orders. Finally a check will be made to ensure that there are no exceptional or compelling reasons that would justify not removing the prisoner. Where there are no such barriers, the Borders and Immigration Agency are notified and asked for confirmation that they can remove the prisoner. Once this confirmation is received, the prisoner is notified that the removal will proceed. In cases where there is a barrier to removal, the prisoner is notified of the decision and the reasons and can make representations or utilise the complaints procedure in the same manner as for HDC refusals (above).[192]

11.131    If the prisoner is subject to an enhanced risk assessment, a check is made to ascertain whether there are any statutory barriers to removal

190  PSO 6000 para 9.6.
191  PSO 6000 para 9.6.5.
192  PSI 19/2008, annex A.

(as for the presumptive scheme) and the governor is required to complete an enhanced risk assessment dossier which is served upon the prisoner so that representations can be made. This is then sent to PPU for a decision to be made. If removal is rejected, the prisoner receives reasons for the decision and the normal parole process will begin.[193]

## Compassionate release

11.132    The Secretary of State retains a general statutory power to release prisoners early from their sentences on compassionate grounds.[194] Compassionate release is only appropriate in cases where the prisoner has not reached the automatic release date or the parole eligibility date of the sentence. In all of these cases, the appropriate method is to have an application for parole considered through the special or early review provisions.

11.133    The statutory power does not proscribe the circumstances in which the power can be exercised and current policy is contained in PSO 6000, chapter 12. The policy limits the exercise of this power to exceptional cases relating to a prisoner's medical condition or where there are tragic family circumstances. Although the policy purports to restrict the exercise of the power to these two grounds, it has been held that the statutory power must be capable of dealing with all situations that fall within the statutory definition. In *R (A) v Governor of Huntercombe YOI and Secretary of State for the Home Department*[195] a young offender had his sentence miscalculated and having prepared for release, was informed on the day of his proposed release that it could not take place. An application was made for compassionate release but this was rejected on the grounds that the case did not raise a medical issue nor did it involve tragic family circumstances. The Prison Service's sentence calculation was found to be correct and so the question of whether the refusal of compassionate release fell to be considered. Stanley Burnton J held that the statutory criteria[196] restrict the power to cases where exceptional circumstances exist, that they must give rise to compassionate grounds for release,

---

193  PSI 19/2008 annex B.
194  CJA 1991 s36; CJA 2003 s248; PCC(S)A 2000 s102(3). For lifers the power derives from C(S)A 1997 s30 – see previous chapter.
195  [2006] EWHC 2544 (Admin).
196  In this case from PCC(S)A 2000 s102(3).

and that those grounds justify release cannot be limited to particular classes of cases. Instead, decisions must address the terms of the power itself:

> The next question is whether these circumstances give rise to compassionate grounds. The governor thought that compassionate grounds would only exist if there was serious or terminal illness of something of equal severity. I do not think that compassion arises only in cases of death or illness. There are compassionate grounds whenever there is pain or suffering or distress or misfortune. The narrow scope of the power under section 102(3) results more from the requirement of exceptional circumstances than the element of compassion. In the present case, the repeated indications of immediate release, or that it would be forthcoming if the judges so recommended, must have given rise to real feelings of upset and disappointment on the part of the claimant, and indeed of his family. It would be an act of compassion to release him in such circumstances[197]

11.134 The policy still recognised that it is most likely that compassionate release will be appropriate in those two limited circumstances, although it does accept that there may be other exceptional circumstances.[198] The general guiding principles for all cases are:

(i) the release of the prisoner will not put the safety of the public at risk;

(ii) a decision to approve release would not normally be made on the basis of facts of which the sentencing or appeal court was aware;

(iii) there is some specific purpose to be served by early release.[199]

11.135 When applied to an application for release on medical grounds, the more detailed guidance explains that release will be only be authorised if:

- the prisoner is suffering from a terminal illness and death is likely to occur soon; or the prisoner is bedridden or similarly incapacitated; *and*
- the risk of re-offending is past; *and*
- there are adequate arrangements for the prisoner's care and treatment outside prison; *and*
- early release will bring some significant benefit to the prisoner or his or her family.[200]

---

197 At para 36.
198 PSO 6000 annex A.
199 PSO 6000 para 12.3.1.
200 PSO 6000 chapter 12, annex A.

11.136   It should be noted that the criteria are cumulative and not alternative. The power is therefore most commonly exercised to allow a terminally ill prisoner to die outside of custody.[201]

11.137   The guidance in relation to compassionate release for tragic family circumstances is that:

- the circumstances of the prisoner or the family have changed to the extent that if he or she served the sentence imposed, the hardship suffered would be of exceptional severity, greater than the court could have foreseen; *and*
- the risk of re-offending is past; *and*
- it can be demonstrated beyond doubt that there is a real and urgent need for the prisoner's permanent presence with his or her family; *and*
- early release will bring some significant benefit to the prisoner or his or her family, which cannot be provided by any other person or agency.[202]

11.138   As with medical release, these criteria are cumulative and would normally relate to factors that were not known or were not apparent at the time the sentence was imposed. Consideration for early release may, for example, be given where a spouse has died or is seriously ill and there is no one to care for young children. It will be necessary to explore the risk to the welfare of the children and the availability of support from other family members, friends or social services.

11.139   In all cases where consideration is to be given to release, the governor of the prison must complete the pro forma application contained in PSO 6000 and provide these the PPU. The statutory requirement is for the Parole Board to be consulted, if possible and their advice will be taken on the issue of the continued risk to the public if release is granted. Applications where the general circumstances are sufficient to meet the compassionate limb of the test but where the prisoner is still considered to pose a risk to the public will therefore be refused. The final decision is a ministerial one and if granted, a normal licence will be issued to run for the statutory period of supervision. Prisoners released under this power are liable to recall for breach of the licence conditions but the PSO makes it clear that a prisoner

201   Although there have been rare examples where continued imprisonment is likely to have such an adverse effect on life expectancy or medical treatment that compassionate release is appropriate. In *Mouisel v France* [2004] 38 EHRR 34 the conditions of detention and treatment for a prisoner receiving treatment for leukaemia were held to be in breach of article 3.
202   PSO 6000 chapter 12, annex A.

will not be recalled if the compassionate circumstances change after release (eg if a recovery is made from the illness).[203]

## The Royal Prerogative of Mercy

11.140 There is one further discretionary power to authorise early release, being the Royal Prerogative of Mercy, otherwise known as special remission. This is an extra-statutory power and its exercise is almost entirely dependent upon Prison Service policy.

11.141 PSO 6650 chapter 13 contains the current policy and states that the power will normally be used where there has been a mistake in sentence calculation or to reward meritorious conduct. In relation to mistaken calculation, it will generally only be granted in cases where the mistake in the calculation has persisted for a long period of time, usually for several months or more, whether there are significant release plans in place that will be frustrated by the change in release date and the length of time or proportion of the sentence that would not be served. Usually, no more than 25 per cent of the sentence or two months would be remitted.[204] Finally, the prisoner's own conduct is relevant, for example, if the prisoner was aware of the mistake and deliberately withheld knowledge of it.

11.142 The policy guidance on when meritorious conduct will justify special remission is set out in the judgment in *R v Secretary of State for the Home Department ex p Quinn*:[205]

> It is established policy that, where a prisoner serving a determinate sentence renders some commendable service to the prison authorities or to the community at large that warrants some tangible recognition, consideration should be given by the area manager to releasing the prisoner earlier than he or she would be released in the usual way.[206]

11.143 Examples of where awards have been made have included situations where the prisoner has assisted other prisoners or members of staff who have been in danger or where helpful information has been provided to the authorities. As might be expected, the prisoner's overall conduct is paramount when a decision is being made. Any suggestion that the prisoner has precipitated the action that leads to the meritorious behaviour (eg starting a fire to put it out) or subsequently

203 PSO 6000 para 12.13.2.
204 PSO 6650 para 13.1.5.
205 [2000] Prison LR 222; [2001] ACD 45.
206 [2000] Prison LR 222 at para 6.

commits offences against prison discipline can lead to an award being reduced or cancelled altogether.

11.144    The procedure for processing applications is that they will be forwarded to the briefing and casework unit and the views of the sentencing court should be sought. For periods of less than one month, a decision can be made by the area manager but longer periods require approval from the justice and victims unit. If an award is made, a Royal Warrant is issued and the prisoner's release dates are amended. As the remedy is entirely discretionary, the decision can be made either to reduce the length of the sentence itself or simply to advance the statutory release date by providing for the licence to commence at an earlier stage.[207] It should also be noted that where a prisoner is released too early from the sentence and the mistake is subsequently identified, an application can be made to exercise the prerogative to prevent the prisoner becoming unlawfully at large and being recalled to custody.

# Discharge from custody

11.145    On release from prison, most prisoners over the age of 18 who are serving a sentence of 14 days or more will be given a discharge grant.[208] The purpose is to provide subsistence for the first week after release.[209] Young offenders who are not returning to the family home will receive individual advice (see below). The following are not eligible to receive a discharge grant:[210]

- Prisoners under the age of 18 years
- Those serving a custodial sentence of 14 days or less
- Those recalled from licence to prison for a period of 14 days or less
- Those serving an Intermittent Custody Sentence
- Licence recalls who were on licence for 14 days or less before recall
- Prisoners awaiting deportation or removal from the United Kingdom
- Anyone travelling to an address outside of the UK

207  R (Ghartey) v Secretary of State for the Home Department [2001] EWHC 199 (Admin).
208  PSO 6400 para 5.1 and PSI 21/2009.
209  Hansard, Written Answers 21 July 2009, Column 620W.
210  PSO 6400 para 5.2.

- Those being discharged to a hospital under a Mental Health Act Section Order
- Fine defaulters and those held on further remand warrants. However, convicted offenders who have completed their sentence and who qualify for a grant but remain in custody in default of payment of a fine or remanded on further charges, will receive the grant on their final release
- Civil prisoners
- Unconvicted prisoners
- Prisoners in resettlement units who are in paid employment in the community

11.146   Eligibility is loosely means tested and sentenced prisoners who are known to have in excess of £8,000 in savings (and would therefore be ineligible for Income Support) are not eligible.

11.147   Prisoners who are released on appeal are still eligible for the payment and so arrangements should be made for the discharge to be taken to court with the prisoner in case release takes place directly from the court.[211] The governor has discretion to make an additional payment of £50 for the purposes of securing accommodation. An application must be made by the prisoner four weeks before the release date and payment can only be made to an approved agency or landlord and not to the prisoner or a friend or relative of the prisoner.[212]

11.148   Once a prisoner is released, they are entitled to access the same range of statutory services provided by local authorities and health care bodies as anyone else in the community. These provisions tend to be chronically underused by prisoners and access to accommodation under the National Assistance Act 1948 or the Housing Act 1996 or the provision of assessments pursuant to the National Health Service and Community Care Act 1990 s47 may be appropriate.[213] The duties to young persons and children are more extensive as a result of the duties imposed by the Children Act (CA) 1989. The Act applies to children in custody, albeit with modified obligations.[214] CA 1989 s17 imposes a duty on local authorities to assess children in

---

211  PSO 6400 para 5.10.
212  PSO 6400 para 5.3.
213  See the articles by Bowen, Markus and Suterwalla, *Legal Action*, January 2008 and February 2008 for a full exploration of these duties.
214  *R (Howard League for Penal Reform) v Secretary of State for the Home Department and Department of Health (Interested Party) (No 2)* [2002] EWHC 2497 (Admin).

need and a failure to carry out an assessment on a child in prison who may potentially be in need is a breach of that duty. The duty may arise simply on discharge or where the Parole Board require certain needs to be assessed.[215] Duties may also be placed upon local authorities to provide accommodation to any child in their area who has been abandoned, or where there is no one with parental responsibility or where that person is prevented from providing suitable accommodation or care.[216]

---

215  *R (K) v Manchester City Council* [2006] EWHC 3164 (Admin).
216  CA 1989 s20.

## CHAPTER 12

# Remedies

*continued*

# Introduction

12.1   The purpose of this chapter is to provide a guide to the main remedies available to prisoners. In relation to claims for judicial review, private law claims and discrimination actions, an overview of the legal framework and the general application to prison issues is provided and it is recommended that this information should be considered in conjunction with legal guides directed specifically at those subject areas.

# Public funding

## The future of public funding

12.2   At the time of writing, the public funding system for prison law work has been under review by the Legal Services Commission (LSC) with a consultation paper having been issued to review the future of public funding in this area. The consultation focuses on the increase in expenditure in this area from 2001–2008 and states that the purpose of the consultation is to devise a strategy for controlling that expenditure. The proposals are that:

- Prison law will become a specialist stand alone contract rather than being part of the general criminal contract.
- Hourly rates will be replaced by fixed or standard fees.
- Fixed matter starts will be introduced.
- A stricter supervisor standard will be put in place for practitioners to obtain a prison law contract requiring the supervisor to practice in prison law for 350 hours a year.
- Future methods of service delivery should include assessing the viability of duty solicitor and telephone advice schemes.

12.3   The likelihood is that some or all of these measures will be in place by the end of 2009 or early 2010. However, the system for public funding as at 30 April 2009 does provide background material on merits and financial eligibility that is likely to be continued into the new scheme.

## The existing scheme

12.4   Prison law as a category is funded by the LSC as part of the Criminal Defence Service (CDS) that was established together with the Community Legal Service (CLS) by the Access to Justice Act 1999 s12.

Firms can have either a general criminal contract (to cover general police station advice and criminal defence work) under which they can take on prison law cases, or a 'stand alone' contract. The supervisor standard includes having carried out 350 hours prison law work in each of the preceding three years.[1]

## Scope of prison law

12.5    The Criminal Defence Service (General) (No 2) Regulations 2001 para 4 states that funding will be provided to any individual who:

(f) requires advice and assistance regarding his treatment or discipline in prison (other than in respect of actual or contemplated proceedings regarding personal injury, death or damage to property);

(g) is the subject of proceedings before the Parole Board;

(h) requires advice and assistance regarding representations to the Home Office in relation to a mandatory life sentence or other parole review.

12.6    The General Criminal Contract which applies to all CDS work determines the circumstances in which Advice and Assistance and Advocacy Assistance can be given. The Contract Specification[2] is somewhat outdated as the specification has not managed to keep up with the changes in the law, such as the harmonisation of early release procedures for lifers. However, the specification explicitly permits advice and assistance and advocacy assistance to be provided to prisoners within all Parole Board procedures.

12.7    Public funding is subject to financial eligibility and as at 1 April 2009, Advocacy Assistance is available where weekly disposable income does not exceed £209 and disposable capital does not exceed £3,000 (for those with no dependents, £3,335 for those with one dependant, £3,535 for those with two dependents with a £100 increase in the limit for each further dependent). Advice and Assistance is available where weekly disposable income does not exceed £99 and disposable capital does not exceed £1,000 (for those with no dependents, £1,335 for those with one dependant, £1,535 for those with two dependents with a £100 increase in the limit for each further dependent). The means of prisoners' partners, married or otherwise, may also need to be considered. The regulations normally require partners' means to be considered where the couple 'normally' live together. If the couple lived together before imprisonment

1  Legal Services Commission Manual para 2B-138
2  Part A 5.2 of the Contract Specification.

and intend to reside together on release, then the means should be taken into account. However, for prisoners serving very long or indeterminate sentences there is so little certainty about release and suitable release addresses that it may be reasonable not to aggregate a partner's means.

## Advice and assistance

12.8   This is the kind of assistance that will be used where there is either no oral hearing, or at the initial stages of a case where it is unclear whether there will be an oral hearing. An application for funding is made on forms CDS 1 and CDS 2 with the supervising solicitor making the assessment as to whether funding is justified. The forms can be completed by post as the solicitor can exercise a devolved power to accept a postal application where there is 'good reason' to do so[3] and the guidance indicates that this includes people detained in custody. Similarly, a claim for telephone advice prior to the signing of the form can be claimed for where there is good reason.[4]

12.9   There is a sufficient benefit test which requires that: 'Advice and Assistance may only be provided on legal issues concerning English law and where there is sufficient benefit to the client, having regard to the circumstances of the matter, including the personal circumstances of the client, to justify work or further work being carried out'.[5] The upper limit of the amount of work that can be undertaken without applying for an extension is £300.[6] Beyond this limit, prior authority to carry out further work can be applied for from the relevant area office on form CDS 5. If authority is granted, further work that is 'actually and reasonably carried out in accordance with the Sufficient Benefit test' can be claimed for up to the maximum agreed extension.[7]

### Advocacy assistance

12.10   This is the type of public funding used in relation to the preparation for and advocacy at oral hearings including prison disciplinary and parole hearings. The forms that have to be used are CDS 1 and CDS 3, although if there has already been provision of advice and assistance in the matter only a CDS 3 needs to be signed by the client. The

---

3   Part B 2.1 of the Contract Specification.
4   Part B 2.3 of the Contract Specification.
5   Part A 5.3, and Part B 2.5 of the Contract Specification.
6   Part B5.5 of the Contract Specification.
7   Part B 2.8 of the Contract Specification.

solicitor can then grant advocacy assistance under devolved powers. As with advice and assistance it is possible to accept a postal application for advocacy assistance where there is good reason and to claim for prior telephone advice.[8]

12.11    In relation to Parole Board applications and hearings, the applicable merits test is that advocacy assistance may not be provided if 'it appears unreasonable that approval should be granted in the particular circumstances of the case'.[9] This is clearly not dependent on the prospects of success, which reflects the fact that Parole Board hearings are the way in which the state is satisfying the duty to have detention based on a perceived risk to the public reviewed in accordance with article 5. There may also be many reasons that it may be in the interests of the prisoner for representation to be provided where there is no prospect of release. The upper limit of the amount of work that can be undertaken without applying for an extension is £1,500.[10] Counsel can be instructed to represent the prisoner at the hearing under devolved powers, although counsel can only be paid at the same rates as apply to solicitors.[11]

## Limits on allowed work

12.12    Unlike with police station or criminal defence work in the courts, there is very little guidance on what the LSC will consider as an appropriate amount of time for specified units of work (the Contract Specification contains no guidance on specific units of work in relation to parole applications or hearings). Clearly it is extremely important to ensure that attendances on the file justify the amount of time recorded for any work claimed for.[12]

12.13    In relation to travel time to visit prisoners, the Contract suggests that travel time of up to three hours one way may be justified to visit a prisoner if the solicitor is already acting and either:

• there is no other local contactor available (including, if necessary, at short notice); or
• the client's problem is so specialised that, in your reasonable view, there is no more local contractor with the expertise to deal with the case; or

---

8  Part B 4.1 of the Contract Specification.
9  Part B 4.3 of the Contract Specification.
10  Part B 5.5 of the Contract Specification.
11  Part B 4.8 of the Contract Specification.
12  See para 4H – 019 of the LSC Manual.

- you have significant previous knowledge of the case or dealings with the client in relation to the issues raised by the case so as to justify renewed involvement even though the client is at a distance.[13]

## Public funding for litigation

12.14  Litigation for prisoners on prison law issues will generally be in public law proceedings for judicial review or private law claims for damages. Public funding is available for both types of action through certificates of public funding issued by the LSC.[14] The LSC's funding code[15] provides comprehensive guidance on the availability of funding for these categories. In order to promote better informed decision making, all funding applications for prisoners' cases are dealt with by the LSC's Special Cases Unit in Brighton. Applications for funding are made on form CLS APP 1 and for people in custody, their financial eligibility is assessed on form CLS MEANS 1.

## Public funding and judicial review

12.15  All solicitors' firms that hold a contract in public law or who hold a general criminal contract[16] can obtain public funding certificates from the LSC for public law work on prison issues as can all those who undertake prison law under the general criminal contract.[17] The general guidance on public funding for all public law challenges, including judicial review and habeas corpus, is contained in the LSC Manual, volume 3, section 7 which must be read in conjunction with the more detailed decision making guidance in volume 3, part C, section 16.

12.16  The guidance provides that applications for funding will normally only be granted where other forms of administrative appeal have already been utilised[18] and where appropriate notification has been

---

13  Part B 7.9 of the Contract Specification.
14  Access to Justice Act 1999 ss 6–11.
15  Issued pursuant to section 8.
16  Although this will be replaced with the specialist prison law contract – see above.
17  Judicial review relating to prison law matters can be carried out as 'Associated CLS work' under the Criminal Contract.
18  LSC Manual Vol 3C para 16.5.1.

given to the proposed defendant by way of a letter before claim.[19] In keeping with the general guidance on funding, the prospects of success will ordinarily have to be greater than 50 per cent and this test refers to the final outcome of the case, not the likelihood of permission being granted.[20] However, the requirement for these prospects of success to be met can be overridden if:

(a) the case has a significant wider public interest;
(b) the case is of overwhelming importance to the client;
(c) the case raises significant human rights issues.[21]

12.17   In cases where permission has already been granted by the Administrative Court, there is a presumption in favour of funding the case, although an assessment of the prospects of success at the full hearing must still be conducted.[22] Certificates will be issued with standard limitations, the first limitation usually permitting an application for permission to be made on the papers alone and thereafter, any amendments need to be supported by an advice from Counsel.[23]

## Public funding for private law claims

12.18   The criteria for funding private law damages claims for prisoners are dealt with in the LSC Manual, volume 3, section 8 to be read in conjunction with the decision making guidance in volume 3, part C, section 17. Only solicitors' firms with a contract to conduct 'Actions against the police and other related claims' are automatically entitled to obtain public funding for these claims and firms that do not hold that contract must obtain permission on a case by case basis from the LSC.[24] Personal injury claims arising from negligence are excluded from scope[25] and clinical negligence is a separate specialist category in its own right for the purposes of public funding.

12.19   Funding for damages claims is available where the case is concerned with 'serious wrongdoing, abuse of position or power or significant breach of human rights' by a public authority.[26] Although personal injury claims are generally out of scope, if the personal

19  LSC Manual Vol 3C para 16.6.2.
20  LSC Manual Vol 3C para 16.6.3(a).
21  LSC Manual Vol 3C para 16.6.4.
22  LSC Manual Vol 3C para 16.7.
23  LSC Manual Vol 3C para 16.8.
24  LSC Manual Vol 3 para 8.4.
25  LSC Manual Vol 3 para 3.2.
26  LSC Manual Vol 3C para 17.1(a).

injury has arisen from a deliberate abuse of power it will fall within this category. Claims that raise mixed allegations including both deliberate abuse of power and negligence can be funded where it is necessary to plead the different causes of action in the alternative.[27] The criteria for funding such cases have more flexibility than for other categories of damages claims and so the normal requirement that the case will attract damages of at least £5,000 does not apply, providing that the case still has good prospects of success and there are other compelling reasons for the claim. As with judicial review, claims may also be funded where the prospects of success are borderline providing:

(a) the case has a significant wider public interest;
(b) the case has overwhelming importance to the client;
(c) the case raises a significant human rights issue.[28]

12.20 Furthermore, cases falling within this area of public funding are not subject to a refusal of public funding because of the availability of a conditional fee agreement, unless the case forms part of a group action.[29]

# Prison complaints procedures

## History

12.21 The right of prisoners to raise complaints about the prison regime or their treatment in prison through a formal set of procedures may seem entrenched but is in fact a relatively recent development. Prior to the introduction of the precursor to the current scheme in 1990, prisoners could raise concerns about their treatment in custody by making a complaint to the governor, although there was no prescribed method for making that complaint; by submitting a complaint to the Board of Visitors (now the Independent Monitoring Board); or by submitting a petition to the Secretary of State. For long periods of time, the guidance issued by the Secretary of State even required prisoners to make use of these procedures at the same time as seeking legal advice (the simultaneous ventilation rule) until the ECtHR held this to be a breach of article 6,[30] or before seeking legal

---

27  LSC Manual Vol 3C para 17.7.
28  LSC Manual Vol 3C para 17.4.1.
29  LSC Manual Vol 3C para 17.5.
30  *Silver v United Kingdom* (1983) 5 EHRR 347.

advice (the prior ventilation rule), a practice that was also found to be unlawful in the domestic courts.[31] The problem with these remedies was that in the absence of any formal procedure, prisoners simply did not know when their complaints would be dealt with or the reasons for the decisions made. The detrimental effect this had on prisoners was spelt out by Lord Bridge in the case of *R v Deputy Governor of HMP Parkhurst ex p Leech*:[32]

> Nothing, I believe, is so likely to generate unrest among ordinary prisoners as a sense that they have been treated unfairly and have no effective means of redress. If a prisoner has a genuine grievance arising from disciplinary proceedings unfairly conducted, his right to petition a faceless authority in Whitehall for a remedy will not be of much comfort to him.[33]

12.22   These observations proved to be prescient and following the Woolf report into the Strangeways riots which recommended that a more formal complaints system be introduced, the government white paper, 'Custody, Care and Justice'[34] recommended that the prison system should give prisoners:

> ... reasons for decisions that affect them; [and have] a fair and just system for resolving disciplinary hearings and for resolving grievances ...[35]

12.23   These recommendations resulted in the introduction of a request/complaints procedure in 1990 and eventually the appointment of the Prisons and Probation Ombudsman. The initial request/complaints system was updated in September 2002 following a review of the procedures by Her Majesty's Chief Inspector of Prisons which found the old system to be slow, cumbersome, difficult to use and sometimes led to prisoners not being able to complain.

## PSO 2510 and complaints

12.24   The statutory underpinning the complaints system can be found in Prison Rules (PR) 1999 rule 11 and YOI Rules (YOIR) rule 8 which provide that:

---

31   *R v Secretary of State for the Home Department ex p Anderson* [1984] QB 778.
32   [1988] 1 AC 533.
33   At p568.
34   Cmn 1647.
35   Page 15.

(1) A request or complaint to the governor or independent monitoring board relating to a prisoner's imprisonment shall be made orally or in writing by the prisoner.

(2) On every day the governor shall hear any requests and complaints that are made to him under paragraph (1).

(3) A written request or complaint under paragraph (1) may be made in confidence.

12.25   PR rule 78(1) and YOIR rule 82(1) also impose a statutory duty on Independent Monitoring Boards to hear complaints from prisoners.

12.26   The aim of the current scheme is to separate out requests or applications from complaints and this aim is described as follows:

> An effective system for dealing with prisoners' requests and complaints underpins much of prison life. It helps to ensure that the Prison Service meets its obligation of dealing fairly, openly and humanely with prisoners. It also helps staff by inspiring in prisoners greater confidence that their needs and welfare are being looked after, by reducing tension and by promoting better relations between prisoners and staff. A prison's equilibrium is more likely to be maintained if prisoners feel they have an accessible and effective means of making a request, an outlet for their grievances and confidence that their requests or complaints will be considered properly, with reasons given for decisions.[36]

12.27   Applications (or requests) are separated out from the complaints process in order to ensure that there is no confusion between the aims of answering grievances and meeting everyday needs.[37] Requests or applications are first dealt with on the wing or landing, usually in an office out of the hearing of other prisoners, with governors holding similar sessions at the weekends.[38] Prisons may use written forms, although this is not mandatory and an applications book should be maintained to record outcomes. Where an application does not resolve a problem, prisoners can then move on to make a complaint.

12.28   In contrast, the complaints process is required to be a formal process in order to meet the overarching requirements of the system. There are four forms that are utilised for making a complaint: COMP 1 for first stage complaints, COMP 1A for confidential matters or second stage complaints, COMP 2 for confidential matters and form ADJ 1 when seeking to have governor's disciplinary

---

36   PSO 2510 para 1.1.1.
37   Para 3.1.5.
38   Para 3.1.2.

hearing reviewed. The aim is for complaints to be dealt with a local level, unless the matter is a reserved subject that must be dealt with at Headquarters and so if the first stage is not resolved by the COMP 1, the prisoner can proceed to appeal the decision on the COMP 1A appeal, again using the form COMP 1A to the governing governor. On this occasion the form will be answered by a member of the prison's management team. This exhausts the internal complaints procedure.

12.29   The first stage requires a form COMP 1 to be completed by the prisoner which is then placed in a locked box on the wing. Forms must be made freely available to prisoners and prisoners cannot be asked to explain why they want access to a form.[39] The old practice of seeking to limit prisoners' access to complaint forms is deprecated but there remains provision to limit access to forms where staff consider that the system is being abused. Guidance suggests that a limit of one form a day might be imposed or alternatively asking the prisoner to prioritise their complaints for reply.[40] Provision should be made to provide complaint forms and leaflets about the complaints procedures in foreign languages for prisoners who do not speak English[41] and to provide suitable access to the complaints process for prisoners with learning, literacy or visual disabilities.[42] The boxes are emptied each working day by an officer designated this task[43] and each prison must have a complaints clerk who is responsible for logging and registering complaints and a complaints co-ordinator responsible for the overall management structure of the complaints processes in the establishment.[44]

## Time limits

12.30   Complaints should normally be made within three months of the incident complained about, although there is discretion to extend this time. The recommended timetable for responding to complaints is:[45]

---

39   Para 6.2.
40   Para 8.7.3.
41   Para 6.5.
42   Para 6.6.
43   Para 5.3.1.
44   Paras 5.1 and 5.2.
45   PSO 2510 para 13.2.

| Stage | Timetable |
|---|---|
| Stage 1 response | 3 weekdays |
| Stage 1 response to complaint against member of staff | 10 weekdays |
| Stage 1 response to complaint involving another establishment | 10 weekdays |
| Stage 2 response | 7 weekdays |
| Stage 2 response to complaint against member of staff | 10 weekdays |
| Stage 2 response to complaint involving another establishment | 10 weekdays |
| Stage 3 response | 7 weekdays |
| Stage 3 response to complaint against member of staff | 10 weekdays |
| Stage 3 response to complaint involving another establishment | 10 weekdays |
| Confidential access to governing governor | 7 weekdays |

## Confidential access

12.31    Once complaints have been collected and registered, they will be allocated for reply. Generally, first stage complaints will be allocated at prison officer level unless the complaint is a confidential access complaint, the complaint is about a reserved subject, the complaint is about a member of staff or the complaint is otherwise inappropriate for a wing officer to deal with (eg a complaint about medical treatment).[46] Where the complaint is submitted on a confidential access scheme it should be given to the person to whom it is addressed without being opened. If it is decided that the subject is not properly one that justifies confidential access, instead of breaching confidentiality (as used to happen), the complaints clerk should return the form to the prisoner with advice that the complaint can be resubmitted under the normal procedures.[47] However, it is important for the prisoner to be aware that confidential access does not mean that the

46   Para 7.4.2.
47   Para 9.2.1.

complaint will be kept confidential whilst it is being investigated[48] and that the confidentiality merely extends to the initial submission of the matter.[49]

## Special categories of complaints

12.32   Certain subject matters require the prison to take additional steps to ensure the complaint is investigated and answered correctly. Those identified in PSO 2510 are as follows:

- The complaint forms have a box to tick to identify whether there is a racial aspect and the form should be passed to the race relations liaison officer (RRLO) to be dealt with.[50] The RRLO should report the matter to the prison's race relations monitoring team and should respond to the complaint unless this aspect of the complaint is 'minor or tangential'[51] in which case the RRLO should pass the matter to an appropriate member of staff to reply (para 12.1.5). Reserved subjects that contain a racial aspect should still be copied to the RRLO before being passed onto the relevant department at headquarters.[52]
- Chapter 11 of PSO 2510 contains guidance on how to deal with complaints against members of staff. The prison remains responsible for instigating formal disciplinary procedures and whether to instigate a formal investigation in accordance with PSO 1300 on Investigations. A central discipline policy team at headquarters provides guidance to local establishments on these matters. In cases where it is decided that the allegations are unfounded, the prisoner can be given a written warning not to repeat the allegations and can even be given a formal order to this effect that can result in disciplinary proceedings if not followed.[53]
- If the form indicates that the complaint concerns bullying, the anti-bullying procedures should be followed.[54]
- Complaints made about matters that have occurred at a different prison should be sent to that prison for a draft reply or for the provision of information to enable the holding prison to provide the

---

48  Para 9.3.1.
49  See for example the Prison Ombudsman's case reports, Issue No 14, Autumn 2004, p4.
50  Para 12.1.
51  Para 12.1.4.
52  Para 12.1.7.
53  Para 11.8.2.
54  Para 12.2.1 and PSO 1702.

response.[55] The holding prison should seek to agree responses with the establishment that is the subject of the complaint.

## Reserved subjects

12.33 Certain matters cannot be dealt with at the prison and have to be forwarded to the relevant department of the Prison Service at their central offices. These will most commonly include complaints about governors' adjudications where form ADJ 1 should be used or complaints about category A matters. COMP 1 forms should still be used for all matters other than adjudications. There is no second stage or right of appeal where the matter is a reserved subject. PSO 2510 contains a full list of reserved subjects at Annex H:

- Adjudications.
- Matters affecting category A prisoners.
- Deportation/repatriation requests.
- Mother and baby units.
- Compassionate release and special remission applications.
- Complaints against the governing governor.
- Artificial insemination and marriage requests.

12.34 The list also includes matters relating to parole and those affecting life sentenced prisoners. In relation to prisoners serving life sentences, most day to day operational matters are now dealt with locally and so complaints should in fact be dealt with at the prison itself. Complaints about parole matters will be passed to the Public Protection Unit for response but it is important for prisoners to remember that the Parole Board is independent of the Prison Service and so the board itself cannot respond to complaints. The practical usefulness of this is therefore limited to procedural errors made by the prison during the parole process.

## Explaining decisions

12.35 As one would expect with a formal, form based system, the Prison Service's own guidance indicates that written responses to complaints are necessary and that the responses must contain sufficient information to enable the prisoner to properly understand how the matter has been considered and resolved:

> The response to a complaint or appeal must properly address the points made by the prisoner, irrespective of whether the complaint is

55  Para 12.3.1.

upheld or rejected. Decisions must not be taken arbitrarily or give the impression that they have been taken arbitrarily.

Responding to a written complaint is an opportunity for the establishment to demonstrate a positive commitment to fairness and to the welfare of prisoners in its care.

A prisoner is more likely to accept a decision if trouble is taken to explain it, even if he or she is still not entirely satisfied.

If a complaint is upheld, either in whole or in part, the response must say what action is being taken to provide any appropriate redress. [56]

## Independent Monitoring Boards

12.36   PR rule 78(1) imposes a statutory requirement on the each prison's IMB to hear any request or complaint made by a prisoner. As the duty falls upon the IMB itself, it is the responsibility of each individual IMB to make necessary arrangements to discharge this duty. Prisons can access the IMB by submitting a complaint and prison staff are under a duty to ensure that any request to speak to a member is passed to the board promptly. [57]

12.37   Although there is a statutory requirement for each prison to have an IMB, their role is that of being a watchdog that is separate from the Prison Service itself and so they do not form part of the formal internal complaints procedures.

12.38   The formation of the Association of Independent Monitoring Boards by the Ministry of Justice has attempted to introduce more uniform practice amongst the different IMBs and also to collate and publish the information that they are able to provide on problems and trends in the prison system. The first annual report indicates that property issues are the biggest single issue raised with them whereas adjudications form the smallest single subject area. [58] This probably reflects both the availability of legal advice on these subjects as well as demonstrating how the more formal complaints procedures are well utilised by prisoners in relation disciplinary matters.

---

56   PSO 2510, introduction to Part 8.
57   PSO 2510 para 2.2.2.
58   *Behind Closed Doors*, Independent Monitoring Boards Annual Report 2008: www.imb.gov.uk/docs/IMB_National_Council_AR09_F1.pdf

# Prisons and Probation Ombudsman

12.39   As well as establishing an internal complaints procedure, the Woolf Report recommended that there should be an external complaints adjudicator providing a final avenue of appeal for prisoners unhappy at the Prison Service's attempts to resolve complaints. This recommendation eventually resulted in the appointment of Prison Ombudsman in October 1994, his jurisdiction being extended to the probation Service in September 2001.

12.40      The Ombudsman is a non-statutory body and as such, he does not have powers to bind the Secretary of State or the Prison Service and can simply make recommendations following investigations into complaints. Although the remit of the Ombudsman has expanded significantly since the creation of the office in 1994, the lack of a statutory footing remains a bone of contention. The first Ombudsman, Sir Peter Woodhead, raised this in his annual report in 1996 and in his 2007/8 annual report the current Ombudsman, Stephen Shaw expressed the:

> ... disappointment that the whole staff team felt when the long anticipated plans to place the PPO office on a statutory footing were abandoned ... Establishing the PPO office as an NDPB could well ensure the conspicuous independence from the Ministry of Justice and Home Office and greater autonomy in the day to day conduct of our business.[59]

# Terms of reference

12.41   The Ombudsman's terms of reference permit him to investigate complaints submitted by:

- individual prisoners; and
- individuals who are, or have been, under the supervision of the National Probation Service or housed in NPS accommodation or who have had pre-sentence reports prepared on them by the NPS;
- individuals held in immigration removal centres.[60]

12.42   In relation to prison complaints, the Ombudsman's remit extends to the actions of prison staff, people working in prisons and agents of the Prison Service. This includes, for example, IMB members and

59  2007/2008 Annual Report, Executive Summary, page 2.
60  As from 2007.

education staff and also encompasses contracted out prisons and escort services.

12.43   The following are excluded from his remit:[61]

- decisions involving the clinical judgments of doctors;
- policy decisions taken by a minister and the official advice to ministers upon which such decisions are based;
- the merits of decisions taken by ministers, save in cases which have been approved by ministers for consideration;
- matters falling outside of the jurisdiction of the Prison Service and National Probation Service such as issues about conviction, sentence or immigration status and the decisions and recommendations of outside bodies including the judiciary, the police, the Crown Prosecution Service and the Parole Board.

12.44   It is worth noting that decisions relating to release on home detention curfew (HDC) are within his remit as they are made by the Prison Service without ministerial involvement.

## The procedure for complaining

12.45   In order for a complaint to be eligible for investigation, the internal complaints mechanisms must first have been exhausted. This will normally entail the submission of the relevant COMP forms (or the probation service's complaints forms) although where the matter has been raised by a legal adviser on behalf of the prisoner at the appropriate level, the Ombudsman will tend to accept the complaint for investigation. In cases where there has been no reply to the final appeal for six weeks, the Ombudsman will treat this as the final determination. The complaint must be made within one month of the final determination although the Ombudsman will exercise discretion to extend that time limit in exceptional circumstances. Conversely:

> ... the Ombudsman may decide not to accept a complaint or to continue any investigation where it is considered that no worthwhile outcome can be achieved or the complaint raises no substantial issue. The Ombudsman is also free not to accept for investigation more than one complaint from a complainant at any one time unless the matters raised are serious or urgent.[62]

12.46   There is no requirement for any particular form to be completed to make a complaint. Prisons are under a duty to provide information

---

61   See PSO 2520, para 1.4.
62   www.ppo.gov.uk/about-us/terms-of-ref/index.html (para 12).

about the Ombudsman to prisoners, including displaying posters and leaflets in prison libraries, in reception and on all prisoner notice boards as well as ensuring that a video is used appropriately, for example on reception or induction at a prison.[63] The Ombudsman has provided a form for prisoners to use if needed and the prison must provide writing materials for complaints and pay the postage.[64] All complaints must be treated as confidential by prison staff as must incoming correspondence from the Ombudsman to the prisoner.[65] The Prison Service has no role in assessing eligibility as this I solely a task for the Ombudsman. The Ombudsman will normally accept letters from legal advisers as the commencement of a complaint. Figures in the 2007/8 Annual report show that around 34 per cent of complaints were eligible for investigation (out of a total number of 4,750 received).

## The investigation

12.47   The Ombudsman is allowed unfettered access to Prison and Probation Service documents for the purposes of assessing the eligibility of complaints and to conduct the investigation itself. The standard investigation procedure will involve the Ombudsman considering the relevant written material although the investigators may decide to interview the prisoner and other relevant parties, either in person on the telephone. One the initial investigation is completed the Ombudsman will submit a draft copy of the report to the Director General of the Prison Service to be checked for factual accuracy and to ensure that disclosure to the prisoner will not breach confidentiality. The draft report is then disclosed to the prisoner to check for factual accuracy. The report disclosed to the prisoner must not contain information that is:

- against the interests of national security;
- likely to prejudice the security of the prison;
- likely to put at risk a third party source of information;
- likely to be detrimental on medical or psychiatric grounds to the mental or physical health of a prisoner;
- likely to prejudice the administration of justice including legal proceedings;
- capable of attracting legal privilege.[66]

63  PSO 2520 para 2.1.
64  PSO 2520 para 3.1.
65  PSO 2520 paras 3.5–3.6.
66  PSO 2520 para 4.17.

12.48    It is aimed to complete investigations within 12 weeks. In an attempt to cope with increasing numbers of complaints, the Ombudsman has increasingly made use of a less formal procedure for determining less serious complaints where the prisoner and the Prison Service are simply sent a letter at the conclusion of the investigation containing the outcome.

12.49    As stated above, the Ombudsman does not have any binding powers and in cases where a complaint is wholly or partially upheld, he can simply issue a recommendation. The Director General of the Prison Service (or the chief probation officer of the relevant probation board) then has four weeks in which to reply. The figures published by the Ombudsman indicate that the largest single area of complaint from prisoners is, as with the IMBs, about property. The Ombudsman does not provide figures for recommendations that are made in relation to compensation, although anecdotal evidence would suggest that outside of compensation for lost property, the Ombudsman generally does not see his role as awarding compensation. This is surprising given the courts' enthusiasm for Ombudsman's schemes as an alternative to litigation[67] but may be indicative of a general lack of confidence arising from the absence of a statutory footing or any binding powers.

12.50    As the Ombudsman cannot bind the Prison and Probation Services, a complaint to his office is not a necessary precursor to applying for judicial review. Surprisingly, the most recent annual reports do not contain the number of recommendations that are rejected although earlier annual reports record that the rejection rate is very small, usually no more than five to six cases a year. However, the LSC is increasingly keen to know whether the Ombudsman can provide a potentially satisfactory remedy and this will need to be addressed on any application for public funding. The Ombudsman is also not confined to the narrow judicial review grounds for reviewing decisions but can also reach a decision about the substantive merits of the case.[68] For matters involving the less serious aspects of the prison regime and prison administration, a complaint to the Ombudsman may well be more pragmatic than resorting to judicial review.

67    For example *Anifrujeva v London Borough of Southwark* [2003] EWCA Civ 140.
68    Although the remit of the investigation extends to the merits of decisions, the Ombudsman's case reports tend to demonstrate a reluctance to genuinely engage with the merits outside of the *Wednesbury* unreasonableness approach.

## Deaths in custody and near fatal incidents

12.51  Since April 2004 and in response to concerns about the proper discharge of the state's duty to investigate deaths in custody[69] in accordance with article 2 of the ECHR, the Ombudsman has had responsibility for investigating all deaths of prisoners, young people held in young offender institutions, residents of probation approved premises, residents of immigration removal centres and those under immigration service managed escort.

12.52  The wider frame of reference in which investigations will be undertaken is explained by the Ombudsman as follows:

- to establish the circumstances and events surrounding the death, especially as regards management of the individual by the relevant service or services, but including relevant outside factors;
- to examine whether any change in operational methods, policy, practice or management arrangements would help prevent a recurrence;
- in conjunction with the NHS where appropriate, examine relevant health issues and assess clinical care;[70]
- to provide explanations and insight for the bereaved relatives;
- to assist the coroner's inquest in achieving fulfillment of the investigative obligation arising under article 2 of the European Convention on Human Rights, by ensuring as far as possible that the full facts are brought to light and any relevant failing is exposed, any commendable action or practice is identified, and any lessons from the death are learned.[71]

12.53  Beyond these overarching principles, the precise terms of reference are set on a case by case basis.

12.54  In addition to the investigation of all deaths in custody, the Ombudsman has also been tasked with conducting inquiries into near deaths where the incident raises an article 2 or 3 issue requiring some form of independent investigation.[72]

---

69  The practical aspect of these investigations is examined in greater detail in chapter 6.

70  The power to investigate clinical issues relevant to the death is in contrast with the normal complaints powers.

71  Ombudsman's terms of reference, Fatal Incidents, para 3.

72  See *R (D) v Secretary of State for the Home Department* [2006] EWCA Civ 143 and *R (JL) v Secretary of State for Justice* [2008] UKHL 68.

## Court proceedings

12.55    The extent to which the courts are able to intervene in prison life has undergone something of a revolution in the last 40 years. As recently as 1972, the Court of Appeal dismissed an application from a prisoner for the return of money deducted from her in relation to her production at court, upholding the almost untrammelled discretion of the Secretary of State in relation to the administration of prisons. In a famous passage Lord Denning explained that:

> If the courts were to entertain actions by disgruntled prisoners, the governor's life would be made intolerable. The discipline of the prison would be undermined. The Prison Rules are regulatory directions only. Even if they are not observed, they do not give rise to a cause of action.[73]

12.56    The suggestion that prison discipline could not be sustained if there was the prospect of decisions being reviewed by the courts reflected a public policy agenda and although the legal analysis is no longer sustainable, there remain echoes of these concerns in relation to judicial intervention into prison life. By and large, however, the main issue to be determined is no longer whether the courts have the jurisdiction in relation to decisions arising from the administration of prisons, but whether the decision under challenge is a matter of public law requiring a judicial review or private law requiring a claim for compensation. The classic exploration of this issue arose in the case of *O'Reilly v Mackman*[74] where the House of Lords held that claims being brought to establish declaratory relief in relation to prison disciplinary issues were public law matters arising from the administration of prisons and should therefore be brought by way of judicial review rather than as private law proceedings. Traditionally, the most common way of distinguishing between these two categories was to ascertain whether the claim was one seeking damages or was a challenge to the exercise of administrative power. These lines have tended to become more blurred in recent years with many private law claims against public authorities requiring the lawfulness of administrative action to be determined as the starting point to a claim.[75]

73    *Becker v Home Office* [1972] 2 WLR 1173.

74    [1983] 2 AC 237.

75    For example *ID v Home Office* [2006] 1 WLR 1003 but the general principle identified by the Lords in *O'Reilly* remains intact, in that public law decisions are to be challenged by way of judicial review and that claims for damages in private law are pursued through the civil courts see also the speech of Lord Diplock in *Council for Civil Service Unions v Minister of the Civil Service* [1985] AC 374 where he explained that to be susceptible to judicial review, the decision maker must be empowered by public law to take or abstain from administrative action.

# Judicial review

12.57　A claim for judicial review can be brought against inferior courts or tribunals (such as decisions of magistrates' courts or the Parole Board) or other public bodies performing public functions. Persons or bodies performing statutory functions are generally seen as public bodies. International law standards support this view with rule 88 of the European Prison Rules stipulating that they apply to privately managed prisons. The UN Human Rights Committee has also made it clear that states remain accountable for violations of prisoners' rights in privatised penitentiaries and must ensure, through effective monitoring, that private contractors respect and protect those rights.[76]

12.58　Civil Procedure Rules (CPR) Rule 54 defines a claim for judicial review as a means to review the lawfulness of an enactment, or a decision, action or failure to act in relation to the exercise of a public function.[77]

12.59　In relation to statutory provisions:

- The courts can determine whether an Act of Parliament is compatible with EU law, and if it is not give precedence to the EU law.[78]
- They can also, in respect of primary legislation, make a declaration that a provision is incompatible with rights under the ECHR.[79]
- Secondary legislation, such as statutory instruments like the Prison Rules 1999, can be declared unlawful on the same grounds as other decisions (see below).
- Policy documents such as Prison Service Orders can be reviewed declared to be unlawful in the same way.

## The development of judicial review and prison law

12.60　Domestic judicial deference to the argument that public policy should inhibit the courts from examining and reviewing the actions of prison administrators was not shared by ECtHR which, in the famous case of *Golder v United Kingdom*, stated that 'justice does not stop at the prison gates'.[80] That decision can, in many ways, be considered the commencement of prison law as it is currently understood as it provided a rebuttal of the view that prisoners were merely allowed privileges at the discretion of the executive by developing

76　Report on New Zealand, ICCPR/CO/75/NZL, at para 13, 26 July 2002.
77　CPR 54.1(2).
78　*R v Secretary of State for Transport ex p Factorframe (No 2)* [1990] 1 AC 603.
79　Human Rights Act 1998 s4 – discussed further below.
80　(1979/80) 1 EHRR 524 – the case was actually decided in 1975.

Prisoners: law and practice / chapter 12

the alternative analysis that the ordinary rights of the citizen are not automatically circumscribed by detention.

12.61     Domestically, the first major judicial incursion into prison life was made by the Court of Appeal in respect of the disciplinary procedures following the riots at Hull prison in 1976 in *R v Board of Visitors of Hull Prison ex p St Germain*.[81] The case involved the review of disciplinary powers exercised by the Boards of Visitors and established that these powers were susceptible to judicial review, as well as holding that the Prison Rules were declaratory of the rules of natural justice. Subsequent decisions of the courts gradually extended this jurisdiction so that the full range of disciplinary powers were found to be amenable to judicial review including: disciplinary transfers;[82] governor's adjudications;[83] and, segregation.[84] It is worth considering Lord Bridge's comments about the unattractive nature of the defence in the *Leech* case at some length as it is not uncommon for the Ministry of Justice to try and persuade the courts that good administration of prisons is undermined by judicial intervention:

> Mr Laws held out the prospect, as one which should make our judicial blood run cold, that opening the door to judicial review of governors' awards would make it impossible to resist an invasion by what he called 'the tentacles of the law' of many other departments of prison administration. My Lords, I decline to express an opinion on any of the illustrations advanced in support of this part of the argument. In a matter of jurisdiction it cannot be right to draw lines on a purely defensive basis and determine that the court has no jurisdiction over one matter which it ought properly to entertain for fear that acceptance of jurisdiction may set a precedent which will make it difficult to decline jurisdiction over other matters which it ought not to entertain. Historically the development of the law in accordance with coherent and consistent principles has all too often been impeded, in diverse areas of the law besides that of judicial review, by the court's fear that unless an arbitrary boundary is drawn it will be inundated by a flood of unmeritorious claims. If there are other circumstances beyond those arising from a governor's disciplinary award where the jurisdiction of the court may be invoked to remedy some injustice alleged to have been suffered by a prisoner consequent upon an abuse of power by those who administer the prison system, I am content to leave those claims for decision as they arise with every confidence in

81 [1979] 1 WLR 1401.
82 *R v Secretary of State for the Home Department ex p McAvoy* [1984] 1 WLR 1408.
83 *R v Deputy Governor of HMP Parkhurst ex p Leech* [1988] 1 AC 533.
84 *R v Deputy Governor HMP Parkhurst ex p Hague; Weldon v Home Office* [1992] 1 AC 58.

the court's ability to protect itself from abuse by declining jurisdiction where no proper basis to establish jurisdiction is shown or by the exercise of discretion to refuse a discretionary remedy for claims within jurisdiction but without substance.[85]

12.62 The fear that judicial intervention into prison life would make the administration of prisons untenable was not borne out and as the later Woolf Report would show, it was the absence of effective scrutiny and remedies that were more likely to result in rendering prisons unmanageable. It is now unimaginable that any administrative action taken by prison administrators would not be amenable to judicial review.

## Formulating challenges

12.63 It is essential to bear in mind that judicial review is not an appeal but is a technical remedy allowing the courts to assess the legality of administrative actions. Lord Hailsham explained this in the following terms:

> It is important to remember in every case that the purpose of ... [judicial review] is to ensure that the individual is given fair treatment by the authority to which he has been subjected and that it is no part of that purpose to substitute the opinion of the judiciary or of individual judges for that authority constituted by law to decide the matters in question.[86]

12.64 The concept of fair treatment is not, however, free floating and is rooted in the classic grounds for judicial review. Broadly speaking, these grounds are that the decision has been taken lawfully, that it has been taken in a procedurally fair manner and that it is not a *Wednesbury* unreasonable decision, or in cases concerning the rights protected by the HRA 1998 that it is proportionate.

12.65 This is reflected in the remedies available if an application for judicial review is successful. These are:

- a mandatory order that requires the public body to do something (formerly known as an order of mandamus);
- a prohibiting order that prevents the public body from doing something unlawful (formerly known as an order of prohibition);
- a quashing order that will quashing the public body's decision (formerly known as an order of certiorari);
- a declaration; and,
- damages (including HRA damages claims).

85  [1988] 1 AC 533 at p566.
86  *Chief Constable of North Wales Police v Evans* [1982] 1 WLR 1155.

12.66    None of these remedies allow for the court to substitute its own opinion for that of the public law decision maker.

12.67    A public body must always act lawfully and a decision made in breach of the law, whether deliberately or accidentally, will be unlawful and will therefore be subject to intervention. The grounds for judicial review have historically been divided into:

(a) Illegality – where a decision maker exceeds their statutory powers (for example a prison governor were to impose a punishment of additional days after a disciplinary hearing). Other misuses of power or discretion may come under this head such as failing to take into account relevant considerations, ignoring relevant considerations, having an improper purpose, improperly delegating a decision or fettering discretion. In exceptional cases there may be a substantive legitimate expectation to continued enjoyment of a benefit, so that removal of it amounts to abuse of power.

(b) Procedural impropriety – or the duty to act fairly. The decision maker must follow any legislative requirements as to fairness. There are also implied principles of fairness (natural justice) that public bodies must adopt depending on the issue to be decided.[87] The minimum will often be disclosure of relevant materials, an opportunity to make representations, and for reasons to be given for a decision. In some case, the importance of the rights at stake may require an oral hearing to be provided.[88] There may be a procedural legitimate expectation that a person enjoying a benefit is consulted prior to the benefit being removed.

(c) Irrationality – or *Wednesbury* unreasonableness.

(d) Breach of Convention rights under the HRA 1998 and proportionality – it is unlawful for public bodies to act in such a way as to breach the rights under the Convention incorporated by the HRA 1998.[89] The court applies proportionality when determining whether there has been a breach of Convention rights.[90]

## Illegality

12.68    This ground of challenge will include decisions where the decision maker has no lawful authority to reach that decision, or those where a wide ranging power has been granted to the decision maker but

---

87  *R v Secretary of State for the Home Department ex p Doody* [1994] 1 AC 531.

88  *R (Smith) v Parole Board* [2005] UKHL 1.

89  HRA 1998 s6.

90  *R (Daly) v Secretary of State for the Home Department* [2001] 2 AC 532.

the decision violates general public law principles by failing to take into account relevant information or to conduct a sufficient inquiry or applying an overly rigid policy. In the prisons context, there have been numerous occasions where the courts have found that decisions taken in relation to prisoners have been taken without lawful authority, either because a Prison Rule has exceeded the limits that might be placed on a prisoner's rights or because the policy contained in Prison Service Orders is itself unlawful. In *R v Secretary of State for the Home Department ex p Leech*[91] for example, a Prison Rule purporting to limit the rights of prisoners to correspond with their lawyers was deemed to be ultra vires the Prison Act 1952. Similarly, Prison Service policies have often come under challenge to establish the extent to which they are compatible with the Prison Act and the Rules. It is equally important that policies are not applied to rigidly or inflexibly that they are incapable of admitting exceptions. In the case of category A prisoners, the policy that they would be detained in category A conditions to protect the public no matter how unlikely an escape might be was held to be unlawful as it failed to take account of cases where highly dangerous prisoners might be physically incapable of an escape.[92]

## Procedural impropriety

12.69 Decisions must also be taken in a manner that is procedurally fair. The leading case on procedural fairness in the context of administrative decision making involved the procedures that had to be followed by the Secretary of State when setting the tariffs for prisoners serving mandatory life sentences.[93] In *R v Secretary of State for the Home Department ex p Doody*[94] the House of Lords held that the failure to allow the prisoners affected to know what material was being considered or to give reasons for the decision reached rendered the process unlawful. In the leading judgment, Lord Mustill set out six principles of fairness in the administrative decision making process. These included:

(i) a presumption that the assumptions that such powers will be exercised in a fair manner;

---

91 [1994] QB 198.
92 *R (Pate) v Secretary of State for the Home Department* [2002] EWHC 1018 (Admin).
93 NB the Secretary of State no longer retains this power since the enactment of the Criminal Justice Act (CJA) 2003, see chapter 10 above.
94 [1994] 1 AC 531.

(ii) a person adversely affected by the decision should generally have the opportunity to make representations before the decision has been made or if that is not possible, after it has been taken to seek to have it modified;

(iii) that fairness will often require the disclosure of the gist of material to be disclosed otherwise it is not possible to make effective representations;

(iv) the standards are no immutable and will vary according to the importance of the right at stake.

12.70    The application of these principles to prison administration has been widespread and most policies promulgated by the Prison Service will allow for prisoners to have the opportunity to know of the information that is being considered and to submit representations.[95] The courts have paid particular attention to the nature of the right at stake as influencing these standards and so higher standards are applied to decisions that have the potential to impact on liberty such category A decisions[96] or the removal of lifers from open conditions[97] than to decisions affecting the categorisation of determinate prisoners[98] or allocation to differential regimes under the Incentives and Earned Privileges Regime.[99] In *R v Secretary of State for the Home Department ex p SP*[100] a juvenile was segregated without being given the opportunity of making representations. The court held that, again as a matter of fairness, that opportunity should have been provided. The decision applied to those in the young offender institution section but not to adults (since the claimant was a young offender) reflecting the additional impact of segregation on a young offender. A further implication of procedural fairness is that reasons should normally be given so that the parties understand why a decision has been taken, that relevant matters have been taken into consideration and why submissions have been rejected.[101]

---

95  Eg the PSOs dealing with Home Detention Curfew and the Incentives and Earned Privileges Regimes.

96  *R v Secretary of State for the Home Department ex p Duggan* [1994] 3 All ER 277; *R (Lord) v Secretary of State for the Home Department* [2003] EWHC 2073 (Admin).

97  *R (Hirst) v Secretary of State for the Home Department* [2002] EWHC 1592 (Admin).

98  *R v Governor of HMP Maidstone ex p Peries* [1998] COD 150.

99  *R (Potter) v Secretary of State for the Home Department* [2001] EWHC 1041 (Admin); *R v Secretary of State for the Home Department ex p Hepworth* [1997] EWHC 324 (Admin).

100  [2004] EWCA Civ 1750.

101  See for example *R v Parole Board ex p Tinney* (2005) EWHC 863 (Admin).

12.71    Where the policy provides for a procedure or a set of criteria to be considered when making a decision, these can create a legitimate expectation that they will be followed, even if the standards are higher than might be ordered by a court. It is important to remember that a legitimate expectation arising in these circumstances can be changed and in the field of imprisonment it is highly unlikely to create a substantive rather than simply creating an expectation that certain procedures or criteria will be applied to decisions. Although prisoners will have a legitimate expectation that the policies and procedures set down in Prison Service documents such as PSOs will be followed, if the policy is subsequently changed then the right is simply to have their case considered under the new policy, even where this has changed to the detriment of the prisoner.[102]

## Human Rights Act and proportionality

12.72    With regards to unreasonableness, the traditional test is called *Wednesbury* unreasonableness, after the case of *AP Picture Houses Limited v Wednesbury Corporation*.[103] The *Wednesbury* test was one by which the court said that they would not interfere with an administrative decision on the grounds of unreasonableness unless it was so unreasonable that no reasonable authority would ever have made it.[104] However, this test has shifted since the advent of the Human Rights Act (HRA) 1998 and in a case which raises a Convention issue the courts will focus on the substance and not just the form of the decision. The courts have accepted that there is a principle of proportionality by which the more important the decision the more anxious scrutiny the courts will give to the decision procedure.

12.73    In the case of *R v Ministry of Defence ex p Smith*[105] a challenge to the government policy prohibiting gays and lesbians from serving in the armed forces the court stated that the more substantial the interference with fundamental rights, the more the courts will require by way of justification before it can be satisfied that the interference is reasonable in a public law sense. In the prisons context, the House of Lords in the case of *R v Secretary of State for the Home Department ex*

---

102  *Re Findlay* [1985] AC 318 and *R v Secretary of State for the Home Department ex p Hargreaves* [1996] COD 168.

103  [1947] 2 All ER 680.

104  Lord Green at p330: 'If a decision on a competent matter is so unreasonable that no reasonable authority could ever have come to it, then the Courts can interfere'.

105  [1996] QB 517.

*p Simms*[106] considered that the Secretary of State's interpretation of a policy prohibiting prisoners contact with the press was found to be unlawful as it interfered with an article 6 rights. Lord Steyn explained that:

> One cannot lose sight that there is at stake a fundamental or basic right, namely the right of a prisoner to seek through oral interviews to persuade a journalist to investigate the safety of the prisoner's conviction and to publicise his findings in an effort to gain access to justice for the prisoner. In these circumstances, even in the absence of an ambiguity there comes into play a presumption of general application operating as a constitutional principle ... this is called 'the principle of legality'.

12.74    Following the enactment of HRA 1998 the case of *R v Secretary of State for the Home Department ex p Daly*[107] examined the Prison Service's policy of searching prisoners' cells by requiring the prisoner to be absent during the entire search. Shortly prior to the enactment of the HRA the Court of Appeal had examined the identical issue in *R v Governor of Whitemoor Prison ex p Main*[108] and concluded that the practice was within the range of reasonable options open to prison governors providing appropriate measures were taken to ensure the free flow of information between a solicitor and a prisoner. Kennedy LJ delivered the classic exposition of the deferential approach that the courts show to decision makers adopting the *Wednesbury* aporoach:

> Once it is accepted that there are powerful arguments for correspondence being examined in the absence of the prisoner, and in my judgment there are, the only remaining issue is how best to reassure prisoners, and especially remand prisoners, that cell searchers are not exceeding their instructions. That is obviously a difficult question, but it is not, in my judgment, a question for decision by this or any other court.[109]

12.75    In contrast, when *Daly* came to be heard, evidence was submitted from a variety of sources including the Prisons Ombudsman explaining how prison security could be maintained with less intrusive searching methods. It was argued that the exclusion of the prisoner when legal documents were searched had the potential to interfere

106 [2000] AC 115.
107 [2001] UKHL 26.
108 [1999] QB 349. This case was heard by the Court of Appeal with the *Simms* case which was also dismissed but unlike Mr Simms, Mr Main did not pursue an appeal to the Lords.
109 [1999] QB 349 at 367.

with article 6 rights as it had the potential to breach legal privilege and in any event that it had 'chilling effect' on the ability to correspond with lawyers confidentially. Lord Bingham gave the main judgment in that case and instead of adopting the deferential approach to the evidence of the prison on the needs of prison security, he allowed the court to for its own view and expressly disagreed with the decision in *Main*:

> In considering these justifications, based as they are on the extensive experience of the Prison Service, it must be recognised that the prison population includes a core of dangerous, disruptive and manipulative prisoners, hostile to authority and ready to exploit for their own advantage any concession granted to them. Any search policy must accommodate this inescapable fact. I cannot however accept that the reasons put forward justify the policy in its present blanket form.[110]

12.76   Lord Bingham reached this conclusion by applying common law principles and went on to say that the same conclusion would be reached by relying on the ECtHR but this might not always be the case. He agreed with Lord Steyn's comments that there was a material difference between the *Wednesbury* and *Smith* grounds of review and the correct approach when reviewing decisions or policies where Convention rights are at stake is proportionality. The proportionality test has been described as comprising three stages:[111] whether the legislative objective is sufficiently important to justify limiting a fundamental right; whether the measures designed to meet the legislative objective are rationally connected to it; and, whether the means used to impair the right or freedom are no more than is necessary to accomplish the objective. The doctrine of proportionality may therefore require the reviewing court to assess the balance which the decision maker has struck, not merely whether it is within the range of rational or reasonable decisions. It will also go further than the traditional grounds of judicial review as it may require attention to be directed to the relevant weight accorded to interests and considerations. Although the reviewing court might be called upon to form a primary view of whether the decisions or actions of public officials are compliant with Convention rights, this does not mean that there has been a shift to merits review.[112]

---

110  [1999] QB 349 at para 19.
111  *de Freitas v Permanent Secretary of Ministry of Agriculture, Fisheries, Land and Housing* [1999] 1 AC 69.
112  *Huang v Secretary of State for the Home Department* [2007] UKHL 11.

## Human Rights Act and primary legislation

12.77    Applications for judicial review relying on HRA 1998 as the main ground of challenge have been an extremely important feature of the recent development of prison law. The *Daly* decision provided the first post-HRA example of how the principle of legality could lead to a different conclusion in respect of the same problem when addressing the fundamental rights a protected by the Convention. Although *Daly* was decided on the application of common law principles, in situations where the primary legislation requires a public authority to act in a particular manner, HRA 1998 makes provision either for the legislation to have words inserted or be read in a manner which will ensure compatibility with Convention rights[113] or for a declaration of incompatibility to be sought.[114] When a court is considering making a declaration of incompatibility, the relevant minister is entitled to be joined as a party to the proceedings.[115]

12.78    There have been many prison law cases where primary legislation has been considered under this framework. In relation to the setting of tariffs for lifers, the provisions of the Criminal Justice Act (CJA) 1991 that required the Secretary of State to set the tariff were held to be in contravention of article 6 and as the Lords did not consider they could be read compatibly with the Convention, a declaration of incompatibility was issued which eventually resulted in the new legislative regime in CJA 2003.[116] In contrast when the new legislation was enacted and it prohibited the High Court from holding oral hearings when re-setting tariffs, the Lords considered that words could be read into the statute under HRA 1998 s3 conferring discretion to convene an oral hearing where necessary.[117]

## Identifying the defendant and exhausting remedies

12.79    Guidance on the procedural requirements of an application for judicial review can be found in CPR Part 54. The general principle is that applications for judicial review must be made promptly and in any event within three months of the decision under challenge (rule 54.5). As all bureaucratic regimes can move very slowly in response to complaints, it is important to be aware of who the decision maker

113  HRA 1998 s3.
114  HRA 1998 s4.
115  HRA 1998 s5.
116  *R (Anderson) v Secretary of State for the Home Department* [2002] UKHL 46.
117  *R (Hammond) v Secretary of State for the Home Department* [2005] UKHL 69.

is and how the decision can be challenged internally in order to ensure that this time limit is not breached.

12.80    The decisions made about prisoners that may be subject to a challenge will generally fall within the powers conferred on the Governor of the prison, the Secretary of State, the Parole Board or in disciplinary cases, the district judge conducting the independent adjudication. It is a general principle of public law that internal remedies should be exhausted before an application for judicial review can proceed. In relation to claims against the Prison Service, the only available internal remedy is to make use of the formal complaints scheme, although as a letter from a solicitor should be treated in the same way as a complaint, abiding by the pre-action protocol on judicial review and sending an appropriate letter before claim will effectively exhaust all available internal remedies. Guidance on the contents of the letter before claim and the pre-action protocol can be found on the Court Service website[118] and on the Ministry of Justice website:[119] Since the rationalisation of the complaints scheme to provide for responses to complaints to be dealt with at the appropriate level, it is necessary to properly identify the legal identity of the decision maker so that the correct defendant can be named.

12.81    An explanation of who has responsibility for particular decisions can be found in chapter 2. Decisions made by the various arms of NOMS and the Prison Service will be either made on the authority of the Secretary of State, or the Governor, or both. The Prison Act 1952 requires and empowers the Secretary of State to make decisions in respect of a range of matters affecting prisoners and all decisions made either at ministerial level or by staff employed centrally by NOMS or at Prison Service Headquarters are done so on the delegated authority of the Secretary of State. As a general rule of thumb, all matters which have to be dealt with on the reserved subject complaint forms (see above) will be decisions taken on or behalf of the Secretary of State. This will include, for example, decisions in relation to category A prisoners, repatriation decisions and compassionate release. Importantly, it will also include challenges to the contents of policy documents such as PSOs.

12.82    In contrast, a number of decisions are either conferred directly upon the governor of a prison, or are devolved to the governor by the Secretary of State. The Prison Rules give the governor direct responsibility for disciplinary matters such as segregation and prison

118 www.hmcourts-service.gov.uk/cms/1220.htm
119 www.justice.gov.uk/civil/procrules_fin/contents/protocols/prot_jrv.htm

adjudications and a range of other decisions are delegated to the Governor as a matter of policy by the Secretary of State including: categorisation other than category A decisions; temporary release; the conduct of visits and other communications with the outside world; the Incentives and Earned Privileges Scheme, Home Detention Curfew; and, the transfer of prisoners. For prisoners held in contracted out prisons, the Offender Management Act 2007 ss16–20 gave Directors powers in relation to formal and informal disciplinary matters[120] and so for the purposes of public law challenges it is possible to simply substitute the director for the governor. Although the director is employed by a private company, he or she is clearly carrying out public functions so as to be challengeable in judicial review proceedings (and will also be a public authority for the purposes of HRA 1998).

12.83    There is inevitably some interplay between the two decision makers. In the case of governor's adjudications, for example, the proceedings are conducted by, or on behalf of, the governor but it is possible to apply to have these decisions reviewed by the Secretary of State. Whilst it could not be said to be an absolute necessity to utilise this review process before applying for judicial review, as a matter of practicality, this is normally a remedy that should be exhausted before commencing legal proceedings. Where an application for review has been made and rejected, the proceedings would fall to be commenced against both the governor and the Secretary of State. There may also be instances where the governor has reached a decision that is in accordance with a policy contained in a PSO but where it is contended that the contents of that policy are unlawful. An example of this has arisen where the PSO on temporary release required prison governors to reject all applications from prisoners with outstanding, unpaid confiscation orders. The challenge made was to the governor for reaching the decision to refuse temporary release and the Secretary of State for promulgating an unlawful policy.[121]

12.84    In relation to adjudications conducted by district judges as independent adjudicators, there is no mechanism for reviewing or appealing findings of guilt and only a limited appeal mechanism against the level of punishment awarded (see chapter 9 on prison discipline). Therefore, in cases where the lawfulness of the finding of guilt is under challenge, it is possible in to proceed directly to the pre-action protocol.

---

120  Ending the distinction between the powers of controllers and directors.
121  *R (Adelana) v Governor of HMP Downview & Secretary of State for Justice* [2008] EWHC 2612 (Admin).

12.85    The Parole Board is a statutory body with its own legal identity (see chapter 2 above) and so challenges to decisions made by the board or its secretariat will name that body as the defendant. There is no process of appealing or reviewing Parole Board decisions internally, other than directions made in advance of oral parole hearings[122] and so it is possible to proceed directly to the pre-action protocol. It is worth bearing in mind that there will be many occasions, especially in delay cases, where responsibility might fall between both the Secretary of State and the Parole Board and so proceedings may need to be contemplated against both.[123]

12.86    Challenges to decisions made by offender managers or on the part of the Probation Service will need to brought against either the relevant probation board or probation trust if it is one of the areas where Trusts have been established by the Offender Management Act (OMA) 2007.[124] As many challenges will involve decisions made in conjunction with either the Secretary of State or the Parole Board, it is necessary to reach a decision whether to have more than one defendant in such cases. The Probation Service does have a formal complaints procedure allowing for a written complaint to be made to the chief probation officer and an appeal against that decision to be made to the secretary of the relevant probation board or trust.[125] Usually, the submission of a letter before claim in accordance with the pre-action protocol will achieve the same aim as a complaint.

## The Ombudsman and other pre-action remedies

12.87    There is no requirement to make complaints to the Independent Monitoring Boards (IMBs) before commencing a judicial review application as although the IMB have the duty to consider prisoners' complaints, they have no power to either adjudicate upon the complaint or take action. Their role is limited to raising the matter with the appropriate authorities on behalf of the prisoner. The right of petition has long since been dismissed as not providing an effective remedy.[126]

---

122  Parole Board Rules 2004 rule 8(3).
123  See for example *R (Craig Smith) v Parole Board and Secretary of State for Justice* [2008] EWHC Civ 2998 (Admin).
124  Both Probation Boards and Probation Trusts are bodies corporate with a separate legal identity: OMA 2007 Sch 1 para 1.
125  For a copy of the complaints procedures see: www.probation.justice.gov.uk/files/pdf/Making%20a%20Complaint%20Leaflet%20English.pdf
126  See the comments of the House of Lords in *R v Deputy Governor of HMP Parkhurst ex p Leech* [1988] 1 AC 533 where Lord Bridge was very dismissive of the value of an application to a 'faceless authority'.

12.88    The question of whether a complaint needs to be made to the Prisons and Probation Ombudsman before commencing judicial review proceedings is slightly more complex from a practical point of view but on a strict legal analysis, his position is little different from that of the IMBs. As the Ombudsman is not a statutory appointment and has no powers to bind the Prison and Probation Services to any course of action, he cannot properly be classed as an effective internal remedy and so it would be very difficult for a court to require this course of action to be taken before proceeding to judicial review. From a practical perspective, there may be occasions where it is in the client's interests to pursue a complaint to the Ombudsman before or instead of a judicial review application. Cases involving matters that will be considered relatively trivial by the courts, such as IEPS decisions or categorisation decisions between category B and C may be better off being dealt with by the Ombudsman in the first instance. Although a complaint to the Ombudsman will take the case outside of the three months time limit for commencing a judicial review, if it still proves necessary to commence legal proceedings it would be very surprising if the court did not consider hat there was 'good reason'[127] to extend time providing proceedings are commenced expeditiously after the conclusion of the Ombudsman's report. The danger in making a complaint to the Ombudsman in these circumstances is that a report that is negative to the prisoner will count quite heavily against them in any subsequent judicial review.

## Judicial review and damages for human rights breaches

12.89    As judicial review is concerned with public law rights, claims for damages arising from any finding of unlawful actions or behaviour will normally be remitted to the Queen's Bench Division or the County Court for determination. The exception to this general principle will arise with HRA 1998 claims where there is a freestanding right to claim damages following a finding that there has been a violation of the rights protected by the Convention.[128] There has tended to be a rather ad hoc approach to the award of damages in ECtHR decisions as the aim of the Convention is to provide 'just satisfaction' where a

---

127  The test under the CPR.
128  HRA 1998 s8.

violation has been established. The decision in *Anufirujeva v London Borough of Southwark*[129] has confirmed that the domestic courts will view such breaches in a similar manner to awards of damages for other tortious acts where there must be proof of loss or damage.[130] Lord Woolf CJ indicated that where there is no domestic equivalent tort, awards made by Ombudsmen for maladministration would provide an appropriate comparator. This was also the approach to damages approved by the House of Lords in *R (Greenfield) v Secretary of State for the Home Department*[131] where an application was made by a prisoner to be compensated for the loss of opportunity arising from disciplinary proceedings that breached article 6 and for his frustration and distress. It was held that as a general principle, just satisfaction under the ECHR did not require the payment of damages and there would have to be a causal connection between the violation and the loss suffered to justify an award being made. In this case, the Lords did not consider that it could be established that representation at the disciplinary hearing would have achieved a different result.

12.90    A particular problem has arisen where breaches of article 5 have been established as article 5(5) states that: 'Everyone who has been the victim of arrest or detention in contravention of the provisions of this article shall have an enforceable right to compensation'. However, this provision would not appear to convey a right to be awarded compensation and merely protects the right to have a mechanism to apply for compensation. In *R (KB) v Mental Health Review Tribunal*[132] a number of mental health act detainees whose MHRT hearings had been postponed or delayed had claims for damages for breach of article 5(4) assessed. The court adopted a very restrictive approach stating that just satisfaction could be achieved without any damages being ordered. Awards were made only in cases where it could be established on the balance of probability that they would have been released if the hearings taken place on time[133] or where there was evidence of significant frustration and distress. No aggravated or exemplary damages were awarded. This approach has now become common place in prison article 5(4) delay cases. Cases where

---

129  [2003] EWCA Civ 1406.
130  See the discussion of damages in misfeasance in public office and the decision of the House of Lords in *Watkins v Home Office* [2006] UKHL 17 below.
131  [2005] UKHL 14.
132  [2004] QB 936.
133  Also see *R (Richards) v Secretary of State for the Home Department* [2004] EWHC 93 (Admin).

the prisoner cannot establish that release would have been granted or where the delay has been in relation to a hearing to allow for movement to open conditions rather than release have not attracted compensation.[134] However, it may be possible to argue that the loss of enjoyment of the residual liberty enjoyed in an open prison represents a ground for damages in domestic law.[135] It is important that claims for damages to be made in judicial review proceedings are pleaded in the claim form, including any application for aggravated or exemplary damages.

## Private law remedies

12.91    The historical developments in public law remedies were also matched by an increasing willingness on the part of the courts to examine private law claims arising from imprisonment. The House of Lords in *Raymond v Honey*[136] affirmed the oft quoted dictum that 'prisoners retain all of their civil rights, other than those expressly or impliedly taken from them by law' and although this decision was concerned with the right of access to the courts, the shift in approach to the nature of the relationship of prisoners to the state was to be profound. However, whilst the decision affirms that prisoners do not automatically lose their right to commence proceedings simply as a result of their detention, it would be wrong to assume that these rights are not in any way circumscribed by imprisonment and it is necessary to look at the various private law rights in the specific context of prisons.

12.92    Issues of identifying the correct defendant also arise in private law claims. This is not problematic where the loss, damage or injury has been caused by Prison Service employees. In such circumstances the defendant will be the Ministry of Justice (rather than the Secretary of State for Justice as in judicial review claims).

12.93    The issue is more complicated where private contractors are involved. If loss is sustained in a contracted out prison, the appropriate defendant will generally be the company which holds the contract. The private contractor will be vicariously liable for the wrongs of its staff in the same way as the Prison Service. Similarly the responsible NHS Trust or private healthcare provider will be the appropriate defendant in straightforward cases of clinical negligence.

---

134  *R (Downing) v Parole Board* [2008] EWHC 3198 (Admin).
135  *Karagozlu v Commissioner of Police for the Metropolis* discussed further below.
136  [1983] 1 AC 1.

12.94    Where however the loss or damage is sustained because of systemic failures, or where the claim for compensation is based on rights under the ECHR, the state may retain or share legal responsibility to compensate (see in particular in relation to clinical negligence claims below).

## Breach of statutory duty

12.95    The classic statements of the law in relation the extent to which prisoners can commence claims for a breach of statutory duty are contained in *Arbon v Anderson*[137] and *Becker v Home Office*[138] both of which held that the Prison Rules did not confer any rights of action on prisoners. Although the overall approach of these two cases to the extent to which civil rights survive imprisonment are no longer good law, the principle that there is no freestanding right for prisoners to commence claims for breach of statutory duty was confirmed by the House of Lords in *R v Secretary of State for the Home Department ex p Hague; Weldon v Home Office*.[139] The claim in *Hague* included a claim for false imprisonment and breach of statutory duty in relation to a period of detention in solitary confinement which was held to be unlawful by reason of procedural unfairness. However, the Lords did not consider that the Prison Act 1952 conferred a right to seek compensation for breaches of the Prison Rules as its purpose was to provide a framework for the administration and management of prisons generally rather than to simply provide prisoners with protection from personal injuries. Consequently, claims for compensation by prisoners have to establish either negligence or some other tortuous breach in order for compensation to be claimed.[140]

## False imprisonment

12.96    In the *Hague* and *Weldon* cases (above), claims were also made for false imprisonment. However, the House of Lords confirmed the longstanding principle[141] that where a prisoner has been lawfully

---

137  [1943] KB 252.
138  [1972] 2 QB 407.
139  [1992] 1 AC 58.
140  For a detailed discussion of this issue see Livingstone, Owen & Macdonald, *Prison Law*, (fourth edition, 2008, OUP) pp61–63.
141  See for example *Williams v Home Office (No 2)* [1981] 1 All ER 1211.

imprisoned, interferences with any 'residual liberty' within the prison could not give rise to a claim for false imprisonment:

> The prisoner is at all times lawfully restrained ... and if he is kept in a segregated cell at a time when, if the rules had not been misapplied, he would be in the company of other prisoners ... this is not the deprivation of his liberty of movement, which is the essence of the tort of false imprisonment, it is the substitution of one form of restraint for another.[142]

12.97    This is a view that has been shared by the ECtHR in the case of *Bollan v United Kingdom*[143] where a claim brought by a prisoner arguing that unlawful confinement to her cell for two hours breached article 5(1) was held to be inadmissible.

12.98    Although there is no claim that can be brought against the Ministry of Justice for false imprisonment on behalf of a prisoner who is lawfully detained,[144] the Lords did indicate that a claim for false imprisonment might arise in situations where there was no statutory authority for the detention, the examples mooted being a prisoner holding another prisoner hostage or against prison staff who have acted outside of their legal authority.[145] In *Toumia v Evans*[146] the Court of Appeal rejected an application to strike out a claim alleging false imprisonment against members of the Prison Officers' Association where their actions had resulted in a prisoner being locked in his cell in contravention of the governor's orders.[147] It is also important to note that in cases where there has been misfeasance in public office, the 'loss' of residual liberty can amount to a loss or damage for the purposes of claiming compensation.[148]

# Negligence

12.99    A successful claim for negligence requires the claimant to establish that 'there has been a failure to exercise the care that the circumstances

---

142  [1992] 1 AC 58 at 163C.
143  Application no 42117/98.
144  Prison Act 1952 s12(1).
145  Thus rendering a claim for vicarious liability against the Ministry of Justice untenable.
146  [1999] Prison LR 153.
147  The question of whether the Hague decision should properly survive the introduction of the HRA 1998 is explored in Lord Steyn's dissenting judgment in *R (Munjaz) v Ashworth Mental Health Trust* [2006] 2 AC 148.
148  *Karagozlu v Commissioner of Police for the Metropolis* [2006] EWCA Civ 1691 which is discussed below.

demand' and compensation can be claimed where the loss resulting from this failure is reasonably foreseeable. The most likely situations where prisoners will seek to pursue negligence claims are where there has been loss or damage to their property, where the prisoner has been the victim of an assault by other prisoners and where an injury has occurred due to unsafe premises or working conditions.

## Property claims

12.100  The duty that exists to prisoners in relation to their property is discussed in detail in chapter 5 above. On one level, litigation in relation to property is becoming less common due to the withdrawal of legal aid funding for this type of action (see the section on public funding at the start of this chapter: public funding is no longer normally available either for advice or legal representation) but this does mean that there is a greater need for prisoners to have ready access to advice on the law in this area that is accessible and comprehensible.[149]

12.101  The policy in relation to prisoners' property is contained in PSO 1250. This distinguishes between stored property and property which is held 'in possession' by the prisoner. All property must be entered on an individual property card for the prisoner. If stored property is lost, either in reception or in transit as a result of a transfer or simply lost at the central store and the property is recorded on the prisoner's property card, then liability to pay compensation will normally be accepted.

12.102  With property that is held in the possession of the prisoner, the normal approach is that liability for loss or damage will not be accepted. The reasoning behind this is that some prisoners may give their property to other prisoners or exchange it for other items or may simply be careless with it. The prisoner will have to establish that there has been some negligence on the part of the prison in order to obtain compensation for loss or damage to property held in possession. The most common examples of where liability might be established are:

- if the prisoner has been removed from normal location without any prior warning and therefore without having had time to secure in-possession property;
- where the prisoner has been temporarily transferred; and
- where the prisoner has absconded or escaped.

149  The Prisoners' Advice Service has printed leaflets available to all prisoners on a range of subjects including property.

12.103　These are all circumstances where, at some point, the prisoner ceases to be able to exercise control over the property held in possession and where control will revert back to the prison. The question to be determined is the point at which the prison effectively resumed control and whether appropriate steps were taken at that time to safeguard the property. In cases where the prisoner is removed from normal location at the behest of prison staff (eg for disciplinary or health reasons), staff will have a duty to take reasonable steps to secure the property as control over it has reverted to them. It will be necessary to ascertain the circumstances around the removal from normal location to determine whether the steps taken to secure the property were prompt and reasonable. A failure to seal a cell for some time after the removal might be an example of where the duty of care has been breached. In cases where the prisoner fails to return from temporary release or absconds/escapes from custody, as the action to relinquish effective control is voluntary (and unlawful), no liability can normally be established between the time of the escape/abscond until the time that the prison have knowledge that it has occurred. Once it has been discovered, the prison should then take reasonable steps to secure the property.

12.104　Where control over a prisoner's property reverts to the prison, the provisions of PR rule 44 apply. This requires an inventory of the property to be kept and if the property remains unclaimed for three years after the prisoner has been discharged, then it can be sold and the proceeds applied to NACRO.[150] PSO 1250 para 2.4 confirms that property not held by the prisoner must be stored at the central store at Branston and that prisoners cannot be required to dispose of property against their will. The Court of Appeal has confirmed that the purpose of Rule 43 is to permit prisoners to be deprived of physical possession of their property but not ownership.[151] This means that even where property has been confiscated from prisoners, unless there is some lawful reason why the property cannot be restored to the prisoner on release, it must be retained in stored property.[152]

12.105　Claims for compensation for property should normally be made through the complaints system with details of how the property came to be lost, a list of what exactly has been lost, where and when the items were purchased and the value of each item. Compensation will

---

150　Rule 44(3).

151　*Duggan v Governor of HMP Full Sutton* [2004] 1 WLR 1010: the case concerned an unsuccessful application by a prisoner to impose an equitable duty on the Governor to invest monies held for the prisoner whilst in custody.

152　*R (Coleman) v Governor of HMP Wayland and Secretary of State for Justice,* (2009) *Times* 23 April.

be based on the value of the item at the time it was lost or damaged and not a replacement item. Where a complaint is made it must at some stage be considered by a member of staff of sufficient seniority to authorise compensation.[153] A wing officer should be able to investigate the basic facts of the case and assess whether the complaint is justified. Any compensation will be paid by the establishment where the loss or damage occurred or by those responsible for transferring the prisoner if the loss or damage occurred in transit.[154] PSO 0150 contains further guidance for prisons on how to respond to contemplated proceedings for lost property. The relevant documentation must be obtained, usually this will be the property sheets and a decision reached on whether to contest the claim or not. Claims under £5,000 will usually be dealt with informally whereas higher value claims are sent to the Treasury Solicitor.[155] If payment of compensation is authorised, this will normally be credited to the prisoner's private cash account.

12.106　　In cases where the prison refuses to provide compensation, a complaint can be made to the Prisons and Probation Ombudsman. As noted above, property matters form the largest single category of complaints received by the Ombudsman each year. The alternative to the Ombudsman is for a claim to be made in the county court, usually through the small claims procedures. This will ordinarily be made against the Ministry of Justice or the in the case of contracted out prisons and escort companies, the private company providing the service. It is possible to obtain a waiver of the court fees on completion of an application form for fee remission available from the county court itself.

## Medical treatment

12.107　Medical care to prisoners is generally provided by Primary Care Trusts although some contracted out prisons buy in medial cover from other sources (see chapter 6 above). The question of whether treatment is adequate is therefore a matter to be determined under general clinical negligence principles. Historically, there had been a train of judicial thought that prisoners were not entitled to the same standard of medical care as those at liberty[156] but this approach is no

---

153　PSO 2510 para 12.4.1.
154　PSO 2510 para 12.4.2.
155　PSO 0150 paras 30–32 and PSO 7500 section 5.
156　*Knight v Home Office* [1990] 3 All ER 237.

longer tenable as a matter of domestic law, nor would such an approach be consistent with HRA 1998 and the principles of the ECHR. In *Brooks v Home Office*[157] the court held that a five-day delay in providing a specialist referral for a pregnant prisoner who subsequently lost her baby fell below the requisite standard of care and that the referral should have been made within two days. However, as the miscarriage occurred within that two day period the failure had not caused the loss and so the claim was dismissed.

12.108    This approach was subsequently confirmed in *R (Brooks) v Secretary of State for Justice*[158] where it was held that prisoners are entitled to the same standards of care as under the National Health Service and that, although there were inevitably some constraints for security reasons, it did not mean that the prisoner should not receive proper medical treatment. Collins J stated that:

> There are, of course, as must be recognised, some constraints which are inevitable because of security considerations, and those have to be taken into account, but they must not result in a situation which means that the prisoner does not receive the proper medical attention that he or she needs.[159]

12.109    Interestingly, the court also held that the Ministry of Justice has a public law duty to a prisoner. The continuing obligation to a prisoner in custody to ensure proper care arose even though it is the PCT and the Ministry of Justice that provides the care and this requires that proper and reasonable arrangements should be made for the care to be provided by the relevant health authority in whatever area the prisoner might be. The duty also carries an obligation to co-operate with the relevant health authority.[160]

12.110    International law standards are also clear that the healthcare offered to prisoners should not fall below those available in the community and this is also explicit in the rule 40 of the European Prison Rules. The ECtHR has made it clear that a failure to provide necessary medical attention cannot be justified for disciplinary reasons.[161] Similarly, preventative action may be necessary to safeguard physical and mental health for prisoners subject to disciplinary action.[162] A

---

157  [1999] 2 FLR 33.
158  [2008] EWHC 2401.
159  At para 6.
160  PSO 3050 contains current prison policy in relation to ensuring a continuity of healthcare for prisoners.
161  *Iorgov v Bulgaria* (2005) 40 EHRR 7.
162  *Keenan v United Kingdom* (2001) 31 EHRR 38.

failure to take appropriate preventative action or to provide adequate medial care can amount to a breach of article 3,[163] although as with the *Brooks* case, the ECtHR have tended to approach the matter very much in the clinical negligence vein.[164] In *S v Secretary of State for the Home Department*[165] the courts also held that article 8 was breached where a detainee in an Immigration Detention Centre developed anaemia and rickets, where there had been no meaningful investigation and where the development of the condition was foreseeable and avoidable. Even though healthcare in the centre was contracted out the court held that the state was responsible for the Convention breach as it was responsible for detention and compliance with the Convention.

## Negligent conditions and supervision

12.111  Prisons must be physically safe and conditions should be consistent with wider statutory provisions concerning safe working environments. As no contractual relationship exists between prisoners and prison governors, a failure to meet these standards does not automatically give rise to a claim for compensation but this does not preclude a prisoner from establishing a claim in negligence where they are required to work in dangerous conditions or with dangerous equipment or where premises are dangerous or defective.[166]

12.112  Poor prison conditions can also potentially give rise to claims for damages for breach of ECHR rights, in particular articles 3 and 8. In *Price v UK*[167] a disabled wheelchair user was held in prison conditions where she was unable to access a toilet without help from male prison officers and she was forced to sleep in her wheelchair. The ECtHR held that although there was no intention to humiliate, the conditions did amount to degrading treatment and compensation was awarded.[168]

---

163  *Hurtado v Switzerland* (1997) Series A, No 280-A.

164  *Lockwood v United Kingdom* (1993) 15 EHRR CD where a four-month deal in obtaining a second medical opinion was not considered to breach article 3 even though the second opinion discovered a malignant tumour.

165  [2007] EWHC 1654 (Admin).

166  *Pullen v Prison Commissioners* [1957] 3 All ER 470; *Christofi v Home Office* (1975) *Times* 31 July; *Ferguson v Home Office* (1997) *Times* 8 July.

167  (2002) 34 EHRR 53.

168  See also *Napier v Scottish Ministers* [2005] UKHRR 268 where the practice of slopping out in Scottish prisons was found to be in breach of article 3.

12.113    The most complex case-law has arisen in relation to the question of providing a safe environment for prisoners in terms of their protection from other prisoners. The importance of this cause of action lies in the fact that prisoners are very unlikely to be able to obtain compensation from the Criminal Injuries Compensation Authority. The scheme is discretionary and awards can be refused if it would be inappropriate to make a payment from public funds because of the person's character or past behaviour.[169] In *R v Criminal Injuries Compensation Board ex p Thompstone*[170] the Court of Appeal upheld a decision to refuse an award to a prisoner who had been assaulted whilst in custody on these grounds, even though the previous convictions were not for violence and had no connection to the injury suffered by the prisoner. It has subsequently been held that general operation of a policy refusing or reducing compensation to people with previous convictions is lawful.[171]

12.114    When a prisoner is the victim of an assault by another prisoner, the Ministry of Justice (or for contracted out prisons, the company that owns and runs the prison) will be liable in negligence if it can be established that:

- the prison had the right to control the proximity of assailant to the victim;
- reasonable care could have prevented the act; and
- it was reasonably foreseeable that loss or injury would occur if reasonable care was not taken.[172]

12.115    A number of cases have explored the circumstances in which liability can occur and have established that the prisoner must be able to demonstrate that there was a danger of an assault occurring, either because the prisoner is particularly vulnerable, or because the assailant is particularly dangerous or because the prison have failed to instigate appropriate steps to maintain prisoner safety. It is difficult to be prescriptive about the circumstances where a claim for damages might occur and each case has to be considered on its own merits.

12.116    The duty on prison staff is particularly acute for vulnerable prisoners and compensation has been awarded to prisoners where an

169  Paragraph 13c of the CICA Scheme, Tariff and Guide 2001.
170  [1984] 1 WLR 1234.
171  *R v CICB ex p Cook* [1996] 1 WLR 1032 where no award was made to the wife of a prisoner who was murdered whilst unlawfully at large from his prison sentence of 16 years for armed robbery.
172  These principles being derived from the speech of Lord Diplock in *Home Office v Dorset Yacht Company Ltd* [1970] AC 174.

escort through the main wing of a prison contrary to the governor's instructions resulted in an assault by other prisoners[173] and where negligence resulted in the disclosure of a prisoner's convictions for sexual offences to other prisoners resulting in him being assaulted.[174] By contrast, a prisoner who had been removed from the protective segregation and who was assaulted by other inmates in the toilets was unable to establish that the failure to notify the officers in the workshop rendered the prison liable for the assault as a spontaneous assault in the lavatory would not have been anticipated in any event.[175]

12.117    This decision illustrates the difficulties in establishing liability even where the prisoner is vulnerable and prison staff may have been less than scrupulous in their oversight and cases seeking to establish liability in relation to prisoners who pose a general danger to others are even more fraught with difficulty. In the case of *Hartshorn v Home Office*,[176] a prisoner succeeded in establishing liability for a failure in the overall supervision of the prison. The governor had identified that there was a heightened risk of violence at particular times and ordered that a date should be closed and guarded. This instruction was not followed and the victim was assaulted by prisoners who had gone though the unguarded gate. The limits of the finding of systemic negligence are perhaps illustrated by the decision of the Court of Appeal to reverse a finding in favour of a young offender who had been attacked with a razor blade finding that the governor had acted within his lawful discretion to adopt a system of issuing razor blades within the prison.[177] On a more positive note for prisoners, a prisoner who had been required to share a cell with another prisoner who committed suicide was permitted to proceed with a claim for psychiatric injury suffered as a result of being present at the incident.[178] The Court of Appeal accepted that there was a duty of care to the prisoner to take reasonable steps to prevent him suffering psychiatric harm.

12.118    In *Hartshorn*, the Court of Appeal were keen to stress that the decision had turned very much on its own facts and that in most cases there will need to be a 'known propensity to violence by the aggressor, known animosity to the victim or particular vulnerability

173  *Burt v Home Office* Norwich County Court, 27 June 1995, unreported.
174  *H v Home Office* (1992) *Independent* 6 May.
175  *Egerton v Home Office* [1978] Crim LR 494.
176  [1999] Prison LR 4.
177  *Thompson v Home Office* [2001] EWCA Civ 331.
178  *Butcthart v Home Office* [2006] EWCA Civ 239.

of the victim.' A series of cases have illustrated how difficult it is to satisfy these requirements in order to establish negligence on the part of the authorities. In *Palmer v Home Office*[179] a prisoner with convictions for three murders and serious convictions for violence stabbed another prisoner in the stomach with a pair of scissors but in the absence of any identifiable threat to the victim, there was no finding of negligence.[180] More recently, the Court of Appeal in *Stenning v Home Office*[181] overruled a damages award to a prisoner who had been held hostage in his cell for five hours and subjected to serious injuries even though the attacker had a custodial history of similar behaviour. Although the judge had first instance had found that there had been 'errors of judgement' that allowed him to make a finding of negligence, the Court of Appeal considered that the decisions were within the range of reasonable decisions available to the prison administrators meaning that negligence had not been made out.

## Assaults

12.119  An assault is any action that 'causes a person to fear the unlawful infliction of violence', and a battery occurs where there is a physical application of force.[182] The application of force by prison officers must be proportionate and necessary and must not persist for longer than is necessary. The use of force for longer than is necessary or without lawful authority can amount to an assault or battery.[183] A deliberate attack by prison staff can also amount to misfeasance in public office (see para 12.121 below).

12.120     In two landmark decisions concerning the use of a pain compliant techniques on young offenders held in secure training centres, it was confirmed that the use of reasonable force authorised by the Criminal Justice and Public Order Act 1994 s9 did not extend to the deliberate infliction of pain and force on children in custody without there being express permission in the Secure Training Centre Rules 1998 for the use of that force. The use of such force to ensure com-

---

179  (1998) *Guardian* 31 March.
180  See also *Porterfield v Home Office* (1988) *Independent* 9 March.
181  [2002] EWCA Civ 793.
182  The classic definition of assault can be found in *Stephens v Myers* [1830] 4 C&P 349 and for a battery in *Cole v Turner* [1704] 6 Mod Rep 149 in which it was defined as 'the least touching of another in anger'.
183  *Rodrigues v Home Office* February 1989 *Legal Action* 14.

pliance with staff orders was found to be unlawful, in breach of the legislation and a violation of article 3.[184]

## Misfeasance in public office

12.121   The *Hague* decision referred to the prospect of a claim for misfeasance in public office as a possible remedy where prison officers had deliberately abused their powers but suggested that their employers could not be vicariously liable for those acts.[185] The rationale for this was that as it is a requirement of the tort that the action is a deliberate abuse of authority, the employer could not be held to account. However, the Lords subsequently rejected this as a blanket approach to the tort in *Racz v Home Office*[186] holding that it is a question of fact and degree whether the unauthorised acts are so unconnected with the authorised duties as to be independent of and outside them.

12.122   In order to establish a claim for misfeasance, it is necessary to establish that a public officer has deliberately acted, or failed to act, in a way intended to cause harm or that the official has been reckless in performing an act knowing that there was no power and that it would cause harm. Where the action is intentional, it can either be within or outwith the lawful powers of the officer but in the case of recklessness, it must be established that the act was outside the officer's lawful powers. The need to establish such a stringent mental element makes it extremely difficult to prove this tort.

12.123   As with other tortious claims, it has been established that it is also necessary to prove loss, the House of Lords in *Watkins v Home Office*[187] having overturned a finding of the Court of Appeal that the tort 'was complete without proof of special damage'.[188] Lord Bingham considered that if the aim of awarding damages was to punish unconstitutional conduct this could be properly achieved through other methods such as judicial review, disciplinary proceedings or

---

184   *R (C) v Secretary of State for Justice* [2008] EWCA Civ 882 and *R (Pounder) v Coroner for Durham* [2009] EWHC 76 (Admin) where an inquest verdict was quashed as the coroner had refused to rule on this issue – see further chapter 8.

185   See Lord Bridge's comments: [1994] 1 AC 58 at 164D.

186   [1994] 2 AC 45.

187   [2006] UKHL 17.

188   This being the finding of of Brooke LJ in the Court of Appeal [2004] EWCA Civ 966 at para 52.

the prosecution of the offending officers.[189] Lord Bingham quoted with approval from *Garrett v Attorney-General* [190] where Blanchard J, at p349 stated:

> ... that it is insufficient to show foreseeability of damage caused by a knowing breach of duty by a public officer. The plaintiff, in our view, must prove that the official had an actual appreciation of the consequences for the plaintiff, or people in the general position of the plaintiff, of the disregard of duty, or that the official was recklessly indifferent to the consequences and can thus be taken to have been content for them to happen as they would.

12.124    An interesting further development in this field has arisen with the possibility that different prison regimes can provide sufficient freedom of movement so as to allow a degree of residual liberty that can then be removed from the prisoner and that the loss of this residual liberty is damage for the purposes of the tort. In *Karagozlu v Commissioner of Police for the Metropolis*[191] a prisoner sought to make a claim against the police for misfeasance in public office in relation to (mis)information that had been supplied to the prison authorities that had resulted in his removal from open prison conditions. The question the Court of Appeal had to determine:

> ... is whether, on the assumption that those allegations of fact are true, he is in principle entitled to general damages for a further restriction on his liberty caused by his removal to HMP Winchester.[192]

12.125    Their conclusion was that the particulars of claim did allege relevant damage:

> It appears to us that those particulars do allege relevant damage. They allege damage special to the appellant and they allege a significant loss of the liberty which he would have enjoyed if he had remained a category D prisoner at HMP Ford. He would have been much less confined both while at Ford and on day release than he was after his transfer to HMP Winchester. That damage is in our opinion a form of the special or material damage to which the House of Lords referred in *Watkins*.[193]

12.126    This decision appears to accept that prisoners held in open conditions enjoy a degree of residual liberty so that unlawful decisions to remove

189  [2006] UKHL 17 at para 26.
190  [1997] 2 NZLR 332.
191  [2006] EWCA Civ 1691.
192  At para 46.
193  Para 51.

prisoners from open conditions may give rise to grounds for damages.[194] It is arguable that if the loss of this residual liberty provides evidence of damage for the purposes of a misfeasance claim, that it can also be damage for other unlawful acts.

## Discrimination and litigation[195]

12.127 There has been surprisingly little private law litigation on behalf of prisoners in relation to discrimination issues,[196] the one reported case remaining that of *Alexander v Home Office*[197] where a black prisoner successfully recovered compensation under the Race Relations Act (RRA) 1976 for being refused employment in a prison kitchen.[198] There has, however, been a growing recognition of the importance of protecting these rights and the different statutory bodies dealing with discrimination issues were brought together with the formation of the Equalities and Human Rights Commission (EHRC) in October 2007. The EHRC is a non-departmental public body established by the Equality Act 2006 with a range of statutory duties including encouraging good practice in relation to equality, diversity and human rights and also to enforce the equality enactments.[199]

12.128 Substantial amendments have also been made to the main anti-disicrimination legislation in recent years significantly extending the scope of both the RRA 1976 and the Disability Discrimination Act (DDA) 1995 through the Race Relations (Amendment) Act 2000 and the Disability Discrimination Act 2005. The original RRA 1976 made

---

194 The House of Lords decision on control orders appears to give further support to this argument as part of the analysis of why the control orders amounted to a deprivation of liberty was because they compared unfavourably with the freedoms enjoyed by prisoners in open conditions: *Secretary of State for the Home Department v JJ and others* [2007] UKHL 45.

195 *Discrimination Law Handbook*, Palmer and others (second edition, 2007, Legal Action Group) provides a detailed practical guide to pursuing remedies in this area.

196 In public law the court in *R (C) v Secretary of State for Justice* referred to above, also held that changes to the Secure Training Centre Rules were unlawful due to a failure to conduct a race equality impact assessment as required by RRA s71 – see further chapter 5.

197 [1988] 1 WLR 968.

198 The claim was not an employment claim as prisoners are not contractually employed but was instead brought in relation to either the provision of goods and services under section 20(1) of the Act and off the management of the prison premises in a discriminatory manner under section 21(2)(a).

199 Equality Act 2006 ss8–9.

direct discrimination unlawful in relation to the provision of employment or goods and services and this has subsequently been extended
to prohibit direct or indirect discrimination by any public authority
in carrying out its public functions.[200] As the Alexander case demonstrated, the RRA 1976 already had some reach into prison establishments but the scope of the legislation now clearly extends into all
aspects of prisoners treatment. Prison Service policy in relation to
racial equality was amended to take account of these obligations and
is set out in PSO 2800 which confirms the statutory duty to prevent
both direct discrimination The legal obligations imposed upon the
Prison Service extend to positive duties to:

(a) eliminate unlawful racial discrimination;
(b) promote race equality;
(c) promote good relations between people of different racial
     groups.[201]

12.129   DDAs 1995 and 2005 provide protection to any person who 'has a
physical, sensory or mental impairment which has a long term and
substantial effect on their ability to carry out normal day to day activities'.[202] Discrimination will occur against a disabled person if that
person is treated less favourably for a reason which relates to their
disability and it cannot be shown that the treatment is justified.[203]
This is a wider description of discrimination than provided for in the
RRA 1976 which refers to less favourable treatment on the grounds of
race. The DDA requires reasonable adjustments to be made by changing practices, policies and procedure, providing aids or services and
by overcoming physical features by removal or modification.[204] However, a statutory defence of justification can be made to DDA claims.

12.130      Claims seeking for compensation for discrimination must ordinarily be brought in the County Court[205] and must be lodged within
six months of the incident that forms the subject of the application
or if the action was continuing, the last incident.[206] Where discrimination is pleaded as part of a claim for judicial review, if the application
for judicial review is successful the consequent claim for damages

200  Section 19B.
201  PSO 2800 para 2.3.
202  PSO 2850 para 2.1.
203  DDA 1995 s3A(1).
204  DDA 1995 s21.
205  RRA 1976 s57, DDA 1995 Sch 3 Part II para 6.
206  RRA 1976 s68; DDA 1995 s25.

will be remitted to the County Court for determination. Where discriminatory treatment is established, it is likely that it will also breach article 3 of the ECHR. Certainly, deliberate racial discrimination will inevitably be a breach of article 3[207] and inadvertent discrimination can amount to such a breach if its effect is to degrade or humiliate, even where that was not the intention.[208]

12.131    In addition to these statutory provisions, article 14 of the ECHR requires that Convention rights must be enjoyed without discrimination on any ground 'such as sex, race, colour, language, religion, political or other opinion, national or social origin, association with a national minority, property, birth or other status'. Article 14 is predicated on the engagement of another Convention right. However, it does not require a substantive breach of another Convention right to be established, merely that the right is engaged and that it has been applied in a discriminatory manner. This was summarised by the ECtHR in the following terms:

> The Court recalls that article 14 complements the other substantive provisions of the Convention and the Protocols. It has no independent existence since it has effect solely in relation to 'the enjoyment of the rights and freedoms' safeguarded by those provisions (see, amongst many authorities, *Sahin v Germany* [GC], (2003) 36 EHRR 765 at [85]. The application of article 14 does not necessarily presuppose the violation of one of the substantive rights guaranteed by the Convention. It is necessary but it is also sufficient for the facts of the case to fall 'within the ambit' of one or more of the Convention articles (see, among many other authorities.[209]

12.132  This has been followed domestically where parole schemes were held to fall within the ambit of article 5 even though they did not substantively engage the article and so the operation of a parole scheme in a discriminatory manner allowed a breach of article 14 to be established.[210] It is of course necessary to establish that the discrimination under article 14 is occuring in relation to someone in a comparable position. So a parole scheme that differentiates between British citizens and foreign nationals serving the same prisons sentences does provide an appropriate comparator by which to assess and measure the difference in treatment. However, it is not so straightforward to

---

207  *Abdulaziz, Cabales and Balkandali v United Kingdom* (1985) 7 EHRR 471.
208  *Price v United Kingdom* (2002) 34 EHRR 53.
209  *Stec v United Kingdom* (2005) 41 EHRR SE 295 at para 38.
210  *R (Clift) v Secretary of State for the Home Department; R (Headley & Hindawi) v Secretary of State for the Home Department* [2006] UKHL 54.

judge people in different situations, for example by trying to compare the facilities that might be available in a women's prison to those in a men's prison.

12.133    The prohibition on discrimination is somewhat wider than in domestic statute and includes the general description of other status. The aim of the article appears to be provide protection against discrimination of the basis of personal characteristics.[211] Whilst this may coincide with a conventional understanding of where discrimination might arise, such as nationality, race, gender or sexual orientation, it arguably extends further. There is very little domestic jurisprudence on this issue and so it is difficult to be confident about what 'other statuses' might be protected, but the House of Lords in *Clift* considered that that the length of a prison sentence cannot be considered a personal characteristic protected by the article. The Lords did postulate that a life sentence might be considered a personal characteristic and the Court of Appeal have been prepared to proceed on that basis, albeit having expressed some concern at the concept.[212] In *R (M) v Secretary of State for Work and Pensions*[213] homelessness was considered to be a characteristic falling within 'other status'.

12.134    Where discriminatory treatment is established, the defence of 'objective justification' is available. The burden of establishing the justification rests with the state and it must be the act of discrimination that is justified rather than the overall scheme itself. In reach this assessment, the court must determine whether the discrimination pursues a legitimate aim and if so, whether the measures are proportionate.[214]

## Obtaining evidence in prison cases

12.135    As prisoners are dependent upon prison officials to prepare documents and to record their complaints, the gathering of evidence can be problematic when preparing litigation. Whilst most documentary evidence held by the prison authorities on prisoners can be obtained, either through the Prison Service's own policies on open reporting

---

211 *Kjeldsen, Busk Madsen and Pedersen v Denmark* (1976) 1 EHRR 711.
212 *R (Waite) v London Borough of Hammersmith & Fulham* [2002] EWCA Civ 482.
213 [2008] UKHL 63.
214 [2008] UKHL 63; the Lords held that the aim of trying to persuade the homeless to seek shelter justified the discrimination.

and disclosure[215] or through Data Protection Act applications (see below), it can still be problematic for prisoners to have accurate contemporaneous records made in relation to issues that may form the subject of future litigation. However, prisoners will have no access to physical evidence that may be relevant to the issues in contention or records such as CCTV recordings. Particular problems can arise when prisoners are seeking to have their concerns recorded by the authorities and when they require injuries to be documented or photographed.

12.136　　The particular disadvantage that prisoners face in this regard means that they need to be pro-active to ensure that contemporaneous evidence is prepared and retained. Prisoners should be encouraged to keep their own records where possible, for example in the form of a diary where a complaint is being made about ongoing behaviour. In cases where distress and frustration are to be pleaded, the lack of a contemporaneous record will significantly weaken the claim. Official complaints forms should be submitted and applications to the IMBs can provide independent verification of a complaint. Where it is alleged that an injury has occurred, access to health care staff should be sought and a complaint made if the injury is not properly recorded. Legal advisers will also need to act promptly by making formal applications for material to be preserved or for complaints to be recorded prior to a visit to the prisoner due to the inevitable time lapse that occurs between an incident taking place and the instructions being received by the solicitor.

# The Data Protection Act 1998

12.137　The Data Protection Act (DPA) 1998 provides a vital tool for obtaining information and evidence from the prison authorities. DPA 1998 operates within a general framework that requires eight principles to be.[216] Personal data must be processed following these principles so that data are:

1) processed fairly and lawfully
2) obtained for specified and lawful purposes
3) adequate, relevant and not excessive
4) accurate and, where necessary, kept up-to-date

---

215 Broadly speaking, records such as disciplinary records, parole reports and sentence planning papers are all disclosed as a matter of routine.
216 Followed DPA 1998 Sch 1 Part 1.

5) not kept for longer than necessary
6) processed in accordance with the subject's rights
7) kept secure
8) not transferred abroad without adequate protection.

12.138    DPA 1998 s7 allows individuals to make a written application for the disclosure of personal data of which that individual is the subject and requires the body or authority holding the data to disclose it in an intelligible form. Data can be withheld if disclosure would cause significant damage or distress,[217] where a certificate is issued by the minister claiming that disclosure is contrary to national security,[218] or where the data has been processed for the prevention or detection of crime or the apprehension or prosecution of offenders.[219] In addition to these grounds for non-disclosure, a request can be refused if disclosure would involve a 'disproportionate effort'.[220] The decision in *R (Lord) v Secretary of State for the Home Department*[221] held that the disclosure of category A reports could not be resisted on these grounds. This prevented the Prison Service from being able to establish a class defence to the disclosure of any prison records and so material can only be withheld or redacted on a document by document basis.

12.139    Applications for information held on prisoners can be made to the Ministry of Justice's information management section[222] on payment of a £10 fee and the provision of a signed authority from the prisoner. The store appears to also hold all historical data prepared by contracted out prisons. The records disclosed should normally include medical records prepared and obtained whilst the person is in custody. Disclosure should take place within 40 days but may be longer if the records are voluminous. The process can be speeded up if the request for information is targeted on particular material, such as security intelligence or wing reports.

12.140    DPA 1998 contains an enforcement procedure if the request is not complied with or if the subject considers that the disclosure made is inadequate. Complaints can be made to the Information Commissioner who can issue enforcement notices and an application can

217  DPA 1998 s9.
218  DPA 1998 s28.
219  DPA 1998 s29.
220  DPA 1998 s8(2)(a).
221  [2003] EWHC 2073 (Admin)
222  Branston Registry, Building 16 S & T Store, Burton Road, Branston, Burton Upon Trent, Staffs DE14 3EG.

be made to the courts under the CPR Part 8.[223] If the information is considered to be inaccurate and the data holder refuses to correct it, this procedure can also be followed.

## The European Court of Human Rights

12.141 The right of individuals to petition the ECtHR still exists and although it is a remedy that is less called upon since the enactment of HRA 1998, it is a right that can still have considerable importance. Applications may be made by any individual in respect of the actions of a member state. The applicant must be a victim of a violation,[224] which generally requires the person or body making the application to be directly affected by the violation, which is somewhat different from the judicial review requirement that the applicant has sufficient interest in the case. The procedure for registering a complaint with the court is far less formal than for domestic proceedings and simply requires a letter of complaint to be sent. The court will normally then supply an application form to be completed and a form of authority for the prisoner to sign. Once an application is registered, the court will reach a preliminary decision as to whether the case discloses a potential violation of the ECHR and if so, whether it should be communicated to the government for comment or whether to simply declare the complaint inadmissible without further investigation. Once a case has been communicated to the government, the court will set time limits for the parties to respond to the questions posed on a case by case basis.

12.142 Applications can only be made after all available domestic remedies have been exhausted and the time limit for introducing an application is six months from that date.[225] Where there is no domestic remedy available, the six months time limit will run from the date of the alleged violation. Although the ECtHR has held on occasion that judicial review is not always an effective remedy, this predated the enactment of HRA 1998, and so applications for judicial review will normally be considered to constitute an effective domestic remedy. It has also been confirmed that domestic remedies are not confined to formal court proceedings and the use of administrative

---

223 Both the county court and the High Court have jurisdiction to deal with Part 8 applications.
224 ECHR art 34.
225 ECHR art 35.

remedies, such as internal prison complaints procedures can be required.[226]

12.143    Although the ability to directly enforce ECHR rights domestically through HRA 1998 has dramatically decreased the number of applications made to the court, there have been a number of significant decisions of the court where the domestic interpretation of ECHR rights has been overruled. In the prison context the court has disagreed with the domestic courts on issues such as the applicability of article 6 to prison discipline,[227] the right of prisoners to vote[228] and the provisions for artificial insemination.[229] These differences in approach have occurred particularly where the domestic provisions have very broad restrictions on fundamental rights. Notwithstanding the margin of appreciation that is afforded to domestic states by the court, there appears to be less deference to domestic policy making and legislation.

226  *McFeely v United Kingdom* (1980) 20 DR 44.
227  *Ezeh and Connors v United Kingdom* (2004) 39 EHRR 1.
228  *Hirst v United Kingdom* (2006) 42 EHRR 41.
229  *Dickson v United Kingdom* (2008) 46 EHRR 41.

# APPENDICES

# Prison Act 1952[1]

## Central administration

### 1 General control over prisons

All powers and jurisdiction in relation to prisons and prisoners which before the commencement of the Prison Act 1877 were exercisable by any other authority shall, subject to the provisions of this Act, be exercisable by the Secretary of State.

### 2 [*Repealed*.]

### 3 Officers and servants of the Secretary of State

(1) The Secretary of State may, for the purposes of this Act, appoint such officers and employ such other persons as he may, with the sanction of the Minister for the Civil Service as to number, determine.

(2) There shall be paid out of moneys provided by Parliament to [the officers and servants appointed under this section such salaries as the Secretary of State may with the consent of the Minister for the Civil Service determine.

### 4 General duties of the Secretary of State

(1) The Secretary of State shall have the general superintendence of prisons and shall make the contracts and do the other acts necessary for the maintenance of prisons and the maintenance of prisoners.

(2) Officers of the Secretary of State duly authorised in that behalf, shall visit all prisons and examine the state of buildings, the conduct of officers, the treatment and conduct of prisoners and all other matters concerning the management of prisons and shall ensure that the provisions of this Act and of any rules made under this Act are duly complied with.

(3) The Secretary of State and his officers may exercise all powers and jurisdiction exercisable at common law, by Act of Parliament, or by charter by visiting justices of a prison.

### 5 Annual report of the Secretary of State

(1) The Secretary of State shall issue an annual report on every prison and shall lay every such report before Parliament.

(2) The report shall contain—

(a) a statement of the accommodation of each prison and the daily average and highest number of prisoners confined therein;

---

1   As amended.

(b) such particulars of the work done by prisoners in each prison, including the kind and quantities of articles produced and the number of prisoners employed, as may in the opinion of the Secretary of State give the best information to Parliament;

(c) a statement of the punishments inflicted in each prison and of the offences for which they were inflicted.

## 5A Appointment and functions of Her Majesty's Chief Inspector of Prisons

(1) Her Majesty may appoint a person to be Chief Inspector of Prisons.

(2) It shall be the duty of the Chief Inspector to inspect or arrange for the inspection of prisons in England and Wales and to report to the Secretary of State on them.

(3) The Chief Inspector shall in particular report to the Secretary of State on the treatment of prisoners and conditions in prisons.

(4) The Secretary of State may refer specific matters connected with prisons in England and Wales and prisoners in them to the Chief Inspector and direct him to report on them.

(5) The Chief Inspector shall in each year submit to the Secretary of State a report in such form as the Secretary of State may direct, and the Secretary of State shall lay a copy of that report before Parliament.

(5A) Subsections (2) to (5) shall apply–

(a) in relation to removal centres within the meaning of section 147 of the Immigration and Asylum Act 1999,

(b) in relation to short-term holding facilities within the meaning of that section, and

(c) in relation to escort arrangements within the meaning of that section.

(5B) In their application by virtue of subsection (5A) subsections (2) to (5)–

(a) shall apply to centres, facilities and arrangements anywhere in the United Kingdom, and

(b) shall have effect–

(i)  as if a reference to prisons were a reference to removal centres, short-term holding facilities and escort arrangements,

(ii) as if a reference to prisoners were a reference to detained persons and persons to whom escort arrangements apply, and

(iii) with any other necessary modifications.

(6) The Chief Inspector shall be paid such salary and allowances as the Secretary of State may with the consent of the Treasury determine.

(7) Schedule A1 to this Act (which makes further provision about the Chief Inspector) has effect.[2]

## Visiting committees and boards of visitors

### 6 Independent monitoring boards

(1) [*Repealed.*]

(2) The Secretary of State shall appoint for every prison a group of independent monitors.

(2A) The groups so appointed are to be known as independent monitoring boards.

2  Subject to transitional provisions specified in Police and Justice Act 2006 s33.

(3) Rules made as aforesaid shall prescribe the functions of independent monitoring boards and shall among other things require members to pay frequent visits to the prison and hear any complaints which may be made by the prisoners and report to the Secretary of State any matter which they consider it expedient to report; and any member of an independent monitoring board may at any time enter the prison and shall have free access to every part of it and to every prisoner.

(4) [*Repealed.*]

### 7 Prison officers

(1) Every prison shall have a governor, a chaplain and such other officers as may be necessary.
(2) Every prison in which women are received shall have a sufficient number of women officers;
(3) A prison which in the opinion of the Secretary of State is large enough to require it may have a deputy governor or an assistant chaplain or both.
(4) The chaplain and any assistant chaplain shall be a clergyman of the Church of England.
(5) [*Repealed.*]

### 8 Powers of prison officers

Every prison officer while acting as such shall have all the powers, authority, protection and privileges of a constable.

### 8A Powers of search by authorised persons

(1) An authorised person] at a prison shall have the power to search any prisoner for the purpose of ascertaining whether he has any unauthorised property on his person.
(2) An authorised person searching a prisoner by virtue of this section—
 (a) shall not be entitled to require a prisoner to remove any of his clothing other than an outer coat, jacket, headgear, gloves and footwear;
 (b) may use reasonable force where necessary; and
 (c) may seize and detain any unauthorised property found on the prisoner in the course of the search.
(3) In this section 'authorised person' means a person working at the prison, of a description for the time being authorised by the governor to exercise the powers conferred by this section.
(4) The governor of a prison shall take such steps as he considers appropriate to notify to prisoners the descriptions of persons who are for the time being authorised to exercise the powers conferred by this section.
(5) In this section 'unauthorised property', in relation to a prisoner, means property which the prisoner is not authorised by prison rules or by the governor to have in his possession or, as the case may be, in his possession in a particular part of the prison.

### 9 Exercise of office of chaplain

(1) A person shall not officiate as chaplain of two prisons unless the prisons are within convenient distance of each other and are together designed to receive not more than one hundred prisoners.

(2) Notice of the nomination of a chaplain or assistant chaplain to a prison shall, within one month after it is made, be given to the bishop of the diocese in which the prison is situated; and the chaplain or assistant chaplain shall not officiate in the prison except under the authority of a licence from the bishop.

## 10 Appointment of prison ministers

(1) Where in any prison the number of prisoners who belong to a religious denomination other than the Church of England is such as in the opinion of the Secretary of State to require the appointment of a minister of that denomination, the Secretary of State may appoint such a minister to that prison.

(2) The Secretary of State may pay a minister appointed under the preceding subsection such remuneration as he thinks reasonable.

(3) The Secretary of State may allow a minister of any denomination other than the Church of England to visit prisoners of his denomination in a prison to which no minister of that denomination has been appointed under this section.

(4) No prisoner shall be visited against his will by such a minister as is mentioned in the last preceding subsection; but every prisoner not belonging to the Church of England shall be allowed, in accordance with the arrangements in force in the prison in which he is confined, to attend chapel or to be visited by the chaplain.

(5) The governor of a prison shall on the reception of each prisoner record the religious denomination to which the prisoner declares himself to belong, and shall give to any minister who under this section is appointed to the prison or permitted to visit prisoners therein a list of the prisoners who

## 11 Ejectment of prison officers and their families refusing to quit

(1) Where any living accommodation is provided for a prison officer or his family by virtue of his office, then, if he ceases to be a prison officer or is suspended from office or dies, he, or, as the case may be, his family, shall quit the accommodation when required to do so by notice of the Secretary of State.

(2) Where a prison officer or the family of a prison officer refuses or neglects to quit the accommodation forty-eight hours after the giving of such a notice as aforesaid, any two justices of the peace, on proof made to them of the facts authorising the giving of the notice and of the service of the notice and of the neglect or refusal to comply therewith, may, by warrant under their hands and seals, direct any constable, within a period specified in the warrant, to enter by force, if necessary, into the accommodation and deliver possession of it to a person acting on behalf of the Secretary of State.

## Confinement and treatment of prisoners

### 12 Place of confinement of prisoners

(1) A prisoner, whether sentenced to imprisonment or committed to prison or remand or pending trial or otherwise, may be lawfully confined in any prison.

(2) Prisoners shall be committed to such prisons as the Secretary of State may from time to time direct; and may by direction of the Secretary of State be removed during the term of their imprisonment from the prison in which

they are confined to any other prison.

(3) A writ, warrant or other legal instrument addressed to the governor of a prison and identifying that prison by its situation or by any other sufficient description shall not be invalidated by reason only that the prison is usually known by a different description.

## 13 Legal custody of prisoner

(1) Every prisoner shall be deemed to be in the legal custody of the governor of the prison.

(2) A prisoner shall be deemed to be in legal custody while he is confined in, or is being taken to or from, any prison and while he is working, or is for any other reason, outside the prison in the custody or under the control of an officer of the prison and while he is being taken to any place to which he is required or authorised by or under this Act or section 95, 98, 99 or 108(5) of the Powers of Criminal Courts (Sentencing) Act 2000 to be taken, or is kept in custody in pursuance of any such requirement or authorisation.[3]

## 14 Cells

(1) The Secretary of State shall satisfy himself from time to time that in every prison sufficient accommodation is provided for all prisoners.

(2) No cell shall be used for the confinement of a prisoner unless it is certified by an inspector that its size, lighting, heating, ventilation and fittings are adequate for health and that it allows the prisoner to communicate at any time with a prison officer.

(3) A certificate given under this section in respect of any cell may limit the period for which a prisoner may be separately confined in the cell and the number of hours a day during which a prisoner may be employed therein.

(4) The certificate shall identify the cell to which it relates by a number or mark and the cell shall be marked by that number or mark placed in a conspicuous position; and if the number or mark is changed without the consent of an inspector the certificate shall cease to have effect.

(5) An inspector may withdraw a certificate given under this section in respect of any cell if in his opinion the conditions of the cell are no longer as stated in the certificate.

(6) In every prison special cells shall be provided for the temporary confinement of refractory or violent prisoners.

## 15 [*Repealed.*]

## 16 Photographing and measuring of prisoners

The Secretary of State may make regulations as to the measuring and photographing of prisoners and such regulations may prescribe the time or times at which and the manner and dress in which prisoners shall be measured and photographed and the number of copies of the measurements and photographs of each prisoner which shall be made and the persons to whom they shall be sent.

---

3   Words in s13(2) substituted by Criminal Justice and Court Services Act (CJCSA) 2000. To be announced.

**16A Testing prisoners for drugs**

(1) If an authorisation is in force for the prison, any prison officer may, at the prison, in accordance with prison rules, require any prisoner who is confined in the prison to provide a sample of urine for the purpose of ascertaining whether he has any drug in his body.

(2) If the authorisation so provides, the power conferred by subsection (1) above shall include power to require a prisoner to provide a sample of any other description specified in the authorisation, not being an intimate sample, whether instead of or in addition to a sample of urine.

(3) In this section—

'authorisation' means an authorisation by the governor;

'drug' means any drug which is a controlled drug for the purposes of the Misuse of Drugs Act 1971;

'intimate sample' has the same meaning as in Part V of the Police and Criminal Evidence Act 1984;

'prison officer' includes a prisoner custody officer within the meaning of Part IV of the Criminal Justice Act 1991; and

'prison rules' means rules under section 47 of this Act.

**16B Power to test prisoners for alcohol**

(1) If an authorisation is in force for the prison, any prison officer may, at the prison, in accordance with prison rules, require any prisoner who is confined in the prison to provide a sample of breath for the purpose of ascertaining whether he has alcohol in his body.

(2) If the authorisation so provides, the power conferred by subsection (1) above shall include power—

(a) to require a prisoner to provide a sample of urine, whether instead of or in addition to a sample of breath, and

(b) to require a prisoner to provide a sample of any other description specified in the authorisation, not being an intimate sample, whether instead of or in addition to a sample of breath, a sample of urine or both.

(3) In this section—

'authorisation' means an authorisation by the governor;

'intimate sample' has the same meaning as in Part V of the Police and Criminal Evidence Act 1984;

'prison officer' includes a prisoner custody officer within the meaning of Part IV of the Criminal Justice Act 1991;

'prison rules' means rules under section 47 of this Act.

**17** [*Repealed.*]

**18** [*Repealed.*]

**19 Right of justice to visit prison**

(1) A justice of the peace assigned to any local justice area may at any time visit any prison in that area and any prison in which a prisoner is confined in respect of an offence committed in that area and may examine the condition of the prison and of the prisoners and enter in the visitors' book, to be kept by the governor of the prison, any observations on the condition of the prison or any abuses.

(2) Nothing in the preceding subsection shall authorise a justice of the peace to communicate with any prisoner except on the subject of his treatment in the prison.

(3) The governor of every prison shall bring any entry in the visitors' book to the attention of the independent monitoring board at their next visit.

**20** [*Repealed.*]

**21 Expenses of conveyance to prison**
A prisoner shall not in any case be liable to pay the cost of his conveyance to prison.

**22 Removal of prisoners for judicial and other purposes**
(1) Rules made under section forty-seven of this Act may provide in what manner an appellant within the meaning of Part I of the Criminal Appeal Act 1968 when in custody, is to be taken to, kept in custody at, and brought back from, any place at which he is entitled to be present for the purposes of that Act, or any place to which the Court of Criminal Appeal or any judge thereof may order him to be taken for the purpose of any proceedings of that court.

(2) The Secretary of State may—
(a) [*Repealed.*]
(b) if he is satisfied that a person so detained requires medical investigation or observation or medical or surgical treatment of any description, direct him to be taken to a hospital or other suitable place for the purpose of the investigation, observation or treatment;
and where any person is directed under this subsection to be taken to any place he shall, unless the Secretary of State otherwise directs, be kept in custody while being so taken, while at that place, and while being taken back to the prison in which he is required in accordance with law to be detained.

**23 Power of constable etc to act outside his jurisdiction**
For the purpose of taking a person to or from any prison under the order of any authority competent to give the order a constable or other officer may act outside the area of his jurisdiction and shall notwithstanding that he is so acting have all the powers, authority, protection and privileges of his office.

## Length of sentence, release on licence and temporary discharge
**24 Calculation of term of sentence**
(1) In any sentence of imprisonment the word 'month' shall, unless the contrary is expressed, be construed as meaning calendar month.
(2) [*Repealed.*]

**25–27** [*Repealed.*]

**28 Power of Secretary of State to discharge prisoners temporarily on account of ill health**
(1) If the Secretary of State is satisfied that by reason of the condition of a prisoner's health it is undesirable to detain him in prison, but that, such condition of health being due in whole or in part to the prisoner's own conduct in prison,

it is desirable that his release should be temporary and conditional only, the Secretary of State may, if he thinks fit, having regard to all the circumstances of the case, by order authorise the temporary discharge of the prisoner for such period and subject to such conditions as may be stated in the order.

(2) Where an order of temporary discharge is made in the case of a prisoner not under sentence, the order shall contain conditions requiring the attendance of the prisoner at any further proceedings on his case at which his presence may be required.

(3) Any prisoner discharged under this section shall comply with any conditions stated in the order of temporary discharge, and shall return to prison at the expiration of the period stated in the order, or of such extended period as may be fixed by any subsequent order of the Secretary of State, and if the prisoner fails so to comply or return, he may be arrested without warrant and taken back to prison.

(4) Where a prisoner under sentence is discharged in pursuance of an order of temporary discharge, the currency of the sentence shall be suspended from the day on which he is discharged from prison under the order to the day on which he is received back into prison, so that the former day shall be reckoned and the latter shall not be reckoned as part of the sentence.

(5) [*Repealed.*]

## Discharged prisoners
29 [*Repealed.*]

### 30[4] Payments for discharged prisoners
The Secretary of State may make such payments to or in respect of person released or about to be released from prison as he may with the consent of the Treasury determine.

## Provision, maintenance and closing of prisons
### 33 Power to provide prisons, etc
(1) The Secretary of State may with the approval of the Treasury alter, enlarge or rebuild any prison and build new prisons.

(2) The Secretary of State may provide new prisons by declaring to be a prison–
  (a) any building or part of a building built for the purpose or vested in him or under his control; or
  (b) any floating structure or part of such a structure constructed for the purpose or vested in him or under his control.

(3) A declaration under this section may with respect to the building or part of a building declared to be a prison make the same provisions as an order under the next following section may make with respect to an existing prison.

(4) A declaration under this section may at any time be revoked by the Secretary of State.

(5) A declaration under this section shall not be sufficient to vest the legal estate of any building in the Secretary of State.

### 34 Jurisdiction of sheriff, etc
(1) The transfer under the Prison Act 1877 of prisons and of the power and jurisdiction of prison authorities and of justices in sessions assembled and visiting

4   Substituted for sections 30–32 by Criminal Justice Act 1967 s66(3).

justices shall not be deemed to have affected the jurisdiction of any sheriff or coroner or, except to the extent of that transfer, of any justice of the peace or other officer.

(2) The Secretary of State may by order direct that, for the purpose of any enactment, rule of law or custom dependent on a prison being the prison of any county or place, any prison situated in that county or in the county in which that place is situated, or any prison provided by him in pursuance of this Act, shall be deemed to be the prison of that county or place.

### 35 Prison property

(1) Every prison and all real and personal property belonging to a prison shall be vested in the Secretary of State for Justice and may be disposed of in such manner as the Secretary of State for Justice, with the consent of the Treasury, may determine.

(2)–(4)[*Repealed.*]

### 36 Acquisition of land for prisons

(1) The Secretary of State may purchase by agreement or compulsorily, any land required for the alteration, enlargement or rebuilding of a prison or for establishing a new prison or for any other purpose connected with the management of a prison (including the provision of accommodation for officers or servants employed in a prison).

(2) The Acquisition of Land Act 1981 shall apply to the compulsory purchase of land by the Secretary of State under this section.

(3) In relation to the purchase of land by agreement under this section, the provisions of Part I of the Compulsory Purchase Act 1965 (so far as applicable) other than sections 4 to 8, section 10, and section 31, shall apply.

### 37 Closing of prisons

(1) Subject to the next following subsection, the Secretary of State may by order close any prison.

(2) Where a prison is the only prison in the county, the Secretary of State shall not make an order under this section in respect of it except for special reasons, which shall be stated in the order.

(3) In this section the expression 'county' a means a county at large.

(4) For the purposes of this and the next following section a prison shall not be deemed to be closed by reason only of its appropriation for use as a remand centre or young offender institution or secure training centre.[5]

### 38 [*Repealed.*]

## Offences

### 39 Assisting a prisoner to escape

(1) A person who–
   (a) assists a prisoner in escaping or attempting to escape from a prison, or
   (b) intending to facilitate the escape of a prisoner–
      (i) brings, throws or otherwise conveys anything into a prison,
      (ii) causes another person to bring, throw or otherwise convey anything into a prison, or

---

5   Words in s37(4) substituted by CJCSA 2000. To be announced.

654    *Prisoners: law and practice  /  appendix A*

(iii) gives anything to a prisoner or leaves anything in any place (whether inside or outside a prison),

is guilty of an offence.

(2) A person guilty of an offence under this section is liable on conviction on indictment to imprisonment for a term not exceeding ten years.

**40** [*Repealed.*]

**40A Sections 40B and 40C: classification of articles**[6]
(1) This section defines the categories of articles which are referred to in sections 40B and 40C.
(2) A List A article is any article or substance in the following list ('List A')–
  (a) a controlled drug (as defined for the purposes of the Misuse of Drugs Act 1971);
  (b) an explosive;
  (c) any firearm or ammunition (as defined in section 57 of the Firearms Act 1968);
  (d) any other offensive weapon (as defined in section 1(9) of the Police and Criminal Evidence Act 1984).
(3) A List B article is any article or substance in the following list ('List B')–
  (a) alcohol (as defined for the purposes of the Licensing Act 2003);
  (b) a mobile telephone;
  (c) a camera;
  (d) a sound-recording device.
(4) In List B–
  'camera' includes any device by means of which a photograph (as defined in section 40E) can be produced;
  'sound-recording device' includes any device by means of which a sound-recording (as defined in section 40E) can be made.
(5) The reference in paragraph (b), (c) or (d) of List B to a device of any description includes a reference to–
  (a) a component part of a device of that description; or
  (b) an article designed or adapted for use with a device of that description (including any disk, film or other separate article on which images, sounds or information may be recorded).
(6) A List C article is any article or substance prescribed for the purposes of this subsection by prison rules.
(7) The Secretary of State may by order amend this section for the purpose of–
  (a) adding an entry to List A or List B;
  (b) repealing or modifying any entry for the time being included in List A or List B;
  (c) adding, repealing or modifying any provision for the interpretation of any such entry.

**40B Conveyance etc of List A articles into or out of prison**
(1) A person who, without authorisation–

---

6  Sections 40A-40C subject to transitional provisions in Offender Management Act 2007 Sch 4 para 5.

    (a) brings, throws or otherwise conveys a List A article into or out of a prison,

    (b) causes another person to bring, throw or otherwise convey a List A article into or out of a prison,

    (c) leaves a List A article in any place (whether inside or outside a prison) intending it to come into the possession of a prisoner, or

    (d) knowing a person to be a prisoner, gives a List A article to him, is guilty of an offence.

(2) In this section 'authorisation' means authorisation given for the purposes of this section–

    (a) in relation to all prisons or prisons of a specified description, by prison rules or by the Secretary of State; or

    (b) in relation to a particular prison, by the Secretary of State or by the governor or director of the prison.

In paragraph (a) 'specified' means specified in the authorisation.

(3) Authorisation may be given to specified persons or persons of a specified description–

    (a) in relation to specified articles or articles of a specified description;

    (b) in relation to specified acts or acts of a specified description; or

    (c) on such other terms as may be specified.

In this subsection 'specified' means specified in the authorisation.

(4) Authorisation given by the Secretary of State otherwise than in writing shall be recorded in writing as soon as is reasonably practicable after being given.

(5) Authorisation given by the governor or director of a prison shall–

    (a) be given in writing; and

    (b) specify the purpose for which it is given.

(6) A person guilty of an offence under this section is liable on conviction on indictment to imprisonment for a term not exceeding ten years or to a fine (or both).

## 40C Conveyance etc. of List B or C articles into or out of prison

(1) A person who, without authorisation–

    (a) brings, throws or otherwise conveys a List B article into or out of a prison,

    (b) causes another person to bring, throw or otherwise convey a List B article into or out of a prison,

    (c) leaves a List B article in any place (whether inside or outside a prison) intending it to come into the possession of a prisoner, or

    (d) knowing a person to be a prisoner, gives a List B article to him, is guilty of an offence.

(2) A person who, without authorisation–

    (a) brings, throws or otherwise conveys a List C article into a prison intending it to come into the possession of a prisoner,

    (b) causes another person to bring, throw or otherwise convey a List C article into a prison intending it to come into the possession of a prisoner,

    (c) brings, throws or otherwise conveys a List C article out of a prison on behalf of a prisoner,

    (d) causes another person to bring, throw or otherwise convey a List C article out of a prison on behalf of a prisoner,

    (e) leaves a List C article in any place (whether inside or outside a prison) intending it to come into the possession of a prisoner, or

(f) while inside a prison, gives a List C article to a prisoner, is guilty of an offence.

(3) A person who attempts to commit an offence under subsection (2) is guilty of that offence.

(4) In proceedings for an offence under this section it is a defence for the accused to show that—

(a) he reasonably believed that he had authorisation to do the act in respect of which the proceedings are brought, or

(b) in all the circumstances there was an overriding public interest which justified the doing of that act.

(5) A person guilty of an offence under subsection (1) is liable—

(a) on conviction on indictment, to imprisonment for a term not exceeding two years or to a fine (or both);

(b) on summary conviction, to imprisonment for a term not exceeding 12 months or to a fine not exceeding the statutory maximum (or both).

(6) A person guilty of an offence under subsection (2) is liable on summary conviction to a fine not exceeding level 3 on the standard scale.

(7) In this section 'authorisation' means authorisation given for the purposes of this section; and subsections (1) to (3) of section 40E apply in relation to authorisations so given as they apply to authorisations given for the purposes of section 40D.

**40D Other offences relating to prison security**

(1) A person who, without authorisation—

(a) takes a photograph, or makes a sound-recording, inside a prison, or

(b) transmits, or causes to be transmitted, any image or any sound from inside a prison by electronic communications for simultaneous reception outside the prison,

is guilty of an offence.

(2) It is immaterial for the purposes of subsection (1)(a) where the recording medium is located.

(3) A person who, without authorisation—

(a) brings or otherwise conveys a restricted document out of a prison or causes such a document to be brought or conveyed out of a prison, or

(b) transmits, or causes to be transmitted, a restricted document (or any information derived from a restricted document) from inside a prison by means of electronic communications, is guilty of an offence.

(4) In proceedings for an offence under this section it is a defence for the accused to show that—

(a) he reasonably believed that he had authorisation to do the act in respect of which the proceedings are brought, or

(b) in all the circumstances there was an overriding public interest which justified the doing of that act.

(5) A person guilty of an offence under this section is liable—

(a) on conviction on indictment, to imprisonment for a term not exceeding two years or to a fine (or both); or

(b) on summary conviction, to imprisonment for a term not exceeding 12 months or to a fine not exceeding the statutory maximum (or both).

**40E Section 40D: meaning of 'authorisation' and other interpretation**

(1) In section 40D (and the following provisions of this section) 'authorisation' means authorisation given for the purposes of that section–

    (a) in relation to all prisons or prisons of a specified description, by prison rules or by the Secretary of State;

    (b) in relation to a particular prison–

        (i) by the Secretary of State;

        (ii) by the governor or director of the prison;

        (iii) by a person working at the prison who is authorised by the governor or director to grant authorisation on his behalf.

In paragraph (a) 'specified' means specified in the authorisation.

(2) Authorisation may be given–

    (a) to persons generally or to specified persons or persons of a specified description; and

    (b) on such terms as may be specified.

In this subsection 'specified' means specified in the authorisation.

(3) Authorisation given by or on behalf of the governor or director of a prison must be in writing.

(4) In section 40D 'restricted document' means the whole (or any part of)–

    (a) a photograph taken inside the prison;

    (b) a sound-recording made inside the prison;

    (c) a personal record (or a document containing information derived from a personal record);

    (d) any other document which contains–

        (i) information relating to an identified or identifiable relevant individual, if the disclosure of that information would or might prejudicially affect the interests of that individual; or

        (ii) information relating to any matter connected with the prison or its operation, if the disclosure of that information would or might prejudicially affect the security or operation of the prison.

(5) In subsection (4)–

'personal record' means any record which is required by prison rules to be prepared and maintained in relation to any prisoner (and it is immaterial whether or not the individual concerned is still a prisoner at the time of any alleged offence);

'relevant individual' means an individual who is or has at any time been–

    (a) a prisoner or a person working at the prison; or

    (b) a member of such a person's family or household.

(6) In section 40D and this section–

'document' means anything in which information is recorded (by whatever means);

'electronic communications' has the same meaning as in the Electronic Communications Act 2000;

'photograph' means a recording on any medium on which an image is produced or from which an image (including a moving image) may by any means be produced; and

'sound-recording' means a recording of sounds on any medium from which the sounds may by any means be reproduced.

**40F Offences under sections 40B to 40D: extension of Crown immunity**
(1) An individual who–
    (a) works at a prison;
    (b) does not do that work as a servant or agent of the Crown; and
    (c) has been designated by the Secretary of State for the purposes of this section,
    shall be treated for the purposes of the application of sections 40B to 40D as if he were doing that work as a servant or agent of the Crown.
(2) A designation for the purposes of this section may be given–
    (a) in relation to persons specified in the designation or persons of a description so specified; and
    (b) in relation to all work falling within subsection (1)(a) or only in relation to such activities as the designation may provide.

**41** [*Repealed.*]

**42 Display of notice of penalties**
The Prison Commissioners shall cause to be affixed in a conspicuous place outside every prison a notice of the penalties to which person committing offences under sections 39 to 40D are liable.

## Remand centres, detention centres and Borstal institutions
**43 Remand centres and young offender institutions[7]**
(1) The Secretary of State may provide–
    (a) remand centres, that is to say places for the detention of persons not less than 14 but under 21 years of age who are remanded or committed in custody for trial or sentence;
    (aa) young offender institutions, that is to say places for the detention of offenders sentenced to detention in a young offender institution or to custody for life or other persons who may be lawfully detained there; and
    (b) [*Repealed.*]
    (c) [*Repealed.*]
    (d) secure training centres, that is to say places in which offenders in respect of whom detention and training orders have been made under section 100 of the Powers of Criminal Courts (Sentencing) Act 2000 may be detained and given training and education and prepared for their release.
(2) The Secretary of State may from time to time direct–
    (a) that a woman aged 21 years or over who is serving a sentence of imprisonment or who has been committed to prison for default shall be detained in a remand centre or a youth custody centre instead of a prison:
    (b) that a woman aged 21 years or over who is remanded in custody or committed in custody for trial or sentence shall be detained in a remand centre instead of a prison;

---

7 Subsections 43(1)(a), (2)(c), (3), (7): repealed by CJCSA 2000 from a date to be announced. Subsections 43(2), (4) have words repealed and substituted by CJCSA 2000 and Criminal Justice and Public Order Act 1994. Date to be announced.

(c) that a person under 21 but not less than 17 years of age who is remanded in custody or committed in custody for trial or sentence shall be detained in a prison instead of a remand centre or a remand centre instead of a prison, notwithstanding anything in section 27 of the Criminal Justice Act 1948 or section 23(3) of the Children and Young Persons Act 1969.

(3) Notwithstanding subsection (1) above, any person required to be detained in an institution to which this Act applies may be detained in a remand centre for any temporary purpose and a person aged 18 years or over may be detained in such a centre for the purpose of providing maintenance and domestic services for that centre.

(4) Sections 5A, 6(2) and (3), 16, 22, 25 and 36 of this Act shall apply to remand centres, detention centres and youth custody centres and to persons detained in them as they apply to prisons and prisoners.

(4A) Sections 16, 22 and 36 of this Act shall apply to secure training centres and to persons detained in them as they apply to prisons and prisoners.

(5) The other provisions of this Act preceding this section, except sections 28 and 37(2) above, shall apply to centres of the descriptions specified in subsection (4) above and to persons detained in them as they apply to prisons and prisoners, but subject to such adaptation and modifications as may be specified in rules made by the Secretary of State.

(5A) The other provisions of this Act preceding this section, except sections 5, 5A, 6(2) and (3), 12, 14, 19, 25, 28 and 37(2) and (3) above, shall apply to secure training centres and to persons detained in them as they apply to prisons and prisoners, but subject to such adaptations and modifications as may be specified in rules made by the Secretary of State.

(6) References in the preceding provisions of this Act to imprisonment shall, so far as those provisions apply to institutions provided under this section, be construed as including references to detention in those institutions.

(7) Nothing in this section shall be taken to prejudice the operation of section 108(5) of the Powers of Criminal Courts (Sentencing) Act 2000.

**44** [*Repealed.*]

**45** [*Repealed.*]

**46** [*Repealed.*]

## Rules for the management of prisons and other institutions
**47 Rules for the management of prisons, remand centres and young offender institutions[8]**

(1) The Secretary of State may make rules for the regulation and management of prisons, remand centres, young offender institutions or secure training centres respectively, and for the classification, treatment, employment, discipline and control of persons required to be detained therein.

(2) Rules made under this section shall make provision for ensuring that a person who is charged with any offence under the rules shall be given a proper opportunity of presenting his case.

---

8 Words in subsections 47(1) and (5) repealed by CJCSA 2000 from a date to be announced.

(3) Rules made under this section may provide for the training of particular classes of persons and their allocation for that purpose to any prison or other institution in which they may lawfully be detained.

(4) Rules made under this section shall provide for the special treatment of the following persons whilst required to be detained in a prison, that is to say–

 (a) [*Repealed.*]

 (b) [*Repealed.*]

 (c) [*Repealed.*]

 (d) any person detained in a prison, not being a person serving a sentence or a person imprisoned in default of payment of a sum adjudged to be paid by him on his conviction or a person committed to custody on his conviction.

(4A) Rules made under this section shall provide for the inspection of secure training centres and the appointment of independent persons to visit secure training centres and to whom representations may be made by offenders detained in secure training centres.

(5) Rules made under this section may provide for the temporary release of persons detained in a prison, remand centre, young offender institution or secure training centre not being persons committed in custody for trial before the Crown Court or committed to be sentenced or otherwise dealt with by the Crown Court or remanded in custody by any court.

**48** [*Repealed.*]

**49 Persons unlawfully at large**

(1) Any person who, having been sentenced to imprisonment or custody for life or ordered to be detained in youth detention accommodation or in a young offenders institution, or having been committed to a prison or remand centre, is unlawfully at a large, may be arrested by a constable without warrant and taken to the place in which he is required in accordance with law to be detained.

(2) Where any person sentenced to imprisonment, or ordered to be detained in youth detention accommodation or in a young offenders institution, is unlawfully at large at any time during the period for which he is liable to be detained in pursuance of the sentence or order, then, unless the Secretary of State otherwise directs, no account shall be taken, in calculating the period for which he is liable to be so detained, of any time during which he is absent from the place in which he is required in accordance with law to be detained:
Provided that—

 (a) this subsection shall not apply to any period during which any such person as aforesaid is detained in pursuance of the sentence or order or in pursuance of any other sentence of any court in the United Kingdom in a prison or remand centre, in youth detention accommodation or in a young offenders institution;

 (b) [*Repealed.*]

 (c) [*Repealed.*]

(3) The provisions of the last preceding subsection shall apply to a person who is detained in custody in default of payment of any sum of money as if he were sentenced to imprisonment.

(4) For the purposes of this section a person who, after being temporarily released in pursuance of rules made under subsection (5) of section forty-seven of this Act, is at large at any time during the period for which he is liable to be detained in pursuance of his sentence shall be deemed to be unlawfully at large if the period for which he was temporarily released has expired or if an order recalling him has been made by the Secretary of State in pursuance of the rules.

(4A) For the purposes of this section a person shall also be deemed to be unlawfully at large if, having been temporarily released in pursuance of an intermittent custody order made under section 183 of the Criminal Justice Act 2003, he remains at large at a time when, by reason of the expiry of the period for which he was temporarily released, he is liable to be detained in pursuance of his sentence.

(5) In this section 'youth detention accommodation' 118 means —
   (a) a young offender institution;
   (b) a secure training centre; or
   (c) any other accommodation that is [youth detention ] 119 accommodation within the meaning given by section 107(1) of the Powers of Criminal Courts (Sentencing) Act 2000 (detention and training orders).

**50 Application of certain provisions to remand homes and attendance centres**
Subsection (1) of section eighteen of this Act shall apply to attendance centres as it applies to prisons.

## Supplemental

**51 Payment of expenses out of moneys provided by Parliament**
All expenses incurred in the maintenance of prisons and in the maintenance of prisoners and all other expenses of the Secretary of State incurred under this Act shall be defrayed out of moneys provided by Parliament.

**52 Exercise of power to make orders, rules and regulations**

(1) Any power of the Secretary of State to make rules or regulations under this Act and the power of the Secretary of State to make an order under section 34, 37 or 40A of this Act or under Schedule A1 to this Act shall be exercisable by statutory instrument.

(2) Any statutory instrument containing regulations made under section sixteen or an order made under section 37 of this Act, shall be laid before Parliament.

(2A) A statutory instrument containing an order under Schedule A1 to this Act shall be subject to annulment in pursuance of a resolution of either House of Parliament.

(2A)⁹ A statutory instrument containing an order under section 40A(7) which relates to List A (whether or not it also relates to List B) shall not be made unless a draft of it has been laid before, and approved by a resolution of, each House of Parliament.

(2B) A statutory instrument containing an order under section 40A(7) which relates only to List B is subject to annulment in pursuance of a resolution of either House of Parliament.

9   This is a possible drafting error. New subsection 2A added by OMA 2007 s22.

(3) The Power of the Secretary of State to make an order under section 6 or section 34 of this Act or under Schedule A1 to this Act shall include power to revoke or vary such an order.

## 53 Interpretation
(1) In this Act the following expressions have the following meanings:—
    'Attendance centre' means a centre provided by the Secretary of State under section 221 of the Criminal Justice Act 2003;
    'Prison' does not include a naval, military or air force prison;
(2) For the purposes of this Act the maintenance of a prisoner shall include all necessary expenses incurred in respect of the prisoner for food, clothing, custody and removal from one place to another, from the period of his committal to prison until his death or discharge from prison.
(3) References in this Act to the Church of England shall be construed as including references to the Church in Wales.
(4) References in this Act to any enactment shall be construed as references to that enactment as amended by any other enactment.

## 54 Consequential amendments, repeals and savings
(1) [*Repealed.*]
(2) [*Repealed.*]
(3) Nothing in this repeal shall affect any rule, order, regulation or declaration made, direction or certificate given or thing done under any enactment repealed by this Act and every such rule, order, regulation, direction, certificate or thing shall, if in force at the commencement of this Act, continue in force and be deemed to have been made, given or done under the corresponding provision of this Act.
(4) Any document referring to any Act or enactment repealed by this Act shall be construed as referring to this Act or to the corresponding enactment in this Act.
(5) The mention of particular matters in this section shall not be taken to affect the general application to this Act of section thirty-eight of the Interpretation Act 1889 (which relates to the effect of repeals).

## 55 Short title, commencement and extent
(1) This Act may be cited as the Prison Act 1952.
(2) This Act shall come into operation on the first day of October, nineteen hundred and fifty-two.
(3) [*Repealed.*]
(4) Except as provided in the Criminal Justice Act 1961, this Act shall not extend to Scotland.
(5) This Act shall not extend to Northern Ireland.
(6) But (despite subsections (4) and (5)) the following shall extend to England and Wales, Scotland and Northern Ireland–
    (a) section 5A(5A) and (5B), and
    (b) section 5A(2) to (5) in so far as they apply by virtue of section 5A(5A).

## SCHEDULE A1: FURTHER PROVISION ABOUT HER MAJESTY'S CHIEF INSPECTOR OF PRISONS

### Section 5A

**1 Delegation of functions**

(1) The Chief Inspector may delegate any of his functions (to such extent as he may determine) to another public authority.

(2) If the carrying out of an inspection is delegated under sub-paragraph (1) above it is nevertheless to be regarded for the purposes of section 5A of this Act and this Schedule as carried out by the Chief Inspector.

(3) In this Schedule 'public authority' includes any person certain of whose functions are functions of a public nature.

**2 Inspection programmes and inspection frameworks**

(1) The Chief Inspector shall from time to time, or at such times as the Secretary of State may specify by order, prepare–

    (a) a document setting out what inspections he proposes to carry out (an 'inspection programme');

    (b) a document setting out the manner in which he proposes to carry out his functions of inspecting and reporting (an 'inspection framework').

(2) Before preparing an inspection programme or an inspection framework the Chief Inspector shall consult the Secretary of State and (subject to sub-paragraph (3) below)–

    (a) Her Majesty's Chief Inspector of Constabulary,

    (b) Her Majesty's Chief Inspector of the Crown Prosecution Service,

    (c) Her Majesty's Chief Inspector of Probation for England and Wales,

    (d) Her Majesty's Chief Inspector of Court Administration,

    (e) Her Majesty's Chief Inspector of Education, Children's Services and Skills,

    (f) [*Repealed.*]

    (g) the Care Quality Commission,

    (h) the Audit Commission for Local Government and the National Health Service in England,

    (i) the Auditor General for Wales, and

    (j) any other person or body specified by an order made by the Secretary of State, and he shall send to each of those persons or bodies a copy of each programme or framework once it is prepared.

(3) The requirement in sub-paragraph (2) above to consult, and to send copies to, a person or body listed in paragraphs (a) to (j) of that sub-paragraph is subject to any agreement made between the Chief Inspector and that person or body to waive the requirement in such cases or circumstances as may be specified in the agreement.

(4) The Secretary of State may by order specify the form that inspection programmes or inspection frameworks are to take.

(5) Nothing in any inspection programme or inspection framework is to be read as preventing the Chief Inspector from making visits without notice.

**3 Inspections by other inspectors of organisations within Chief Inspector's remit**

(1) If–
  (a) a person or body within sub-paragraph (2) below is proposing to carry out an inspection that would involve inspecting a specified organisation, and
  (b) the Chief Inspector considers that the proposed inspection would impose an unreasonable burden on that organisation, or would do so if carried out in a particular manner, the Chief Inspector shall, subject to sub-paragraph (7) below, give a notice to that person or body not to carry out the proposed inspection, or not to carry it out in that manner.
(2) The persons or bodies within this sub-paragraph are–
  (a) Her Majesty's Inspectorate of Probation for England and Wales;
  (b) Her Majesty's Chief Inspector of Education, Children's Services and Skills;
  (c) [*Repealed.*]
  (d) the Care Quality Commission;
  (e) the Audit Commission for Local Government and the National Health Service in England.
(3) The Secretary of State may by order amend sub-paragraph (2) above.
(4) In sub-paragraph (1)(a) above 'specified organisation' means a person or body specified by an order made by the Secretary of State.
(5) A person or body may be specified under sub-paragraph (4) above only if it exercises functions in relation to any prison or other institution or matter falling with the scope of the Chief Inspector's duties under section 5A of this Act.
(6) A person or body may be specified under sub-paragraph (4) above in relation to particular functions that it has. In the case of a person or body so specified, sub-paragraph (1)(a) above is to be read as referring to an inspection that would involve inspecting the discharge of any of its functions in relation to which it is specified.
(7) The Secretary of State may by order specify cases or circumstances in which a notice need not, or may not, be given under this paragraph.
(8) Where a notice is given under this paragraph, the proposed inspection is not to be carried out, or (as the case may be) is not to be carried out in the manner mentioned in the notice. This is subject to sub-paragraph (9) below.
(9) The Secretary of State, if satisfied that the proposed inspection–
  (a) would not impose an unreasonable burden on the organisation in question, or
  (b) would not do so if carried out in a particular manner, may give consent to the inspection being carried out, or being carried out in that manner.
(10) The Secretary of State may by order make provision supplementing that made by this paragraph, including in particular–
  (a) provision about the form of notices;
  (b) provision prescribing the period within which notices are to be given;
  (c) provision prescribing circumstances in which notices are, or are not, to be made public;
  (d) provision for revising or withdrawing notices;
  (e) provision for setting aside notices not validly given.

#### 4 Co-operation

The Chief Inspector shall co-operate with–
(a) Her Majesty's Inspectors of Constabulary,
(b) Her Majesty's Chief Inspector of the Crown Prosecution Service,
(c) Her Majesty's Inspectorate of Probation for England and Wales,
(d) Her Majesty's Inspectorate of Court Administration,
(e) Her Majesty's Chief Inspector of Education, Children's Services and Skills,
(f) the Commission for Healthcare Audit and Inspection,
(g) the Commission for Social Care Inspection,
(h) the Audit Commission for Local Government and the National Health Service in England,
(i) the Auditor General for Wales, and
(j) any other public authority specified by an order made by the Secretary of State,

where it is appropriate to do so for the efficient and effective discharge of his functions.

#### 5 Joint action

(1) The Chief Inspector may act jointly with another public authority where it is appropriate to do so for the efficient and effective discharge of his functions.
(2) The Chief Inspector, acting jointly with the chief inspectors within sub-paragraph (3) below, shall prepare a document (a 'joint inspection programme') setting out–
  (a) what inspections he proposes to carry out in the exercise of the power conferred by sub-paragraph (1) above, and
  (b) what inspections the chief inspectors within sub-paragraph (3) below (or their inspectorates) propose to carry out in the exercise of any corresponding powers conferred on them.
(3) The chief inspectors within this sub-paragraph are–
  (a) Her Majesty's Chief Inspector of Constabulary;
  (b) Her Majesty's Chief Inspector of the Crown Prosecution Service;
  (c) Her Majesty's Chief Inspector of Probation for England and Wales;
  (d) Her Majesty's Chief Inspector of Court Administration.
(4) A joint inspection programme shall be prepared from time to time or at such times as the Secretary of State, the Lord Chancellor and the Attorney General may jointly direct.
(5) Sub-paragraphs (2), (3) and (5) of paragraph 2 above apply to a joint inspection programme as they apply to a document prepared under that paragraph.
(6) The Secretary of State, the Lord Chancellor and the Attorney General may by a joint direction specify the form that a joint inspection programme is to take.

#### 6 Assistance for other public authorities

(1) The Chief Inspector may if he thinks it appropriate to do so provide assistance to any other public authority for the purpose of the exercise by that authority of its functions.
(2) Assistance under this paragraph may be provided on such terms (including terms as to payment) as the Chief Inspector thinks fit.

FIRST SCHEDULE [*Repealed.*]

SECOND SCHEDULE [*Repealed.*]

THIRD SCHEDULE [*Repealed.*]

FOURTH SCHEDULE [*Repealed.*]

# Prison Rules 1999[1]

## PART I

**1 Citation and commencement**

These Rules may be cited as the Prison Rules 1999 and shall come into force on 1st April 1999.

**2 Interpretation**

(1) In these Rules, where the context so admits, the expression–

'adjudicator' means a District Judge (Magistrates' Courts) or Deputy District Judge (Magistrates' Courts) approved by the Lord Chancellor for the purpose of inquiring into a charge which has been referred to him;

'communication' includes any written or drawn communication from a prisoner to any other person, whether intended to be transmitted by means of a postal service or not, and any communication from a prisoner to any other person transmitted by means of a telecommunications system;

'controlled drug' means any drug which is a controlled drug for the purposes of the Misuse of Drugs Act 1971;

'convicted prisoner' means, subject to the provisions of rule 7(3), a prisoner who has been convicted or found guilty of an offence or committed or attached for contempt of court or for failing to do or abstain from doing anything required to be done or left undone, and the expression 'unconvicted prisoner' shall be construed accordingly;

'fixed term prisoner' has the meaning assigned to it by section 237(1) of the Criminal Justice Act 2003;

'governor' includes an officer for the time being in charge of a prison;

'health care professional' means a person who is a member of a profession regulated by a body mentioned in section 25(3) of the National Health Service Reform and Health Care Professions Act 2002 and who is working within the prison pursuant to rule 20(3);

'information technology equipment' includes any laptop or notebook computer, desktop computer, gaming console, handheld computing device, personal organiser or any electronic device containing a computer processor and capable of connecting to the internet, and any reference to information technology equipment includes a reference to–

(a) a component part of a device of that description; or

(b) any article designed or adapted for use with any information technology

1 SI No 728. As amended.

equipment (including any disk, film or other separate article on which images, sounds, computer code or other information may be stored or recorded);

'intercepted material' means the contents of any communication intercepted pursuant to these Rules;

'intermittent custody order' has the meaning assigned to it by section 183 of the Criminal Justice Act 2003;

'legal adviser' means, in relation to a prisoner, his counsel or solicitor, and includes a clerk acting on behalf of his solicitor;

'officer' means an officer of a prison and, for the purposes of rule 40(2), includes a prisoner custody officer who is authorised to perform escort functions in accordance with section 89 of the Criminal Justice Act 1991;

'prison minister' means, in relation to a prison, a minister appointed to that prison under section 10 of the Prison Act 1952;

'registered medical practitioner' and 'registered nurse' mean a practitioner or nurse who is working within the prison pursuant to rule 20(3);

'short-term prisoner' and 'long-term prisoner' have the meanings assigned to them by section 33(5) of the Criminal Justice Act 1991, as extended by sections 43(1) and 45(1) of that Act;

'telecommunications system' means any system (including the apparatus comprised in it) which exists for the purpose of facilitating the transmission of communications by any means involving the use of electrical or electro-magnetic energy;

'the 2003 Act' means the Criminal Justice Act 2003.

(2) In these Rules–

(a) a reference to an award of additional days means additional days awarded under these Rules by virtue of section 42 of the Criminal Justice Act 1991 or by virtue of section 257 of the 2003 Act;

(b) a reference to the Church of England includes a reference to the Church in Wales; and

(c) a reference to a numbered rule is, unless otherwise stated, a reference to the rule of that number in these Rules and a reference in a rule to a numbered paragraph is, unless otherwise stated, a reference to the paragraph of that number in that rule.

## PART II: PRISONERS

### GENERAL

**3 Purpose of prison training and treatment**

The purpose of the training and treatment of convicted prisoners shall be to encourage and assist them to lead a good and useful life.

**4 Outside contacts**

(1) Special attention shall be paid to the maintenance of such relationships between a prisoner and his family as are desirable in the best interests of both.

(2) A prisoner shall be encouraged and assisted to establish and maintain such relations with persons and agencies outside prison as may, in the opinion of the governor, best promote the interests of his family and his own social rehabilitation.

**5 After care**
From the beginning of a prisoner's sentence, consideration shall be given, in consultation with the appropriate after-care organisation, to the prisoner's future and the assistance to be given him on and after his release.

**6 Maintenance of order and discipline**
(1) Order and discipline shall be maintained with firmness, but with no more restriction than is required for safe custody and well ordered community life.
(2) In the control of prisoners, officers shall seek to influence them through their own example and leadership, and to enlist their willing co-operation.
(3) At all times the treatment of prisoners shall be such as to encourage their self-respect and a sense of personal responsibility, but a prisoner shall not be employed in any disciplinary capacity.

**7 Classification of prisoners**
(1) Prisoners shall be classified, in accordance with any directions of the Secretary of State, having regard to their age, temperament and record and with a view to maintaining good order and facilitating training and, in the case of convicted prisoners, of furthering the purpose of their training and treatment as provided by rule 3.
(2) Unconvicted prisoners:
  (a) shall be kept out of contact with convicted prisoners as far as the governor considers it can reasonably be done, unless and to the extent that they have consented to share residential accommodation or participate in any activity with convicted prisoners; and
  (b) shall under no circumstances be required to share a cell with a convicted prisoner.
(3) Prisoners committed or attached for contempt of court, or for failing to do or abstain from doing anything required to be done or left undone:
  (a) shall be treated as a separate class for the purposes of this rule;
  (b) notwithstanding anything in this rule, may be permitted to associate with any other class of prisoners if they are willing to do so; and
  (c) shall have the same privileges as an unconvicted prisoner under rules 20(5), 23(1) and 35(1).
(4) Nothing in this rule shall require a prisoner to be deprived unduly of the society of other persons.

**8 Privileges**
(1) There shall be established at every prison systems of privileges approved by the Secretary of State and appropriate to the classes of prisoners there, which shall include arrangements under which money earned by prisoners in prison may be spent by them within the prison.
(2) Systems of privileges approved under paragraph (1) may include arrangements under which prisoners may be allowed time outside their cells and in association with one another, in excess of the minimum time which, subject to the other provisions of these Rules apart from this rule, is otherwise allowed to prisoners at the prison for this purpose.
(3) Systems of privileges approved under paragraph (1) may include arrangements under which privileges may be granted to prisoners only in so far as

they have met, and for so long as they continue to meet, specified standards in their behaviour and their performance in work or other activities.

(4) Systems of privileges which include arrangements of the kind referred to in paragraph (3) shall include procedures to be followed in determining whether or not any of the privileges concerned shall be granted, or shall continue to be granted, to a prisoner; such procedures shall include a requirement that the prisoner be given reasons for any decision adverse to him together with a statement of the means by which he may appeal against it.

(5) Nothing in this rule shall be taken to confer on a prisoner any entitlement to any privilege or to affect any provision in these Rules other than this rule as a result of which any privilege may be forfeited or otherwise lost or a prisoner deprived of association with other prisoners.

### 9 Temporary release

(1) The Secretary of State may, in accordance with the other provisions of this rule, release temporarily a prisoner to whom this rule applies.

(2) A prisoner may be released under this rule for any period or periods and subject to any conditions.

(3) A prisoner may only be released under this rule:
   (a) on compassionate grounds or for the purpose of receiving medical treatment;
   (b) to engage in employment or voluntary work;
   (c) to receive instruction or training which cannot reasonably be provided in the prison;
   (d) to enable him to participate in any proceedings before any court, tribunal or inquiry;
   (e) to enable him to consult with his legal adviser in circumstances where it is not reasonably practicable for the consultation to take place in the prison;
   (f) to assist any police officer in any enquiries;
   (g) to facilitate the prisoner's transfer between prisons;
   (h) to assist him in maintaining family ties or in his transition from prison life to freedom.
   (i) [*Revoked.*]

(4) A prisoner shall not be released under this rule unless the Secretary of State is satisfied that there would not be an unacceptable risk of his committing offences whilst released or otherwise failing to comply with any condition upon which he is released.

(5) The Secretary of State shall not release under this rule a prisoner serving a sentence of imprisonment if, having regard to:
   (a) the period or proportion of his sentence which the prisoner has served or, in a case where paragraph (10) does not apply to require all the sentences he is serving to be treated as a single term, the period or proportion of any such sentence he has served; and
   (b) the frequency with which the prisoner has been granted temporary release under this rule, the Secretary of State is of the opinion that the release of the prisoner would be likely to undermine public confidence in the administration of justice.

(6) If a prisoner has been temporarily released under this rule during the relevant period and has been sentenced to imprisonment for a criminal offence com-

mitted whilst at large following that release, he shall not be released under this rule unless his release, having regard to the circumstances of this conviction, would not, in the opinion of the Secretary of State, be likely to undermine public confidence in the administration of justice.

(7) For the purposes of paragraph (6), 'the relevant period':

    (a) in the case of a prisoner serving a determinate sentence of imprisonment, is the period he has served in respect of that sentence, unless, notwithstanding paragraph (10), the sentences he is serving do not fall to be treated as a single term, in which case it is the period since he was last released in relation to one of those sentences under Part II of the Criminal Justice Act 1991 ('the 1991 Act') or Chapter 6 of Part 12 of the 2003 Act;

    (b) in the case of a prisoner serving an indeterminate sentence of imprisonment, is, if the prisoner has previously been released on licence under Part II of the Crime (Sentences) Act 1997 or Part II of the 1991 Act or Chapter 6 of Part 12 of the 2003 Act, the period since the date of his last recall to prison in respect of that sentence or, where the prisoner has not been so released, the period he has served in respect of that sentence; or

    (c) in the case of a prisoner detained in prison for any other reason, is the period for which the prisoner has been detained for that reason;

save that where a prisoner falls within two or more of sub-paragraphs (a) to (c), the 'relevant period', in the case of that prisoner, shall be determined by whichever of the applicable sub-paragraphs produces the longer period.

(8) A prisoner released under this rule may be recalled to prison at any time whether the conditions of his release have been broken or not.

(9) This rule applies to prisoners other than persons committed in custody for trial or to be sentenced or otherwise dealt with before or by any Crown Court or remanded in custody by any court.

(10) For the purposes of any reference in this rule to an inmate's sentence, consecutive terms and terms which are wholly or partly concurrent shall be treated as a single term.

(11) In this rule:

    (a) any reference to a sentence of imprisonment shall be construed as including any sentence to detention or custody; and

    (b) any reference to release on licence or otherwise under Part II of the 1991 Act includes any release on licence under any legislation providing for early release on licence.

## 10 Information to prisoners

(1) Every prisoner shall be provided, as soon as possible after his reception into prison, and in any case within 24 hours, with information in writing about those provisions of these Rules and other matters which it is necessary that he should know, including earnings and privileges, and the proper means of making requests and complaints.

(2) In the case of a prisoner aged less than 18, or a prisoner aged 18 or over who cannot read or appears to have difficulty in understanding the information so provided, the governor, or an officer deputed by him, shall so explain it to him that he can understand his rights and obligations.

(3) A copy of these Rules shall be made available to any prisoner who requests it.

## 11 Requests and complaints

(1) A request or complaint to the governor or independent monitoring board relating to a prisoner's imprisonment shall be made orally or in writing by the prisoner.

(2) On every day the governor shall hear any requests and complaints that are made to him under paragraph (1).

(3) A written request or complaint under paragraph (1) may be made in confidence.

## WOMEN PRISONERS

### 12 Women prisoners

(1) Women prisoners shall normally be kept separate from male prisoners.

(2) The Secretary of State may, subject to any conditions he thinks fit, permit a woman prisoner to have her baby with her in prison, and everything necessary for the baby's maintenance and care may be provided there.

## RELIGION

### 13 Religious denomination

A prisoner shall be treated as being of the religious denomination stated in the record made in pursuance of section 10(5) of the Prison Act 1952 but the governor may, in a proper case and after due enquiry, direct that record to be amended.

### 14 Special duties of chaplains and prison ministers

(1) The chaplain or a prison minister of a prison shall–
   (a) interview every prisoner of his denomination individually soon after the prisoner's reception into that prison and shortly before his release; and
   (b) if no other arrangements are made, read the burial service at the funeral of any prisoner of his denomination who dies in that prison.

(2) The chaplain shall visit daily all prisoners belonging to the Church of England who are sick, under restraint or undergoing cellular confinement; and a prison minister shall do the same, as far as he reasonably can, for prisoners of his denomination.

(3) The chaplain shall visit any prisoner not of the Church of England who is sick, under restraint or undergoing cellular confinement, and is not regularly visited by a minister of his denomination, if the prisoner is willing.

### 15 Regular visits by ministers of religion

(1) The chaplain shall visit the prisoners belonging to the Church of England.

(2) A prison minister shall visit the prisoners of his denomination as regularly as he reasonably can.

(3) Where a prisoner belongs to a denomination for which no prison minister has been appointed, the governor shall do what he reasonably can, if so requested by the prisoner, to arrange for him to be visited regularly by a minister of that denomination.

### 16 Religious services

(1) The chaplain shall conduct Divine Service for prisoners belonging to the Church of England at least once every Sunday, Christmas Day and Good Fri-

day, and such celebrations of Holy Communion and weekday services as may be arranged.
(2) Prison ministers shall conduct Divine Service for prisoners of their denominations at such times as may be arranged.

### 17 Substitute for chaplain or prison minister
(1) A person approved by the Secretary of State may act for the chaplain in his absence.
(2) A prison minister may, with the leave of the Secretary of State, appoint a substitute to act for him in his absence.

### 18 Sunday work
Arrangements shall be made so as not to require prisoners of the Christian religion to do any unnecessary work on Sunday, Christmas Day or Good Friday, or prisoners of other religions to do any such work on their recognised days of religious observance.

### 19 Religious books
There shall, so far as reasonably practicable, be available for the personal use of every prisoner such religious books recognised by his denomination as are approved by the Secretary of State for use in prisons.

## MEDICAL ATTENTION
### 20 Medical attendance
(1) The medical officer of a prison shall have the care of the health, mental and physical, of the prisoners in that prison.
(2) Every request by a prisoner to see a registered medical practitioner, a registered nurse or other health care professional such as is mentioned in paragraph (3) shall be recorded by the officer to whom it is made and promptly passed on to the medical officer.
(3)[2] The medical officer may consult–
 (a) a registered medical practitioner,
 (b) a registered nurse, or
 (c) any other health care professional,
and such a person may work within the prison under the general supervision of the medical officer.
(4) [*Revoked.*]
(5) If an unconvicted prisoner desires the attendance of a registered medical practitioner or dentist, and will pay any expense incurred, the governor shall, if he is satisfied that there are reasonable grounds for the request and unless the Secretary of State otherwise directs, allow him to be visited and treated by that practitioner or dentist in consultation with a registered medical practitioner such as is mentioned in paragraph (3).
(6) Subject to any directions given in the particular case by the Secretary of State, a registered medical practitioner selected by or on behalf of a prisoner who is a party to any legal proceedings shall be afforded reasonable facilities for examining him in connection with the proceedings, and may do so out of hearing but in the sight of an officer.

2   Words inserted by SI 2002 No 3135. Has effect from a date to be announced.

**21 Special illnesses and conditions**
(1) A registered medical practitioner such as is mentioned in rule 20(3) shall report to the governor on the case of any prisoner whose health is likely to be injuriously affected by continued imprisonment. The governor shall send the report to the Secretary of State without delay together with his own recommendations.
(2) [*Revoked.*]

**22 Notification of illness or death**
(1) If a prisoner dies, becomes seriously ill, sustains any severe injury or is removed to hospital on account of mental disorder, the governor shall, if he knows his or her address, at once inform the prisoner's spouse or next of kin, and also any person who the prisoner may reasonably have asked should be informed.
(2) If a prisoner dies, the governor shall give notice immediately to the coroner having jurisdiction, to the independent monitoring board and to the Secretary of State.

## PHYSICAL WELFARE AND WORK
**23 Clothing**
(1) An unconvicted prisoner may wear clothing of his own if and in so far as it is suitable, tidy and clean, and shall be permitted to arrange for the supply to him from outside prison of sufficient clean clothing:
    Provided that, subject to rule 40(3):
    (a) he may be required, if and for so long as there are reasonable grounds to believe that there is a serious risk of his attempting to escape, to wear items of clothing which are distinctive by virtue of being specially marked or coloured or both; and
    (b) he may be required, if and for so long as the Secretary of State is of the opinion that he would, if he escaped, be highly dangerous to the public or the police or the security of the State, to wear clothing provided under this rule.
(2) Subject to paragraph (1) above, the provisions of this rule shall apply to an unconvicted prisoner as to a convicted prisoner.
(3) A convicted prisoner shall be provided with clothing adequate for warmth and health in accordance with a scale approved by the Secretary of State.
(4) The clothing provided under this rule shall include suitable protective clothing for use at work, where this is needed.
(5) Subject to rule 40(3), a convicted prisoner shall wear clothing provided under this rule and no other, except on the directions of the Secretary of State or as a privilege under rule 8.
(6) A prisoner may be provided, where necessary, with suitable and adequate clothing on his release.

**24 Food**
(1) Subject to any directions of the Secretary of State, no prisoner shall be allowed, except as authorised by a health care professional such as is mentioned in rule 20(3), to have any food other than that ordinarily provided.

(2) The food provided shall be wholesome, nutritious, well prepared and served, reasonably varied and sufficient in quantity.

(3) Any person deemed by the governor to be competent, shall from time to time inspect the food both before and after it is cooked and shall report any deficiency or defect to the governor.

(4) In this rule 'food' includes drink.

## 25 Alcohol and tobacco

(1) No prisoner shall be allowed to have any intoxicating liquor.

(2) No prisoner shall be allowed to smoke or to have any tobacco except as a privilege under rule 8 and in accordance with any orders of the governor.

## 26 Sleeping accommodation

(1) No room or cell shall be used as sleeping accommodation for a prisoner unless it has been certified in the manner required by section 14 of the Prison Act 1952 in the case of a cell used for the confinement of a prisoner.

(2) A certificate given under that section or this rule shall specify the maximum number of prisoners who may sleep or be confined at one time in the room or cell to which it relates, and the number so specified shall not be exceeded without the leave of the Secretary of State.

## 27 Beds and bedding

Each prisoner shall be provided with a separate bed and with separate bedding adequate for warmth and health.

## 28 Hygiene

(1) Every prisoner shall be provided with toilet articles necessary for his health and cleanliness, which shall be replaced as necessary.

(2) Every prisoner shall be required to wash at proper times, have a hot bath or shower on reception and thereafter at least once a week.

(3) A prisoner's hair shall not be cut without his consent.

## 29 Physical education

(1) If circumstances reasonably permit, a prisoner aged 21 years or over shall be given the opportunity to participate in physical education for at least one hour a week.

(2) The following provisions shall apply to the extent circumstances reasonably permit to a prisoner who is under 21 years of age–

    (a) provision shall be made for the physical education of such a prisoner within the normal working week, as well as evening and weekend physical recreation; the physical education activities will be such as foster personal responsibility and the prisoner's interests and skills and encourage him to make good use of his leisure on release; and

    (b) arrangements shall be made for each such prisoner who is a convicted prisoner to participate in physical education for two hours a week on average.

(3) In the case of a prisoner with a need for remedial physical activity, appropriate facilities will be provided.

(4) [*Revoked.*]

## 30 Time in the open air

If the weather permits and subject to the need to maintain good order and discipline, a prisoner shall be given the opportunity to spend time in the open air at least once every day, for such period as may be reasonable in the circumstances.

## 31 Work

(1) A convicted prisoner shall be required to do useful work for not more than 10 hours a day, and arrangements shall be made to allow prisoners to work, where possible, outside the cells and in association with one another.

(2) A registered medical practitioner or registered nurse such as is mentioned in rule 20(3) may excuse a prisoner from work on medical grounds, and no prisoner shall be set to do work which is not of a class for which he has been passed by a registered medical practitioner or registered nurse such as is mentioned in rule 20(3) as being fit.

(3) No prisoner shall be set to do work of a kind not authorised by the Secretary of State.

(4) No prisoner shall work in the service of another prisoner or an officer, or for the private benefit of any person, without the authority of the Secretary of State.

(5) An unconvicted prisoner shall be permitted, if he wishes, to work as if he were a convicted prisoner.

(6) Prisoners may be paid for their work at rates approved by the Secretary of State, either generally or in relation to particular cases.

## EDUCATION AND LIBRARY

## 32 Education

(1) Every prisoner able to profit from the education facilities provided at a prison shall be encouraged to do so.

(2) Educational classes shall be arranged at every prison and, subject to any directions of the Secretary of State, reasonable facilities shall be afforded to prisoners who wish to do so to improve their education by training by distance learning, private study and recreational classes, in their spare time.

(3) Special attention shall be paid to the education and training of prisoners with special educational needs, and if necessary they shall be taught within the hours normally allotted to work.

(4) In the case of a prisoner of compulsory school age as defined in section 8 of the Education Act 1996, arrangements shall be made for his participation in education or training courses for at least 15 hours a week within the normal working week.

## 33 Library

A library shall be provided in every prison and, subject to any directions of the Secretary of State, every prisoner shall be allowed to have library books and to exchange them.

## COMMUNICATIONS

## 34 Communications generally

(1) Without prejudice to sections 6 and 19 of the Prison Act 1952 and except as

provided by these Rules, a prisoner shall not be permitted to communicate with any person outside the prison, or such person with him, except with the leave of the Secretary of State or as a privilege under rule 8.

(2) Notwithstanding paragraph (1) above, and except as otherwise provided in these Rules, the Secretary of State may impose any restriction or condition, either generally or in a particular case, upon the communications to be permitted between a prisoner and other persons if he considers that the restriction or condition to be imposed–

   (a) does not interfere with the convention rights of any person; or
   (b) (i) is necessary on grounds specified in paragraph (3) below;
       (ii) reliance on the grounds is compatible with the convention right to be interfered with; and
       (iii) the restriction or condition is proportionate to what is sought to be achieved.

(3) The grounds referred to in paragraph (2) above are–

   (a) the interests of national security;
   (b) the prevention, detection, investigation or prosecution of crime;
   (c) the interests of public safety;
   (d) securing or maintaining prison security or good order and discipline in prison;
   (e) the protection of health or morals;
   (f) the protection of the reputation of others;
   (g) maintaining the authority and impartiality of the judiciary; or
   (h) the protection of the rights and freedoms of any person.

(4) Subject to paragraph (2) above, the Secretary of State may require that any visit, or class of visits, shall be held in facilities which include special features restricting or preventing physical contact between a prisoner and a visitor.

(5) Every visit to a prisoner shall take place within the sight of an officer or employee of the prison authorised for the purposes of this rule by the governor (in this rule referred to as an 'authorised employee'), unless the Secretary of State otherwise directs, and for the purposes of this paragraph a visit to a prisoner shall be taken to take place within the sight of an officer or authorised employee if it can be seen by an officer or authorised employee by means of an overt closed circuit television system.

(6) Subject to rule 38, every visit to a prisoner shall take place within the hearing of an officer or authorised employee, unless the Secretary of State otherwise directs.

(7) The Secretary of State may give directions, either generally or in relation to any visit or class of visits, concerning the day and times when prisoners may be visited.

(8) In this rule–

   (a) references to communications include references to communications during visits;
   (b) references to restrictions and conditions upon communications include references to restrictions and conditions in relation to the length, duration and frequency of communications; and
   (c) references to convention rights are to the convention rights within the meaning of the Human Rights Act 1998.

## 35 Personal letters and visits

(1) Subject to paragraph (8), an unconvicted prisoner may send and receive as many letters and may receive as many visits as he wishes within such limits and subject to such conditions as the Secretary of State may direct, either generally or in a particular case.

(2) Subject to paragraphs (2A) and (8), a convicted prisoner shall be entitled–

    (a) to send and to receive a letter on his reception into a prison and thereafter once a week; and

    (b) to receive a visit twice in every period of four weeks, but only once in every such period if the Secretary of State so directs.

(2A) A prisoner serving a sentence of imprisonment to which an intermittent custody order relates shall be entitled to receive a visit only where the governor considers that desirable having regard to the extent to which he has been unable to meet with his friends and family in the periods during which he has been temporarily released on licence.

(3) The governor may allow a prisoner an additional letter or visit as a privilege under rule 8 or where necessary for his welfare or that of his family.

(4) The governor may allow a prisoner entitled to a visit to send and to receive a letter instead.

(5) The governor may defer the right of a prisoner to a visit until the expiration of any period of cellular confinement.

(6) The independent monitoring board may allow a prisoner an additional letter or visit in special circumstances, and may direct that a visit may extend beyond the normal duration.

(7) The Secretary of State may allow additional letters and visits in relation to any prisoner or class of prisoners.

(8) A prisoner shall not be entitled under this rule to receive a visit from:

    (a) any person, whether or not a relative or friend, during any period of time that person is the subject of a prohibition imposed under rule 73; or

    (b) any other person, other than a relative or friend, except with the leave of the Secretary of State.

(9) Any letter or visit under the succeeding provisions of these Rules shall not be counted as a letter or visit for the purposes of this rule.

## 35A Interception of communications

(1) The Secretary of State may give directions to any governor concerning the interception in a prison of any communication by any prisoner or class of prisoners if the Secretary of State considers that the directions are–

    (a) necessary on grounds specified in paragraph (4) below; and

    (b) proportionate to what is sought to be achieved.

(2) Subject to any directions given by the Secretary of State, the governor may make arrangements for any communication by a prisoner or class of prisoners to be intercepted in a prison by an officer or an employee of the prison authorised by the governor for the purposes of this rule (referred to in this rule as an 'authorised employee') if he considers that the arrangements are–

    (a) necessary on grounds specified in paragraph (4) below; and

    (b) proportionate to what is sought to be achieved.

(3) Any communication by a prisoner may, during the course of its transmission in a prison, be terminated by an officer or an authorised employee if he con-

siders that to terminate the communication is–
  (a) necessary on grounds specified in paragraph (4) below; and
  (b) proportionate to what is sought to be achieved by the termination.
(4) The grounds referred to in paragraphs (1)(a), (2)(a) and (3)(a) above are–
  (a) the interests of national security;
  (b) the prevention, detection, investigation or prosecution of crime;
  (c) the interests of public safety;
  (d) securing or maintaining prison security or good order and discipline in prison;
  (e) the protection of health or morals; or
  (f) the protection of the rights and freedoms of any person.
(5) Any reference to the grounds specified in paragraph (4) above in relation to the interception of a communication by means of a telecommunications system in a prison, or the disclosure or retention of intercepted material from such a communication, shall be taken to be a reference to those grounds with the omission of sub-paragraph (f).
(6) For the purposes of this rule 'interception'–
  (a) in relation to a communication by means of a telecommunications system, means any action taken in relation to the system or its operation so as to make some or all of the contents of the communications available, while being transmitted, to a person other than the sender or intended recipient of the communication; and the contents of a communication are to be taken to be made available to a person while being transmitted where the contents of the communication, while being transmitted, are diverted or recorded so as to be available to a person subsequently; and
  (b) in relation to any written or drawn communication, includes opening, reading, examining and copying the communication.

## 35B Permanent log of communications
(1) The governor may arrange for a permanent log to be kept of all communications by or to a prisoner.
(2) The log referred to in paragraph (1) above may include, in relation to a communication by means of a telecommunications system in a prison, a record of the destination, duration and cost of the communication and, in relation to any written or drawn communication, a record of the sender and addressee of the communication.

## 35C Disclosure of material
The governor may not disclose to any person who is not an officer of a prison or of the Secretary of State or an employee of the prison authorised by the governor for the purposes of this rule any intercepted material, information retained pursuant to rule 35B or material obtained by means of an overt closed circuit television system used during a visit unless–
  (a) he considers that such disclosure is–
    (i) necessary on grounds specified in rule 35A(4); and
    (ii) proportionate to what is sought to be achieved by the disclosure; or
  (b) (i) in the case of intercepted material or material obtained by means of an overt closed circuit television system used during a visit, all parties to the communication or visit consent to the disclosure; or

(ii) in the case of information retained pursuant to rule 35B, the prisoner to whose communication the information relates, consents to the disclosure.

## 35D Retention of material

(1) The governor shall not retain any intercepted material or material obtained by means of an overt closed circuit television system used during a visit for a period longer than 3 months beginning with the day on which the material was intercepted or obtained unless he is satisfied that continued retention of it is—

(a) necessary on grounds specified in rule 35A(4); and

(b) proportionate to what is sought to be achieved by the continued retention.

(2) Where such material is retained for longer than 3 months pursuant to paragraph (1) above the governor shall review its continued retention at periodic intervals until such time as it is no longer held by the governor.

(3) The first review referred to in paragraph (2) above shall take place not more than 3 months after the decision to retain the material taken pursuant to paragraph (1) above, and subsequent reviews shall take place not more than 3 months apart thereafter.

(4) If the governor, on a review conducted pursuant to paragraph (2) above or at any other time, is not satisfied that the continued retention of the material satisfies the requirements set out in paragraph (1) above, he shall arrange for the material to be destroyed.

## 36 Police interviews

A police officer may, on production of an order issued by or on behalf of a chief officer of police, interview any prisoner willing to see him.

## 37 Securing release

A person detained in prison in default of finding a surety, or of payment of a sum of money, may communicate with and be visited at any reasonable time on a weekday by any relative or friend to arrange for a surety or payment in order to secure his release from prison.

## 38 Legal advisers

(1) The legal adviser of a prisoner in any legal proceedings, civil or criminal, to which the prisoner is a party shall be afforded reasonable facilities for interviewing him in connection with those proceedings, and may do so out of hearing but in the sight of an officer.

(2) A prisoner's legal adviser may, subject to any directions given by the Secretary of State, interview the prisoner in connection with any other legal business out of hearing but in the sight of an officer.

## 39 Correspondence with legal advisers and courts

(1) A prisoner may correspond with his legal adviser and any court and such correspondence may only be opened, read or stopped by the governor in accordance with the provisions of this rule.

(2) Correspondence to which this rule applies may be opened if the governor has

reasonable cause to believe that it contains an illicit enclosure and any such enclosures shall be dealt with in accordance with the other provision of these Rules.

(3) Correspondence to which this rule applies may be opened, read and stopped if the governor has reasonable cause to believe its contents endanger prison security or the safety of others or are otherwise of a criminal nature.

(4) A prisoner shall be given the opportunity to be present when any correspondence to which this rule applies is opened and shall be informed if it or any enclosure is to be read or stopped.

(5) A prisoner shall on request be provided with any writing materials necessary for the purposes of paragraph(1).

(6) In this rule, 'court' includes the European Commission of Human Rights, the European Court of Human Rights and the European Court of Justice; and 'illicit enclosure' includes any article possession of which has not been authorised in accordance with the other provisions of these Rules and any correspondence to or from a person other than the prisoner concerned, his legal adviser or a court.

## REMOVAL, SEARCH, RECORD AND PROPERTY

### 40 Custody outside prison

(1) A person being taken to or from a prison in custody shall be exposed as little as possible to public observation, and proper care shall be taken to protect him from curiosity and insult.

(2) A prisoner required to be taken in custody anywhere outside a prison shall be kept in the custody of an officer appointed or a police officer.

(3) A prisoner required to be taken in custody to any court shall, when he appears before the court, wear his own clothing or ordinary civilian clothing provided by the governor.

### 41 Search

(1) Every prisoner shall be searched when taken into custody by an officer, on his reception into a prison and subsequently as the governor thinks necessary or as the Secretary of State may direct.

(2) A prisoner shall be searched in as seemly a manner as is consistent with discovering anything concealed.

(3) No prisoner shall be stripped and searched in the sight of another prisoner, or in the sight of a person of the opposite sex.

### 42 Record and photograph

(1) A personal record of each prisoner shall be prepared and maintained in such manner as the Secretary of State may direct.

(2) Every prisoner may be photographed on reception and subsequently, but no copy of the photograph or any other personal record shall be given to any person not authorised to receive it.

(2A) In this rule 'personal record' may include personal information and biometric records (such as fingerprints or other physical measurements).

### 43 Prisoners' property

(1) Subject to any directions of the Secretary of State, an un convicted prisoner

may have supplied to him at his expense and retain for his own use books, newspapers, writing materials and other means of occupation, except any that appears objectionable to the independent monitoring board or, pending consideration by them, to the governor.

(2) Anything, other than cash, which a prisoner has at a prison and which he is not allowed to retain for his own use shall be taken into the governor's custody. An inventory of a prisoner's property shall be kept, and he shall be required to sign it, after having a proper opportunity to see that it is correct.

(2A) Where a prisoner is serving a sentence of imprisonment to which an intermittent custody order relates, an inventory as referred to in paragraph (2) shall only be kept where the value of that property is estimated by the governor to be in excess of £100.

(3) Any cash which a prisoner has at a prison shall be paid into an account under the control of the governor and the prisoner shall be credited with the amount in the books of the prison.

(4) Any article belonging to a prisoner which remains unclaimed for a period of more than 3 years after he leaves prison, or dies, may be sold or otherwise disposed of; and the net proceeds of any sale shall be paid to the National Association for the Care and Resettlement of Offenders, for its general purposes.

(5) The governor may confiscate any unauthorised article found in the possession of a prisoner after his reception into prison, or concealed or deposited anywhere within a prison.

**44 Money and articles received by post**

(1) Any money or other article (other than a letter or other communication) sent to a convicted prisoner by post shall be dealt with in accordance with the provisions of this rule, and the prisoner shall be informed of the manner in which it is dealt with.

(2) Any cash shall, at the discretion of the governor, be–
  (a) dealt with in accordance with rule 43(3);
  (b) returned to the sender; or
  (c) in a case where the sender's name and address are not known, paid to the National Association for the Care and Resettlement of Offenders; for its general purposes:
      Provided that in relation to a prisoner committed to prison in default of payment of any sum of money, the prisoner shall be informed of the receipt of the cash and, unless he objects to its being so applied, it shall be applied in or towards the satisfaction of the amount due from him.

(3) Any security for money shall, at the discretion of the governor, be–
  (a) delivered to the prisoner or placed with his property at the prison;
  (b) returned to the sender; or
  (c) encashed and the cash dealt with in accordance with paragraph (2).

(4) Any other article to which this rule applies shall, at the discretion of the governor, be–
  (a) delivered to the prisoner or placed with his property at the prison;
  (b) returned to the sender; or
  (c) in a case where the sender's name and address are not known or the article

is of such a nature that it would be unreasonable to return it, sold or otherwise disposed of, and the net proceeds of any sale applied in accordance with paragraph(2).

## SPECIAL CONTROL, SUPER VISION AND RESTRAINT AND DRUG TESTING

### 45 Removal from association

(1) Where it appears desirable, for the maintenance of good order or discipline or in his own interests, that a prisoner should not associate with other prisoners, either generally or for particular purposes, the governor may arrange for the prisoner's removal from association accordingly.

(2) A prisoner shall not be removed under this rule for a period of more than 72 hours without the authority of the Secretary of State and authority given under this paragraph shall be for a period not exceeding 14 days but it may be renewed from time to time for a like period.

(3) The governor may arrange at his discretion for a prisoner removed under this rule to resume association with other prisoners at any time, and in exercising that discretion the governor must fully consider any recommendation that the prisoner resumes association on medical grounds made by a registered medical practitioner or registered nurse such as is mentioned in rule 20(3).

(4) This rule shall not apply to a prisoner the subject of a direction given under rule 46(1).

### 46 Close supervision centres

(1) Where it appears desirable, for the maintenance of good order or discipline or to ensure the safety of officers, prisoners or any other person, that a prisoner should not associate with other prisoners, either generally or for particular purposes, the Secretary of State may direct the prisoner's removal from association accordingly and his placement in a close supervision centre of a prison.

(2) A direction given under paragraph(1) shall be for a period not exceeding one month, but may be renewed from time to time for a like period, and shall continue to apply notwithstanding any transfer of a prisoner from one prison to another.

(3) The Secretary of State may direct that such a prisoner as aforesaid shall resume association with other prisoners, either within a close supervision centre or elsewhere.

(4) In exercising any discretion under this rule, the Secretary of State shall take account of any relevant medical considerations which are known to him.

(5) A close supervision centre is any cell or other part of a prison for the time being used for holding a prisoner who is subject to a direction given under paragraph (1).

### 47 Use of force

(1) An officer in dealing with a prisoner shall not use force unnecessarily and, when the application of force to a prisoner is necessary, no more force than is necessary shall be used.

(2) No officer shall act deliberately in a manner calculated to provoke a prisoner.

## 48 Temporary confinement

(1) The governor may order a refractory or violent prisoner to be confined temporarily in a special cell, but a prisoner shall not be so confined as a punishment, or after he has ceased to be refractory or violent.

(2) A prisoner shall not be confined in a special cell for longer than 24 hours without a direction in writing given by an officer of the Secretary of State. Such a direction shall state the grounds for the confinement and the time during which it may continue.

## 49 Restraints

(1) The governor may order a prisoner to be put under restraint where this is necessary to prevent the prisoner from injuring himself or others, damaging property or creating a disturbance.

(2) Notice of such an order shall be given without delay to a member of the independent monitoring board, and to a registered medical practitioner or to a registered nurse such as is mentioned in rule 20(3).

(3) On receipt of the notice, the registered medical practitioner or registered nurse referred to in paragraph (2), shall inform the governor whether there are any medical reasons why the prisoner should not be put under restraint. The governor shall give effect to any recommendation which may be made under this paragraph.

(4) A prisoner shall not be kept under restraint longer than necessary, nor shall he be so kept for longer than 24 hours without a direction in writing given by a member of the independent monitoring board or by an officer of the Secretary of State (not being an officer of a prison). Such a direction shall state the grounds for the restraint and the time during which it may continue.

(5) Particulars of every case of restraint under the foregoing provisions of this rule shall be forthwith recorded.

(6) Except as provided by this rule no prisoner shall be put under restraint otherwise than for safe custody during removal, or on medical grounds by direction of a registered medical practitioner or of a registered nurse such as is mentioned in rule 20(3). No prisoner shall be put under restraint as a punishment.

(7) Any means of restraint shall be of a pattern authorised by the Secretary of State, and shall be used in such manner and under such conditions as the Secretary of State may direct.

## 50 Compulsory testing for controlled drugs

(1) This rule applies where an officer; acting under the powers conferred by section 16A of the Prison Act 1952 (power to test prisoners for drugs), requires a prisoner to provide a sample for the purpose of ascertaining whether he has any controlled drug in his body.

(2) In this rule 'sample' means a sample of urine or any other description of sample specified in the authorisation by the governor for the purposes of section 16A of the Prison Act 1952.

(3) When requiring a prisoner to provide a sample, an officer shall, so far as is reasonably practicable, inform the prisoner:

    (a) that he is being required to provide a sample in accordance with section 16A of the Prison Act 1952; and

(b) that a refusal to provide a sample may lead to disciplinary proceedings being brought against him.

(4) An officer shall require a prisoner to provide a fresh sample, free from any adulteration.

(5) An officer requiring a sample shall make such arrangements and give the prisoner such instructions for its provision as may be reasonably necessary in order to prevent or detect its adulteration or falsification.

(6) A prisoner who is required to provide a sample may be kept apart from other prisoners for a period not exceeding one hour to enable arrangements to be made for the provision of the sample.

(7) A prisoner who is unable to provide a sample of urine when required to do so may be kept apart from other prisoners until he has provided the required sample, save that a prisoner may not be kept apart under this paragraph for a period of more than 5 hours.

(8) A prisoner required to provide a sample of urine shall be afforded such degree of privacy for the purposes of providing the sample as may be compatible with the need to prevent or detect any adulteration or falsification of the sample; in particular a prisoner shall not be required to provide such a sample in the sight of a person of the opposite sex.

**50A Observation of prisoners by means of an overt closed circuit television system**

(1) Without prejudice to his other powers to supervise the prison, prisoners and other persons in the prison, whether by use of an overt closed circuit television system or otherwise, the governor may make arrangements for any prisoner to be placed under constant observation by means of an overt closed circuit television system while the prisoner is in a cell or other place in the prison if he considers that–

(a) such supervision is necessary for–
   (i) the health and safety of the prisoner or any other person;
   (ii) the prevention, detection, investigation or prosecution of crime; or
   (iii) securing or maintaining prison security or good order and discipline in the prison; and
(b) it is proportionate to what is sought to be achieved.

(2) If an overt closed circuit television system is used for the purposes of this rule, the provisions of rules 35C and 35D shall apply to any material obtained.

**50B Compulsory testing for alcohol**

(1) This rule applies where an officer, acting under an authorisation in force under section 16B of the Prison Act 1952 (power to test prisoners for alcohol), requires a prisoner to provide a sample for the purpose of ascertaining whether he has alcohol in his body.

(2) When requiring a prisoner to provide a sample an officer shall, so far as is reasonably practicable, inform the prisoner–

(a) that he is being required to provide a sample in accordance with section 16B of the Prison Act 1952; and
(b) that a refusal to provide a sample may lead to disciplinary proceedings being brought against him.

(3) An officer requiring a sample shall make such arrangements and give the

prisoner such instructions for its provision as may be reasonably necessary in order to prevent or detect its adulteration or falsification.

(4) Subject to paragraph (5) a prisoner who is required to provide a sample may be kept apart from other prisoners for a period not exceeding one hour to enable arrangements to be made for the provision of the sample.

(5) A prisoner who is unable to provide a sample of urine when required to do so may be kept apart from other prisoners until he has provided the required sample, except that a prisoner may not be kept apart under this paragraph for a period of more than 5 hours.

(6) A prisoner required to provide a sample of urine shall be afforded such degree of privacy for the purposes of providing the sample as may be compatible with the need to prevent or detect any adulteration or falsification of the sample; in particular a prisoner shall not be required to provide such a sample in the sight of a person of the opposite sex.

## OFFENCES AGAINST DISCIPLINE
### 51 Offences against discipline
A prisoner is guilty of an offence against discipline if he–

(1) commits any assault;

(1A) commits any racially aggravated assault;

(2) detains any person against his will;

(3) denies access to any part of the prison to any officer or any person (other than a prisoner) who is at the prison for the purpose of working there;

(4) fights with any person;

(5) intentionally endangers the health or personal safety of others or, by his conduct, is reckless whether such health or personal safety is endangered;

(6) intentionally obstructs an officer in the execution of his duty, or any person (other than a prisoner) who is at the prison for the purpose of working there, in the performance of his work;

(7) escapes or absconds from prison or from legal custody;

(8) fails to comply with any condition upon which he is temporarily released under rule 9;

(9) is found with any substance in his urine which demonstrates that a controlled drug has, whether in prison or while on temporary release under rule 9, been administered to him by himself or by another person (but subject to rule 52);

(10) is intoxicated as a consequence of consuming any alcoholic beverage (but subject to rule 52A);

(11) consumes any alcoholic beverage whether or not provided to him by another person (but subject to rule 52A);

(12) has in his possession–
    (a) any unauthorised article, or
    (b) a greater quantity of any article than he is authorised to have;

(13) sells or delivers to any person any unauthorised article;

(14) sells or, without permission, delivers to any person any article which he is allowed to have only for his own use;

(15) takes improperly any article belonging to another person or to a prison;

(16) intentionally or recklessly sets fire to any part of a prison or any other property, whether or not his own;

(17) destroys or damages any part of a prison or any other property, other than his own;

(17A) causes racially aggravated damage to, or destruction of, any part of a prison or any other property, other than his own;

(18) absents himself from any place he is required to be or is present at any place where he is not authorised to be;

(19) is disrespectful to any officer, or any person (other than a prisoner) who is at the prison for the purpose of working there, or any person visiting a prison;

(20) uses threatening, abusive or insulting words or behaviour;

(20A) uses threatening, abusive or insulting racist words or behaviour;

(21) intentionally fails to work properly or, being required to work, refuses to do so;

(22) disobeys any lawful order;

(23) disobeys or fails to comply with any rule or regulation applying to him;

(24) receives any controlled drug, or, without the consent of an officer, any other article, during the course of a visit (not being an interview such as is mentioned in rule 38);

(24A) displays, attaches or draws on any part of a prison, or on any other property, threatening, abusive or insulting racist words, drawings, symbols or other material;

(25) (a) attempts to commit,
    (b) incites another prisoner to commit, or
    (c) assists another prisoner to commit or to attempt to commit, any of the foregoing offences.

## 51A Interpretation of rule 51

(2) For the purposes of rule 51 words, behaviour or material are racist if they demonstrate, or are motivated (wholly or partly) by, hostility to members of a racial group (whether identifiable or not) based on their membership (or presumed membership) of a racial group, and 'membership', 'presumed', 'racial group' and 'racially aggravated', shall have the meanings assigned to them by section 28 of the Crime and Disorder Act 1998.

## 52 Defences to rule 51(9)

It shall be a defence for a prisoner charged with an offence under rule 51(9) to show that:

(a) the controlled drug had been, prior to its administration, lawfully in his possession for his use or was administered to him in the course of a lawful supply of the drug to him by another person;

(b) the controlled drug was administered by or to him in circumstances in which he did not know and had no reason to suspect that such a drug was being administered; or

(c) the controlled drug was administered by or to him under duress or to him without his consent in circumstances where it was not reasonable for him to have resisted.

## 52A Defences to rule 51(10) and rule 51(11)

It shall be a defence for a prisoner charged with an offence under rule 51(10) or (11) to show that–

(a) the alcohol was consumed by him in circumstances in which he did not know and had no reason to suspect that he was consuming alcohol; or

(b) the alcohol was consumed by him without his consent in circumstances where it was not reasonable for him to have resisted.

(c) [*Revoked.*]

## 53 Discplinary charges

(1) Where a prisoner is to be charged with an offence against discipline, the charge shall be laid as soon as possible and, save in exceptional circumstances, within 48 hours of the discovery of the offence.

(2) Every charge shall be inquired into by the governor or, as the case may be, the adjudicator

(3) Every charge shall be first inquired into not later, save in exceptional circumstances or in accordance with rule 55A(5), than:

(a) where it is inquired into by the governor, the next day, not being a Sunday or public holiday, after it is laid;

(b) where it is referred to the adjudicator under rule 53A(2), 28 days after it is so referred.

(4) A prisoner who is to be charged with an offence against discipline may be kept apart from other prisoners pending the governor's first inquiry or determination under rule 53A.

## 53A Determination of mode of inquiry

(1) Before inquiring into a charge the governor shall determine whether it is so serious that additional days should be awarded for the offence, if the prisoner is found guilty.

(2) Where the governor determines:

(a) that it is so serious, he shall:

(i) refer the charge to the adjudicator forthwith for him to inquire into it;

(ii) refer any other charge arising out of the same incident to the adjudicator forthwith for him to inquire into it; and

(iii) inform the prisoner who has been charged that he has done so;

(b) that it is not so serious, he shall proceed to inquire into the charge.

(3) If:

(a) at any time during an inquiry into a charge by the governor; or

(b) following such an inquiry, after the governor has found the prisoner guilty of an offence but before he has imposed a punishment for that offence, it appears to the governor that the charge is so serious that additional days should be awarded for the offence if (where sub-paragraph (a) applies) the prisoner is found guilty, the governor shall act in accordance with paragraph (2)(a)(i) to (iii) and the adjudicator shall first inquire into any charge referred to him under this paragraph not later than, save in exceptional circumstances, 28 days after the charge was referred.

## 54 Rights of prisoners charged

(1) Where a prisoner is charged with an offence against discipline, he shall be informed of the charge as soon as possible and, in any case, before the time when it is inquired into by the governor or, as the case may be, the adjudicator.

(2) At an inquiry into a charge against a prisoner he shall be given a full opportunity of hearing what is alleged against him and of presenting his own case.

(3) At an inquiry into a charge which has been referred to the adjudicator, the prisoner who has been charged shall be given the opportunity to be legally represented.

## 55 Governor's punishments

(1) If he finds a prisoner guilty of an offence against discipline the governor may, subject to paragraph (2) and to rule 57, impose one or more of the following punishments:
   (a) caution;
   (b) forfeiture for a period not exceeding 42 days of any of the privileges under rule 8;
   (c) exclusion from associated work for a period not exceeding 21 days;
   (d) stoppage of or deduction from earnings for a period not exceeding 84 days;
   (e) cellular confinement for a period not exceeding 21 days;
   (f) [*Revoked.*]
   (g) in the case of a prisoner otherwise entitled to them, forfeiture for any period of the right, under rule 43(1) , to have the articles there mentioned;
   (h) removal from his wing or living unit for a period of 28 days.

(2) A caution shall not be combined with any other punishment for the same charge.

(3) If a prisoner is found guilty of more than one charge arising out of an incident, punishments under this rule may be ordered to run consecutively but, in the case of a punishment of cellular confinement, the total period shall not exceed 21 days.

(4) In imposing a punishment under this rule, the governor shall take into account any guidelines that the Secretary of State may from time to time issue as to the level of punishment that should normally be imposed for a particular offence against discipline.

## 55A Adjudicator's punishments

(1) If he finds a prisoner guilty of an offence against discipline the adjudicator may, subject to paragraph (2) and to rule 57, impose one or more of the following punishments:
   (a) any of the punishments mentioned in rule 55(1);
   (b) in the case of a short-term prisoner or long-term prisoner or fixed-term prisoner, an award of additional days not exceeding 42 days.

(2) A caution shall not be combined with any other punishment for the same charge.

(3) If a prisoner is found guilty of more than one charge arising out of an incident, punishments under this rule may be ordered to run consecutively but, in the case of an award of additional days, the total period added shall not exceed 42 days and, in the case of a punishment of cellular confinement, the total period shall not exceed 21 days.

(4) This rule applies to a prisoner who has been charged with having committed an offence against discipline before the date on which the rule came into force, in the same way as it applies to a prisoner who has been charged with

having committed an offence against discipline on or after that date, provided the charge is referred to the adjudicator no later than 60 days after that date.
(5) Rule 53(3) shall not apply to a charge where, by virtue of paragraph (4), this rule applies to the prisoner who has been charged.

### 55B Review of adjudicator's punishment
(1) A reviewer means the Senior District Judge (Chief Magistrate) or any deputy of such a judge as nominated by that judge.
(2) Where a punishment is imposed by an adjudicator under rule 55A(1), a prisoner may, within 14 days of receipt of the punishment, request in writing that a reviewer conducts a review.
(3) The review must be commenced within 14 days of receipt of the request and must be conducted on the papers alone.
(4) The review must only be of the punishment imposed and must not be a review of the finding of guilt under rule 55A.
(5) On completion of the review, if it appears to the reviewer that the punishment imposed was manifestly unreasonable he may–
   (a) reduce the number of any additional days awarded;
   (b) for whatever punishment has been imposed by the adjudicator, substitute another punishment which is, in his opinion, less severe; or
   (c) quash the punishment entirely.
(6) A prisoner requesting a review shall serve any additional days awarded under rule 55A(1)(b) unless and until they are reduced.

### 56 Forfeiture of remission to be treated as an award of additional days
(1) In this rule, 'existing prisoner' and 'existing licensee' have the meanings assigned to them by paragraph 8(1) of Schedule 12 to the Criminal Justice Act 1991.
(2) In relation to any existing prisoner or existing licensee who has forfeited any remission of his sentence, the provisions of Part II of the Criminal Justice Act 1991 shall apply as if he had been awarded such number of additional days as equals the numbers of days of remission which he has forfeited.

### 57 Offences committed by young persons
(1) In the case of an offence against discipline committed by an inmate who was under the age of 21 when the offence was committed (other than an offender in relation to whom the Secretary of State has given a direction under section 13(1) of the Criminal Justice Act 1982 that he shall be treated as if he had been sentenced to imprisonment) rule 55 or, as the case may be, rule 55A shall have effect, but–
   (a) the maximum period of forfeiture of privileges under rule 8 shall be 21 days;
   (b) the maximum period of stoppage of or deduction from earnings shall be 42 days;
   (c) the maximum period of cellular confinement shall be ten days;
   (d) the maximum period of removal from his cell or living unit shall be 21 days.
(2) In the case of an inmate who has been sentenced to a term of youth custody or detention in a young offender institution, and by virtue of a direction of the

Secretary of State under section 99 of the Powers of Criminal Courts (Sentencing) Act 2000, is treated as if he had been sentenced to imprisonment for that term, any punishment imposed on him for an offence against discipline before the said direction was given shall, if it has not been exhausted or remitted, continue to have effect:
(a) if imposed by a governor, as if made pursuant to rule 55;
(b) if imposed by an adjudicator, as if made pursuant to rule 55A.

**58**

Before deciding whether to impose a punishment of cellular confinement the governor, adjudicator or reviewer shall first enquire of a registered medical practitioner or registered nurse, such as is mentioned in rule 20(3), as to whether there are any medical reasons why the punishment is unsuitable and shall take this advice into account when making his decision.

## 59 Prospective award of additional days
(1) Subject to paragraph (2), where an offence against discipline is committed by a prisoner who is detained only on remand, additional days may be awarded by the adjudicator notwithstanding that the prisoner has not (or had not at the time of the offence) been sentenced.
(2) An award of additional days under paragraph (1) shall have effect only if the prisoner in question subsequently becomes a short-term or long-term prisoner or fixed-term prisoner whose sentence is reduced, under section 67 of the Criminal Justice Act 1967 or section 240 of the 2003 Act, by a period which includes the time when the offence against discipline was committed.

## 59A Removal from a cell or living unit
Following the imposition of a punishment of removal from his cell or living unit, a prisoner shall be accommodated in a separate part of the prison under such restrictions of earnings and activities as the Secretary of State may direct.

## 60 Suspended punishments
(1) Subject to any directions given by the Secretary of State, the power to impose a disciplinary punishment (other than a caution) shall include power to direct that the punishment is not to take effect unless, during a period specified in the direction (not being more than six months from the date of the direction), the prisoner commits another offence against discipline and a direction is given under paragraph (2).
(2) Where a prisoner commits an offence against discipline during the period specified in a direction given under paragraph (1) the person dealing with that offence may–
(a) direct that the suspended punishment shall take effect;
(b) reduce the period or amount of the suspended punishment and direct that it shall take effect as so reduced;
(c) vary the original direction by substituting for the period specified a period expiring not later than six months from the date of variation; or
(d) give no direction with respect to the suspended punishment.
(3) Where an award of additional days has been suspended under paragraph (1)

and a prisoner is charged with committing an offence against discipline during the period specified in a direction given under that paragraph, the governor shall either:
(a) inquire into the charge and give no direction with respect to the suspended award; or
(b) refer the charge to the adjudicator for him to inquire into it.

## 61 Remission and mitigation of punishments and quashing of findings of guilt
(1) Except in the case of a finding of guilt made, or a punishment imposed, by an adjudicator under rule 55A(1) the Secretary of State may quash any finding of guilt and may remit any punishment or mitigate it either by reducing it or by substituting another award which is, in his opinion, less severe.
(2) Subject to any directions given by the Secretary of State, the governor may, on the grounds of good behaviour, remit or mitigate any punishment already imposed by an adjudicator or governor.

## PART III: OFFICERS OF PRISONS

## 62 General duty of officers
(1) It shall be the duty of every officer to conform to these Rules and the rules and regulations of the prison, to assist and support the governor in their maintenance and to obey his lawful instructions.
(2) An officer shall inform the governor promptly of any abuse or impropriety which comes to his knowledge.

## 63 Gratuities forbidden
No officer shall receive any unauthorised fee, gratuity or other consideration in connection with his office.

## 64 Search of officers
An officer shall submit himself to be searched in the prison if the governor so directs. Any such search shall be conducted in as seemly a manner as is consistent with discovering anything concealed.

## 65 Transactions with prisoners
(1) No officer shall take part in any business or pecuniary transaction with or on behalf of a prisoner without the leave of the Secretary of State.
(2) No officer shall without authority bring in or take out, or attempt to bring in or take out, or knowingly allow to be brought in or taken out, to or for a prisoner, or deposit in any place with intent that it shall come into the possession of a prisoner, any article whatsoever.

## 66 Contact with former prisoners
No officer shall, without the knowledge of the governor, communicate with any person whom he knows to be a former prisoner or a relative or friend of a prisoner or former prisoner.

## 67 Communications to the press
(1) No officer shall make, directly or indirectly, any unauthorised communica-

tion to a representative of the press or any other person concerning matters which have become known to him in the course of his duty.

(2) No officer shall, without authority, publish any matter or make any public pronouncement relating to the administration of any institution to which the Prison Act 1952 applies or to any of its inmates.

## 68 Code of discipline

The Secretary of State may approve a code of discipline to have effect in relation to officers, or such classes of officers as it may specify, setting out the offences against discipline, the awards which may be made in respect of them and the procedure for dealing with charges.

## 69 Emergencies

Where any constable or member of the armed forces of the Crown is employed by reason of any emergency to assist the governor of a prison by performing duties ordinarily performed by an officer of a prison, any reference in Part II of these Rules to such an officer (other than a governor) shall be construed as including a reference to a constable or a member of the armed forces of the Crown so employed.

## PART IV: PERSONS HAVING ACCESS TO A PRISON

## 70 Prohibited articles

No person shall, without authority, convey into or throw into or deposit in a prison, or convey or throw out of a prison, or convey to a prisoner, or deposit in any place with intent that it shall come into the possession of a prisoner, any article whatever. Anything so conveyed, thrown or deposited may be confiscated by the governor.

## 70A List C Articles

A List C article is any article or substance in the following list–
(a) tobacco;
(b) money;
(c) clothing;
(d) food;
(e) drink;
(f) letters;
(g) paper;
(h) books;
(i) tools;
(j) information technology equipment.

## 71 Control of persons and vehicles

(1) Any person or vehicle entering or leaving a prison may be stopped, examined and searched and in addition any such person may be photographed, fingerprinted or required to submit to other physical measurement.

(1A) Any such search of a person shall be carried out in as seemly a manner as is consistent with discovering anything concealed about the person or their belongings.

(2) The governor may direct the removal from a prison of any person who does not leave on being required to do so.

## 72 Viewing of prisons

(1) No outside person shall be permitted to view a prison unless authorised by statute or the Secretary of State.
(2) No person viewing the prison shall be permitted to take a photograph, make a sketch or communicate with a prisoner unless authorised by statute or the Secretary of State.

## 73 Visitors

(1) Without prejudice to any other powers to prohibit or restrict entry to prisons, or his powers under rules 34 and 35, the Secretary of State may prohibit visits by a person to a prison or to a prisoner in a prison for such periods of time as he considers necessary if the Secretary of State considers that such a prohibition is—
   (a) necessary on grounds specified in rule 35A(4); and
   (b) is proportionate to what is sought to be achieved by the prohibition.
(2) Paragraph (1) shall not apply in relation to any visit to a prison or prisoner by a member of the independent monitoring board of the prison, or justice of the peace, or to prevent any visit by a legal adviser for the purposes of an interview under rule 38 or visit allowed by the independent monitoring board under rule 35(6).

## PART V: INDEPENDENT MONITORING BOARD

## 74 Disqualification for membership

Any person, directly or indirectly interested in any contract for the supply of goods or services to a prison, shall not be a member of the independent monitoring board for that prison and any member who becomes so interested in such a contract shall vacate office as a member.

## 75 Independent monitoring board

(1) A member of the board of visitors for a prison appointed by the Secretary of State under section 6(2) of the Prison Act 1952 shall subject to paragraphs (3) and (4) hold office for three years, or such lesser period as the Secretary of State may appoint.
(2) A member—
   (a) appointed for the first time to the independent monitoring board for a particular prison; or
   (b) reappointed to the board following a gap of a year or more in his membership of it, shall, during the period of 12 months following the date on which he is so appointed or (as the case may be) reappointed, undertake such training as may reasonably be required by the Secretary of State.
(3) The Secretary of State may terminate the appointment of a member if he is satisfied that—
   (a) he has failed satisfactorily to perform his duties;
   (b) he has failed to undertake training he has been required to undertake under paragraph (2), by the end of the period specified in that paragraph;

(c) he is by reason of physical or mental illness, or for any other reason, incapable of carrying out his duties;

(d) he has been convicted of such a criminal offence, or his conduct has been such, that it is not in the Secretary of State's opinion fitting that he should remain a member; or

(e) there is, or appears to be or could appear to be, any conflict of interest between the member performing his duties as a member and any interest of that member, whether personal, financial or otherwise.

(4) Where the Secretary of State:

(a) has reason to suspect that a member of the independent monitoring board for a prison may have so conducted himself that his appointment may be liable to be terminated under paragraph (3)(a) or (d); and

(b) is of the opinion that the suspected conduct is of such a serious nature that the member cannot be permitted to continue to perform his functions as a member of the board pending the completion of the Secretary of State's investigations into the matter and any decision as to whether the member's appointment should be terminated,

he may suspend the member from office for such period or periods as he may reasonably require in order to complete his investigations and determine whether or not the appointment of the member should be so terminated; and a member so suspended shall not, during the period of his suspension, be regarded as being a member of the board, other than for the purposes of this paragraph and paragraphs (1) and (3).

(5) A board shall have a chairman and a vice chairman who shall be members of the board.

(6) The Secretary of State shall—

(a) upon the constitution of a board for the first time, appoint a chairman and a vice chairman to hold office for a period not exceeding twelve months;

(b) thereafter appoint, before the date of the first meeting of the board in any year of office of the board, a chairman and vice chairman for that year, having first consulted the board; and

(c) promptly fill, after first having consulted the board, any casual vacancy in the office of chairman or vice chairman.

(7) The Secretary of State may terminate the appointment of a member as chairman or vice chairman of the board if he is satisfied that the member has—

(a) failed satisfactorily to perform his functions as chairman (or as the case may be) vice chairman;

(b) has grossly misconducted himself while performing those functions.

## 76 Proceedings of boards

(1) The independent monitoring board for a prison shall meet at the prison once a month or, if they resolve for reasons specified in the resolution that less frequent meetings are sufficient, not fewer than eight times in twelve months.

(2) The board may fix a quorum of not fewer than three members for proceedings.

(3) The board shall keep minutes of their proceedings.

(4) The proceedings of the board shall not be invalidated by any vacancy in the membership or any defect in the appointment of a member.

## 77 General duties of boards
(1) The independent monitoring board for a prison shall satisfy themselves as to the state of the prison premises, the administration of the prison and the treatment of the prisoners.
(2) The board shall inquire into and report upon any matter into which the Secretary of State asks them to inquire.
(3) The board shall direct the attention of the governor to any matter which calls for his attention, and shall report to the Secretary of State any matter which they consider it expedient to report.
(4) The board shall inform the Secretary of State immediately of any abuse which comes to their knowledge.
(5) Before exercising any power under these Rules the board and any member of the board shall consult the governor in relation to any matter which may affect discipline.

## 78 Particular duties
(1) The independent monitoring board for a prison and any member of the board shall hear any complaint or request which a prisoner wishes to make to them or him.
(2) The board shall arrange for the food of the prisoners to be inspected by a member of the board at frequent intervals.
(3) The board shall inquire into any report made to them, whether or not by a member of the board, that a prisoner's health, mental or physical, is likely to be injuriously affected by any conditions of his imprisonment.

## 79 Members visiting prisons
(1) The members of the independent monitoring board for a prison shall visit the prison frequently, and the board shall arrange a rota whereby at least one of its members visits the prison between meetings of the board.
(2) A member of the board shall have access at any time to every part of the prison and to every prisoner, and he may interview any prisoner out of the sight and hearing of officers.
(3) A member of the board shall have access to the records of the prison, except that members of the board shall not have access to any records held for the purposes of or relating to conduct authorised in accordance with Part 2 of the Regulation of Investigatory Powers Act 2000.

## 80 Annual report
(1) The independent monitoring board for a prison shall, in accordance with paragraphs (2) and (3) below, from time to time make a report to the Secretary of State concerning the state of the prison and its administration, including in it any advice and suggestions they consider appropriate.
(2) The board shall comply with any directions given to them from time to time by the Secretary of State as to the following matters:
   (a) the period to be covered by a report under paragraph (1);
   (b) the frequency with which such a report is to be made; and
   (c) the length of time from the end of the period covered by such a report within which it is to be made;
   either in respect of a particular report or generally; providing that no direc-

tions may be issued under this paragraph if they would have the effect of requiring a board to make or deliver a report less frequently than once in every 12 months.

(3) Subject to any directions given to them under paragraph (2), the board shall, under paragraph (1), make an annual report to the Secretary of State as soon as reasonably possible after 31st December each year, which shall cover the period of 12 months ending on that date or, in the case of a board constituted for the first time during that period, such part of that period during which the board has been in existence.

## PART VI: SUPPLEMENTAL

### 81 Delegation by governor

The governor of a prison may, with the leave of the Secretary of State, delegate any of his powers and duties under these Rules to another officer of that prison.

### 82 Contracted out prisons

(1) Where the Secretary of State has entered into a contract for the running of a prison under section 84 of the Criminal Justice Act 1991 ('the 1991 Act') these Rules shall have effect in relation to that prison with the following modifications—

(a) references to an officer in the Rules shall include references to a prisoner custody officer certified as such under section 89(1) of the 1991 Act and performing custodial duties;

(b) references to a governor in the Rules shall include references to a director approved by the Secretary of State for the purposes of section 85(1)(a) of the 1991 Act except—

(i) in rule 81 the reference to a governor shall include a reference to a controller appointed by the Secretary of State under section 85(1)(b) of the 1991 Act;

(ii) in rules 62(1), 66 and 77 where references to a governor shall include references to the director and the controller; and

(iii) in rules 45, 48, 49, 53, 53A, 54, 55, 57, 60 and 61 where references to a governor shall include a reference to the director or the controller;

(c) rule 68 shall not apply in relation to a prisoner custody officer certified as such under section 89(1) of the 1991 Act and performing custodial duties.

(1A) The director of a prison may, with the leave of the Secretary of State, delegate any of his powers and duties under rules 45, 48, 49, 53, 53A, 55, 57, 60 and 61 to another officer of that prison.

(2) [*Revoked.*]

### 83 Contracted out parts of prisons

Where the Secretary of State has entered into a contract for the running of part of a prison under section 84(1) of the Criminal Justice Act 1991, that part and the remaining part shall each be treated for the purposes of Parts II to IV and Part VI of these Rules as if they were separate prisons.

**84 Contracted out functions at directly managed prisons**

(1) Where the Secretary of State has entered into a contract under section 88A(1) of the Criminal Justice Act 1991 ('the 1991 Act') for any functions at a directly managed prison to be performed by prisoner custody officers who are authorised to perform custodial duties under section 89(1) of the 1991 Act, references to an officer in these Rules shall, subject to paragraph (2), include references to a prisoner custody officer who is so authorised and who is performing contracted out functions for the purposes of, or for purposes connected with, the prison.

(2) Paragraph (1) shall not apply to references to an officer in rule 68.

(3) In this rule, 'directly managed prison' has the meaning assigned to it by section 88A(5) of the 1991 Act.

**85 Revocations and savings**

(1) Subject to paragraphs (2) and (3) below, the Rules specified in the Schedule to these Rules are hereby revoked.

(2) Without prejudice to the Interpretation Act 1978, where a prisoner committed an offence against discipline contrary to rule 47 of the Prison Rules 1964 prior to the coming into force of these Rules, those rules shall continue to have effect to permit the prisoner to be charged with such an offence, disciplinary proceedings in relation to such an offence to be continued, and the governor to impose punishment for such an offence.

(3) Without prejudice to the Interpretation Act 1978, any award of additional days or other punishment or suspended punishment for an offence against discipline awarded or imposed under any provision of the rules revoked by this rule, or those rules as saved by paragraph (2), or treated by any such provision as having been awarded or imposed under the rules revoked by this rule, shall have effect as if awarded or imposed under the corresponding provision of these Rules.

## SCHEDULE

Rule 85

| *Rules Revoked* | *SI No* |
|---|---|
| The Prison Rules 1964 | 1964/388 |
| The Prison (Amendment) Rules 1968 | 1968/440 |
| The Prison (Amendment) Rules 1971 | 1971/2019 |
| The Prison (Amendment) Rules 1972 | 1972/1860 |
| The Prison (Amendment) Rules 1974 | 1974/713 |
| The Prison (Amendment) Rules 1976 | 1976/503 |
| The Prison (Amendment) Rules 1981 | 1981/70 |
| The Prison (Amendment) Rules 1982 | 1982/260 |
| The Prison (Amendment) Rules 1983 | 1983/568 |
| The Prison (Amendment) Rules 1987 | 1987/1256 |
| The Prison (Amendment) Rules 1988 | 1988/89 |
| The Prison (Amendment) (No 2) Rules 1988 | 1988/747 |
| The Prison (Amendment) (No 3) Rules 1988 | 1988/1421 |
| The Prison (Amendment) Rules 1989 | 1989/330 |

# Young Offender Institution Rules 2000[1]

## PART I: PRELIMINARY

### 1 Citation and commencement

(a) These Rules may be cited as the Young Offender Institution Rules 2000 and shall come into force on 1st April 2001.

(b) The Rules set out in the Schedule to this Order are hereby revoked.

### 2 Interpretation

(1) In these Rules, where the context so admits, the expression–

'adjudicator' means a District Judge (Magistrates' Courts) or Deputy District Judge (Magistrates' Courts) approved by the Lord Chancellor for the purpose of inquiring into a charge which has been referred to him.

'communication' includes any written or drawn communication from an inmate to any other person, whether intended to be transmitted by means of a postal service or not, and any communication from an inmate to any other person transmitted by means of a telecommunications system;

'compulsory school age' has the same meaning as in the Education Act 1996;

'controlled drug' means any drug which is a controlled drug for the purposes of the Misuse of Drugs Act 1971;

'fixed-term prisoner' has the meaning assigned to it by section 237(1) of the Criminal Justice Act 2003;

'governor' includes an officer for the time being in charge of a young offender institution;

'health care professional' means a person who is a member of a profession regulated by a body mentioned in section 25(3) of the National Health Service Reform and Health Care Professions Act 2002 and who is working within the young offender institution pursuant to rule 27(3);

'information technology equipment' includes any laptop or notebook computer, desktop computer, gaming console, handheld computing device, personal organiser or any electronic device containing a computer processor and capable of connecting to the internet, and any reference to information technology equipment includes a reference to–

(a) a component part of a device of that description; or

(b) any article designed or adapted for use with any information technology equipment (including any disk, film or other separate article on which images, sounds, computer code or other information may be stored or recorded) ;

'inmate' means a person who is required to be detained in a young offender institution;

'intercepted material' means the contents of any communication intercepted pursuant to these Rules;

'legal adviser' means, in relation to an inmate, his counsel or solicitor, and includes a clerk acting on behalf of his solicitor;

'minister appointed to a young offender institution' means a minister so appointed under section 10 of the Prison Act 1952;

'officer' means an officer of a young offender institution;

'registered medical practitioner' and 'registered nurse' mean a practitioner or nurse who is working within the young offender institution pursuant to rule 27(3);

'short-term prisoner' and 'long-term prisoner' have the meanings assigned to them by section 33(5) of the Criminal Justice Act 1991, as extended by sections 43(1) and 45(1) of that Act;

'telecommunications system' means any system (including the apparatus comprised in it) which exists for the purpose of facilitating the transmission of communications by any means involving the use of electrical or electro-magnetic energy;

'the 2003 Act' means the Criminal Justice Act 2003.

(2) In these Rules a reference to–

   (a) an award of additional days means additional days awarded under these Rules by virtue of section 42 of the Criminal Justice Act 1991 or by virtue of section 257 of the 2003 Act;

   (b) the Church of England includes a reference to the Church of Wales; and

   (c) a reference to a numbered rule is, unless otherwise stated, a reference to the rule of that number in these Rules and a reference to a numbered paragraph is in a rule, unless otherwise stated, a reference to the paragraph of that number in that rule.

## PART II: INMATES

### GENERAL

**3 Aims and general principles of young offender institutions**

(1) The aim of a young offender institution shall be to help offenders to prepare for their return to the outside community.

(2) The aim mentioned in paragraph (1) shall be achieved, in particular, by–

   (a) providing a programme of activities, including education, training and work designed to assist offenders to acquire or develop personal responsibility, self-discipline, physical fitness, interests and skills and to obtain suitable employment after release;

   (b) fostering links between the offender and the outside community; and

   (c) co-operating with the services responsible for the offender's supervision after release.

**4 Classification of inmates**

Inmates may be classified, in accordance with any directions of the Secretary of State, taking into account their ages, characters and circumstances.

## 5 Temporary release
(1) The Secretary of State may, in accordance with the other provisions of this rule, release temporarily an inmate to whom this rule applies.

(2) An inmate may be released under this rule for any period or periods and subject to any conditions.

(3) An inmate may only be released under this rule:
   (a) on compassionate grounds or for the purpose of receiving medical treatment;
   (b) to engage in employment or voluntary work;
   (c) to receive instruction or training which cannot reasonably be provided in the young offender institution;
   (d) to enable him to participate in any proceedings before any court, tribunal or inquiry;
   (e) to enable him to consult with his legal adviser in circumstances where it is not reasonably practicable for the consultation to take place in the young offender institution;
   (f) to assist any police officer in any enquiries;
   (g) to facilitate the inmate's transfer between the young offender institution and another penal establishment;
   (h) to assist him in maintaining family ties or in his transition from life in the young offender institution to freedom.
   (i) [*Revoked.*]

(4) An inmate shall not be released under this rule unless the Secretary of State is satisfied that there would not be an unacceptable risk of his committing offences whilst released or otherwise of his failing to comply with any condition upon which he is released.

(5) Where at any time an offender is subject concurrently:
   (a) to a detention and training order; and
   (b) to a sentence of detention in a young offender institution, he shall be treated for the purposes of paragraphs (6) and (7) as if he were subject only to the one of them that was imposed on the later occasion.

(6) The Secretary of State shall not release under this rule an inmate if, having regard to:
   (a) the period or proportion of his sentence which the inmate has served or, in a case where paragraph (10) does not apply to require all the sentences he is serving to be treated as a single term, the period or proportion of any such sentence he has served; and
   (b) the frequency with which the inmate has been granted temporary release under this rule,
   the Secretary of State is of the opinion that the release of the inmate would be likely to undermine public confidence in the administration of justice.

(7) If an inmate has been temporarily released under this rule during the relevant period and has been sentenced to any period of detention, custody or imprisonment for a criminal offence committed whilst at large following that release, he shall not be released under this rule unless his release, having regard to the circumstances of his conviction, would not, in the opinion of the Secretary of State, be likely to undermine public confidence in the administration of justice; and for this purpose 'the relevant period':
   (a) in the case of an inmate serving a determinate sentence of imprisonment,

detention or custody, is the period he has served in respect of that sentence, unless, notwithstanding paragraph (10), the sentences he is serving do not fall to be treated as a single term, in which case it is the period since he was last released in relation to one of those sentences under Part II of the Criminal Justice Act 1991 ('the 1991 Act') or section 100 of the Powers of the Criminal Courts (Sentencing) Act 2000 ('the 2000 Act') or Chapter 6 of Part 12 of the 2003 Act; or

(b) in the case of an inmate serving an indeterminate sentence of imprisonment, detention or custody, is, if the inmate has previously been released on licence under Part II of the 1991 Act or Part II of the Crime (Sentences) Act 1997 [ or Chapter 6 of Part 12 of the 2003 Act, the period since the date of his last recall to a penal establishment in respect of that sentence or, where the inmate has not been so released, the period he has served in respect of that sentence,

save that where an inmate falls within both of sub-paragraphs (a) and (b) above, the 'relevant period', in the case of that inmate, shall be determined by whichever of the applicable sub-paragraphs that produces the longer period.

(8) An inmate released under this rule may be recalled at any time whether the conditions of his release have been broken or not.

(9) This rule applies to inmates other than persons committed in custody for trial or to be sentenced or otherwise dealt with before or by the Crown Court or remanded in custody by any court.

(10) For the purposes of any reference in this rule to an inmate's sentence, consecutive terms and terms which are wholly or partly concurrent shall be treated as a single term.

(11) In this rule, any reference to release on licence under Part II of the 1991 Act includes any release on licence under any earlier legislation providing for early release on licence.

## CONDITIONS
### 6 Privileges

(1) There shall be established at every young offender institution systems of privileges approved by the Secretary of State and appropriate to the classes of inmates thereof and their ages, characters and circumstances, which shall include arrangements under which money earned by inmates maybe spent by them within the young offender institution.

(2) Systems of privileges approved under paragraph (1) may include arrangements under which inmates may be allowed time outside the cells and in association with one another, in excess of the minimum time which, subject to the other provisions of these Rules apart from this rule, is otherwise allowed to inmates at the young offender institution for this purpose.

(3) Systems of privileges approved under paragraph (1) may include arrangements under which privileges may be granted to inmates only in so far as they have met, and for so long as they continue to meet, specified standards in their behaviour and their performance in work or other activities.

(4) Systems of privileges which include arrangements of the kind referred to in paragraph (3) shall include procedures to be followed in determining whether or not any of the privileges concerned shall be granted, or shall continue to be granted, to an inmate; such procedures shall include a requirement that the

inmate be given reasons for any decision adverse to him together with a statement of the means by which he may appeal against it.

(5) Nothing in this rule shall be taken to confer on an inmate any entitlement to any privilege or to affect any provision in these Rules other than this rule as a result of which any privilege may be forfeited or otherwise lost or an inmate deprived of association with other inmates.

## 7 Information to inmates

(1) Every inmate shall be provided, as soon as possible after his reception into the young offender institution, and in any case within 24 hours, with information in writing about those provisions of these Rules and other matters which it is necessary that he should know, including earnings and privileges, and the proper method of making requests and complaints.

(2) In the case of an inmate aged under 18, or an inmate aged 18 or over who cannot read or appears to have difficulty in understanding the information so provided, the governor, or an officer deputed by him, shall so explain it to him that he can understand his rights and obligations.

(3) A copy of these Rules shall be made available to any inmate who requests it.

## 8 Requests and complaints

(1) A request or complaint to the governor or [independent monitoring board] relating to an inmate's detention shall be made orally or in writing by that inmate.

(2) On every day the governor shall hear any oral requests and complaints that are made to him under paragraph (1).

(3) A written request or complaint under paragraph (1) may be made in confidence.

## 9 Communications generally

(1) Without prejudice to sections 6 and 19 of the Prison Act 1952 and except as provided by these Rules, an inmate shall not be permitted to communicate with any person outside the young offender institution, or such person with him, except with the leave of the Secretary of State or as a privilege under rule 7.

(2) Notwithstanding paragraph (1), and except as otherwise provided in these Rules, the Secretary of State may impose any restriction or condition, either generally or in a particular case, upon the communications to be permitted between an inmate and other persons if he considers that the restriction or condition to be imposed–

(a) does not interfere with the Convention rights of any person; or

(b) is necessary on grounds specified in paragraph (3) below, provided that:

(i) reliance on the grounds is compatible with the Convention right to be interfered with; and

(ii) the restriction or condition is proportionate to what is sought to be achieved.

(3) The grounds referred to in paragraph (2) are–

(a) the interests of national security;

(b) the prevention, detection, investigation or prosecution of crime;

(c) the interests of public safety;

(d) securing or maintaining security or good order and discipline in the young offender institution;

(e) the protection of health or morals;

(f) the protection of the reputation of others;

(g) maintaining the authority and impartiality of the judiciary; or

(h) the protection of the rights and freedoms of any person.

(4) Subject to paragraph (2), the Secretary of State may require that any visit, or class of visits, shall be held in facilities which include special features restricting or preventing physical contact between an inmate and a visitor.

(5) Every visit to an inmate shall take place within the sight of an officer or employee of the young offender institution authorised for the purposes of this rule by the governor (in this rule referred to as an 'authorised employee'), unless the Secretary of State otherwise directs, and for the purposes of this paragraph a visit to an inmate shall be taken to take place within the sight of an officer or authorised employee if it can be seen by an officer or authorised employee by means of an overt closed circuit television system.

(6) Subject to rule 13, every visit to an inmate shall take place within the hearing of an officer or authorised employee, unless the Secretary of State otherwise directs.

(7) The Secretary of State may give directions, either generally or in relation to any visit or class of visits, concerning the day and times when inmates may be visited.

(8 In this rule–

(a) references to communications include references to communications during visits;

(b) references to restrictions and conditions upon communications include references to restrictions and conditions in relation to the length, duration and frequency of communications; and

(c) references to Convention rights are to the Convention rights within the meaning of the Human Rights Act 1998.

## 10 Personal letters and visits

(1) Subject to paragraph (7) an inmate shall be entitled–

(a) to send and to receive a letter on his reception into a young offender institution and thereafter once a week; and

(b) to receive a visit twice in every period of four weeks, but only once in every such period if the Secretary of State so directs.

(2) The governor may allow an inmate an additional letter or visit as a privilege under rule 6 or when necessary for his welfare or that of his family.

(3) The governor may allow an inmate entitled to a visit to send and to receive a letter instead.

(4) The governor may defer the right of an inmate to a visit until the expiration of any period of confinement to a cell or room.

(5) The independent monitoring board may allow an inmate an additional letter or visit in special circumstances, and may direct that a visit may extend beyond the normal duration.

(6) The Secretary of State may allow additional letters and visits in relation to any inmate or class of inmates.

(7) An inmate shall not be entitled under this rule to receive a visit from–

(a) any person, whether or not a relative or friend, during any period of time that person is the subject of a prohibition imposed under rule 77; or

(b) any other person, other than a relative or friend, except with the leave of the Secretary of State.

(8) Any letter or visit under the succeeding provisions of these Rules shall not be counted as a letter or visit for the purposes of this rule.

## 11 Interception of communications

(1) The Secretary of State may give directions to any governor concerning the interception in a young offender institution of any communication by any inmate or class of inmates if the Secretary of State considers that the directions are—

(a) necessary on grounds specified in paragraph (4); and

(b) proportionate to what is sought to be achieved.

(2) Subject to any directions given by the Secretary of State, the governor may make arrangements for any communication by an inmate or class of inmates to be intercepted in a young offender institution by an officer or an employee of the young offender institution authorised by the governor for the purposes of this rule (referred to in this rule as an 'authorised employee') if he considers that the arrangements are—

(a) necessary on grounds specified in paragraph (4); and

(b) proportionate to what is sought to be achieved.

(3) Any communication by an inmate may, during the course of its transmission in a young offender institution, be terminated by an officer or an authorised employee if he considers that to terminate the communication is—

(a) necessary on grounds specified in paragraph (4); and

(b) proportionate to what is sought to be achieved by the termination.

(4) The grounds referred to in paragraphs (1)(a), (2)(a) and (3)(a) are—

(a) the interests of national security;

(b) the prevention, detection, investigation or prosecution of crime;

(c) the interests of public safety;

(d) securing or maintaining security or good order and discipline in the young offender institution;

(e) the protection of health or morals; or

(f) the protection of the rights and freedoms of any person.

(5) Any reference to the grounds specified in paragraph (4) in relation to the interception of a communication by means of a telecommunications system in a young offender institution, or the disclosure or retention of intercepted material from such a communication, shall be taken to be a reference to those grounds with the omission of sub-paragraph (f).

(6) For the purposes of this rule 'interception'–

(a) in relation to a communication by means of a telecommunications system, means any action taken in relation to the system or its operation so as to make some or all of the contents of the communications available, while being transmitted, to a person other than the sender or intended recipient of the communication; and the contents of a communication are to be taken to be made available to a person while being transmitted where the contents of the communication, while being transmitted, are diverted or recorded so as to be available to a person subsequently; and

(b) in relation to any written or drawn communication, includes opening, reading, examining and copying the communication.

## 12 Permanent log of communications

(1) The governor may arrange for a permanent log to be kept of all communications by or to an inmate.

(2) The log referred to in paragraph (1) may include, in relation to a communication by means of a telecommunications system in a young offender institution, a record of the destination, duration and cost of the communication and, in relation to any written or drawn communication, a record of the sender and addressee of the communication.

## 13 Disclosure of material

(1) Except in accordance with paragraph (2), the governor may not disclose to any person who is not

(a) an officer of a young offender institution;

(b) an officer of the Secretary of State;

(c) an officer of the Youth Justice Board for England and Wales, where the Board has entered into a contract for the provision or running, or both, of the young offender institution; or

(d) an employee of the young offender institution authorised by the governor for the purpose of this rule, any intercepted material, information retained pursuant to rule 12 or material obtained by means of an overt closed circuit television system used during a visit.

(2) The governor may disclose the material and information identified in paragraph (1) to persons, other than those mentioned in that paragraph, if:

(a) he considers that such disclosure is–
  (i) necessary on the grounds specified in rule 11(4); and
  (ii) proportionate to what is sought to be achieved by the disclosure;

(b) in the case of intercepted material or material obtained by means of an overt closed circuit television system used during a visit, all parties to the communication or visit consent to the disclosure; or

(c) in the case of information retained pursuant to rule 12, the inmate to whose communication the information relates, consents to the disclosure.

## 14 Retention of material

(1) The governor shall not retain any intercepted material or material obtained by means of an overt closed circuit television system used during a visit for a period longer than 3 months beginning with the day on which the material was intercepted or obtained unless he is satisfied that continued retention of it is–

(a) necessary on grounds specified in rule 11(4); and

(b) proportionate to what is sought to be achieved by the continued retention.

(2) Where such material is retained for longer than three months pursuant to paragraph (1) the governor shall review its continued retention at periodic intervals until such time as it is no longer held by the governor.

(3) The first review referred to in paragraph (2) shall take place not more than three months after the decision to retain the material taken pursuant to para-

graph (1) and subsequent reviews shall take place not more than three months apart thereafter.

(4) If the governor, on a review conducted pursuant to paragraph (2) or at any other time, is not satisfied that the continued retention of the material satisfies the requirements set out in paragraph (1), he shall arrange for the material to be destroyed.

### 15 Police interviews

A police officer may, on production of an order issued by or on behalf of a chief officer of police, interview any inmate willing to see him.

### 16 Legal advisers

(1) The legal adviser of an inmate in any legal proceedings, civil or criminal, to which the inmate is a party shall be afforded reasonable facilities for interviewing him in connection with those proceedings, and may do so out of hearing of an officer.

(2) An inmate's legal adviser may, with the leave of the Secretary of State, interview the inmate in connection with any other legal business.

### 17 Correspondence with legal advisers and courts

(1) An inmate may correspond with his legal adviser and any court and such correspondence may only be opened, read or stopped by the governor in accordance with the provisions of this rule.

(2) Correspondence to which this rule applies may be opened if the governor has reasonable cause to believe that it contains an illicit enclosure and any such enclosure shall be dealt with in accordance with the other provisions of these Rules.

(3) Correspondence to which this rule applies may be opened, read and stopped if the governor has reasonable cause to believe its contents endanger prison or young offender institution security or the safety of others or are otherwise of a criminal nature.

(4) An inmate shall be given the opportunity to be present when any correspondence to which this rule applies is opened and shall be informed if it or any enclosure is to be read or stopped.

(5) An inmate shall on request be provided with any writing materials necessary for the purposes of paragraph (1).

(6) In this rule, 'court' includes the European Court of Human Rights and the European Court of Justice; and 'illicit enclosure' includes any article possession of which has not been authorised in accordance with the other provisions of these Rules and any correspondence to or from a person other than the inmate concerned, his legal adviser or a court.

### 18 Securing release of defaulters

An inmate detained in a young offender institution in default of payment of a fine or any other sum of money may communicate with, and be visited at any reasonable time on a weekday by, any relative or friend for payment in order to secure his release.

## 19 Clothing
(1) An inmate shall be provided with clothing adequate for warmth and health in accordance with a scale approved by the Secretary of State.
(2) The clothing provided under this rule shall include suitable protective clothing for use at work, where this is needed.
(3) Subject to the provisions of rule 45(3), an inmate shall wear clothing provided under this rule and no other, except on the directions of the Secretary of State or as a privilege under rule 6.
(4) An inmate shall where necessary be provided with suitable and adequate clothing on his release.

## 20 Food
(1) Subject to any directions of the Secretary of State, no inmate shall be allowed, except as authorised by a health care professional as is mentioned in rule 27(3), to have any food other than that ordinarily provided.
(2) The food provided shall be wholesome, nutritious, well prepared and served, reasonably varied and sufficient in quantity.
(3) Any person deemed by the governor to be competent, shall from time to time inspect the food both before and after it is cooked, and shall report any deficiency or defect to the governor.
(4) In this rule, 'food' includes drink.

## 21 Alcohol and tobacco
(1) No inmate shall be allowed to have any intoxicating liquor.
(2) No inmate shall be allowed to smoke or to have any tobacco except in accordance with any directions of the Secretary of State.

## 22 Sleeping accommodation
(1) No room or cell shall be used as sleeping accommodation for an inmate unless it has been certified by an officer of the Secretary of State (not being an officer of a young offender institution) that its size, lighting, heating, ventilation and fittings are adequate for health, and that it allows the inmate to communicate at any time with an officer.
(2) A certificate given under this rule shall specify the maximum number of inmates who may sleep in the room or cell at one time, and the number so specified shall not be exceeded without the leave of the Secretary of State.

## 23 Beds and bedding
Each inmate shall be provided with a separate bed and with separate bedding adequate for warmth and health.

## 24 Hygiene
(1) Every inmate shall be provided with toilet articles necessary for his health and cleanliness, which shall be replaced as necessary.
(2) Every inmate shall be required to wash at proper times, have a hot bath or shower on reception and thereafter at least once a week.
(3) An inmate's hair shall not be cut without his consent.

## 25 Female inmates
The Secretary of State may, subject to any conditions he thinks fit, permit a

female inmate to have her baby with her in a young offender institution, and everything necessary for the baby's maintenance and care may be provided there.

**26 Library books**

A library shall be provided in every young offender institution and, subject to any directions of the Secretary of State, every inmate shall be allowed to have library books and to exchange them.

## MEDICAL ATTENTION

**27 Medical attendance**

(1) The medical officer of a young offender institution shall have the care of the health, mental and physical, of the inmates of that institution.

(2) Every request by an inmate to see a registered medical practitioner, a registered nurse or other health care professional such as is mentioned in paragraph (3) of this rule shall be recorded by the officer to whom it is made and promptly passed on to the medical officer.

(3)[2] The medical officer may consult–

   (a) a registered medical practitioner,
   (b) a registered nurse, or
   (c) any other health care professional, and such a person may work within the young offender institution under the general supervision of the medical officer.

(4) [*Revoked.*]

(5) Subject to any directions given in the particular case by the Secretary of State, a registered medical practitioner selected by or on behalf of an inmate who is a party to any legal proceedings shall be afforded reasonable facilities for examining him in connection with the proceedings, and may do so out of hearing but in the sight of an officer.

**28 Special illnesses and conditions**

(1) A registered medical practitioner such as is mentioned in rule 27(3) shall report to the governor on the case of any inmate whose health is likely to be injuriously affected by continued detention or any conditions of detention. The governor shall send the report to the Secretary of State without delay, together with his own recommendations.

(2) [*Revoked.*]

**29 Notification of illness or death**

(1) If an inmate dies, or becomes seriously ill, sustains any severe injury or is removed to hospital on account of mental disorder, the governor shall, if he knows his or her address, at once inform the inmate's spouse or next of kin, and also any person who the inmate may reasonably have asked should be informed.

(2) If an inmate dies, the governor shall give notice immediately to the coroner having jurisdiction, to the independent monitoring board and to the Secretary of State.

---

2  Words inserted by The Medical Act 1983 (Amendment) Order 2002 SI No 3135. Insertion has effect from date to be announced.

## RELIGION

### 30 Religious denomination

An inmate shall be treated as being of the religious denomination stated in the record made in pursuance of section 10(5) of the Prison Act 1952, but the governor may, in a proper case after due inquiry, direct that record to be amended.

### 31 Special duties of chaplains and appointed ministers

(1) The chaplain or a minister appointed to a young offender institution shall–

(a) interview every inmate of his denomination individually as soon as he reasonably can after the inmate's reception into that institution and shortly before his release; and

(b) if no other arrangements are made, read the burial service at the funeral of any inmate of his denomination who dies in that institution.

(2) The chaplain shall visit daily all inmates belonging to the Church of England who are sick, under restraint or confined to a room or cell; and a minister appointed to a young offender institution shall do the same, as far as he reasonably can, for inmates of his own denomination.

(3) If the inmate is willing, the chaplain shall visit any inmate not of the Church of England who is sick, under restraint or confined to a room or cell, and is not regularly visited by a minister of his own denomination.

### 32 Regular visits by ministers of religion, etc

(1) The chaplain shall visit regularly the inmates belonging to the Church of England.

(2) A minister appointed to a young offender institution shall visit the inmates of his denomination as regularly as he reasonably can.

(3) The governor shall, if so requested by an inmate belonging to a denomination for which no minister has been appointed to a young offender institution do what he reasonably can to arrange for that inmate to be visited regularly by a minister of that denomination.

(4) Every request by an inmate to see the chaplain or a minister appointed to a young offender institution shall be promptly passed on to the chaplain or minister.

### 33 Religious services

(1) The chaplain shall conduct Divine Service for inmates belonging to the Church of England at least once every Sunday, Christmas Day and Good Friday, and such celebrations of Holy Communion and weekday services as may be arranged.

(2) A minister appointed to a young offender institution shall conduct Divine Service for inmates of his denomination at such times as may be arranged.

### 34 Substitute for chaplain or appointed minister

(1) A person approved by the Secretary of State may act for the chaplain in his absence.

(2) A minister appointed to a young offender institution may, with the leave of the Secretary of State, appoint a substitute to act for him in his absence.

### 35 Sunday work

Arrangements shall be made so as not to require inmates to do any unnecessary work on Sunday, Christmas Day or Good Friday nor inmates of religions other than the Christian religion to do any unnecessary work on their recognised days of religious observance (as in alternative, but not in addition, to those days).

### 36 Religious books

There shall, so far as reasonably practicable, be available for the personal use of every inmate such religious books recognised by his denomination as are approved by the Secretary of State for use in young offender institutions.

## OCCUPATION AND LINKS WITH THE COMMUNITY

### 37 Regime activities

(1) An inmate shall be occupied in a programme of activities provided in accordance with rule 3 which shall include education, training courses, work and physical education.

(2) In all such activities regard shall be paid in individual assessment and personal development.

(3) The medical officer or a medical practitioner such as is mentioned in rule 27(3) may excuse an inmate from work or any other activity on medical grounds; and no inmate shall be set to participate in work or any other activity of a kind for which he is considered by the medical officer or a medical practitioner such as is mentioned in rule 27(3) to be unfit.

(4) An inmate may be required to participate in regime activities for no longer than the relevant period in a day, 'the relevant period' for this purpose being–

  (a) on a day in which an hour or more of physical education is provided for the inmate, 11 hours;

  (b) on a day in which no such education is provided for the inmate, ten hours; or

  (c) on a day in which a period of less than an hour of such education is provided for the inmate, the sum of ten hours and the period of such education provided,

  provided that he may not be required to participate in any one regime activity for more than eight hours in a day.

(5) Inmates may be paid for their work or participation in other activities at rates approved by the Secretary of State, either generally or in relation to particular cases.

### 38 Education

(1) Provision shall be made at a young offender institution for the education of inmates by means of programmes of class teaching or private study within the normal working week and, so far as practicable, programmes of evening and weekend educational classes or private study. The educational activities shall, so far as practicable, be such as will foster personal responsibility and an inmate's interests and skills and help him to prepare for his return to the community.

(2) In the case of an inmate of compulsory school age, arrangements shall be

made for his participation in education or training courses for at least 15 hours a week within the normal working week.

(3) In the case of an inmate aged 17 or over who has special educational needs, arrangements shall be made for education appropriate to his needs, if necessary within the normal working week.

(4) In the case of a female inmate aged 21 or over who is serving a sentence of imprisonment or who has been committed to prison for default and who is detained in a young offender institution instead of a prison, reasonable facilities shall be afforded if she wishes to improve her education, by class teaching or private study.

## 39 Training courses

(1) Provision shall be made at a young offender institution for the training of inmates by means of training courses, in accordance with directions of the Secretary of State.

(2) Training courses shall be such as will foster personal responsibility and an inmate's interests and skills and improve his prospects of finding suitable employment after release.

(3) Training courses shall, so far as practicable, be such as to enable inmates to acquire suitable qualifications.

## 40 Work

(1) Work shall, so far as practicable, be such as will foster personal responsibility and an inmate's interests and skills and help him to prepare for his return to the community.

(2) No inmate shall be set to do work of a kind not authorised by the Secretary of State.

## 41 Physical education

(1) Provision shall be made at a young offender institution for the physical education of inmates within the normal working week, as well as evening and weekend physical recreation. The physical education activities shall be such as will foster personal responsibility and an inmate's interests and skills and encourage him to make good use of his leisure on release.

(2) Arrangements shall be made for each inmate, other than one to whom paragraph (3) and (5) applies, to participate in physical education for at least two hours a week on average or, in the case of inmates detailed in such institutions or parts of institutions as the Secretary of State may direct, for at least 1 hour each weekday on average, but outside the hours allotted to education under rule 38(2) in the case of an inmate of compulsory school age.

(3) If circumstances reasonably permit, a female inmate aged 21 years or over shall be given the opportunity to participate in physical education for at least one hour a week.

(4) In the case of an inmate with a need for remedial physical activity, appropriate facilities shall be provided.

(5) If the weather permits and subject to the need to maintain good order and discipline, a female inmate aged 21 years or over shall be given the opportunity to spend time in the open air at least once every day, for such period as may be reasonable in the circumstances.

## 42 Outside contacts

(1) The governor shall encourage links between the young offender institution and the community by taking steps to establish and maintain relations with suitable persons and agencies outside the institution.

(2) The governor shall ensure that special attention is paid to the maintenance of such relations between an inmate and his family as seem desirable in the best interests of both.

(3) Subject to any directions of the Secretary of State, an inmate shall be encouraged, as far as practicable, to participate in activities outside the young offender institution which will be of benefit to the community or of benefit to the inmate in helping him to prepare for his return to the community.

## 43 After-care

(1) From the beginning of his sentence, consideration shall be given, in consultation with the appropriate supervising service, to an inmate's future and the help to be given to him in preparation for and after his return to the community.

(2) Every inmate who is liable to supervision after release shall be given a careful explanation of his liability and the requirements to which he will be subject while under supervision.

## 44 Maintenance of order and discipline

(1) Order and discipline shall be maintained, but with no more restriction than is required in the interests of security and well-ordered community life.

(2) Notwithstanding paragraph (1), regimes may be established at young offender institutions under which stricter order and discipline are maintained and which emphasise strict standards of dress, appearance and conduct; provided that no inmate shall be required to participate in such a regime unless he has been first assessed as being suitable for it and no inmate shall be required to continue with such a regime if at any time it appears that he is no longer suitable for it.

(3) For the purposes of paragraph (2), whether an inmate is suitable for a stricter regime is to be assessed by reference to whether he is sufficiently fit in mind and body to undertake it and whether, in the opinion of the Secretary of State, experience of the regime will further his rehabilitation.

(4) In the control of inmates, officers shall seek to influence them through their own example and leadership, and to enlist their willing co-operation.

## 45 Custody outside a young offender institution

(1) A person being taken to or from a young offender institution in custody shall be exposed as little as possible to public observation and proper care shall be taken to protect him from curiosity and insult.

(2) An inmate required to be taken in custody anywhere outside a young offender institution shall be kept in the custody of an officer appointed under section 3 of the Prison Act 1952 or of a police officer.

(3) An inmate required to be taken in custody to any court shall, when he appears before the court, wear his own clothing or ordinary civilian clothing provided by the governor.

## 46 Search
(1) Every inmate shall be searched when taken into custody by an officer, on his reception into a young offender institution and subsequently as the governor thinks necessary or as the Secretary of State may direct.
(2) An inmate shall be searched in as seemly a manner as is consistent with discovering anything concealed.
(3) No inmate shall be stripped and searched in the sight of another inmate or in the sight of a person of the opposite sex.

## 47 Record and photograph
(1) A personal record of each inmate shall be prepared and maintained in such manner as the Secretary of State may direct, but no part of the record shall be disclosed to any person not authorised to receive it.
(2) Every inmate may be photographed on reception and subsequently, but no copy of the photograph or any other personal record shall be given to any person not authorised to receive it.
(2A) In this rule 'personal record' may include personal information and biometric records (such as fingerprints or other physical measurements).

## 48 Inmates' property
(1) Anything, other than cash, which an inmate has at a young offender institution and which he is not allowed to retain for his own use shall be taken into the governor's custody.
(2) Any case which an inmate has at a young offender institution shall be paid into an account under the control of the governor and the inmate shall be credited with the amount in the books of the institution.
(3) Any article belonging to an inmate which remains unclaimed for a period of more than three years after he is released, or dies, may be sold or otherwise disposed of; and the net proceeds of any sale shall be paid to the National Association for the Care and Resettlement of Offenders, for its general purposes.
(4) The governor may confiscate any unauthorised article found in the possession of an inmate after his reception into a young offender institution, or concealed or deposited within a young offender institution.

## 49 Removal from association
(1) Where it appears desirable, for the maintenance of good order or discipline or in his own interests, that an inmate should not associate with other inmates, either generally or for particular purposes, the governor may arrange for the inmate's removal from association accordingly.
(2) An inmate shall not be removed under this rule for a period of more than 72 hours without the authority of the Secretary of State and authority given under this paragraph shall be for a period not exceeding 14 days but it may be renewed from time to time for a like period.
(3) The governor may arrange at his discretion for an inmate removed under this rule to resume association with other inmates at any time, and in exercising that discretion the governor must fully consider any recommendation that the inmate resumes association on medical grounds made by a registered medical practitioner or registered nurse such as is mentioned in rule 27(3).

## 50 Use of force

(1) An officer in dealing with an inmate shall not use force unnecessarily and, when the application of force to an inmate is necessary, no more force than is necessary shall be used.

(2) No officer shall act deliberately in a manner calculated to provoke an inmate.

## 51 Temporary confinement

(1) The governor may order an inmate who is refractory or violent to be confined temporarily in a special cell or room, but an inmate shall not be so confined as a punishment, or after he has ceased to be refractory or violent.

(2) A cell or room shall not be used for the purpose of this rule unless it has been certified by an officer of the Secretary of State (not being an officer of a young offender institution) that it is suitable for the purpose, that its size, lighting, heating, ventilation and fittings are adequate for health, and that it allows the inmate to communicate at any time with an officer.

(3) In relation to any young offender institution, section 14(6) of the Prison Act 1952 shall have effect so as to enable the provision of special rooms instead of special cells for the temporary confinement of refractory or violent inmates.

(4) An inmate shall not be confined under this rule for longer than 24 hours without a direction in writing given by an officer of the Secretary of State.

## 52 Restraints

(1) The governor may order an inmate to be put under restraint where this is necessary to prevent the inmate from injuring himself or others, damaging property or creating a disturbance.

(2) The governor may not order an inmate aged under 17 to be put under restraint, except that he may order such an inmate be placed in handcuffs where this is necessary to prevent the inmate from injuring himself or others, damaging property or creating a disturbance.

(3) Notice of such an order shall be given without delay to a member of the independent monitoring board and to the registered medical practitioner or registered nurse such as is mentioned in rule 27(3).

(4) On receipt of the notice, the registered medical practitioner or registered nurse referred to in paragraph (3), shall inform the governor whether there are any reasons why the inmate should not be put under restraint. The governor shall give effect to any recommendation which may be made under this paragraph.

(5) An inmate shall not be kept under restraint longer than necessary, nor shall he be so kept for longer than 24 hours without a direction in writing given by a member of the independent monitoring board or by an officer of the Secretary of State (not being an officer of a young offender institution). Such a direction shall state the grounds for the restraint and the time during which it may continue.

(6) Particulars of every case of restraint under the foregoing provisions of this rule shall be forthwith recorded.

(7) Except as provided by this rule no inmate shall be put under restraint otherwise than for safe custody during removal, or on medical grounds by direction of the registered medical practitioner or registered nurse such as is mentioned in rule 27(3). No inmate shall be put under restraint as a punishment.

(8) Any means of restraint shall be of a pattern authorised by the Secretary of State, and shall be used in such manner and under such conditions as the Secretary of State may direct.

## 53 Compulsory Testing for controlled drugs

(1) This rule applies where an officer, acting under the powers conferred by section 16A of the Prison Act 1952 (power to test inmates for drugs), requires an inmate to provide a sample for the purposes of ascertaining whether he has any controlled drug in his body.

(2) In this rule 'sample' means a sample of urine or any other description of sample specified in the authorisation by the governor for the purposes of section 16A.

(3) When requiring an inmate to provide a sample, an officer shall, so far as is reasonably practicable, inform the inmate:
(a) that he is being required to provide a sample in accordance with section 16A of the Prison Act 1952; and
(b) that a refusal to provide a sample may lead to disciplinary proceedings being brought against him.

(4) An officer shall require an inmate to provide a fresh sample, free from any adulteration.

(5) An officer requiring a sample shall make such arrangements and give the inmate such instructions for its provision as may be reasonably necessary in order to prevent or detect its adulteration or falsification.

(6) An inmate who is required to provide a sample may be kept apart from other inmates for a period not exceeding one hour to enable arrangements to be made for the provisions of the sample.

(7) An inmate who is unable to provide a sample of urine when required to do so may be kept apart from other inmates until he has provided the required sample, save that an inmate may not be kept apart under this paragraph for a period of more than five hours.

(8) An inmate required to provide a sample of urine shall be afforded such degree of privacy for the purposes of providing the sample as may be compatible with the need to prevent or detect any adulteration or falsification of the sample; in particular an inmate shall not be required to provide such a sample in the sight of a person of the opposite sex.

## 54 Supervision of inmates by means of an overt closed circuit television system

(1) Without prejudice to his powers to make arrangements for the supervision of inmates in his custody, the governor may make arrangements for any inmate to be placed under constant supervision by means of an overt closed circuit television system placed in a cell, dormitory or other place in the young offender institution if he considers that–
(a) such supervision is necessary for–
  (i) the health and safety of the inmate or any other person;
  (ii) the prevention, detection or prosecution of crime; or
  (iii) securing or maintaining security or good order and discipline in the young offender institution; and
(b) it is proportionate to what is sought to be achieved.

(2) If an overt closed circuit television system is used for the purposes of this rule, the provisions of rules 13 and 14 shall apply to any material obtained.

## 54A Compulsory testing for alcohol

(1) This rule applies where an officer, acting under an authorisation in force under section 16B of the Prison Act 1952 (power to test prisoners for alcohol), requires an inmate to provide a sample for the purpose of ascertaining whether he has alcohol in his body.

(2) When requiring an inmate to provide a sample an officer shall, so far as is reasonably practicable, inform the inmate–

    (a) that he is being required to provide a sample in accordance with section 16B of the Prison Act 1952; and

    (b) that a refusal to provide a sample may lead to disciplinary proceedings being brought against him.

(3) An officer requiring a sample shall make such arrangements and give the inmate such instructions for its provision as may be reasonably necessary in order to prevent or detect its adulteration or falsification.

(4) Subject to paragraph (5) an inmate who is required to provide a sample may be kept apart from other inmates for a period not exceeding one hour to enable arrangements to be made for the provision of the sample.

(5) An inmate who is unable to provide a sample of urine when required to do so may be kept apart from other inmates until he has provided the required sample, except that an inmate may not be kept apart under this paragraph for a period of more than 5 hours.

(6) An inmate required to provide a sample of urine shall be afforded such degree of privacy for the purposes of providing the sample as may be compatible with the need to prevent or detect any adulteration or falsification of the sample; in particular an inmate shall not be required to provide such a sample in the sight of a person of the opposite sex.

## 55 Offences against discipline

An inmate is guilty of an offence against discipline if he–

(1) commits any assault;

(2) commits any racially aggravated assault;

(3) detains any person against his will;

(4) denies access to any part of the young offender institution to any officer or any person (other than an inmate) who is at the young offender institution for the purpose of working there;

(5) fights with any person;

(6) intentionally endangers the health or personal safety of others or, by his conduct, is reckless whether such health or personal safety is endangered;

(7) intentionally obstructs an officer in the execution of his duty, or any person (other than an inmate) who is at the young offender institution for the purpose of working there, in the performance of his work;

(8) escapes or absconds from a young offender institution or from legal custody;

(9) fails to comply with any condition upon which he was temporarily released under rule 5 of these rules;

(10) is found with any substance in his urine which demonstrates that a controlled drug has, whether in prison or while on temporary release under rule 5, been administered to him by himself or by another person (but subject to rule 56);

(11) is intoxicated as a consequence of consuming any alcoholic beverage (but subject to rule 56A);

(12) consumes any alcoholic beverage whether or not provided to him by another person (but subject to rule 56A);
(13) has in his possession–
(a) any unauthorised article, or
(b) a greater quantity of any article than he is authorised to have;
(14) sells or delivers to any person any unauthorised article;
(15) sells or, without permission, delivers to any person any article which he is allowed to have only for his own use;
(16) takes improperly any article belonging to another person or to a young offender institution;
(17) intentionally or recklessly sets fire to any part of a young offender institution or any other property, whether or not his own;
(18) destroys or damages any part of a young offender institution or any other property other than his own; (19) causes racially aggravated damage to, or destruction of, any part of a young offender institution or any other property, other than his own;
(20) absents himself from any place where he is required to be or is present at any place where he is not authorised to be;
(21) is disrespectful to any officer, or any person (other than an inmate) who is at the young offender institution for the purpose of working there, or any person visiting a young offender institution;
(22) uses threatening, abusive or insulting words or behaviour;
(23) uses threatening, abusive or insulting racist words or behaviour;
(24) intentionally fails to work properly or, being required to work, refuses to do so;
(25) disobeys any lawful order;
(26) disobeys or fails to comply with any rule or regulation applying to him;
(27) receives any controlled drug or, without the consent of an officer, any other article, during the course of a visit (not being an interview such as is mentioned in rule 16);
(28) displays, attaches or draws on any part of a young offender institution, or on any other property, threatening, abusive, or insulting racist words, drawings, symbols or other material;
(29) (a) attempts to commit,
(b) incites another inmate to commit, or
(c) assists another inmate to commit or to attempt to commit,
any of the foregoing offences.

## 56 Defences to rule 55(10)
It shall be a defence for an inmate charged with an offence under rule 55(10) to show that–
(a) the controlled drug had been, prior to its administration, lawfully in his possession for his use or was administered to him in the course of a lawful supply of the drug to him by another person;
(b) the controlled drug was administered by or to him in circumstances in which he did not know and had no reason to suspect that such a drug was being administered; or
(c) the controlled drug was administered by or to him under duress or to him without his consent in circumstances where it was not reasonable for him to have resisted.

**56A Defences to rule 55(11) and rule 55(12)**

It shall be a defence for an inmate charged with an offence under rule 55(11) or (12) to show that–

(a) the alcohol was consumed by him in circumstances in which he did not know and had no reason to suspect that he was consuming alcohol; or

(b) the alcohol was consumed by him without his consent in circumstances where it was not reasonable for him to have resisted.

(c) [*Revoked.*]

**57 Interpretation of rule 55**

For the purposes of rule 55 words, behaviour or material shall be racist if they demonstrate or are motivated (wholly or partly) by hostility to members of a racial group (whether identifiable or not) based on their membership (or presumed membership) of a racial group, and 'membership', 'presumed', 'racial group' and 'racially aggravated', shall have the meanings assigned to them by section 28 of the Crime and Disorder Act 1998

**58 Disciplinary charges**

(1) Where an inmate is to be charged with an offence against discipline, the charge shall be laid as soon as possible and, save in exceptional circumstances, within 48 hours of the discovery of the offence.

(2) Every charge shall be inquired into by the governor or, as the case may be, the adjudicator

(3) Every charge shall be first inquired into not later, save in exceptional circumstances or in accordance with rule 60A(5) or rule 65(4), than:

(a) where it is inquired into by the governor, the next day, not being a Sunday or public holiday, after it is laid;

(b) where it is referred to the adjudicator under rule 58A(2), 28 days after it is so referred.

(4) An inmate who is to be charged with an offence against discipline may be kept apart from other inmates pending the governor's first inquiry or determination under rule 58A.

**58A Determination of mode of inquiry**

(1) Before inquiring into a charge the governor shall determine whether it is so serious that additional days should be awarded for the offence, if the inmate is found guilty.

(2) Where the governor determines:

(a) that it is so serious, he shall:

(i) refer the charge to the adjudicator forthwith for him to inquire into it;

(ii) refer any other charge arising out of the same incident to the adjudicator forthwith for him to inquire into it; and

(iii) inform the inmate who has been charged that he has done so;

(b) that it is not so serious, he shall proceed to inquire into the charge.

(3) If:

(a) at any time during an inquiry into a charge by the governor; or

(b) following such an inquiry, after the governor has found the inmate guilty of an offence but before he has imposed a punishment for that offence, it appears to the governor that the charge is so serious that additional days should be awarded for the offence if (where sub-paragraph (a) applies) the inmate is found guilty, the governor shall act in accordance with paragraph (2)(a)(i) to (iii) and the adjudicator shall first inquire into any charge referred to him under this paragraph not later than, save in exceptional circumstances, 28 days after the charge was referred.

## 59 Rights of inmates charged

(1) Where an inmate is charged with an offence against discipline, he shall be informed of the charge as soon as possible and, in any case, before the time when it is inquired into by the governor or, as the case may be, the adjudicator.
(2) At an inquiry into charge against an inmate he shall be given a opportunity of hearing what is alleged against him and of presenting his own case.
(3) At an inquiry into a charge which has been referred to the adjudicator, the inmate who has been charged shall be given the opportunity to be legally represented.

## 60 Governor's punishments

(1) If he finds an inmate guilty of an offence against discipline the governor may, subject to paragraph (3) and rule 65, impose one or more of the following punishments:
 (a) caution;
 (b) forfeiture for a period not exceeding 21 days of any of the privileges under rule 6;
 (c) removal for a period not exceeding 21 days from any particular activity or activities of the young offender institution, other than education, training courses, work and physical education in accordance with rules 37, 38, 39, 40 and 41;
 (d) extra work outside the normal working week for a period not exceeding 21 days and for not more than two hours on any day;
 (e) stoppage of or deduction from earnings for a period not exceeding 42 days of;[3]
 (f) in the case of an offence against discipline committed by an inmate who was aged 18 or over at the time of commission of the offence, other than an inmate who is serving the period of detention and training under a detention and training order pursuant to section 100 of the Powers of Criminal Courts (Sentencing) Act 2000 , confinement to a cell or room for a period not exceeding ten days;
 (g) removal from his wing or living unit for a period not exceeding 21 days.
 (h) [*Revoked.*]
(2) If an inmate is found guilty of more than one charge arising out of an incident punishments under this rule may be ordered to run consecutively, but in the case of a punishment of cellular confinement the total period shall not exceed ten days.

---

3 Possible drafting error. Sentence does not make sense when only these words are repealed by Young Offender Institution (Amendment) Rules 2002 SI No 2117 Sch 1 para 5(b).

(3) A caution shall not be combined with any other punishment for the same charge.

(4) In imposing a punishment under this rule, the governor shall take into account any guidelines that the Secretary of State may from time to time issue as to the level of punishment that should normally be imposed for a particular offence against discipline.

### 60A Adjudicator's punishments

(1) If he finds a inmate guilty of an offence against discipline the adjudicator may, subject to paragraph (2) and to rule 65, impose one or more of the following punishments:
  (a) any of the punishments mentioned in rule 60(1);
  (b) in the case of an inmate who is a short-term prisoner or long-term prisoner or fixed-term prisoner, an award of additional days not exceeding 42 days.

(2) A caution shall not be combined with any other punishment for the same charge.

(3) If an inmate is found guilty of more than one charge arising out of an incident, punishments under this rule may be ordered to run consecutively but, in the case of an award of additional days, the total period added shall not exceed 42 days and, in the case of a punishment of cellular confinement, the total period shall not exceed ten days.

(4) This rule applies to an inmate who has been charged with having committed an offence against discipline before the date on which the rule came into force, in the same way as it applies to an inmate who has been charged with having committed an offence against discipline on or after that date, provided the charge is referred to the adjudicator no later than 60 days after that date.

(5) Rule 58(3) shall not apply to a charge where, by virtue of paragraph (4), this rule applies to the inmate who has been charged.

### 60B Review of adjudicator's punishment

(1) A reviewer means the Senior District Judge (Chief Magistrate) or any deputy of such a judge as nominated by that judge.

(2) Where a punishment is imposed by an adjudicator under rule 60A(1) or rule 65(1A) an inmate may, within 14 days of receipt of the punishment, request in writing that a reviewer conducts a review.

(3) The review must be commenced within 14 days of receipt of the request and must be conducted on the papers alone.

(4) The review must only be of the punishment imposed and must not be a review of the finding of guilt.

(5) On completion of the review, if it appears to the reviewer that the punishment imposed was manifestly unreasonable, he may–
  (a) reduce the number of any additional days awarded;
  (b) for whatever punishment has been imposed by the adjudicator, substitute another punishment which is, in his opinion, less severe; or
  (c) quash the punishment entirely.

(6) An inmate requesting a review shall serve any additional days awarded under rule 60A(1)(b) or 65(1A)(b) unless and until they are reduced.

## 61 Confinement to a cell or room

(1) Before deciding whether to impose a punishment of confinement to a cell or room, the governor, adjudicator or reviewer shall first enquire of a registered medical practitioner or registered nurse, such as is mentioned in rule 27(3), as to whether there are any medical reasons why the punishment is unsuitable and shall take this into account when making his decision.

(2) No cell or room shall be used as a detention cell or room for the purpose of a punishment of confinement to a cell or room unless it has been certified by an officer of the Secretary of State (not being an officer of a young offender institution) that it is suitable for the purpose; that its size, lighting, heating, ventilation and fittings are adequate for health; and that it allows the inmate to communicate at any time with an officer.

## 62 Removal from wing or living unit

Following the imposition of a punishment of removal from his wing or living unit, an inmate shall be accommodated in a separate part of the young offender institution under such restrictions of earnings and activities as the Secretary of State may direct.

## 63 Suspended punishments

(1) Subject to any directions of the Secretary of State, the power to impose a disciplinary punishment (other than a caution) shall include a power to direct that the punishment is not to take effect unless, during a period specified in the direction (not being more than six months from the date of the direction), the inmate commits another offence against discipline and a direction is given under paragraph (2).

(2) Where an inmate commits an offence against discipline during the period specified in a direction given under paragraph (1), the person dealing with that offence may–
  (a) direct that the suspended punishment shall take effect; or
  (b) reduce the period or amount of the suspended punishment and direct that it shall take effect as so reduced; or
  (c) vary the original direction by substituting for the period specified therein a period expiring not later than six months from the date of variation; or
  (d) give no direction with respect to the suspended punishment.

(3) Where an award of additional days has been suspended under paragraph (1) and an inmate is charged with committing an offence against discipline during the period specified in a direction given under that paragraph, the governor shall either:
  (a) inquire into the charge and give no direction with respect to the suspended award; or
  (b) refer the charge to the adjudicator for him to inquire into it.

## 64 Remission and mitigation of punishments and quashing of findings of guilt

(1) Except in the case of a finding of guilt made, or a punishment imposed, by an adjudicator under rule 60A(1)(b) or rule 65(1A)(b); the Secretary of State may quash any findings of guilt and may remit a disciplinary punishment or mitigate it either by reducing it or by substituting a punishment which is, in his opinion, less severe.

(2) Subject to any directions given by the Secretary of State, the governor may, on the grounds of good behaviour, remit or mitigate any punishment already imposed by an adjudicator or governor.

### 65 Adult female inmates: disciplinary punishments

(1) In the case of a female inmate aged 21 years or over, rule 60 shall not apply, but the governor may, if he finds the inmate guilty of an offence against discipline, impose one or more of the following punishments:
  (a) caution;
  (b) forfeiture for a period not exceeding 42 days of any of the privileges under rule 6;
  (c) removal for a period not exceeding 21 days from any particular activity or activities of the young offender institution, other than education, training courses, work and physical education in accordance with rules 37, 38, 39, 40 and 41;
  (d) stoppage of or deduction from earnings for a period not exceeding 84 days;
  (e) confinement to a cell or room for a period not exceeding 21 days.
  (f) [*Revoked.*]
(1A) In the case of a female inmate aged 21 years or over, where a charge has been referred to the adjudicator, rule 60A shall not apply, but the adjudicator may if he finds the inmate guilty of an offence against discipline, impose one or more of the following punishments:
  (a) any of the punishments mentioned in paragraph (1);
  (b) in the case of an inmate who is a short-term or long-term prisoner or fixed-term prisoner, an award of additional days not exceeding 42 days.
(2) If an inmate is found guilty of more than one charge arising out of an incident, punishments under this rule may be ordered to run consecutively, but in the case of an award of additional days, the total period added shall not exceed 42 days.
(3) Paragraph (1A) applies to an inmate who has been charged with having committed an offence against discipline before the date on which that paragraph came into force, in the same was as it applies to an inmate who has been charged with having committed an offence against discipline on or after that date, provided the charge is referred to the adjudicator no later than 60 days after that date.
(4) Rule 58(3) shall not apply to a charge where, by virtue of paragraph (3), paragraph (1A) applies to the inmate who has been charged.

### 66 Forfeiture of remission to be treated as an award of additional days

(1) In this rule, 'existing prisoner' and 'existing licensee' have the meanings assigned to them by paragraph 8(1) of Schedule 12 to the Criminal Justice Act 1991.
(2) In relation to any existing prisoner or existing licensee who has forfeited any remission of his sentence, the provisions of Part II of the Criminal Justice Act 1991 shall apply as if he had been awarded such number of additional days as equals the number of days of remission which he has forfeited.

## PART III

## OFFICERS OF YOUNG OFFENDER INSTITUTIONS

### 67 General duty of officers

(1) It shall be the duty of every officer to conform to these Rules and the rules and regulations of the young offender institution, to assist and support the governor in their maintenance and to obey his lawful instructions.

(2) An officer shall inform the governor promptly of any abuse or impropriety which comes to his knowledge.

### 68 Gratuities forbidden

No officer shall receive any unauthorised fee, gratuity or other consideration in connection with his office.

### 69 Search of officers

An officer shall submit himself to be searched in a young offender institution if the governor so directs. Any such search shall be conducted in as seemly a manner as is consistent with discovering anything concealed.

### 70 Transactions with inmates

(1) No officer shall take part in any business or pecuniary transaction with or on behalf of an inmate without the leave of the Secretary of State.

(2) No officer shall, without authority, bring in or take out, or attempt to bring in or take out, or knowingly allow to be brought in or taken out, to or for an inmate, or deposit in any place with intent that it shall come into the possession of an inmate, any article whatsoever.

### 71 Contact with former inmates, etc

No officer shall, without the knowledge of the governor, communicate with any person who he knows to be a former inmate or a relative or friend of an inmate or former inmate.

### 72 Communications to the press, etc

(1) No officer shall make, directly or indirectly, any unauthorised communication to a representative of the press or any other person concerning matters which have become known to him in the course of his duty.

(2) No officer shall, without authority, publish any matter or make any public pronouncement relating to the administration of any institution to which the Prison Act 1952 applies or to any of its inmates.

### 73 Code of discipline

The Secretary of State may approve a code of discipline to have effect in relation to officers, or such classes of officers as it may specify, setting out the offences against discipline, the awards which may be made in respect of them and the procedure for dealing with charges.

## PART IV

## PERSONS HAVING ACCESS TO A YOUNG OFFENDER INSTITUTION

### 74 Prohibited articles

No person shall, without authority, convey into or throw into or deposit in a young offender institution, or convey to an inmate, or deposit in any place with intent that it shall come into the possession of an inmate, any article whatsoever. Anything so conveyed, thrown or deposited may be confiscated by the governor.

### 74A

List C Articles

A List C article is any article or substance in the following list–

(a) tobacco;
(b) money;
(c) clothing;
(d) food;
(e) drink;
(f) letters;
(g) paper;
(h) books;
(i) tools;
(j) information technology equipment.

### 75 Control of persons and vehicles

(1) Any person or vehicle entering or leaving a young offender institution may be stopped, examined and searched and in addition any such person may be photographed, fingerprinted or required to submit to other physical measurement.

(1A) Any such search of a person shall be carried out in as seemly a manner as is consistent with discovering anything concealed about the person or their belongings.

(2) The governor may direct the removal from a young offender institution of any person who does not leave on being required to do so.

### 76 Viewing of young offender institutions

(1) No outside person shall be permitted to view a young offender institution unless authorised by statute or the Secretary of State.

(2) No person viewing a young offender institution shall be permitted to take a photograph, make a sketch or communicate with an inmate unless authorised by statute or the Secretary of State.

### 77 Visitors

(1) Without prejudice to any other powers to prohibit or restrict entry to young offender institutions, or his powers under rules 9 and 10, the Secretary of State may prohibit visits by a person to a young offender institution or to an inmate in a young offender institution for such periods of time as he considers necessary if the governor considers that such a prohibition is–

(a) necessary on grounds specified in rule 11(4); and

(b) is proportionate to what is sought to be achieved by the prohibition.

(2) Paragraph (1) shall not apply in relation to any visit to a young offender institution or inmate by a member of the independent monitoring board of the young offender institution, or justice of the peace, or to prevent any visit by a legal adviser for the purposes of an interview under rule 16 or visit allowed by the independent monitoring board under rule 10(5)

## PART V

## INDEPENDENT MONITORING BOARD

### 78 Disqualification for membership

Any person directly or indirectly interested in any contract for the supply of goods or services to a young offender institution shall not be a member of the independent monitoring board for that institution and any member who becomes so interested in such a contract shall vacate office as a member.

### 79 Appointment

(1) A member of the independent monitoring board for a young offender institution appointed by the Secretary of State under section 6(2) of the Prison Act 1952 shall subject to paragraphs (3) and (4) hold office for three years or such shorter period as the Secretary of State may appoint.

(2) A member–

(a) appointed for the first time to the independent monitoring board for a particular young offender institution; or

(b) re-appointed to the board following a gap of a year or more in his membership of it,

shall, during the period of 12 months following the date on which he is so appointed or (as the case may be) re-appointed, undertake such training as may reasonably be required by the Secretary of State.

(3) The Secretary of State may terminate the appointment of a member if satisfied that–

(a) he has failed satisfactorily to perform his duties;

(b) he has failed to undertake training he has been required to undertake under paragraph (2), by the end of the period specified in that paragraph;

(c) he is by reason of physical or mental illness, or for any other reason, incapable of carrying out his duties;

(d) he has been convicted of such a criminal offence, or his conduct has been such, that it is not in the Secretary of State's opinion fitting that he should remain a member; or

(e) there is, or appears to be, or could appear to be, any conflict of interest between the member performing his duties as a member and any interest of that member, whether personal, financial or otherwise.

(4) Where the Secretary of State:

(a) has reason to suspect that a member of the independent monitoring board for a young offender institution may have so conducted himself that his appointment may be liable to be terminated under paragraph (3)(a) or (d); and

(b) is of the opinion that the suspected conduct is of such a serious nature that the member cannot be permitted to continue to perform his functions as a member of the board pending the completion of the Secretary of State's investigations into the matter and any decision as to whether the member's appointment should be terminated,

he may suspend the member from office for such period or periods as he may reasonably require in order to complete his investigations and determine whether or not the appointment of the member should be so terminated; and a member so suspended shall not, during the period of the suspension, be regarded as being a member of the board, other than for the purposes of this paragraph and paragraphs (1) and (2).

(5) A board shall have a chairman and a vice chairman, who shall be members of the board.

(6) The Secretary of State shall–
  (a) upon the constitution of a board for the first time, appoint a chairman and a vice chairman to hold office for a period not exceeding 12 months;
  (b) thereafter appoint, before the date of the first meeting of the board in any year of office of the board, a chairman and a vice chairman for that year, having first consulted the board; and
  (c) promptly fill, after having first consulted the board, any casual vacancy in the office of chairman or vice chairman.

(7) The Secretary of State may terminate the appointment of a member as chairman or vice chairman of the board if he is satisfied that the member has–
  (a) failed satisfactorily to perform his functions as chairman or (as the case may be) vice-chairman; or
  (b) has grossly misconducted himself whilst performing those functions.

## 80 Proceedings of boards

(1) The independent monitoring board for a young offender institution shall meet at the institution at least once a month.

(2) The board may fix a quorum of not fewer than three members for proceedings.

(3) The board shall keep minutes of their proceedings.

(4) The proceedings of the board shall not be invalidated by any vacancy in the membership or any defect in the appointment of a member.

## 81 General duties of boards

(1) The independent monitoring board for a young offender institution shall satisfy themselves as to the state of the premises, the administration of the institution and the treatment of the inmates.

(2) The board shall inquire into and report upon any matter into which the Secretary of State asks them to inquire.

(3) The board shall direct the attention of the governor to any matter which calls for his attention, and shall report to the Secretary of State any matters which they consider it expedient to report.

(4) The board shall inform the Secretary of State immediately of any abuse which comes to their knowledge.

(5) Before exercising any power under these Rules, the board and any member of the board shall consult the governor in relation to any matter which may affect discipline.

## 82 Particular duties

(1) The independent monitoring board for a young offender institution and any member of the board shall hear any complaint or request which an inmate wishes to make to them or him.

(2) The board shall arrange for the food of the inmates to be inspected by a member of the board at frequent intervals.

(3) The board shall inquire into any report made to them, whether or not by a member of the board, that an inmate's health, mental or physical, is likely to be injuriously affected by any conditions of his detention.

## 83 Members visiting young offender institutions

(1) The members of the independent monitoring board for a young offender institution shall visit the institution frequently, and the board shall arrange a rota for the purpose.

(2) A member of the board shall have access at any time to every part of the institution and to every inmate, and he may interview any inmate out of the sight and hearing of officers.

(3) A member of the board shall have access to the records of the prison, except that members of the board shall not have access to any records held for the purposes of or relating to conduct authorised in accordance with Part 2 of the Regulation of Investigatory Powers Act 2000.

## 84 Annual report

(1) The independent monitoring board for a young offender institution shall, in accordance with paragraphs (2) and (3), from time to time make a report to the Secretary of State concerning the state of the institution and its administration, including in it any advice and suggestions they consider appropriate.

(2) The board shall comply with any directions given to them from time to time by the Secretary of State as to the following matters–

(a) the period to be covered by a report under paragraph (1);

(b) the frequency with which such a report is to be made; and

(c) the length of time from the end of the period covered by such a report within which it is to be made, either in respect of a particular report or generally;

provided that no directions may be issued under this paragraph if they would have the effect of requiring a board to make or deliver a report less frequently than once in every 12 months.

(3) Subject to any directions given to them under paragraph (2), the board shall, under paragraph (1), make an annual report to the Secretary of State as soon as reasonably possible after 31st December each year, which shall cover the period of 12 months ending on that date or, in the case of a board constituted for the first time during that period, such part of that period during which the board has been in existence.

## PART VI

**SUPPLEMENTAL**
### 85 Delegation by governor
The governor of a young offender institution may, with the leave of the Secretary of State, delegate any of his powers and duties under these Rules to another officer of that institution.

### 86 Contracted out young offender institutions
(1) Where the Secretary of State has entered into a contract for the running of a young offender institution under section 84 of the Criminal Justice Act 199183 (in this rule 'the 1991 Act') these Rules shall have effect in relation to that young offender institution with the following modifications–
  (a) references to an officer shall include references to a prisoner custody officer certified as such under section 89(1) of the 1991 Act;
  (b) references to a governor shall include references to a director approved by the Secretary of State for the purposes of section 85(1)(a) of the 1991 Act except–
    (i)  in rule 85 the reference to a governor shall include a reference to a controller appointed by the Secretary of State under section 85(1)(b) of the 1991 Act;
    (ii) in rules 67(1), 71 and 81 where references to a governor shall include references to a director and a controller; and
    (iii) in rules 49, 51, 52, 58, 58A, 60, 63, 64 and 65 where references to a governor shall include a reference to the director or the controller;
  (c) rule 73 shall not apply in relation to a prisoner custody officer certified as such under section 89(1) of the 1991 Act and performing custodial duties.
(1A) The director of a prison may, with the leave of the Secretary of State, delegate any of his powers and duties under rules 49, 51, 52, 58, 58A, 60, 63, 64 and 65 to another officer of that prison.
(2) [*Revoked.*]

### 87 Contracted out parts of young offender institutions
Where the Secretary of State has entered into a contract for the running of part of a young offender institution under section 84(1) of the Criminal Justice Act 1991, that part and the remaining part shall each be treated for the purposes of Parts I to IV and Part VI of these Rules as if they were separate young offender institutions.

### 88 Contracted out functions at directly managed young offender institutions
(1) Where the Secretary of State has entered into a contract under section 88A(1) of the Criminal Justice Act 1991 for any functions at a directly managed young offender institution too be performed by prisoner custody officers who are authorised to perform custodial duties under section 89(1) of that Act, references to an officer in these Rules shall, subject to paragraph (2), include references to a prisoner custody officer who is so authorised and who is performing contracted out functions for the purposes of, or for purposes connected with, the young offender institution.

(2) Paragraph (1) shall not apply to references to an officer in rule 73.

(3) In this rule 'directly managed young offender institution' means a young offender institution which is not a contracted out young offender institution.

## 89 Revocations and savings

(1) Subject to paragraphs (2) and (3), the Rules specified in the Schedule to these Rules are hereby revoked.

(2) Without prejudice to the Interpretation Act 1978 ('the 1978 Act'), where an inmate committed an offence against discipline contrary to rule 50 of the Young Offender Institution Rules 1988 ('the 1988 Rules') prior to the coming into force of these Rules, the 1988 Rules shall continue to have effect to permit the prisoner to be charged with such an offence, disciplinary proceedings in relation to such an offence to be continued, and the governor to impose punishment for such an offence.

(3) Without prejudice to the 1978 Act, any award of additional days or other punishment or suspended punishment for an offence against discipline awarded or imposed under any provision of the Rules revoked by this rule, or the 1988 Rules as saved by paragraph (2), or treated by any such provision as having been awarded or imposed under the Rules revoked by this rule, shall have effect as if awarded or imposed under the corresponding provision of these Rules.

## SCHEDULE: REVOCATIONS

Rule 89(1)

| *Rules Revoked* | *SI No* |
| --- | --- |
| The Young Offender Institution Rules 1988 | 1988/1422 |
| The Young Offender Institution (Amendment) Rules 1989 | 1989/331 |
| The Young Offender Institution (Amendment) (No 2) Rules 1989 | 1989/2142 |
| The Young Offender Institution (Amendment) Rules 1990 | 1990/1763 |
| The Young Offender Institution (Amendment) Rules 1992 | 1992/513 |
| The Young Offender Institution (Amendment) (No 2) Rules 1992 | 1992/2081 |
| The Young Offender Institution (Amendment) Rules 1993 | 1993/3076 |
| The Young Offender Institution (Amendment) Rules 1994 | 1994/3194 |
| The Young Offender Institution (Amendment) Rules 1995 | 1995/984 |
| The Young Offender Institution (Amendment) (No 2) Rules 1995 | 1995/1599 |
| The Young Offender Institution (Amendment) Rules 1996 | 1996/1662 |
| The Young Offender Institution (Amendment) Rules 1997 | 1997/789 |
| The Young Offender Institution (Amendment) Rules 1998 | 1998/1545 |
| The Young Offender Institution (Amendment) (No 2) Rules 1999 | 1999/962 |
| The Young Offender Institution (Amendment) Rules 2000 | 2000/700 |
| The Young Offender Institution (Amendment) (No 2) Rules 2000 | 2000/1795 |
| The Young Offender Institution (Amendment) (No 3) Rules 2000 | 2000/2642 |

# Index